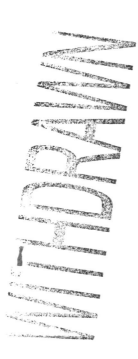

THE ROUTLEDGE INTERNATIONAL HANDBOOK TO VEILS AND VEILING PRACTICES

Veils and veiling are controversial topics in social and political life, generating debates across the world. The veil is enmeshed within a complex web of relations encompassing politics, religion and gender, and conflicts over the nature of power, legitimacy, belief, freedom, agency and emancipation. In recent years, the veil has become both a potent and unsettling symbol and a rallying point for discourse and rhetoric concerning women, Islam and the nature of politics.

Early studies in gender, doctrine and politics of veiling appeared in the 1970s following the Islamic revival and 're-veiling' trends that were dramatically expressed by 1979's Iranian Islamic revolution. In the 1990s, research focused on the development of both an 'Islamic culture industry' and greater urban middle-class consumption of 'Islamic' garments and dress styles across the Islamic world. In the last decade academics have studied Islamic fashion and marketing, the political role of the headscarf, the veiling of other religious groups such as Jews and Christians, and secular forms of modest dress. Using work from contributors across a range of disciplinary backgrounds and locations, this book brings together these research strands to form the most comprehensive book ever conceived on this topic.

As such, this handbook will be of interest to scholars and students of fashion, gender studies, religious studies, politics and sociology.

Anna-Mari Almila is a Postdoctoral Research Fellow in Sociology of Fashion at London College of Fashion, University of the Arts London.

David Inglis is Professor of Sociology at the University of Exeter, UK.

'Through an impressive array of thought-provoking essays, the reader is presented with contemporary, and historical, understandings of veils and veiling in various parts of the world. We hear the stories of women—contextualized by scholars from a variety of disciplines—and in listening to their voices we begin to understand the complexity of meaning hidden behind the veil.'
—*Nancy Nason-Clark, University of New Brunswick, Canada*

THE ROUTLEDGE INTERNATIONAL HANDBOOK TO VEILS AND VEILING PRACTICES

Edited by Anna-Mari Almila and David Inglis

Routledge
Taylor & Francis Group

LONDON AND NEW YORK

First published 2018
by Routledge
2 Park Square, Milton Park, Abingdon, Oxon OX14 4RN

and by Routledge
711 Third Avenue, New York, NY 10017

Routledge is an imprint of the Taylor & Francis Group, an informa business

British Library Cataloguing in Publication Data
A catalogue record for this book is available from the British Library

Library of Congress Cataloging in Publication Data
A catalog record for this book has been requested

ISBN: 978-1-4724-5536-9 (hbk)
ISBN: 978-1-315-61373-4 (ebk)

Typeset in Bembo and Minion Pro
by Florence Production Ltd, Stoodleigh, Devon, UK

Printed in the United Kingdom
by Henry Ling Limited

CONTENTS

List of figures   viii

List of tables   ix

Notes on contributors   x

1   Introduction: The veil across the globe in politics, everyday life
and fashion   1
Anna-Mari Almila

PART I
Politics

2   Neoliberalization and *Homo Islameconomicus*: The politics of women's
veiling in Turkey   29
Yıldız Atasoy

3   Discourses of veiling and the precarity of choice: Representations
in the post-9/11 US   44
Tabassum F. Ruby

4   Wearing a veil in the French context of *laïcité*   53
Anne Fornerod

5   2007/8: The winter of the veiled women in Israel   63
Tamar Elor

6   Veiling narratives: Discourses of Canadian multiculturalism, acceptability
and citizenship   73
Shelina Kassam and Naheed Mustafa

7   Veiling and unveiling in Central Asia: Beliefs and practices,
tradition and modernity   84
Marianne Kamp and Noor Borbieva

Contents

PART II
From politics to fashion

8 Iran's compulsory hijab: From politics and religious authority
to fashion shows 97
Faegheh Shirazi

9 The fashions and politics of facial hair in Turkey: The case
of Islamic men 116
Nazlı Alimen

10 Representing the veil in contemporary Australian media:
From 'ban the burqa' to 'hijabi' bloggers 125
Branka Prodanovic and Susie Khamis

PART III
Fashion and anti-fashion

11 Modest fashion and anti-fashion 139
Reina Lewis

12 Veiling, fashion and the (per)formative role of dress in Niger 152
Adeline Masquelier

13 The 'discipline of the veil' among converts to Islam in France
and Quebec: Framing gender and expressing femininity 163
Géraldine Mossière

14 Muslim youth practising veiling in Berlin: Modernity, morality
and aesthetics 174
Synnøve Bendixsen

15 Fashioning selves: Biographic pathways of hijabi women in
Rio de Janeiro, Brazil 184
Gisele Fonseca Chagas and Solange Riva Mezabarba

PART IV
Industries, images, materialities

16 Culture industries and marketplace dynamics 197
Özlem Sandıkçı

17 Images of desire: Creating virtue and value in an Indonesian
    Islamic lifestyle magazine   213
    Carla Jones

18 Smart-ening up the hijab: The materiality of contemporary
    British Muslim veiling in the physical and the digital   222
    Shehnaz Suterwalla

PART V
Gender, space, community

19 Veiling, gender and space: On the fluidity of 'public' and 'private'   231
    Anna-Mari Almila

20 Hindu and Muslim veiling in north India: Beyond the Public/Private
    Dichotomy   246
    Janaki Abraham

21 Hui women and the headscarf in China   255
    Xiaoyan Wang

22 Constructions and reconstructions of 'appropriate dress' in the
    diaspora: Young Somali women and sartorial social control in Finland   267
    Anu Isotalo

23 Cover their face: Masks, masking, and masquerades in historical-
    anthropological context   278
    David Inglis

24 The Amish prayer cap as a symbol that bounds the community   292
    Jana M. Hawley

25 Veiling studies and globalization studies: The promise of
    historical sociologies   301
    David Inglis and Anna-Mari Almila

Index   306

FIGURES

7.1	Typical Kyrgyz or Kazakh woman's headwear	85
7.2	A woman wearing *paranji* and *chachvon*	86
8.1	Fine ticket for improper hijab	107
8.2	One of the earlier efforts to create government fashion shows dates to 2001. Photo Credit: FARS News Agency, Iran	110
8.3	This particular example is a reminiscent style of Qajar woman's hijab (*chador va chaghchor*) that Reza Khan abolished by *kashf e hejab* edict. Photo Credit: Sina Shiri, FARS News Agency, Iran. 2013	111
10.1	Delina on the streets of Newtown. Image from 'Muslim Street Fashion', reproduced courtesy of Delina Darusman-Gala	132
10.2	Delina on the streets of Sydney. Image from 'Muslim Street Fashion', reproduced courtesy of Delina Darusman-Gala	132
10.3	Delina on the streets of Jakarta. Image from 'Muslim Street Fashion', reproduced courtesy of Delina Darusman-Gala	133
12.1	Nigérien woman wearing *hijabi* over a head scarf	157
12.2	Nigérien women wearing *hijabai*	158
14.1	At the Muslim youth summer camp	175
14.2	Young Muslim women in Berlin	180
15.1	Veiled women praying in Rio de Janeiro. Photograph Solange Riva Mezabarba	187
15.2	Al-amira style veil	191
16.1	Advertisement for Altın İğne, Turkey, circa 1990	201
16.2	Tekbir, Turkey, 2005 catalog	203
16.3	Setre, Turkey, 2004 catalog	204
21.1	Hui housewives with white hats. Photograph Jinsuo Zhao	256
21.2	Hui woman with headscarf. Photograph Xuejun Ma	257
21.3	Hui women with headscarves at an Arabic language school. Photograph Linsuozhao	262
21.4	A girl wearing a headscarf in a Muslim-articles store. Photograph Xuejun Ma	262
24.1	Styles of prayer caps vary by community. Illustration by Jonathan Garcia Gutierrez, 2016.	297

TABLES

24.1   Companies that sell Amish clothing   298

NOTES ON CONTRIBUTORS

Editors

Anna-Mari Almila is a Postdoctoral Research Fellow in Sociology of Fashion at London College of Fashion, University of the Arts London. She writes in the field of cultural sociology, and her topics range from space, materiality and history of dress and fashion to wine, food and gender. She is the author of *Veiling in Fashion: Space and the Hijab in Minority Communities* (forthcoming with I.B.Tauris).

David Inglis is Professor of Sociology at the University of Exeter, UK. He holds degrees in Sociology from the universities of Cambridge and York. He writes in the areas of cultural sociology, the sociology of globalization, historical sociology, the sociology of food and drink, and social theory, both modern and classical. He has written and edited various books in these areas, most recently *An Invitation to Social Theory*, published by Polity (2nd edition, 2016). He is founding editor of the Sage/BSA journal *Cultural Sociology*. His current research concerns the sociological analysis of the global wine industry.

Contributors

Janaki Abraham, MA, MPhil, PhD (Delhi), is Associate Professor in Sociology at the University of Delhi. Her research interests include the study of kinship, gender and caste, visual anthropology, and gender and space, particularly the study of towns. She is finalizing her manuscript entitled 'Gender, Caste and Matrilineal Kinship: Shifting Boundaries in Twentieth-Century Kerala', based on her doctoral research. An exhibition entitled 'Exploring the Visual Cultures of North Kerala: Photographs, Albums and Videos in Everyday Life' showed at the Arts and Aesthetics gallery in JNU, New Delhi and was based on her postdoctoral research.

Nazlı Alimen received her PhD in Cultural Studies and Marketing at the London College of Fashion, University of the Arts London. Her research interests include Islamic fashions and consumer cultures, and fast fashion consumption.

Yıldız Atasoy is Professor of Sociology and Associate Member in the School for International Studies and Department of Geography at Simon Fraser University in Vancouver, Canada. She received her PhD (Sociology) from the University of Toronto in 1998. Her recent publications include *Global Economic Crisis and the Politics of Diversity* (Palgrave Macmillan, 2014, editor); Islam's *Marriage with Neoliberalism: State Transformation in Turkey* (Palgrave Macmillan, 2009); *Hegemonic Transitions, the State and Crisis in Neoliberal Capitalism* (Routledge, 2009, editor); *Turkey, Islamists and Democracy: Transition and Globalization in a Muslim State* (I.B.Tauris, 2005); and *Global Shaping and Its Alternatives* (Garamond Press, 2003, co-editor with William K. Carroll). Her latest book, *Supermarkets and Global Agrifood Systems: Shifting Relations of Food Provisioning in Turkey* (Routledge) is forthcoming. Her current research focuses on Islamic politics and neoliberal agency, supermarkets and global agrifood systems, and land commodification.

Synnøve Bendixsen is a Postdoctoral Research Fellow at the Department of Social Anthropology, University of Bergen (Norway). Her research interests include Islam and Muslims in Europe, forms of inclusion and exclusion, and processes of marginalization, irregular migration and political mobilization. She has written a number of articles and book chapters, and one monograph: *The Religious Identity of Young Muslim Women in Berlin* (Brill, 2013). Bendixsen has been a visiting scholar at COMPAS, Oxford University, and New York University. Since 2013 she has been the co-editor of the *Nordic Journal of Migration Research*.

Noor O'Neill Borbieva is Associate Professor of Anthropology and an affiliated faculty member with Women's Studies at Indiana University-Purdue University Fort Wayne. She has a PhD from Harvard University (2007) and a BA from Princeton University (1996). Her research on religious change and development in the former Soviet Union has been published in *Central Asian Studies*, *Slavic Review*, *Anthropological Quarterly*, and other journals. She is currently working on a manuscript entitled 'Being Foreign, Being Local: Culture, Identity, and Hierarchy in the Kyrgyz Republic'.

Tamar Elor is Sarah Allen Shaine Professor of Anthropology at the Hebrew University in Jerusalem. Her academic interests lie at the intersection between gender, culture and knowledge. El Or's PhD dissertation was a pioneering study of ultra-Orthodox women in Israel. The research was published as the book, *Educated and Ignorant*, in both Hebrew and English. El Or's fieldwork and findings on the ultra-Orthodox community led to research on the modern (national) Orthodox and Sephardic Mizrahi communities in Israel. The results are a trilogy of monographs on gender, religion and the meanings of knowing. She is currently conducting research on material culture and style.

Gisele Fonseca Chagas is Professor of Anthropology at Fluminense Federal University (Brazil), where she was a Postdoctoral Fellow previously (2011–2013). She has written several articles and book chapters in Portuguese and English based on her anthropological research on Muslim communities in Brazil and on Female Sufism in Damascus, Syria.

Anne Fornerod, PhD (Public Law), has been a researcher at the National Centre for Scientific Research since 2011 (DRES Centre of Research, CNRS/University of Strasbourg). Her research interests are within law and religion: religious heritage, the principle of *laïcité*, public funding for religious groups and religious pluralism. She is a member of the editorial board of the newly created journal, *Revue du droit des religions*. She is currently supervising a research project on French case law pertaining to religious issues. Her main publications are: *Annotated Legal Documents on Islam in Europe: France* (Brill, 2016), *Funding Religious Heritage* (Ashgate, 2015, editor) and *Le régime juridique du patrimoine religieux* (L'Harmattan, 2013).

Jana M. Hawley, PhD, is Director of the Norton School of Family and Consumer Sciences at University of Arizona. Hawley earned her PhD at the University of Missouri in Human Environmental Sciences with an emphasis in Textile and Apparel Management. She is a Fulbright Scholar to India, HERS Fellow, International Textile Apparel Association (ITAA) Fellow, and Global Scholar to Thailand, India and Turkey. She has served as president of ITAA. Trained in cultural anthropology, she has expertise in sustainability and cultural studies of dress. She has authored or co-authored more than 100 publications, several of which have received honours.

Anu Isotalo is a Researcher in the Finnish Youth Research Network. She is currently working in the project 'Generational Negotiations, Social Control and Gendered Sexualities' (GENESO) financed by The Academy of Finland. Her postdoctoral research based on police crime reports deals with dating violence among young people in Finland. Isotalo received her PhD in Comparative Religion at the University of Turku, Finland in 2015. Her dissertation focused on meanings and consequences of good and bad reputation for young Somali women living in Finland. Her research was based on extensive ethnographic fieldwork among Somali women with refugee migrant background in Turku.

Carla Jones is Associate Professor of Anthropology at the University of Colorado, Boulder. Her research analyses the cultural politics of appearance in urban Indonesia, with particular focus on femininity, domesticity, aesthetics and Islam. She has written extensively on self-improvement programmes and middle-class respectability during the Suharto and post-Suharto periods in Yogyakarta and Jakarta, and is the co-editor, with Ann Marie Leshkowich and Sandra Niessen, of *Re-Orienting Fashion: The Globalization of Asian Dress* (Berg, 2003). Her current work situates anxieties about Islamic style in the context of broader debates about corruption and exposure.

Marianne Kamp is Associate Professor of Central Eurasian Studies at Indiana University, where she teaches about gender and society in contemporary Central Asia. Her research concerns social change in Uzbekistan, focusing on women, labour and agriculture. Her book, *The New Woman in Uzbekistan: Islam, Modernity, and Unveiling under Communism*, was published by Indiana University Press (2006). She and co-editor Mariana Markova published *Muslim Women of the Fergana Valley: A Nineteenth Century Ethnography from Central Asia*, their translation of an 1886 book by the Nalivkins, with Indiana University Press (2016).

Shelina Kassam is a PhD candidate at the Department of Social Justice Education, Ontario Institute for Education (OISE) at the University of Toronto. She received an MA (McGill, 1993) and a BA (Simon Fraser, 1985), both of which focused on contemporary social and political Muslim movements. Her current research concentrates on Muslims in contemporary Western multicultural nation states, and, in particular, on the figure of the 'acceptable' or 'moderate' Muslim in contemporary discourses. She is an instructor in the Division of Women and Gender Studies at the University of Toronto, Mississauga. In her previous professional life, Kassam worked with numerous academic, educational and social justice organizations, both in Canada and internationally, including those related to global development, human rights and anti-oppression.

Susie Khamis, PhD, is a Senior Lecturer in the School of Communication at the University of Technology Sydney. Her doctoral thesis 'Bushells and the Cultural Logic of Branding' won the Sydney Harbour Foreshore Heritage Prize in 2007, and in 2011 she was founding editor of *Locale: The Australasian-Pacific Journal of Regional Food Studies*. Dr Khamis joined UTS in 2015 as part of the Public Communication discipline. Her research areas are branding, representations of cultural diversity, marketing media and consumer cultures. She has published widely in these areas and her current research focuses on how successful global brands represent cultural diversity in their advertising, marketing and public relations.

Reina Lewis is Professor of Cultural Studies at London College of Fashion, UAL. Her books include *Muslim Fashion: Contemporary Style Cultures* (2015); *Rethinking Orientalism: Women, Travel and the Ottoman Harem* (2004); and *Gendering Orientalism: Race, Femininity and Representation* (1996). Edited volumes include *Modest Fashion: Styling Bodies, Mediating Faith* (2013); *Gender, Modernity and Liberty: Middle Eastern and Western Women's Writings: A Critical Reader* (with Nancy Micklewright, 2006); *Feminist Postcolonial Theory: A Reader* (with Sara Mills, 2003); and *Outlooks: Lesbian and Gay Visual Cultures* (with Peter Horne, 1996). Lewis co-edits two book series: 'Dress Cultures' with Elizabeth Wilson and 'Cultures in Dialogue' with Teresa Heffernan. Lewis convenes the public talk series 'Faith and Fashion', available at www.arts.ac.uk/research/research-projects/current-projects/faith-and-fashion/.

Adeline Masquelier is Professor of Anthropology at Tulane University (New Orleans, Louisiana, USA). She has published extensively on issues of religion, gender and medicine in Niger. She is the author of *Prayer Has Spoiled Everything: Possession, Power, and Identity in an Islamic Town of Niger* (2001) and *Women and Islamic Revival in a West African Town* (2009), winner of the 2010 Herskovits Award for best scholarly book on Africa and the 2012 Aidoo-Snyder prize for best scholarly book about African women. She is the editor of *Dirt, Undress, and Difference: Critical Perspectives on the Body's Surface* (2005) and *Muslim Youth and the 9/11 Generation* (2016). Her current research interests focus on youth in Niger.

Géraldine Mossière holds a PhD in anthropology from Université de Montréal. She is Assistant Professor in the Faculty of Theology and Religious Studies at the Université de Montréal. She is regular member of the Centre d'Études Ethniques des Universités Montréalaises (CEETUM) where she is responsible for research activities on religious pluralism. She works on religion in secular societies as well as on individual religious trajectories. She has written on religion, migration and transnationality, in particular Pentecostal churches, as well as on issues related to gender, youth and ethnicity. She is interested in modern religious subjectivities and mobilities, notably on processes of conversion. In 2013, she published *Converties à l'islam. Parcours de femmes en France et au Québec*. She currently conducts ethnographic research on changes of religion, new ritualities and on religion in life cycles.

Naheed Mustafa is an award-winning broadcaster, producer and writer based in Canada. She has a special interest in media discourse around Muslims, and its impact.

Branka Prodanovic is a PhD candidate in the Department of Media, Music, Communications and Cultural Studies at Macquarie University, Sydney, Australia. Her PhD thesis focuses on the shifting representations of Muslims in the Australian media. Specifically, it looks at how representations change given the socio-political context of Australia as a nation and how it deals with issues of ethnicity, immigration and border protection. Other research interests for Prodanovic include politics, ethnic studies, popular culture, gender studies, celebrity studies and fashion. She is also a freelance writer and has written on lifestyle, spirituality and popular culture.

Solange Riva Mezabarba received her PhD in Anthropology at Fluminense Federal University (UFF, Brazil) and was a Postdoctoral Fellow at the École des Hautes Etudes en Sciences Sociales

(EHESS, Paris, France) from 2014 to 2016. Her research focuses on consumption studies with emphasis on fashion. She is an Associated Researcher to the Center for Modernity Studies (NEMO/UFF) and to the Associação de Estudos do Consumo (Consumption Studies). Currently, she is a Professor at UCAM-ABGC (Universidade Candido Mendes and Associação Brasileira de Gestão Cultural), at Senai Cetiqt and at IED-Rio (Instituto Europeo di Design Rio de Janeiro). She has published numerous articles and is one of the editors of *Etnografias Possiveis*, a book that addresses urban ethnography and fieldwork on consumption.

Tabassum F. Ruby, PhD, is an Assistant Professor at West Chester University of Pennsylvania. Her research focuses on Islam and gender discourses and applies post-colonial, anti-racist and transnational feminist studies. Based on her PhD research, she is completing a manuscript that examines how liberal-secular normative values have shaped and informed the question of Muslim women's rights. She also has conducted research on Canadian immigrant Muslim women to explore the meanings of the hijab. She has published articles in peer reviewed journals and edited volumes. Among others, she teaches *Representations of Muslim Women in Western Discourses* and *Islam, Gender, and the Media* courses.

Özlem Sandıkçı is Professor of Marketing at the School of Management and Administrative Sciences, Istanbul Şehir University, Turkey. Her research addresses sociocultural dimensions of consumption and focuses on the relationship between globalization, marketing and culture. Her work is published in various journals including the *Journal of Marketing*, *Journal of Consumer Research*, *Journal of Business Research*, *Marketing Theory*, *Business History Review*, and *Fashion Theory*, and in several books. She is the co-editor of *The Handbook of Islamic Marketing* (Edward Elgar, 2011) and *Islam, Marketing and Consumption: Critical Perspectives on the Intersections* (Routledge, 2016).

Faegheh Shirazi is Professor in the Department of Middle Eastern Studies, the Islamic Studies program, University of Texas, Austin. She is the author of *The Veil Unveiled: Hijab in Modern Culture* (2001); *Velvet Jihad: Muslim Women's Quiet Resistance to Islamic Fundamentalism* (2009); *Muslim Women in War and Crisis: From Reality to Representation* (2010, editor); and *Brand Islam: The Commodification of Piety* (forthcoming). Her research interests include Islamic popular religious practices, rituals and their influence on gender identity and discourse in Muslim societies, Islamic veiling, material culture, textile and clothing.

Shehnaz Suterwalla, PhD, is a design historian, writer and critic. She is Tutor at the Royal College of Art. Previously Suterwalla was a journalist at Newsweek International, and an editor at *The Economist*. Her research and writing has focused on the contemporary body, with regard to gender and race, and the embodied relationship of individuals with popular and subcultural material, visual and digital culture. She is particularly interested in personal experiences, identities and representation in the design of digital life as well as digital senses: how might we smell, taste and hear data? She presents her work globally at symposia and conferences; she has also presented at the ICA, and will be a participant at the 2016 Being Human Festival of the Humanities in London.

Xiaoyan Wang, PhD, is Associate Professor of Ethnology at the Center for Studies of Education and Psychology of Ethnic Minorities in Southwest China, Southwest University. She is currently Visiting Scholar in Cross-Cultural Psychology in the Department of Human Development and Women's Studies at California State University, East Bay. Her primary research interest is cultural anthropology of minorities, and her field research is located among the Hui societies of Gansu, northwest China, and the Miao of Guizhou, southwest of China.

1

INTRODUCTION

The veil across the globe in politics, everyday life and fashion

Anna-Mari Almila

Introduction

Veil – what is it, where does it come from, how and why is it worn, what does it mean? From a minor subject of study, veiling has grown into a significant topic of a field of studies during the recent two decades. Global political changes have contributed to this development, but behind political and legislative battles, there is a whole world of everyday experiences, religious debates and garment markets that increasingly have drawn the attention of those who study veils and veiling practices. As a versatile topic, the veil has also inspired a versatile body of literature, drawing upon philosophy, anthropology, political science, sociology, law, urban geography, gender studies, cultural studies, fashion studies, religious studies, marketing and consumption studies, and history. This handbook aims to do two things: first, show the richness and variation in ways of studying veiling; and second, to present veiling as a global phenomenon, not limited to any specific religion, to one gender only, or to particular garments, styles, or appearances.

While Muslim veiling is the most politically heated topic globally, many Jews (Chapter 5), Christians (Chapter 24), and Hindus (Chapter 20) also practise forms of veiling. Veiling is also a fundamentally global phenomenon today: it is practised in North Africa (Chapter 19), Sub-Saharan Africa (Chapter 12), Asia Minor (Chapters 2, 9 and 16), the Middle East (Chapters 5 and 8), Central Asia (Chapters 3 and 7), South Asia (Chapter 20), South East Asia (Chapter 17), Far East Asia (Chapter 21), Australia (Chapter 10), Latin America (Chapter 15), North America (Chapters 3, 6, 13 and 24), and Europe (Chapters 2, 4, 9, 11, 14, 16, 18, 19 and 22) in many forms and shapes. Beyond the obvious forms of veiling, other phenomena, such as male facial hair (Chapter 9) and masks (Chapter 23) can also be studied within the framework of veiling. Veiling is a phenomenon that is simultaneously symbolic, material, spatial, gendered and discursive.

This introduction offers an outline of veiling phenomena from three points of view: (1) international and state politics; (2) everyday veiling and its politics; and (3) fashion and fashion industries. In such a rapidly expanding field as veiling studies, such an introduction can never hope to be comprehensive, so what we are seeking to offer is a wider historical and contemporary context in which to locate the individual case studies that follow. Also the case studies are far from covering the whole field of research; instead they are chosen to represent a rich variety of locations – from obvious ones, such as Turkey, Iran and France, to less obvious, such as

China, Brazil and Uzbekistan – and approaches. In the end of the book, the reader will find a chapter discussing veiling studies through the lense of globalization studies (Chapter 25).

What is veiling?

In this book, veiling is understood in a wide sense, encompassing material, social, spiritual and spatial elements. Veil and veiling are used as generic terms to describe practices, garments and elements of appearance, which seek to both unite and separate groups and individuals. According to El-Guindi:

> the meanings assigned in general reference to the Western term veil comprise four dimensions: the material, the spatial, the communicative, and the religious. The material dimension consists of clothing and ornament, i.e. veil in the sense of [a] clothing article covering head, shoulders, and face or in the sense of ornamentation over a hat drawn over the eyes. In this usage 'veil' is not confined to face covering, but extends to the head and shoulders.
>
> (El-Guindi 1999, 6)

But the word does not come without problems. According to Allievi (2006, 120), '[t]he word veil itself dramatizes the debate [happening in Europe], referring at least implicitly and certainly psychologically to something that separates, conceals, masks, or blocks the view'. Scott's (2007, 16) analysis of the French usage of 'voile' seems to make a similar point:

> Muslim women in France wear what they refer to as a hijab; in French the word is foulard; in English, headscarf. Very quickly, this head covering was referred to in the media as a veil (voile), with the implications that the entire body and face of its wearer were hidden from view.

Admittedly, to use the word veil is to introduce a potentially Eurocentric, Western viewpoint. As Neuburger points out, '[h]istorically, the concept of the "veil" has been and remains the quintessential metaphor for all that the "East" purportedly represents in contrast to a "Western" norm' (2014, 253). The term is also very generic, risking the blurring of differences between garments and phenomena.

Today Muslim women often refer to their veils and veiling practices as 'hijab'. Hijab can mean a barrier, something that prevents, conceals, covers or protects. In the Qur'an, it has both positive and negative connotations; it may refer to a metaphoric obstacle or division, as well as spatial separation, but it is actually not used to refer to women's dress codes (Ruby 2006, 55–6). Another related term, common in Central and South Asia, is 'purdah'. Purdah means 'curtain', and it is the word most commonly used for the system of secluding women and enforcing high standards of female modesty in parts of Asia. Purdah is an important part of the life experience of many South Asians, both Muslim and Hindu, and is a central feature of the social systems of the area (Papanek 1973, 289).

Both these terms have their own specific problems as well, for they are associated with a certain religion in the case of hijab, and geographic area in the case of purdah. As Ruby (2006, 56) points out, 'the distinction between the words veil and hijab is important, as the latter has Islamic association that differentiates it from the former term'.

Therefore veil as a term allows for certain possibilities that these two terms do not. It allows the crossing of geographical distances, and it allows for seeing similarities and differences between practices in different parts of the globe. To talk about 'veils' is not intended to blur differences and generalize, but is instead meant to help the reader to see the enormous richness and variation that is associated with veiling across the globe.

Veiling in Abrahamic religions

The holy scriptures of the three Abrahamic religions – the Torah, the Bible and the Qur'an – all contain phrases that indicate veiling, or at least have been interpreted as either recommending or ordaining veiling for women. In the Torah, Rebecca veils herself when she first sees her husband-to-be Isaac (Genesis 24:65), and therefore Jewish women from sects often considered 'orthodox' cover themselves when married. According to Rabbinic interpretation, this usually means wearing a wig to cover one's hair, and a dress that covers the body so that the collar bones, elbows and knees are covered. Headgears and veils are worn by some in addition to wigs (Carrel 2008), and also more covering dress styles, including face-veils, appear, but particularly face-veils are often condemned by religious patriarchs (Vakulenko 2012). The male orthodox dress is far more stylistically restricted than the female dress, and the doctrinal restrictions of it come in an extremely detailed form (Carrel 2008).

In the New Testament, Paul touches upon the topic of veiling, stating that women should cover their heads when praying or prophesying (1 Corinthians 11:4–5). Paul also recommends women's veil as a sign of hierarchical status where women are categorically lower than men, and a woman's unveiled head shames her husband. Elsewhere in the Bible, women are instructed to 'pray without ceasing' (1 Thessalonians 5:17). When taken together, these statements have been taken by some Christian groups to mean that women should cover their heads constantly. Christian theologians of the early Church elaborated upon the topic of veiling. Virgins had been exempt from the veiling requirement, highlighting their high spiritual position in the early Church. Tertullian took an issue with this practice in the third century CE, and by the fourth century, veiling had come to be associated with virginity, and women's opportunities to gain spiritual position within the Church had been weakened (D'Angelo 1995). While Christian veiling is today far more limited a phenomenon than Muslim veiling, there nevertheless are groups, old and new, who practise forms of it (e.g. Cameron 2013; Graybill and Arthur 1999; Hawley 2008; Lafontaine 2008).

There are three Qur'anic lines associated with veiling, one of which specifically refers to the wives of Muhammed, who should talk to the believers from behind a curtain (hijab) (Qur'an 33:53, see e.g. Mernissi 1991 for a discussion of the circumstances related to the revelation of the verse). Elsewhere, all believers are ordained the following advice:

> Say to the believing men that they lower their gaze and restrain their sexual passions. That is purer for them. Surely Allah is Aware of what they do.
>
> And say to the believing women that they lower their gaze and restrain their sexual passions and do not display their adornment except what appears thereof.
>
> *(Qur'an 24:30–1)*

A further statement tells women to draw their cloaks (jilbab) around their bodies 'so that they are recognized and thus not harmed' (Qur'an 33:59). Thus the Qur'an gives very little guidance as regards female dress. Also the hadiths (oral tradition of Muhammed) have little to say about women's clothing: their dress focus is on male garments and materials considered appropriate for believing men rather than women (El-Guindi 1999, 135).

Veiling is not restricted to Abrahamic religions only, nor is veiling practised by women only, or by all women who identify as Jews, Christians or Muslims. Sikh men cover their heads with turbans (Walton-Roberts 1998), Muslim Tuareg men practise veiling (Murphy 1964), Hindu women veil and follow related spatial customs (Abraham 2010). Also within Abrahamic religions there are disagreements about veiling. Catholic nuns were allowed to unveil only in the 1960s, but some nuns rebelled against their convention's order to unveil (Lafontaine 2008). Some Jewish women practise face-veiling despite the condemnation of such a practice by rabbis and family members (Vakulenko 2012). Muslim scholars and individual Muslims alike are engaged in debates as to whether veiling is necessary at all, and if it is, to what degree women should veil. In what follows, we seek to show some very general trends that veiling phenomena have followed throughout history. Such approach allows for little detail, but detail is exactly what all the other chapters in this book offer.

Politics and law: A struggle over female bodies

It is nothing new that dress is regulated by law or religious doctrine. History knows a number of attempts to stop lower classes wearing garments 'above their station', and clerical orders to restrain cross-dressing (Ribeiro 2003 [1986]). Veiling is no exemption, nor is it a very special case until relatively recently. The veil has been legally and socially regulated for thousands of years in different contexts, but it only emerges as a powerfully political symbol since late colonial and post-colonial times. Veiling is strongly connected to gender and the regulation of sexuality at the individual level, and reproductive capacity at the collective level, categories of regulation that communities, states and institutions have been keen on controlling throughout human history (Turner 2008 [1984]).

The veil before the twentieth century

Veiling goes back a long time in history. Practised in a number of cultures, kingdoms and areas, the veil was no property of a specific religion. While, for example, both Jews and early Christians practised veiling in ancient Rome, so did Romans more generally follow certain veiling customs (d'Angelo 1995; Levine 1995). The veil in its early history tends to be linked to urbanization, and is aimed at making two specific distinctions. It separates gender, creating women as different from men (and often also spatially separating these groups), and it distinguishes 'honourable' women, that is, women belonging to free men through marriage or kinship, from slaves and prostitutes, that is, women sexually available to any man (Ahmed 1992). The distinction of veiling between slaves and free women, whereby slaves were forbidden to veil, survived at places in Africa until the late nineteenth century when slavery was formally abandoned (Fair 2013).

Therefore the veil was for a long time fundamentally linked to social status and social standing, and was a privilege. So, for example, Assyrian law stated heavy punishments to women who wore the veil without being entitled to it, and to men who allowed them to do so (Ahmed 1992). In the Christian Middle East, veiling was well established by the time of Muhammed. Veiling did also not come to be widely practised among Muslims during Muhammed's life, but was rather established afterwards. By the medieval era, gender seclusion had been established in Muslim urban centres (Hämeen-Anttila 2004), and while elite women rarely left their domestic dwellings, and if they did, did so fully veiled or in closed carriages, lower-class and rural women often practised less restrictive forms of veiling (Sedghi 2007).

During the colonial times, new discourses about veiling emerged, first prompted by representors of colonial power who used their views of 'women's position' as proof of inferiority of local cultures. Veil in such arguments played an important part as a visible marker of 'oppression', a theme that is powerfully and repeatedly reproduced today. Yet, while these male advocates of unveiling claimed to liberate Muslim women, they were curiously reluctant to allow any political rights for women in their home countries, firmly opposing such demands as suffrage for women (Abu-Lughod 2002). Colonial, essentializing discourses about Muslim women and men were and are repeated also in art and literature throughout several centuries, enforcing the association of Muslim women as sexualized victims (Haddad 2007) and the veil as imposed by men (Behiery 2012). While some European travellers felt true sympathy, and attempted to understand local customs, and restrictions of their own culture (Lewis 1999), the idea of unveiling, promoted also by many female travellers and missionaries to North Africa and the Middle East, took root in local discourses. At the same time, alternative narratives defending the veil, and arguing that European female dress was morally inferior also emerged (Hirschmann 1998).

Unveiling in the early twentieth century

While some liberated slaves in Africa were embracing their legal right to finally veil (Fair 2013), local elites across North Africa and the Middle East were engaged in European-inspired debates about the necessity and meaning of veiling (Ghumkhor 2012; Kejanlioğlu and Taş 2009). Many minority Christian women were persuaded to unveil by missionaries in the early twentieth century, and towards the end of the nineteenth century, and particularly in the early twentieth century, debates emerged across Muslim Arab countries, as well as in Central Asia, that considered women's rights in a new light (Ahmed 2011; Kamp 2014). Education was of primary importance in these debates, but the veil also got its share of attention. From the 1920s on, women's public, symbolic unveiling occurred in various places, led by local elite women (or in some cases by their husbands) (Hoodfar 1997; Kamp 2014; Wide 2014; Zahedi 2007). These were quite different from the political spectacles arranged by colonialists, for example in Algeria, where French women collected local lower-class women to public places and ceremoniously unveiled them (Fanon 1989 [1959]).

While the Egyptian intellectual circles were crucial for these developments, Turkey, Iran and Afghanistan were the places where unveiling took most radical forms, mostly due to state interference. It is important to remember that in all these places, male dress was the first and primary focus of regulation by the state. The Turkish dress reform addressed male dress well before it focused on women's attire, legislating against Ottoman headgears in 1925 ('Hat Law', see e.g. Adak 2014; Libal 2014). In Afghanistan, only male dress was regulated by actual legislation, although unveiling was debated and the king publicly unveiled his wife in the 1920s (Wide 2014). Also in Iran a Europeanized male dress code was introduced in the late 1920s (Rostam-Kolayi and Matin-Asgari 2014).

Campaigns to unveil women typically only targeted urban women, and specifically those in state employment (Metinsoy 2014; Rostam-Kolayi and Matin-Asgari 2014). These were campaigns to 'modernize' the state and its subjects, following European ideals of secularism and modernity (Onar and Müftüler-Baç 2011), and therefore it was crucial that individuals close to state institutions unveiled. In rural settings, veiling often persisted, and also in urban environments women found ways to rebel against legislations, which often targeted only certain kinds of veils (Metinsoy 2014). When talking of unveiling, it is important to remember that the actual success of these movements was limited, and many women either found ways to adapt their veiling, or were restrained in their mobility due to the enforcement of law (Zahedi 2007).

New veiling in the 1970s

In the 1970s, new developments in veiling practices occurred (Duval 1997; Saktanber and Çorbacioğlu 2008), which culminated in the Islamic Revolution of Iran in 1979, and the consequent enforced veiling in the early 1980s (see e.g. Gould 2014; Hirschmann 1998; Sedghi 2007; Shirazi 2001; Zahedi 2007). These changes were driven by a variety of factors. There were economic changes, often related to the liberalization of markets. There was a high level of unemployment in some locations, increased possibilities of geographic mobility, and at the same time new job markets funded through oil money emerging in the Gulf countries. Young rural women with limited economic means were increasingly moving to cities and gaining education. New Islamic movements emerged, often critical of secular state systems, and preaching religious alternatives. Many of these movements were highly critical of 'European' ideas, such as secularism and feminism. Many also considered veiling a religiously ordained obligation for Muslim women. As part of these movements, women's movements also gained ground, and these movements demanded to be allowed into mosques – previously a male domain – and considered women as spiritually equal to men and subject only to God (Ahmed 2011; MacLeod 1987; Patel 2012).

As part of these changes, new forms of veiling also appeared (Zahedi 2007). The veil was appealing particularly to women who participated in education or work life outside home, a new situation whereby many women felt vulnerable. The veil also liberated women from fashion competition, which they were unable to afford, and appeased their families and husbands who may have otherwise restricted their spatial mobility (Abaza 2007; Duval 1997; MacLeod 1987; 1992).

Because the new veil emerged particularly in the setup of (lower) middle-class women participating in work life and education, it was a very different form of practice from the old veiling associated with (elite) seclusion and gender segregation. This new veil precisely enabled women's entry into mixed-gender spaces, and therefore granted to them economic opportunities and more freedom of movement than may have otherwise been the case. They were able to retain their respectability, and to demand their right to work at the same time. While for some, work was an unfortunate necessity to provide for their family, for others it offered a new spatial and economic liberty which they did not wish to give up even upon marriage (MacLeod 1987; 1992).

One contributing factor towards new veiling were the male guest workers who went to the Gulf countries. Upon their return, they were more economically affluent than their peers who stayed at home, and thus in a better position to provide for their families. They also often brought back with them religious ideas they had picked up while abroad (Abaza 2007; Amrullah 2008; Osella and Osella 2007). Therefore a Saudi-influenced religious interpretation started to gain ground throughout the Muslim world, and this trend was further supported by the funding of mosques around the world, as well as the wide distribution of religious leaflets, tapes and other religious materials that Saudi Arabia actively undertook (de Castro 2014; Rabine 2013; Stoica 2013; van Santen 2013). Persuading women to veil is an important part of such religious influence, and many women's mosque movement members are very active in urging their unveiled peers to don the veil (Ali 2005; Brenner 1996; de Castro 2014).

Soviet countries, the Balkans and China

Anti-veiling debates and campaigns appeared also in Central Asia in the early twentieth century. These often initiated as women-led campaigns, and many women were keen to embrace new, liberating developments. Many of these women were political activists, and they campaigned for education and women's rights more generally. But after the establishment of Soviet rule in many Central Asian states, women's movements were put under state control, and also the anti-veiling campaigns were made state-led and state-ordained. The paradoxical result of this was that the campaigns targeted men rather than women, and required party members to demonstrate their loyalty to the party by unveiling their wives. This took the initiative away from women, but it also caused serious problems for women whose families were opposed to unveiling. Between state demands and family resistance, women faced violence and even death in the hands of family members (Kamp 2014).

In many Balkan countries, unveiling campaigns and bans on veiling were linked to building an independent state with loyal subjects (Clayer 2014; Neuburger 2014). Veiling was constructed as a 'backwards' practice, and in an attempt to belong in the 'modern', 'developed' world, states actively encouraged their citizens to give up veiling and conform to secular norms promoted by the state. For example, Albania banned veiling in 1929, and made the ban a part of formal legislation in 1937 (Clayer 2014), and Yugoslavia enforced a face-veiling ban in early 1950s (Brunner 1989). In many Balkan countries, the state strategy was also a conscious part of arguing a belonging in Europe, rather than belonging in the 'backwards' Orient. As former parts of the Ottoman empire, these countries had internalized the Orientalist discourses and struggled to establish themselves as 'modern' through enforcing 'European' ideologies (Neuburger 2014).

In the early twentieth century, all Chinese living in regions with significant Muslim populations covered their heads, irrespective of religion and gender, as part of 'decent' dress. Yet debates about appropriate dress occurred at this time in China as well, and some 'radical' women wore male robes. From the 1940s onwards, the Communist Party actively promoted gender neutral dress, and since the late 1950s, headgears, with the exception of workers' caps, were declared feudal and un-modern. This is when the majority of Muslim women unveiled, continuing the practice only when praying in private: veils in public were censored. In the post-Mao era (since 1976), the focus on gender neutrality of dress lessened, and many women donned skirts again. But Muslim women still often favoured trousers, which they considered as fitting both religious modesty, and modernity. There was also an increased official tolerance of religious and minority groups, and some Muslim men started covering their heads. Working women typically preferred not to veil, for the veil was considered an inconvenience in work life. Veiling was typically practised occasionally – during religious ceremonies, in mosques, while praying – with a white 'cap' that women carried with them in their bags in order to quickly put it on when necessary (Gillette 2005). Today, there is a renewed state regulation of religious practice, targeting particularly Muslims. Recently, 'abnormal' beards and veils have been banned in Xinjiang region that is home to a significant Muslim population. The battle over secularization of citizens' bodies continues.

The European headscarf disputes

Despite the colonial discourses about veiling that shaped European understandings of it, the topic remained irrelevant to most European states until very recently. Work migration, particularly after the Second World War, to many Western European countries from various Muslim-majority countries transformed the host countries' demographic and cultural maps for a much longer term than was planned. Often no effort towards integrating the workers was made, for they were supposed to return home eventually. Instead, many brought their families to Europe and settled down for good.

The first headscarf controversies in Europe surfaced in late 1980s. In France, Germany and UK, there were disagreements over veils in schools. Schools have been one of the most central venues over which political and legislative battles have been fought in Europe (see e.g. Batur 2012; Bowen 2007; Duits and van Zoonen 2006; Edmunds 2012; Lentin 2012; McGoldrick 2006; Scott 2007; Weber 2012). Other venues include court rooms and workplaces. The most publicized, and strictest, anti-veiling legislation has been introduced by France, by banning head-scarves (and other 'conspicuous' religious symbols) in public schools in 2004, and by banning the covering of the face in public spaces altogether in 2011 (Body-Gendrot 2007; Edmunds 2012; Tissot 2011). These, as well as other legislative regulations to veiling in Europe, have been repeatedly challenged in the European Court of Human Rights (ECtHR). The ECtHR prac-tises a policy of so-called 'wide margin of appreciation' for states, and therefore has often declared that while an individual woman's religious rights may have been offended, the state nevertheless has the right to regulate its citizens in these ways (Edmunds 2012). The United Nations Human Rights Committee has taken a different approach (Vakulenko 2012). As they practise no margin of appreciation in these questions, they tend to judge for the individual more often than the ECtHR. But they have significantly less enforcing power, if any at all, than has the ECtHR.

Headscarves have also been, and are still, debated in European countries that have not banned them. Across the region, strikingly similar discursive strategies have emerged, applied by both sides of the debate. The most powerful frames directing, and also limiting, the debate are questions to do with 'free choice' and agency, and with gender equality (Bracke and Fadil 2012; Vakulenko 2012). The 'headscarf' is typically seen as a symbol of religion, rather than as (mandatory) religious practice (Shadid and Van Koningsveld 2005). The headscarf debates are directed by local understandings of citizenship and integration politics, relationships between the state and the national church, and traditions of anti-discrimination. But most importantly, the debates are about framing gender oppression and otherness, and often serve to claim the superiority of 'European' gender relations over 'Islamic' ones (Kiliç *et al.* 2008). All ideological frames applied in the debate are, of course, historically constructed concepts rather than universal and neutral ones. They can also potentially limit debates, and the possibilities on both sides of the divide. If anti-veil arguments about gender oppression are often colonialist and racist, many pro-hijab arguments tend to be uncritical of Islam and women's role in the religion.

North America and Australia

One game-changing moment in the recent history of politics of veiling was September 11, 2001, and the New York terror attacks. The attacks were followed by a rhetorical wave which directly evoked old colonialist ideas and concepts. Once again, Muslim women needed to be saved from Muslim men. The 'war on terror' rhetoric was astonishingly similar to the nineteenth-century colonial commentary on women's position in Muslim countries. Through extensive media coverage focusing on specific topics (while not focusing on others), the war was made to look like a result of a fundamental cultural conflict, rather than due to economic or political issues (Abu-Lughod 2002). Similarly, European societies have made questions to do with Islam and Muslims appear as 'cultural', by insisting that they are so (Lentin and Titley 2012).

The Anglo-Saxon mainstream media is remarkably united when it comes to 'Islam' and 'women'. Similar narratives circulate from North America to Australia and the UK, and vice versa (Fitzpatrick 2009). Ever since the end of the Cold War, 'Islam' has been created as the ultimate other, drawing upon historical narratives of women, harems and veiling. For example in Austra-lia, this has happened in the context of Muslim presence in the beach, a national symbol central to national identity and pride (Khamis 2010). Yet, for example in the US, the legislative stance against workplace discrimination of Muslim women is often stronger than in Europe (Greene 2013; Moore 2007), and a wide legislative ban against veiling seems like an impossibility (Westerfield 2006). But while an individual's freedom to choose her faith and clothing is formally defended, and European veiling bans considered too extreme, there are jobs, such as police officer, in which veiling is forbidden in many states (Byng 2010). Debates about the veil have emerged also across the border: Canadian veiling cases go back to mid-1990s, and often involve school venues (Shakeri 1998; Todd 1998). Particularly in the French-speaking part of Canada, the debates are still ongoing, and touch upon issues of migration, belonging, and French-Canadian identity (Al-Saji 2010).

Politics of face-veiling

Hardly had the situation cooled down after the headscarves-in-schools debates, when a new 'threat' to European states emerged, in the form of face-veiling (Brems 2014b; Ferrari and Pastorelli 2013). Taking many by surprise (for the number of face-veiling women in Europe is estimated to be very low indeed), legislative regulations to covering face in public were introduced in quick succession in France and Belgium in 2011. There are also local bans on face-veiling in effect in the Netherlands, Italy and Spain, and many other European countries have debated a face-veil ban (Brems 2014a). An EU-wide ban has also been suggested.

Typical arguments in these debates evoke not only the themes familiar already from the headscarf debates, but also questions to do with safety and security, communication problems, and voluntary disintegration (Meer, Dwyer and Modood 2010; Moors 2014). Claims that the face-veil can be (and has been) used to hide identity for criminal and terrorist purposes (Magnet and Rodgers 2012), combined with the discomfort that many Europeans (including many Muslims) experience with a fully veiled woman (Tarlo 2010), make the question of the face-veil not only a symbolic one, but also a question experienced at the everyday level in terms of personal comfort and a sense of security. Through political and media discourses, the 'burqa' (not that many women wear the burqa in Europe; the most common face-veil is the niqab) has emerged as an ultimate threat to 'European' values and way of life (see e.g. Moors 2007b; 2009b; Tissot 2011). Yet, at the same time, illustrations of the 'burqa' have emerged as tool of critique in political cartoons, used to challenge neo-colonialist politics (Rantanen 2005). Ever since the Afghan burqa came to be associated with extreme oppression of women under the Taleban, its political uses and fetishization have been extreme (McLarney 2009).

In Europe, but also elsewhere, the face-veil is also associated with extremism and even terrorism. The wearers of it deny such a charge. For many, the face-veil is a highly spiritual choice, a result of individual religious commitment and conviction. It is commonly acknowledged fact among Muslims that wearing the face-veil in Europe is extremely challenging, due to hostility and violence targeted at face-veiling women (Bouteldja 2014; Brems *et al.* 2014; Moors 2014; Østergaard *et al.* 2014). During political debates about the veil, and especially when a ban is introduced, such hostility tends to increase even more (Amnesty International 2012).

While the Western European cases of debating and/or banning the face-veil have been more visible in the global media than many others, it is the case that the topic has been debated also elsewhere. A Bulgarian town has recently banned face-veils (Aljazeera 2016), Congo and Chad have introduced a general ban (Aljazeera 2015a; 2015b), and Senegal has debated such a measure (Aljazeera 2015c). The African states all voice security concerns, particularly in respect to Boko Haram, as the reason for the bans. In 2014 Australia overturned a controversial decision to make face-veiled women sit separately when following parliamentary sessions (Aljazeera 2014). It is likely that the face-veiling debates are far from over yet.

Politics of sport

One curious realm of veiling disagreements is that of competitive sport, the most publicized example of which is football. FIFA (The International Football Federation) first introduced a ban on headscarves in 2007, but the issue eventually provoked a statement even from the United

Nations when the national Iranian women's team was prevented from playing in 2011. The Federation was forced to reconsider its decision and finally overturned the ban in 2012, having been convinced of a Dutch design company's sport-scarf's suitability for the players, (Joseph 2013). What is interesting about this eventual decision is that it considered only the safety of players, whereas the initial ban also concerned the neutrality on football fields, whereby religious, political and personal messages were forbidden (Ayub 2011). If such a policy were really to be enforced, it would of course mean the banning of, for example, religious gestures and tattoos, too.

Also swimming, gender and veils have created controversy. Gender-segregated swimming and the wearing of burkinis have provoked debates and bans especially in Europe and Australia (Karlsson Minganti 2013; Khamis 2010; Amara 2012). In summer 2016, several French towns panned the burkini on their beaches - a decision that was declared unlawful by French courts. While 'Western' media coverage of burkini swimwear has both celebrated and mocked, the garment (Fitzpatrick 2009), a constructive collaboration between designer Aheda Zanetti and the Surf Lifesaving Australia, resulted in the graduation of the first veiled lifesaver in 2007. She wore the Burqini (registered trademark, as opposed to 'burkini') when graduating, and intense media attention and massive global sales followed. Such a development can be seen as making the Australian beach a more accommodating space (Khamis 2010).

Everyday life: Debated and experienced

Even though the veil is highly politicized today, it is nevertheless the case that this political aspect is very recent when reflected against the long history of veiling practices. And despite these political complexities, for many women, the veil remains an everyday item, something that indicates religious belonging and facilitates religious practice, ensures appropriate gender relations and moral purity. These aspects of veiling cannot be fully separated from the political elements, but nevertheless are the guiding principle of veiling practices to many religious women, not only Muslims.

The major change in individual veiling practices that has happened during recent decades is primarily related to 'awareness', religious 'knowledge' and individual consciousness. From the realm of social customs and obligations, the requirements for veiling have shifted towards individual conviction, and internal purity of motivations and intentions. Yet this ideal of integrity and individual commitment to veiling does not remove social pressures and coercion, nor does it nullify the fact that in some countries, law requires women to veil, and in some environments unveiling can cause a serious risk of violence and even death. The global and local politics of veiling shape the everyday experiences of Muslim women, and strikingly similar trends in styles of veiling and discourses about veiling appear across the continents.

Islamic movements and 'pure' Islam

What had begun as re-Islamization movements in the 1970s (El-Guindi 1981; Hochel 2013) had by the 1990s developed into various reform movements – across Asia, Africa, Latin and North America and Europe – demanding the 'purification' of Islam from cultural influences (Ali 2005; Atasoy 2006; Renne 2013, Tong and Turner 2008; van Santen 2013). These movements appealed especially to young Muslims, often more cosmopolitan than their parents' generation. Religious education provided by various reform movements stressed the need for 'knowledge' of religious doctrine and religious responsibilities, framing their religious interpretations as 'pure' and 'real' Islam (Ali 2005; Alvi 2013, Brenner 1996; Fair 2013). Veiling is often advocated by (the male leaders of) such movements as a religious obligation, yet one to be chosen freely by believing women out of internal conviction and submission to God's will (Bullock 2000; de Castro 2014;

Göle 2003; Read and Bartkowski 2000; Williams and Vashi 2007). Young women who veil in a more fully covering manner than their mothers did or do, justify their choices in terms of 'knowing more' about religion than the previous generations did, thus utilizing the rhetoric common within the reform movements (Brenner 1996; Osella and Osella 2007; Tong and Turner 2008).

Women are often active in these religious movements, and although the male leaders make statements about veiling, and (male) family members may exercise levels of pressure (Body-Gendrot 2007; Gurbuz and Gurbuz-Kucuksari 2009; Killian 2003), it is often the female peer group that influences decisions to veil (Ali 2005; Atasoy 2006; Brenner 1996; Furseth 2011; Stoica 2013). Veiling in these contexts is framed as something that the woman will eventually do, once she is 'ready', and decisions to don the veil are hailed as courageous and mature (MacLeod 1987; Siraj 2011). More or less subtle peer pressure towards veiling is not seen as contradictory to the requirement of individual choice. This is not to say that veiling women would not be sincere when they say that their decision to veil was a freely made choice. The idea of freely chosen religious duty is central to new discourses about veiling, and it also allows women to resist veiling, by stating that it is too great a 'responsibility', or that they are not 'ready' (Hochel 2013).

The veil, the internal, and behaviour

The decision to don the veil may be a challenging one to make. While in many contexts and for many ethnic groups and communities, veiling is a custom casually followed, increasingly donning the veil, or donning a certain kind of veil, is associated with a requirement of honesty and purity of intentions (Brenner 1996; MacLeod 1987; Ruby 2006). A veiled woman must be internally pious and her behaviour must reflect her piety. Donning the veil and behaving in an inappropriate manner is frowned upon. Dressing in a 'modest' way means that one must also behave in a 'modest' manner (Gökarıksel and Secor 2012; Hochel 2013; Omair 2009; Tarlo 2007). What such modest behaviour means varies from one cultural context to another, but certain things, such as openly sexual relations with men, and consuming alcohol, are generally considered unfitting for a veiled woman. Through veiling, pious selves are both created and expressed. The veil, and the consciousness of its recognizability and visibility, prevent certain activities and thus function as tools for self-discipline and self-improvement (Gökarıksel and Secor 2012; Mahmood 2001; 2005; Winchester 2008).

Yet the veil functions differently in contexts where veiled women are a majority than it does where veiled women are in a minority position. A fully veiled woman may use her anonymity in order to engage in clandestine activities in countries where veiling is common (Billaud 2009; Fair 2013; Moors 2007a), but in another contexts her full veil renders her extremely visible and therefore places even more demand on her 'good' behaviour. In a minority context, a 'misbehaving' veiled woman may be seen as representing the Muslim community as a whole and therefore endangering the community's reputation (Bendixsen 2013; Zine 2006), but elsewhere she would be seen as representing her family, and her behaviour would be linked to family honour and reputation (Moors 2007a).

Yet the justifications and motivations for veiling are very similar from one place to another. Veiling is seen as an indicator of Muslim identity, as facilitating the wearer's relation to God, as providing women access to spaces and activities that might otherwise be denied from them, and as a preventer of sexual harassment (Cole and Ahmadi 2003; Furseth 2011; Heyat 2008; Maia Marques 2009; Masquelier 2013; Omair 2009; Patel 2012; Read and Bartkowski 2000; Siraj 2011; Zine 2006). Veiling women associate their form of dress with respectability and dignity. There is also a certain demand for consistency as it comes to new veiling. Many say that once the veil has been donned, it should not be removed anymore (Brenner 1996; Read and Bartkowski 2000; Smith-Hefner 2007). Such ideas have recently been challenged by women who view unveiling as part of their individual spiritual path (Lewis 2015b). It must be remembered that many Muslim women who do not veil still are practising Muslims who hold similar ideas of virtuous womanhood as their veiled peers (Fadil 2011; Killian 2007; Ruby 2006). As religion and veiling both have become more individual and individualistic, also the variety of arguments to be used for and against veiling has become widely available and usable by individual women.

Feminist arguments

Secular feminism has been critical of veiling for a long time, considering it a tool of controlling women, their bodies, and their sexuality (see e.g. Marshall 2005; Mernissi 2003 [1975]; Naghibi 1999). Many early unveilings were associated with secular feminism (although others were associated with the secularization of state), and consequently, re-Islamization and reform movements have been highly critical of feminism as external, European influence that undermines Islam and Muslim cultures. Yet Muslim feminists have defended veiling as 'liberating' (Khan 2014), and many who do not identify as feminists, or are in fact anti-feminist, use feminist arguments to justify the veil. These arguments typically include a critique of 'Western' objectification and commercialization of the female body (Franks 2000; Tarlo 2005; Williams and Vashi 2007). For many veiling women, the veil is a liberator that forces others to pay attention to the woman's character, her inner capacities, rather than focusing on external attributes and appearance (Droogsma 2007; Gurbuz and Gurbuz-Kucuksari 2009; Weitz 2001). According to such interpretations, the veil desexualizes the female body and makes her equal to men in public spaces and everyday communication, particularly where spaces are not gender-segregated (Byng 2004). The veil prevents the female body from being used for commercial or objectifying purposes.

Yet one can also argue that the veil in fact ultimately hypersexualizes the female body, and essentializes male sexuality, if the justification for it is that it prevents men from thinking sexual thoughts or experiencing sexual desire towards women in public spaces (Gould 2014; Marshall 2005; Mernissi 2003 [1975]; 1991, Ruby 2006; Zine 2006). Therefore many veiled women stress that they do not veil in order to protect men from sin, for it is men's own responsibility to lower their gaze, as the Qur'an mandates, and to control their thoughts, desires and behaviour (Furseth 2011; Haddad and Esposito 1998). Many also stress that whether they veil or not is between themselves and the God, and no business of (male) relatives or husbands (Brenner 1996; Moors 2009a).

Effects of veiling on self and others

As already indicated above, the veil is a tool of self-discipline, a means of shaping the self and behaviour. It is a reminder of one's religious status, and therefore an important part of the cultivation of pious, religious self. One important aspect of this is that the veil is supposed to prevent certain activities and forms of behaviour, such as flirting (Droogsma 2007; Fair 2013). Men are expected to recognize veiling through respectful behaviour, including averting their gaze (Alvi 2013; Billaud 2009). Many women experience a change in male attitudes towards them after donning the veil, and report a more respectful behaviour towards them especially from the part of men (Odoms-Young 2008; Williams and Vashi 2007). How well this functions will always be dependent on particular environments and contexts. In a minority context, simply wearing a scarf may be enough to communicate to men that the woman is not interested in flirting, while in some other context, a full-body veil indicating a more religious status may be necessary for the same message to get through (Patel 2012). Yet many women complain that although Muslim men should know that the hijab indicates piety and chastity, it does not prevent them from attempting to engage in flirtation with the woman. Although Muslim men may consider veiled women more 'marriageable' than their unveiled peers (Hawkins 2008; Tong and Turner 2008), they may also be cynical of the veiled woman's motivations to veil, and express this through less respectful behaviour. In such situations, a more covering form of veil may be desirable for the woman (Patel 2012).

The veil also opens and closes certain spaces for women. Many women consider it a means through which their participation in work life is enabled while they retain their respectability in the eyes of their family and community (Carvalho 2013; MacLeod 1978, 1992). Thus the veil provides economic possibilities, and certain freedom from constant family surveillance. But some public spaces are closed for a veiled woman, for she may be expected to not enter bars or even cafes and cinemas (Cole and Ahmadi 2003; Droogsma 2007; Gökarıksel and Secor 2012). In some cities, different areas are differently accessible for veiled and unveiled women since the majority dress style in each area renders a differently dressed woman highly visible, thus creating discomfort and a desire to avoid such areas that do not 'fit' with one's dress (Secor 2002; Tarlo 2007). Other areas are denied to veiled women through more formal regulations, such as legislative bans (Secor 2002).

The veil also influences the woman's relationship to her own body. Veiling seems to a certain degree to prevent the internalization of 'Western' beauty ideals, such as idealization of thinness Dunkel *et al.* 2010). Veiling also protects women against experiences of objectification, and may promote a healthier attitude towards one's body size (Swami *et al.* 2014; Tolaymat and Moradi 2011). On the other hand, veiling is particularly in Europe and North America associated with experiences of discrimination and hostility. Veiling changes others' interpretations about the veiled woman (El-Geledi and Bourhis 2012): she may be seen less an individual and more a representor of her religion, and she may even be considered less educated or less intelligent by others due to her choice of dress (Mahmud and Swami 2010). Veiled women have also been subject to workplace discrimination (or veiling bans), both in Muslim majority and minority contexts (Ali 2005; Brenner 1996; Jelen 2011; Unkelbach *et al.* 2010; Zine 2006). On the other hand, veiled women are often perceived as more attractive by veiling and non-veiling Muslim peers alike (Pasha-Zaidi 2015).

Global politics have direct consequences for veiling women in their everyday lives. One visible marker of this is the increased hostility and risk of verbal and physical attack that tends to follow well-publicized terror attacks and other incidents associated with radical Islamism (Allen and Nielsen 2002; Amnesty International 2012; Human Rights First 2007). Veiling women are often the ones most vulnerable to Islamophobic attacks following radical political violence. Yet also solidarity movements to support veiling women have appeared recently – and these have, in their turn, been criticized by some Muslim women who consider demands for veiling as overly 'conservative' (see Nomani and Arafa 2015).

Style preferences

Veils come in an extremely varied range of shapes, colours, patterns and materials. While one can make certain kinds of distinctions, such as 'conservative', 'moderate', 'fashionable', and so forth, it is the case that as styles and influences mix, it is increasingly difficult to interpret religious belongings and affiliations at any general level. As communities become increasingly cosmopolitan when people, goods and ideas travel across borders, dress styles become highly mixed, and reading motivations behind a dress style becomes increasingly difficult (Lewis 2015a; Masquelier 2013, see also Albrecht *et al.* 2015).

One trend noticeable in almost all Muslim communities is the presence of Arab influences, particularly driven by the spread of Saudi-influenced religious movements, but also influenced by Egyptian styles. These styles are often considered more 'conservative' than other styles, and they come in sober colours, and in shapes that completely cover all body shapes. These are also styles that are more covering than the 'traditional' forms of veiling in certain areas, and they are often rejected by local religious authorities and others as 'external' influences (Górak-Sosnowska and Lyszczarz 2013; Schulz 2007; van Santen 2013). Yet wearing a more covering dress may have nothing to do with more conservative religious beliefs. A woman may don a more conservative dress as a result of a heightened status following the hajj pilgrimage (van Santen 2013), she may consider the face-veil a fashionable garment that communicates her economic affluence (Fair 2013), or she may simply be accustomed with such styles of veiling among her family and acquaintances, and therefore prefer them herself (Bouteldja 2014).

Mixing and matching local styles and garments with imported goods happens both in Muslim majority and minority contexts. European hijab styles mixing high street fashions with garments imported from the Middle East, or produced by local Muslim entrepreneurs, sub-Saharan African styles drawing upon 'Western', 'African' and 'Arab' styles (Rabine 2013), and Asian fashions, combining local colourful elements with Arab sober styles (Jones 2007) are all examples of hybrid veiling fashions increasingly popular today. Consciously fashionable veiling is also a means of indicating certain kinds of belonging, in which the local context and global Muslim community are both seen as important parts of individual identity (Schulz 2007). The choice of not donning an 'Arab' veil may also be a conscious critique against 'Arab culture' in a local context (Almila 2018, Smith-Hefner 2007).

Despite the great variation between styles, Muslim veiling styles and fashions are highly distinctive, and differ from Jewish and Christian forms of veiling and modest dress (even if this may not always be recognized by 'outsiders'). Indeed, it is often important for these women that their veiling style is distinctively recognizable as representing a certain religion (Tarlo 2013). More and less covering styles, more and less 'modest' styles often indicate the level of religious commitment among Jews, and differentiate between different sects of Judaism. Details such as whether the wig a Jewish woman uses to cover her hair is made of human or artificial hair, and how 'natural' it looks indicate religious belonging and religious divisions (Carrel 2008). Veils not only draw borders between religious and non-religious people, but also between religions, affiliations and sects.

The Internet

Veiling not only draws borders but also evokes forms of solidarity. The Internet in particular has emerged as a realm where religious interpretations, similarities and differences are discussed and debated (Akou 2010). New religious discourses have developed due to access to a variety of sources that are no longer bound to local clerical authority. The Internet has enabled individuals' active participation both in searching for religious information and in creating new interpretations of religious doctrines. Veiling women change opinions, pick preferred interpretations, and encourage and critique each other in their veiling choices.

One interesting element in these discourses is that they at least potentially enhance understanding and support between religions. Cross-faith discourses are facilitated due to free access of many women to discussion fora, blogs and visual materials. While some of these discussions reflect the conflict-ridden situation between, for example, Jews and Muslims, there are also openings which stress solidarity, support and understanding between religious veiling women (Tarlo 2013).

Through the Internet, new role models for veiling women surface. Peer support and inspirational veiling narratives are widely available, but some individuals become more visible than others due to their online activities. Many of these women are reluctant to make authoritative statements about 'correct' ways of veiling but instead state that God knows best, and each woman's choice of veiling is between herself and her creator (Lewis 2015a, 2015b; Moors 2013). Such 'disclaimers' not only protect the individual woman against criticism, but also reflect the individualistic ideas of religion and veiling as personal choices based on individual faith and conviction.

Fashion and aesthetics: Production and consumption

Dress styles are intimately connected to production systems and economic conditions. The state-issued dress reforms in the Middle East created enormous demand for new garments practically overnight, and the supply markets both struggled to respond, and suffered and benefited from the changes (Wide 2014). Women's unveiling in many countries created economic possibilities for international and local garment producers alike (Kashani-Sabet 2014), but at the same time, makers of 'traditional' garments lost at least part of their clientele (Metinsoy 2014). While the 1970s new veiling was associated with solidarity, rejection of sartorial competition between women, and anti-fashion (fashion being primarily associated with 'western' garments and styles at the time), by the 1990s, the increased affluence of young veiling women had created a new market segment, which some Muslim entrepreneurs, particularly in Turkey, were quick to respond to (Navaro-Yashin 2002; Sandıkçı and Ger 2007; White 1999). Muslim fashion has recently been in the spotlight in Europe, with an increasing number of international brands consciously providing goods and collections for veiling women, acknowledging the staggering $230bn market that currently exists (Thompson Reuters 2015). Yet the history of such a garment production system is much longer, and Muslim entrepreneurs in Muslim majority and minority contexts alike have contributed to the production and distribution of Muslim fashions for decades. Similarly, for example, Paris fashion houses have for a long time already taken into account the tastes of their affluent clientele in the Gulf countries (Balasescu 2003; 2007). What seems like a very recent phenomenon has in fact been going on for some decades already.

Cultural industries

The women participating in the new veiling movements in the 1970s often found it necessary to sew their own garments for the lack of suitable supply. They were not a prime target group for fashion producers, for their interest laid in cheap and uniform clothes, rather than in conspicuous styles. But as veiling has become more common, as veiling women have gained increasing economic capital, and as veiling in a fashionable manner has increased in popularity, a significant supply market has developed to respond to the needs and desires of these women (Abaza 2007; Gökarıksel and Secor 2010; Jones 2007; Kelly 2010; Moors and Tarlo 2007). Producers and distributors in this market serve both local communities and international audiences alike. As a consequence of these new circulation systems, fashion systems have also come to overlap so that Muslim fashions in particular locations may be influenced simultaneously by 'Western', 'Arab', and local (e.g. 'African', Chinese and so forth) fashion markets (Gillette 2005; Rabine 2013). These trade routes follow historical trade connections (of import and export), the migration routes of individuals (for work and education), and tourism (such as hajj pilgrimage). Online shops are also important, especially in contexts where the local availability of suitable garments is limited (Tarlo 2010). Thus work migration to Gulf countries (Abaza 2007; Moors 2007a; Osella and Osella 2007), as well as increasing opportunities to perform the hajj (Gillette 2005; Renne 2013; van Santen 2013), have contributed to the spreading of 'Arab' styles to other countries. The significant Muslim fashion industry that has appeared in Turkey in the late twentieth century has, for example, shaped German Turkish diaspora fashions and influenced the Somali diaspora in the US too (Akou 2007; Gökarıksel and Secor 2013). Asian students in Egyptian universities have brought with them Egyptian styles when returning home (Amrullah 2008). Therefore when 'Western' brands seek to enter the field, there are two things that are useful to keep in mind. First, young Muslim women have been shopping high street brands, such as H&M, for a long time already (Moors 2009a). It seems rather slow of the brand to consider them an important enough group of consumers only now. Second, many local Muslim entrepreneurs have worked for years creating and distributing fashions for their peers (e.g. Koskennurmi-Sivonen *et al.* 2004; Mossière 2012; Österlind 2013). These business will now increasingly face competition from large mainstream high street brands targeting veiling women. Some of these small brands and shops have also contributed to the employment of Muslim women in contexts where their position in the labour market is extremely weak, as is the case in many European countries, for example. Therefore the recent trend of 'including' veiling women by some high street shops may be more controversial than it seems at first glance.

Along with fashion production and retail, fashion mediation systems also appear. Fashion advertisements (e.g. Kılıçbay and Binark 2002), fashion shows (e.g. Sandıkçı and Ger 2007), lifestyle media (e.g. Kassam 2011; Lewis 2010) and fashion blogging (e.g. Lewis 2015b; Moors 2013) are some of the new phenomena necessarily linked to the 'Islamic' fashion system. Muslim fashion imagery first appeared in a conservative form, shops and online stores self-censoring female faces and bodies in order to pacify the conservative groups among local communities (Gökarıksel and Secor 2010; Tarlo 2010). But recently, fashion blogging, video blogging, and numerous hijab tutorials widely available online, along with increasingly 'professionalized' webstores, have transformed visual imagery of 'Islamic' fashions online (Lewis 2013). With increasing diversity, cosmopolitan identification, and selective religious interpretations, local communities have less power to influence online representations of Islam and appropriate female Muslim dress. In contexts where the state controls such representations, such as in Iran, fashion shows necessarily come in a more restricted form (Balasescu 2007), yet extremely fashionable abaya styles have appeared and been exhibited, for example in the conservative Gulf States (Al-Qasimi 2010).

While the market for Jewish fashion is smaller than Muslim fashion, mostly because there is a longer history of accommodating Jewish veiling, and because only certain Jewish groups veil, it is nevertheless the case that some mainstream brands, such as Topshop, locally cater to Hasidic women's needs, for example in New York City. The Torah-observant Jewish women draw upon European and North American mainstream fashions, modifying, customizing and combining garments as appropriate (Carrel 2013). Yet the consumers' challenges are often the same for Jews and Muslims: layering and matching clothes, seeking suitable garments that can be worn in a religiously appropriate manner, and seeking to present an appearance that balances religious requirements and 'modern', fashionable styles (Almila 2018; Carrel 2013; Sandıkçı and Ger 2001, 2005).

Along with the fashion production system that supplies modest garments for everyday wear, more specific branches of the clothing industry have also developed. Some examples of these are brands producing sportswear such as sports scarves and swimwear. Modest swimwear is available for both Muslims and Jews, and has been known to be worn also by others (Fitzpatrick 2009; Shavit and Wiesenbach 2012; Tarlo 2013). For those seeking to communicate their identity through verbal or image messages, a wide variety of Muslim and Jewish T-shirts have appeared, with slogans such as '100% Muslim' or 'Jews Kick Ass' (see Silverman 2013; Tarlo 2010). Islamic alternatives for the popular Barbie doll have also been marketed in various locations (Yaqin 2007). As religious identity seems to be an increasingly important and defining factor of many individuals' identities, such industries aiming to fulfil the needs and desires of religiously identifying individuals is tapping into a vast market segment.

Fashion and anti-fashion

So new forms of conspicuous consumption have developed of late, especially among young Muslim women. The increased opportunities to shop, mix and match have also created more heterogeneous styles, often developed in contexts of increasingly cosmopolitan identities, and a consciousness of global Muslim community and belonging. Yet as fashionable veiling increases, questions as to whether fashion and religion are compatible, and whether consumption and religion can work together, abound (Gökarıksel and McLarney 2010; Kılıçbay and Binark 2002; Sandıkçı and Ger 2011). Some veiling women explicitly denounce fashion and wasteful consumption, while others see no contradiction between fashion and modesty (Almila 2016; Stoica 2013). Some consider fashionable veiling as attracting too much attention and therefore as not being in accordance with religious requirements of modesty. Some condemn certain styles, such as specific scarf-enhancing techniques, or 'too tight' garments (Sandıkçı and Ger 2005). And yet others consider explicitly anti-fashion styles, such as black abayas, as too conspicuous and therefore not religiously appropriate in certain local contexts (Almila 2016).

The compatibility of religion and fashion has been debated by both religious and secular people. First 'Islamic' fashion shows in the 1990s in Turkey were severely criticized for commercializing religion, by religious and non-religious commenters alike (Navaro-Yashin 2002; Sandıkçı and Ger 2007). Some consider the 'wasteful' consumption associated with fashion to be in discord with religious ideals. For others, Muslim fashion entrepreneurship is a positive matter, for Muhammed himself was a tradesman and as long as trade and consumption are performed in a religiously appropriate manner, there is no contradiction with religious teachings. This involves certain ethical principles such as donating to charity, and guaranteeing living wages (Akou 2007), and the idea of consumption that is not 'wasteful' (Gökarıksel and McLarney 2010). Some Jewish groups have similarly been concerned about fashionable female dress, which they see as corrupting and dangerous (Carrel 2013). Yet others, both Muslims and Jews, consider modest, fashionable styles not only acceptable but also desirable expressions of religious, yet modern identity. To be dressed in an aesthetically pleasing manner is not per se in contradiction with religion for these individuals. Rather, they want to dress fashionably within the limits of religion. For some Muslims, indeed, an aesthetic appearance is a religious duty (Kejanlioğlu and Taş 2009). They stress that 'God loves beauty', and that Muhammed was known for being handsome and taking care of his appearance.

Thus, arguments for and against fashionable veiling are multiple and varied. Similarly, arguments for and against anti-fashion veiling are mixed. Further, anti-fashion statements of many Muslim women are increasingly mixed up with secular anti-fashion arguments, including Marxist and feminist views (Moors and Tarlo 2013). Given all these possibilities, it is no surprise that individual expressions of style preference can be framed in a highly complex manner. In fact, it is often the case that no individual woman can be placed exclusively on one side of the debate only, for individual dress strategies and preferences are usually more nuanced than religious doctrines and theoretical statements (Almila 2016).

Conclusion

This chapter has sought to represent the extreme complexity of veiling phenomena around the world today, bound as they are by political, economic, social, religious, spatial and individual aspects. The rest of the chapters in this book offer more detailed, contextual analyses of specific phenomena. Each section begins with a longer, more detailed study, and is followed by a number of shorter case studies. The aim of this handbook is to offer a wide range of possible ways of understanding veils and veiling, while drawing attention to the similarities across times and locations. Particularly in terms of the latter goal, the concluding chapter will return to key questions about those global forces which influence veils and veiling across the planet today.

Veiling will not disappear. It has been practised in a rich variety of forms for thousands of years, and is today more prominent and visible than it has ever been. Veiling studies, which has developed and expanded vastly in recent years, and will likely continue to do so in the future, is in a position to touch upon a number of extremely important socioeconomic issues. What the future of the field needs, is more systematic mappings and analyses as to how the enormous amount of knowledge collected and created by researchers across the globe so far relates to globalization and globality. Veiling is a global phenomenon, as this book clearly demonstrates. Studying veiling as a truly transnational phenomenon will open new domains of enquiry within the field, and will further increase the field's relevance to other areas of study.

References

Abaza, Mona. 2007. 'Shifting Landscapes of Fashion in Contemporary Egypt'. *Fashion Theory* 11(2/3): 281–98.

Abraham, Janaki. 2010. 'Veiling and the Production of Gender and Space in a Town in North India: A Critique of the Public/Private Dichotomy'. *Indian Journal of Gender Studies* 17(2):191–222.

Abu-Lughod, Lila. 2002. 'Do Muslim Women Really Need Saving? Anthropological Reflections on Cultural Relativism and Its Others'. *American Anthropologist* 104(3):783–90.

Adak, Sevgi. 2014. 'Anti-Veiling Campaigns and Local Elites in Turkey of the 1930s: A View from the Periphery'. In *Anti-Veiling Campaigns in the Muslim World*, edited by Stephanie Cronin, 59–85. London: Routledge.

Ahmed, Leila. 1992. *Women and Gender in Islam: Historical Roots of a Modern Debate*. London: Yale University Press.

Ahmed, Leila. 2011. *A Quiet Revolution: The Veil's Resurgence, from the Middle East to America*. London: Yale University Press.

Akou, Heather Marie. 2007. 'Building a New "World Fashion": Islamic Dress in the Twenty-First Century'. *Fashion Theory* 11(4):403–22.

Akou, Heather Marie. 2010. 'Interpreting Islam through the Internet: Making Sense of Hijab'. *Contemporary Islam* 4(3):331–46.

Albrecht, Milde, Bertha Jacobs, Arda Retief and Karien Adamski. 2015. 'The Role of Important Values and Predominant Identity in the Dress Practices of Female Muslim Students Attending a South African University'. *Clothing and Textiles Research Journal* 33(4):248–64.

Ali, Syed. 2005. 'Why Here, Why Now? Young Muslim Women Wearing *Hijab*'. *The Muslim World* 95(4):515–30.

Aljazeera. 2014. 'Australia Parliament Reverses Face Veil Rule'. 20 October. Available at www.aljazeera. com/news/asia-pacific/2014/10/australia-parliament-reverses-ace-veil-rule-20141020122821122202. html (accessed 28 January 2017).

Aljazeera. 2015a. 'Congo-Brazzaville Bans Women from Wearing Full Veil'. 3 May. Available at www.aljazeera.com/news/2015/05/congo-brazzaville-bans-women-wearing-full-veil-150503172028326.html (accessed 28 January 2017).

Aljazeera. 2015b. 'Chad Arrests 62 Women for Wearing Veil after Bombings'. 15 October. Available at www.aljazeera.com/news/2015/10/chad-arrests-62-women-wearing-veils-bombings-boko-haram-151015224151781.html (accessed 28 January 2017).

Aljazeera. 2015c. 'Senegal Considers Veil Ban as Boko Haram Fears Escalate'. 19 November. Available at www.aljazeera.com/news/2015/11/senegal-considers-veil-ban-boko-haram-fears-escalate-151119081653206.html (accessed 28 January 2017).

Aljazeera. 2016. 'Bulgarian Town Bans Women from Wearing Full-Face Veils'. 27 April. Available at www.aljazeera.com/news/2016/04/bulgarian-town-bans-women-wearing-full-face-veils-160427172412993.html (accessed 28 January 2017).

Allen, Christopher and Jorgen S. Nielsen. 2002. *Summary Report on Islamophobia in the EU after 11 September 2001*. European Monitoring Centre on Racism and Xenophobia.

Allievi, Stefano 2006. 'The Shifting Significance of the Halal/Haram Frontier: Narratives on the Hijab and Other Issues'. In *Women Embracing Islam: Gender and Conversion in the West*, edited by Karin van Nieuwkerk, 120–49. Austin, TX: University of Texas Press.

Almila, Anna-Mari. 2016. 'Fashion, Anti-Fashion, Non-Fashion and Symbolic Capital: The Uses of Dress among Muslim Minorities in Finland'. *Fashion Theory* 20(1):81–102.

Almila, Anna-Mari. 2018. *Veiling in Fashion: Space and the Hijab in Minority Communities*. London: I.B.Tauris.

Al-Qasimi, Noor. 2010. 'Immodest Modesty: Accommodating Dissent and the "Abaya-as-Fashion in the Arab Gulf"'. *Journal of Middle East Women's Studies* 6(1):46–74.

Al-Saji, Alia. 2010. 'The Racialization of Muslim Veils: A Philosophical Analysis'. *Philosophy and Social Criticism* 36(8):875–902.

Alvi, Anjum 2013. 'Concealment and Revealment: The Muslim Veil in Context'. *Current Anthropology* 54(2):177–99.

Amara, Mahfoud. 2012. 'Veiled Women Athletes in the 2008 Beijing Olympics: Media Accounts'. *The International Journal of the History of Sport* 29(4):638–51.

Amnesty International. 2012. *Choice and Prejudice: Discrimination against Muslims in Europe*. London: Amnesty International.

Amrullah, Eva. 2008. 'Indonesian Muslim Fashion: Styles and Designs'. *ISIM Review* 22:22–3.

Atasoy, Yıldız. 2006. 'Governing Women's Morality: A Study of Islamic Veiling in Canada'. *European Journal of Cultural Studies* 9(2):203–21.

Ayub, Awista. 2011. 'A Closer Look at FIFA's Hijab Ban: What It Means for Muslim Players and Lessons Learned'. *SAIS Review* 31(1):43–50.

Balasescu, Alexandru. 2003. 'Tehran Chic: Islamic Headscarves, Fashion Designers, and New Geographies of Modernity'. *Fashion Theory* 7(1):39–56.

Balasescu, Alexandru. 2007. 'Haute Couture in Tehran: Two Faces of an Emerging Fashion Scene'. *Fashion Theory* 11(2/3):299–318.

Batur, Ayse Lucie. 2012. 'Mythology of the Veil in Europe: A Brief History of a Debate'. *Comparative Studies of South Asia, Africa and the Middle East* 32(1):156–68.

Behiery, Valerie. 2012. 'Alternative Narratives of the Veil in Contemporary Art'. *Comparative Studies of South Asia, Africa and the Middle East* 32(1):130–46.

Bendixsen, Synnøve. 2013. '"I Love my Prophet": Religious Taste, Consumption and Distinction in Berlin'. In *Islamic Fashion and Anti-Fashion*, edited by Emma Tarlo and Annelies Moors, 272–90. London: Bloomsbury.

Billaud, Julie. 2009. 'Visible under the Veil: Dissimulation, Performance and Agency in an Islamic Public Space'. *Journal of International Women's Studies* 11(1):120–35.

Body-Gendrot, Sophie. 2007. 'France Upside Down over a Head Scarf?'. *Sociology of Religion* 68(3):298–304.

Bouteldja, Naima. 2014. 'France vs. England'. In *The Experiences of Face Veil Wearers in Europe and the Law*, edited by Eva Brems, 115–60. Cambridge: Cambridge University Press.

Bowen, John. 2007. *Why the French Don't Like Headscarves: Islam, the State, and Public Space*. Princeton, NJ: Princeton University Press.

Bracke, Sarah and Nadia Fadil. 2012. 'Is the Headscarf Oppressive or Emancipatory? Field Notes from the Multicultural Debate'. *Religion and Gender* 2(1):36–56.

Brems, Eva. 2014a. 'Introduction to the Volume'. In *The Experiences of Face Veil Wearers in Europe and the Law*, edited by Eva Brems, 1–16. Cambridge: Cambridge University Press.

Brems, Eva, ed. 2014b. *The Experiences of Face Veil Wearers in Europe and the Law*. Cambridge: Cambridge University Press.

Brems, Eva, Yaiza Janssense, Kim Lecoyer, Saïla Ouald Chaib, Victoria Vandersteen and Jogchum Vrielink. 2014. 'The Belgian "Burqa Ban" Confronted with Insider Realities'. In *The Experiences of Face Veil Wearers in Europe and the Law*, edited by Eva Brems, 77–114. Cambridge: Cambridge University Press.

Brenner, Suzanne. 1996. 'Reconstructing Self and Society: Javanese Muslim Women and "The Veil"'. *American Ethnologist* 23(4):673–97.

Brunner, Georg. 1989. 'The Status of Muslims in the Federative Systems of the Soviet Union and Yugoslavia'. In *Muslim Communities Re-emerge*, edited by Edward Allworth, 183–213. Durham, NC: Duke University Press.

Bullock, Katherine. 2000. 'Challenging Media Representation of the Veil: Contemporary Muslim Women's Re-veiling Movement'. *American Journal of Islamic Social Sciences* 17(3):22–53.

Byng, Michelle D. 2004. 'Sexism, Racism and African American Muslim Women: What Does Wearing *Hijab* Mean to Them?'. In *Race and Ethnicity – Across Time, Space and Discipline*, edited by Rodney Coates, 351–64. Boston, MA: Brill Academic Publishers.

Byng, Michelle D. 2010. 'Symbolically Muslim: Media, Hijab, and the West'. *Critical Sociology* 36(1):109–29.

Cameron, Jane. 2013. 'Modest Motivations: Religious and Secular Contestation in the Fashion Field'. In *Modest Fashion*, edited by Reina Lewis, 137–56. London: I.B.Tauris.

Carrel, Barbara Goldman. 2008. 'Shattered Vessels That Contain Divine Sparks: Unveiling Hasidic Women's Dress Code'. In *The Veil: Women Writers on Its History, Lore, and Politics*, edited by Jennifer Heath, 44–59. Berkeley, CA: University of California Press.

Carrel, Barbara Goldman. 2013. 'Hasidic Women's Fashion Aesthetic'. In *Modest Fashion*, edited by Reina Lewis, 91–117. London: I.B.Tauris.

Carvalho, Jean-Paul. 2013. 'Veiling'. *The Quarterly Journal of Economics* 128(1):337–70.

Clayer, Nathalies. 2014. 'Behind the Veil: The Reform of Islam in Interwar Albania or the Search for a "Modern" and "European" Islam'. In *Anti-Veiling Campaigns in the Muslim World*, edited by Stephanie Cronin, 231–51. London: Routledge.

Cole, Darnell and Shafiqa Ahmadi. 2003. 'Perspectives and Experiences of Muslim Women Who Veil on College Campuses'. *Journal of College Student Development* 44(1):47–66.

de Castro, Cristina Maria. 2014. 'The Construction of Muslim Identities: A Comparative Perspective between Two São Paulo Communities'. *Dados* 57(4):1043–76.

Droogsma, Rachel Anderson. 2007. 'Redefining Hijab: American Muslim Women's Standpoints on Veiling'. *Journal of Applied Communication Research* 35(3):294–319.

Duits, Linda and Liesbet van Zoonen. 2006. 'Headscarves and Porno-Chic: Disciplining Girls' Bodies in the European Multicultural Society'. *European Journal of Women's Studies* 13(2):103–17.

Dunkel, Trisha M., Denise Davidson and Shaji Qurashi. 2010. 'Body Satisfaction and Pressure to Be Thin in Younger and Older Muslim and non-Muslim Women: The Role of Western and non-Western Dress Preferences'. *Body Image* 7:56–65.

Duval, Soroya. 1997. 'New Veils and New Voices: Islamist Women's Groups in Egypt'. In *Women and Islamization*, edited by Karin Ask and Marit Tjomsland, 43–72. Oxford: Berg.

Edmunds, June. 2012. 'The Limits of Post-national Citizenship: European Muslims, Human Rights and the Hijab'. *Ethnic and Racial Studies* 35(7):1181–99.

El-Geledi, Shaha and Richard Y. Bourhis. 2012. 'Testing the Impact of the Islamic Veil on Intergroup Attitudes and Host Community Acculturation Orientations toward Arab Muslims'. *International Journal of Intercultural Relations* 36:694–706.

El-Guindi, Fadwa. 1981. 'Veiling Infitah with Muslim Ethic: Egypt's Contemporary Islamic Movement'. *Social Problems* 28(4):465–85.

El-Guindi, Fadwa. 1999. *Veil: Modesty, Privacy and Resistance*. Oxford: Berg.

Fadil, Nadia. 2011. 'Not-/unveiling as an Ethical Practice'. *Feminist Review* 98:83–109.

Fair, Laura. 2013. 'Veiling, Fashion and Social Mobility: A Century of Change in Zanzibar'. In *Veiling in Africa*, edited by Elisha P. Renne, 15–33. Bloomington: Indiana University Press.

Fanon, Frantz. 1989 [1959]. *Studies in a Dying Colonialism*. London: Earthscan.

Ferrari, Alessandro and Sabrina Pastorelli, eds. 2013. *The Burqa Affair across Europe: Between Public and Private Space*. London: Routledge.

Fitzpatrick, Shanon. 2009. 'Covering Muslim Women at the Beach: Media Representations of the Burkini'. *Thinking Gender Papers*, UCLA Center for the Study of Women, UC Los Angeles.

Franks, Myfanwy. 2000. 'Crossing the Borders of Whiteness? White Muslim Women Who Wear the Hijab in Britain Today'. *Ethnic and Racial Studies* 23(5):917–29.

Furseth, Inger. 2011. 'The Hijab: Boundary Work and Identity Negotiations among Immigrant Muslim Women in the Los Angeles Area'. *Review of Religious Research* 52(4):365–85.

Ghumkhor, Sahar. 2012. 'The Veil and Modernity: The Case of Tunisia'. *Interventions: International Journal of Postcolonial Studies* 14(4):493–514.

Gillette, Maris. 2005. 'Fashion among Chinese Muslims'. *ISIM Review* 15:36–7.

Gökarıksel, Banu and Ellen McLarney. 2010. 'Introduction: Muslim Women, Consumer Capitalism, and the Islamic Culture Industry'. *Journal of Middle East Women's Studies* 6(3):1–18.

Gökarıksel, Banu and Anna Secor. 2010. 'Between Fashion and Tesettür: Marketing and Consuming Women's Islamic Dress'. *Journal of Middle East Women's Studies* 6(3):118–48.

Gökarıksel, Banu and Anna Secor. 2012. '"Even I Was Tempted": The Moral Ambivalence and Ethical Practice of Veiling-Fashion in Turkey'. *Annals of the Association of American Geographers* 102(4):847–62.

Gökarıksel, Banu and Anna Secor. 2013. 'Transnational Networks of Veiling-Fashion between Turkey and Western Europe'. In *Islamic Fashion and Anti-Fashion*, edited by Emma Tarlo and Annelies Moors, 157–67. London: Bloomsbury.

Göle, Nilüfer. 2003. 'The Voluntary Adoption of Islamic Stigma Symbols'. *Social Research* 70(3):809–28.

Górak-Sosnowska, Katarzyna and Michael Lyszczarz. 2013. 'Perspectives on Muslim Dress in Poland: A Tatar View'. In *Islamic Fashion and Anti-Fashion*, edited by Emma Tarlo and Annelies Moors, 93–104. London: Bloomsbury.

Gould, Rebecca. 2014. 'Hijab as Commodity Form: Veiling, Unveiling, and Misveiling in Contemporary Iran'. *Feminist Theory* 15(3):221–40.

Graybill, Beth and Linda B. Arthur. 1999. 'The Social Control of Women's Bodies in Two Mennonite Communities'. In *Religion, Dress and the Body*, edited by Linda B. Arthur. Oxford: Berg.

Greene, D. Wendy. 2013. 'A Multidimensional Analysis of What Not to Wear in the Workplace: Hijabs and Natural Hair'. *FIU Law Review* 8:331–62.

Gurbuz, Mustafa E. and Gulsum Gurbuz-Kucuksari. 2009. 'Between Sacred Codes and Secular Consumer Society: The Practice of Headscarf Adoption among American College Girls'. *Journal of Muslim Minority Affairs* 29(3):387–99.

Haddad, Yvonne Yazbeck. 2007. 'The Post 9/11 Hijab as Icon'. *Sociology of Religion* 68(3):253–67.

Hämeen-Anttila, Jaakko. 2004. *Islamin käsikirja*. Helsinki: Otava.

Hawkins, Simon. 2008. 'Hijab: Feminine Allure and Charm to Men in Tunis'. *Ethnology* 47(1):1–21.

Hawley, Jana M. 2008. 'The Amish Veil: Symbol of Separation and Community'. In *The Veil: Women Writers on Its History, Lore, and Politics*, edited by Jennifer Heath, 90–8. Berkeley, CA: University of California Press.

Hirschmann, Nancy J. 1998. 'Western Feminism, Eastern Veiling, and the Question of Free Agency'. *Constellations* 5(3):345–68.

Hochel, Sandra. 2013. 'To Veil or Not to Veil: Voices of Malaysian Muslim Women'. *Intercultural Communication Studies* 22(2):40–57.

Hoodfar, Homa. 1997. 'The Veil in Their Minds and on Our Heads'. In *The Politics of Culture in the Shadow of Capital*, edited by Lisa Lowe and David Lloyd, 248–79. Durham, NC: Duke University Press.

Human Rights First. 2007. *Islamophobia: 2007 Hate Crime Survey*. New York: Human Rights First.

Jones, Carla. 2007. 'Fashion and Faith in Urban Indonesia'. *Fashion Theory* 11(2/3):211–32.

Joseph, Suad. 2013. *Muslim Women in Sports: Participation worldwide*. EWIC Staff Report.

Kamp, Marianne. 2014. 'Women-Initiated Unveiling: State-Led Campaigns in Uzbekistan and Azerbaijan'. In *Anti-Veiling Campaigns in the Muslim World*, edited by Stephanie Cronin, 205–28. London: Routledge.

Karlsson Minganti, Pia. 2013. 'Burqinis, Bikinis and Bodies: Encounters in Public Pools in Italy and Sweden'. In *Islamic Fashion and Anti-Fashion*, edited by Emma Tarlo and Annelies Moors, 33–54. London: Bloomsbury.

Kashani-Saget, Firoozeh. 2014. 'Dressing Up (or Down): Veils, Hats and Consumer Fashions in Interwar Iran'. In *Anti-Veiling Campaigns in the Muslim World*, edited by Stephanie Cronin, 149–62. London: Routledge.

Kassam, Shelina. 2011. 'Marketing an Imagined Muslim Woman: Muslim Girl Magazine and the Politics of Race, Gender and Representation'. *Social Identities: Journal for the Study of Race, Nation and Culture* 17(4):543–64.

Kejanlioğlu, D. Beybin and Oğuzhan Taş. 2009. 'Regimes of Un/veiling and Body Control: Turkish Students Wearing Wigs'. *Social Anthropology* 17(4):424–38.

Kelly, Marjorie. 2010. 'Clothes, Culture, and Context: Female Dress in Kuwait'. *Fashion Theory* 14(2):215–36.

Khamis, Susie. 2010. 'Braving the BurqiniTM: Re-branding the Australian Beach'. *Cultural Geographies* 17(3):379–90.

Khan, Masood. 2014. 'The Muslim Veiling: A Symbol of Oppression or a Tool of Liberation?'. *UMASA Journal* 32:1–11.

Kılıçbay, Barış and Mutlu Binark. 2002. 'Consumer Culture, Islam and the Politics of Lifestyle: Fashion for Veiling in Contemporary Turkey'. *European Journal of Communication* 17(4):495–511.

Killian, Caitlin. 2003. 'The Other Side of the Veil: North African Women in France Respond to the Headscarf Affair'. *Gender & Society* 17(4):567–90.

Killian, Caitlin. 2007. 'From a Community of Believers to an Islam of the Heart: "Conspicuous" Symbols, Muslim Practices, and the Privatization of Religion in France'. *Sociology of Religion* 68(3):305–20.

Koskennurmi-Sivonen, Ritva, Jaana Koivula and Seija Maijala. 2004. 'United Fashions – Making a Muslim Appearance in Finland'. *Fashion Theory* 8(4):443–60.

Lafontaine, Laurence M. 2008. 'Out of the Cloister: Unveiling to Better Serve the Gospel'. In *The Veil: Women Writers on Its History, Lore, and Politics*, edited by Jennifer Heath, 75–89. Berkeley, CA: University of California Press.

Lentin, Alana and Gavan Titley. 2012. 'The Crisis of Multiculturalism in Europe: Mediated Minarets, Intolerable Subjects'. *European Journal of Cultural Studies* 15(2):123–38.

Lentin, Ronit. 2012. 'Turbans, *Hijabs* and Other Differences: "Integration from below" and Irish Interculturalism'. *European Journal of Cultural Studies* 15(2):226–42.

Levine, Molly Myerowitz. 1995. Gendered Grammar of Ancient Mediterranean Hair. In *Off with Her Head!*, edited by Howard Eilberg-Schwartz and Wendy Doniger, 76–130. Berkeley, CA: University of California Press.

Lewis, Reina. 1999. 'On Veiling, Vision and Voyage'. *Interventions: International Journal of Postcolonial Studies* 1(4):500–20.

Lewis, Reina. 2010. 'Marketing Muslim Lifestyle: A New Media Genre'. *Journal of Middle East Women's Studies*, 6(3):58–90.

Lewis, Reina. 2013. 'Fashion Forward and Faith-tastic: Online Modest Fashion and the Development of Women as Religious Interpreters and Intermediaries'. In *Modest Fashion*, edited by Reina Lewis, 41–66. London: I.B.Tauris.

Lewis, Reina. 2015a. *Muslim Fashion: Contemporary Style Cultures*. Durham, NC: Duke University Press.

Lewis, Reina. 2015b. 'Uncovering Modesty: Dejabis and Dewigies Expanding the Parameters of the Modest Fashion Blogosphere'. *Fashion Theory* 19(2):243–70.

Libal, Kathryn. 2014. 'From Face Veil to Cloche Hat: The Backward Ottoman versus New Turkish Woman in Urban Public Discourse'. In *Anti-Veiling Campaigns in the Muslim World*, edited by Stephanie Cronin, 39–58. London: Routledge.

McGoldrick, Dominic. 2006. *Human Rights and Religion: The Islamic Headscarf Debate in Europe*. Oxford: Hart.

McLarney, Ellen. 2009. 'The Burqa in Vogue: Fashioning Afghanistan'. *Journal of Middle East Women's Studies* 5(1):1–23.

MacLeod, Arlene Elowe. 1987. *Accommodating Protest: Working Women, the New Veiling and Change in Cairo*. New York: Columbia University Press.

MacLeod, Arlene Elowe. 1992. 'Hegemonic Relations and Gender Resistance: The New Veiling as Accommodating Protest in Cairo'. *Signs* 17(3):533–57.

Magnet, Shoshana and Rodgers, Tara. 2012. 'Stripping for the State'. *Feminist Media Studies* 12(1):101–18.

Mahmood, Saba. 2001. 'Feminist Theory, Embodiment, and the Docile Agent: Some Reflections on the Egyptian Islamic Revival'. *Cultural Anthropology* 16(2):202–36.

Mahmood, Saba. 2005. *Politics of Piety: The Islamic Revival and the Feminist Subject*. Princeton, NJ: Princeton University Press.

Mahmud, Yusr and Viren Swami. 2010. 'The Influence of the Hijab (Islamic Head-Covering) on Perceptions of Women's Attractiveness and Intelligence'. *Body Image* 7(1):90–3.

Maia Marques, Vera Lúcia. 2009. 'Sobre Práticas Religiosas e Culturais Islâmicas no Brasil e em Portugal: Notas e Observações de Viagem', PhD thesis, Universidade Federal de Minas Gerais.

Masquelier, Adeline. 2013. 'Modest Bodies, Stylish Selves: Fashioning Virtue in Niger'. In *Veiling in Africa*, edited by Elisha B. Renne, 110–36. London: Bloomsbury.

Marshall, Gül Aldikaçti. 2005. 'Ideology, Progress, and Dialogue: A Comparison of Feminist and Islamist Women's Approaches to the Issues of Head Covering and Work in Turkey'. *Gender & Society* 19(1):104–20.

Meer, Nasar, Claire Dwyer and Tariq Modood. 2010. 'Embodying Nationhood: Conceptions of British national identity, citizenship, and Gender in the "Veil Affair"'. *The Sociological Review* 58(1):84–111.

Mernissi, Fatima. 1991. *Women and Islam: An Historical and Theological Enquiry*. Oxford: Blackwell.

Mernissi, Fatima. 2003 [1975]. *Beyond the Veil: Male–Female Dynamics in Modern Muslim Society*. London: Saqi.

Metinsoy, Murat. 2014. 'Everyday Resistance to Un-veiling and Flexible Secularism in Early Republican Turkey'. In *Anti-Veiling Campaigns in the Muslim World*, Stephanie Cronin, 86–118. London: Routledge.

Moore, Kathleen M. 2007. 'Visible through the Veil: The Regulation of Islam in American Law'. *Sociology of Religion* 68(3):237–51.

Moors, Annelies. 2007a. 'Fashionable Muslims: Notions of Self, Religion, and Society in San'a'. *Fashion Theory* 11(2/3):319–46.

Moors, Annelies. 2007b. '"Burka" in Parliament and on the Catwalk'. *ISIM Review* 19:5.

Moors, Annelies. 2009a. '"Islamic Fashion" in Europe: Religious Conviction, Aesthetic Style and Creative Consumption'. *Encounters* 1:175–201.

Moors, Annelies. 2009b. 'The Dutch and the Face-Veil: The Politics of Discomfort'. *Social Anthropology* 17(4):393–408.

Moors, Annelies. 2013. '"Discover the Beauty of Modesty": Islamic Fashion Online'. In *Modest Fashion*, edited by Reina Lewis, 17–40. London: I.B.Tauris.

Moors, Annelies. 2014. 'Face Veiling in the Netherlands: Public Debates and Women's Narratives'. In *The Experiences of Face Veil Wearers in Europe and the Law*, edited by Eva Brems, 19–41. Cambridge: Cambridge University Press.

Moors, Annelies and Emma Tarlo. 2007. 'Introduction'. *Fashion Theory* 11(2/3):133–42.

Moors, Annelies and Emma Tarlo. 2013. 'Introduction'. In *Islamic Fashion and Anti-Fashion*, edited by Emma Tarlo and Annelies Moors, 1–29. London: Bloomsbury.

Mossière, Géraldine. 2012. 'Modesty and Style in Islamic Attire: Refashioning Muslim Garments in a Western Context'. *Contemporary Islam* 6(2):115–34.

Murphy, Robert F. 1964. 'Social Distance and Veil'. *American Anthropologist* 66(6):1257–74.

Naghibi, Nima. 1999. 'Bad Feminist or Bad-Hejabi?'. *Interventions: International Journal of Postcolonial Studies* 1(4):555–71.

Navaro-Yashin, Yael. 2002. 'The Market for Identities: Secularism, Islamism, Commodities'. In *Fragments of Culture: The Everyday of Modern Turkey*, edited by Deniz Kandiyoi and Ayşe Saktanber, 221–53. New Brunswick, NJ: Rutgers University Press.

Neuburger, Mary. 2014. 'Difference Unveiled: Bulgarian National Imperatives and the Re-Dressing of Muslim Women, 1878–1989'. In *Anti-Veiling Campaigns in the Muslim World*, edited by Stephanie Cronin, 252–66. London: Routledge.

Nomani, Asra Q. and Hala Arafa. 2015. 'As Muslim Women, We Actually Ask You Not to Wear the Hijab in the Name of Interfaith Solidarity'. *Washington Post*, 21 December. Available at www.washington post.com/news/acts-of-faith/wp/2015/12/21/as-muslim-women-we-actually-ask-you-not-to-wear-the-hijab-in-the-name-of-interfaith-solidarity/ (accessed 28 January 2017).

Odoms-Young, Angela. 2008. 'Factors that Influence Body Image Representations of Black Muslim Women'. *Social Science & Medicine* 66:2573–84.

Omair, Katlin. 2009. 'Arab Women Managers and Identity Formation through Clothing'. *Gender in Management: An International Journal* 24(6):412–31.

Onar, Nora Fisher and Meltem Müftüler-Baç. 2011. 'The Adultery and Headscarf Debates in Turkey: Fusing "EU-niversal" and "alternative" modernities?'. *Women's Studies International Forum* 34:378–89.

Osella, Caroline and Filippo Osella. 2007. 'Muslim Style in South India'. *Fashion Theory* 11(2/3):233–52.

Østergaard, Kate, Margit Warburg and Birgitte Schepelern Johansen. 2014. 'Niqabis in Denmark: When Politicians Ask for a Qualitative and Quantitative Profile of a Very Small and Elusive Subculture'. In *The Experiences of Face Veil Wearers in Europe and the Law*, edited by Eva Brems, 42–76. Cambridge: Cambridge University Press.

Österlind, Leila Karin. 2013. 'Made in France: Islamic Fashion Companies on Display'. In *Islamic Fashion and Anti-Fashion*, Emma Tarlo and Annelies Moors, 168–80. London: Bloomsbury.

Papanek, Hanna. 1973. 'Purdah: Separate Worlds and Symbolic Shelter'. *Comparative Studies in Society and History* 15(3):289–325.

Pasha-Zaidi, Nausheen. 2015. 'The Hijab Effect: An Exploratory Study of the Influence of Hijab and Religiosity on Perceived Attractiveness of Muslim Women in the United States and the United Arab Emirates'. *Ethnicities* 15(5):1–17.

Patel, David S. 2012. 'Concealing to Reveal: The Informational Role of Islamic Dress'. *Rationality and Society* 24(3):295–323.

Rabine, Leslie. 2013. 'Religious Modesty, Fashionable Glamour, and Cultural Text: Veiling in Senegal'. In *Veiling in Africa*, edited by Elisha B. Renne, 85–109. London: Bloomsbury.

Rantanen, Pekka. 2005. 'Non-documentary Burqa Pictures on the Internet Ambivalence and the Politics of Representation'. *International Journal of Cultural studies* 8(3):329–51.

Read, Jen'Nan Ghazal and John P. Bartkowski. 2000. 'To Veil or Not to Veil? A Case Study of Identity Negotiation among Muslim Women in Austin, Texas'. *Gender and Society* 14(3):395–417.

Renne, Elisha. 2013. 'Intertwined Veiling Histories in Nigeria'. In *Veiling in Africa*, edited by Elisha B. Renne, 58–81. London: Bloomsbury.

Ribeiro, Aileen. 2003 [1986]. *Dress and Morality*. Oxford: Berg.

Rostam-Kolayi, Jasamin and Afshin Matin-Asgari. 2014. 'Unveiling Ambiguities: Revisiting 1930s Iran's kashf-i hijab Campaign'. In *Anti-Veiling Campaigns in the Muslim World*, Stephanie Cronin, 121–48. London: Routledge.

Ruby, Tabassum F. 2006. 'Listening to the Voices of Hijab'. *Women's Studies International Forum* 29(1):54–66.

Saktanber, Ayşe and Gül Çorbacioğlu. 2008. 'Veiling and Headscarf-Skepticism in Turkey'. *Social Politics* 15(4):514–38.

Sandıkçı, Özlem and Güliz Ger. 2001. 'Fundamental Fashions: The Cultural Politics of the Turban and the Levi's'. In *Advances in Consumer Research*, Vol. 28, edited by Mary C. Gilly and Joan Meyers-Levy, 146–50. Valdosta, GA: Association for Consumer Research.

Sandıkçı, Özlem and Güliz Ger. 2005. 'Aesthetics, Ethics and Politics of the Turkish Headscarf'. In *Clothing as Material Culture*, edited by Susanne Küchler and Daniel Miller, 61–82. Oxford: Berg.

Sandıkçı, Özlem and Güliz Ger. 2007. 'Constructing and Representing the Islamic Consumer in Turkey'. *Fashion Theory* 11(2/3):189–210.

Sandıkçı, Özlem and Güliz Ger. 2011. 'Islam, Consumption and Marketing: Going beyond the Essentialist Approaches'. In *The Handbook of Islamic Marketing*, edited by Özlem Sandıkçı and Gillian Rice, 484–502. Cheltenham: Edward Elgar Publishing.

Scott, Joan Wallach. 2005. 'Symptomatic Politics: The Banning of Islamic Head Scarves in French Public Schools'. *French Politics, Culture & Society* 23(3):106–27.

Scott, Joan Wallach. 2007. *The Politics of the Veil*. Princeton, NJ: Princeton University Press.

Secor, Anna J. 2002. 'The Veil and Urban Space in Istanbul: Women's Dress, Mobility and Islamic Knowledge'. *Gender, Place & Culture* 9(1):5–22.

Sedghi, Hamideh. 2007. *Women and Politics in Iran: Veiling, Unveiling, and Reveiling*. Cambridge: Cambridge University Press.

Shakeri, E. 1998. 'Muslim Women in Canada: Their Role and Status as Revealed in the *Hijab* Controversy'. In *Muslims on the Americanization Path?*, edited by Y. Y. Haddad and J. L. Esposito, 129–44. Atlanta, GA: Scholars Press.

Shavit, Uriya and Frederic Wiesenbach. 2012. 'An "Integrating Enclave": The Case of Al-Hayat, Germany's First Islamic Fitness Center for Women in Cologne'. *Journal of Muslim Minority Affairs* 32(1):47–61.

Shirazi, Faegheh. 2001. *The Veil Unveiled: The Hijab in Modern Culture*. Gainesville, FL: University Press of Florida.

Silverman, Eric. 2013. *A Cultural History of Jewish Dress*. London: Bloomsbury.

Siraj, Asifa. 2011. 'Meanings of Modesty and the *Hijab* amongst Muslim Women in Glasgow, Scotland'. *Gender, Place & Culture* 18(6):716–31.

Smith-Hefner, Nancy J. 2007. 'Javanese Women and the Veil in Post-Soeharto Indonesia'. *The Journal of Asian Studies* 66(2):389–420.

Stoica, Daniela. 2013. 'The Clothing Dilemmas of Transylvanian Muslim Converts'. In *Islamic Fashion and Anti-Fashion*, edited by Emma Tarlo and Annelies Moors, 260-71. London: Bloomsbury.

Swami, Viren, Jusnara Miah, Nazerine Noorani. and Donna Taylor. 2014. 'Is the Hijab Protective? An Investigation of Body Image and Related Constructs among British Muslim Women'. *British Journal of Psychology* 105:352–63.

Tarlo, Emma. 2005. 'Reconsidering Stereotypes: Anthropological Reflections on the Jilbab Controversy'. *Anthropology Today* 21(6):13–7.

Tarlo, Emma. 2007. 'Hijab in London: Metamorphosis, Resonance and Effects'. *Journal of Material Culture* 12(2):131–56.

Tarlo, Emma. 2010. *Visibly Muslim: Fashion, Politics, Faith*. Oxford: Berg.

Tarlo, Emma. 2013. 'Meeting through Modesty: Jewish–Muslim Encounters on the Internet'. In *Modest Fashion: Styling Bodies, Mediating Faith*, edited by Reina Lewis, 67–90. London: I.B.Tauris.

Thompson Reuters. 2015. 'State of the Global Islamic Economy'. *Thompson Reuters's Zawya*. Available at www.zawya.com/ifg-publications/IslamicEconomy15–251114170832G/ (accessed 28 January 2017).

Todd, Sharon. 1998. 'Veiling the "Other," Unveiling Our "Selves": Reading Media Images of the Hijab Psychoanalytically to Move beyond Tolerance'. *Canadian Journal of Education* 23(4):438–51.

Tolaymat, Lana D. and Bonnie Moradi. 2011. 'U.S. Muslim Women and Body Image: Links among Objectification Theory Constructs and the Hijab'. *Journal of Counseling Psychology* 58(3):383–92.

Tong, Joy Kooi-Chin and Bryan S. Turner. 2008. 'Women, Piety and Practice: A Study of Women and Religious Practice in Malaysia'. *Contemporary Islam* 2(1):41–59.

Turner, Bryan S. 2008 [1984]. *The Body & Society*, 3rd edition. London: Sage.

Unkelbach, Christian, Hella Schneider, Kai Gode and Miriam Senft. 2010. 'A Turban Effect, Too: Selection Biases against Women Wearing Muslim Headscarves'. *Social Psychological and Personality Science* 1(4):378–83.

Vakulenko, Anastasia. 2012. *Islamic Veiling in Legal Discourse*. Oxon: Routledge.

van Santen, José C. M. 2013. ' "Should a Good Muslim Cover Her Face?" Pilgrimage, Veiling, and Fundamentalisms in Cameroon'. In *Veiling in Africa*, edited by Elisha P. Renne, 137–63. London: Bloomsbury.

Walton-Roberts, Margaret. 1998. 'Three Readings of the Turban: Sikh Identity in Greater Vancouver'. *Urban Geography* 19(4):311–31.

Weber, Beverly M. 2012. 'Hijab Martyrdom, Headscarf Debates: Rethinking Violence, Secularism, and Islam in Germany'. *Comparative Studies of South Asia, Africa and the Middle East* 32(1):102–15.

Webster, Sheila K. 1984. 'Harīm and Hijāb: Seclusive and Exclusive Aspects of Traditional Muslim Dwelling and Dress'. *Women's Studies International Forum* 7(4):251–7.

Weitz, Rose. 2001. 'Women and Their Hair: Seeking Power through Resistance and Accommodation'. *Gender and Society* 15(5):667–86.

Westerfield, Jennifer M. 2006. 'Behind the Veil: An American Legal Perspective on the European Headscarf Debate'. *The American Journal of Comparative Law* 54(3):637–78.

PART I

Politics

2

NEOLIBERALIZATION AND *HOMO ISLAMECONOMICUS*

The politics of women's veiling in Turkey[1]

Yıldız Atasoy

This chapter locates the politics of women's veiling in Turkey within the process of 'neoliberalization'. This process reflects a *gradual shift* from the state-led developmentalist model, implemented in various forms since the 1930s, to the institutionalization of the neoliberal model of capitalist development which began in the 1980s. During this period there has been a significant shift in the government's attitude toward female students wearing the headscarf at university. A ban on the headscarf was imposed on women in schools after the 1980 military coup. Eventually, the Justice and Development Party (AKP) government implemented a two-stage partial lifting of the ban in 2012 and 2013. This chapter explores the relationship between a 'neoliberal turn' in the economy and the lifting of the ban. I use the term veil and veiling to refer to women's headscarf-wearing practices in Turkey.

The following analysis is based on data drawn from the published documents of various Islamic organizations and trade unions, as well as official statistics, and interviews which I conducted with 20 headscarf-wearing university students in 2009 and 2011 (a period when the headscarf ban was strictly enforced). The students were in their 20s.

The incorporation of the religious realm into a neoliberal remaking of the social is a theoretically significant empirical question. However, the chapter avoids a narrow identification of religious concerns with the economic interests of people who are religious – an analytical position dominant in the 'sociology of knowledge' (Mannheim 1986 [1929]). From the perspective of this chapter, then, Muslim women's veiling is not exterior to the neoliberal process of restructuring capitalism but lies *within* that process of making a neoliberal history (cf. Callinicos 2009). That is to say, it cognitively enables people to 'sense-make' within a specific ontological orientation. This is also significant because it responds to the inadequacy of existing research which continues to place women's veiling within the old modernization paradigm, often evoking emotionally charged and divergent reactions as to the modernity (or traditionalism) of women who wear, or are opposed to wearing, the veil.

There is a large body of literature which reflects similar and contrasting views in its examination of local circumstances that affect women's individual choices regarding the veil. Those who focus on state-required 'compulsory veiling' in Iran (Afshar 1998; Moghadam 1991) have analysed the veil as a symbol of women's subordination to men which restricts personal freedom and is inimical to women's agency. Others who examine 'voluntary veiling' in Egypt where the dominant cultural ideology is seen as not being conducive to women's education and paid employment (Hoodfar 1997; MacLeod 1991) develop the opposite argument. They conceptualize veiling as a personal strategy adopted by Muslim women to gain access to the public sphere of paid employment and education while maintaining their honour and religiosity. In contrast to the first group of scholars who examine the subordinating effects of cultural practices whereby women appear to passively accept their own subordination, the second group of researchers attributes greater *autonomy* to women, conceptualizing their voluntary veiling as an outcome of purposeful deliberation intended to bypass culturally subordinating norms.

Although there is no commonly shared understanding of the meaning of Muslim women's veiling practices, it is widely accepted in the literature that Muslim women are subordinate to men and that they should choose to act against their conditions of subordination and inequality. This subordination is often linked to the religion of Islam, which is portrayed as inherently misogynistic and a threat to the egalitarian, democratic principles of modernity (Ho 2007). Women's subordination is also explained as historically specific to the Muslim cultural politics of reconfiguring dominant gender norms, which supposes women to be obedient, submissive and humble in society (Ahmed 1992; Mernissi 1996). Regardless of the perspective, Muslim women are generally expected to make a choice between accepting their condition of subordination and acting as '*agentic religious subjects*' committed to advancing individual agendas (Korteweg 2008) against those conditions. The donning of the veil, then, is viewed either as a symbol of women's subordination to traditional culture or of women's strategic empowerment.

This sort of theorizing is built on the discursive tradition of essentializing Islam and the West in a cultural dichotomy, where the values and practices of Islam are seen to embody a backward culture requiring women's passivity, while European cultural norms and the liberal tradition enable women to achieve freedom and self-realization (Mohanty 2003). Many liberal feminists, including those with a Muslim cultural background (i.e. Manji 2010), reinforce this dichotomy, suggesting that veiled women are largely unaware of their oppression and docility toward the subordinating practices of Islam, and therefore, are in need of assistance. By proposing that women must resist Islamic norms and practices that privilege men if they wish to be free, 'Western feminists' have generalized their particular perspective as universal while categorizing non-Western women as tradition-bound victims of patriarchal cultures (Abu-Lughod 2013).

Apart from insights into geo-historical variation and the local diversity of women's lives,[2] existing research makes further contributions. It illustrates the importance of theorizing women's veiling (and/or opposition to veiling) as part of a larger discussion on state-making, national unity and homogeneity (Atasoy 2009), and as integral to the making of a 'Muslim modernity' with claims to cultural authenticity (Korteweg and Yurdakul 2014). Ultimately, new questions arise about Islam's incorporation into the global political economy and its power dynamics to determine what this means for gender politics.

These questions require a different methodological and theoretical orientation from earlier studies on the global hierarchy, including colonial encounters between Muslim societies and European powers. Colonial encounters have been examined by reference to the dominant discursive tradition of essentialism noted above (Yeğenoğlu 1998). Ahmed (1992), for example, has theorized women's veiling as signalling a distinct historical, cultural experience embedded in Muslim anti-colonial resistance to Western domination. On the other hand, after establishing independence, Westernization came to be seen as a necessary modernizing precondition for 'catching-up' to European levels of development. This was certainly the case in Turkey. Westernization was deployed by state-ruling cadres to promote the cultural emulation of European lifestyles and turn citizens into loyal subjects of the state and its development project (cf. Fanon 1963). For Abu-Lughod (1998), the state's modernist disciplining of its subjects introduced a Western ideal of female domesticity into Muslim societies, expressed by the Victorian gender ideology which relegated women to the private domain of the home. For Ahmed (1992) and Mernissi (1996), it is this form of modernization which consolidated the embodiment of European gender norms and female domesticity in Muslim societies, replacing Islamic and other local standards.

My own research suggests that it is through a historical understanding of a shift in the development project itself that we can better appreciate the shaping of a Muslim politics of veiling. This politics of veiling represents a moment in the broader relations of the diffusion of capital and the role of the state in that moment where local practices and global projects of development are intertwined.

I situate religious issues in Turkey, including women's veiling, within the conflictual relations of a modernization path taken by state-ruling civil–military cadres in their institutionalization of national developmentalism. This path has historically shaped the particular content of political struggles over inclusion, exclusion, domination and subordination. While neoliberal reasoning allows various Muslim groups to articulate their position in the social hierarchy of developmentalism as unequally endowed groups, neoliberalization of the economy also enables them to work their way into the middle class, as they become educationally equipped with the necessary technical skills to be competitively engaged in the economy.

Rather than delineate what neoliberalism means in terms of economic policies and outcomes, I draw from scholarship which focuses on neoliberal reasoning and a neoliberal ontology (Brown 2015; Çalışkan and Callon 2009; Gill 2000). These concepts are essential for understanding the reorganization of the social hierarchy of developmentalism. This reorganization relates to various dimensions of power (cf. Mann 1986), which do not necessarily overlap or manifest a single economic logic of neoliberalism. They are separate but intertwined. The politics of women's veiling is situated within the contingent conjunction of economic, political-military[3] and cultural-religious dimensions of power at play in Turkey's neoliberalization. It has little or no relevance to debates on the modernity (or traditionalism) of women who wear it. However, it does point to the possibility that the established cultural fundamentals of the state can be revised to permit political renegotiation around the relations between rulers and ruled.

The AKP's lifting of the ban expresses an entirely historical and deeply 'messy' phenomenon of turning away from statist-developmentalism. The main problem in making sense of this messiness lies in the interconnectivity between individuals (expressed in women's desire to don the veil) and neoliberal restructuring. This sort of sense-making helps us avoid *methodological individualism* (Hodgson 2007), which takes Muslim women solely as independent decision makers.

Human capital and religion

Although the European Union (EU) has never referred to the headscarf ban[4] as an individual human rights and freedoms issue, the AKP government (in power since 2002) initially framed its policies on the headscarf ban in relation to EU membership requirements set by Copenhagen political criteria. The EU has a two-pronged approach to membership requirements – the adoption of a neoliberal capitalist economy, and state-restructuring in line with liberal-democratic principles (Atasoy 2009; van der Pijl 2006). The neoliberal model has been a dominant policy perspective in Turkey since the early 1980s. Therefore, the EU-imposed economic policy reorientation has caused little friction in Turkey. However, the liberal-democratic restructuring of the state constitutes a major source of political tension among various contenders for power who wish to control the direction of change.

The pursuit of democratization as an EU requirement by the AKP has involved a shift from the state-centric principles of the Kemalist path adopted since the 1920s.[5] This has been a highly contentious process affecting state-citizen relations and bargaining between various groups and social classes over a social-change trajectory. Those who mobilized themselves to protect the Kemalist fundamentals of the state (civil–military bureaucratic cadres and the old bourgeoisie) generated cultural meanings in favour of the headscarf ban through ideological adherence to *laiklik* (Turkish secularism). The AKP, on the other hand, framed the lifting of the ban around the EU-required 'individual rights and freedoms' discourse of liberal democracy, asserting that the ban violates Muslim women's citizenship and human rights (Atasoy 2011). The question remains, however, as to how a liberal-democratic orientation was framed for lifting the ban within a general process of economic neoliberalization.

I argue that the AKP has integrated religious issues with neoliberalization through the *human-capital* perspective (cf. Becker 1962; Coleman 1988) spelled out in its Development and Democratization Programme (AKP 2002). According to the AKP (2002, 34), 'combining world economic and European democratic normative standards with Turkish cultural values and moral precepts can produce an ethics that would apply in all aspects of the economy as a precondition for permanent and perpetual growth'. The AKP saw the combining of global and European standards with Islamic moral principles as a means for *asset building* in human capital, but it required the removal of state-imposed political, cultural and administrative constraints as expressed in the Kemalist tradition of state-centrism (Atasoy 2007, 123). The *human capital* perspective was significant in the AKP's consideration of the discriminatory nature of the headscarf ban which has adversely affected the higher education, occupational attainment and employment prospects of thousands of women who wear the headscarf.

There is no statistical data which indicates the actual number of women affected by the headscarf ban in relation to their education and employment opportunities. However, given that approximately 64 per cent of Muslim women wear a headscarf when outside the home (*Milliyet Newspaper* 27 May 2003), the ban appears to have affected many families in Turkey. *Zaman Newspaper* (1 October 2004) reported that 80,000 university students were expelled from school in 2004 as a direct outcome of the ban. That number may have increased until the partial lifting of the ban in 2012 and 2013. While those who did not wish to jeopardize their education decided to expose their hair by not wearing the headscarf, many others chose the humiliating practice of wearing a wig over their hair or headscarf, or taking their head-cover off on the street before entering school (Atasoy 2009, chapters 6 and 7). My interview with Zehra, who decided to continue her schooling by wearing a wig, conveys this humiliation:

> I do not want to think that a Muslim should live her life like a turtle withdrawn from life in her shell. We should be out there active in society. Therefore, I decided to attend classes with a wig. You are putting it over your headscarf. Does the headscarf show underneath the wig? Of course it does. When I see girls dressed like me wearing wigs . . . even I find them funny-looking and strange . . . We carry the wigs in our bags and put them over our headscarves just before entering the university. As a result, these wigs often look uncombed and frizzled, as if they are shocked by electricity. But they let you into the school as long as they see some hair on your head.
>
> *(Interview 25 May 2009)*

The number of students who were expelled from school might even be higher given that many students wearing headscarves did not attend classes regularly because of the ban. Moreover, many were not allowed to write their final examinations while wearing the headscarf, thereby disqualifying them from continuing their education. Still others decided to leave school rather than expose their hair. Students who could not complete their formal education were effectively pushed out of public-sector employment. Even if they completed their education by choosing to wear a wig over their hair or headscarf, they were still excluded from employment as headscarf-wearing individuals. The students whom I interviewed saw these restrictions as irreconcilable with liberal-democratic values and free-market economic principles.

Students who could not complete their education, and therefore were unemployable in the public sector, could only hope to find jobs in the private sector, often informally as precarious, marginalized workers without registration or access to social-security coverage and benefits (cf. Standing 2011). The informal sector made up approximately 28 per cent of Turkey's GDP between 2008 and 2011 (Kearney 2011, 15). For 2015, the Turkish Statistics Institute estimates that 34 per cent of total employment in Turkey is in the informal sector (TÜİK 2015). Women occupy a significant position within this category. Given that approximately 71 per cent of women are absent from the formal workforce (Sönmez 2013),[6] it would seem that women's informal, unregistered employment has become normalized in Turkey.

Before the ban was lifted, headscarf-wearing women were probably forced into the domestic sphere of marriage and family life. In 2013 approximately 61 per cent of women above the age of 15 (11.4 million) were classified as 'housewives' in Turkey (Sönmez 2013). This does not mean that these women are not productively involved in the economy (cf. Mies 1982), but it is indicative of an increasingly precarious mode of living for many of them in unregistered, informal jobs. Until 2001, married women's participation in the labour force was conditional on their husbands' approval, even though this was not legally enforced (Akyol 2014). It is reasonable to assume that headscarf-wearing women with few prospects for completing their education and securing public-sector employment became even more dependent on their husbands for participation in paid-work.

Headscarf-wearing women who *were* employed in the public sector were subject to various disciplinary measures, including layoffs and forced resignation. There are no official statistical data on headscarf-wearing public employees who were laid off. The following data come from the Eğitimciler Birliği Sendikası (Union for Educational Workers). Approximately 3,527 teachers were laid off between 1997 and 2001. During the same period, an estimated 11,000 teachers were forced to resign. This is approximately 11 per cent of the total number of teachers required by the educational system between 1996 and 1999, and approximately 3 per cent of the 414,774 teachers employed at that time. In addition, 33,271 teachers were subject to disciplinary investigation for wearing a headscarf (Eğitimciler Birliği Sendikası 2014).

The adverse effects of the ban were pronounced, causing widespread anxiety among students, their families and other members of society, particularly when it became strictly enforced on campuses after the military's ousting of a democratically elected, pro-Islamic Welfare Party-led collation government in 1997. The government was accused of being Islamist and a threat to the secular foundations of the state. Although official data is unavailable, it is well known that the 'Islamist' accusation was extended to the husbands of headscarf-wearing women, as well as their brothers and fathers employed in the public sector. Some of these men were exiled or expelled while others were forced to resign from their positions (Eğitimciler Birliği Sendikası 2014).

The lifting of the ban by the AKP after years of struggle with the judicial and military bureaucracy (Atasoy 2009) has created the conditions for women's increased access to education, work experience and occupational attainment, and, consequently, greater formal participation in the economy. It has also helped to improve the emotional health of younger generations dealing with the anxiety caused by the ban. McFadden (2008) has investigated the role of health as a dimension of the human capital of individuals in relation to the life-cycle, and as a factor in the acquisition of performance values and maintenance of cognitive skills. The AKP's lifting of the ban is likely to have boosted young Muslim women's morale, motivating them to complete their education, to gain and implement their skills more efficiently and to become more productively integrated into the economy. The lifting of the ban may also contribute to improvements in previously tenuous employment patterns which had governed the material conditions of many women. Human-capital creation and accumulation by Muslim women, possibly strengthened through the lifting of the ban, may be seen as an integral part of growth-oriented economic development projects.

Barro (1999) and Cannon (2000), among others, have developed arguments on the relationship between human-capital accumulation and economic growth. Despite differences, all conceptualize human capital as a significant input in shaping economic behaviour and the productivity of individuals, with resulting effects on economic growth. Their research indicates that the accumulation of human capital enhances 'flexibly bundled' productive skills and the efficiency of individuals to reflexively manage their fit into the market logic of neoliberalism (cf. Gershon 2011). In the absence of research on the relationship between women's veiling and human capital, the relevance of this argument to the AKP's lifting of the ban remains speculative. Nonetheless, it is strongly suggestive as a factor in women claiming greater access to higher education and public-sector employment.

Although religious issues cannot be properly understood from the economically reductionist perspective of human capital, the AKP's emphasis on human-capital growth melded with EU-imposed democratization policies has generated a market-integration mechanism for religious women who wear the headscarf. In Weberian terms, there may be an 'elective affinity' (Gerth and Mills 1946, 62) between religious ideas and the economic behaviour of individuals.

However, for Weber:

> [T]here is no pre-established correspondence between the content of an idea and the interests of those who follow them from the first hour . . . Ideas, selected and reinterpreted from the original doctrine, do gain an affinity with the interests of certain member of special strata; if they do not gain such an affinity they are abandoned.
>
> *(Gerth and Mills 1946, 63)*

Weber's notion of 'elective affinity' raises questions about the meaning of ideas which find an affinity in economic behaviour, without assuming that ideas express specific interests. Through neoliberal policy, the AKP did generate an affinity between religiosity and market economic integration, as reflected in individual accumulation of productivity-enhancing skills and entrepreneurial activity. Although external factors cannot be solely responsible for this 'affinity', the EU-required 'individual rights and freedoms' discourse of liberal democracy fuelled the process.

The human-capital approach is premised on a different theoretical foundation than Weber's notion of elective affinity, which places the economic and non-economic in separate spheres. The human-capital hypothesis presupposes a pre-existing market rationality in human behaviour that can advance human-capital accumulation through education and training. This accumulation is functional in that it enables people to better integrate into a market economy by generating wealth and growth outcomes (Piketty 2014, 21–2). McIntosh and Islam (2010) argue, in their example of Bahrain, that Muslim women's practice of Islamic customs, including veiling, enhances their human capital, with which they can better access funding and business networks and thereby find acceptance as entrepreneurs in a male-dominated Muslim context. *Religious human capital* enhanced by the practice of veiling becomes functional in helping to create a Muslim category of economically active citizens, encouraging women to seek greater 'equality' in the economy.

I believe that the 'religious human capital' (Iannaccone 1990) argument merely reduces religious issues to economic considerations of self-interested individuals seeking greater market-integration and economic success. Capitalism does not operate under the rule of self-regulating, self-adjusting markets into which self-interested individuals with religious human capital are integrated for capital accumulation and wealth generation (cf. Polanyi 1944). Such an approach identifies religion, together with education, in terms of its *functions*, which are presupposed to empower Muslim women in the market economy (cf. Coleman 1988). However, religion in *substantive* terms operates within a distinct realm of human social experience, and an attempt to identify it with its presupposed functions requires certain assumptions about *human nature* (Wuthnow 1988). These assumptions are consistent with a seventeenth-century discursive tradition exemplified by John Locke, who developed an understanding of society as an aggregate of independent and free actors making rational choices. This discursive tradition presses our analytical categories into the mold of ahistorical analysis. I utilize a more historical, social-relational approach. Thus, the question remains as to how these two distinct fields (religion and economy) intersect within the general neoliberalization process in relation to women's desire to wear the headscarf and participate in the economy.

Brown (2015) associates the process of neoliberalization with governance of everything by market metrics and rationality. If so, how does a neoliberal deepening of market metrics and rationality intersect with religiosity?

The intersection of religion and neoliberal reason is conjunctural, embedded in an ontological concern centred on the political reorganization of the past and the present. It calls into question the legitimacy of the institutional framework of state-centric national developmentalism which has dominated Turkey since the 1930s. This questioning involves the elevation of a market economic rationality to the status of 'epistemic privilege' (Somers and Block 2005, 265) within the strategic thinking of neoliberal reorganization. In the name of stimulating economic growth, this kind of thinking conceptualizes individuals as human capital fitted into the accumulation process. It focuses on the convergence of the moral-religious and economic-market spheres at a moment in history which is witnessing the reorganization of society through the expansion and deepening of neoliberalism. I have captured the essence of this convergence in my 2009 book, *Islam's Marriage with Neoliberalism*.

A generic individual and *homo economicus*

By forging a *neoliberal discursive synthesis* in the early 2000s between a Muslim cultural orientation and European standards in the context of Turkey's membership bid for the EU, the AKP launched a 'liberal' platform which has redefined the economic, cultural and political tensions in society in relation to existential inequalities and insecurities (cf. Therborn 2006). For the AKP, these inequalities were at the heart of the historical injustices generated under developmentalism, disadvantaging large segments of the Anatolian population, including women who wear the headscarf, and small- and medium-scale capital groups from smaller towns and cities. The rhetoric of 'historical injustices' aimed at developmentalism effectively framed the 'moral' argument for the reshaping of the economy and also connected women's veiling to a neoliberal ontology.

My use of the term 'neoliberal ontology' follows that of Brown (2015) and Çalışkan and Callon (2009) who conceptualize it as something much more comprehensive than an economic project and set of policy measures that emphasize market mechanisms for bolstering growth. These authors view the concept as a *normative* project which justifies the elevation of market principles to the status of an organizing principle of society and the state. By bringing economization to all aspects of social relationships through the principles of entrepreneurialism and responsibilization, neoliberalism rests on specific assumptions about the nature of lived reality. For Gill (2000, 49), these assumptions constitute 'the knowledge structures of political economy'. From the perspective taken in this chapter, the AKP's reshaping of a neoliberal knowledge structure incorporates women's veiling as a means of claims-making for greater justice and social inclusion. The result is a *restructuring* of the social, which figures humans as entrepreneurial and self-investing capital seeking to maximize their performance values and competitively reposition in society.

Alongside the AKP, other Islamically oriented social groups including the Fethullahçılar (an influential mass-based religious civil society movement) have participated in the institutional-ization of a neoliberal ontology under the banner of enlarging civic engagement in the economy. Resonant with Adam Smith's (1759/1976) insistence on the need for moral regulation in the pursuit of capitalist self-interest, the Fethullahçılar has formulated a notion of *homo economicus* with an Islamic twist, which I call *homo Islameconomicus*. It reflects a mentality for correcting 'historical distortions' of the economy in order that Muslim individuals can take part in eco-nomic growth and accumulation. *Homo Islameconomicus* ties the wealth creation activities of Muslim individuals to a supportive normative orientation for ethically grounded behaviour – 'doing good' for society which is typically described as '*hizmet*' or dedicated vocational work (Atasoy 2009, 127–30).

In 'doing good', the Fethullahçılar's *homo Islameconomicus* has two primary objectives: to reconstruct individual thought in accordance with the ideas, moral values and normative standards of Islam; and to connect individualized pious belief to the transformation of behaviour in the public sphere. In setting these objectives, the Fethullahçılar claims that Islam is more than a religion. It is a 'civilization for individual growth', concerned with individuals becoming better, socially responsible citizens (Şirin 2005). Fethullahçılar advocates greater piety, to be realized through high quality education that connects the spiritual and material worlds within the individual freedoms and rights discourse of liberal democracy and a neoliberal market economy. This worldview has been embraced by others as well, including MÜSİAD (the Independent Industrialists' and Businessmen's Association).

MÜSİAD supports the notion of individual autonomy and human economic rationality, coupled with the idea that Islam 'requires only those individuals with reason, intelligence and freedom to fulfil their religious duties' (Özdemir 2006, 162). MÜSİAD has expressed its ideals in the periodical *Homo-Islamicus* (1993–97), whose title represents the incorporation of *homo economicus* into an Islamic orientation. The association sees itself as the champion of 'Muslimness', believed to be a political category made up of those who were marginalized in the develop-mentalist hierarchy of the state which privileged İstanbul-based large industrial capitalists. MÜSİAD often cites statements attributed to the Prophet Muhammed such as 'God loves those who earn' (Atasoy 2007, 128). In a section of its website called 'compass' (*pusula* in Turkish) MÜSİAD includes a Turkish translation of Qur'anic surah and statements attributed to 'Eastern' philosophy. One such philosophical statement indicates: 'there is no continuation of property without trade'.[7] A surah included in the website reads:

> 'Oh Allah! Owner of sovereignty [*mülk*]![8] Thou givest sovereignty [*mülk*] unto whom you wilt, and Thou withdrawest sovereignty [*mülk*] from whom you wilt. Thou exaltest whom Thou wilt and Thou abasest whom Thou wilt. In Thy hand is the good. Lo! Thou art able to do all things'
>
> (*The Glorious Qur'an 3:26*)

This surah highlights the importance of Islamic ethical virtue in framing the economic behaviour of Muslims. To be chosen by God for the endowment of *mülk* (property), individual moral renewal is a prerequisite.

For Fethullah Gülen (1941–), the founder of Fethullahçılar, wearing the headscarf is not essential to faith. He states:

> [The head-covering is] not as significant as the obligation of worship and servanthood to God in [a] general sense. [It belongs] to the secondary level, the level of details . . . [L]et us not be drowned in details. Let us not sacrifice big things for the sake of the small . . . (t)hen, we, the people . . . can choose any style of dress with our own free will . . . Going into standardization would kill the flexibility and therefore the universality to be found in the spirit of the religion.
>
> *(Ergil 2015a)*

For Gülen, the headscarf ban was a bad administrative decision which deprived students of their right to an education. This decision only amplified authoritarian rule in Turkey which, for tens of years, had suppressed the political and cultural demands of the Anatolian population, pushing the country with 'enormous . . . potential, having human resources and power of labour' into backwardness and poverty (Ergil 2015a).

To view the headscarf as an issue of secondary importance is not a rhetorical device, but an integral part of *homo Islameconomicus*, which is necessary to encourage the autonomy of individuals and to awaken the latent potential within them. According to Gülen, the ban suppresses women's freedom and therefore limits their potential. But, women should not be belligerent about their head-covering as it only constitutes a small detail in Islamic faith. For Gülen (2003), 'the new man and woman':

> will rely equally on reason and experience, but give as much importance to conscience and inspiration . . . [They] will be individuals of integrity who, free from external influences, can manage independently of others . . . Rather than imitating others, they will rely on their original dynamics rooted in the depths of history and try to equip their faculties of judgment with authentic values of their own . . . Having no attachment to worldly things . . . they will be the dynamism of history that initiates and shapes events. With due perception of their age and surrounding conditions . . . they will be in a state of continuous self renewal.

Gülen (2015a) asserts that 'the new' individuals are to act as 'children of their time'. They need to know the requirements of their time, follow appropriate methods and improve their behaviour and performance. In the current neoliberal age:

> [i]t is possible to . . . use time efficiently by alternating between acts of worship and worldly tasks . . . we first need to tell about the necessity of understanding work, offer due rehabilitation, make people accustomed to it, and after all of these, entrust the notion of self-sacrifice to their freewill . . . It should not be forgotten that all of those achievements are Divine favours granted in return for making serious efforts and working diligently, night and day, with an understanding of work surpassing the norms.
>
> *(Gülen 2015b)*

The suggestion here is that disciplined, free-willed individuals can use their time efficiently to combine spiritual and worldly work that is well suited to the business-led neoliberal market economy model of wealth generation. Moreover, Gülen sees wealth creation as a means for restructuring society and the global economic hierarchy. He states:

everywhere in the world and all the time Muslims have to be a wealthy and dominant force . . . it is not possible for the Muslim to face the challenge in the world without having superiority, economically and scientifically. [God] will not appreciate to see the domination of Muslims by the unbelievers.[9] . . . a nation which does not search for means and ways to become wealthier against poverty is bound to be under the domination of another . . . Starting from this fundamental thinking, every believer to be sure remaining within the legitimate boundaries has to find a way to become rich by any means possible . . . through the help of people, raised with positive sciences and disciplines of religious studies . . . God almighty states in the Qur'an: "*We . . . wrote down in the Psalms after the Torah that My righteous servants will inherit the earth.*" (Al-Anbiya 21:105)[10] . . . the believers have to search for the ways inside the country as well as outside, to discover the ways to get richer, and become wealthy.

(*Ergil 2015b*)

Significantly, the rationality circumscribing the intentionality of human behaviour here is a means for restructuring the dominant forms of power which historically subordinated and oppressed Muslims within and between states. In the *homo Islameconomicus* formulation there appears to be a call for the mobilization of the *agentic power* of individuals *within* a social-change movement where agency belongs to the *movement itself* rather than the intention of individual Muslims (cf. Gramsci 1971 [1928], 123–205). Women's struggle for the right to cover their hair represents an instance in the remaking of the social through demands for the restoration of human and citizenship rights by *homo Islameconomicus*. Groups such as the Fethullahçılar argue for the activation of *homo Islameconomicus* through an appeal to responsible, religiously disciplined individuals to participate productively in the market economy and thereby restructure the social.

The mobilization of *religiously responsible human capital* (as opposed to 'religious human capital') in generating and accumulating wealth assumes a generic individual in much Islamic thinking. *Homo Islameconomicus* appears to be a Muslim man, given that groups such as Fethullahçılar and MÜSİAD make no specific reference to women in their articulation of a neoliberal economic imaginary. What follows centres on the question of where women's struggle for 'access rights' in education and employment fits into the Islamically oriented neoliberal ascendancy of *homo economicus*. The personal narratives of several women are included.

Women's access rights to higher education and employment

Students who were affected by the headscarf ban demanded that university administrations and the government restore their individual right to freedom of expression and conscience. They also waged a legal battle on the grounds that their human rights were violated by the state, challenging the ban in both Turkish courts and the European Court of Human Rights (Atasoy 2009, 182–200). In addition, students became involved in various non-governmental Muslim women's human rights organizations, such as Ak-Der, to advance their struggle against the ban.

Women who wore the headscarf were well aware that the abstract idea of *humanity* does not in and of itself guarantee 'the right to have rights, or the right of every individual to belong to humanity', as Arendt (1973 [1951], 298) wrote in *The Origins of Totalitarianism*. However, at the same time, they saw within neoliberalism's 'generic individual' a medium for the recognition of normative authority by an individual to deliberate and act – the most essential human freedom outside state-led projects (cf. Arendt 1958, 177). The generic individual is 'economic man', an 'acting being' furnished with the necessary skills and qualities of human capital (cf. Smith 1976 [1759]). Muslim women's normative embodiment of the generic individual is expressed through commonly upheld headscarf narratives. According to one student, Emine:

> Islamic knowledge should help Muslims better understand the meaning of individual freedoms and how to connect this with the religious demand for a moral life. A Muslim must reflect on the material conditions of his or her existence . . . and find innovative solutions to problems. Unless these issues are discussed extensively, Muslims will continue to focus on religion in a limited sense confined to issues of personal piety. Piety is a matter of faith between God and the individual. It really doesn't concern me. What is most important is to realize the connection between the way I think and the way I live as an autonomous, well-educated and skilled individual to succeed in the economy and society.
>
> *(Interview 3 June 2010)*

For Selvi:

> A Muslim should acquire the capacity to develop a more disciplined and refined self. These are important for personal growth and in order to flourish in society. Wearing a headscarf is important for spiritual growth but not a fundamental requirement.
>
> *(Interview 4 June 2010)*

Other students also said that covered women should be independent, hard-working and actively engaged in the economy. Zeliha's insights are illuminating here:

> There are three categories of women in Turkey. One category consists of traditional women from smaller Anatolian towns and villages. They cover their hair in a traditional way . . . They are Muslims but not very knowledgeable on religious matters. The second category of women consists of those who are highly knowledgeable on religious matters but are not active in public life. They are rather withdrawn from society. The third category of women includes those of us who are not only interested in religious science but also in the natural sciences, technical engineering, economics, history, society. I accept the humiliation of opening and closing my hair on the streets if this is what I have to do to get my education and fully participate in the economy and the society.
>
> *(Interview 1 June 2010)*

Yasemin expresses much the same idea:

> We should have a different flair in our look. In addition to striving towards being good . . . in our personal lives, we should also strive towards building a capacity in the sciences and other professions. We need to strengthen and live our faith; our work in the sciences should help us to find Allah as the creator of the best.
>
> *(Interview 15 June 2010)*

For many of the students whom I interviewed, the ban was a social class issue, supported by those who wished to maintain the privileged positions they established during the state-led developmentalist era. For them, headscarf-wearing students portrayed a new image of Anatolian women with new goals and high aspirations. This became a visible reminder to state bureaucrats that the *laik* cultural hierarchy was gradually being turned upside down. The old elite now felt threatened by the social mobilization of Muslim groups *repositioning* themselves in society as a culturally distinct fraction of the newly emerging Anatolian upper classes. According to Hatice:

> In the past the state educational system helped *laik* women in higher social status to professionally advance in the economy. They had no interest in wearing the headscarf. In the past, those who wanted to be more religious stayed away from public life. They were more interested in issues of moral uprightness, character formation and domestic matters than higher education in sciences and professional employment. But, now we are more aware of our secondary social status in society, and we want to change it. We are more conscious that our head coverage and our religiosity should not prevent us from improving our social position in life . . . As we put this heightened awareness at the centre of our mobilization, opposition against our headscarves has become more rigid. It is because those who oppose our head covering do not want to see us up there with them in the higher institutional positions of the state and the economy.
>
> *(Interview 29 May 2010)*

The students clearly agree that the headscarf ban serves to protect the privileged position of the traditional upper classes in society. For them, the religion of Islam cultivates 'a regulative sensibility' (Mahmood 2005, 47) through its values and norms that shapes one's overall conduct in economic and social life. Religion is not relegated to a distinct, separate sphere, but viewed as a regulative standard of moral, ethical behaviour. The religious restoration of personal self-growth, autonomy and self-determination was therefore a social-change project with a close affinity to the ontology of neoliberalism. The *neoliberal turn* in the economy provides these women with an opportunity to claim a heightened sense of their self-worth as active, religiously equipped individuals. However, considerable ambiguity remains regarding the interpretive valuation of Islam in regard to the neoliberal normative logic. One of my respondents expressed this ambiguity in the following way:

> Being learned is the highest form of religious worship. A good Muslim will be trustworthy, hardworking and reflective of the meaning of his or her actions. In the West, they also reflect on the meaning of their actions but only for the purpose of realizing their own self-interest. In Islam, reflection cannot be directed towards maximization of self-interest for economic gain.
>
> *(Interview 15 May 2010)*

Interestingly, the emphasis here on critical thinking and reflection on the meaning of faithful action draws attention to Islamic pedagogy which is built on the *separateness* of the religious from the economic realm. This last point suggests the divergence of an Islamic ethos from what an economic calculative logic entails in relation to the freedom of the economically self-interested to maximize gain. This divergence reveals a potential normative conflict in the affinity between Islam and neoliberalism as articulated within *homo Islameconomicus*.

Conclusion

My research departs from questions on women's reasons for wearing the headscarf, the political effects of their decisions and generalizations concerning the ideas of their opponents. My research also avoids the assumption that Muslim women (or men) involved in the headscarf issue possess a single, unified form of 'agency' which enables them to change the conditions of their experience (cf. Emirbayar and Mische 1998; Hitlin and Johnson 2015). It is through the political agency of a social-change *movement* (Gramsci 1971 [1928]) that Muslims have positioned themselves in support of neoliberalization and against tight state control.

As an 'economic policy regime' (Callinicos 2012) and a 'class project' (Harvey 2005), neoliberalism in Turkey represents the repositioning of various Muslim groups in society and the economy and the reorganization of state-society relations. The process of neoliberalization embodies highly conflictual relations. The headscarf ban and associated violations of human and citizenship rights (in terms of education and employment) are an example of the tensions involved in the neoliberal remaking of the social. This remaking hinges on the activation of a market logic operating in opposition to historically rooted state discipline.

Neoliberalization in Turkey is also a normative project directed toward the economization of the social sphere. An important question requiring further research is what kind of 'value system' or normative order emerges as state-centrism is gradually replaced by a mode of thinking which deepens market principles in society. My interviews suggest that women are struggling with an interpretive valuation of what it means for religious women to be inserted into the deep structures of the neoliberal economy. It seems that a calculative logic of interest maximization and a utilitarian ethic of capital accumulation have not been fully internalized by Muslim women. Male-dominated Muslim economic groups would appear to be more drawn to wealth accumulation through competitive growth and adherence to the practices and principles of entrepreneurialism. This raises a further question as to how differences in Islamic valuations may interact with existing gender inequalities in society. Additional research is needed here as well to advance our understanding of how such differences are intertwined with the neoliberal order of reason and economization motives in relation to gender outcomes. An improved understanding can only deepen our appreciation for the historically variable and contingent meanings of citizenship as a multilayered concept embodying a multiplicity of normative influences, struggles and interpretive positions. It is this very complexity which enables neoliberalism to be reconfigured as a flexible restructuring ethos, extending beyond the economic realm into that of religion. The headscarf issue in Turkey offers us many insights into that complexity.

Notes

1. I would like to thank Ken Jalowica of Kwantlen Polytechnic University in Surrey, BC, Canada, for his invaluable comments on the chapter.
2. For immigrant Muslim women's veiling practices in Canada, France, Germany and the United States, among others, see Atasoy (2006); Korteweg and Yurdakul (2014); Read and Bartkowski (2000).
3. The military dimension of power includes the state-bureaucratic disciplinary practices of citizenship (Mitchell 2002).
4. There has never been a law in Turkey which officially forbids women from wearing the headscarf or other forms of Islamic dress. There are only administrative by-laws or regulations on a dress code accepted by governments and established at public institutions (Atasoy 2009, chapter 6).
5. Kemalism, named after the founder of the Republic of Turkey, Mustafa Kemal, is an ideological referent for Turkey's modernity. Its specific principles include republicanism, nationalism, *laiklik* (secularism), populism, statism and revolutionism/reformism. They are the unchangeable founding principles of the Turkish republic.
6. This is the case despite the fact that there was a 45 per cent increase in the employment of women from 5.3 million to 7.7 million between 2005 and 2013 (Sönmez 2013).
7. Available at http://erdemlihayat.com/category/hayatimiz/erdemsizhayat (accessed 16 September 2015).
8. The website includes a Turkish translation of the surah. For an English translation, I have used Pickthall's *The Glorious Qur'an*. The MÜSİAD website uses the term *mülk* in Turkish which translates into English as property, landed property, real estate, domain or territory. However, various English translations of the Qur'an use the interpretation of sovereignty, power or rule. Sovereignty translates as *hakimiyet*

Yıldız Atasoy

in Turkish. Therefore, it is noteworthy that MÜSİAD used the term *mülk* rather than *hakimiyet* in its Turkish translation of the surah.

9. 'Unbelievers' here does not refer to Christians or Jews as they are believers in God, according to Gülen.
10. This statement strengthens the Turkish translation of the Qur'anic term sovereignty as *mülk* (property).

References

Abu-Lughod, L., ed. 1998. *Remaking Women*. Princeton, NJ: Princeton University Press.
Abu-Lughod, L. 2013. *Do Muslim Women Need Saving?* Cambridge, MA: Harvard University Press.
Afshar, H. 1998. *Islam and Feminisms*. London: Macmillan.
Ahmed, L. 1992. *Women and Gender in Islam*. New Haven, CT: Yale University Press.
AKP. 2002. *Development and Democratization Program*. Ankara: *AK Parti* Yayınları.
Aksoy, M. 2005. *Başörtüsü-Türban*. İstanbul: Kitap Yayınevi.
Akyol, R. A. 2014. 'Turkish Women's Informal Work'. *Aljazeera*. Available at www.aljazeera.com/indepth/opinion/2014/08/informal-female-work-turkey-com-201481163535208284.html (accessed 14 September 2015).
Arendt, H. 1958. *The Human Condition*. Chicago, IL: University of Chicago Press.
Arendt, H. 1973 [1951]. *The Origins of Totalitarianism*. London: Andre Deutsch.
Atasoy, Y. 2006. 'Governing Women's Morality'. *European Journal of Cultural Studies* 9(2):203–21.
Atasoy, Y. 2007. 'The Islamic Ethic and the Spirit of Turkish Capitalism Today'. In *Socialist Register 2008*, edited by L. Panitch and C. Leys, 121–40. London: The Merlin Press.
Atasoy, Y. 2009. *Islam's Marriage with Neoliberalism*. London: Palgrave Macmillan.
Atasoy, Y. 2011. 'Two Imaginaries of Citizenship in Turkey'. *International Journal of Politics, Culture and Society* 24(3–4):105–23.
Barro, R. J. 1999. 'Human Capital and Growth in Cross-Country Regressions'. *Swedish Economic Policy Review* 6:237–77.
Becker, G. S. 1962. 'Investment in Human Capital'. *Journal of Political Economy* 70(5):9–49.
Brown, W. 2015. *Undoing the Demos*. New York: Zone Books.
Çalışkan, K. and M. Callon. 2009. 'Economization, Part I'. *Economy and Society* 38(3):369–98.
Callinicos, A. 2009. *Making History*. Chicago, IL: Haymarket Books.
Callinicos, A. 2012. 'Commentary: Contradictions of Austerity'. *Cambridge Journal of Economics* 36(1): 65–77.
Cannon, E. 2000. 'Human Capital'. *Oxford Economic Papers* 52(4):670–76.
Coleman, J. S. 1988. 'Social Capital in the Creation of Human Capital'. *American Journal of Sociology* 94(Supplement):S95–120.
Eğitimciler Birliği Sendikası. 2014. 'Bir Daha Asla: 17 Yıl Sonra 28 Şubat'. (Şubat 2014). Available at www.egitimbirsen.org.tr (accessed 14 September 2015).
Emirbayar, M. and A. Mische. 1998. 'What is Agency?'. *American Journal of Sociology* 103(4):962–1023.
Ergil, D. 2015a. 'How Can the Headscarf Issue Be Resolved?'. (2 April). Available at http://fgulen.com/en/gulen-movement/fethullah-gulen-and-the-gulen-movement-in-100-questions/48132-how-can-the-headscarf-issue-banning-of-headscarves-in-the-public-sector-in-turkey-be-resolved (accessed 16 September 2015).
Ergil, D. 2015b. 'What is Fethullah Gülen's View of the Market Economy?'. (16 April). Available at http://fgulen.com/en/gulen-movement/fethullah-gulen-and-the-gulen-movement-in-100-questions/48357-what-is-fethullah-gulens-view-of-the-market-economy-where-would-he-place-the-state-and-private-enterprise-in-the-economy (accessed 16 September 2015).
Fanon, F. 1963. *The Wretched of the Earth*. New York: Grove Press.
Gershon, I. 2011. 'Neoliberal Agency'. *Current Anthropology* 52(4):537–55.
Gerth, H. H. and C. W. Mills. 1946. *From Max Weber*. New York: Oxford University Press.
Gill, S. 2000. 'Knowledge, Politics, and Neo-Liberal Political Economy'. In *Political Economy and the Changing Global Order*, edited by R. Stubbs and G. R. D. Underhill, 48–59. Toronto, ON: Oxford University Press.
Gramsci, A. 1971 [1928]. *Selections from the Prison Notebooks*. New York: International Publishers.
Gülen, F. 2003. 'The New Man and Woman'. (5 November). Available at http://fgulen.com/en/fethullah-gulens-life/1305-gulens-thoughts/25094-the-new-man-and-woman (accessed 3 October 2015).
Gülen, F. 2015a. 'Getting to See Important Responsibilities as Mundane Tasks and the Qur'anic Method of Tasrif'. (18 May). Available at http://fgulen.com/en/fethullah-gulens-works/thought/endeavor-for-

renewal/48669-getting-to-see-important-responsibilities-as-mundane-tasks-and-the-qur-anic-method-of-tasrif-renewal-of-format (accessed 16 September 2015).

Gülen, F. 2015b. 'Working Hours of the Devoted Souls'. (13 May). Available at http://fgulen.com/en/fethullah-gulens-works/thought/endeavor-for-renewal/48623-working-hours-of-the-devoted-souls (accessed 16 September 2015).

Harvey, D. 2005. *A Brief History of Neoliberalism*. Oxford: Oxford University Press.

Hitlin, S. and M. K. Johnson. 2015. 'Reconceptualizing Agency within the Life Course'. *American Journal of Sociology* 120(5):1429–72.

Ho, C. 2007. 'Muslim Women's New Defenders'. *Women's Studies International Forum* 30(4):290–98.

Hodgson, M. G. 2007. 'Meanings of Methodological Individualism'. *Journal of Economic Methodology* 14(2):211–26.

Hoodfar, H. 1997. 'Return to the Veil'. In *The Women, Gender & Development Reader*, edited by Nalini Visvanathan *et al.*, 320–26. London: Zed.

Iannaccone, L. R. 1990. 'Religious Practice'. *Journal for the Scientific Study of Religion* 29(3):297–314.

Kearney, A. T. 2011. 'The Shadow Economy in Europe'. Available at www.visaeurope.com (accessed 13 February 2013).

Korteweg, A. C. 2008. 'The Sharia Debate in Ontario'. *Gender & Society* 22(4):434–54.

Korteweg, A. C. and G. Yurdakul. 2014. *The Headscarf Debates*. Stanford, CA: Stanford University Press.

MacLeod, A. E. 1991. *Accommodating Protest*. New York: Columbia University Press.

Mahmood, S. 2005. *Politics of Piety*. Princeton, NJ: Princeton University Press.

Manji, I. 2010. *The Trouble with Islam Today*. Toronto, ON: Vintage.

Mann, M. 1986. *The Sources of Social Power*. Cambridge: Cambridge University Press.

Mannheim, K. 1986 [1929]. *Ideology and Utopia*. New York: Anchor.

McFadden, D. 2008. 'Human Capital Accumulation and Depreciation'. *Review of Agricultural Economics* 30(3):379–85.

McIntosh, J. C. and S. Islam. 2010. 'Beyond the Veil'. *International Management Review* 6(1):103–09.

Mernissi, F. 1996. *Women's Rebellion & Islamic Morality*. London & New Jersey: Zed.

Mies, M. 1982. *Lace Makers of Narsapur*. London: Zed.

Milliyet Newspaper. 2003. 'Türban Dosyası'. 27 May–18 June.

Mitchell, T. 2002. *Rule of Experts*. Berkeley, CA: University of California Press.

Moghadam, V. 1991. 'The Islamist Movements and Women's Responses in the Middle East'. *Gender and History* 3:268–84.

Mohanty, C. T. 2003. *Feminism without Borders*. Durham, NC: Duke University Press.

Özdemir, O. 2006. *MÜSİAD*. Ankara: Vadi Yayınları.

Piketty, T. 2014. *Capital in the Twenty-First Century*. London: The Belknap Press of Harvard University Press.

Polanyi, K. 1944. *The Great Transformation*. Boston, MA: Beacon Press.

Read, G. and J. Bartkowski. 2000. 'The Veil or Not to Veil?'. *Gender & Society* 4(3):395–417.

Şirin, T. 2005. *Kişisel Gelişim Medeniyeti*. İstanbul: Armoni.

Smith, A. 1976 [1759]. *The Theory of Moral Sentiments*. New York: Penguin Books.

Somers, M. and F. Block. 2005. 'From Poverty to Perversity'. *American Sociological Review* 70(1):260–87.

Sönmez, M. 2013. 'Women Employment in Turkey Shows High Rise but Low Quality'. *Hürriyet Daily News* (23 November). Available at www.hurriyetdailynews.com/women-employment-in-turkey-shows-high-rise-but-low.aspx?pageID=238&nID=58384&NewsCatID=347 (accessed 14 September 2015).

Standing, G. 2011. *The Precariat*. London: Bloomsbury Academic.

The Glorious Qur'an, translated by Marmaduke Pickthall. 1999. İstanbul: Çağrı Yayınları.

Therborn, G. 2006. *Inequalities of the World*. London & New York: Verso.

TÜİK. 2015. 'Labour Force Statistics, May 2015'. Press Release No. 18640 (17 August). Available at www.turkstat.gov.tr/PreHaberBultenleri.do?id=18640 (accessed 14 September 2015).

van der, Pijl, K. . 2006. 'A Lockean Europe?'. *New Left Review* 37:9–37.

Wuthnow, R. J. 1988. 'Sociology of Religion'. In *Handbook of Sociology*, edited by N. J. Smelser, 473–509. Newbury Park, CA: Sage.

Yeğenoğlu, M. 1998. *Colonial Fantasies*. Cambridge: Cambridge University Press.

Zaman Newspaper. 2004. 'Ağar: Başörtülüleri Kazansak Fena Mı Olur?'. 1 October.

3

DISCOURSES OF VEILING AND THE PRECARITY OF CHOICE

Representations in the post-9/11 US

Tabassum F. Ruby

Introduction

Hello, Sunshine: A young woman in Kabul takes advantage of the sudden opportunity to move about unveiled. The Taliban, which was particularly brutal to women, required them to wear the head-to-toe burka. Now those who stuck with the traditional costume did so by choice.

(Behakis 26 November 2001)

The full-length *Time* magazine article from which this quote is drawn is accompanied by exotic pictures of Afghan women, both veiled and unveiled. The excerpt and the pictures are powerful. The sunshine bursts with life, energy, joy; the caption *Hello, Sunshine* expresses the new confidence that Afghan women (ostensibly) achieved immediately following the United States' invasion of Afghanistan in September 2001. As the young woman who 'takes advantage of the sudden opportunity' still covers her hair loosely, while others remain in head-to-toe burqas, the photograph presents a contrast between women who are relatively free and those who are constrained. Yet the traditional costume is now one choice among others, the author suggests, for the invasion has granted women a certain agency. Such a characterization of the burqa dehistoricizes the veiling practice, of course, but also offers a rationale for the United States' invasion of the country.

While fixation on the veil is not new in Western discourses (Ahmed 1992; Kahf 1999; Andrea 2007), in post-9/11 America certain nuances require critical examination. To that end, this depiction is only one example of how the bodies of Muslim women who veil (the headscarf, abaya, niqab, burqa, and so forth – I refer to these together as 'veiling', because the problematic of representation that I address in this chapter does not essentially differentiate among types or cuts of cloth) were made a contested terrain in the post-9/11 era. Veiling practice is frequently interpreted as proof of women's subjugation, despite a growing body of literature which challenges such representations. Yet either interpretation often hinges on an opposition between freedom and coercion (is the veil imposed on women? or do they choose to wear it?). This discursive contour is problematic at a number of registers. In particular, and disregarding social and historical context, it presumes that a liberal conception of choice will adequately determine whether or not the practice is voluntarily embraced. As Saba Mahmood (2005, 11–2) critically notes, freedom in liberalism is constituted as the ability to autonomously 'choose one's desires' and that an individual's actions must be established to be the consequence of her 'own will', rather than of custom, tradition, or social coercion. Similarly, Carol Hay (2013, 12) observes that liberals agree that individuals should be free 'from the unwanted interferences of others', should 'live the life of one's choosing', and should choose 'one's own conception of the good'. Joan Scott (2007) also underscores the problematics of such liberalism. This liberal perspective passes over how a subject's social and cultural upbringing shapes their interests and desires; how presumably free choices are attained within power relations and asymmetries; and how the hegemony of certain representations already constitutes certain practices as signifying one thing or another.

Keeping in mind these aspects of the liberal conception of free will, this chapter first examines burqa representations against the backdrop of the 'war on terror' in US news media, and then analyses the notion of 'choice'. I chart the manner in which the practice of veiling points to problematic liberal assumptions and their fraught relationships to female Muslim emancipation – since the ostensible liberation is already punctuated within colonial and imperial discourses. I then discuss how some Muslim women themselves understand veiling. For not only does the mainstream mediatized landscape render Muslim women through the vocabulary of choice, but also the discursive logics of self-representation re-inscribe this vocabulary in the name of reclaiming agency. To underscore problematic aspects of agency, I also draw attention to US women's bodily patriarchal practices. In the final section, I discuss the discrimination Muslim women often face in the United States while conducting their daily business, because of their clothing. Such intolerance points to a fragmentation as well as an ethnocentrism regarding veiling. To present these arguments, I begin with former First Lady Laura Bush's radio address, and then draw upon articles that appeared in *Time* magazine and the *Washington Post*, widely read news media in the US.

Representations of burqas

In her radio address of 17 November 2001, former First Lady Laura Bush contended that as a result of the United States invasion, much of the Taliban regime had retreated, 'and the people of Afghanistan – especially women – are rejoicing'. These two events, according to her, are directly related, because 'the brutal oppression of women is a central goal of the terrorists' and 'the Taliban and its terrorist allies were making the lives of children and women in Afghanistan miserable'. This misery is profound: 'Seventy percent of the Afghan people are malnourished. One in every four children won't live past the age of five because health care is not available. Women have been denied access to doctors . . . Women cannot work outside the home, or even leave their homes by themselves.' This description blurs suffering of women and children as a result of poverty (Afghanistan is one of the poorest countries of the world), three years of severe drought, inadequate healthcare resources, and the restrictions imposed by the Taliban regime during the five years of rule – all into a single frame of immiseration. Yet one distinction does emerge: that between the civilized and the uncivilized. For not only do the civilizeds 'hearts break for the women and children in Afghanistan, but also . . . we see the world the terrorists would like to impose on the rest of us'. The invasion of Afghanistan thus has world-historical significance beyond addressing the stated suffering of Afghan children and women. It is about saving the world: 'All of us have an obligation to speak out.' And this 'speech' yields results: 'because of our recent military gains . . . women are no longer imprisoned in their homes. They can listen to music'.

Some crucial historical information is missing here, of course. While the former First Lady proudly declares the United States' military gains, she neglects to note how 'over the course of just one month, the US dropped over half a million tons of bombs – approximately 20 kilograms of high explosive for every man, woman, and child in the country' (Khattak 2002, 19). Women may not be imprisoned in their homes, but many may have simply died or been injured and disabled because of the bombing. Indeed, many of them may have been 'put at greater risk of starvation because US bombing severely restricted the delivery of food aid' (Hirschkind and Mahmood 2002, 341). The celebratory radio address also omits the well-documented history of how the CIA and various Western countries, to weaken the Soviet Union, supported the Taliban in the 343 refugee camps that were established across the North West Frontier Province and Baluchistan in Pakistan (Khattak 2002, 19). Shahnaz Khan (2006, 120) writes that in 1998, Zbigniew Brzezinski, Secretary of State under President Jimmy Carter, admitted that he and CIA director Bill Casey 'had helped create the conditions for the Soviet intervention in Afghanistan'. They believed that 'the resistance in camps in Pakistan would hasten the fall of the Soviet empire'. In the aftermath of 9/11, when Brzezinski was asked about 'the wisdom of supporting radical Islamists in Afghanistan', he remarked: 'What is more important to the history of the world? The Taliban or the collapse of the Soviet empire?' (For further information on the United States' role in these events, see Hirschkind and Mahmood 2002). This admission puts Laura Bush's contrast between civilized and uncivilized in a different light. The people whose 'hearts break' for Afghan suffering actually bear clear responsibility for their suffering. This does not allow for benevolent intervention.

Wrapping the generic sufferings of Afghan women around the brutality of the Taliban is frequent in American news media – often as bolstered by Afghan women themselves, though no less problematic for it. A common pattern has an Afghan woman who left Afghanistan long ago identify the practice of veiling as alien, recalling the freedom women enjoyed prior to Taliban rule. One article reports that an Afghan women's rights activist, Fahima Vorgetts, who fled Afghanistan in 1979 and now lives in the United States, showed despair upon her return to Afghanistan. Before leaving, she wore mini-skirts; now women had to wear burqas to feel safe (Hernandez 2002). Another article features an Afghan woman who returns to Kabul after 23 years living in the United States. She is shocked to see women 'shrouded in burqas', because 'in the Kabul of her childhood, no one wore the enveloping shrouds' (Sheridan 2002). Although such nostalgic, selective autobiographical accounts identify the burqa as a Taliban-imposed practice, they ignore the long-standing veiling tradition in Afghanistan and inadequately address why women did not feel safe leading up to the fall of the Taliban regime. My intention here is certainly not to minimize women's sufferings caused by the Taliban, but to underscore the problematic framing that obscures (rather than clarifies) the stakes and context of the veiling practice.

It is well documented that forms of veiling for women in the subcontinent of Central Asia are long-standing. Pashtun women, one of several ethnic groups in Afghanistan, traditionally wore a burqa when they went out (Abu-Lughod 2013, 35). The practice symbolizes women's modesty and respectability, and separates men's and women's spheres, including making a distinction between *mahram* (close relatives with whom marriage is not permissible) and non-mahram (individuals with whom marriage is permissible). It also allows women to move into the public sphere without jeopardizing religious and cultural expectations of moral and sexual behaviour. The burqa thus performs multiple symbolic and physical functions. But if it has been part of the social fabric of Afghanistan, 'Why would women suddenly want to give up the burqa in 2001? Why would they throw off the markers of their respectability?' (Abu-Lughod 2013, 35). In other words, while Afghan women no longer live under the Taliban-imposed rulings on the burqa, the Taliban did not invent it in the first place. Whilst they imposed a particular style of veiling 'on everyone as "religiously" appropriate' (Abu-Lughod 2013, 37), it is unreasonable to expect a renouncing of traditional clothing in the wake of American invasion of the region.

In fact, although the burqa discourse often makes media headlines, it may not be among the greatest worries of Afghan women. One article even states that 'the burka is the least of their concerns' (Lacayo 2001). The same article interviews Dr Rahima Zafar Staniczia, the head of the Rabia Balhi hospital for women, who says: 'What women wear is a secondary issue . . . first we need peace. Then we need central government. Then we need education. After all that, we will be in a position to make a decision on the burka' (36–7). This account counters the popular depiction of the burqa. In fact, as Dr Staniczia states, it is only conditions of sustained law and order that will enable women to decide about the burqa. From this perspective, if one is genuinely concerned about women's rights in Afghanistan, she needs to sincerely explore 'the history of the development of repressive regimes in the region and the United States' role in this history' (Abu-Lughod 2013, 31). One also needs to ask if US tax dollars put toward the war in Afghanistan will bring peace, security, and education closer to women or rip them further away. The role of the burqa is not amplified in this discussion.

In the aftermath of the 'war on terror', issues related to security and women's covering are greatly intertwined in both Afghanistan and Iraq (after the US invasion in 2003). Several news reports indicate women are reluctant to take off their veils in both countries, for safety reasons. Several Iraqi women, mostly university students, tell an interviewer that more and more women wear the hijab 'simply out of fear' (Spinner 2004). An Iraqi woman remarks, 'I put on the scarf because I wanted to walk in the street without fearing someone will kill me or kidnap me . . . I heard rumors about killing women without a scarf. Why should I risk my life?' The article continues:

> This is the new reality for many women in Iraq . . . As the months have passed since the U.S.-led attack, fewer women are daring to venture out without wearing a . . . head scarf . . . In Baghdad, moderate Muslim women used to feel they had a choice whether to wear the scarf, even as religious oppression under Saddam Hussein grew over the past decade. Now, in many neighborhoods, it is hard to find a woman outdoors without a head scarf.

Thus Iraqi women (subjected to the violence engendered by the war and beyond) have to wear the hijab for safety reasons after the American invasion. That Iraqis increasingly withdraw to their cultural, ethnic, and religious affiliations, and commit sectarian violence, must be understood in relation to the American invasion which ended an entire regime of social life. More directly, this whole discourse (increased veiling, what this is taken to signify, etc.) must be critically situated in relation to the 'war on terror' that created such conditions, rather than simply recoursing to the popular rhetoric of Islamists imposing rigid and conservative clothing on women.

Other news articles report on how the war hinders Iraqi women's daily life and robs them of opportunities they had previously enjoyed: 'Iraqi women had been earning university degrees since the 1920s . . . and became physicians, engineers and lawyers' (Trejos 2006). It continues: 'as a college student in 1974, Nouri showed off her long black hair . . . wore short skirts . . . walked around campus with friends who happened to be boys . . . [Women] took walks around their neighborhood . . . wearing whatever they wanted.' However, after the United States' invasion, all of this was changed. 'The younger women say they fear being snatched on their way to school and wonder whether their college degrees will mean anything in the new Iraq.

Older women, proud of their education and careers, are watching their independence slip away. "We're suffering right now . . . The war took all our rights."' Once again, these women's lived experiences call for a critical assessment of the popular discourse that suggests that Muslim women live constrained and secluded lives, either voluntarily or otherwise, and wear the hijab because of the influence of radical Islamists.

Situating choice

As discussed above, in the US news media, veiling is often portrayed as a practice imposed on women. In particular, it is frequently juxtaposed with Western-style clothing, signifying the former as a symbol of conformity and the latter as a symbol of autonomy. One article states: 'The burka is still universal . . . even in Kabul, where Western-style skirts were not uncommon before the Taliban' (Lacayo 2001, 36). Another article reports that a tailor in Kabul is now busy making women's pants that were banned under the Taliban. The article also states that 'skirts cut just below the knee are particularly popular for indoor wear' (Baker 2001). Likewise, another journalist remarks: 'Although Iraq is predominantly Muslim, for many decades its capital was a trendy, modern city. In the 1960s, women wore short skirts and blouses with low necklines. But their daughters say they do not have such freedom today. They blame a post-war insurgency bolstered by conservative hard-liners' (Spinner 2004). While the Taliban and the conservative hardliners are here blamed for restricting women from wearing pants, skirts, and low necklines, women seem to have only two options: Western-style attire, modernity, autonomy – or 'traditional' clothes, conservatism, confinement. Such casual oppositions are neither remarkable nor recent, for such representations of Muslim women and their veiling practices are embedded in classical Orientalist discourses. As Edward Said's (1978, 7) landmark work demonstrated, Europe produced the Orient as its contrasting image to assert its own superiority. Further, as Uma Narayan (1997, 45) states, '[a] colonial representation is one that replicates problematic aspects of Western representations of Third-World nations and communities', and it can be 'produced' by those outside the 'West', too, including 'Third-World' subjects. Viewed from this perspective, the veil stands between tradition and modernity, East and West, suppression and autonomy. This formulation constructs Islam as an oppressive religion and proposes that Muslim women must be liberated from the veil.

When such accounts emphasize that women cannot wear Western-style outfits because of conservative hardliners, they imply that Western women choose their clothing freely. This implicit assumption appears similar to the category of the 'average Third World woman', in contrast to the self-representation of the 'Western' woman that Chandra Mohanty (2003, 22) has examined. That is, while the former supposedly leads an essentially truncated, sexually constrained, and tradition-bound life, the latter presumably has control over her body and sexuality. This portrayal is built upon a racial and geographical hierarchy, and uncritically situates 'Western' women as agents of their own destiny. Of course, a serious look at the massive Western fashion, advertising and cosmetic industries, which incessantly proclaim the 'imperfections' of women's bodies, declaring what they must wear to get a perfect man or job, swiftly collapses the mirage of freedom on offer.

Indeed, seeking to intelligently understand the practice of veiling also requires situating Western women's choices in social context. Consider the banal examples of high-heeled shoes and plastic surgery. Many women continue to wear high-heeled shoes despite the fact that they cause health problems, for 'high heels have a long history of social status, sexuality, and power. It is not really surprising, by the time girls are four years old they know that Disney's high-heeled glass slipper does not fit the ugly women' (Head of Oxfordshire Podiatry Services, cited in Chambers

2008, 2). A steady increase of cosmetic surgeries in the US also demonstrates the internalization of certain beauty standards and gendered behaviours. The American Society of Plastic Surgeons (2013) reported performing 290,224 breast augmentations in 2013, a 37 per cent increase since 2000. It can be argued, as Clare Chambers (2008) has remarked, that a woman may want breast implants because she herself likes the way they look, and not to please a man or to submit to patriarchal norms. However, 'it would be impossible to say that a woman's desire for breast implants were independent of patriarchal norms unless she lived in a nonpatriarchal society . . . Why on earth would anyone want to have surgery to insert heavy and dangerous alien objects into her body if there were no social meaning to, or social payoff from, the practice?' (39–40) In other words, rather than problematically assuming Western women have control over their bodies and sexualities, one must consider that 'all choices take place in a cultural context, and depend in large part on that context for their meaning' (40). These body modifications and others are embedded in a social script that devalues women's natural bodies and represents them as objects for the male gaze.

To further appreciate the limits of agency, assumed for American women, is also to consider how women in other parts of the globe view their autonomy. Courtney Smith (2011) conducted research in which she compared practices of female genital cutting and breast implantation. Although in her study, the American interviewees emphasized that 'in the U.S. women are free to make whatever choice they want regarding their bodies', her African participants articulated a very different response to breast implantation. One interviewee remarked, 'I have never heard of this practice and never in my life do I want to know about it. Women who do it aren't really women. It must be caused by a sickness.' Commenting on the statement, Smith writes that her participant is clear that 'not everybody believes American women are, in fact, free' and that their 'bodily integrity clashed directly with Western notions of liberty and rights' (34, 37). Smith's study illustrates the limitations of freedom afforded to American women, given the perspective of those who have not internalized similar social meanings. American women's choices and autonomy are indeed shaped and curtailed by patriarchal culture.

And women elsewhere are critical of Western values and hegemony. One article (Mcgirk 2002) discusses the ways some elite Pakistani female students who study in very modern and expensive American-style schools, and who have been to the US, express concerns regarding the American invasion of Afghanistan. One student remarks, '[a]nd what's so great about these American values that they're trying to impose on us? . . . Is it really liberty? I watched *Oprah* the other day. She was talking to pregnant 13-year-old girls who were unmarried. I'm glad I don't have those complications in my life.' Following her lead, another student states: 'That's right . . . Americans talk about protecting women's rights. But have you seen that George Michael video where he has these women on leashes like dogs? Give me a burqa any day [instead].' These students are attentive to American supremacy and do not seem inspired by presumed liberal American values. Their observations regarding mainstream media demeaning women resonates with critical scholarship. As many scholars argue, media images suggest 'how women in general, specific women and groups of women in particular, are seen, treated and received. [They construct] their status as unequal and their reputation as inferior' (MacKinnon 2011, 14). Since the objectification of women's bodies in the media points to a certain violence that women in the US are subjected to, the student cited above juxtaposes it with the burqa and considers the latter, sarcastically, a better disparity.

Even so, people often do not reflect on diverse forms of social inequalities that women face in the US. They seem to have internalized the liberal notion of choice and draw on it to assert a certain autonomy. A newspaper editorial, 'Veils as a Matter of Choice', is a case in point. 'To mandate . . . that I must or must not wear a veil, robs a woman of her inherent freedom . . . I may choose to wear a habit, a veil, a chador, a niqab. I have that freedom, as well as the freedom to respect another person's choice' (Ugolini 2006). Similarly, a Muslim woman argues elsewhere that although she would never herself wear a burqa, she 'must agree with Afghanistan's new minister for women's affairs, who told the *New York Times Magazine* recently that it was not about the burqa but about choice'. The author continues:

> I have met women who choose to cover their entire body, including their face. We must support that choice . . . Isn't that what it's about for women all over the world, be it the choice to vote, have an abortion, drive a car, wear a miniskirt or wear a scarf? When it becomes about what women wear rather than what they choose to wear then we infantilize women as much as the Taliban did.
>
> *(Eltahawy 2002)*

These accounts are critical of the popular representations of veiling, and argue that women must be free to choose their dress. Denying women that right is seen equal to the Taliban-imposed restrictions. Everything – the salvation of the world, as in Laura Bush's idiom above – seems to hinge on this right. However, these descriptions, too, disregard the social context in which women make their decisions. For 'if we accept the fundamental premise that humans are social beings, raised in certain social and historical contexts and belonging to particular communities that shape their desires and understandings of the world' (Abu-Lughod 2013, 40), then one has to consider the significance of cultural practices to individual choices.

Veiling encounters intolerance

The notion of freedom also needs to be understood against the power relations which shape it and which it sustains. In the US, the practice of veiling is not seen as a sign of cultural and religious aspiration but a practice belonging to the Other. Within this context, many Muslim women experienced discrimination at different venues in the post-9/11 era. One article reports that in Atlanta, police arrested a Muslim woman because she refused to remove her head scarf before attending a hearing (*Washington Post* 2008). Thereafter, a judge ordered her to serve ten days in jail for contempt of court. Though she was released in less than a day, the incident sparked a protest, ending up requiring court workers to undergo sensitivity training. However, as Council on American-Islamic Relations spokesman Ibrahim Hooper argues, training does not address the problem behind the behaviour. Elsewhere, a journalist reports that '[a] Muslim woman was asked to leave her place in line at a credit union in Southern Maryland and be served in a back room because the head scarf she wore for religious reasons violated the institution's "no hats, hoods or sunglasses" policy' (Zapotosky 2009). Commenting on the event in the article, Hooper reiterates that '[t]his may be the tip of the iceberg . . . There's got to be a way to work it out so that this security concern does not lead to violations of constitutional rights'. Indeed, such discrimination remains part of the social fabric of the society.

Other articles report on discrimination regarding employment opportunities faced by head scarf-wearing women. The Supreme Court was to hear the case of whether Abercrombie & Fitch 'violated anti-discrimination laws when it denied a job to a Muslim applicant because her head scarf conflicted with the company's dress code' (Barnes 2015). When the applicant was interviewed, 'she scored high enough on the company's ratings to qualify for a job'. Another Muslim woman describes her experience: 'When I walk into interviews, I find that literally interviewers' jaws drop. They are excited on the phone, but in person they lose the energy'. This woman sent a post-interview email, explaining that 'she hopes no one was taken aback by her manner of dress and that her faith has nothing to do with how well she works or what level of commitment she brings to a job'. The journalist reports that the woman is 'born and raised in this country (not that this should matter) and is well educated, with a master's degree in public policy. She has had a solid six years of work in international development.' The woman's friends also had similar discriminatory experiences (Joyce 2005). Overall, religion-based discriminations have increased in the post-9/11 America. According to the Equal Employment Opportunity Commission, 'the number of charges filed by Muslims alleging discrimination doubled from the four years before the September 11, 2001, terrorist attacks to the four years after' (Joyce 2005). These incidents expose prejudice that Muslim women face in the United States, despite the fact that Title VII of the Civil Rights Act of 1964 prohibits workplace discrimination based on religion, national origin, race or gender. Muslim women's choice to wear or to not wear a veil, thus, must be situated within this broader social context, this wider terrain of prejudice. The discourse of choice regarding veiling is clearly insufficient: whether concerning women in the West or elsewhere, whether framed in the language of choice or not, it cannot be understood without understanding the social context and relevant power relations.

Conclusion

This chapter has discussed post-9/11 representations of the veil in the US. While the practice of veiling continues to be freighted with negative connotations, it needs to be situated within socio-historical context. I have discussed how the 'War on Terror', and related rhetoric, has subjected Muslim women to new violence and restrictions, while veiling has been framed by a problematic liberal notion of choice. After all, 'ideology and beliefs limit and shape what are perceived as available and viable options for all individuals in a society' (Fineman 2004, 41). Since the practice of veiling already has a negative trajectory in the US, any discussion regarding it cannot be consigned outside such discourse: it must speak to (if not from) this discursive formation. When the media represent the veil as an imposed (rather than freely chosen) practice, this rhetorical and discursive move epitomizes Muslim women as docile, powerless, and vulnerable victims. This has a distributed effect, 'because the Western definition of what makes one human depends on the notion of agency and the ability to make rational choice' (Volpp 2001, 1192). To throw Muslim women into a world where their dress codes are determined by conservative hardliners, as such interpretations do, erases the long and variegated history of the veil, reducing it to a foil for the freedoms signified by Western clothing. Furthermore, one cannot ignore discriminations Muslim women continue to face because of their clothing in the US. To that end, one has to account for US ethnocentrism in order to comprehend Muslims' veiling discourse. This notion of choice, after all, does not carry some innate, objective reality; it remains precarious.

References

Abu-Lughod, Lila. 2013. *Do Muslim Women Need Saving?* Cambridge, MA: Harvard University Press.

Ahmed, Leila. 1992. *Women and Gender in Islam: Historical Roots of a Modern Debate*. New Haven, CT: Yale University Press.

American Society of Plastic Surgeons. 2013. 'Plastic Surgery Statistic Report'. Available at www.plastic surgery.org/Documents/news-resources/statistics/2013-statistics/plastic-surgery-statistics-full-report-2013.pdf (accessed 28 January 2017).

Andrea, Bernadette. 2007. *Women and Islam in Early Modern English Literature*. Cambridge: Cambridge University Press.

Baker, Peter. 2001. 'In a New Kabul, Feelings of "Freedom in the Air"'. *Washington Post*, 25 November.

Barnes, Robert. 2015. 'Supreme Court to Hear Case of Woman Who Wasn't Hired Because of Head Scarf'. *Washington Post*, 24 February.

Behakis, Yannis. 2001. 'Hello, Sunshine'. *Time*, 26 November.

Bush, Laura. 2001. 'Radio Address by Mrs. Bush'. *The American Presidency Project*. 17 November. Available at www.presidency.ucsb.edu/ws/?pid=24992 (accessed 28 January 2017).

Chambers, Clare. 2008. *Sex, Culture, and Justice: The Limits of Choice*. University Park, PA: The Penn State University Press.

Eltahawy, Mona. 2002. 'When Women Cannot Choose'. *Washington Post*, February 5.

Fineman, Martha. 2004. *The Autonomy Myth: A Theory of Dependency*. New York: The New Press.

Hay, Carol. 2013. *Kantianism, Liberalism, and Feminism: Resisting Oppression*. London: Palgrave Macmillan.

Hernandez, Nelson. 2002. 'Returning and Rebuilding; Arnold Store Owner Founds a School for Afghan Refugees'. *Washington Post*, 7 March.

Hirschkind, Charles and Saba Mahmood. 2002. 'Feminism, the Taliban, and Politics of Counter-Insurgency'. *Anthropological Quarterly* 75(2):339–54.

Joyce, Amy. 2005. 'Discriminating Dress; External Symbols of Faith Can Unfairly Add to Interview Stress'. *Washington Post*, 25 September.

Kahf, Mohja. 1999. *Western Representations of the Muslim Woman: From Termagant to Odalisque*. Austin, TX: University of Texas Press.

Khan, Shahnaz. 2008. 'From Rescue to Recognition: Rethinking the Afghan Conflict'. *TOPIA: Canadian Journal of Cultural Studies*, 19 (Spring):115–36.

Khattak, Saba Gul. 2002. 'Afghan Women: Bombed to Be Liberated?' *Middle East Report* 222 (Spring):18–23.

Lacayo, Richard. 2001. 'About Face: An Inside Look at How Women Fared under Taliban Oppression and What the Future Holds for Them Now'. *Time*, 3 December.

MacKinnon, Catharine. 2011. 'X-Underrated: Living in a World the Pornographers Have Made'. In *Big Porn INC: Exposing the Harms of the Global Pornography Industry*, edited by Melinda Tankard Reist and Abigail Bray, 9–15. Melbourne: Spinifex.

Mahmood, Saba. 2005. *Politics of Piety: The Islamic Revival and the Feminist Subject*. Princeton, NJ: Princeton University Press.

Mcgirk, Tim. 2002. 'MTV or the Muezzin'. *Time*, 9 September.

Mohanty, Chandra Talpade. 2003. *Feminism without Borders: Decolonizing Theory, Practicing Solidarity*. Durham, NC: Duke University Press.

Narayan, Uma. 1997. *Dislocating Cultures: Identities, Traditions, and Third World Feminism*. New York: Routledge.

Said, Edward. 1978. *Orientalism*. New York: Pantheon.

Scott, Joan. 2007. *The Politics of the Veil*. Princeton, NJ: Princeton University Press.

Sheridan, Mary Beth. 2002. 'Woman Visits Kabul with Gifts, Hopes'. *Washington Post*, 20 May.

Smith, Courtney. 2011. 'Who Defines "Mutilation"? Challenging Imperialism in the Discourse of Female Genital Cutting'. *Feminist Formations* 23(1):25–46.

Spinner, Jackie. 2004. 'Head Scarves Now a Protective Accessory in Iraq: Fearing for Their Safety, Muslim and Christian Women Alike Cover Up before They Go Out'. *Washington Post*, 30 December.

Trejos, Nancy. 2006. 'Women Lose Ground in the New Iraq: Once They Were Encouraged to Study and Work; Now Life Is "Just Like Being in Jail"'. *Washington Post*, 16 December.

Ugolini, Joanne. 2006. 'Veils as a Matter of Choice'. *Washington Post*, 28 October.

Volpp, Leti. 2001. 'Feminism versus Multiculturalism'. *Columbia Law Review* 101(5):1181–1218.

Washington Post. 2008. 'Around the Nation'. *Washington Post*, 25 December.

Zapotosky, Matt. 2009. 'Muslim Woman Asked to Leave Line at Bank over Head Scarf'. *Washington Post*, 10 March.

4

WEARING A VEIL IN THE FRENCH CONTEXT OF *LAÏCITÉ*

Anne Fornerod

Introduction

When addressing the veil issue in France, it has become very common to start with speaking of three girls refusing to remove their Islamic headscarves before attending classes in a Parisian suburban secondary school.[1] This 'Creil case' is usually depicted as the initiating event that triggered a year-long social, political and legal process leading to the passing of the 2004 Act banning the wearing of religious signs and clothes at school. In itself, and through its implementation, this Act resulted in widespread questioning of the law applicable at that time, which was governed by clear and well-established principles. Indeed, whereas the legal principle of *laïcité* imposes religious neutrality only on public institutions, citizens should benefit, either in the public or the private sphere, of the freedom of religion within the limits of public order. Since the passing of the 2004 Act, however, the exact scope of the principle of *laïcité* has been constantly discussed as to whether it applies beyond the sphere of public institutions and civil servants.

This actually reflects the fact that *laïcité* carries another meaning beyond secularity of public institutions, as it also represents a core social and political value allegedly embodying national identity, and therefore goes beyond the limits of public institutions and their activities. Within this meaning, *laïcité* corresponds to various relations to religion, including a clear sense of distrust towards it (Willaime 2005). It is often synonymous with the idea of extensive neutrality, in that manifestations of freedom of religion should be confined to the private sphere only.

Relations between these two ways of understanding *laïcité* can be considered from two angles. On the one hand, these conceptions of *laïcité* are not separate: the 'ideological' or 'philosophical' *laïcité* clearly influences the narrower legal notion as it eventually did in 2004. This explains why the veil, like religious clothing in general, belongs to the expression of freedom of religion, but some limits have been put on its wearing in the name of *laïcité*, as is the case in public institutions. On the other hand, the legal – and more liberal – approach of *laïcité* is based on a more balanced relation between neutrality and freedom of religion resulting in a discrepancy between how *laïcité* is handled in case law and in public debates. The latter conveys a conception of *laïcité* that is ill-disposed towards the visible expression of religious beliefs in the public sphere that should be religiously neutral. In such a context, the balanced legal discourse on *laïcité* and the related freedom of religion implications becomes less audible. Religious dress code and the veil precisely constitute a key element of analysis of the relations, including tensions and overlaps between both approaches. This is particularly tangible regarding the veil in the workplace. Lastly, though its banning by the 2010 Act, the full veil illustrates an approach based on a large scale religious mentality.

The veil in public institutions

As a rule, the principle of *laïcité* applies to people involved in the carrying out of public service activities, be they civil servants or not. Religious neutrality, however, does not impose upon the users of public service activities. In this regard, pupils in public schools are an exception to the rule.

Incompatibility between the veil and the status of civil servants

Civil servants enjoy the right to freedom of conscience but the principle of *laïcité* prevents them from expressing their beliefs. The principle of religious – as well as political or ideological – neutrality of the state is deeply rooted in the French tradition (see van Ooijen 2012). Public institutions must run public service activities without any consideration of religion, so that users addressing such services do not feel discriminated.

As regards civil servants, it has been established by case law before it is inscribed in the Act of 20 April 2016 on deontology, rights and duties of civil servants. In an opinion dated 3 March 2000, the Council of State clearly held that civil servants are subject to the principle of *laïcité* and religious neutrality in a case involving a student monitor in a state school, who was dismissed by a regional chief education officer. According to this opinion, it follows from the constitutional and legislative provisions, that the principles of freedom of conscience and of *laïcité* of the state, apply to all public services. Moreover, the principle of *laïcité* prevents all civil servants from manifesting their religious beliefs within a public service. Lastly, a civil servant of the education public service manifesting his/her religious beliefs, particularly through a sign, amounts to a breach of obligation. The Court of cassation – which is the highest court for matters of civil law – even held that the ban depends on the public service activity carried out and not on the public or private status of the company the employees work for (Court of Cassation, 19 March 2013, no. 12–11.690).

The users of public services are not bound by the duty of religious neutrality, but, rather, benefit from the general right to freedom of religion within the limits of what is required by the proper functioning of the public service. In this regard, pupils in public schools are submitted to a derogatory status.

The veil in public schools

Dealing with the veil in public schools – i.e. state-run and funded schools – implies a start of a long story between school and *laïcité*. In the 1880s, the governing Republican Party's fight against the moral and intellectual influence of the Catholic Church mainly took place at school. Public schools are still governed by the principle of *laïcité*, inherited from the 'school Acts' adopted at that time.[2]

The Education Code, however, establishes the guarantee of freedom of education (Article L. 151–1), which derives from the Act of 31 December 1959 on the relationship between the state and private schools,[3] the majority of them denominational. This point is worth mentioning as the debate on the relationship between school and religion has been for years precisely marked by the issue of the public funding of private schools. In this regard, the issue of religious signs worn by pupils constitutes a turning point as the focus is henceforth on the place of religion at public school again.

The process took 15 years from the 'Creil case' mentioned in the introduction to the adoption of the Act of 15 March 2004 governing, pursuant to the principle of *laïcité*, the wearing in public schools of symbols or clothing denoting religious adherence (whose provisions are now entrenched in Article L. 141–5-1 of the Education Code), and went through various stages from the assertion of the pupils' freedom of religion to the eventual limitation of their related right to express their religious beliefs through clothing. Throughout this process, the focus was clearly on the Islamic veil, although some appeals involving Sikh pupils were lodged with judicial courts under the 2004 Act.

Shortly after the Creil case, the Council of State issued an opinion upon request of the Ministry of Education in which it declares that the wearing of signs or dress by which pupils demonstrate a religious belonging is not in itself incompatible with the principle of *laïcité* (Conceil d'État 1989).[4] Later on, the Council of State also intervened, this time as the highest administrative court, and took a similar view. As an example, it held in 1992 that a school internal regulation act forbidding the wearing of any distinctive religious, political or philosophical sign amounts to a breach in the freedom of expression of the pupils, which is guaranteed by the principles of neutrality and *laïcité* of public school (Council of state, 2 November 1992, *Kherouaa*, no. 130394).

The ultimate critical stage was the report issued in 2003 by the Commission for Reflection on the Application of the Principle of *Laïcité* in the Republic (Stasi 2003), commonly called the Stasi Commission. Notwithstanding its large title and scope, this report rapidly turned out to be analysed and commented on through the solitary issue of the wearing of the Islamic headscarf and particularly whether a bill banning the Islamic veil at state schools would be passed afterwards. On this point, the Stasi report justifies the need for a legislative text regulating religious dress code in public schools. The situation in public schools would have outpaced the rules defined earlier by the Council of state as it is attested by the lack of mention of the gender equality challenge in its 1989 opinion (Stasi 2009). In this report, the Islamic headscarf is perceived as a failure of social integration and incompatible with gender equality (Stasi 2003, 45ff.). The Commission eventually recommends that:

> with respect for freedom of conscience and the individual character of private establishments under contracts, ban clothing and symbols that express religious or political affiliation from schools, colleges, and high schools. Any sanction should be proportionate and taken after the student was asked to comply with these obligations; this provision should be inseparable from the motivations of the following statement: 'Interdicted religious clothing and symbols consist of overt signs such as the large cross, veil, or kippah. Discreet signs such as medallions, small crosses, Stars of David, Hands of Fatima, or small Qurans are not regarded as symbols pointing to religious belonging'.
>
> *(Stasi 2003, 68, author's translation)*

Such details do not appear in the legislative text but can be found in the implementing administrative circular of the Ministry of public education of 18 May 2004 which provides further details on the interpretation to be given to 'symbols or clothing denoting religious belonging': they are those 'whose wearing leads one to be immediately recognised by religious affiliation, such as the Islamic veil, whatever name it is given, the kippah, or a cross of manifestly excessive dimension'.

Moreover, the Act would be applicable to all religions and likely to new symbols or any attempts to circumvent its provisions. Such provisions allow interpretation of the signs worn by pupils in that these do not need to be directly and in themselves religious to be prohibited. In this regard, two rulings are worth mentioning which upheld the decisions of the expulsion of pupils who respectively wore a bandana-like headscarf (Council of State 5–12–2007, *Ghazal* no. 295671) and a long skirt (Council of State, 19–03–2013, no. 366749) but interpreted like religious clothing and then falling within the scope of the prohibition contained in Article L. 141–5-1 of the Education Code.

The 2007 Ghazal case was then brought before the European Court of Human Rights thus giving the opportunity for conventionality review of the ban on religious signs (*Ghazal v. France*, no. 29134/08). According to the Court, the restriction on her freedom of religion was in accordance with the law and pursued the legitimate aim of protecting the rights and freedoms of others, public order and the constitutional principle of *laïcité*. Moreover, the Court relied on the margin of appreciation left to the national authorities in this area and accordingly found the application manifestly ill-founded. As for five other very similar applications (*Aktas v. France* (no. 43563/08), *Bayrak v. France* (no. 14308/08), *Gamaleddyn v. France* (no.18527/08), *Jasvir Singh v. France* (no. 25463/08) and *Ranjit Singh v. France* (no. 27561/08)), it was unsurprisingly held inadmissible.

The conventionality review of the ban on religious garments had actually occurred before the adoption of the 2004 Act. Through the cases Dogru and Kervanci (*Dogru v. France*, no. 27058/05, 4 December 2008, *Kervanci v. France*, no. 31645/04), the Court of Strasbourg had explored the law applicable at that time, in order to decide whether the school head had been entitled to exclude pupils wearing the Islamic veil during physical education lessons. In the cases at hand, the Court held that the impugned measures of exclusion had sufficient legal basis (laws and regulations pertaining to the requirement of assiduity in attending lessons, safety concerns and the need to dress in a manner compatible with the practice of sports).

The discussion about whether the ban on religious signs at public school is applicable only to pupils deserves attention here as it emphasizes once again the sensitivity of the veil issue, especially in this republican space embodied by public school. Though the above mentioned 2004 circular made it clear that the ban on religious signs at school does not apply to parents, the subsequent 2011 circular by Education Ministry interprets the 2004 Act as also preventing women wearing the veil from accompanying pupils and teachers on school trips. The administrative court of Montreuil adopted a similar stance by ruling the same year that this is 'an application of the constitutional principle of neutrality of the public service to supervision during school trips by parents' who are, in such circumstances, considered to be auxiliary civil servants. The Council of State intervening as an advisory body overturned such a solution in 2013: mothers offering additional adult supervision are public service users and should consequently not be submitted to the requirements of religious neutrality (Conseil d'État 2013). The ruling of the Administrative Court of Nice of 9 June 2015 echoes this position putting an – provisional? – end to this question. This shows, however, that the veil issue blurred the lines of the scope of the principle of *laïcité*. The discussion on whether and how wearing the veil is compatible with the Republican value of *laïcité* does not stop at the public school gates, showing that this is an ongoing issue in public debate.

The veil in the workplace

The veil is undeniably an issue in the workplace but is regulated through common law applicable to all religious practices. The main debate took place regarding childcare structures.

Overall legal framework for wearing the veil in the workplace

Like for other religious garments, Islamic veil regulation falls within the scope of the general provisions of the Labour code regulating the exercise of rights and freedom in the workplace. Article L. 1121–1 of this code provides that no limit on employees' rights and freedoms can be brought unless such a limit is justified by the nature of the task to be carried out and proportionate to the aim pursued. Although it does not reflect the whole picture of how religious practices are dealt with in the workplace, case law shows that when it comes to applying these provisions to religious signs and practices the veil is regularly at the heart of the litigations.

Among the most quoted cases, the decision of the court of appeal of Paris 'société téléperformance' dealt with a telephone interviewer dismissed because of her refusal to remove her veil, even after she was suggested to wear it tied as a hat (Court of appeal of Paris, 19 June 2003, *Société Téléperformance*, no. S03/30212). The dismissal was declared void by the court on the ground that the employer did not provide evidence of the existence of objective elements unrelated to any discrimination based on religious beliefs to justify the dismissal. He argued that the new conditions of activity after transfer of the employee to another site justified the decision to prohibit the wearing of headscarf. However, the employee, a telephone interviewer, was already in contact with customers in his former position without any reported problem with them in connection with the headscarf.

The contact with customers was also a key element in a more recent case for which a request for a preliminary ruling from the *Cour de cassation* was lodged on 24 April 2015 with the Court of Justice of the European Union. The question pertained to the compatibility between the European Council Directive 78/2000 establishing a general framework for equal treatment in employment and occupation and the wish of a customer of an information technology consulting company no longer to have the information technology services of that company provided by an employee, a design engineer, wearing an Islamic headscarf (Case *Asma Bougnaoui, Association de défense des droits de l'homme (ADDH) v Micropole Univers SA*; Cour de cassation, 9 April 2015, no. 13–19.855).[5]

Lastly, the role of the High Authority for the Struggle against Discrimination and for Equality (*Haute autorité de lutte contre les discriminations et pour l'égalité*, hereinafter HALDE) is worth mentioning.[6] This equality body has left a significant set of decisions pertaining to discrimination on religious grounds thus providing examples of how the veil is dealt with in the workplace and beyond. As an example, an employee working in the catering service a retirement home had been required to wear a hairnet instead of the veil. The HALDE decided that this amounted to a refusal to comply with hygiene rules imposed by the task and that such rules met the objective justification required by the labour code (Articles L.1121–1 and L. 1321–3; Decision of 18/10/2010, no. 2010–166).

A case in particular further illustrates the key role of the veil in this case law, involving an employee of a private nursery.

Wearing the veil in childcare structures

The amazingly heated debate triggered by the Baby Loup case started in 2008 with the dismissal of an employee of a private nursery due to her refusal to remove her headscarf in breach of the nursery internal regulations. These regulations actually imposed the employees to abide by the principle of *laïcité* and religious neutrality. The legal saga was initiated by the employee who referred the matter to the HALDE in 2009 and ended with the ruling of the Court of cassation of June 2014.[7]

The HALDE originally supported the employee by holding that both principles of *laïcité* and neutrality do not apply to the employees of a private association in the absence of public service activity. In addition, the internal regulation amounted to an unlawful general and absolute forbidding of religious freedom. Consequently, the dismissal was discriminatory on grounds of religion. The highest civil court eventually held that the general clause on *laïcité* and neutrality in the internal regulations of the Baby Loup Association limiting the employees' freedom of religion comply with the provisions of Article L. 1121–1 of the Labour Code. This limitation was justified owing to the small number of employees likely to be in relation with children and their parents.

The decision of the Court of cassation of June 2014 is the final point of this very controversial case as it has raised an important debate on the enforceability of the principle of *laïcité* in private companies, while both principles of *laïcité* and neutrality normally do not apply to the employees of a private association in the absence of public service activity (Court of cassation, 25 June 2014, *Association Baby Loup*, no. 13–28.369). The activity of the Baby Loup association, however, would make it specific for it addresses young children and this is likely to explain the impact of this case. Besides the media's large coverage and parallel to the judicial process, the public debate took the form of parliamentary interventions. Before the Senate a bill aiming at extending the duty of neutrality to certain individuals or private structures welcoming young children was submitted in October 2011 (Senat 2011) and a similar text was submitted before the National Assembly in January 2013 (Assemblée Nationale 2013).

The full veil issue

At the time when the bill banning the full veil was written, the issue was not entirely topical, for it had been dealt with before in case law.[8] The adoption of the Act of 11 October 2010 prohibiting the concealment of the face in public space, however, amounts to a peak in the discussion about this specific garment, which was later extended before the European Court of Human Rights.

The full veil issue before the Parliament: The Act of 11 October 2010

The full veil issue stands apart in at least two ways. First, compared with hijab, the full veil wearing is above all quite a limited practice.[9] Whether it corresponds to a religious requirement was seriously discussed and even denied (Gérin and Raoult 2010, 22). Second, the gap between the whole political and parliamentary process and the legislation eventually passed on this issue is worth emphasizing. Indeed, although the Act of 11 October 2010 formally relates to concealing the face in public space, 'the background to the provision makes very clear that the full-face veil worn by some Muslim women was its main target' (Vickers 2014). Although it was introduced, discussed and publicized as 'the Act on burqa', the legislation that eventually passed in 2010 does not refer to Islamic dress. Article 1 of the 2010 Act provides that 'No-one shall, in public space, wear clothing designed to conceal one's face'. In addition, Article 2 defines public space, which is 'composed of public streets and places open to the public or dedicated to a public service'. A number of exceptions to the ban lie in Article 2: the ban does not apply 'if the garment is required or permitted by law or regulations, if it is justified for health or professional reasons, or if it is part of sporting practices, festivals or artistic or traditional events'. Finally, Article 4 introduces new provisions in the Penal Code (Article 225–4-10) creating the criminal penalty for concealment of the face or coercion of a person to hide his face.

The explanation of such a wording lies again in the dual faceted *laïcité*. It emerges from political and parliamentary debates preceding the Act that the full veil is perceived as a dressing contradicting Republican values like gender equality and, in the first place, laïcité.[10] *Laïcité* is conceived and used in public debate led by politicians as a core Republican value likely to bring people together. Hence, emphasizing the threat on *laïcité* makes it easier to justify a ban on the full veil. A legal approach of *laïcité* makes the scope of *laïcité* narrower. In this regard, the government called on the advice of the Council of State which has been a determining factor prior to the discussion of the bill before the Parliament in that it clearly asserted that it 'found it impossible to recommend a ban on the full veil alone (as a garment representing values incompatible with those of the Republic), in that such a ban would be legally weak and difficult to apply in practice' (Conseil d'État 2010, 8 and ff.). In a similar vein, the Council considered that '*laïcité* could not provide the basis for a general restriction on the expression of religious convictions in the public space'. The Council eventually advocated a ban on the covering of the face beyond the simple case of a full veil, but in a limited way, namely 'to safeguard public order when it is threatened' or 'when identification is needed for access or movement in certain places and for performing certain procedures'. The Council then deems that, in general, banning face concealment in public space would entail restrictions on several fundamental rights and freedoms and refers to the justifications of limitations which may be applied to liberties which are generally part of public order. Although the opinion of the Council of State on the lawfulness of the bill sounds classically formulated, it introduces a key element when it comes to deal with public order. Indeed, the Council of State reminds that 'public order has a substantive dimension, which has to do with its three traditional components: public security, peace and health', but it also includes, a 'non-substantive' dimension (Conseil d'État 2010, 24–5). There lies a critical element of the whole process to be found again before the Constitutional Council, the administrative circulars and subsequently the European Court of Human Rights in the case *SAS v. France*.

In its (short) ruling of 7 October 2010, the Constitutional Council held the bill to be in conformity with the Constitution. Despite the cautious terminology and apparent classical reasoning, it sanctioned this non-substantive public policy by referring to the 'minimum requirements for living in society'. These requirements would find their origin in Article 5 of the Declaration of the Rights of Man and of the Citizen (Verpeaux 2010, 2373), according to which 'The Law has only the right to defend actions harmful to Society. Anything that is not forbidden in Law cannot be prevented, and no one can be forced to do anything that is not required in Law'. An indirect reference to the full veil lies in the assertion that 'women hiding their faces, voluntarily or not, find themselves in a situation of exclusion and inferiority clearly inconsistent with the constitutional principles of freedom and equality'. The administrative circular of 2 March 2011 enacted by the prime minister and providing details on the scope of the Act is clearer in its reference to the actual object of the ban and entails a reference to the non-substantive public order by providing that 'concealing one's face amounts to undermining the minimum requirements of social life'. According to this circular of March 2011 – banned – 'garments used to conceal the face' should be understood as those 'that make it impossible to identify the person', which expectedly include the 'full veils (burqa, niqab)'.

The 2010 Act before the European Court of Human Rights

From the very beginning of the legislative process, the question arose of the fate of an act introducing an overall ban on the full veil before the European Court of Human Rights. The Grand Chamber of the European Court of Human Rights handled this issue in the case *SAS v. France* on 1 July 2014 (no. 43835/11). Following the usual structure of the reasoning of the Court the interference with the freedom of religion, the aim pursued and the proportionality between both, with regard to the necessity of the impugned measure in a democratic society, ought to be successively considered. The applicant argued that the 2010 Act infringed her right to private life and, above all, her freedom of religion (Article 9 of the European Convention of Human Rights), as wearing a full veil amounted to dressing in accordance to her religious beliefs. Hence, the Court unsurprisingly held that there had been an interference with her freedom of religion.

In respect with the aims pursued by the French Parliament when passing the Act, the Court first upholds the aim of public safety though it 'wonders whether the lawmaker granted significance to such concerns' (§ 115). The second aim invoked by the French government was the compliance with the minimum common set of values in a democratic and open society, including gender equality, dignity and the minimum requirements of life in society. The first two elements were dismissed by the Court. As regards gender equality, the Court deemed that this principle cannot be the basis for 'prohibiting a practice that women – like the applicant – claim in the context of the exercise of rights' (§119). On this point, the Grand Chamber interestingly departs from the case *Dahlab v. Switzerland* in which it was held that 'it cannot be denied outright that the wearing of a headscarf might have some kind of proselytising effect', seeing that it appears to be imposed on women by a precept which is laid down in the Qu'ran and which, as the Federal Court noted, is 'hard to square with the principle of gender equality' (ECtHR, *Dahlab v. Switzerland*, no. 42393/98, 15/02/2001) and echoes the position of Judge Françoise Tulkens in her dissenting opinion on the case *Leyla Şahin* (ECtHR, Grand Chamber, 10 November 2005, *Leyla Şahin v. Turkey*, no. 44774/98). In the eyes of judge Tulkens, it is very hard to consider that:

> the principle of sexual equality can justify prohibiting a woman from following a practice which, in the absence of proof to the contrary, she must be taken to have freely adopted. Equality and non-discrimination are subjective rights which must remain under the control of those who are entitled to benefit from them. 'Paternalism' of this sort runs counter to the case-law of the Court, which has developed a real right to personal autonomy on the basis of Article 8.
>
> *(§ 12)*

The flexible nature of the third element 'the living-together' called for an in-depth proportionality review of the impugned measure, in order to assess whether the latter is necessary in a democratic society. At this stage, the Court expresses strong reservations with regard to the adoption of a large scope ban against the limited number of women wearing the full veil. Moreover, it expresses a great concern about the Islamophobic statements that accompanied the passing of the Act. Despite these reservations, the Court eventually held, however, that given the wide margin of appreciation applicable in religious freedom cases, the ban was proportionate to be aim pursued, namely the preservation of the 'living together' (§ 157), and that there had been no violation of Articles 8 and 9.

Conclusion

Despite the reservations expressed and the wording of the 2010 Act, the European Court of Human Rights has repeatedly validated the lasting political choice (irrespective of the party affiliation) that consists in resorting to *laïcité* as a value to regulate religious practices legally covered by freedom of religion. It is no surprise, then, that the veil regularly comes in the news as a discussed and even questionable religious practice. In an interview given to the newspaper *Libération* in April 2016, the prime minister declared that he is in favour of a ban on the veil in universities, thus triggering again discussions on this point, although such a practice is legally permitted. No other religious dress code gives rise to such large-scale public debate as the veil does. Moreover, one observes a constant discrepancy between how the veil is handled in public debate and how it is generally regulated in law.

Notes

1. See, among many others, Mercier (2016). The 'Creil case' is considered to be one of the two cases at the origin of the 'Muslim issue' in France (along with Salman Rushdie's book *The Satanic Verses*) – see Beaugé and Abdellali (2014).
2. Compulsory, free and *laïque* education was set up by the Act of 28 March 1882. Thus under the Act of 30 October 1886, education is entrusted to *laïque* teachers only in public primary schools (today Article L. 141–5 of the Education Code).
3. The 1959 Act endorses the principle of freedom of education enshrined in several Acts adopted during the nineteenth century: the Guizot Act of 28 June 1833 applies to primary schools, while the Falloux Act of 15 March 1850 affirms the freedom of education for secondary schools, and notably provides that public authorities can grant premises and subsidies to private schools.
4. The French Council of State exercises a dual function: it acts as an advisory body to the government, and as the highest administrative jurisdiction.
5. In its decision of 14 March 2017 (C-188/15, Bougnaoui and ADDH) the Court of Justice of the European Union held that "the willingness of an employer to take account of the wishes of a customer no longer to have the services of that employer provided by a worker wearing an Islamic headscarf cannot be considered a genuine and determining occupational requirement".
6. This equality body was created in 2004 and its main task consists in assisting all individuals facing allegedly discriminatory practices by providing advice on legal options and helps establish proof of discrimination. It was suppressed and included in the powers of a new body, the *Défenseur des droits* (Rights supporter), in 2011.
7. This chapter is not the place to report on all the judicial stages of the case. Over 50 papers have been published in French legal literature alone. In English, see e.g. Hunter-Henin (2015).
8. As an example, the widely publicized case of Madame M. from 2008: the applicant, a Moroccan woman married to a French man, sought the annulment of the decree preventing her from acquiring French nationality (Articles 21–2 and 21–4 of the Civil Code). However, the Council of State considered that the applicant, by wearing the full veil, had 'adopted a radical practice of her religion, incompatible with the key values of the French community, notably with the principle of gender equality and, therefore, she did not satisfy the condition of assimilation' (Council of State, 27–06–2008, Madame M., no. 286798).
9. For the year 2009, which marks the beginning of the process that led to the passing of the Act, the data provided by the newspapers ranges from several thousands to less than 400. According to the parliamentary report that preceded the legislative process, although the Ministry of Interior evaluated to '1900 the number of women wearing the full veil, that is the *niqab*, that is however a phenomenon uneasy to quantify even if increasing. However, the Ministry of Interior cannot provide information on women wearing the burqa' (Gérin and Raoult 2010, 28).
10. As an example, the explanatory memorandum to the bill of 19 May 2010 expressed the idea that the concealment of the face and wearing of the full veil in particular are detrimental to the values which 'guarantee the cohesion of the Nation' and constitute 'a manifestation of a rejection by a community of Republican values' (Assemblée Nationale 2010).

References

Assemblée Nationale. 2010. *Project de loi interdisant la dissimulation du visage dans l'espace public*. Available at www.assemblee-nationale.fr/13/projets/pl2520.asp (accessed 28 January 2017).

Assemblée Nationale. 2013. *Proposition de Loi visant à étendre l'obligation de neutralité à certaines personnes ou structures privées accueillant des mineurs et à assurer le respect du principe de laïcité*. Available at www.assemblee-nationale.fr/14/pdf/propositions/pion0593.pdf (accessed 28 January 2017).

Beaugé, Julien and Hajjat Abdellali. 2014. 'Élites françaises et construction du "problème musulman". Le cas du Haut Conseil à l'intégration (1989–2012)'. *Sociologie* 5(1):31–59.

Conseil d'État. 2010. *Study of Possible Legal Grounds for Banning the Full Veil*. Available in English at: www.conseil–etat.fr/content/download/1910/5758/version/1/file/etude_voile_integral_anglais.pdf (accessed 28 January 2017).

Conseil d'État. 2013. *Étude demandée par le Défenseur des droits le 20 septembre 2013*. Available at www.defenseurdesdroits.fr/sites/default/files/atoms/files/ddd_avis_20130909_laicite.pdf (accessed 28 January 2017).

Dieu, Frédéric. 2010. 'Le droit de dévisager et l'obligation d'être dévisagé: vers une moralisation de l'espace public?'. *La Semaine juridique administrations et collectivités territoriales* 48:2355.

Gérin, André and Éric Raoult. 2010. *Rapport d'information au nom de la mission d'information sur la pratique du port du voile intégral sur le territoire national*. Assemblée nationale 2262.

Hunter-Henin, Myriam. 2015. 'Religion, Children and Employment: The Baby Loup Case'. *International and Comparative Law Quarterly* 64:717–31.

Mercier, Charles. 2016. 'Laïcités, écoles, intégration'. *Études* 1:43–53.

Senat. 2011. *Proposition de loi visant à étendre l'obligation de neutralité aux structures privées en charge de la petite enfance et à assurer le respect du principe de laïcité*. Available at www.senat.fr/leg/ppl11–056.pdf (accessed 28 January 2017).

Stasi, Bernard. 2003. *Commission de réflexion sur l'application du principe de laïcité dans la République: rapport au Président de la République*. Paris: La documentation française.

Van Ooijen, Hana. 2012. *Religious Symbols in Public Functions: Unveiling State Neutrality: A Comparative Analysis of Dutch, English and French Justifications for Limiting the Freedom of Public Officials to Display*. School of Human Rights Research Series. Cambridge: Intersentia Ltd.

Verpeaux, Michel. 2010. 'Dissimulation du visage, la délicate conciliation entre la liberté et un nouvel ordre public'. *Actualité Juridique. Droit Administratif*, 2373.

Vickers, Lucy. 2014. 'S.A.S. v France: The French Burqa Ban and Religious Freedom'. 10 September. Available at www.e-ir.info/2014/09/10/sas-v-france-the-french-burqa-ban-and-religious-freedom/ (accessed 28 January 2017).

Willaime, Jean-Paul. 2005. '1905 et la pratique d'une *laïcité* de reconnaissance sociale des religions'. *Archives de sciences sociales des religions* 129:67–82.

5

2007/8

The winter of the veiled women in Israel

Tamar Elor[1]

Introduction

This chapter revolves around Jewish, rather than Muslim, veiled women. It dwells upon a short period of time in winter 2007/8, when a tangential point was created between the worldwide manifestations of the global 'problem' and its Israeli variants. The joining in of Jewish women to the camp of veiled women[2] may serve as a platform for various theoretical queries. The most recurrent subjects deserving attention can be found on a bipolar axis: on the one hand, veiling is portrayed as an act of submission to a patriarchal regime; and on the other hand, it is conceived as provocative and subversive.

The veiled women from Beit Shemesh

In November 2007, Tamar Rotem published a short article in the *Haaretz* newspaper under the title: 'This is not Kabul, it is Beit Shemesh' (Rotem 2007). She described a 'new phenomenon' among ultra-Orthodox women who, according to her, 'turned modesty into a flag, self-expression, obsession. Of their own accord, unguided by a rabbi, they pray and recite Psalms very often and believe that modestly dressed women will bring redemption' (Rotem 2007). These women, whose total number in Ramat Beit Shemesh, Jerusalem, Safad and other places is estimated at about 150, are usually associated, in one way or another, with one woman, their purported leader, who assumed for herself the title 'Rabbanit'. Besides their prayers and dress codes, they also take vows of silence. Some of them opt to stay at home as much as possible, and many cover the house's hallways with various fabrics to create an atmosphere of a tent. All keep a healthy dietary regime, and the Rabbanit also practices alternative medicine. The multilayered garments are meant to emulate or revive the appearance of biblical mother figures. Most of the attention is drawn to the veil-like fabric covering their heads. This external piece of cloth is thrown over another scarf or several scarves tied under the chin (and not on the back of the neck as is the custom among other Orthodox Jewish women). Several women also cover one eye or both eyes and need to be guided through the streets by their children. Rotem visited Keren in her home and joined her and her followers in some of their study sessions. The veiled women from Beit Shemesh had their '15 minutes' of media glory in winter 2008. Sari Makover-Belikov (2008) wrote about them in detail in *NRG*, *Ma'ariv* newspaper's online edition, in January 2008. The numerous phone calls I received from foreign reporters stationed in Israel indicated that the phenomenon certainly caught their attention as a potentially interesting piece of news for their readers. Taking it at face value, they might have rushed to conclude that it represented a leakage of the European 'problem' to Israel's Jewish society.

As Rotem rightly mentions, we are dealing here with the independent initiative and move of women who did not consult their rabbis, or ask their husbands' permission. Moreover, in some cases their choice even prompted their husbands to divorce them. The group's leaders advise novices how to fend off their husbands' objections. They tell them to avoid arguments and confrontations. Modesty, they say, is their own business, not their husbands'. They are advised to answer comments thrown at them with 'all is done for the sake of God'.

If we were to locate the phenomenon in the vast field of managing the Jewish-Orthodox female body, veiled women would be at its centre. Not the accepted or conventional, canonical, legitimate centre, but at the eye of the storm. They are surrounded by various communities that manage their bodies and clothing in different ways and recoil from the origin of the swirl like centrifugal circles. Nevertheless, they are aware of the modesty tornado, of the vortex moving toward its new targets: tights for girls, gender-separated buses, stitching up *schlitzes* (clothing slits), wig-burning, declaring tricot fabric spawn of the devil, and so on and so forth.

Various transformations take place in the ultra-Orthodox world, opening up increasingly more options for participating in non-Orthodox arenas (work, leisure, studies, communication, etc.). Alongside these easy but rather constant breezes, rages the modesty tornado as it looks for creative responses to its self-styled challenge. Of course, it is men who control the bellows channelling the tornado and mark its route. The veiled women of Beit Shemesh only took control of one of the bellows and accelerated its pace to such a degree that it seemed to outside observers to radicalize the situation *ad absurdum* or *ad obsessionem* as suggested by Rotem (2007).

The relentless imperative of 'chastity' imposed upon women has been widely discussed in sociological literature (see Elor 1992; Oryan 1994), and has become a meta-narrative of the life of women and girls. Chastity is the yardstick, the ethics and aesthetics of their existence. The veiled women resorted to the original text and appropriated the story. Actually, there is nothing new about it. Women, and other weakened groups, always knew how to make the most of the oppressive component by identifying it and working through it, by surviving through the kitchen, through their children, their sexuality. The feminist attempt to identify in these tactics remnants of empowering is not new either. Identifying the oppressive element and choosing a way to deal with and resist it are certainly a kind of agency. Yet the feminist endeavour usually strives to find out where a certain conduct places women. For instance, whether ultra-Orthodox women who have increasingly more children, more than their spouses would have wished, are performing a subversive act; can their appropriation of the *baleboste* icon of a perfect housewife, who also works outside her home, raises 14 children and looks amazing, be interpreted as *Haredi* feminism?

In contrast to MacLeod (1991) and other scholars who perceive the Muslim veiling as a liberating practice in an oppressive environment, we can safely say that the veiling did not provide the women of Beit Shemesh with opportunities to venture into new public spheres of action. The plethora of fabrics entrenched them in their castles/homes, confined to their innermost rooms, in which some of them keep their vows of silence. They are not to be seen outside, nor heard at home: thus subversiveness assumes different connotations here. These women wanted to disappear, as it were, to duck all surveillance devices, to operate in the dark. But their refusal to be seen and heard was not easily accepted; many elements, both private and public, called the authorities to intervene in the acts of covering and uncovering outlined by the women from Beit Shemesh. The authorities, in their turn, were not too keen to intervene. Perplexed as they were, inner authorities (local rabbis, the town's public leaders) waited for this lunatic fringe phenomenon to vanish over time. Turning a blind eye to it, the peace of the *Haredi* public was only interrupted by occasional neighbourly harassment.

Constructing the subversive stance domestically shifts the veil debate from the universal level and brings it nearer to the female body. The debates in France, Turkey and Belgium revolved around the *laïcité* of the state and its public spaces and around prohibitions and permissions pertaining to both men and women, although their main issue was with girls and women. In her analysis of Mona Jbareen's case in Israel, Gilly Hamer (2006) too claimed that it was tried with regard to the state and its institutions and away from the female body. The veiled women of Beit Shemesh deny this illusion. The 'domestication' of the issue created an interface between the woman qua normative citizen and her body, sexuality, children, spouse and immediate environment. Should the state wish to intervene in Jewish women's acts of covering and uncovering, it will have to follow a different course than the one taken in France. In France, women are required to reveal their faces qua citizens, whereas in Israel, as we shall find out shortly, they are ordained to do so by virtue of their nationality and their motherhood.

'These are ways of the Gentiles, this is how Arab women walk around the Old City': The spectacles of the nation

In front of the rabbinical court discussing the divorce case of a 'veiled' woman, stood a woman who refused to bare her face and communicated with the *dayanim* (religious judges) via written messages delivered by her (female) attorney. Court-ordered personality tests refuted their assumption that she was a 'mental case' (Rotem 2007). Among other reasons, the court ordered the divorce, citing that 'these are ways of the Gentiles, this is how Arab women walk around the Old City' of Jerusalem.

The discontent with the 'veiled' women phenomenon is interwoven with the Arab 'issue', and this theme runs throughout the texts written about them and said to them. The title of Rotem's (2007) article alluding to Taliban women and reports of the women themselves indicate that the first phase of the veil's politicization and the attempts to regiment it were nationally biased. This should not come as a surprise, as this is the most significant societal-political parameter in Israel (not unlike the *laïcité* in France and Turkey, or the Belgian preservation of ethnic difference), and in the case of veiling it is, in fact, self-evident. To quote the women's own words, as recorded by journalists: 'They called me smelly Arab and told me to get lost . . . they pushed me . . . I'm stopped at the central bus station and asked to present my papers. I don't want men seeing my [ID] photo, so I show them my son to prove I'm not an Arab' (Rotem 2007). 'Neighbours scribbled on my mailbox "chuck out the Taliban", and address me in Arabic'; 'Once I was stopped by policemen who scattered my bags all over the place'; 'People say about me, "Who is she? A Moslem? An Arab?"'; 'It is most hurtful when we are insulted among ultra-Orthodox public' (Makover-Belikov 2008).

The veiled women of Beit Shemesh introduced a new game of (defying) visibility. Like early twentieth-century *halutzim* (Zionist pioneers), they wished, as it were, to reproduce the appearance of the nation's Canaanite forefathers/foremothers, to dress like our foremothers in their tents. They, too, relied on the Orientalist assumption that the Bedouin prototype accurately represents the appearance of our ancestors. Thus they perceive the clothes of the Arab rural woman as an authentic and outright restoration of those worn by our mother Sarah. In a way . . . they have dissociated the 'veil' from its Arabness, and thereby differentiated between Arabness and Islamism. For them, the veil is an article of clothing that had characterized the female dwellers of the tents of Kedar and has nothing to do with any decree of religious law (be it Jewish or Muslim).

But they do not stop there. By resorting to the 'desert source', they wish to accumulate power and bring it home, in order to transform the principal arena allotted to the activity of Orthodox women. This is a completely different arena from that of the Muslim female agents. The latter wish *to go out into the world* as Muslims, whereas the veiled women of Beit Shemesh want to entrench themselves *inside*, to dig into the walls of their homes and shake their pillars. They do it in a way familiar to women and fundamentalists – the 'right' and 'acceptable' way.

Their use of the code of decency should protect them from criticism: one cannot easily denounce veiling or silence, since 'the king's daughter is all glorious within' (Psalm 45:13) and 'a voice in a woman is licentiousness' (TB Ber. 24a). Therefore the criticism directed against them has emerged within safer locations – the national and motherly (as distinct from gendered-sexualized) arenas.

It is one thing to stand firmly against the perplexed patriarchy, and say: 'I follow to its conclusion your moralization about decency'; and quite another thing to be labelled as an 'Arab' and accused of stepping out of the perimeters of the nation and faith and betraying the conceived duties of motherhood (we shall return to that shortly). The ultra-Orthodox world maintains a strict regime of covering and uncovering. Some of the criticism associates their 'Arabness' with their marginality in the *Haredi* society and with their hallucinatory image, as is evidenced in the following passage:

> Several weeks ago I travelled to Rachel's Tomb. I was standing in the crowded bus by a Breslov Hasidic woman. In front of me sat two *Haredi* Yeshiva students and one of them said to his friend: 'Here comes the Nach-Nach-Nachmanit to greet the Arab woman'. I could not control myself anymore. I said to them, out loud, so that the whole bus would hear: 'I don't speak to men, but Sarah our mother was dressed like me, and Rachel our mother too, and at least you can appreciate it instead of mocking it'. I told them, 'Your women's wigs are better, right? Promiscuity is better, no?' They kept silent and didn't answer me.
>
> *(Makover-Belikov 2008)*

Boundaries of the freedom to play with the body

While collecting my materials on the 2007/8 occurrences of veiled women, the Beit Shemesh (and two other cases) plot had thickened, introducing care-taking and motherhood into the picture of managing the covered body. The act that was described above as an entrenching in the castle/home and undermining its foundations turned out to be more daring than one might imagine. It also included new and different perceptions of pedagogy, proper parenthood and motherhood.

Deviant

On 25 March 2008, a *Haredi* woman from Beit Shemesh was arrested on suspicion of child abuse and failing to report incest in her family. Press photos and television footage had shown a woman completely covered. It took another look to realize it was not one more case of a detainee hiding his/her face to avoid identification. The woman's lawyer argued that she was arrested because her neighbours, who perceived her as aberrant, connived against her.

In an article published in the *Haaretz* newspaper on the day following the arrest, reporter Tamar Rotem provided details linking the detained mother (whose name was suppressed) to the 'veiled women's Rabbanit', about whom she had written several months before. Rotem searched her memory for incriminating signs she might have noticed during her visits to the veiled woman's home (Rotem 2008a). She remembered a 13-year-old boy, who seemed underdeveloped for his age, and a girl who did not attend school regularly. In her article were interwoven sentences indicating that an open and cheerful atmosphere reigned in the Rabbanit's house, and that the girl had sat until the small hours of the night with the women gathered there and was treated by them with warmth. Alongside Rotem's article, the newspaper published an item by crime journalists who reported that welfare officers had known the family for quite some time.

Neighbours hearing sounds of beating and crying summoned the welfare authorities, and at least one boy was removed from the house and sent to a boarding school. The journalists described a dominant mother (the father spent a lot of time abroad on fundraising), who did not want the authorities to intervene in her children's upbringing. One winter night, the article reported, a woman who was praying in the Rabbanit's house refused to let in one of her children who was standing outside wearing only an undershirt. Her son (who did not look like a religious boy) appeared on televised news and denied on camera the things attributed to his mother. Unable to show the boy's face, the camera operator focused time and again on his bruised hands.

On 26 March 2008, Nativ Nahmani reported on the Walla! web portal that the police confronted one of the brothers with his sister, and that the boy admitted to having had different sexual relations with her, some consensual, some enforced. It was also mentioned that the police were continuing to investigate whether he had had similar relations with his younger sister also (Nahmani 2008). Tamar Rotem cited again, beside the crime article, some of the mother's friends and followers, who told her that she was a dedicated mother, albeit not necessarily a normative one. Following the Rabbanit's arrest, the facts of the affair were gradually becoming clear, but in the meantime her arrest had already marked her (even though her name was not published as yet), her initiative and her flock as deviant, deviance and deviants, respectively.

At the beginning of May 2008, *Ynet* reporter Neta Sela returned to the veiled woman from Beit Shemesh. The woman, now subjected to house arrest, agreed to respond in writing and a few sentences to the charges brought against her. Denying the offences attributed to her in the indictment, she nevertheless confessed that she believed in the proverb 'He that spareth his rod hateth his son' and learned from a *midrash* of our sages that King Solomon's mother tied him to the pole of the bed and had him whipped. She explained her inward withdrawal with the alternative psychological economy she had devised: 'I saw that they [her children] don't really listen to me and that I'm wasting precious time arguing with them that they should go to bed on time . . . [so] I've decided that instead of talking to the wall, I should dedicate my time to prayers'.

She told the reporter that she was on a mission in the service of the people of Israel, that her actions were hastening the redemption and the coming of the Messiah. When asked if she would want the reporter to give any message to her children, she consented and said: 'I love you very much and I'm not angry at anyone, but most of all I love the Holy One Blessed be He' (Sela 2008).

A total of 327 responses were registered to this article, most of which slandered the veiled woman, complained about her misuse of the title 'Rabbanit', recommended to send her to psychiatric treatment and prevent her from seeing any of her 12 children. The fact that she had presented herself as a righteous woman, who chose to distance herself from worldly vanities, to withdraw to a world of prayer and silence, to reduce the body and hide it, did not elicit a single empathic response, let alone a word of respect. Her deviant behaviour toward herself and her body was perceived as a betrayal of her role as a mother. The fact that she drove a wedge between her body and her children and did not treat them with warmth was interpreted (also by her daughter in an interview) as the reason that drove her children to seek warmth and intimacy with each other.

Tossed out of the boundaries of the Jewish collective as Taliban-Arabic, the covered body is now hurled further. This time outside the boundaries of humanity. Betraying the role of a mother, child abuse and self-withdrawal were conceived as all-out rebellion. Her attempt to present her behaviour as alternative pedagogy and as a proposal for motherhood of a different kind failed miserably. The state's intervention was received with glee by the ultra-Orthodox public. They reserve to themselves the right to deal with their own women and men; with the others the state is more than welcome to deal as it sees fit.

Freakin' deviant

Just as the narratives relating to the 'Beit Shemesh abuser' were swirling and twisting, a story about a 'Jerusalem abuser' unfolded in late winter 2008 (Rotem 2008b). Newspapers sometimes referred to her as the 'woman in white' – the symbolically opposite colour of that of the woman from Beit Shemesh who covered herself with very dark fabrics. Her 'veil' was a white-covered Book of Psalms in which she always buried her head in front of journalists and camera operators who waited for her at the courthouse. She and her husband submitted themselves to the unconventional leadership of Elior Chen, a young practitioner of practical Kabbalah. On his orders she had separated from her husband and let into her home two of Chen's adherents to help her raise her eight children. The indictment against her was filed in spring 2008 and included charges of severe child abuse, such as burning the children, pouring alcohol on their wounds, locking them in suitcases and other such tortures. The woman was arrested after one of her children was taken to a hospital unconscious, probably due to violent shaking. The story of the woman and her ex-husband unfolded alongside that of Elior Chen, who fled Israel as soon as the police began investigating the case. Newspapers published several detailed profiles of Chen's personality, but her profile featured large in them, always hidden behind a prayer book. At the same time, an ultra-Orthodox woman from Netivot was arrested for sexually abusing her minor sons. She, too, appeared at her remand hearings with her head buried in a Book of Psalms, and hid her hair under a traditional Sephardi head-covering.

As mentioned above, winter 2007/8 had brought with it another wave of global preoccupation with the 'phenomenon of the veil', which also had a local expression with contexts of its own: forging links between revealing and covering, faith, multi-children families, economic adversity, incest and child abuse. The threat of the veil that in Europe was perceived as economic-cultural and also political, imploded domestically and undermined the belief that homes and families can be run according to criteria other than those of the middle class, that a mother can divide her love and attention between many children, keep an eye on all of them and commit herself to the work of motherhood without collapsing. This implosion spills over and by far overreaches the 'veiled' women. It questions the ability of others in general (*Haredim*, Arabs, newcomers) to take care of their children.

The recurring incidents increased the suspicions that there might be quite a few endangered children of women who cover themselves to various degrees, suggesting that twisted minds and cruel hands might be hiding beneath the long sleeves, wigs and scarves. Suspicions of this kind prompted the Welfare and Social Services Ministry to appoint a revision committee to look into events in Beit Shemesh. The committee was meant to investigate, first of all, the performance of the municipal Welfare Department in its dealing with the case of Bruria Keren, who was known to welfare authorities from her previous place of residence, Bnei Brak. However, the Ministry sought to harness the committee's report to a broader debate on the limits of the country's 'radar' and its ability to detect deviations of *Haredi* families and especially *Haredi* mothers.

The revision committee

About a month after the publication of the internal report, a multi-participant brainstorming conference was held at the School for Educational Leadership in Jerusalem to discuss the report findings and related issues. The district director conveyed her hope that the debate would assist in devising modes of operation to sharpen the signals caught by the radar in the *Haredi* society. It was there that I heard for the first time the radar metaphor in this context. Members of the top echelon of the Welfare Ministry in the Jerusalem district were present in the room; and on the academic-professional side, David Tene, professor of social work and clinical therapist, and I attended the meeting. Psychiatrist Professor Eliezer Witstum contributed to the debate via a videotaped interview conducted by Dr Neri Horowitz, who initiated and chaired the debate.

Horowitz also wrote a summary report and submitted it to the Ministry in early October 2008. The report's opening sentences clearly stated the aim of that document:

> This paper seeks to grapple with the difficulty of social services officials to identify abuse and endangerment in helpless individuals, and attempts to pinpoint groups from the same circle of induction that present potential danger and to offer directions and procedures that would better the chances of locating endangered groups and individuals.
>
> *(Horowitz 2008, 1)*

The report was based on a comprehensive and diversified research made specifically for that purpose. 'Identification and locating' were targeted for research – namely, the marking of potential internal factors that might endanger and harm helpless individuals within ultra-Orthodox circles. The document implicitly indicates that not only children are helpless and suggests that women, too, may fall near this category. For instance, an examination of the history of the woman suspected of abusive behaviour reveals that she herself was a victim of abuse:

> Her increasing dysfunctionality, the revelation that she was severely abused by her father and that some of her behavioural patterns imply personality disorders raise the question of the need to deal with the suspect beyond the legal, public aspect . . . the deterioration of the suspect, with respect to her parental functionality, is not examined over a period of time, but rather emerges, contrary to the testimonies, as a constant state of abuse and neglect that has evaded the 'radar' of various services.
>
> *(Horowitz 2008, 5)*

The report, therefore, attempts to outline access routes to 'barred' areas, in the words of its author. State authorities find it difficult to penetrate these areas, and the signals they emit are not caught regularly on the welfare radar. Only when one of Keren's children was removed from the home and sent to a boarding school, did the signals begin to routinely pulsate. The standard work of welfare officers revealed what needed to be revealed. The simultaneous publications on the 'freakish cult' that have radicalized the imperatives of chastity and have taken the law into its hands provided the event with a colourful sub-communal context. Therein was also made the acute connection between marginal groups (newly religious, New Age, etc.), women's freedom and sexuality, and the quality of motherhood.

Details, cited in the meeting and the report, indicate that the accused was known to the welfare authorities, and not for her tendencies to cover herself. These emerged in recent years. Outgrowing her traditional Jewish background, she went on a search for a specialization niche of her own. Her sister said about her that she had tried to be all kind of things before she became a natural therapist. In Bnei Brak she had initiated *pashkevils* against wigs, and spoke against rabbis. While still living there, she had already taken vows of silence. The hegemonic fabric of the ultra-Orthodox society of Bnei Brak could not tolerate such behaviour, and she had to move to the *Haredi* borderland – Beit Shemesh. She had developed the concept of multiple veils in the four years preceding her arrest, drawing her inspiration from the 'shawl movement'.[3]

Based on the input of the clinical experts, the ensuing conversion took a pronounced psychological turn, organizing the veiled women's deviance around sex and violence. These were the facts; these were the grounds for the arrests. Sexual deviance and violence were caught on the radar. Horowitz's report balanced the psychologic bias and introduced the sociological aspect.

I'd like to use the final paragraphs of this chapter to propose a broader sociological reading of the unusual events concerning the veiled women. One should bear in mind that Jewish veiled women represent a marginal episode, but their marginality can certainly be extended into the feminine context of *Haredi* society, as well as into Israeli political contexts, in light of what has been said here about other veiled women.

Lifting the curtain, peeping, and closing

Situations in which the state lets women be 'what they are' should not be taken at face value. It is worthwhile to first check whether the state actually means to let them enjoy cultural freedom of action, or whether it actually means to create a public sphere that would include various forms of presence.

Perhaps the state simply 'does not see them', and is rather satisfied with what it sees and for that reason is not inclined to intervene in and change the public spectacles of their bodies. Bodily markers may serve a given political-social-cultural situation, and it is in the best interest of the state not to blur them.

In Israel, as it turns out, the state finds it convenient to let Arabs be Arabs, and ultra-Orthodox be ultra-Orthodox. Trespassing into these seemingly unmarked public spaces, without bodily markers, is undesirable. Israeli universities do not even consider stipulating conditions for the outward presentation of identity of those who enter their gates. They have other means to manage the quantity and quality of these potential admittees.

Prevailing games of power make it easier to deal with a female student who looks like an Arab than with her inconspicuous friend who does not particularly look like an Arab. And this is true also in the case of Orthodox Jewish female students. Ambiguity could lead to confusion. A Jewish woman from Beit Shemesh perceived as an Arab would have her belongings scattered all over the place by people whose job is to protect and uphold the law. A female Palestinian student would get a job, or be able to rent a flat, because 'she doesn't look Arab and speaks accentless Hebrew'. Identity games, disruptions of appearance, walking around the Israeli public space with a body bearing no national/religious label, are all privileges reserved for other people . . . Thus, the assertion of Scott (2007) – or O'Brien after her – that the objection to the veil in France and elsewhere is *only* a matter of racism is somewhat problematic. It may very well be that this objection *also* represents the remnants of an increasingly corroded attempt at creating spaces in which immigrants could be 'French'. Since no one is really French, everyone could be French. Since no one was really European, Jews could become excellent Europeans for a short while in early twentieth-century Europe. It is precisely the licence to be 'Muslim' that implies the abandonment of creating potentially egalitarian public space and leeway, since such a licence is predicated on the existence of authentic Islamism on the one hand, and proper Frenchhood that rejects diversification on the other. A multicultural project would want, of course, to deconstruct conventional Frenchhood and reconstruct it from interminable equivalent possibilities. But such a project would have to be essentialist – namely, believe in (miscible) cultural essences.

In spite, or maybe because, of the acknowledgment of the power of religion, the ancient idea to create an artificial religion-free space is replete with the potential to benefit many, and has benefited quite a few people, but probably not nearly enough. In France matters have reached such a state that some Muslim women would have fared better had they covered their heads. Invisible transparent walls strewn all over the *laïcité* are all the harder to pass. The promised possibilities to move freely in the public sphere were not entirely realized, either by the state or by the women. Covering the head offered a more rewarding, empowering, immediate route.

In Israel, standard veiled women are treated leniently. The Jewish religious/ultra-Orthodox or Muslim woman may be whatever she chooses to be. The state allows women to deal with their own identity within familial spaces, the village or the community. A religious Jewish woman is required to pay a price for covering her head in the public sphere, but not a steep one. This price rises if the woman is ultra-Orthodox or an Arab who covers her head. Her preliminary ethnic marking draws the boundaries of her activity. But she can cross them, and often does, not always unsuccessfully. However, each head-cover has an expected and accepted habitat of its own. The veiled women of winter 2007/8 started a new game. Their game forced the state to join in. Inner patriarchies (husbands, rabbis, extended families) collaborated with state authorities to regiment them, to reveal their true face.

The state lifts the cover only when sexual deviance and violence against children are involved. Once the matter is dealt with, the curtain descends once again on the *Haredi* society. Now a sign is attached to it, saying: 'Behind this piece of cloth, terrible things transpire'. *Quod erat demonstrandum*: raising large families entails neglect, deviance, violence and lack of love. This boosts our (people who are not religious, not Arab and do not have multi-children families) confidence in our conception of mental and familial normalcy. Thus the ultra-Orthodox woman's head-cover continues to signal to us what is right and what is wrong. The fact that it functions as a marker within the various *Haredi* communities makes no difference to the state.

The women of Beit Shemesh limited the political potential of managing the body to the domestic sphere, and thus helped the state and their husbands to relegate this game to the realms of psychological treatment. If they ventured out, they were dealt with like 'Arab' women, ousted from mainstream citizenship and pushed into the margins. Time and again, their message was reduced to different forms of madness and obsession, to something that should and could be locked at home or behind bars. Their excessive covering has demonstrated that the State of Israel is at ease with a body that marks one's affiliation as long as it does not fool the radar as in the case of a Jewish body that signals 'Arabness', or child abuser's body that signals benign 'multi-children motherhood'.

In France, the state demands: 'Reveal your head so that we would know that you're alright, a woman like any other French woman'. In Israel, the state demands: 'Cover your head so that you would appear as who you are, not like any other woman'.

Translated by Aya Breuer.

Notes

1. This is an extract of an article originally published in Hebrew as 'Hahoref shel ha're'ulot: Kissui vegilui be-20007/08' [2007/8: The Winter of the Veiled Women] *Theory and Criticism* 37(Autumn 2010):37–68.
2. This, of course, is not the first time that Jews are affected by the veil issue. In France, for example, the ban on publicly wearing conspicuous religious symbols or garbs has a bearing on Jews and their ability to abide by their own dress codes, wear necklaces with the Star of David or *yarmulkes*. In January 2004, the Knesset held a special session on the implications of the Stasi Commission recommendations on the Jewish community of France. The Chief Rabbi of France and other Jewish leaders from that country attended the session.
3. The 'shawl' movement is a broader boundary-crossing movement associated with the Keter Malchut organization headed by Rabbi Benyamin Rabinovitz. The women cover their upper body with a kind of shawl or cloak when they go out, call for replacing the wigs with scarves, and completely avoid tricot and spandex garments (Rotem 2007). On the margins of the shawl group, there is a group of *Haredi* women belonging to Chassidut Toldot Aharon (but not only), who cover their whole body with a hooded cloak (somewhat resembling a monk's habit). Most of the women wearing shawls and black cloaks belong to the ultra-Orthodox Ashkenazi society. Most of the veiled women, on the other hand, are newly observant Sephardi women. The three groups keep in touch with each other and meet on festive and other occasions.

References

Elor, Tamar. 1994. *Educated and Ignorant: On Ultraorthodox Women and Their World*. Boulder, CO: Lynne Rienner. (First published in 1992 in Hebrew).

Hamer, Gilli. 2006. 'Gender Transparency of the Court– Regarding Veiling at Israeli and French Schools'. Unpublished. (Hebrew).

Horowitz, Neri. 2008. 'The Challenge of Identifying Vulnerability in Clustered Environments: Jerusalem Agura'. (Hebrew).

MacLeod, Arlene Elwoe. 1991. *Accommodating Protest: Working Women, the New Veiling and Change in Cairo*. New York: Columbia University Press.

Makover-Belikov, Sari. 2008. 'The Women of the Veil'. *NRG*. Available at www.nrg.il/11/ART1/684/453.html (accessed 28 January 2017).

Nahmani, Nativ. 2008. 'The Abuser from Beit Shemesh'. *Walla* online news (Hebrew). Available at www.news.walla.co.il/?w=/1/1267424 (accessed 28 January 2017).

Oryan, Slomit. 1994. 'Nothing is More Beautiful than Modesty'. MA dissertation, Department of Communication, Haifa University (Hebrew).

Rotem, Tamar. 2007. 'This is not Cabool, its Beit Semesh'. *Haaretz*, 23 November (Hebrew).

Rotem, Tamar. 2008a.' The Suspect is a Saint who Speaks Only One Hour a Week'. *Haaretz*, 26 March (Hebrew).

Rotem, Tamar. 2008b. 'A Child Looked in a Suit Case'. *Haaretz*, 11 April (Hebrew).

Scott, Joan Wallach. 2007. *The Politics of the Veil*. Princeton, NJ: Princeton University Press.

Sela, Netta. 2008. 'It's a Crazy Lie'. Available at www.ynet.co.il/articles/0,7340,L-3539024,00.html (Hebrew) (accessed 28 January 2017).

6

VEILING NARRATIVES

Discourses of Canadian multiculturalism, acceptability and citizenship

Shelina Kassam and Naheed Mustafa

Introduction

In June 1993, Canada's *Globe and Mail* newspaper printed a short essay entitled: 'My Body is my Own Business'. One of the authors of this chapter (Mustafa) wrote about what it was like being young, Canadian and Muslim. I outlined my reasons for choosing to wear the hijab and how the people around me, from parents to strangers, responded and reacted. The essay caused a stir, eliciting responses and challenges from a variety of sources.

Popular access to the Internet gave the essay new life and 23 years later it continues to circulate and is regularly re-printed in high school and university textbooks. We bring up the essay not as a quaint stroll down memory lane but, rather, to illustrate that in the last two decades, the conversation about Muslim women, veiling and the varied reasons for choosing to veil has not pushed much past that short essay. The fact that the essay has essentially held up over time is a testament to the reality that we are in a conversational rut about Muslim women and the choices they make. What is fascinating, however, is that the conversation has become so central to national debates about citizenship and belonging and how the issue of veiling has been used politically and ideologically to illuminate key boundaries in the Canadian national imaginary.

Setting the context: Muslims and hegemonic discourse in the post–9/11 world

The post-9/11 discourse about Muslims has been taken up in two broad ways: using Muslim men (the 'dangerous Muslim man') as an entry point into stories about terrorism and the threat to national security, and using Muslim women (the 'imperilled Muslim woman') as an entry point into narratives about multiculturalism and fear of the erosion of Canadian values. As in other western multicultural nation-states, Muslims in Canada have become trigger points for discourses relating to citizenship, multiculturalism and secularism and have often been targeted for national, social, political and cultural exclusion. The position of Muslim women in these discourses is particularly precarious. Situated as she is at the ideological fault lines of community and society, the spectre of 'the Muslim woman' looms large in contemporary discourses.

In the Canadian context, public discourse has focused on the Muslim body, in particular on Muslim women and their clothing. This discourse has fixated on the racialized and gendered Muslim body, one that stubbornly insists (or so the story goes) on 'traditional' (and public) ways of living, whether through the wearing of veils while testifying or voting (the latter an invented problem), a desire for Shari'ah law, or cases of domestic violence that are perceived to be 'honour-based'. In such cases, the media lens invariably shifts to discourses of 'traditional' thinking and gravitates towards veiling practices as symbolic of all that is presumed to be in conflict with 'modern' notions of freedom and secularism.

Canadian public, media and political discourse about veiling has become an increasingly fraught, sometimes polarized, debate over the past decade. This national conversation has been strongly contested, with the issue gaining prominence also in legal challenges and political campaigns. Seen as a so-called 'wedge issue' in the 2015 federal election, Muslim women's veiling has become an iconic signifier of Canadian conversations on multiculturalism, secularism and integration. The predominant public and political discourse is underwritten by a triad of allegorical figures: 'the dangerous Muslim male, the imperilled Muslim woman and the civilized European, the latter a figure who is seldom explicitly named but who nevertheless anchors the first two figures' (Razack 2008, 5). The vociferous debates about veiling in the Canadian context illuminate the boundaries of 'acceptable' Canadian citizenship, with certain types of bodies (e.g. niqabi women) falling outside these boundaries.

In this chapter, we trace the issue of Muslim women's veiling in Canada over the past ten years, and provide an analysis of the political, media and public discourses regarding the veil. We argue that Canadian narratives about veiling are a telling reinforcement of the neo-Orientalist discourse of 'saving Muslim women' which positions some figures as outside the boundaries of 'acceptability' of Canadian citizenship and society. Hence, veiling narratives are utilized ideologically both to reinforce and to render invisible exclusionary practices of citizenship through which some – in this case, veiled Muslim women – are excluded from the Canadian national narrative.

Theoretical imperatives

Orientalist tropes about Islam and Muslims have a powerfully resilient history and have fuelled western fascination with the exotic 'other'. Said describes Orientalism as 'a western style for dominating, restructuring and having authority' (2003 [1978], 3) over the so-called 'primitive other'. Orientalist thought depicts Muslims as exotic, primitive, irrational, depraved, child-like, different – the other – while Europeans are seen as civilized, rational, mature, virtuous and normal (40). Such a binary constitutes the boundaries of the 'western' subject and the 'other', a codification that must continually be reinscribed. Orientalist notions of Islam are reified, essentialized and present a 'universalized Islam', a set of common beliefs, principles and cultural practices that represent the heterogeneous ways of life of Muslims everywhere. Latent Orientalist perspectives, embedded in contemporary discourse, infuse contemporary understandings about Muslims who are often juxtaposed against the so-called rational, modern, enlightened and 'normal' western subject. It is against this backdrop of (neo) Orientalist symbolism that Muslim bodies are measured and through which some Muslims are deemed to fall outside 'acceptable' boundaries of (western) citizenship.

The western fascination with the exotic Oriental woman necessitates a re-reading of Orientalist thought, a rethinking which centres gender at the heart of this discourse. Yeğenoğlu (1998, 11) maintains that the Orient is 'a fantasy built upon sexual difference ... the 'veiled Oriental woman' has a particular place in these texts, not only as signifying Oriental women as mysterious and exotic but also as signifying the Orient as feminine, always veiled, seductive and dangerous'. Such a gendered reading of Orientalism is critical in analyses of Muslims and especially in considering how and why veiling has become a crucial battleground for contemporary public and political debates. It is, after all, on the bodies of Muslim women that the most fervent ideological battles are waged in the contemporary context; it is these bodies that are often the specific targets for the gendered (neo) Orientalist logic of 'saving and rescue'.

Scholarship on race, citizenship and belonging in western multicultural societies is key to our analysis. Volpp (2007, 574) suggests that citizenship is not a neutral notion and that culture and citizenship are inextricably intertwined. Citizenship, she argues, 'emerges through its distinction from the cultural other'. Volpp further suggests that the cultural content of western citizenship is far from neutral: embedded in the notion of the 'citizen' are key values or virtues that are culturally specific, such as 'the Protestant work ethic or the spirit of capitalism, mould-ing the values of socially dominant groups into the identity of the citizen' (577). In this respect, Volpp suggests that so-called cultural attachments are perceived to inhibit the practice of citizenship. She uses the example of gender equality as a key value of citizenship in the western democratic states, a commitment which is perceived to enforce shared moral commitments and which demarcates the national body into zones of inclusion and exclusion.

These differential notions of citizenship are embedded in national narratives, in which ideas about 'the nation', its origins and contemporary manifestations (including ideas about citizenship, belonging, and multiculturalism) are played out. Thobani (2007) suggests that there are three types of subjects in the Canadian national narrative: the exalted (the white so-called legitimate subject), the extinct (the Aboriginal subject, marked for physical or cultural extinction), and the estranged (the 'visible' or racialized immigrant, granted conditional inclusion). In many cases, the conditional inclusion or acceptance of the estranged subject in the national space is contingent upon notions of culture. In the post 9/11 context, the Muslim body is the one through which the most fraught debates are occurring and upon whom ideas of 'culture' and 'other' are most often imprinted.

The idea of culture is used to reinforce these notions of differential subjecthood, thereby justifying which subjects fall within and outside the boundaries of the national narrative. Mamdani suggests that 'culture talk' (2004, 17) provides a convenient shorthand way to represent those considered pre-modern as those who 'made culture only at the beginning of creation' (18). Embedded in hegemonic ideas about culture is the view that 'bad' Muslims are those that refuse to be 'liberated' from their 'ancient' cultures, the values of which oppress and do not evolve. In this view, 'good' Muslims are those willing to be 'modernized' and practice their cultural traditions only in certain (mostly private) areas of their lives. Those Muslims willing to suppress their traditions and cultures for the so-called higher values embedded in 'being Canadian' are welcomed to the inner circle. Those who insist on holding on to their past, orbit on the outside. This demarcation between the 'good' and 'bad' Muslim (Mamdani 2004) becomes the dividing line between the 'acceptable' and 'unacceptable' in the national polity, with the good/acceptable Muslim often defined as 'moderate' and being granted qualified inclusion in society.

The 'imperilled Muslim woman' (Razack 2004) is central to veiling narratives in Canada. Jiwani (2005a; 2009) suggests that Muslim women are often represented as 'helpless victims' with western bodies positioned as 'chivalrous knights'. She further suggests that the 'rescue-ability' of Muslim women 'comes to be defined through terms that reveal how these women have become "ours" or more like us' (2009, 736). These figures stand at the heart of veiling discourses – many debates about the veil depict the Muslim woman as being under threat from Muslim men and requiring the saving intervention of the western subject. Such a narrative is founded on differential and racialized notions of citizenship, in which the 'saving' discourse is central.

The figure of the cultural other is a crucial dimension of a differentiated and racialized citizenship. Volpp states that 'the citizen is assumed to be modern and motivated by reason; the cultural other is assumed to be traditional and motivated by culture. In order to be assimilated into citizenship, the cultural other needs to shed his excessive and archaic culture' (2007, 574). Thus, citizenship rights are perceived in the national imagination to be centred on the acceptance of key (supposedly shared) values. Gender equality is seen as one such value. As Volpp observes, 'the immigrant other must be emancipated from the group or group values of gender subordination to qualify as a citizen' (2007, 580). Gender stands at the heart of intense debates about Muslims in Canadian public life, issues that often become viewed – explicitly or otherwise – as a key value of (racially coded) belonging to the Canadian national imaginary. Veiling – depicted as an equality issue – has become an iconic signifier through which notions of acceptability are explored within the multicultural Canadian nation-state.

This boundary of acceptability is illuminated in the differential treatment of niqabi women, versus those who choose other so-called acceptable ways of expressing their cultural and religious commitments (e.g. hijabs or other forms of clothing deemed to be 'cultural' or 'religious'). These boundaries have shifted in the public and political discourse in Canada: for example, while hijabs were previously hotly debated, they are now viewed as more acceptable and the debate has shifted to the niqab or full face-veils. The boundaries of acceptable Canadian citizenship have, therefore, shifted to 'permit' the wearing of certain acceptable symbols of religious or cultural commitment while seeking to exclude (sometimes forcibly) the 'bad' or 'unacceptable' racialized Muslim body.

These boundaries of citizenship in post 9/11 Canada rely heavily on Muslim bodies and it is especially on Muslim women that these demarcations in the body politic are made yet clearer. The veiling narrative in the Canadian context is an important signifier – perhaps the key signifier – to illuminate these boundaries and to demarcate the 'acceptable' from the 'unacceptable'.

Veiling in Canadian political and media discourse

Canadian political and media discourses have increasingly focused on the issue of Muslim women – and in particular veiling – as trigger points in larger national conversations about multi-culturalism, immigration and integration. Media searches reveal that Muslim women are a dominant theme, and perhaps more tellingly, that the issue of veiling elicits heated commentary. Furthermore, even when the topic of commentary is multiculturalism, veiling is most often the issue that triggers the commentary.

Such an overwhelming focus on veiling illuminates the symbolic, political and ideological importance of the veil in Canadian public discourse. The veil is often utilized, politically and ideologically, as a symbol of Muslim women's inequity. The strong focus on veiling in Canadian discourse is certainly an indication that this issue has struck a chord. Some of the media coverage was a reflection of current events (e.g. niqab in the courts, veiling and voting, niqab and the Citizenship Oath, etc.). However, many commentaries (including editorials) have utilized veiling as a starting point for broader issues related to multiculturalism, 'Canadian identity', 'security', and 'our values'.

Data analysis of searches that one of the authors (Kassam) conducted of the coverage in 19 Canadian newspapers spanning a decade from 1 January 2005 to 31 December 2014 (Kassam 2015) reveals the breadth of the media obsession with veiled Muslims women.[1] The decade includes key events in Canadian news and current affairs, including the arrests of the so-called Toronto 18 (2006), the debates about the Shari'ah (2005–2006), various veiling-related controversies (2007–2015), debates on 'reasonable accommodation' and Quebec's 'Charter of Values' (2007–2008, 2010 and 2013), and anti-terrorism measures such as the use of security certificates.

The data (Kassam 2015) reveal that Canadian press discourse about Muslims focused predominantly on Muslim women. Of the four searches conducted (each with a different search term relating to Muslims), the one on Muslim women elicited the most number of articles (4,224 articles) over the ten-year period. In comparison, the search on Muslim men elicited 2,061 articles, the search on 'moderate Muslim' elicited 540 articles, and the one on 'Muslims and multiculturalism' elicited 1,161 articles, all for the same time period. In other words, the search on Muslim women in the Canadian press coverage elicited more than twice as many articles than on Muslim men, and significantly more coverage than in the other searches. In fact, the media search on Muslim women elicited more articles than all the other three searches combined.

Such a focus on women is not surprising, given that Muslim women constitute perhaps the most urgent arena in the contemporary post-9/11 ideological war. While the ideological use of Muslim women is not new, given the long history of Orientalist representations, the battleground has been reconfigured in the post-9/11 era, in which positions of gender equality are central to determining 'acceptability' within public discourse. Perhaps more illuminating is that the veil was the predominant lens through which Muslim women were depicted in Canadian media coverage. Media discourse extended time and again to commentaries and editorials about the 'acceptable' use of the veil in Canadian public space, and the so-called limits to multiculturalism. Hence the veil has become an iconic signifier in public discourse about questions of identity, multiculturalism, citizenship and belonging. Such an overwhelming focus on veiling illuminates the symbolic, political and ideological importance of the veil in Canadian public discourse, and is a telling indication that the issue has struck a powerful chord in the public imagination.

The dominant framing in Canadian media discourse about veils focused on the manner in which veils (and in particular, niqabs or burkas) are contrary to Canada's shared values of openness, tolerance, and gender equality. This framing was dominant also in political and public discourse, especially in light of debates around the banning of the niqab/burqa in public spaces, including proposed legislation in Quebec (Bill 94, 2010; the Charter of Values 2013), the restriction against face-veils while taking the Oath of Canadian Citizenship (2011–2014), and other similar debates. Commentaries and editorials focused time and again on how 'Canadian values' (however defined) did not include the covering of faces, an act which was perceived to be an 'intolerable custom' in Canadian public space. For example, one commentator, writing about the prohibition on niqab-wearing women taking the Oath of Canadian Citizenship, argued:

> There is not a single positive thing to be said for the niqab, burka or any other visible sign of one's gender submission to another. Notwithstanding liberal handwringing about diversity and tolerance, it should have no place – none – on any official Canadian stage . . .
>
> This is not mere clothing we're talking about, some colorful expression of ethnic background. No, the face veil is a powerful symbol of subjugation or, at best, second-class citizenship. It is an aggressive, overt denial of full personhood.
>
> It really doesn't matter how its wearers feel about it. Some Muslim women, including Canadian-born converts and young women who have grown up here, have adopted the niqab in an earnest embrace of traditionalism. They like how they feel in it, they say.

So what? Their misguided attachment doesn't redeem what is essentially irredeemable: a tangible public statement that women are less than men.

(Kennedy 2011, B6)

What is especially striking in this excerpt is that the commentator, a self-avowed feminist, is openly dismissive of the opinions and views – the choices – of niqab-wearing women. Indeed, in first situating the niqab as an 'aggressive, overt denial of full personhood' and then dismissing the views of niqabi women, she is denying the very personhood she claims to defend. Such are the contradictions of the 'eternal triangle' (Razack 2004): the 'civilized' European seeks to 'save' the imperilled Muslim woman from the 'barbaric' customs of Islam. In her haste to 'save' Muslim women, she fails to respect (or even care about) the opinions and rights of those she seeks to save. Such a discourse has an undercurrent of redemption: 'Save them from themselves, for they know not what they do'. It is especially noteworthy that such discourses are reminiscent of age-old Orientalist and colonial perspectives, an echo of those earlier, but equally fervent appeals to 'civilize the natives'.

A particularly telling, and important, aspect of Canadian public and media discourse about veiling was the focus on the 'Islamic credentials' of the niqab. This manoeuvre shifts the discussion *away* from rights protected under the Charter of Rights and Freedoms, and *towards* the perspectives of Islamic religious requirements, a discursive shift which renders invisible the actual rights (and citizenship) of niqab-wearing Muslim women. In using the argument that the niqab is not a religious requirement, such commentators become, unwittingly, and perhaps unknowingly, arbiters of Islamic religious law rather than defenders of the Canadian Charter of Rights and Freedoms. Inherent in such a position is a contradiction: on the one hand, some commentators argue that religious symbols have no place in Canadian public life but, on the other hand, they resort to religious perspectives to make the argument that these symbols are not 'religiously mandated'.

Canadian discourse about veiling is often framed as being about women's rights versus religious/cultural rights, a narrative that is echoed in other debates about Muslim women, such as the Shari'ah law debates (2004), and discussions on the 'limits of multiculturalism'. Such narratives place Muslim women at the centre of a 'saving' discourse, in which Muslim women, seen as oppressed by their 'primitive' men and/or religious/cultural traditions, can be brought into civilization through the abandoning of their so-called archaic cultural traditions. Often depicted as 'helpless victims' (Jiwani 2009), Muslim women are sometimes perceived in the public discourse as requiring the rescue efforts of 'chivalrous knights' (Jiwani 2009). For example, making a submission to the Bouchard–Taylor Commission in 2007, the Quebec Council for the Status of Women argued for a ban on visible religious symbols amongst public-sector workers. The Council and its supporters argued that veils are symbolic of women's subjugation, and therefore should be banned. Similarly, the 2013 Quebec Charter of Values, was supported by prominent women's rights advocates. The Charter of Values, strikingly similar to the 2007 proposal by the Quebec Council for the Status of Women, proposed to ban conspicuous symbols of religious expression in the public sector, arguing that these symbols contradict the principles of state secularism and gender equality. While male and non-Muslim expressions of faith were also included, it is clear that the real intended targets in both proposals were the head coverings and veils of Muslim women. In debating these proposals, many women's groups, both within and outside Quebec, argued that veils are unacceptable symbols of oppression and inequality. Embedded in these positions is the 'rescue-motif': the presumption that Muslim women are compelled to veil is central to the argument that it is the responsibility of 'true feminists' (and the government) to 'save' Muslim women from such an 'unequal existence'.

Veiling, Quebec, reasonable accommodation and the Rest of Canada

The Quebec context is important in analysing Canadian veiling narratives as it highlights key themes and presents a juxtaposition to the national debates. The debates in Quebec illuminate an important demarcation in public discourse: some feel that Quebec's policies are appropriate and should be emulated nationally, while others argue that these policies have 'gone too far' and that Canadians are too sophisticated to emulate them.

The debates on reasonable accommodation in Quebec began in late 2006, with the debate over accommodating religious sensibilities of Hasidic Jewish communities in Montreal. Very quickly, however, the debate became focused on the customs, practices and traditions of Muslim communities. In 2007, the small Quebec town of Hérouxville passed a 'code of living norms' which explicitly forbade 'stoning of women, the donning of burqas, wearing Sikh ceremonial daggers in school' (Gordon 2007). The Hérouxville code, along with other issues (e.g. wearing of hijab in sports, statutory holidays for non-Christian groups, etc.), inflamed the debate about the 'reasonable accommodation' of minority rights. In addition, there was an intense and significant discussion about the issue of voting while veiled. The debate began in Quebec, but soon became a national one, in which elections officials, politicians and the public became embroiled. At issue was whether Muslim women with niqab should be compelled to unveil before being permitted to vote. Election officials, both in Quebec and nationally, indicated that niqabi women could vote as long as they met identification requirements (at the time, not requiring photographs). Some political leaders, including then-Prime Minister Harper, vehemently disagreed, igniting a vociferous debate and media frenzy.

The Quebec reasonable accommodation debates – and specifically on Muslim women and veiling – were re-ignited between 2010 and 2013, with the introduction of two pieces of legislation by the then-provincial government. In 2010, the government introduced Bill 94, which proposed a prohibition on face coverings for those working in the public sector or wishing to access government services. In 2013, the government introduced Bill 60, colloquially known as the 'Quebec Charter of Values', which proposed the prohibition of 'conspicuous' religious symbols for state employees, imposing on them a duty of religious neutrality. It further proposed to ban face coverings for those providing or receiving government services. The Quebec Charter of Values incited vociferous debate throughout Canada, including in Quebec, and resulted in intense public discourse about the Charter, its assumptions, motivations, and whether it violated Canadian principles of multiculturalism, human rights and secularism.

Media discourse on Quebec's reasonable accommodation debates were often framed within the context of larger Canadian debates. The debates on minority rights in Quebec, like those in the Rest of Canada (RoC), often led to debates about multiculturalism, secularism and Canadian (or Quebec) identity. However, it is noteworthy how often the Canadian discourse made reference, either explicitly or implicitly, to the idea of 'Quebec vs. RoC'. Embedded in such narratives was the argument that Quebec was more xenophobic and racist than the rest of the country, which was perceived as a 'beacon of multicultural tolerance'. This framing of Quebec is significant as it reinforces the Canadian national narrative of benevolence, and lack of complicity for past (and present) racist policies. An editorial in the *Globe and Mail*, for example, stated:

> If the charter is adopted in the form that many fear it will be, its enshrinement will mark Quebec's departure from Canada's well-established consensus on religious freedoms ... Quebec is heading for a showdown unless political leaders there find the courage to challenge this ill-advised project ... Quebeckers are proud of the fact

they have separated church and state that were once interlaced more tightly than the stitching on a priest's cassock. It is an essential Quebec value. So what must they do to accommodate in others what they no longer wish to accommodate in themselves?

They already have the answer: Canada. The so-called Rest of Canada has gone through its own upheavals related to religious accommodation . . . Canada has for the most part arrived at a consensus in which the expression of one's religion is protected as long as it doesn't harm society's basic values.

(The Globe and Mail 2013)

Embedded in such commentaries is the narrative of Quebec vs. RoC; Quebeckers (and their political leaders) are advised to learn from Canada's example and 'consensus'. What is noteworthy in this editorial is the silence on the various challenges to the 'consensus' on accommodation of minority rights. There is no mention, for example, of the debates about veils in Canadian public space (including legal challenges about wearing niqab in the judicial system or during the Oath of Citizenship). What is highlighted instead in this editorial is the image of a Canadian consensus on the issue of minority rights, a consensus which is considered more or less settled. A cursory glance at the public discourse regarding minority rights, and especially with respect to Muslims and veiling, reveals that the debate is far from settled.

While some commentators and political leaders argue that the Charter of Quebec Values went farther than other legislation (in that it banned not just the niqab but other religious symbols including the hijab and the turban), we argue that the essential principles underlying such legislation and policies are problematic. Proposals to limit the rights of women in religious or cultural expression are very much about power and privilege rather than about gender equality. We contend that there is no difference between the power dynamic of compulsory *uncovering* and compulsory *covering* of Muslim women. Gender equality is not safeguarded by policies that determine how women, Muslim or otherwise, should live, dress, express faith, and behave. Such power dynamics underlie the 'saving discourse', in which certain types of bodies, behaviour, dress or perspectives are deemed to be 'unacceptable' and in need of 'rescue'.

Canadian federal election 2015

The Canadian federal election in October 2015 illuminates the public and political anxieties in relation to veiling, Canadian identity and the demarcation of 'acceptable' boundaries in the Canadian nation-state. Some of these anxieties were focused on Zunera Ishaq and her legal challenge to permit the wearing of her niqab during her Oath of Canadian Citizenship.

Ishaq's challenge began in 2012, when she applied to take her Oath of Citizenship wearing a niqab. In 2011, the then-Immigration Minister, Jason Kenney, had made administrative changes to the citizenship process to prohibit face coverings during the Citizenship Oath (some women had previously been permitted to wear their niqabs after having confirmed their identities in private with officials). Ishaq argued that this prohibition violated her religious rights, according to the Canadian Charter of Rights and Freedoms (McKeon 2015).

As Ishaq's case made its way through various levels of the justice system, the popular discourse around her choice of religious expression and her challenge of the federal government's policy sometimes expressed itself in open bigotry and xenophobia. The media commentary held a variety of views about what Ishaq's decisions ought to have been. There was the minority position of 'everybody mind their own business', to 'niqab is awful but I support her right to wear it', to the shriller 'we need to help women who are oppressed', to the openly xenophobic 'if she wants to live that way why did she come to Canada?'. Racist online commentary was not only directed at Ishaq but at Muslims in general. Ishaq and her niqab became the symbol for everything that was wrong and dangerous about multiculturalism.

Finally, in February 2015, the Federal Court decided in favour of Ishaq and her right to wear her niqab during her Oath of Citizenship. The government appealed against the ruling which was heard in September 2015 by the Federal Court of Appeal, which decided in Ishaq's favour. The government declared its intention to take the case to the Supreme Court of Canada, although the appeal has been abandoned by the current government.

Ishaq's case, while already a talking point in media discourse during her long legal challenge, was thrust into the spotlight during the Canadian federal election campaign (October 2015). The issue became a flashpoint for anxieties about multiculturalism, terrorism, Canadian values, secularism and citizenship, with veiling as a sensitive trigger point for these debates and fears. During the election campaign, numerous members of the then-government expressed their hostility toward the niqab, and the then-Prime Minister Stephen Harper referred to the niqab as being 'rooted in a culture that is anti-woman' (Anonymous 2015).

Furthermore, some two weeks before the election, the government announced its intention to establish a telephone service (a 'tip line') for Canadians to report on 'barbaric cultural practices' (such as forced marriage, polygamy and 'honour killings') presumably being practised by their neighbours, acquaintances and colleagues. At the press conference announcing the tip line, the Minister of Citizenship and Immigration, Chris Alexander, stated: 'We need to stand up for our values. We need to do that in citizenship ceremonies. We need to do that to protect women and girls from forced marriage and other barbaric practices' (Powers 2015). Many Canadians interpreted this service as a direct criticism of Muslim communities (as Muslims are presumed to adhere to such practices), through these practices are certainly not followed by all Muslims, and are also practised by some non-Muslims. Perhaps more importantly, the practices identified as examples through the proposed 'tip line' service are already prohibited by Canadian law – in other words, the proposed 'barbaric practices' label was being applied in a particular way to identify certain cultural practices (though already deemed illegal) seemingly targeted in the popular imagination as being 'Muslim practices'. Such was the use of 'culture talk' (Mamdani 2004) which identifies certain practices, groups or ideas as 'pre-modern' and 'barbaric' in order to demarcate 'them' from 'us'. The proposed 'barbaric practices' tip line was clearly one of the low points in the election campaign, reflecting a coded appeal to xenophobic and racist elements within the Canadian electorate.

The various coded appeals crystallized the swirling discontent, highlighting the anxieties some Canadians were feeling about Muslim women, their veils, and the presumed 'primitive' thinking and cultural practices represented by the veil. Embedded in this election discourse was, once again, the spectre of the 'imperilled Muslim woman' (Razack 2004) who needed to be 'saved' from her misogynistic and 'primitive' cultural/religious traditions.

While the niqab and Muslim women became a powerful focus during the 2015 election campaign, the rhetoric eventually dissipated, after hitting its peak during the last weeks of the campaign. Ishaq became a citizen, wearing her niqab during the Oath; the election on 19 October resulted in the defeat of the Conservative government, which had initiated much of the furore about veiling and Muslim women.

While the new government of Prime Minister Justin Trudeau has changed the official narrative about Muslim women in Canada, the election campaign and its tone have affected popular rhetoric in damaging ways. The election campaign sparked intense debate and fears among Canadians about Muslim women, fears that were ready to be exploited by some members of the political elite. Furthermore, while the desire of the media (and Canadians) to move on from Ishaq and her niqab was welcomed, the election campaign and its heated rhetoric left behind a public narrative that is now perhaps part of mainstream discourse. What seems like an extreme point of view when first uttered, soon becomes normalized and 'permissible' through repetition. There is a prevailing sense, especially amongst the political right, but also in some quarters on the left, that those who do not subscribe to the view that hijabs and niqabs (especially the latter) are anti-democratic and anti-women, are simply succumbing to 'political correctness'. Such a narrative further suggests that multiculturalism is problematic as it encourages people to remain aloof from so-called Canadian values, even though such 'values' are rarely defined and if they are, they simply reaffirm the national narrative that positions some Canadians (those of European descent) as 'exalted subjects' (Thobani 2007) and other Canadians as 'outsiders'.

Conclusion

The issue of veiling continues to be an important and recurrent narrative in Canadian political, public and media discourse. Time and again, the discourse has focused on what Muslim women are wearing and debates have become a lightning rod for intense conversations about gender equality, Canadian identity, and the limits of multiculturalism. The 2005-2015 public debates on Muslim women's clothing centred on various issues: voting while wearing niqabs, the possible banning of niqabs in Canadian public spaces, Quebec's proposed Bill 94 and Charter of Values, the prohibition of niqab at the Canadian citizenship ceremonies, niqabs in legal proceedings and the court, and even the wearing of hijabs in educational, athletic and public settings. What is common to all of these debates is the fascination with the choices made by Muslim women with respect to clothing and, more importantly, how these choices either fall within or outside the 'acceptable' boundaries of Canadian citizenship, igniting furious discussion on issues related to multiculturalism and Canadian identity.

Canadian narratives about veiling are shaped by the discourses embedded in the national psyche. These discourses are challenged by the issue of veiling, which reveals the divergences of Canadian understandings of multiculturalism, diversity, and 'Canadian' identity. Veiling narratives illuminate the boundary of acceptability within the national narrative, in which some are exalted (Thobani 2007) while others are either granted conditional inclusion or excluded entirely from the symbolic boundaries of the nation-state. Simultaneously, Canadian narratives about veiling hide (or veil?) the underlying racialized dimensions of the national imaginary.

Rendered invisible and silenced in these discourses are the voices of the great majority of Canadian Muslim women, veiled or not, who fashion responses to the varied issues of their lives. Against the backdrop of the surveillance state, where Islamophobia and anti-Muslim violence (or the threat of it) are regular occurrences, and the good/bad Muslim dichotomy is entrenched, Muslim women must often make difficult choices. Demonstrating one's 'good' or 'acceptable' Muslimness may constrain the articulation of diverse Muslim women's voices – perspectives that could challenge the one-dimensional images embedded in Canadian political, media and public discourses. In this sense, while Canadian narratives on veiling illuminate fault lines within the national imaginary, they also silence more nuanced perspectives on the diversity of Canadian Muslim women's experiences and lives.

Note

1. The data was collected in 2015, as part of a larger, as-yet-unpublished research project. The research project is primarily concerned with how Muslims are presented in Canadian media, public and political discourses, with a particular focus on the figure of the Acceptable Muslim. The searches were focused on the major daily newspapers in Canada and utilized the Canadian Newsstands Database.

References

Anonymous. 2013. 'Beware the Charter of Values'. *The Globe and Mail*, 15 June.

Anonymous. 2015. '"Niqabs" rooted in a Culture that is Anti-Women,'' Harper Says'. *The Globe and Mail*, 10 March. Available at www.theglobeandmail.com/news/politics/niqabs-rooted-in-a-culture-that-is-anti-women-harper-says/article23395242 (accessed 15 January 2016).

Gordon, Sean. 2007. 'Quebec Town Spawns Uneasy Debate'. *Toronto Star*, 5 February.

Jiwani, Yasmin. 2005a. 'The Eurasian: Sydney Fox as Relic Hunter'. *Journal of Popular Film and Television* 32(4):182–91.

Jiwani, Yasmin. 2009. 'Helpless Maidens and Chivalrous Knights: Afghan Women in the Canadian Press'. *University of Toronto Quarterly* 78(2):728–44.

Kassam, Shelina. Forthcoming. *Mapping the Terrain: Canadian Media Discourse on Muslims 2005–2014.* Toronto, ON: University of Toronto. Unpublished.

Kennedy, Janice. 2011. 'Gender Equality Trumps Apparel'. *Ottawa Citizen*, 17 December, B6.

Mamdani, Mahmood. 2004. *Good Muslim, Bad Muslim: America, the Cold War and the Roots of Terror.* New York: Pantheon Books.

McKeon, Lauren. 2015. 'Zunera's War'. *Toronto Life*. Available at http://torontolife.com/city/toronto-politics/zunera-ishaq-niqab-ban/ (accessed 15 January 2016).

Powers, Lucas. 2015. 'Conservatives Pledge Funds, Tip Line to Combat "Barbaric Cultural Practices"'. Available at www.cbc.ca/news/politics/canada-election-2015-barbaric-cultural-practices-law-1.3254118 (accessed 15 January 2016).

Razack, Sherene. 2004. 'Imperilled Muslim Women, Dangerous Muslim Men and Civilised Europeans: Legal and Social Responses to Forced Marriages'. *Feminist Legal Studies* 12:129–74.

Razack, Sherene. 2008. *Casting Out: The Eviction of Muslims from Western Law and Politics.* Toronto, Buffalo and London: University of Toronto Press.

Said, Edward. 2003 [1978]. *Orientalism.* New York and Toronto, ON: Random House.

Thobani, Sunera. 2007. *Exalted Subjects: Studies in the Making of Race and Nation in Canada.* Toronto, Buffalo and London: University of Toronto Press.

Volpp, Leti. 2007. 'The Culture of Citizenship'. *Theoretical Inquiries in Law* 8(2):571–602.

Yeğenoğlu, Meyda. 1998. *Colonial Fantasies: Towards a Feminist Reading of Orientalism.* Cambridge: Cambridge University Press.

7

VEILING AND UNVEILING IN CENTRAL ASIA

Beliefs and practices, tradition and modernity

Marianne Kamp and Noor Borbieva

Among the Central Asian Muslim cultures that became subject to Russian Imperial control in the late nineteenth century, women who belonged to farming and urban communities covered their body, head, and faces when they were outside the home. Women who belonged to nomadic pastoralist communities covered their hair and occasionally their faces. By the 1920s, when the Soviet Union drew the boundaries that became Uzbekistan, Kyrgyzstan, and the other Central Asian republics, women's veiling (covering head, face, and body) and seclusion became topics of social debate and targets for government intervention. Veiling largely disappeared during the Soviet period, but after the Central Asian republics became independent in 1991, many Central Asian women began practicing new forms of veiling. This chapter explores both trends, asking what unveiling meant to Central Asian women in the 1920s and what veiling means to them in the 2000s.

Traditional veiling and unveiling

Until the late 1920s, hijab implied a complex of practices, including that a woman seclude herself in private spaces of the home, and that she wear a veil when staying at home was not possible. Women who belonged to Central Asia's urban and agricultural Uzbek and Tajik ethnic groups always wore headscarves to cover their hair, and when going outside their homes, covered themselves head-to-toe in a long veiling robe, *paranji* (see Figure 7.2). They draped a black horsehair net, *chachvon*, from the crown of the head to waist, concealing much more than their faces. Women from traditionally nomadic Kazakh and Kyrgyz ethnic groups did not wear *paranji*s; they appeared in public with uncovered faces (see Figure 7.1).

Although there is little direct evidence regarding how Central Asian women thought about the *paranji*, one male school teacher's 1907 letter to a women's newspaper made clear that veiling was subject to social discussion (Hasanov 1907). He wrote:

> Discussions about the 'hijab issue' are being written about in every newspaper and book. Some say hijab is necessary and others say it is not . . . To people of penetration

and discernment, there is a hijab issue that must be considered even more important than the robe-hijab. Among the women of tribes of our Russian Islam, there is also a hijab called ignorance (jahilat) . . . Even if the hijab robe is removed, can this hijab be removed?

Hasanov, writing about the Uzbek and Kazakh women around the small city of Toqmoq, which is in present-day Kyrgyzstan, noted that women of sedentary groups wore very thorough forms of veiling. When he asked why, Hasanov was told that removing the *paranji* would be a great sin, because women must be separated from men, and that these customs are what differentiate people from animals. In Hasanov's view, the absence of modern schools for girls kept them in a veil of darkness. 'We have to lift the hijab of ignorance before lifting the hijab-robe . . . among Kazakh and Kyrgyz women there is no hijab but their lack of hijab apparently does not provide them with progress; the point is that education brings progress' (3–4). Like religious scholars of the early twentieth century, Hasanov used 'hijab' in its Qur'anic sense (33:53) of curtain, implying separate spaces for women where unrelated men could not see them. His 'hijab question' linked forms of dress that covered the face and body with the social practice of women's seclusion; seclusion and its associated social attitudes prevented girls from attending schools with boys. In an era when Muslims in the Russian Empire advocated modernizing and expanding girls' education, hijab posed an obstacle.

Figure 7.1 Typical Kyrgyz or Kazakh woman's headwear

Figure 7.2 A woman wearing *paranji* and *chachvon*

Unveiling in the 1920s

In the mid-1920s, as the Soviet Union's Communist Party was spreading its plans for social and economic transformation across Central Asia, the early twentieth-century critiques of hijab as an obstacle to progress expanded into politicized condemnations of veiling and seclusion. The 1917 Bolshevik Revolution had set off a cascade of dramatic changes in the social and economic order, and in cultural practices. In Uzbekistan, the Communist Party launched a campaign called the *Hujum* [Attack] to convince women to 'throw off' their *paranji*s and participate in school, work, politics, and mixed-gender social spaces. A writer for the Uzbek women's journal *Yangi Yo'l* expressed *Hujum*-era ideas about veiling and seclusion in a story about Zulfiya, who was forcibly married at age 15 to Ibrahim, who insisted she stay secluded in his home. A neighbor woman told Zulfiya:

> According to Soviet government, women and girls are equal to men; they have the same rights. If a woman or girl wants to, she can throw off her *paranji*. Men who oppose her will be punished. Women who separate from husbands who oppress them will be given work in collectives, and the opportunity to go to school for literacy.

Disobeying her husband's orders, Zulfiya left home to visit her ailing mother. Ibrahim followed her and challenged her: 'Who gave you permission to come here?' (Bashir 1928, 19) Bashir's account of one of the *Hujum*'s many cases of femicide articulates the connection between veiling and seclusion; through her intent to unveil and by leaving her house, Zulfiya rejected her husband's dominance. This *Hujum*-era critique of hijab injected an emphasis on individual rights: a woman had the right to choose not to veil, whether or not her family or society approved.

During the 1920s and 1930s, most young Central Asian women stopped wearing the *paranji* and *chachvon*. Rather than covering head, body and face with a robe and veil, young Uzbek and Tajik women instead wore long dresses and loose pants covering the body, and large scarves that covered their head, hair, and shoulders. Activist women wore small embroidered caps in an ethnically specific style, letting hair show. Those women who removed their *paranji* and *chachvon* were called 'open' or 'uncovered', because their faces were showing. No one associated the new style of scarves with earlier norms of hijab, which implied covering one's face and remaining secluded.

The connection between covering the face and secluding women had been based on a widely accepted interpretation of the Qur'an, but during the *Hujum* some Central Asian mullahs offered new interpretations to encourage unveiling. Their religious arguments are recorded indirectly, in hostile words of Uzbek Communist Party members. In a lengthy tract addressed to Uzbek anti-religion activists, the activist 'Aliullin (1929) argued that mullahs were teaching that Islam and socialism were compatible in an effort to keep religion relevant in a rapidly changing society. 'The Qur'anic verses and hadith clearly say' that women must cover up in the *paranji*, 'Aliullin wrote, but 'in Tatarstan, Bashqordstan, and Uzbekistan, fatwas are made that women and girls are allowed to go out with uncovered faces . . . Mullahs who see current progress and who fear that women will escape from religion's influence' have quickly reinterpreted the Qur'an, making veiling optional, proclaiming women's equality with men, and encouraging women to pray in the mosque. The activist asked provocatively: 'Where were those mullahs hiding these fatwas ten or fifteen years ago?' (1929: 17–21).

Although Communist reports about changing Islamic teachings were inherently distorted, 'Aliullin's comments reflect the fact that mullahs and society thought of veiling as related to social interaction. The reformist mullahs linked their unveiling option with male–female equality and with invitations to women to join men in worship. Contrary to the anti-religion activists' accusations, some mullahs and women religious teachers had preached these innovations for several decades (Kamp 2015). Nonetheless, the *Hujum* and its attack on veiling may have stimulated wider acceptance of new Islamic interpretations that regarded face-veiling as optional.

Veiling after socialism

In the 1920s, many Uzbek women associated removing the *paranji* and *chachvon* with freedom. By contrast, in the 2000s many Central Asian Muslim women embrace the freedom to veil as a 'modern' privilege, one that distinguishes their lives today from the lives women lived during the Soviet era. In many communities, growing interest in Islam has created a demand for basic information about how to live Islamically, and by extension, how to veil. Jamal Frontbek kyzy, leader of a high-profile Muslim women's NGO in Kyrgyzstan, has been known to give popular public lectures on Islam to women. In one lecture, she explained that there is often confusion about the correct way to veil. Women often think they must cover their faces, she began. According to Islamic law, however, hijab (covering all but the face and hands) is obligatory, while wearing a veil across the face, called nikab, is not an obligatory action but a recommended action, which earns the wearer spiritual merit. She reminded her audience to observe obligatory practices first before practices like nikab. 'If I wear nikab but commit sin, what is the use of my nikab?' she asked. 'Worry first about avoiding sin and fulfilling your [religious obligations.] Only if you are sure about these things, can you think about nikab' (Borbieva forthcoming).

Central Asian religious authorities such as Frontbek kyzy teach that veiling is God's commandment, meaning that the Muslim woman should spend less time thinking about why she veils and more time thinking about how to veil correctly. One Kyrgyz pamphlet reads:

> God has given you much fortune, so you should also be grateful. Shouldn't you obey God's commands? . . . Wearing hijab, like prayer and fasting, is considered obligatory. It is God's command. Instead of discussing the things God has commanded, saying 'I like this one or don't like that one', we must try to adopt them all immediately.
>
> *(Ryskulov and Möküyeva 2012, 11–18)*

This is not to say religious authorities like Frontbek kyzy and the authors of this pamphlet do not offer commentary to address the 'why' question. One common argument they articulate is that veiling protects social harmony; it allows women and men who are unmarried and unrelated to interact without inciting desire – specifically male desire. Seeing a woman uncovered provokes lustful thoughts in men, and this can lead to sinful behavior, which in turn threatens social harmony and stability. Some religious tracts specifically mention the West as a cautionary example; in the West women do not veil, and for that reason the West has many social problems, such as high rates of divorce, teen pregnancy, abandoned children, and abortion (Chotonov 2002, 12, 182, 268; Ryskulov and Möküyeva 2012, 3–4, 31; see also Schwab 2012, 174).

Ethnographers who have studied women in the Muslim world debate how appropriate it is to approach veiling as a symbolic act. Saba Mahmood (2001, 2005) has argued that to reduce the veil to a symbol neglects the ways veiling is also a disciplinary process and mode of agency. In Central Asia, according to available research, veiling both facilitates a woman's adoption of additional Islamic attitudes and behaviors and announces her intensified religious commitment to the public; in other words, it is both practice and symbol (McBrien 2009; Peshkova 2006, 2013; Stephan 2010). Many women who adopt the veil do so as part of broader lifestyle changes. These changes include praying five times a day, reading religious books, not socializing with unrelated men, and avoiding impure thoughts. Religious texts point out that veiling makes these other obligatory observances easier. These texts also mention that being seen wearing a veil can encourage religiosity in others. The Kyrgyz pamphlet tells the reader that if she veils, her friends will notice, and '[i]f you are a reason they start on the true path, you will earn much spiritual reward' (Ryskulov and Möküyeva 2012, 16).

Veiling and modernity

For many Central Asian Muslim women, the freedom to veil intersects in complex ways with concerns about modernity. Julie McBrien (2009) has written about Mukadas, a young woman in southern Kyrgyzstan, who agonized over whether or not to veil. She wanted to practice her religion, but she also wanted to be modern, and she thought of the veil as 'backward'. In the end, Mukadas decided to veil because she realized that although the veil might be inconsistent with Western visions of modernity, it asserted an alternative modernity that implicitly questioned the idea that one region or ideology can claim to be modernity's defining voice (McBrien 2009, S140). Similarly, Manja Stephan (2010, 478) interviewed pious young women in Dushanbe, among whom the veil symbolized 'a new female imagination of modernity' and helped them 'see themselves as obedient, modest, pious and modern at the same time'.

The ethnographic literature also suggests that many Central Asian women, especially young women, associate the veil and Islamic piety with female beauty. Women in Dushanbe told Stephan (2010) they were drawn to particular veiled religious teachers because they found these teachers' Islamic dress attractive. One informant described veiling as 'intriguing', saying it gave women an enviable 'aura of beauty' (Stephan 2010, 477). The Brazilian soap opera, *The Clone*, which aired on Russian TV in 2004 and featured a wealthy Moroccan family, reinforced painfully Orientalist stereotypes of the Middle East and North Africa. In Central Asia, it also inspired broad interest in veiling because it linked veiling with glamour and privilege (McBrien 2007, 2012; Montgomery 2007, 201). Female religious leaders encourage similar associations by organizing Islamic fashion shows and supporting Islamic fashion designers (e.g. Islam Ajary 2009).

In Central Asian public spaces, the veil has taken on new meanings and functions since the five republics became independent. Ethnographic literature and international news sources suggest that veiling both discourages and incites harassment (Abramson 2004; Borbieva 2012, 298; McBrien 2009, S139; Peshkova 2006; Shodiyev 2007). Young women have reported increased social pressure to dress modestly. This pressure can take the form of rude comments from men (Abramson 2004, 71). It can also take more subtle forms; one university student recalls that her instructors openly expressed their frustrations about women's provocative styles of dress and urged female students to dress more modestly (Shodiyev 2007). Women who adopt the veil claim they suffer less sexual harassment, but veiling can attract other forms of negative attention. McBrien's Mukadas recalled being approached by a woman in a bazaar who told Mukadas she hated women who cover (2009, S139). The nature of a community's response to a woman who veils is influenced by ethnicity, region, and family reputation. If Uzbek and Tajik women experience pressure to veil in many urban and rural neighborhoods, Kazakh and Kyrgyz women may hear parents, husbands, and neighbors tell them not to veil. In an interview, Jamal Frontbek kyzy told Borbieva about being harassed constantly when she began to veil, as she was one of the first to do so in Bishkek, the capital of Kyrgyzstan. Sitting in the audience at a large conference, she was singled out by a speaker who demanded she explain why she was covered. 'I had to stand up in front of two hundred people and answer for myself', she recalled. Those who choose to veil despite harassment and objections from family find solace in the knowledge that by veiling they are avoiding possible punishment from God. Another of Borbieva's informants told her 'my husband doesn't want me to wear a veil. He wants me to dress openly. He likes how I used to be. I say to him, "but if I show myself, that is sin"' (Borbieva 2012, 298).

In some regions, public responses to veiling may divide along generational lines. If young women in Dushanbe see veiling as a sign of female beauty and virtue, some elders believe it calls unneeded attention to the sexual reputation of the wearer and suggests a wearer feels insecure about past indiscretions (Stephan 2010). One middle aged informant commented, 'you see lots of young girls on the street today wearing Islamic clothes (*islomy fason*). They pray and live by the rules (*qoida*). But who's to say they are pure (*dilashon toza*) within as well? . . . They cover their dark inner self (*darunash*) with the white scarf (*rumoli safed*)' (Stephan 2010, 478).

Devout women across Central Asia often veil in a style David Abramson has called 'transnational', as it explicitly connects the wearer to a 'transnational Islamic community' (2004, 72). This is the style Frontbek kyzy promoted: the hair and neck are covered completely with one or several pieces of material, and long, loose clothing covers the rest of the body, except the hands. This style stands in opposition to recognizably local styles of covering. Local styles persist, such as among the female religious teachers Svetlana Peshkova worked with in Uzbekistan. These women continue the age-old practice of wearing *paranji* and *chachvon* when they leave their homes. They view these traditional, pre-Soviet styles as effective ways to communicate their spiritual authority and protect their sacredness (Peshkova 2006, 149–50).

Garments reminiscent of the *paranji* and *chachvon* are sometimes worn by Uzbek brides at wedding feasts, as an expression of ethnic pride and female virtue (Peshkova 2006, 107). Among Kazakhs, only married women are expected to wear a headscarf, and it is traditionally white. Unmarried women who wear headscarves for religious reasons, however, also often wear white scarves. This attracts the criticism of elders who believe pious women are undermining a useful social convention that allows a woman's marital status to be read from her apparel (Schwab 2012, 175).

Limitations and legislation

Central Asian Muslim women articulate many reasons for veiling (e.g. RFERL 2010), but their freedom to veil is often circumscribed by external factors, such as international concerns about terrorism and governing regimes' concerns about religious extremism. The most common limitation is on students' rights to veil. In Kazakhstan, Kyrgyzstan, Tajikistan, and Uzbekistan educators and lawmakers have banned the veil in educational institutions.

Uzbekistan has long prohibited students from wearing religious garb in universities, and in 1998 a law on religion restricted the wearing of religious clothing in public (HRW 1999; Peshkova 2006, 312–313). Regime propaganda that links certain Islamic observances with extremism and jihadism has influenced public opinion, and in many communities, people are suspicious of those who wear a veil. Although female modesty is celebrated in Uzbekistan, the state promotes forms of modest dress that reflect Uzbek ethnic heritage, such as brightly colored loose dresses and pants made from locally produced silk and loose kerchiefs worn around the top of the head. In such a context, Islamic veiling can be intended and interpreted less as an expression of modesty and more as defiance against the regime (Abramson 2004; Peshkova 2006).

In southern Kyrgyzstan, beginning in 2003, numerous school districts prohibited students from wearing veils to school. Although national politicians, such as Ombudsman Tursunbai Bakir uulu, released statements supporting the rights of girls to wear veils to school, these did not appear to have had an impact at the local level. In February 2009, the Minister of Education released a decree that banned students from wearing religious clothing in public schools. In March of that year, after extensive public protest, the decree was reverted to a recommendation (USDS 2009). Similar tensions emerged in Kazakhstan, beginning in 2011. International news agencies document discrimination against veiled women by universities and other institutions. President Nursultan Nazarbayev expressed his support for these measures, stating 'I am categorically against the hijab, and especially don't want female students wearing it' (Najibullah 2011).[1]

In Tajikistan, the Ministry of Education decreed in 2007 that female students in colleges were not allowed to wear veils, and a federal court upheld the decree when it was challenged by religious leaders (Shodiyev 2007). Although many young women removed their veils, international attention focused on the case of one student, Dovlatmo Ismailova, who challenged the decision to suspend her from the Institute of Foreign Languages. In an interview with Ferghana.ru, she explained her decision to veil despite the fact that it meant she had to stop her education:

> I'm not going to follow these orders that humiliate me and encroach on my rights
> . . . The Ministry of Education does not permit hijab wearing, the so called Ulem
> Council does not permit us to attend Friday prayer. All of that is against the norms
> or democracy and Shar'ah [sic] law.
>
> *(Shodiyev 2007)*

This interview and other stories in international outlets about the struggles of Central Asian women who want to veil and study reveal that in the international context, veiling's significance is highly contextual; in these reports, women's ability (or lack thereof) to veil freely has become an indicator of the status of human rights, women's rights, and democratic reforms in post-Soviet Central Asia.

Hijab as seclusion, hijab as pious self-expression

Over the course of a century, meanings and practices of hijab changed dramatically in Central Asia. Until the 1920s, most Uzbek and Tajik women who lived in cities or farming communities practiced a very thorough veiling of face and body, and lived in houses constructed to create physical separation of women from men who did not belong to their family. These related practices of hijab were the unmarked position, accepted as ordinary and proper until Muslim modernizers challenged the *paranji* and women's seclusion as obstacles to women's education and to social progress (Kamp 2006). Early twentieth-century defenses of veiling focused on preventing *fitna*, the social chaos that was sure to erupt if unmarried men and women interacted. That is, hijab served a social purpose in a Muslim community. Early twentieth century discussions did not connect face-veiling or modest dress with fashion, freedom, or women's personal piety (Halili 1917).

When they challenged veiling and seclusion, Muslim modernizers and Communists sought to change social patterns, believing that women's seclusion and its mobile extension, face-veiling, prevented women from becoming educated members of a modernizing society. Veils became a topic of debate among Muslims, and Communist activists interpreted them as extensions of feudalism, symbols of religion's tyranny, and barriers to all forms of equality. Advocates for unveiling promoted rationales, from individual freedom to improved health, to convince Uzbek and Tajik women to abandon their *paranji*s and *chachvon*s. The combination of propaganda and coercion ended the *paranji*'s status as the normal and unmarked form of women's dress. Although many Soviet-period Uzbek and Tajik women maintained aspects of modesty, covering hair partially with scarves and wearing long-sleeved, loose dresses over loose pants, they did not call those forms of dress 'hijab' (Kamp 2006).

In the 1990s and 2000s, Muslims in all of the Central Asian republics embraced opportunities for religious expression that had been limited or suppressed under the Soviet government, and veiled women can be seen in communities throughout Uzbekistan, Tajikistan, Kyrgyzstan and Kazakhstan. Forms of modest dress and head- or face-covering vary but frequently reflect the trends in modern veiling fashion found in Turkey, Iran, the Arab world, and South East Asia. The traditional *paranji* and *chachvon* are rarities; so are the all-encompassing Saudi-style abaya, Iranian chador, and Afghan burka, though each of these is occasionally seen in Central Asia.

Frontbek kyzy's teachings about hijab reflect a reversal in discourse. In present-day Central Asia, not wearing a veil is the unmarked position, while veiling is the subject of discussion, persuasion, and active propaganda. Seemingly no woman has to explain why she does not veil or needs to link her exposed hair to an identity or ideology, but those who consciously adopt modest dress, cover their heads, and occasionally cover their faces articulate multifaceted reasons for doing so. Unlike the early twentieth-century defenders of hijab, twenty-first century Central Asian women who veil see hijab as doing more than helping to ensure morality when women and men interact. While they do not deny this function of the veil, veiled women in Central Asia also value wearing a headscarf as sign of their own faith and their connection to a community of belief, and as a respectable way to enjoy fashion and be beautiful.

Finally, the state has always weighed in on veiling in Central Asia. During the *Hujum*, Central Asian modernizers associated unveiling with freedom and with women's individual rights.

The Soviet state supported unveiling by pressuring Uzbek and Tajik men to unveil their wives (Northrup 2001), and reactionary community members threatened unveiled women with death; both of these forces rendered moot women's freedom of choice (Kamp 2011). In the twenty-first century, Central Asian women who veil associate that choice with religious freedom and individual rights. Central Asian governments have come to regard women's veiling with suspicion, associating the practice with violent or extremist Islamic movements. Government efforts to limit veiling today are not as harsh as they were in the early Soviet decades, but reveal that religious freedom is incomplete, while stimulating some Muslim women toward greater determination and a strong defense of their own choices.

Note

1. We would like to express our gratitude to Wendell Schwab for sharing with us his thoughts on veiling in Kazakhstan, and for helping us locate this and other useful sources.

References

Abramson, David. 2004. 'Engendering Citizenship in Postcommunist Uzbekistan'. In *Post-Soviet Women Encountering Transition: Nation Building, Economic Survival, and Civic Activism*, edited by Kathleen Kuehnast and Carol Nechemias, 65–84. Washington, DC: Woodrow Wilson Center Press.

'Aliullin. 1929. *Xotin-qizlar urtasida dinga qarshi tashviqot* [Propaganda against religion among women]. Samarqand and Tashkent: O'z Nashr.

Bashir, Zarifa. 1928. 'Ozodliq qurbonsiz bo'lmaydi: bo'lg'an voqe'adan oling'an hikoya' [Freedom is not without sacrifices: A story based on real events]. *Yangi Yo'l* 3:18–20.

Borbieva, Noor O'Neill. 2012. 'Empowering Muslim Women: Independent Religious Fellowships in the Kyrgyz Republic'. *Slavic Review* 71(2):288–307.

Borbieva, Noor O'Neill. 2017. 'The Ascendance of Orthodoxy: Nation Building and Religious Pluralism in Central Asia'. In *Islam, Society, and Politics in Central Asia*, edited by Pauline Jones. Pittsburgh, PA: Pittsburgh University Press.

Chotonov, Özübek ajy. 2002. *Ÿïman Sabagy* [Faith class]. Bishkek: Tekhnologiia basma borboru.

Halili. 1917. 'Qazondaghi 'umumi Mulimalar isiezdi' [The all Muslim women's congress in Kazan]. *Suyum Bike*, May 10, 166–74.

Hasanov. 1907. 'Qayuv hijab zararli?' [What makes hijab harmful?]. *Alem-i Nisvan* (Bakhcheserai) 7:3–4.

H[uman] R[ights] W[atch]. 1999. "Uzbekistan. Class Dismissed: Discriminatory Expulsions of Muslim Students." Reports, volume 11, no. 12. October. https://www.hrw.org/legacy/reports/1999/uzbekistan/ (accessed April 14, 2017).

Islam Ajary. 2009. 'Musul'manskoye stil' v mode' [Islamic style is in fashion]. *Islam Ajary*, No.04(019):6.

Kamp, Marianne. 2006. *The New Woman in Uzbekistan: Islam, Modernity, and Unveiling under Communism.* Seattle, WA: University of Washington Press.

Kamp, Marianne. 2011. 'Femicide as Terrorism: The Case of Uzbekistan's Unveiling Murders'. In *Sexual Violence in Conflict Zones: From the Ancient World to the Era of Human Rights*, edited by Elizabeth D. Heineman, 56–70. Philadelphia, PA: University of Pennsylvania Press.

Kamp, Marianne. 2015. 'Debating Sharia: The 1917 Muslim Women's Congress in Russia'. *Journal of Women's History* 27(4):13–37.

McBrien, Julie. 2007. 'Brazilian TV and Muslimness in Kyrgyzstan'. *ISIM Review* 19:16–7.

McBrien, Julie. 2009. 'Mukadas's Struggle: Veils and Modernity in Kyrgyzstan'. *Journal of the Royal Anthropological Institute* 15:S127–44.

McBrien, Julie. 2012. 'Watching Clone: Brazilian Soap Operas and Muslimness in Kyrgyzstan'. *Material Religion: The Journal of Objects, Art and Belief* 8(3):374–97.

Mahmood, Saba. 2001. 'Rehearsed Spontaneity and the Conventionality of Ritual: Disciplines of Ṣalāt'. *American Ethnologist* 28(4):827–53.

Mahmood, Saba. 2005. *Politics of Piety: The Islamic Revival and the Feminist Subject.* Princeton, NJ, and Oxford: Princeton University Press.

Montgomery, David. 2007. 'The Transmission of Religious and Cultural Knowledge and Potentiality in Practice: An Anthropology of Social Navigation in the Kyrgyz Republic'. PhD thesis, Boston University.

Najibullah, Farangis. 2011. 'Hijab Now a Hot Topic in Kazakhstan'. Radio Free Europe Radio Liberty. March 20. Available at http://www.rferl.org/a/islamic_hejab_head_scarf_hot_topic_kazakhstan/2344 233.html (accessed April 14, 2017).

Northrup, Douglas. 2001. 'Subaltern Dialogues: Subversion and Resistance in Soviet Uzbek Family Law'. *Slavic Review* 60(1):115–39.

Peshkova, Svetlana. 2006. '*Otinchalar* in the Ferghana Valley: Islam, Gender and Power'. PhD thesis, Syracuse University.

Peshkova, Svetlana. 2013. 'A Post-Soviet Subject in Uzbekistan: Islam, Rights, Gender, and Other Desires'. *Women's Studies* 42:667–95.

R[adio] F[ree] E[urope] R[adio] L[iberty]. 'Project Hijab.' August 12. Available at http://www.rferl.org/z/3248 (accessed April 14, 2017).

Ryskulov, Nimatulla and Rahat Möküyeva. 2012. *Men emne üchün hijab kiyishim kerek?!!!* [Why must I wear hijab?!]. Bishkek: Kyrgyzstan Musulmandarynyn Din Bashkarmasy.

Schwab, Wendell. 2012. 'Traditions and Texts: How Two Young Women Learned to Interpret the Qur'an and Hadiths in Kazakhstan'. *Contemporary Islam* 6(2):173–97.

Shodiyev, Shuhrat. 2007. 'Tajik Student Prepared to Seek Help from International Court'. Ferghana.ru: Central Asia News. Available at http://enews.fergananews.com/articles/2070 (accessed April 14, 2017).

Stephan, Manja. 2010. 'Education, Youth and Islam: The Growing Popularity of Private Religious Lessons in Dushanbe, Tajikistan'. *Central Asian Survey* 29(4):469–83.

US D[epartment of] S[tate]. 2009. 'International Religious Freedom Report 2009: Kyrgyz Republic'. Under Secretary for Democracy and Global Affairs; Bureau of Democracy, Human Rights, and Labor. Available at https://www.state.gov/j/drl/rls/irf/2009/127367.htm (accessed April 14, 2017).

PART II

From politics to fashion

8

IRAN'S COMPULSORY HIJAB

From politics and religious authority to fashion shows

Faegheh Shirazi

[M]any women in our society who do not respect our hijab laws are virtuous. Our emphasis should be on the virtue, not on the mere outward appearance.

(President Ruhani of Iran, cited in Boboltz 2013)

Introduction

When I published my first academic article on the subject of the hijab, I never envisioned that 20 years later I still would be dealing with the same topic. Of course within this span of time, I have published numerous articles on hijab and niqab, including a book called *The Veil Unveiled* (Shirazi 2001a). What I initially concluded in my book about the veil is still very valid regarding the semantic versatility of the veil. This one piece of cloth holds many meanings that change from original context due to politics, social, cultural and economic issues, and a host of other important reasons such as religious fatwas (decrees).

The expansion of the Internet has provided a large depository of online discussions, up-to-date news, and global happenings on this topic, and contradictory opinions are plentiful. In this mix, the reader must carefully discern what is an 'objective' truth on the topic. In this chapter, I have chosen to address only one small portion of this global issue: the compulsory hijab in Iran. I will be looking into the recent history of the hijab from the era of *kashf e hejab* (compulsory unveiling) to the era of compulsory veiling, and a host of many other related events still happening in Iran, all of which profoundly affect Iranian women.

This chapter specifically examines (1) the hijab and women's emancipation in Reza Khan's era of kashf e hejab (compulsory unveiling); (2) the Islamic Revolution and its effect on compulsory hijab; (3) Iranian religious fatwas and the hijab; (4) the Islamic Republic and its effort to control hijab fashion designs and fashion shows; and (5) street hijab fashion, underground fashion shows, and the thriving online fashion markets.

Dress and appearance have always been significant themes discussed when speaking of the emancipation of women, and empowerment. For example, post-Victorian women freed themselves from restrictive corsets and rigidities of clothing and stepped into the new era of 'rational dress movement' which is considered as one of the positive achievements of women during this era. Once women started to actively participate in sports, the dress emancipation gained greater momentum.

Relatedly, much has been written and discussed regarding the emancipation and empowering of Muslim women, including the hijab and dress codes. Muslim women have for a long time participated in movements for women's rights in the Middle East, North Africa, and South Asia (Moghadam 2007). Ettehadieh (2004) speaks about one such women's movement. This movement started in 1946 when the Iranian population was dissatisfied, and wanted to limit the Shah's controlling power by enacting constitutional laws and ending foreign dominance by establishing a parliament (*Majlis*). The conflict was partially related to secularization, which meant prohibition of the hijab:

> Most ulama (religious scholars) joined the ranks of the constitutionalists, but when the ulterior aims of the revolutionaries, such as secularizing legal and educational system, became apparent, an internal conflict developed, one group siding with the shah and the constitution's enemies and the other with the parliament.
>
> *(2004, 86–7)*

The compulsory hijab is reflected in Iranian movies and has been dealt with in various ways depending on the politics in post-revolution Iran. Iranian authorities are still very sensitive about the proper 'Islamic' behaviour and the image of Iranian women in public, including censorship of movies. The censorship committee, after agreeing on the content and images of any new movie, issues a permission license for public viewing (Al-Marashi 2007; Shirazi 2001b; Naficy 1993; Semati 2008; Moore 2005; Bahar 2012).

How Iranian women's hijab and 'emancipation' are meshed together

In Iranian social and political history, for the past 100 years, the hijab and dress codes play a significant role in the lives of women. 'This veiling history deals with the various process of veiling, unveiling and re-veiling' (Ettehadieh 2004, 86–7) with two opposite emancipation regimens: 1) Reza Khan's forced unveiling and 2) the Islamic Republic's forced veiling.

Under Reza Shah, better known as Reza Khan, the police authorities carried out the first *Kashf e hejab* (unveiling) of Iranian women by forcefully unveiling them. On 8 January 1936, Reza Khan ruled that women must not wear a hijab of any kind, including the chador, niqab and headscarf. Well known in the history of Iranian women is that the Women's Awakening in the era comprising 1936–1941 was a conflict between the modernization policies of Reza Khan and the religious clerks and patriarchal forces who were opposed to the unveiling of women. Women were caught in between the two forces. Women in public without the hijab were castigated, while women in public wearing the hijab were subject to its forceful removal. The removal of a hijab in public was understood as a form of insult and public shaming. In the veiling battle, many women chose to stay at home, safe from the forms of harassment caused by the pro- and anti-veiling camps. Ironically, the homebound women were absent from the public, contradicting the 'emancipation' dialogue. Soon after the inauguration of the second Pahlavi Shah (Mohammad Reza Shah) on 16 September 1941, the compulsory unveiling edict was lifted because of strong public opposition. During the time of his ruling as the Shah of Iran, women were left alone to be veiled or unveiled in public.

The policy of unveiling had given elite, and perhaps a number of middle-class women from urban areas, the ability to follow Western fashion. Veiled women in many situations were associated with backwardness, lack of education, lower social status, and belonging to a religious, traditional family backgrounds. Veiled women were often banned from entering movie theatres and other events by the authorities, who discriminated against them, and whose disapproving stares alone made it clear that they did not belong in that specific space. Further complications occurred with younger girls who would have unveiled if it were not for their backgrounds in strict, traditional households. In some cases, they arrived to public schools or university grounds veiled, in the ladies' room removed their hijab, folded it in their bag, combed their hair, and entered the classrooms. At the end of the school day they reapplied their hijabs in the washrooms and returned home. This type of behaviour (unveiling for the duration of the school day) was a secret between the student and her trustworthy friends. These young women often lived in fear of exposure to their traditional families.

'*Kashf e Hejab*' policies during the Reza Khan period

Soon after the Pahlavi Monarchy was toppled by the Islamic Republic (on 1 April 1979), the new government began publishing numerous archival records of so-called secrets belonging to the reign of both Pahlavi Shahs. One of the most exclusive secret records dealt with Reza Khan's direct orders communicated by telegraph and official correspondence between various ministries, municipalities, and head mistresses of institutions about the plan and implementation of the unveiling programme (Violence and Culture Confidential Records about the Abolition of Hijab, 1990). During my trips to Iran, I have collected a series of such published documents from the earlier phase of the Islamic Revolution publications under the auspices of the organization called Ershad e Eslami/Irshad Islami (Islamic Guidance) of the Islamic Government of Iran. Several items published by Ershad e Eslami (Islamic Guidance) reveal some of the brutalities related to the unveiling process and the correspondence between different government agencies that resulted due to the *kashf e hejab* edict. Salah (2005) states that news of the unveiling initially did not seem new since much discussion and talks transpired before the unveiling episode was implemented and seriously followed. Another facet of the event was that the authorities, who were sympathetic to veiling women, were at the same time forced to enact the order of *kashf e hejab* and were therefore misperceived to have turned against the *muhajabas* (ladies wearing the hijab) (Salah 2005). Women realized that not only must they remove their facial niqab, but were no longer permitted to be in the public eye even with their full-length chadors.[1]

The rule was absolute about the requirement of uncovering the face and the hair. The women experienced acute discomfort for exposing their hair in public, since they believed that revealing hair to *na mahram*[2] is a sinful act. This unveiling in public was also the concern of men who felt that their spouses and female relatives appearing in public unveiled were dishonourable. In the Iranian tradition, women preserved the honour of their men by veiling, by not attracting attention to their bodies, and by behaving modestly. Removing the chador and niqab was unacceptable, because all their lives these women had been taught that no strange man should look at their hair and faces. Appearing in the public unveiled counted as degrading themselves, or even being equated with prostitutes who revealed their hair and wore their chadors in a much more relaxed way – such behaviour was understood as inviting the gaze of men. Naturally, the women's reaction was not positive.

Reza Khan clashed with Iran's clergy and devout Muslims on many occasions. For example, among the memorable events was his violation during March 1928 of the sanctuary of Qom's Fatima Al-Masumeh Shrine, 'to beat a cleric who had angrily admonished Reza Shah's wife for temporarily exposing her face a day earlier while on pilgrimage to Qom' (Mackey 1996). The religious class was frustrated by the government policies to unveil their women. In a report originating from the Ministry of the Interior, the Central Police Office was alerted to the fact that in Tehran and other cities, the ulama (the body of religious scholars) and preachers inside mosques were giving sermons against unveiling, and were emphasizing the importance of veiling for Muslim women. The religious class was puzzled as to why people did not follow Islamic regulations anymore (*Vagheh e kashf e hejab*, 1990).

Reza Khan implemented another rule in 1928, referred to as the dress reform law, that required men to dress in Western clothes while in public. The only exception to this rule were the Shia legal scholars, who had passed a special qualifying examination. This dress reform for men included a hat with a brim. The hat is known as *Kolah Pahlavi* or Pahlavi Hat. According to Mackey (1996), Muslim men were annoyed by this dress code, but most of all they did not like the hat with a 'brim which prevented the devout from touching their foreheads on the ground during the salat [praying] required by Islamic law' (Mackey 1996, 184). Mackey's comments about the brimmed Pahlavi hat raises some doubts, as it is hard to imagine that men would be praying with their hats on, or would not be aware that they could remove their hats during prayer time.

School was one of the primary locations for the forced unveiling of women in large numbers. Women – head mistresses, staff and teachers – could no longer attend school with head coverings. At the same time, students, if veiled, no longer could attend classrooms or even register for school. Yet there was resistance. A report from the principality of Kerman to the office of the prime minister reported, 'with the exception of the principal of the school and only four students, the rest of the students, the entire staff and teachers are veiled and refuse to follow the order of *kashf e hejab*' (*Vagheh e kashf e hejab* 1996, 100). In another report, teachers in Qom resigned from their posts because of the order of unveiling, and religious clerks were influential in convincing students' parents to stop the girls from attending school unveiled (102). Following is an sample of a correspondence between local authorities and the central government about issues regarding the forced unveiling. The correspondence reveals the chaotic situation that *kashf e hejab* created at the time:

#88. Arak (a note from the governor of Arak to the Prime Minister, dated Khorad, 18, 1315 HS (1936 CE)

The Internal Government of Arak, No. 1061

Honourable Prime Minister, the note No. 2970 arrived in which the subject was training of the ladies to unveil. We are progressing fast about this matter; both the police and municipality of Arak are working hard. There are no covered/veiled (*mastoreh*) ladies visible in public spaces, even though we are having a number of public celebrations and parties in which a large number of women are present. However, there are a group of women who are poor, and disturbed [mentally retarded], and that are mostly bald [*kachal*]. This group of women uses a small thin headscarf. There is no need to stop these women to unveil.

Signed: Acting Governor of Arak (signature illegible)

P.S. Please respond to this note. We are striving for daily progress regarding unveiling.
(Khoshonat va Farhang 1996, 52)

The above document illustrates unpredicted issues for those pressed by the central government to impose the rules. In another correspondence between the governor of Bandar Langeh and the surrounding small southern coast municipalities, we read an extract of the events and the report prepared for the central government:

#129. Bandar Langeh

Day, 9, 1314 HS (1935)

The Governance of Bandar Langeh and Governor of the southern coast region, No. 170

Secret and Directive

The Governor of the southern coast region received the secret telegraph no.448, a training and progress of ladies' action report about Bandar Abbas. We are directly reporting about the local condition of Bandar Langeh (that was reported previously). The majority of local citizens of Bandar Langeh are Bahraini, Lari, Bestaki, Avazi, and Blooki. These groups are usually very poor and the ladies are accustomed to wear the burqa at all times. In fact, the burqa they use in this part of the country is locally known as *batolah*, which leaves only the two eyes open and the rest of the face is hidden by *batolah*. In addition to the *batolah*, these ladies use another layer of hijab on the top of *batolah*. Their sincere belief in keeping their *batolah* on all the time is so strong that even when ladies are visiting other ladies as guests, or entertain other women at home, they keep the *batolah* on their face all the time, and when they are in the public their faces are covered at all times. The same is true even for the poor and deprived class who are working as maids inside houses. They never remove their *batolah* from their faces even when there is no man present inside the house. It is known that these ladies believe that removing their *batolah* even in front of other women is shameful. Thus, hopefully after the explanation of the local culture of Bandar Langeh and the rest of southern coasts I am hoping that you can delay the *kashf e hejab* ordinance for some time, hence hoping that within a short period of time when the local people mingle and see the tourist, hear and read more about it they become more familiar with the unveiling concept. So they would be prepared to make the change and comply with the rules. Of course your Excellency, this delay in action is absolutely dependent upon your agreement in this matter.

Signed: Mohammad Karim Navab – The Governance of Bandar Langeh

(Khoshonat va Farhang 1996, 75–6)

The following report is an example of how the compulsory unveiling order hurt the poor population who were unable to afford the new dress code for going outdoors, composed of Western-style clothing and hat styles:

#159. From Mashhad Municipality to Eastern Region Police Authority Station

Tir, 14, 1315 (1936 CE)

Mashhad Municipality No. 7209. Secret

From the Municipality of the city of Mashhad of the Eastern Region

After discussions with Mashhad city committee members and the mayor, it was decided that the city would like to help the poor ladies who are not able to purchase [Western] hats. Thus, the office of the mayor would purchase 200 hats to deliver to the ladies in need. Please order to receive the hats and distribute them properly.

Signed: Ebrahim Sharifi-Mashhad Municipality

(Khoshonat va Farhang 1996, 92–93)

The poverty among the women of various regions is a common theme in the correspondence from these recorded documents. The locations mentioned in the aforementioned records are Arak in central west, Bandar Langeh on the south coast of the Persian Gulf south, and Mashhad in the northwest – geographically diverse localities with different cultural backgrounds. One could gain a better understanding of why, in addition to the religious resistance and modesty issues mentioned earlier, so many was opposed to the *kashf e hejab*. The imposition of unveiling for traditional women were an economic burden. Western hats and clothes and the types of suitable textiles for manufacturing such clothes were unaffordable for many women. Ample official reports showed how textile merchants and hat suppliers, benefiting from the *kashf e hejab* order, price gouged the customers. The Ministry of Interior wrote to all the Counties and Governors (1935), addressing public complaints about unfair prices. Following is a partial translation of this document written by the prime minister discussing the idea of expense 'used to disobey the unveiling order':

Document No. 212.

Directive to all the Counties and Governors

It is surprising to learn that some claim that women's continued usage of chador is due to the scarcity and exorbitant prices for the cloth needed to make the proper outer-gown/over-gown/mantua required by law. In reality a chador requires more yardage to make than a mantua. In addition, the traditional black chador (suitable to be worn in public) is made of the fine Crepe de Chine fabrics that are much more expensive than ordinary fabrics. Hence, the expense or scarcity of fabric is not the issue and has no validity as an excuse. It is the duty of each county to keep up with the law and see that the order is properly carried out.

Signed: The Prime Minister

(Vagheh kashf e hejab 1990, 438)

Other correspondence between the Ministry of Interior and the local governors reveals more information about the unveiling process. For example, the prime minister in 1936 had sent a letter to the Minister of Transportation warning him that some of the inspectors who had visited various locations around Tehran and its surroundings reported seeing numerous veiled ladies in some train compartments. Thus, the bus stations, carriage stations, taxis, trains, and entrance to cinemas were closely watched and veiled women were turned away from using the services or the facilities.

In carrying out the unveiling order, authorities did not hesitate to attack women in public to grab, remove, and snatch the chador away from them. The act was violent, constituting physical abuse, and most of all dishonourable and unacceptable behaviour forbidden by the religion and the culture. In an ironic twist, some 50 years later after the *kashf e hejab*, the Islamic Republic of Iran used similar techniques of harassing and abusing women publicly to force them to wear the hijab. The Islamic Republic also published secret documents of *kashf e hejab* as a proof of the violence used against women in the name of emancipation during the Pahlavi reign.

In 1941 the Ministry of Interior (document no. 194) directly instructed the police to avoid clashing with people, and warning that they must behave respectfully towards veiled ladies in their business of reminding women of the *kashf e hejab* order (*Vagheh kashf e hejab* 1990, 404). In a document presented by women of Yazd to Majles e Shoriay Meli (Legislative Assembly/ Parliament) in 1941 (document no. 185), women collectively complained about the rough treatment, physical and verbal abuse in addition to public humiliations they had received from the authorities carrying out *kashf e hejab*:

> While the newspapers and radio programs only present the happy and positive side of the unveiling order and its success, it ignores the dark side of it. The news never speaks of brutality and unkind behaviour of the police towards us, which includes using foul language, hitting us with batons, and kicking us with their boots. Some women seriously injured or became paralyzed, while some even lost their lives . . . they even beat on pregnant and sick women.
>
> *(Vaegheh e Kashf e Hejab 1996, 386)*

The report also spoke of theft by the police in the name of carrying out the unveiling order. The women complained that the police:

> confiscated our personal property in the name of confiscating our chadors and head scarves . . . and god forbid if we confronted the police, they would treat us like captives or slaves and if we could not afford to pay the fines for our freedom, or could not come up with a bribe to be free from their harassments they would take us to the police station which would be more painful and tortuous and it would cost us more to be released.
>
> *(Vaegheh e Kashf e Hejab 1996, 386)*

The letter ends with pleading and request for women's freedom to wear the hijab and a cessation of the abuse and unkindness. In a note (labelled secret) to the prime minister from the governor of the State of Khorasan, a similar episode is reported:

Document No. 136

Secret – State of Khorasan

Tir, 27, 1315 SH (1936 CE)

From the Governor of the State of Khorasan addressed to the Prime Minister.

Based on several reports it has become evident that the police and the authorities use unnecessary and excess force when dealing with veiled ladies and even in some cases police misused their authoritative power for their own personal gains. Your Honour, we would like to report and express our concerns about the continuation of such unpleasant events, which may cause migration of a large number of people (living close to the borders) to migrate to Afghanistan.

Signed: The Governor of State of Khorasan.

(Vaegheh e Kashf e Hejab 1996, 286)

Several facts become clear based on the documents presented here from the Reza Khan era. Resistance to *kashf e hejab* came from all social strata, but particularly from those not belonging to the upper class and elite members of society. Clerks were influential in working against *kashf e hejab* by publishing and distributing flyers among the populace condemning the unveiling rule as an un-Islamic and sinful act. Police authorities at times became violent against women, both physically and mentally. Merchants engaged in price gouging for the required Western-style hats and fabrics. Sometimes women bribed police to turn a blind eye to veiled ladies. The regime of unveiling Iranian women in order to 'modernize' and 'emancipate' them was in reality unfeasible in a culture largely opposed to unveiling in public during the time.

The Islamic Revolution, compulsory hijab, and the fatwas

The issue of compulsory hijab has been an ongoing discussion since the establishment of the Islamic theocracy in Iran at 1979. For every social, political, cultural, gender-related, economic and religious discussion about Iran, one must be ready to hear about the hijab, which is always linked to a simple sentence: women must wear the hijab. At the beginning of the Islamic Republic of Iran, Ayatollah Khomeini 'recommended that working women wear modest dress (1979); coeducational activities in sports and education above primary levels are banned; women are encouraged to take early retirement in professions that put them in close contact with men' (cited in Beck and Nashat 2004: xii). After the first Islamic Parliament and the election of the first president (January 1980), Islamic dress (which required covering the hair and the entire body) became a mandatory, law-ordained rule for female employees of the state. Of course, most Iranian women in public spaces were already afraid to venture out unveiled because they had been attacked by revolutionary guards. Veiling started as a recommendation for female state employees in Iran, but soon became a strict law, and a related struggle. Much has been written about this compulsory veiling in Iran, with its own dark history of abuse and violence. Ironically when the Islamic Republic of Iran was exposing the violence and abuse of Reza Khan's unveiling scheme, *kashf e hejab*, they turned a blind eye to what the new government of Iran was doing. The new Islamic government practically perpetrated the same abuse towards women in an even more brutal way to force women to veil in public.

The mental and physical abuse of Iranian women for forced veiling under the Islamic Republic is by far greater, compared to Reza Khan's *kashf e hejab* time of forced unveiling. Reza Khan did not give orders to lash women as a punishment for a failure to unveil. Islam never advocated 74 lashes on the body of a woman to teach her to wear her hijab in an 'interpretive' conservative form, the ideal veiling imagined by the government. And examples are plentiful of the use of foul language toward women, referring to them as 'prostitutes', 'lustful women', or even making them wear a sign in Persian that says 'I am a prostitute' (*man yek fahesheh hastam*). As opposed to the Reza Khan regime, the present government uses God to justify its physical and mental abuse in order to keep the hijab on women.

Thus women have become the subject of the political battle between the religious and secular camps. Both the Pahlavi and the Islamic Republic eras use women's bodies for political goals and agendas. Both regimes, relating to the compulsory unveiling and compulsory re-veiling, use a piece of cloth, the hijab, in their argument for the 'freedom' and 'emancipation' of women. And after 80 years between the two regimes, one thing has not changed, and that is that men 'know' for sure what is good for women, including their dress code.

Religious fatwas about the hijab

Ample literature is still published in the form of fatwas (religious rulings) and *ahkam* (orders) issued for Iranian women. Khomeini's fatwa for women's hijab is still one of the most followed and quoted fatwas in Iran. In his fatwa, Khomeini instructs that the face and hands are not covered, dark colours are best suited for women working in offices, and the traditional chador is the best hijab for Iranian women. While rules are presented about when a woman is religiously excused from praying or her responsibilities towards her family, duties as wife, and many other daily life matters, dress code and the hijab comprise a large aspect of these rules. Following are samples of related fatwas:

No. 30 coverage of [women's] body during praying

A woman must be completely covered, even her hair and head (in the same manner as seen in public). However, it is not required for her to cover her face (only as much that requires for ablution) or covering her hands (from the wrist to the end of the fingers) or no need to cover her feet from ankles to the toes.

(Sanaei, fatwa and ahkam 2000, 99)

Because of the clash of various political powers in Iran who are pro-reformist and the hardliners aligned with the Supreme Leader Ayatollah Khamenei, a recent fatwa has been issued by the Supreme Leader:

Iran: Fatwa orders women to keep wearing the Islamic veil

Tehran, 29 January 2014 (AKI) – Iran's most senior Shia clerics including the nation's supreme leader, Ayatollah Ali Khamenei, have decreed that women will be punished under Islamic law if they don't wear the veil.

'The veil remains obligatory for all Iranian women and the Islamic Republic has the right to imposed this norm across the whole country.'

'Any woman who rebels against this ordinance will be appropriately punished under Islamic Sharia law', continued the fatwa.

The edict was signed by Khamenei and other grand ayatollahs including Nuri Hamedani and Makarem Shirazi.

This fatwa regarding the obligatory hijab is a direct reaction to what President Ruhani had stated during the same time period (See Boboltz 2013).

In 1995 the forty-first edition of Morteza Motahhari's famous book *Masaleh Hejab* (The Issue of Hijab) was published. Motahhari (a disciple of Ayatollah Khomeini) is considered to be among the important influential members on the formation of ideologies of the Islamic Republic. This book is written in a very appealing manner using both logical arguments and Qur'anic verses and *tafsirs* (interpretations) to put the issue of women's veiling in a much larger scope and perspective. Ayatollah Khomeini has written much about the virtues of the hijab for women, in addition to numerous negative portraits of *Kashf e Hejab* of Reza Khan. *Simay e Zan dar Kalam e Imam Khomeini* (Images of women according to Imam Khomeini) is a good place to start, in order to understand the Grand Ayatollah Khomeini's opinion about women. In this volume are contained unedited speeches and parts of speeches, which he has delivered to the public regarding the hijab and a woman's responsibilities towards her family and society. In the following section I have translated several passages that reveal his opinion on the subject.

Ayatollah Khomeini describes two eras in history during which women were abused: the *jahelia* (pre-Islamic) era where women were treated worse than animals[3] and were rescued by Islam. The second era where women were abused was during the two Pahlavi Shah regimes. 'In the name of freeing the woman they inflected pain, toppled woman from her high honourable standing made her a commodity – in the name of freedom, the freedom of "freed women," and "freed men" was taken away, they spoiled the minds of our youth' (Khomeini

1993, 13). The Shah, pretending he wanted to give women greater status in society, instead made her into a doll, not recognizing that she is a human being and a worthy teacher of society (Khomeini 1993).

In another section, Khomeini writes that 'a woman should be the source of all the happiness and hope for all. Unfortunately, this father and son [Reza Khan and Mohammad Reza Shah Pahlavi], particularly the son, committed much greater crimes against women compared to men' (1993, 15). This statement refers to Mohammad Reza Shah's push for advancement to be in line with the West. Khomeini's negative opinion about the idea of freedom for woman and man is mostly argued from his condemnation of the sexual revolution during the time of the second Pahlavi Shah, making numerous references to mixed-gender gatherings, swimming on beaches, and the freedom of having boyfriends and girlfriends. Khomeini questions the proclaimed freedom of secular Iran as bogus since no freedom of speech was granted to media or people during the Shah's time – an ironic claim since freedom of speech and the status of women in theocratic Iran is the same as was during the second Pahlavi's time. Khomeini writes:

> God is our witness what happened to Iran during that era of *Kashf e Hejab*. They [agents of Reza Khan] tore down the human honour [a reference to hijab as an honour for woman to maintain aligned in keeping the man's honour], they forced the ulama under the spearheads, to attend parties [a reference to mixed gendered gatherings usually held in the evenings] with their wives, and forced ulama's wives to give similar parties. Such gatherings were done under force, the guests were honourable men and women, who were not happy attending such gatherings, however they had no choice. Many of the guests end up crying in these gathering, as they did not like to see or to be part of such [sinful] activities.
>
> *(Simay e zan 1993, 43)*

Khomeini adds, '[i]t is not possible to be a Muslim and be in agreement with kashfe Hejab. The Iranian women showed Shah their dissatisfaction by protesting against his unveiling, they shouted "we want to be free, and this man [Reza Khan] says you are free only if you remove your chadors and headscarves when you are attending schools. Tell me, is this what you call azadi [freedom]?"' (1993, 43). He then explains what he means by freedom:

> The purpose of our revolution is for saving our souls, due to the fact that they [Reza Khan's regime] removed the chadors from the head of our pious, honourable Muslim women. Today to do that [unveiling] is against the religion [Islam] and the law of the land. There is no one who speaks against it' (1993). But who could speak against it when the consequence was lashings, jail sentences, or charged for the 'crime of bad hijabi'?

Khomeini believed a true Muslim (man or woman) would never accept an unveiled woman in public, and that the meaning of freedom for Iranian woman meant veiling. Thus Reza Khan and Ayatollah Khomeini both argued the meaning of *azadi* (freedom) from opposite poles using force to unveil and to veil. Both of these powerful politically motivated men, one with secular Westernized ideology and the other with a religious ideology, defined for women their 'freedom'.

Throughout the history of the Islamic Republic since 1979, the government's anxiety surrounding the hijab and its enforcement has been constant, and the subject of veiling has been amongst the most important in the Parliament. Political and economic situation, conditions of war and sanctions, all have interwoven into the issue of veiling and corresponding arrests, verbal harassment or even physical attacks. The number of hijab arrests is seasonal with more arrests in late spring and summer relating to the heat (see Figure 8.1 for an illustration of a fine ticket for improper hijab). Victims of rape are often accused for improper wearing of the hijab. Improperly veiled women with repeated offences may be treated more harshly, paying a fine and sometimes are forced to attend guidance classes. The subject of women's reform is continuously debated and discussed by the government. An internal battle about the status of women is evident within the political power structure in Iran.

Top right reads:

Ticket number: 1546
Date: 21 Khordad 1389 (11 June 2010)
Bill No. 47563
Type of disorderly conduct: Nail polish on 4 and half fingers
Disorderly Code: 4
Amount of fine: 22,500.00 Toman
First and last name: _____
National ID Card NO. 258610562
Location that the fine was issued: Khiyaban Golsar, Next to Golsar Business Complex
Issuing Institution: Gasht e Ershad (the Guidance force)
Officer's Code No: 0543
Type of payment: Cash

Top left reads:

Chadour the superior hejab (*chadour hejab e bartar*)
The text next to the woman's face reads: *hejab*
The text below the woman's face reads: rare jewel (*gohar e naab*)

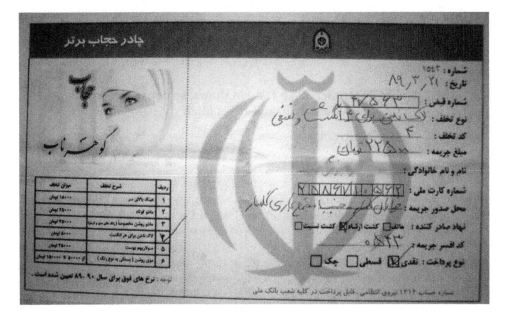

Figure 8.1 Fine ticket for improper hijab

The chart with six columns is a reference to the type of disorderly conduct and the amount of fine for each disobedience:

1 – Placing (wearing) glasses on the top of the head.
2 – Short Mantou (outer gown).
3 – Light-coloured Mantou, particularly those in green or red.
4 – Nail polish for each finger.
5 – Tanned face.
6 – Light-coloured hair, depending on the type of colour (dyed hair)

For example, President Ruhani, on the occasion of Women's Day in 2014, stated: 'We will not accept the culture of sexual discrimination . . . Women must enjoy equal opportunity, equal protection and equal social rights . . . [and] according to the Islamic rules, man is not the stronger sex and woman is not the weaker one'. Shortly after, the Supreme Leader Ayatollah Ali Khamenei in a speech stated that gender equality was 'one of the biggest mistakes of the Western society thought . . . Justice is a right . . . But equality is sometimes right and sometimes wrong'. Regarding the intensification of hijab patrols (*gasht e hejab*) to enforce public obedience to the dress code, Ruhani addressed the hardliners' ideas on the subject of 'the path to paradise', including forcing people to wear conservative dress, by stating 'You can't force people to heaven with whips and threats . . . We shouldn't interfere in people's lives to such an extent, even out of compassion. Let them choose their own path to heaven'. In a response to Ruhani's 'forced heaven' statement, a conservative imam in a sermon addressing the people of Mashhad said, 'Forget the whip, we will stand with all our force in the way of those who prevent people from going to heaven' (Kamali Dehghan 2014).

As we can see, many contradictory factions and clashes of ideas exist in Iran. One might think that the religious class of *mo'ammem* (meaning: those wearing the turban) is not only conservative but anti-women's rights. But as we had witnessed, also the former president of Iran, Ahmadinejad, was not from the religious class, wore Western suit and trousers, has an advance degree in engineering, but behaved very conservatively. At times he was an open misogynist without shame, when compared to the former president of Iran Mohammad Khatami or the current president, Ruhani, who are from a religious class and both are *mo'ammem*.

Government-controlled hijab fashion shows, secretive underground fashion hijab, and street hijab styles

Young Iranians have rebelled for decades against veiling and religious dictates, against the harshly and continuously imposed 'pious and heavenly garb'. Of course, when it comes to the idea of Islamic fashion, one must assume that there is more to 'Muslim Dress'[4] than the traditional abaya, chador and burka. Young Muslim women use an array of multiple fashion systems to create not only their own fashion, but also to negotiate ethnicity, identity and religion. Malaysia was the first Muslim nation that held an Islamic Fashion Festival in 2006 in Kuala Lumpur. Dato' Raja Rezza Shah was the original founder of this festival:

[P]artly to combat received stereotypes about Islam, the festival is part of a wider movement within a slice of the Muslim world – most often Muslims living in minority contexts, or non-Arab Muslim majority countries – that has seized on fashion as a means to reshape the cultural narrative.

(Friedmannov 2015)

The interest and growth in Islamic fashion are due to several reasons, one of which is population growth. According to the Pew Research (2015), Muslims may number almost 3 billion by 2050, as compared to 1.6 billion now. Another factor in the rise of Muslim fashion is Muslim spending power and contribution to economy:

> Muslim consumers spent about $266 billion on clothing in 2013, the latest year for which data is available, according to the State of the Global Islamic Economy 2014–2015 report commissioned by Thomson Reuters and Dinar Standard. They are expected to spend about $484 billion by 2019.
>
> *(Gorman 2015)*

Muslim youth are now more educated and better-travelled than the previous generations, and certainly global communication technology has played a big part in consumerism, and in inciting a desire for luxury goods. In addition to regular Islamic fashion shows, a number of high fashion houses create Hijab Couture for elite clientele, just as couture fashions operate based on design exclusivity, fine workmanship, and finer textiles in the production. The government of Malaysia supports the local designers, and textile and apparel industry, and forms partnerships with fashion houses to promote Malaysia on the top of global fashion.

In contrast to the Malaysian government, the Iranian government has always projected a negative attitude towards fashion inspired by the West. The Islamic Republic promotes unfashionably long, loose garments in dark and sober colours. Hijab patrols (*gasht e hejab*) walk the streets, looking to catch anyone in unauthorized hijab. At the same time, the Iranian government wants to be part of the lucrative Islamic fashion industry. The Iranian government has always had a hand in the apparel business through governmental cooperative shops known as *taavoni*, which produce simple outer gowns made in standard plain darker fabrics, and are aimed at the price conscious rather than the fashion-conscious consumer. However, the government obviously took notice of other Muslim nation fashion festivals that had become generators of revenue. Malaysia and Turkey are considered the hub for seasonal Islamic fashion with good design, and creative use of colours and textiles.

Government-sponsored fashion festivals in Iran

On 7 March 2013 the Islamic Republic of Iran hosted an Islamic fashion and clothing festival. The festival, according to the Iranian source, 'is aimed at increasing national pride, promote innovations in Islamic-Iranian designs and to raise the standards of the designs' (Tehran hosts 2 Fair Intl. fashion & clothing festival 2013). Qaraguzlu, an Iranian fashion designer, stated: 'I choose modernity and tradition . . . we should choose colours which fit our culture, skin, life and manner'. In a press interview, Hamid Shahabadi, Iran's Deputy Minister of Culture, said:

> Iranian people are very proud of what symbolizes their Islamic Iranian values and design, culture and their civilization . . . But some people in the west like to impose their own style of clothes on our nation that is quite different from our traditions and values that is based on the Iranian taste, culture and values.

This interview makes clear that although the government of Iran is celebrating fashion festivals, designers must remember that designs must follow 'Islamic Iranian value' (Tehran hosts 2 Fair Intl. 2013). This is a key phrase reflecting back to Ms Qaraguzlu's carefully chosen words about 'colours, which fit our culture, skin, and manner'.

A close examination of published exhibition pictures and a video clip of the event indicated clearly that the collection lacked innovative ideas, because this type of fashion is government-controlled with strictly imposed guidelines. Restrictive governmental directives in the name of 'Islamic Iranian values' are counter to a dynamic creative product (see Figures 8.2 and 8.3).

Underground private fashion shows, online hijab fashion sales, and Iranian street fashion

Despite prohibitions on women's dress and make-up, Iranian women account for almost one-third of all cosmetics bought in the two-dozen countries of the Middle East, again led by youth.

(Memarian, and Nesvaderani, 2010)

Figure 8.2 One of the earlier efforts to create government fashion shows dates to 2001.
Photo Credit: FARS News Agency, Iran

Figure 8.3 This particular example is a reminiscent style of Qajar woman's hijab (*chador va chaghchor*) that Reza Khan abolished by *kashf e hejab* edict.
Photo Credit: Sina Shiri, FARS News Agency, Iran. 2013

Iranian youth are connected to the external world despite governmental restrictions and censorship of the Internet, and the exchange of ideas among the global youth is undeniable. Thus, there are underground fashion shows of Western styles with catwalk models without hijab or restrictions on body coverage. This class of creation is only for a certain clientele in private home parties and not to be seen in public.

To showcase the creativity and talent of Iranian designers to the world, a joint collaborative effort transpired between Alangoo (an online website) and an Edinburgh fashion festival. The Edinburgh Iranian Festival fashion show, Persian Chic, was created. This show was held at the National Museum of Scotland in the Grand Gallery. Jessica Howarth, an acclaimed British jewellery designer, reported that in addition to the Iranian designers both inside and outside Iran:

> There will be eight designers including myself from around the world, whose work is influenced by Iran. Not only will there be a catwalk and Jewellery exhibition there, you will also get to listen to some wonderful Iranian music.
>
> *(Howarth 2015)*

Alangoo website states that this was a great opportunity for the 'Iran based designers who would otherwise have limited ways to share their talent with the world . . . there was a common thread among all, an influence and admiration for their Persian history and culture' (2015). It is a rare opportunity for the underground fashion designers, but there is also a worry about arrest not only for the designer but also the models and the attending audience, including even the people who rented the facility for the show:

> The *LA Times* goes behind the scenes of a fashion show in Tehran where women and men mix freely and models flash plentiful skin.
>
> Sadaf, the designer, rented out an acquaintance's basement and flew in four of the six models. One described herself as 'a little terrified', but the show went on to a warm reception from an enthusiastic crowd. The mullahs, presumably, were none the wiser. Said Azita, a designer in the audience: 'We love it so much because the clerics hate it.'
>
> *(Rosen 2007)*

Examples of underground fashion shows in Iran tell the story of the youth in Iran who are taking risks to rebel against government controls, including the control of fashion.

The street fashion scene in Iran

Street fashions are created individually by Iranian men and women, and are not part of an organized underground fashion show. Street fashion seen everywhere is a unique phenomenon with no particular style or individual designer. Generally, the designers are individuals wearing carefully selected garments that can include not only the headscarf, and the outer gown (mantua) but also the hair partially visible under fashionably draped scarves. Also included are accessories: shoes and handbags all tastefully matched together. The look is markedly different from the government-prescribed styles that encourage women not to wear colourful garments, sandals, make-up, nail polish, or leggings, which are also banned by the fashion police (*gasht e hejab*). Since 2011, the traffic police have also joined in to crack down on both men and women for the crime of improper clothing (*Bad Pooshi*):

> Iran's road and safety police have been handed a new responsibility. They have the power to fine Iranians who are not dressed according to the rules of Islam.
>
> Traditionally this had been the job of the moral police, but now a traffic police officer can give Iranians two fines in one, a speeding fine and an un-Islamic dress code fine.
>
> *(Zarindast 2011, see Figure 8.1)*

Those appearing in street fashion are often hunted down with sometimes-serious consequences. And yet, the street fashion scene is thriving, and during the hot days of summer, one can observe in street fashions creative ways to wear the hijab and clothes in cool and light-coloured fabrics in a less formal way.

Conclusion

The hijab has no equal – at least among other items of clothing – in terms of generating interest, curiosity and discussion in contemporary global Muslim society and beyond. Both Muslim-majority and non-Muslim-majority nations have created regulations and laws to forcefully adopt or to not adopt the hijab. In Iran, the hijab is not only a religious symbol exclusively related to women, but also is a symbol defining control over women. Woman's body and veiling have been discussed from opposite polarities while women themselves had no say in the matter. Reza Khan attempted to forcefully remove the veil from women in public spaces to 'emancipate them', Ayatollah Khomeini forced women to cover their bodies for the same 'emancipation'. The mental and physical violence and abuse of women have been amply documented during both of these 'emancipation' periods. In the vocabulary of the hardliners in Iran, fashion and the hijab are mutually exclusive, and combining the two is an insult associated with Western culture. Thus, referring to a colourful mantua worn with large, printed colourful scarves, as 'Westernized hijab' in effect meant no hijab at all.

Global social media have made it possible now for youth to demand more freedom in their lives. And meanwhile the Islamic Government of Iran is doing its best to control public fashion scenes by arranging annual fashion festivals, hoping that controlled hijabi fashions under the auspices of Iranian Islam will divert the attention of those women not interested in the uninspiring colours and loose-fitting outer garments promoted by the government.

Notes

1. *Chador* is an Iranian traditional form of veil/hijab; it is a long, enveloping piece of cloth covering the entire head and body.
2. *Na mahram* means men who are haram, forbidden to women by religious law.
3. This statement is not clear as if this is a reference to pre-Islamic Arabia or it is a general reference to women's condition around the world including Iran.
4. In reality there is no such terminology that could be true since Muslim means a person (not an object) who follows the religion of Islam. Thus, a dress does not have a religion and a veil is not equated with Islam either. However, for better or worse, today we are stocked with this term, which describes a form of dress in concept not necessary in a particular look that is modest in its coverage and accompanied with a form of head-covering.

References

Adnkronos. 2014. 'Iran: Fatwa Orders Women to Keep Wearing the Islamic Veil'. 29 January. Available at http://www1.adnkronos.com/IGN/Aki/English/Religion/Iran-Fatwa-orders-women-to-keep-wearing-the-Islamic-veil_321163607685.html (accessed 2 July 2015).

Al-Marashi, Ibrahim. 2007. 'Feminism and Censorship in an Islamic Republic, Women Filmmakers in Iran'. In *From Patriarchy to Empowerment*, edited by Valentine M. Moghadam, 230–40. Syracuse, NY: Syracuse University Press.

Bahar, Mehri. 2012. 'Religious Identity and Mass Media: The Situation of Women in Iranian Cinema Following the Islamic Revolution'. *OIDA International Journal of Sustainable Development* 4(11):35–44.

BBC. 2014. 'Iran President Rouhani Urges Equal Rights for Women'. 20 April. Available at www.bbc.com/news/world-middle-east-27099151 (accessed 1 July 2015).

Beck, Lois and Nashat Guity. 2004. 'Chronology'. In *Women in Iran from 1800 to the Islamic Republic*, edited by Lois Beck and Guity Nashat, xii. Chicago, IL: University of Illinois Press.

Boboltz, Sara. 2013. 'These Stylish Iranian Women Won't Let A Dress Code Hold Them Back'. *Huffington Post*, 20 December. Available at www.huffingtonpost.com/2013/12/20/tehran-street-style_n_4467366.html (accessed 7 July 2015).

Friedmannov, Vanessa. 2015. 'Reading the Subtleties of Islamic Fashion'. *New York Times*, 25 November. Available at www.nytimes.com/2014/11/27/fashion/reading-between-the-seams-at-the-islamic-fashion-festival-in-malaysia.html?_r=0 (accessed 3 July 2015).

Gorman, Ryan. 2015. 'The Islamic Fashion Business is Booming'. *Business Insider*, 9 April. Available at www.businessinsider.com/the-islamic-fashion-business-is-booming-2015-4 (accessed 2 July 2015).

Howarth, Jessica. 2015. 'Iranian Fashion Show: Persian Chic'. February 2015. Available at http://jessicahowarth.com/iranian-fashion-show-persian-chic/ (accessed 5 July 2015).

Kamali, Dehghan, Saeed. 2014. 'Iran's Rouhani Locks Horns with Hardliners over Path to Paradise'. 3 June 2014. Available at www.theguardian.com/world/iran-blog/2014/jun/03/iran-rouhani-locks-horns-hardliners-path-paradise (accessed 23 December 2015).

Khomeini, Ayatollah. 1993. *Simay e Zan dar Kalam e Imam Khomein*. Tehran, Iran: Sazman e Chaap e Enteshaarat Vezarat Farhang va Ershad Eslami.

Khoshonat va Farhang: Asnad e Mahramaneh Kashf e Hejab.1313–1322 HS [Violence and culture confidential records about the abolition of hijab 1934–1943]. 1990. Iran, Tehran: Department of Research Publication and Education National Archives, Iran.

Mackey, Sandra. 1996. *The Iranians: Persia, Islam and the Soul of a Nation*. New York: Dutton.

'Malaysia Showcases Its Diverse Fashion at the World Fashion Week'. Malaysia Fashion Week; The FACIT @INTRADE 2014. 30 September 2014. Available at www.prnewswire.com/news-releases/malaysia-showcases-its-diverse-fashion-at-the-world-fashion-week-277579641.html (accessed 3 July 2015).

Moghadam, Valentine M., ed. 2007. *From Patriarchy to Empowerment*. New York: Syracuse University Press.

Moore, L. C. 2005. 'Women in a Widening Frame: (Cross-) Cultural Projection, Spectatorship and Iranian Cinema'. *Camera Obscura: Feminism, Culture and Media Studies* 20(2):1–33.

Motahhari, Morteza. 1995. *Masaleh Hejab*. Tehran: Sadra Publisher.

Naficy, Hamid. 1993. 'Veiled Vision/Powerful Presence: Women in Post –Revolutionary Iran and Cinema'. In *In the Eye of the Storm: Women in Post-Revolutionary Iran*, edited by Mahnnaz Afkhami and Erika Friedle, 131–50. Syracuse, NY: Syracuse University Press.

Rosen, Sam Gale. 2007. 'Iranians Embrace Underground Fashion Shows'. 11 May. Available at www.newser.com/story/2109/iranians-embrace-underground-fashion-shows.html (accessed 7 July 2015).

Saanei, Ayatollah. 2000. *Ahkam e Banovan: Motabegh ba Fatwa e Hazrat Ayatollal al Ozma Sanaaei*. Qom, Iran: the publication office of Ayatollah Saanei.

Sadat Paak, Neda. Nahad, Attorney at Law. Available at www.tebyan.net/newmobile.aspx/index.aspx?pid=267614/.
Also see:
www.asriran.com/fa/news/123865/.
http://hadafonline.com/dinaandishe/shobahat/304-hijab/.
http://alef.ir/vdccsoqm.2bqmo8laa2.html/?7txt/.

Salah, Mahdi. 2005. *Kashf e Hejab, zamineh ha, vakeneshha, va paymadha* [Unveil: Ground works, reactions and conclusions]. Tehran: Political Studies & Research Institute (PSRI).

Semati, Mehdi. 2008. *Media, Culture and Society in Iran: Living with Globalization and the Islamic State*. New York: Routledge.

Shirazi, Faegheh. 2001a. *The Veil Unveiled: Hijab in Modern Culture*. Gainesville, FL: University Press of Florida.

Shirazi, Faegheh. 2001b. 'Tools of Persuasion: Images of Iranian Women'. *Studies in Contemporary Islam* 2(1):1–27.

Shirazi, Faegheh. 2004. 'Overview of Traditional and Modern Clothes'. In *Encyclopedia of the Modern Middle East and North Africa*, 2nd revised edition. New York: Macmillan Library Reference.

Shirazi, Faegheh. 2006. 'Hijab and Women's Clothing in the Middle East Cultures'. In *Encyclopedia of Women & Islamic Cultures*. Leiden: Brill.

Shirazi, Faegheh. 2008. 'The Veil and Veiling in Iranian Culture'. In *Iran Today: An Encyclopedia of Life in the Islamic Republic*. Santa Barbara, CA: Greenwood Press.

Shirazi, Faegheh. 2010. 'Islam and Barbie: The Commodification of Hijabi Dolls'. *Islamic Perspective* (3):10–23.

Shirazi, Faegheh. 2012. 'The Islamic Veil in Civil Societies'. *Kufa Review* 1(1):19–40.

Shirazi, Faegheh and Mishra Smeeta. 2010. 'Young Muslim Women on the Face Veil (Niqab): A Tool of Resistance in Europe but Rejected in the United States'. *The International Journal of Cultural Studies* 13(1):43–62.

Shirazi-Mahajan, Faegheh. 1995. 'A Dramaturgical Approach to Hijab in Post-Revolutionary Iran'. *Critique: Critical Middle Eastern Studies* 4(7):34–51.

Simay e Zan dar Kalam e Imam Khomein. 1993. Tehran, Iran: Sazman e Chaap e Enteshaarat Vezarat Farhang va Ershad Eslami.

'Tehran hosts 2 Fair Intl. Fashion & Clothing Festival'. 3 March 2013. Available at www.presstv.ir/detail/2013/03/03/291765/tehran-festival-attracts-fashion-lovers (accessed July 4, 2015).

'Textiles and Apparel Overview. The Official Portal of Malaysia External Trade Development Corporation'. n.d. Available at www.matrade.gov.my/en/foriegn-buyers-section/69-industry-write-up--products/722-textiles-and-apparel- (accessed 2 July 2015).

Pew Research. *The Future of World Religions: Population Growth Projections, 2010–2050.* 2 April 2015. (accessed 2 July 2015) Available at www.pewforum.org/2015/04/02/religious-projections-2010–2050/ (accessed 28 January 2017).

Vagheh e kashf e hejab-Asnad e montasher nashodeh az vagheh kashf e hejab dar asr e Reza Khan [The events of Kashf e Hjab: Unpublished documents for the event of Kashf e Hejab during Reza Khan's rule]. 1990. Tehran: Vezarat e Farhang e Ershad e Eslami.

YouTube. 2013. 3 March, 2013. Reported by Press TV. Available at www.youtube.com/watch?v=gSSL p1NEm8g (accessed 2 July, 2015).

Zarindast, Karen. 2011. 'Traffic Police Regulate Iran's Dress Code'. 8 June 2011. Available at www. bbc.co.uk/news/world-middle-east-13703848 (accessed 7 July 2015).

9

THE FASHIONS AND POLITICS OF FACIAL HAIR IN TURKEY

The case of Islamic men

Nazlı Alimen

Introduction

Fashion is a powerful social phenomenon that reflects aesthetic, social, economic, political and cultural changes and affects our lives in many ways. In popular understanding, fashion is more often associated with women (see Craik 1993; Frierson 2000). Even though men and women have been influenced by trends in styles and fashions both historically and globally, 'male fashion has received less attention than women's' (Craik 1993, 170). Similarly, scholarly works and socio-political arguments on (appropriate) Islamic attires and Islamic fashions have focused mostly on women. One reason for this is that Islamic identity has been most easily and spectacularly visible via the hijab.

Nonetheless, there are Islamic rules of modesty not only for women but also for men. In Turkey, Muslim men can provide some indications of their observant identity, such as loose trousers and silver wedding rings worn on the right hand. In addition, facial hair, both moustache and beard, is also a common Islamic signifier, although in the Turkish context the moustache is predominant in general. Moreover, as this chapter explains, facial hair possesses different meanings which are linked to different Islamic sects and faith-inspired communities as well as Islamist politics. Consequently, much like the veil of Muslim women, men's facial hair in Turkey has been a subject of numerous socio-political events and discussions, such as nation-building, religious revival, community affiliation, dress and appearance regulations in the public sphere, as well as fashion.

In order to examine the facial hair of Muslim men, an under-investigated issue (see e.g. Shirazi 2008), this chapter focuses on Turkish men's facial hair practices and fashions as well as the Islamic rules related to moustaches and beards. Since Turkey is a predominantly Muslim country and also a secular state, this chapter refers to practising/devout Muslims as 'Islamic' in order to distinguish them from less observant/secular Muslims in the country.

This chapter is divided into five parts, the first of which briefly presents men's facial hair practices around the world and introduces the Islamic rules related to men's facial hair. The following part examines men's facial hair in the religious and socio-political context of Turkey and meanings associated with specific types of facial hair. The third part investigates the politicization of particular types of facial hair during the left and right political polarization in the 1970s. In addition, it explains facial hair and the stigmatization of several facial hair types in the sociocultural context of the 1980s and 1990s. The fourth part begins with the exploration of the 'Islamic' forms of facial hair with the rise of Islamist political parties in the 1990s, and focuses on facial hair practices during the 2000s when the state was being ruled by a right wing Islamic political party. In addition, it examines the diffusion of facial hair trends in the 2010s. The last part presents concluding remarks.

Men and facial hair

Men's facial hair can indicate different meanings, such as nationalism, manliness and ideological stance, in different cultures. The meanings attached to a particular type of facial hair in one society also change across different times. At times shaving is linked to effeminacy while facial hair is associated with manliness (see Walton 2008). Moreover, there might be different facial hair styles worn by different generations of men. As men get older, they may adopt a different style of facial hair (see Daoud 2000). There might also be intercultural influences in men's facial hair practices. For instance, the British military moustache in the early twentieth century originated from 'the style of the Croatian hussars of the Austrian Imperial forces' (Oldstone-Moore 2011, 49). Also historical figures, such as Gandhi and Stalin, and celebrities, such as Douglas Fairbanks, have influenced facial hair trends as well as personal choices (Daoud 2000; Oldstone-Moore 2011).

Facial hair can be in vogue at times or considered tasteless and outdated at other times (see Walton 2008). Starting in the early twentieth century, the beauty industry, with the invention of the safety razor and spread of advertising images of shaving products and clean-shaven men, has enormously influenced men's facial hair practices around the world (Robinson 1976). In addition to this, 'a growing concern about disease and hygiene' and 'a shift in the cultural formation of masculinity itself . . . from an individualist/patriarchal model of manhood toward a corporate/professional ideal' resulted in the shift towards being clean-shaven (Oldstone-Moore 2011, 50).

Facial hair can signify either elite or lower social status. Moreover, as this chapter shows, particular types of facial hair can be linked to negative connotations and become stigmatized. Facial hair can also be an object of cultural stereotyping. For example, starting in the sixteenth century in Europe, 'Turks' came to be imagined and depicted as the ones with moustaches (see Kolb 2011; Wunder 2003). Even today in Western societies, a thick, black moustache is the symbol of the 'Turk' (see Öz 2013).

Practices in and the symbolism of facial hair occur not only in a culture-specific and region-specific manner, but also in a religion-specific manner. Rules and practices associated with men's facial hair differ among religions and religious groups (see Hostetler 1995; Shirazi 2008). Historically, facial hair practices among Jews, Christians and Muslims are 'used as distinctive signs to emphasise the gap between neighboring associations or groups, or as an essential element to identify oneself or caricature others' (Bromberger 2008, 386). In other words, intra- and inter-faith distinctions are expressed through facial hair.

Islamic rules relating to facial hair derive from the *hadith*, the prophet Muhammad's deeds and sayings. Several hadiths regard a moustache and beard as a man's *fitra* (nature or the natural order) and outline what may and may not be done in each case (Schick 2011, 26). One hadith lists five practices belonging to the men's fitra: 'circumcision, shaving the pubes, paring the nails, plucking the armpits, and clipping the moustache' (Juynboll 2007, 605). Another hadith states, the prophet ordered the moustache to be clipped and to let the beard grow (Juynboll 2007, 339). Moreover, some hadiths indicate that Muslims should not look like non-Muslims and that Muslim women and Muslim men should not look alike (Al-Bukhari 1997). According to interpretations of these hadiths, Muslim men should grow a beard in order to distinguish themselves from women and non-Muslim men (Al-Bukhari 1997). Nonetheless, interpretations and practices of Islamic rules and how they are practised vary with respect to numerous factors, such as sect (Sunni or Shi'a), sub-sect (*madhab*), tradition and geographical region, and individual tastes and preferences. Consequently, there is no single form of Islamically appropriate moustache and beard, and facial hair practices as well as their significance among Muslims all around the world can differ.

Men's facial hair in Turkey

In Turkey, traditionally, facial hair, particularly wearing a moustache, is not solely a religious practice or specific to religious men. Rather, it has for many generations been a widespread cultural generic. Beards, for example, might signify a life event – aging and pilgrimage status – and demonstrate the wearer's maturity and wisdom as well as authority in sociocultural and religious matters. Traditionally, older men, particularly those who have completed the religious ritual of *hajj* (visited Mecca), grow a beard. Moreover, shaving a man's moustache was a punishment for a crime and subsequent public humiliation in the previous centuries, and this was practised even in the twentieth century in some rural areas of eastern Turkey (see Yıldız 2011).

Following the foundation of the secular republic in 1923, the modernization project aimed to rapidly transform the Turkish nation into a part of the Western world because Western modernity was regarded as superior to the traditional culture (Azak 2010). These modernization reforms prioritized the transformation of the appearance and manners of society, and included the hat law, which came into force in 1925 and obliged all men to wear Western-style hats, and the dress reform, which was introduced in 1934 with the law that banned the wearing of traditional and religious garments. These reforms were strictly implemented until the shift from the single-party to multi-party political system in 1946, and those who did not obey the hat and dress laws were punished, some even with the death penalty (see, for example, Nereid 2011). Moreover, the founder-leaders of the new state, Mustafa Kemal Atatürk (1881–1938) and İsmet İnönü (1884–1973) were very influential on the bodily attires and lifestyles of politicians and bureaucrats as well as other civil servants. Nonetheless, even though Atatürk ('father of the state') was usually clean-shaven after 1923, İnönü (*Milli Şef* [National Chief]) kept his moustache. One of the witnesses of the early republican era, Nadir Nadi (1908–1991), a renowned journalist, narrates an anecdote from the İnönü era (1938–1950):

> One day in early 1943, I ran across Hasan Ali Yücel, Minister of Education, in the grand salon of the Ankara Palas [a hotel]. There was something strange, in fact, something missing on his face. When I looked at it carefully, I realized that his moustache was missing.
>
> 'What's the matter, master; why did you shave your beautiful moustache?'
> 'Don't mention it! National Chief [İsmet İnönü] ordered so.'
> He [İsmet İnönü] ordered not only Hasan Ali, but all MPs who had the symbol of manhood above their lips to get their moustaches shaved.
>
> *(Nadi 1979, 237–8)*

Despite İnönü's strict no moustache policy in the Parliament and public offices, the moustaches of the general public were not seen to pose much of a problem. Therefore, men, except those doing their military services, usually kept their traditional facial hair, which is related to culture-specific understandings and traditions of Islam. Although predominantly Sunni, there is also *Alevism*, which is a syncretistic interpretation of Islam, 'combining Sufi mysticism, elements of pre-Islamic shamanism' and the central tenets of Shi'a Islam (Tee 2014, 25). However, some view Alevism as heterodoxy and some Alevis do not refer to themselves as Muslims. In his ethnographic study of Sunni and Alevi rural/traditional lives in Turkey, Shankland (2003) states that:

> men of both Alevi and Sunni villages grow moustaches, but Alevi men trim their moustaches in a way quite distinct from the Sunnis. The Sunni Men cut a slight nick so that the centre of the upper lip is exposed. The Alevis, on the other hand, allow the moustache to grow.
>
> (Shankland 2003, 6)

The Alevi moustache is a bushy one that covers the upper lip and extends along the sides of the mouth. The significance of this moustache among Alevis derives from Hurufism,[1] a mystical Jewish Kabbalistic doctrine. According to Hurufism, every human bears the signs of God's speech in the form of lines of hair, such as the hairline, eyebrows, eyelashes and the body parts such as the nose and ears (Bashir 2005). Each part of the face, for instance, eyebrows, eyelashes and nose line, symbolizes an Arabic letter and forms the names of God, the prophet and of several *sahaba* (the companions of the prophet) (see Bashir 2005). In order to have the name of 'Ali' on their faces, Alevi men need to have a moustache. Therefore, an eyebrow, nose line and a moustache line stand for the Arabic letters of ''ayn', 'lām', and 'yā'', respectively; and constitute the name 'Ali' on both sides of the face. The first stanza of a famous *nefes* (hymn) by an Alevi *dede* (socio-religious leader), Mehmet Ali Hilmi (1842–1907), reflects this belief:

> I held the mirror up to my face,
> Ali appeared to my eyes.
> I considered my essence,
> Ali appeared to my eyes.

The politicization and stigmatization of facial hair

With the political polarization and growing tension between the leftist and rightist groups during the Cold War era, ideological positions were prominently reflected through facial hair with particular moustache styles becoming markers of political views (Yumul 2010). The horseshoe moustache (a full moustache with vertical extensions grown down the sides of the mouth to the jawline) symbolized the nationalist movement. The bushy, Walrus moustache, called a 'communist' or 'Stalin' moustache in Turkey, was emblematic of the leftists. Like the Alevi moustache, it covers the upper lip, so that both Alevi and communist moustaches can be pejoratively referred as *pis bıyık* (dirty moustache) or *kaşık süpüren* (spoon sweeper). In addition, since the Alevis have long supported leftist politics, the terms Alevi and communist have come to be used interchangeably, especially by Sunnis and right-wingers, for the bushy moustache covering the upper lip.

With the emergence of political Islam in the 1970s, a specific moustache style began to be associated with Islamist men. Unlike the bushy 'communist' moustache, this moustache style is thin and well-trimmed; thus in line with the understandings of the Islamic rules. An illustration of this is the moustache of Necmettin Erbakan, who initiated the Islamist movement in Turkish politics in the early 1970s. On the other hand, a well-trimmed moustache is not unique to

Islamist politicians and supporters of Islamist politics. Since it is in line with the interpretations of the Islamic rules in the country, it is a common moustache type among observant men. Therefore, a well-trimmed moustache can be seen by some as a more generic symbol of Islamic male identity in Turkey. For instance, most male members of the Süleymanlı, a faith-inspired community, wear a well-trimmed moustache (Alimen 2014). Furthermore, even though well-trimmed moustaches may all seem the same to 'the untrained eye', there are different forms of well-trimmed moustache varying with respect to personal preferences as well as faith-inspired communities (Öğret 2010).

Following the 1980 military intervention, the 'communist' and 'nationalist' moustaches became less and less common, though these moustache styles still hold the same connotations today. Furthermore, the military regime introduced a 'Dress and Appearance Regulation' which prohibited civil servants (including MPs) while on duty in public agencies, offices and institutions, and university students while at the premises of universities, from wearing, in the case of women, headscarves, mini-skirts and low-necked dresses; and in the case of men, beards, sideburns and long hair. Moreover, the regulation specified the 'acceptable' moustache type and listed its details which are similar to those of the 'Islamic' moustache:

> Men must shave every day and not grow a beard. A moustache can be grown, but it must not cover the upper lip. The hair on the top of the moustache must not be trimmed. The sides must be in line with the corners of the mouth and the ends must be trimmed by the lip line.
>
> *(Dress and Appearance Regulation, Article 5[2])*

According to Çınar (2005), this regulation aimed to end the polarization between the left and the right, which had affected all domains of public life during the 1970s, and to eliminate the bodily signs of leftist and rightist identities in the public space. As she notes, 'the ban on the beard elicited a reaction from among left-wing intellectuals and was not perceived as a secularist measure against a mark of Islam' (Çınar 2005, 186). Nonetheless, in 2013 there were several changes in this regulation. Together with the end of the headscarf ban for female employees, male employees are now permitted to grow long hair, but beards and sideburns are still rigorously enforced at certain times.

Furthermore, as a result of the shift from state-controlled to liberal economic policies starting in the 1980s, Turkey witnessed rapid economic and social changes, such as an increase in income per capita, a dramatic shift in class structures, and an increase in products offered in the Turkish consumption space (Emrence 2008; Eser *et al.* 2007). These changes, together with the global trend towards clean-shaven faces in the 1990s, resulted in 'clean-shaven' (ideal) images of men (see Sumer 2003). In other words, a 'modern' man was considered to be one without a moustache, which was a common form of facial hair whereas, as mentioned previously, mostly older men had beards. The clean-shaven trend spread from higher to lower social classes. Initially, in the 1980s and 1990s, for urban and educated men from middle and upper social classes, the moustache became a symbol of 'wild', undisciplined masculinity. Therefore, in order not to bear this 'undesired' image, these men, especially young ones, did not grow a moustache (Yumul 2000). Nonetheless, these 'new' men who shaved their moustaches in order to represent a 'civilized' image claimed that 'wild' masculinity is, in fact, related not to the appearance. According to them, having a clean-shaven face and long hair would not eliminate 'macho' characteristics of Turkish men because as 'the descendants of the Ottomans', 'machismo is in their blood'. They concluded that 'new' Turkish men are the ones with the Western appearances and the Eastern mentality (Yumul cited in Yumul, 2000).

In popular culture (for example, in humour magazines), men from lower socioeconomic levels have come to be depicted with thick, black moustaches which show the wearer to be rude, uncivilized, uneducated and macho (see Apaydin 2005). On the other hand, in 2003, an advertising campaign of a soft drink brand, *Cola Turka*, showed a clean-shaven American man who, after taking a sip of Cola Turka, suddenly got a black, bushy moustache and was thus Turkified: the ad campaign was a huge success in the country (see Ogan *et al.* 2007; Sandıkçı and Ekici 2009).

The growing support for the Islamist parties in the Turkish local and general elections in the 1990s created bipolarity, namely the Islamist and secular division, which replaced the left–right polarization of the 1970s. Like the headscarf (see Sandıkçı and Ger 2010), the thin and well-trimmed moustache worn by Islamic men became stigmatized. This moustache style and also a person with this moustache have been called *badem bıyık* (almond moustache[3]) by secular individuals who tend to categorize them as one homogeneous group wanting to overthrow the secular regime and declare an Islamic state ruled by *shariah* law. After the 28 February 1997 military intervention, which consisted of 'a list of measures designed to nullify the supposed Islamization of Turkey and fortify the secular system' (Cizre Sakallıoğlu and Çınar 2003, 309), some Islamic men, including politicians as well as members of faith-inspired communities, such as the Gülen community (see Alimen 2014; Rasim 2012), shaved their moustaches in an attempt to hide their pious identities.

The rise of (Islamic) facial hair and the diffusion of facial hair fashions

Despite its stigmatization, the visibility of the well-trimmed moustache has increased since 2002 as a result of the electoral victories of the Justice and Development Party (*Adalet ve Kalkınma Partisi* – AKP), the Islamic-oriented, right wing party. This party has had various MPs with a well-trimmed moustache, for example, Recep Tayyip Erdoğan (president now, prime minister 2002–2014). Moreover, as previously mentioned, MPs are also subject to the Dress and Appearance Regulation. Nonetheless, between the years 2002–2015, the Parliament had a 'bearded' minister, Taner Yıldız (MP [2002–2015] and Minister of Energy and Natural Resources [2009–2015]). Although there were some rumours that he would cut his beard when he was appointed as a minister, he proved them wrong and kept his beard (see Şahin 2012).

Moreover, during the era of AKP rule (2002–), Islamic identities, such as women with the veil and men with the well-trimmed moustache, have become increasingly visible in the secular sphere. In addition, as I elaborate below, new Islamic identities have been created through the blending of religious/political ideologies, and popular culture elements and trends. These identities, adapted particularly by young Islamic men, are in line with the (neo)Ottomanist discourses and politics of the AKP (see Ongur 2015) that are extensively built upon Ottoman revival/Ottoman nostalgia.

Most of the young Islamic men today, except those belonging to some religious groups, for example, the Süleymanlı community, do not wear a well-trimmed moustache. They may be clean-shaven or make a choice from a wide range of moustache and beard styles, such as the handlebar and hammer-cut moustaches, full beard and Verdi beard, which is a combination of a full beard, short and rounded at the bottom, and 'a full, upturned moustache' that is distinct from the beard (Peterkin and Burns 2010, 92). Since the early 2010s, facial hair has been fashionable for two reasons: the hipster trend and Turkish historical costume dramas. With the global 'hipster' trend, more and more urban, young men (between the ages of 20 and 35, including both Islamic and secular) have grown moustaches or beards. Also some characters from famous costume dramas have initiated facial hair fashions. For instance, the actors Burak Özçivit and

Halit Ergenç have been very influential on men's facial hair trends in the last four years.[4] Özçivit had the same moustache style in two famous Turkish historical costume dramas, as *Malkoçoğlu Bali Bey* in *Magnificent Century*[5] (based on a fictional narration of the reign of the Ottoman Sultan, Suleiman the Magnificent, and which aired in 2011–2014) and as *Kâmran* in *Çalıkuşu*[6] (adapted from Reşat Nuri Güntekin's famous novel of the same name, and which aired in 2013–2014). Ergenç starred as *Süleyman the Magnificent* in *Magnificent Century*. The 'Malkoçoğlu' moustache and the 'Süleyman' beard have been among the most famous ones in men's facial hair fashions recently. However, these fashionable moustache and beard styles do not reflect an ideological standpoint or religious piety, but rather mark the wearer as a fashion-conscious person. In addition, as stated above, not only Islamic but also secular men in Turkey wear them. Consequently, unlike in the past, Islamic men, particularly those who are young, urban, educated and from upper-middle and higher income levels, follow trends and tend to choose styles that do not conflict with Islamic rules and/or the values of their family and social environment. Moreover, their clothing choices become 'secularized' and 'fashionable', for example, skinny trousers and shirts, and loafers without socks, instead of 'classical', 'Islamically appropriate' Islamic male looks, such as a suit with or without a tie, and loose trousers and shirts (Alimen 2014). Thus, unlike in the past, it is now no longer possible to assign a specific facial hair style to Islamic men and distinguish the wearer's religious identity from his facial hair.

Conclusion

As this chapter demonstrates, men's facial hair in Turkey is linked to numerous factors including but not limited to Islamic sects, faith-inspired communities, and fashion trends. Facial hair can be regarded as the man's veil since, much like the woman's veil, it is open to politicization and stigmatization in the socio-political context. Moreover, as shown above, the Dress and Appearance Regulation can be neglected or enforced flexibly for civil servants at higher levels of the state, namely in the Parliament. This illustrates how, depending on their managers as well as their work and social environment, civil servants at various ranks can grow beards or wear moustaches that are not in line with the regulation. However, this might be limited to a few cases since the regulation is widely known to the general public. Therefore, in Turkey, a man with a beard, or with a moustache that does not accord with the regulation is immediately recognizable as not being a civil servant, but probably someone who works in a 'liberal' workplace or with business sector, such as advertising and fashion, or is self-employed, unemployed, or a student.

Arguably, as a result of the long-term governance of the AKP as well as the increased visibility and prevalence of the well-trimmed (i.e. *badem* – 'almond') moustache, its connotations related to Islamism have shifted. On the other hand, this type of moustache is still politicized and stigmatized so that both the terms *badem bıyık* ('almond moustache') and *badem* ('almond') are employed, especially by opponents of the AKP, to ridicule the wearer(s) and the party. It might be fruitful to compare connotations of this moustache type within the future socio-political context of Turkey. Moreover, it will be interesting to see whether young Islamic men who are now followers of facial hair trends will still follow facial hair trends in the following years, or grow well-trimmed moustaches or full beards as their predecessors have done, or favour a shaven face.

Notes

1. Available at http://www.alevice.net/alevilik-ve-bektasilikte-biyigini-onemi (accessed 15 August 2015).
2. Kamu Kurum ve Kuruluşlarında Çalışan personelin Kılık ve Kıyafetine Dair Yönetmelik. Available at www.mevzuat.gov.tr/MevzuatMetin/3.5.85105.pdf (accessed 15 August 2015).

3. It should be noted that this term was also used in the past while referring to different 'stigmatized' groups, for instance, in the 1950s, for newly rich men from Anatolian cities and towns.
4. Available at www.frmmagazin.com/erkeklerde-kanuni-sakali-modasi (accessed 15 August 2015).
5. Available at http://en.muhtesemyuzyil.tv (accessed 15 August 2015).
6. Available at http://calikusudizi.tv/en/ (accessed 15 August 2015).

References

Al-Bukhari, Muhammed ibn Ismail. 1997. *Sahih Al-Bukhari: The Translation of the Meanings of Sahih Al-Bukhari*, translated by Muhammad Muhsin Khan. Riyadh: Dar-us-Salam Publications.

Alimen, Nazlı. 2014. 'Islamic Masculinities in Turkey'. Paper presented at the 1st International Symposium on Men and Masculinities: Identities, Cultures, Societies, 11–13 September, Izmir, Turkey.

Apaydin, Gökçen Ertuğrul. 2005. 'Modernity as Masquerade: Representations of Modernity and Identity in Turkish Humour Magazines'. *Identities: Global Studies in Culture and Power* 12:107–42.

Azak, Umut. 2010. *Islam and Secularism in Turkey: Kemalism, Religion and the Nation State*. London: I.B. Tauris.

Bashir, Shahzad. 2005. *Fazlallah Astarabadi and the Hurufis*. Oxford: One World.

Bromberger, Christian. 2008. 'Hair: From the West to the Middle East through the Mediterranean'. *Journal of American Folklore* 121:379–99.

Çınar, Alev. 2005. *Modernity, Islam, and Secularism in Turkey: Bodies, Places, and Time*. Minneapolis, MN: The University of Minnesota Press.

Cizre Sakallıoğlu, Ümit and Menderes Çınar. 2003. 'Turkey 2002: Kemalism, Islamism, and Politics in the Light of the February 28 Process'. *The South Atlantic Quarterly* 102:309–32.

Craik, Jennifer. 1993. *The Face of Fashion: Cultural Studies in Fashion*. London: Routledge.

Daoud, Hassan. 2000. 'Those Two Heavy Wings of Manhood: On Moustaches'. In *Imagined Masculinities: Male Identity and Culture in the Modern Middle East*, edited by Mai Ghoussoub and Emma Sinclair-Webb, 273–80. London: Saqi.

Emrence, Cem. 2008. 'After Neoliberal Globalization: The Great Transformation of Turkey'. *Comparative Sociology* 7:51–67.

Eser, Zeliha, Servet Mutlu and Mehmet Cakar. 2007. 'Changing Environment and Consumer in Turkey'. *Journal of Euromarketing* 16:67–79.

Frierson, Elizabeth B. 2000. 'Cheap and Easy: The Creation of Consumer Culture in Late Ottoman Society'. In *Consumption Studies and the History of the Ottoman Empire, 1550–1922: An Introduction*, edited by Donald Quataert, 243–60. New York: State University of New York Press.

Hostetler, John A. 1995. 'Dress as a Language of Protest'. In *Dress and Identity*, edited by Marry Ellen Roach-Higgins, Joanne Bubolz Eicher and Kim K. P. Johnson, 218–20. New York: Fairchild Publications.

Juynboll, G. H. A. 2007. *Encyclopedia of Canonical Hadith*. Leiden: Brill.

Kolb, Justin. 2011. '"A Turk's Mustachio": Anglo-Islamic Traffic and Exotic London in Ben Johnson's *Every Man Out of His Humour* and *Entertainment at Britain's Burse*'. In *Early Modern England and Islamic Worlds*, edited by L. McJannet and A. Bernadette, 197–214. New York: Palgrave Macmillan.

Nadi, Nadir. 1979. *Perde Aralığından*. Istanbul: Çağdaş.

Nereid, Camilla T. 2011. 'Kemalism on the Catwalk: The Turkish Hat Law of 1925'. *Journal of Social History* 44:707–28.

Ogan, Christine, Filiz Çiçek and Yesim Kaptan. 2007. 'Reverse Glocalization? Marketing a Turkish Cola in the Shadow of a Giant'. *Journal of Arab and Muslim Media Research* 1:47–62.

Öğret, Özgür. 2010. 'Facial Hair in Turkish Politics: A Tale of Mustaches and Men'. *Hürriyet Daily News*, 6 August. Available at www.hurriyetdailynews.com/default.aspx?pageid=438&n=facial-hair-in-turkish-politics-a-tale-of-moustaches-and-men-2010-08-06 (accessed 15 August 2015).

Oldstone-Moore, Christopher. 2011. 'Mustaches and Masculine Codes in Early Twentieth-Century America'. *Journal of Social History* 45:47–60.

Ongur, Hakan Ovunc. 2015. 'Identifying Ottomanisms: The Discursive Evolution of Ottoman Pasts in the Turkish Presents'. *Middle Eastern Studies* 51:416–32.

Öz, Senem. 2013. 'The Construction of "the Turk" and Entextualization of Historical Stereotypes Political Cartoons in French'. MA dissertation, Simon Fraser University.

Peterkin, Allan D. and Nick Burns. 2010. *The Bearded Gentleman: The Style Guide to Shaving Face*. Vancouver, BC: Arsenal Pulp Press.

Rasim, Ramazan. 2012. 'Cemaatçi ile İslâmcı Arasındaki 27 Fark'. *Taraf*, 17 February. Available at http://arsiv. taraf.com.tr/yazilar/ramazan-rasim/cemaatci-ile-islamci-arasindaki-27-fark/19991/ (accessed August, 15 2015).

Robinson, Dwight E. 1976. 'Fashions in Shaving and Trimming of the Beard: The Men of the *Illustrated London News*, 1842–1972'. *American Journal of Sociology* 81:1133–41.

Şahin, Ömer. 2012. ' "Sinekkaydı" Lügatinde Yok'. *Radikal*, 3 June. Available at www.radikal.com.tr/ politika/sinekkaydi_lugatinde_yok-1089934 (accessed 15 August 2015).

Sandıkçı, Özlem and Ahmet Ekici. 2009. 'Politically Motivated Brand Rejection'. *Journal of Business Research*, 62:208–17.

Sandıkçı, Özlem and Güliz Ger. 2010. 'Veiling in Fashion: How does a Stigmatized Practice Become Fashionable?'. *Journal of Consumer Research* 37:15–36.

Schick, Irvin Cemil. 2011. 'Some Islamic Determinants of Dress and Personal Appearance in Southwest Asia'. *Khil'a* 3:25–53.

Shankland, David. 2003. *The Alevis in Turkey: The Emergence of a Secular Islamic Tradition*. London and New York: Routledge.

Shirazi, Faegheh. 2008. 'Men's Facial Hair in Islam: A Matter of Interpretation'. In *Hair: Styling, Culture and Fashion*, edited by Geraldine Biddle-Perry and Sarah Cheang, 111–22. Oxford: Berg.

Sumer, Beyza. 2003. 'White vs. Black Turks: The Civilising Process in Turkey in the 1990s'. MA dissertation, Middle East Technical University.

Tee, Caroline. 2014. 'On the Path of Pir Sultan? Engagement with Authority in the Modern Alevi Movement'. In *Contemporary Turkey at a Glance: Interdisciplinary Perspectives on Local and Translocal Dynamics*, edited by Kristina Kamp, Ayhan Kaya, E. Fuat Keyman and Özge Onursal Beşgül, 25–39. Heidelberg: Springer. Available at www.springer.com/us/book/9783658049157 (accessed 15 August 2015).

Walton, Susan. 2008. 'From Squalid Impropriety to Manly Respectability: The Revival of Beards, Moustaches and Martial Values in the 1850s England'. *Nineteenth-Century Contexts* 30:229–45.

Wunder, Amanda. 2003. 'Western Travelers, Eastern Antiquities, and the Image of the Turk in Early Modern Europe'. *Journal of Early Modern History* 7:89–119.

Yıldız, Alpay Doğan. 2011. 'Şevket Bulut'un Hikâyelerinde Aleviler ve Alevilik Algısı'. *Türk Kültürü ve Hacı Bektaş Veli Araştırma Dergisi* 59:341–52.

Yumul, Arus. 2000. 'Bitmemiş Bir Proje Olarak Beden'. *Toplum ve Bilim* 84:37–50.

Yumul, Arus. 2010. 'Fashioning the Turkish Body Politic'. In *Turkey's Engagement with Modernity*, edited by Celia Kerslake, Kerem Oktem and Philip Robins, 349–69. Basingstoke: Palgrave Macmillan.

Zelinsky, Wilbur. 2004. 'Globalization Reconsidered: The Historical Geography of Modern Western Male Attire'. *Journal of Cultural Geography* 22:83–134.

10

REPRESENTING THE VEIL IN CONTEMPORARY AUSTRALIAN MEDIA

From 'ban the burqa' to 'hijabi' bloggers

Branka Prodanovic and Susie Khamis

Introduction

Over the last 15 years, the hijab has been one of the most contentious symbols of Islam in Australia. It has underpinned political debates and cultural anxieties and, particularly in mainstream media, been used to associate Islam with a suite of negative connotations, particularly oppression, misogyny and violence. This is largely attributable to global events linked to Islamist terrorists; most notably the attacks in New York on 11 September 2001, but also subsequent and similarly inspired attacks in Bali (2002), Madrid (2004), London (2005), Sydney (2014) and Paris (2015). This terrorism has sponsored fear, alarm and paranoia in predominantly non-Muslim countries such as Australia, and veiled Muslim women have thus become easy targets for discrimination and hostility.

This chapter surveys how certain assumptions have framed veiled Muslim women in Australia's mainstream media, with the recurrence of certain motifs and narratives tied to burgeoning unease around Islam's compatibility with Australian values (Hebbani and Wills 2012, 88). There is a sub-text at play in many of these representations: that a religion so widely considered an anachronistic theocracy does not belong in a pluralistic, egalitarian and ostensibly secular nation like Australia. Since the veil marks its wearer so conspicuously, it has become convenient visual shorthand for rationalizing Islam's clash with 'modern' Australia. While this is a worldwide phenomenon (Syed and Pio 2010, 120), this chapter shows how, over the last five years or so, the range of representations has broadened in at least one key way: young veiled Muslim Australian women – 'hijabis' – have assumed a compelling and provocative role in the media-sphere, specifically: blogs and social media are now powerful means by which these women 'speak back' to each other and to the wider community. By exchanging styling tips, fostering a sense of camaraderie, and exploiting the conversational, interactive nature of participatory media, they cue a seminal shift in how the veil is represented in Australian media.

Islam and the Australian media

One of the most salient narratives in contemporary Australian media, with regards to Muslim women that choose to veil, is that the practice is anathema to Australian values and the 'Australian way of life' – a nebulous concept and phrase that both punctuates and anchors many of these discussions. Often, the veil seemingly 'proves' that Islam undermines the reigning tenets of a modern democracy, especially gender equality (Aly and Walker 2007, 210). Several politicians (including Fred Nile, Michaelia Cash, Robyn McSweeny and Bronwyn Bishop) have argued that some forms of veiling, especially the burqa and the niqab, should be banned from public spaces because they seem such emphatic symbols of female servitude and actively mitigate cultural assimilation. Some have even argued that such veils constitute risks to the nation's security since they could be used to conceal weapons, a notion that clearly trades on widespread fears that all Muslims have terrorist tendencies (Amer 2014; Ho 2010). For this reason, and as Julie Posetti argues, 'Muslim women are both highly visible members of one of the most marginalised groups in Western society and the most vulnerable to vilification and media stereotyping, suffering the "triple-whammy" effect of sexism, racism and religious bigotry' (2010, 69). In a country where under 1 per cent of the population wear the veil (Awad 2013), those that do stand out visually and have become over-identified with an already-feared religion, and thus suffer accordingly.

The treatment of veiled Muslim women in Australia sits within a wider story about how Islam has been depicted over the last few decades in predominantly non-Muslim nations, in particular: the UK, the USA, Australia and parts of Western Europe. After several terrorist attacks attributed first to al-Qaeda and more recently to ISIS, ignorance and/or anxiety about Islam has morphed into widespread perceptions that it supports (or at least justifies) violent extremism. In turn, a veiled Muslim woman superficially confirms the proximity of terror. According to Nahid Kabir (2006, 316), the US-led 'War on Terror' (which Australia joined under former Prime Minister John Howard) triggered a tendency in newspaper coverage of Islam whereby images of known terrorists were placed alongside imagery of veiled Muslim women, a semiotic slide that clearly encouraged readers to conflate Islam and violence. Veiled women were thus paradoxically positioned as both victims and aggressors, oppressed by a sexist religion yet still sympathetic to its aims. That veiled women became widely invested with such disparate meanings surfaced in 2011 with changes to the Law Enforcement Act in New South Wales, to allow police officers (and later prison guards and court officials) to demand removal of all forms of face-covering for the purposes of identification. Whilst these pertained to all types of face-covering (including helmets and masks), it was widely referred to as the 'burqa removal law' (ABC 2011).

Central to how mainstream media depicts Islamic veiling are implicit assumptions about what the veil means and what it does to the wearer. Ironically, conclusions are usually drawn and convictions confirmed regardless of (or oblivious to) what veiled Muslim Australians actually say. In her interviews with Muslim women, Posetti (2010, 76) found them increasingly tired of clichéd representations that rest almost exclusively on a few misconceptions (regarding misogyny, oppression and polygamy) and thus present the veil as irredeemably 'un-Australian'. Much of this frustration stems from how their opinions are so often filtered through (and then flattened by) dominant mainstream narratives. As Susan Carland (2012) found, even when Muslim women did appear in mainstream media, their appearance and input was almost always drawn back to the question of veiling – as though nothing else they said or did mattered more than this one, 'problematic' piece of clothing. Put simply, argues Carland, 'Muslim women are defined by and reduced to what they wear' (149). Not only is it difficult to speak out as a veiled woman in Australia, but also it is rendered futile when what is said is then cast in terms that seemingly reinforce negative perceptions. One participant in Posetti's study explained it liked this: 'I won't try because they won't or don't understand, and whatever I said, there is a risk to be misquoted or being taken out of context. So I prefer to remain silent, and I think everyone should be unless they are absolutely 100 per cent sure that their words will not be abused' (quoted in Posetti 2010, 94).

The 'burqa ban'

In Australia the most common form of veiling by Muslim women is the hijab, which refers to a veil that covers the hair and neck, but not the face. Less common, but often confused with a burqa, is the niqab, a veil that covers the head and face (but not the eyes) and is usually paired with a loose garment, often black (an abaya) that covers from the head to the feet. The burqa, which consists of a veil that covers the entire body and face, with mesh fabric over the eyes, is the least common type of veil worn by Muslim women in Australia (Vyver 2015). Specific data regarding the prevalence and/or percentage of each style in Australia is notoriously difficult to find; even informed guesses place the number of Australian women that wear the niqab as only a few hundred, and the burqa as practically negligible (Aly 2014). Yet despite the fact that such a tiny proportion of Australian Muslims actually wear a burqa, it has become the dominant prism through which popular anxieties are channelled, and therefore the issue most mined by politicians for populist mileage. The issue pivots on why the burqa should be banned in Australia, a discourse that found traction in the wake of similarly construed French legislation – the 'French ban' – in 2010 (Hewitt and Koch 2011, 16; Carland 2011, 469). In Australia, calls for a 'burqa ban' have featured most prominently on news and current affairs programmes on commercial television, especially *Today Tonight*, *Sunday Night* and *A Current Affair*. The issue has also been widely covered on the two public service broadcasters (PSB) on discussion-based forums such as SBS's *Insight* and ABC's *Q&A*. Unlike the commercial networks, though the PSB programmes have tended to include more diverse perspectives, this does not necessarily disavowal dominant preconceptions. This has much to do with how cultural antipathy and unease towards the burqa is considered the natural setting within which the women's sartorial choices must be rationalized or defended. For example, in 2010 the host of SBS's *Insight* programme Jennie Brockie asked women wearing the burqa and niqab when and why they decided to veil, if they had reasons besides Islam for veiling, and whether they understood how it may be seen as a symbol of oppression and inequality (SBS 2010). Similar questions were posed on *Sunday Night*, a weekly current affairs programme on the Seven Network (*Sunday Night* 2012). This is how the 'debate' has been framed on Australian television: within a context of latent suspicion that the women lack agency or volition, and that they are actively persisting with a cultural practice that inspires social antagonism and political anxiety. In turn, public regulation of what they wear functions as de facto regulation of Islam (Sotsky 2013, 798).

The question of veiling in general and the burqa specifically has also fuelled animated debates on Australian radio. In particular, it has energized numerous heated exchanges on commercial stations hosted by the so-called 'shock-jocks' – that is, (usually) male talkback hosts that rely on polarizing, provocative topics, populist rhetoric, and a stridently parochial sensibility and audience. Generally, these hosts draw on (and give airtime to) high-profile guests, especially politicians, which have made public calls for a 'burqa ban'. One such politician is Liberal senator Cory Bernadi. Since 2010, Bernadi has been one of the most outspoken critics of the burqa, arguing that the 'un-Australian' item had become the preferred guise for bank bandits, that it hindered 'normal' interaction, and that it reinforced antiquated gender roles – all of which threatened Australia's 'hitherto homogeneous society' (Bernadi 2010). In 2014, after a series of anti-terrorism raids in Sydney and Brisbane, Bernadi renewed his calls for a 'burqa ban', calling the burqa 'a flag for fundamentalism' and a 'shroud of oppression'. As news broke of the raids, Bernadi Tweeted: 'Note burqa wearers in some of the houses raided this morning?' (Bourke 2014). Such simplistic, reductionist commentary finds much support on commercial talkback radio. Radio station 2GB in Sydney, for instance, has covered the 'burqa ban' numerous times over the last decade. Although the talkback genre celebrates open dialogue, on this topic there is rarely any airtime parity between opposing viewpoints. In October 2014, a Muslim listener named Ajay called in to speak to 2GB talkback host Ray Hadley, to explain (and inevitably defend) Muslim women's right to veil. Hadley's response was lamentably predictable, a mere repetition of Bernadi's position – which by then had become talkback orthodoxy: Hadley maintained that it was too easy to conceal weapons or a bomb under a hijab and that, at a time when Australians were in a permanent mode of terror alert, any concession meant capitulation. The caller persisted that his female relatives *chose* to veil – that is, whatever liberty or freedom that Hadley was defending was already at work in how these women expressed their faith. Hadley, however, remained unconvinced (2GB 2014).

In terms of discursive latitude, Australian press has been slightly more generous in its coverage of veiling. In 2003, the popular *Daily Telegraph* published an article titled 'The Silent Sufferers', a reference to women under Islam. Author Ann Beveridge argued that men have 'always' played a dominant role in Muslim society and that 'women obey' (Beveridge 2003, 47). She claimed gender oppression was a core principle of Islam, and this manifests most vividly through the veil. Still, and far more than other mainstream media, Australian newspapers have also provided opportunities for Muslim women to present their positions. For instance, in 2004, Fatima Shah, who wears a burqa, wrote for *The Age* and stressed how her freedom is served (not constrained) by her decision to do so: 'Like every other veiled woman, I am exercising that same personal choice and using the same freedoms that everyone else has, to decide what to wear' (Shah 2004, 11). In 2006, in *The Sun-Herald*, Taghred Chandab reminded readers that, while experiences of veiling differ among Muslim women, especially those who decide not to veil (or decide to remove their veil), there was a symbolic violence at work in how the issue had dominated popular understanding of both Islam and the veil. In turn, she wrote 'let's give Muslim women a break and stop using them as political scapegoats' (Chandab 2006, 31). In 2010, writing for the *Sydney Morning Herald*, Maeve McCarthy and Christina Ho reflected on how the 'made-for-media' burqa debate played on public emotions and triggered three key reactions. These were fear that the burqa constituted a security risk; anger that, in equating the burqa with modesty, its advocates were implying that anything less was immoral; and compassion for women who, were it not for the burqa, would otherwise enjoy a higher quality of life. For McCarthy and Ho, though, a more balanced public attitude would be civil indifference, 'the most ethical response to a debate that has been framed by extremists on all sides, who have elevated the burqa issue to a level out of all proportion to its significance in the lives of most Australian Muslims' (Ho and McCarthy 2010, 13). Clearly, the amount of energy and angst spent on the burqa debate is patently disproportionate to its presence in Australia, which suggests that it has become the preferred means by which key prejudices are distilled and articulated. Moreover, in terms of media visibility, coverage of the 'burqa debate' has been at the expense of the average Muslim woman in Australia – which ultimately secures for her the inequality that the burqa has been associated with.

Modest changes in mainstream media

Before turning to how social media has opened up opportunities hitherto denied to veiled Muslim women in Australia, it is worth noting here that, over the last two or so years, mainstream media have started to represent veiling in slightly more nuanced ways. On commercial television for instance, Network Ten's top-rating reality cooking show *Masterchef Australia* has twice featured a veiled Muslim contestant, Amina Elshafei in 2012 and Samira El Khafir in 2013. Their appearance spotlighted not just their culinary flair; for the estimated 2 million viewers that tuned in every night, the hijab was at least temporarily disconnected from dominant cultural anxieties regarding Islam, or at least in how the show was encoded by its producers. The centrality of food and cooking shifted the focal beam away from politicized and/or parochial assumptions, so at the very least the women signified something other than what they were wearing. Similarly, in 2012, the *Encounter* programme on ABC's Radio National broadcast a documentary about Muslims and Australian football (ABC 2012). This highlighted these women's interest in sport, a topic otherwise ignored by most media in 'sports mad' Australia. And, in 2013, the *Compass* programme on ABC TV looked at emerging hijab trends in Australia, with a particular focus on the burgeoning market for local hijabi fashions, from Australian-based designers sensitive to which colours and fabrics worked best for the Australian climate (ABC 2013).

The tendency to dichotomize Islam and Australia had become so entrenched in public discourse that these 'normalizations', albeit infrequent and partial, matter. In 2011, the *Macquarie Dictionary* deemed 'burqini' the 'Word of the Year'. Invented by Sydney-based Muslim designer Aheda Zanetti, the 'burqini' is an innovative two-piece swimsuit that preserves the wearer's modesty whilst ensuring complete comfort and mobility. It has drawn worldwide acclaim (Nigella Lawson has been photographed in one; and it appeared in the movie *Sex & the City 2*) and was such a success that Zanetti had to shut down her website for several months to keep pace with the orders. Yet what bears stressing here is the glaring logic that this design should first surface in Australia. For many international visitors, Australia is synonymous with the beach. Yet in the absence of appropriate swimwear, many Muslim Australian women reluctantly forfeited the pastime lest they compromised their modesty or, as often happened, were ridiculed for fashioning swimwear out of something other than a swimsuit (like a leotard). The burqini has become an iconic marker of cross-cultural dialogue, staking a provocative and ironic claim on a distinctly 'Aussie' pastime. With its catchy, intriguing and highly marketable name (an obvious portmanteau of 'bikini' and 'burqa'), the burqini found wide and mostly positive coverage across Australian media. While this was largely attributable to its clever design, it was also a post-Cronulla salve: after the ugly race-based riots on Cronulla beach in December 2005, the burqini appeared as a succinct and elegant rebuttal (Khamis 2010).

Another way that dominant perceptions of veiling were challenged in Australia was through a seminal exhibition at Sydney's Powerhouse Museum. The 'Faith Fashion Fusion' exhibition in 2013, a showcase of Muslim women's style in Australia, was the first time a major cultural venue both spotlighted practices of veiling and gave a voice to veiled Australian women (Meacham 2012, 10). Through interviews, photographs, personal stories and interactive projects, the exhibition was devoted almost entirely to these women – that is, the veil was discussed by women that wear it, and not journalists, clerics or politicians. In turn, visitors to the museum heard *directly* from these women, a rare insight given the extent to which the practice is routinely discussed in mainstream media without their input. According to curator Glynis Jones, this involvement was integral to the authenticity and appeal of the event: 'In the course of research for this project we spoke to a number of Australian women who are actively working to dispel [these] misconceptions but are frustrated by being constantly asked to justify Muslim women's dress choices' (Jones 2012, 7). What emerged was a picture of diverse, accomplished women for whom veiling was a cherished part of their cultural identity in what were often difficult circumstances, including: Mecca Laalaa, the first veiled Muslim woman to become a surf life saver (thanks to the burqini); Constable Maha Sukkar, Australia's first veiled police officer; and

Kath Fry and Eisha Saleh, owners of the modest fashion label Baraka – which was named Muslim Business of the Year in 2009.

As much as the exhibition confronted much of the hysteria and bigotry around veiling, key events both around the world and within Australia continue to shape how Islam and therefore its adherents are viewed. After a series of ISIS-related terrorist attacks (particularly on the *Charlie Hebdo* magazine headquarters in January 2015, and the Paris attacks of November 2015), as well as the December 2014 Martin Place siege in Sydney by ISIS-sympathizer Man Haron Monis, high-profile veiled Australian women remain targets for vilification and abuse – much of which is carried by Twitter and Facebook. This has been the case for academic and social commentator Susan Carland, a regular and popular guest across Australian media. In November 2015, Carland announced that for every hateful Tweet she received she would donate one dollar to UNICEF, (half) joking that she might go broke in the process (Mannix 2015). Carland's response to the abuse – through Twitter – highlights how social media has become an increasingly powerful and salient means by which veiled Muslim women claim some autonomous space in an otherwise cacophonous and often hostile media environment. Indeed, it has become the dominant way that veiled Muslim women in Australia confront and confound their misrepresentation in mainstream media. In particular, the popularity of blogs run by young, stylish and charismatic 'hijabis' shows how social media empowers users to present imagery and narratives that are independently authored and is thus a potent force for those that are most marginalized and/or maligned in mainstream media.

The rise of 'hijabi' blogs

That social media drives new ways for ordinary users to produce, distribute and consume media has been amply documented. Its use by young Australian 'hijabis' though is far from ordinary. Generally, women tend to use social media more frequently and actively than men, and do so for social engagement, to find information, and for recreation (Chen 2015, 26–7). Despite the extent to which veils in Australia have been largely framed as symbolic markers of extremism, terrorism, misogyny and submission, social media also provides a powerfully liberating means by which these women speak back – both to each other and to society at large. By 'owning' these media spaces, these women problematize and/or debunk many of the assumptions around veiling. At the same time, they show just how myopic so much of the media coverage around veiling has been: as cosmopolitan, articulate agents in control of their own representation, these women are connected to global conversations about veiling, Islam, feminism, fashion and popular culture in general (Prodanovic 2014). One of the most successful for instance is Sydney-based blogger Delina Darusman-Gala, who is also known as 'Haiina Love' (see Figures 10.1–10.3). The 31-year old blogger, designer and mother of three created the first Muslim fashion blog in Australia in 2010, 'Muslim Street Fashion' (MSF). Characteristic of this genre, she posted 'outfit of the day' (OOTD) images of herself; unlike most fashion blogs though, these always included a hijab. In every other way, MSF looked like most other personal fashion blogs, self-reflective and self-referential blends of individual dress practices and collective fashion narratives (Titton 2015, 202): the artfully composed outfits, sunny streetscapes, and atmospheric, urban locations. As Darusman-Gala sees it:

> Wearing hijab connects me to my religion and fills me with a sense of peace, but underneath it all I'm just like any other thirty-something woman trying to make the most of her life and career. The only difference between you and me? I just happen to have a scarf addiction.
>
> *(Quoted in Yasa 2014)*

Yet in a country and time when the hijab still signifies much more than just modesty, the 'only difference' is a loaded and iconic visual marker, which makes her blog's worldwide popularity all the more significant. Indeed, according to popular website Buzzfeed, Darusman-Gala was one of the top 12 Muslim Australians who 'crushed it' in 2014 (Wray and Esposito 2014).

The 'street style' aesthetic of MSF shifts the veil from one set of associations (politics, religion, and terrorism) to another: style, fashion and youth. Similarly, Mya Arafin (of 'MyazFashionSpot') and Ange (of 'Diary of Ange') have found social media fame through blogs that fuse their love of fashion, advice for other 'hijabis', and particularly in the case of Perth-based Ange, general lifestyle tips (including food, travel and décor). As she told the *Independent Fashion Bloggers* website in 2012, online platforms provide a much-needed resource for women like her:

> Most of the Muslim bloggers I know are from the UK, USA, Middle East, Indonesia, Malaysia, etc. There really aren't that many Australian Muslim bloggers that I know of. We have a few nationwide, but in my state as far as I know there is only me. There are so many Muslim fashion bloggers out there! In TV/magazine type media we are definitely underrepresented (or more likely not represented at all) but we have definitely taken the matter into our own hands when it comes to online media. There is a huge community for us to share ideas and show off our style.
>
> *(Quoted in Davies 2012)*

These blogs problematize conventional critiques of social media that are largely cynical of its capacity to dislodge or destabilize dominant media structures and/or conventions. As numerous analysts have noted, social media have allowed 'ordinary' users to generate extra-ordinary fame and success through strategies of 'micro-celebrity', whereby users strategically cultivate online fan-bases that can then be leveraged offline for wider celebrity. For some, this phenomenon is at least partly responsible for an epidemic of narcissism (Engholm and Hansen-Hansen 2014: 146–7), as social media users become increasingly self-absorbed in their quest for important metrics (the number of Facebook 'Likes', re-Tweets, shares and so forth). Viewed thus, the blog is little more than an overly contrived vanity project, which rewards style over substance and adds little of value to the broader society. Others see in fashion blogs mere replication of the codes and practices of the established fashion industry. Specifically, whatever independent spirit these bloggers profess readily bends to commercial forces once the bloggers achieve a certain level of marketable influence (Findlay 2015, 172). As such, their blogs fail to expand fashion media in subversive or provocative ways (Duffy 2015, 50).

Whilst barely a fraction of the content published on social media poses any serious challenge to the social, political or economic status quo, the case of MSF *et al.* is distinctive and different. These women are not 'just' chasing fame or celebrity but are creating safe spaces where their cultural identities are not subjected to others' interpretations and deliberations. In the context of widespread Islamophobia, this media presence is both provocative and necessary. In their obvious focus on 'hijabi' fashion, replete with video tutorials and styling tips, these blogs link to at least three significant global developments. First is the growing popularity of blogs run by and for women for whom modest attire is important for religious and/or personal reasons. For instance, besides the fame enjoyed by their hijabi counterparts in other countries (such as UK-based Dina Tokio or US-based Asma of 'Haute Muslimah'), there are now blogs that cater for various faiths that require modest attire for female followers, including Jewish, Mormon and Orthodox Christian (Sherman 2015). This online media has vitalized lively forums for women who have been largely ignored by mainstream media in terms of their fashion and lifestyle interests

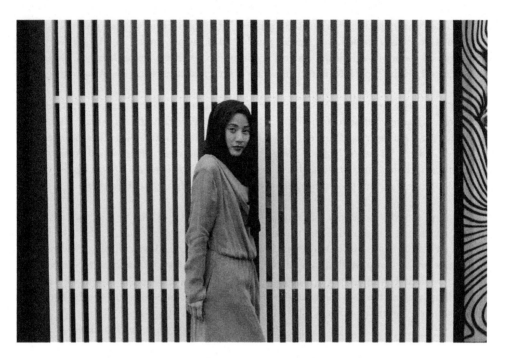

Figure 10.1 Delina on the streets of Newtown. Image from 'Muslim Street Fashion', reproduced
courtesy of Delina Darusman-Gala

Figure 10.2 Delina on the streets of Sydney. Image from 'Muslim Street Fashion', reproduced courtesy
of Delina Darusman-Gala

Figure 10.3 Delina on the streets of Jakarta. Image from 'Muslim Street Fashion', reproduced courtesy of Delina Darusman-Gala

(Lewis 2015, 243). That such blogs have widened fashion coverage and commentary beyond traditional experts, key cities and established designers is widely noted (Rocamora 2012, 101). More important here though is how these blogs create *new* spaces and opportunities in fashion media rather than just challenge or replace existing ones. Second, and with regards to hijabi blogs, there is growing appreciation of just how lucrative quality modest clothing is: to cite just three recent examples, there has been a 'Ramadan' line from US designer Donna Karan in mid-2014, a veiled Muslim model (Mariah Idrissi) featured in advertisements for the Swedish fashion chain H&M in September 2015, and a hijab and abaya collection from Italian fashion house Dolce & Gabbana in early 2016. Clearly, the potential for the fashion industry to profit from the world's fastest growing religion (Lipka and Hackett 2015) is formidable. For hijabi blogger and CEO of Haute Hijab, Melanie Elturk (2015): 'It's no wonder *Fortune* magazine deemed Muslim women as the next big untapped fashion market' – which has flow-on effects for those best placed to review and critique this phenomenon (such as hijabi bloggers). Third and finally: these bloggers are clearly engaged in a worldwide conversation about hijabi fashion, and regularly credit each other for inspiration (Pham 2015).

Conclusion

Australia's hijabi bloggers represent the cultural creativity that is required (and rewarded) in the postmillennial digital economy (Pham 2013, 245). These women symbolically transcend the categories assigned to them by mainstream media, which still seems mostly tied to inflexible, Orientalist assumptions and fears. Instead, they assume control of their representation, and communicate directly with their audiences. As Minh-Ha T. Pham (2011, 10) argues, the fashion blogger is both the agent and object of her own representation; for Muslim bloggers in particular, this is all the more important – since their stories are so often told for them (Echchaibi 2013, 862). As Salam Al-Mahadin writes: 'it is essential to deconstruct the western gaze by querying both its fears and anxieties and questioning the meaning of the object that is being gazed upon, from the perspective of the woman this time' (Al-Mahadin 2013, 16). Herein lies the significance of Australia's 'hijabi' bloggers: the representation of veiling had hardened around negative and mostly inaccurate assumptions about Islam and was almost always mediated without the considered or balanced input from women that choose the practice. Through social media, these women reclaim some discursive autonomy and negotiate their own cultural identities. As such, they actively subvert categorizations that are condescending, demeaning and presumptuous, whilst engaging with global conversations that allow for more nuanced and ultimately empowering understanding of what veiling actually means.

References

2GB. 2014. 'Ray Hadley: The Burqa Debate'. 2 October. Available at www.2gb.com/article/ray-hadley-burqa-debate (accessed January 2016).

ABC. 2011. 'Burqa Removal Law Extended beyond Police'. 19 August. Available at www.abc.net.au/news/2011-08-19/burka-removal-law-extended-beyond-police/2846916 (accessed January 2016).

ABC. 2012. 'Bridging Codes'. *Encounter Radio National*, 4 February. Available at www.abc.net.au/radio national/programs/encounter/new-document/3801094 (accessed January 2016).

ABC. 2013. 'Fashion and Faith: Muslim Style'. *Compass*, 20 June. Available at www.abc.net.au/compass/s3785995.htm (accessed January 2016).

Al-Mahadin, Salam. 2013. 'The Social Semiotics of Hijab: Negotiating the Body Politics of Veiled Women'. *Journal of Arab & Muslim Media Research* 6(1):3–18.

Aly, Anne and David Walker. 2007. 'Veiled Threats: Recurrent Cultural Anxieties in Australia'. *Journal of Muslim Minority Affairs* 27(2):203–14.

Aly, Waleed. 2014. 'Burqa Ban a Political Excuse for Persecution'. *Sydney Morning Herald*, 3 October. Available at www.smh.com.au/comment/burqa-ban-a-political-excuse-for-persecution-20141002-10p0mc.html (accessed February 2016).

Amer, Sahar. 2014. 'Burqa and Niqab: They Cover the Face, not the Mind'. *The Conversation*, 3 October. Available at https://theconversation.com/burqa-and-niqab-they-cover-the-face-not-the-mind-31558 (accessed January 2016).

Awad, Amal. 2013. 'Everything You Know about Burqas is Probably Wrong'. *Daily Life*, 7 May. Available at www.dailylife.com.au/news-and-views/dl-opinion/everything-you-know-about-burqas-is-probably-wrong-20130507-2j59r.html (accessed January 2016).

Bernadi, Cory. 2010. 'For Australia's Sake, We Need to Ban the Burqa'. *Sydney Morning Herald*, 6 May. Available at www.smh.com.au/it-pro/for-australias-sake-we-need-to-ban-the-burqa-20100506-ubun.html (access January 2016).

Beveridge, Ann. 2003. 'The Silent Sufferers'. *Daily Telegraph*, 20 February, p. 47.

Bourke, Latika. 2014. '"Stupid and Ignorant": Cory Bernadi's Comments Linking Terrorism with a Push to Ban Burqa Slammed'. *Sydney Morning Herald*, 18 September. Available at www.smh.com.au/federal-politics/political-news/stupid-and-ignorant-cory-bernardis-comments-linking-terrorism-raids-with-a-push-to-ban-burqa-slammed-20140918-10iltb.html (accessed January 2016).

Carland, Susan. 2011. 'Islamophobia, Fear of Loss of Freedom, and the Muslim Woman'. *Islam and Christian-Muslim Relations* 22(4):469–73.

Carland, Susan. 2012. 'Silenced: Muslim Women Commentators in the Australian Media'. *The La Trobe Journal* 89:140–51.

Chandab, Taghred. 2006. 'Burqa Debate's Veiled Bigotry'. *The Sun-Herald*, 15 October, 31.

Chen, Gina M. 2015. 'Why Do Women Bloggers Use Social Media? Recreation and Information Motivations Outweigh Engagement Motivations'. *New Media & Society* 17(1):24–40.

Davies, Taylor. 2012. 'Balancing Fashion & Faith: A Look at Muslim Style Bloggers'. *Independent Fashion Bloggers*, 9 March. Available at https://heartifb.com/2012/03/09/balancing-fashion-faith-a-look-at-muslim-style-bloggers (accessed January 2016).

Duffy, Brooke. 2015. 'Amateur, Autonomous, and Collaborative: Myths of Aspiring Female Cultural Producers in Web 2.0'. *Critical Studies in Media Communication* 32(1):48–64.

Echchaibi, Nabil. 2013. 'Muslimah Media Watch: Muslim Activism and Muslim Choreographies of Social Change'. *Journalism* 14(7):852–67.

Elturk, Melanie. 2015. 'What H&M's Hijab-Wearing Model Means for Muslim Women'. *Elle Magazine*, 29 September. Available at www.elle.com/culture/career-politics/news/a30845/hm-campaign-hijab-wearing-model (accessed January 2016).

Engholm, Ida and Erik Hansen-Hansen. 2014. 'The Fashion Blog as Genre – between User-Generated Bricolage Design and the Reproduction of Established Fashion System'. *Digital Creativity* 25(2):140–54.

Findlay, Rosie. 2015. 'The Short, Passionate, and Close-Knit History of Personal Style Blogs'. *Fashion Theory* 19(2):157–78.

Hebbani, Aparna and Charise-Rose Wills. 2012. 'How Muslim Women in Australia Navigate through Media (Mis)Representations of Hijab/burqa'. *Australian Journal of Communication* 39(1):87–100.

Hewitt, Anne and Cornelia Koch. 2011. 'Can and Should Burqas Be Banned? The Legality and Desirability of Bans of the Full Veil in Europe and Australia'. *Alternative Law Journal* 36(1):16–20.

Ho, Christina. 2010. 'Responding to Orientalist Feminism'. *Australian Feminist Studies* 25(66):433–9.

Ho, Christina and M. McCarthy. 2010. 'The Burqa Should Not Be an Issue'. *The Sydney Morning Herald*, 13 October.

Jones, Glynis. 2012. 'Introduction'. In *Faith Fashion Fusion: Muslim Women's Style in Australia*, edited by Glynis Jones, 1–7. Sydney: Powerhouse Museum Publishing.

Kabir, Nahid. 2006. 'Representations of Islam and Muslims in the Australian Media, 2001–2005'. *Journal of Muslim Minority Affairs* 26(3):313–28.

Khamis, Susie. 2010. 'Braving the Burqini: Re-branding the Australian Beach'. *Cultural Geographies* 17(3):379–90.

Lewis, Reina. 2015. 'Uncovering Modesty: Dejabis and Dewigies Expanding the Parameters of the Modest Fashion Blogosphere'. *Fashion Theory: The Journal of Dress, Body and Culture* 19(2):243–69.

Lipka, Michael and Conrad Hackett. 2015. 'Why Muslims Are the World's Fastest Growing Religious Group'. *Pew Research Center* 23 April. Available at www.pewresearch.org/fact-tank/2015/04/23/why-muslims-are-the-worlds-fastest-growing-religious-group (accessed January 2016).

Mannix, Liam. 2015. 'Academic Susan Carland, Wife of Waleed Aly, Donating $1 to Charity for Each Hate Tweet'. *Sydney Morning Herald*, 13 November. Available at www.smh.com.au/national/waleed-alys-wife-susan-carland-donating-1-to-charity-for-each-hate-tweet-20151112-gkx38b.html (accessed January 2016).

Meacham, Steve. 2012. 'Cover Girls'. *The Sydney Morning Herald* (*Spectrum* section), 5 May, 10.

Pham, Sheila. 2015. 'What is Australian Fashion?'. *Australia Plus*, 26 November. Available at http://australiaplus.com/international/2015–11–25/what-is-australian-fashion/1518492 (accessed January 2016).

Pham, Minh-Ha T. 2011. 'Blog Ambition: Fashion, Feelings, and the Political Economy of the Digital Raced Body'. *Camera Obscura* 26(1):1–37.

Pham, Minh-Ha T. 2013. ' "Susie Bubble is a Sign of the Times" '. *Feminist Media Studies* 13(2):245–67.

Posetti, Julie. 2010. 'Jihad Sheilas or Media Martyrs? Muslim Women and the Australian Media'. In *Islam and the Australian News Media*, edited by H. Rane, J. Ewart and M. Abdalla, 69–104. Melbourne: Melbourne University Press.

Prodanovic, Branka. 2014. 'The Big Players in the Growth of Islamic Fashion Online'. *The Conversation*, 29 August. Available at https://theconversation.com/the-big-players-in-the-growth-of-islamic-fashion-online-30031 (accessed January 2016).

Rocamora, Agnès. 2012. 'Hypertextuality and Remediation in the Fashion Media'. *Journalism Practice* 6(1):92–106.

SBS. 2010. 'Banning the Burka'. 21 September. SBS. Available at www.sbs.com.au/news/insight/tv episode/banning-burqa (accessed January 2016).

Shah, Fatima. 2004. 'There's Enough Room under the Burqa for Personal Choice'. *The Age*, 8 January, 11. Available at http://www.theage.com.au/articles/2004/01/07/1073437342609.htm (accessed February 2017).

Sherman, Lauren. 2015. 'How Bloggers Made the Fashion Industry Pay More Attention to Minorities'. *Fashionista*, 25 March. Available at http://fashionista.com/2015/03/fashion-blogging-diversity (accessed January 2016).

Sotsky, Jennifer. 2013. 'They Call Me Muslim: Muslim Women in the Media through and beyond the Veil'. *Feminist Media Studies* 13(5):791–9.

Sunday Night. 2012. 'Behind the Veil'. *Sunday Night*, 25 June. Available at https://au.news.yahoo.com/sunday-night/transcripts/a/14033076/behind-the-veil (accessed January 2016).

Syed, Jawad and Edwina Pio. 2010. 'Veiled Diversity? Workplace Experiences of Muslim Women in Australia'. *Asia Pacific Journal of Management* 27:115–37.

Titton, Monica. 2015. 'Fashionable Personae: Self-identity and Enactments of Fashion Narratives in Fashion Blogs'. *Fashion Theory: The Journal of Dress, Body and Culture* 19(2):201–20.

Vyver, James. 2014. 'Explainer: Why Do Muslim Women Wear a Burka, Niqab or Hijab?'. *ABC News*, 2 October. Available at www.abc.net.au/news/2014-09-23/why-do-muslim-women-wear-a-burka-niqab-or-hijab/5761510 (accessed January 2016).

Wray, Nick and Brad Esposito. 2014. '12 Muslim Australians Who Crushed It in 2014'. *Buzzfeed*. Available at www.buzzfeed.com/nicholaswray/muslim-australia#.lcw8N1bqr (accessed January 2016).

Yasa, Dilvin. 2014. 'Keeping the Faith: What It Means to Be a Young Muslim Woman in Australia Today'. *Daily Telegraph*, 12 November. Available at www.dailytelegraph.com.au/news/keeping-the-faith-what-it-means-to-be-a-young-muslim-woman-in-australia-today/news-story/c3a65f5306ff4623cd923ea150d61faf (accessed January 2016).

PART III

Fashion and anti-fashion

11

MODEST FASHION AND ANTI-FASHION

Reina Lewis

Introduction

Modest fashion has emerged as a commercial term, an ideological concept, and a category of critical analysis. For some who participate in forms of modest fashion the term also signals a style of dressing; an attitude to covering and displaying the body. But although some religious adherents would argue that for their faith there are particular ways of achieving modesty, few would think that modesty denotes a specific aesthetic. In contrast, despite the oft-voiced injunctions against revealing certain parts of the body and against certain colours or degrees of pattern or embellishment, the variety of ways in which modest presentation has been achieved in the past and in the burgeoning and highly varied contemporary commercial niche market for modest fashion today reveal the variety and creativity with which modest fashion is achieved around the world and across the faiths. These developments in modes and styles of modest dress are rarely without controversy: in-group and out-group attempts at surveillance, regulation, and control are a constant feature of how women, and men, plan, discuss, and experience their modest self-presentation.

This chapter discusses the commercial market that has emerged to support practices in Muslim veiling and other forms of modest dressing among Muslim women and those of other faiths. Focusing on the increase in Muslim head-covering from the second half of the twentieth century onwards, the chapter explores how the commercial market for modest fashion grew dramatically at the turn of the twenty-first century in the context of the Internet. Arguing that modest fashion can be considered a form of everyday religious practice and that modest fashion pioneers can be regarded as influencers within and beyond their religious communities, the chapter begins by discussing the changing and contested terms used in relation to modest Muslim fashion and veiling, evaluating the political impact of changes in intra- and extra-Muslim definitions of the veil. The development of a creative industry for modest fashion in countries of Muslim majority and minority is contextualized in relation to the role of the market and media, in legitimating and encouraging veiling and modest dressing. Reviewing the discourse of choice that underpins much modest fashion discourse and exploring how some modest dressers wish to use fashion as a mode of communication, the chapter considers how social media have also increased the offline surveillance that greets the modestly dressed body from co-religionists and external observers and agencies. I conclude by identifying potential avenues for future research.

Terms, terrains, and tensions

Women have been dressing with (different definitions of) modesty in mind for centuries. Often the same garment has been worn by women of different religions, and for example the forms of veiling that covered the face in the Middle East, the veil often signalled social status rather than personal piety (Micklewright 2000; Graham-Brown 1988). In my own research on the Middle East and on Euro-American imperial cultures and Orientalism, I had generally referred to forms of veiling and unveiling to encompass the diverse modes of head, face and body covering seen in the late Ottoman empire (Lewis 2004; Lewis and Micklewright 2006). When I started writing about contemporary Muslim fashion in the early 2000s, I used the term veil to refer generically to the then more prevalent practice of head-covering in Western Europe and North America. At that time, face-covering could be distinguished by referring colloquially to face-veils, or niqabs, or more rarely burqas. But as legislation in France and court cases in Britain from the mid-2000s began to focus on face-covering, the term shifted again, with British English-language usage increasingly understanding veil to refer to face-covering rather than head-covering. The rapid changes in nomenclature within my own research practice, publications and public engagement repeatedly reminds me that terminology in relation to modest dress is inherently unstable and frequently controversial. Particular garments have different names. Names for garments change. And the ideological significance of how things are named is itself highly charged and also changeable. For example, as veiling shifted in British English discourse from head- to face-covering, I began to use the term 'hijab' as a generalized category for the diverse forms of head-covering I could see about me. In this I was following the popular use of the term in Muslim modest fashion blogs and social media, and among the young women that I interviewed for my book *Muslim Fashion* between 2005 and 2015.

But, the near hegemonic status of this term in Anglophone discourse about Muslim dress is challenged by Asra Q. Nomani and Hala Arafa in the *Washington Post* who, tracing the etymology of the word from the Qur'an and hadiths, argue that it has never meant simply 'headscarf'.[1] Emptying the term of its apparent neutrality, they position hijab as a descriptor that has been mobilized by repressive forms of Islam in Saudi Arabia and Iran which seek to promote head-covering as a 'virtual "sixth pillar" of Islam' in order to normalize it as a required practice for Muslim women. The discursive impact of this repositions as immoral or immodest the women who do not cover their heads, with attendant judgement and sanctions. Advocating that hijab be avoided in media terminology and that well-meaning non-Muslim women should certainly not don the hijab for a day in shows of solidarity, they propose instead that feminists should join in supporting Muslim women in the pursuit of rights to cover or not cover and for full participation in religious spaces, practices and politics. Many feminists, Muslim and non-Muslim, do indeed take this approach, but it may be that framing the argument about choice in religio-cultural expression through the language of hijab serves unwittingly to promulgate a world view that is not gender inclusive or egalitarian.

Nomani herself faces criticism for rendering hijab as always and only a sign of women's oppression ('Orientalist' for Hoda Katebi, 2016). But, that some of the young women speaking to me of their hijab fashions would not themselves be aware of this argument about terminology is precisely the point; a timely reminder that the academic researcher is herself part of the discursive construction of values and judgements. Terms that seem or seemed to be preferable for their ability to be inclusive or non-judgemental may take on new valences in new circumstances, or when used with different audiences.

In the late twentieth and early twentieth-first century the commercial manufacture and distribution of modest fashion brought a new set of associations to the composite term 'modest fashion'. Following the popularization of the term online in commerce and commentary from the mid-2000s, I use modest fashion as a catch-all classification to describe the many different ways in which women dress in relation to concepts of modest body management and behaviour.

For many modest dressers of all faiths, and at the core of what can be seen as a cross-faith modest fashion 'movement', there is an emphasis on women's choice (hence the timely reminder from Nomani and Arafa to encompass all choices). For many women, forms of modest dress are inauthentic if they are not freely chosen. An ideal of respect for women's individual choices is widespread even if it is sometimes difficult to maintain (Lewis 2013b). For Muslim women it is perfectly clear in Muslim-minority settings in Europe, North and South America or Australia that there is indeed a cohort of youngish women who are in a position to choose to wear hijab, just as there are some, fewer, who choose to wear a face-veil. But it is also clear that there are many women who exercise little choice in when, how or whether to cover their heads, faces and bodies. In some cases, social class or wealth is a guiding factor in determining degrees of choice, but this is not the only factor. Location can change the way that women feel about their presentation, with new observers exerting different types of pressure. Migration can bring new norms of Muslim embodiment, such as with the South Asian migrants to London who, as Tarlo discusses, find themselves wearing abayas rather than clothes conventional to their community in order to fit in with local, hegemonic definitions of good modest presentation, a dress decision driven more by their lack of social capital than by individual piety (Tarlo 2010). For others, including young women of affluent social status, arrival at college or university can be a time of pressure to fit in with the sometimes conservative dress norms fostered by student Islamic societies. Even for women who elect to engage in modest dress, the sometimes oppressive forms of dress surveillance undertaken by their female peers as a form of da'wa[2] or encouragement to pious behaviour can be, as Asma T. Uddin writes, deeply off-putting (Uddin 2011).

Whatever the individual reasons behind particular forms of Muslim dressed embodiment, the observer cannot tell if a mode of dressing is 'freely' chosen. Neither can the observer tell what was intended. Muslim dress, Muslim fashion, like all dress and fashion is polyvalent, generating different meanings to different observers and rarely if ever communicating directly the intention of the wearer. For Muslims, for people of other faiths, as for everyone, choice is always contingent and constrained.

Modest fashion may be an expression of religious or spiritual commitment and it may be worn for a multitude of other reasons. Wearing a form of hijab or of dress coded as Muslim, such as an abaya or jilbab robe, may serve as a social alibi for women wanting to be in gender-mixed environments, a way to reassure family and onlookers of their respectability; it may be a political riposte to anti-Muslim prejudice; it may be an amalgam of Muslim dress with other local dress codes that secure preferred forms of gender presentation donned in relation to local politics rather than individual faith. As Adeline Masquelier explains in relation to the increase in revivalist forms of the veil in Niger, innovations in Muslim dress promoted, sometimes coercively, by the revivalist elite have been grafted onto existing forms of head-covering within a culture in which 'sartorial modesty was already critical to women's definition of propriety and piety' (Masquelier this volume pp. 154). Within prevailing gendered codes of respectability, women's dress and body management was already highly surveilled in ways not experienced by men and boys. As the tailored revivalist 'hijabi' over-garment became hegemonic, it replaced, and invalidated, local forms of Muslim dress previously deemed suitably modest. This example illustrates the tensions between culture and religion that underwrite so many of the contestations about appropriate forms of dress in daily life: British South Asian teenagers challenge the equation of 'ethnic' dress with Muslim dress (Dwyer 1999) and young women and men mobilize personal study of the holy texts to argue that Islam supports individual autonomy in matters such as marriage or education, positioning parental or community norms as 'cultural not religious'. For most young people, new religious practices emerge through negotiation with rather than in direct repudiation of existing religious and cultural norms (Amir-Moazami and Salvatore 2003). A similar argument can be made about the commercial sector of modest Muslim fashion, where multiple religious interpretations and aesthetic conventions are melded by designers and entrepreneurs and made afresh again in their moment of styling and display on the bodies of consumers.

Modest fashion: The development of a category and of a market

The commercial market in modest fashion has facilitated and encouraged modes of modest dressing for women from diverse religious and, to a lesser extent, secular backgrounds. As Fonseca Chagas and Riva Mezabarba (this volume) discuss, the lack of market offer for the relatively small Muslim population in Brazil may be experienced as an obstacle to the successful development of the 'individual aesthetic project' of hijab styling that for some women is an integral part of their ability to become and be devout Muslim women. The need for garments and style inspiration for creating modest or covered dress in the context of Brazilian body conscious cultural fashion norms was thrown into relief for one informant whose move to London brought her into the orbit of a multicultural and multi-ethnic Muslim fashionscape.

As a descriptor of a niche commercial market, and as a category of diverse forms of religiously informed dressing, modest fashion includes and goes beyond veiling in all the many forms that are discussed in this book. It is worth pointing out, therefore, that in the commercial sector modest fashion can denote church dresses with short sleeves and just-above-the-knee skirt lengths marketed to Mormon women just as easily as it can refer to high-necked long-sleeved floor-length party gowns sold to be worn by Muslim women with matching headscarves. Any of these garments might also be utilized for forms of body covering and styling by women from other faith backgrounds and by women who do not consider themselves religious. Therefore, as a term within critical research, modest dressing should be understood to refer to clothes and forms of body management and behaviour utilized by women (and to a lesser extent men) for reasons of religious and religio-ethnic consideration *and* where relevant to behaviours and modes of dressing deployed for reasons that are apparently 'secular'. This last would include workplace considerations (such as wanting longer T-shirts to tuck into trousers when working in day-care with young children), age-specific attitudes to which parts of the body might be covered (such as 'older' women wanting occasion wear with sleeves to cover upper arms that become less toned with age), and spatial factors which include clothing deemed appropriate for particular spaces (whether the synagogue or the courtroom) to be seen by particular people (whether elders, juniors, or ingroup or outgroup observers). Those dressing in modest fashion can also include women who consider themselves to be people of faith and spirituality but do not see this as the motivating factor in how they dress, even if other parts of their lives are strongly marked by conscious religious adherence. For women who do see their dress as motivated by religion, the factors listed above might also be determinants in how they present themselves at different moments in different spaces and to different observers.

As these examples suggest, modest dressing, like all clothing, can be understood as a form of embodiment that is spatially and temporally contingent and changeable. Although broadly accepted as an approach within fashion studies (Entwistle 2000), especially within the sociology of fashion, it is worth emphasizing spatiality in relation to modest fashion (Secor 2002). The inclusion of religion into the frame of fashion can often lead non-specialist observers to exceptionalize the modestly dressed body, regarding the body dressed in relation to religion as somehow intrinsically outside the vagaries of the fashion industry and as emblematic of unchanging ahistorical collective religious or religio-ethnic identities rather than as part of the modern world marked by fashion as change and bound up in processes of individuation.

The commitment to understand modest dressing as something that is mutable, individuated, and liable to change over the course of an individual lifetime is a cornerstone of my research approach, informed by sociological approaches to everyday religion. Work by scholars such as Ammerman (2007) and McGuire (2008), not specifically on fashion, are valuable to the researcher of modest fashion because they emphasize that daily religious practices are syncretic and are often developed though interaction with, rather than rejection of, the market. I find this framework helpful even when considering instances of modest dress that position themselves against the quotidian and commercial concerns of the fashion industry. Saba Mahmood's influential study (2005) of Egyptian women in the early piety movements of the Islamic Revival in the mid-twentieth century makes clear that the repeated act of putting on the hijab and modest dress was integral to the process of cultivating and maintaining a pious disposition. The clothing was part of, not an addition to, the creation of the pious gendered self in a chosen submission to perceived divine will which, Mahmood argues, is a form of individuated agency. For those who favoured plain modest robes, sewn at home or by local seamstresses, piety could be integrated with a social agenda that presented displays of conspicuous consumption as a form of divisive social status-seeking typical of the post-colonial elite's patronage of 'Western' capitalist fashion industry (see also Moors 2007).

This anti-fashion and anti-consumer culture ideal is part of a long-established pattern in which proponents and opponents of consumer cultures have used religious values to support their case (see introduction and essays in Tarlo and Moors 2013). Fashion – with women positioned as key consumers – has often served as the paradigmatic example in debates about the evils or benefits of non-essential spending, tying concern about the morality of unnecessary consumption of fashion commodities to the morality of the women who wear them.

The market itself has at times been directly related to sacralized space, and to religious cultures. In early department store fashion retail in the USA in the second half of the nineteenth century, the commercialization of Christian festivals for marketing purposes raised considerable concern, with products such as Easter bonnets used to lure women consumers into the habits of consumption as leisure in the elaborate spaces of the store (Leach 1989). In the Middle East, the tradition of men as the controller of family expenditure was facilitated in some locations when markets were situated within the grounds of mosques. For middle- and upper-class women in the modernizing centres of the late Ottoman empire, it was similarly the advent of the department store that facilitated shopping as a respectable activity, though Muslim codes of gender seclusion had sometimes to be accommodated for early shoppers. One such was upper-class teenager Hoda Shaarawi, later to become a leading Egyptian feminist and nationalist, whose first visit to the department store in Alexandria was made only after her guardians had negotiated a temporary 'harem' section (Shaarawi 1987 [n.d]; Lewis 2007); when her mother realized the financial autonomy, and pleasure, that could accrue from doing her own shopping, she too followed suit.

How the market reflects and revises religious practice

Modest fashion as a sector of commercial activity has emerged as a niche market. For designers, brands and marketers within this sector comprehending the variability of individual dressing preferences and the overlap of different interpretations within and between faiths can be valuable knowledge. Most modest fashion brands emerged from within particular religious communities, often led by women designers and creative entrepreneurs who could not find the products that they or their daughters wanted in the stores and so set up small businesses to meet those needs (Moors 2013). Selling online and offline, entrepreneurs soon discovered that they had consumers from different faith groups and were quick to respond with changes in their offering to meet those needs: for example, when Utah-based Mormon company ModBod learned that they had ultra-orthodox Jewish consumers in California who wanted long sleeves even in summer (something not considered necessary by their core Mormon consumers who only required long sleeves for warmth in winter and considered a short above elbow sleeve sufficient for modesty in summer), they decided to produce an additional long-sleeved run of the summer seasonal colours in lighter weight summer jersey for their Jewish clientele (see Shellie Slade in Lewis 2013c). Other religiously-originated brands implemented or considered similar adjustments to their offering or to their marketing in order to reach consumers from other, or no, faith backgrounds.

Sometimes, the term 'modest' became an obstacle to commercial success or community connection, indicating the intense mobility of the concept and the ways it is conceptualized. For many in the first cohort of entrepreneurs in the mid-2000s, the label modest fashion was preferred over more religiously specific categories such as Muslim fashion or Islamic fashion or Jewish fashion: a way to signal a vision of dressing that could extend beyond the boundaries of a given religion. As I discuss below, such a preference was driven by both commercial good sense (marketing that could reach more consumers) and an ideological and spiritual/religious commitment to supporting practices of modest dressing across communities. However, the intended inclusivity of the phrase modest fashion did not always translate well in the wider fashion industry, and some designers keen to get their product adopted by buyers for 'mainstream' stores learned to avoid any reference to religion or modesty in their marketing. Designers, entrepreneurs and bloggers across the faiths have also struggled to reconcile the sometimes self-abnegating associations of the term modesty with their feminist and social emancipatory world views (Cameron 2013).

It is not only that these associations do not play well externally in mainstream fashion marketing. Internal to religious communities, women who participate in modest dressing may find themselves challenged by conservative women or men who disparage them for covering in a 'wrong' way, or using 'immodest' bright colours or patterns. Simply covering parts of the body is rarely sufficient; the form of a particular garment and how cloth becomes part of an individual's embodiment are subject to scrutiny within and without religious communities. The terms and limits of these boundary disputes change constantly in relation to internal and external community – cultural politics, and to macro-political changes in the ways that particular religions are viewed, such as the association of Muslim women's clothing (or Muslim men's beards) with religious extremism in the securitising discourse prevalent after the attacks of 9/11 in 2001.

When co-religionists discuss and evaluate forms of modest dressing, a variety of definitions are applied, with much scope for disagreement. As is evident from other chapters in this book, the religious value or meaning of a garment does not lie in the garment itself. In some cases this seems self-evident: Turkish manufacturers in the tesettür sector may produce a square silk scarf that can be worn as a hijab or as a fashionable accessory draped loosely around the neck of a woman with her hair uncovered. But this is also true of garments that may be seen as intrinsically Muslim, such as the abaya or long robe worn by many Muslims in non-gender-segregated spaces such as the public street. Whilst many Emirati women wear an abaya in the Gulf, they do not wear one when visiting Europe. Why? Because wearing an abaya in the Emirates signals nationality and imbues the wearer with the local social and class privileges of the Emirati citizen in a context where Emiratis make up a small minority of the overall population. Whilst a woman in Britain or France wearing an abaya would more likely be (understood to be) making a statement about religious identity, in the Emirates, the same garment is worn to signal social distinction within the state-sanctioned Islamicate public culture. When in winter 2016 Dolce

& Gabbana announced that they were to launch a range of abayas aimed at the high-end luxury Gulf consumer, the story went viral on social and news media because this was one of the first times that a global luxury brand had produced garments specifically for Muslim dressing and had promoted it as part of their global marketing campaign. Outside the fact that most Muslim women, like most women in the world, could not afford to buy a designer garment of any sort, it did not seem to be the case that the Italian design duo had realized that their loyal clients among, for example, the Emirati super-rich would not necessarily be wearing the abaya over their Dolce & Gabbana dress when they stepped off the plane in Milan, London or New York: seen often as a cultural rather than religious garment, the reason for wearing the abaya is located in the social distinctions it achieves in the Muslim-majority context of the Gulf, unnecessary for many when in the West.

Veiled meanings: The illegibility of modest fashion

Just as observers cannot deduce the wearer's motivation in wearing or not wearing forms of modest fashion, so too are the details of particular garments or ways of dressing differently legible to different observers from inside and outside religious communities. In Turkey and the Turkish diaspora, distinctive ways of wearing a headscarf (sometimes paralleled in facial hair or jewellery for men, see Alimen this volume) have signified affiliation to particular religious communities, with varying degrees of legibility to secular compatriots (Saktanber 2002). In Kenya, Oromo Muslim women from Ethiopia, alongside women of other faiths, tactically don the all-covering abaya and sometimes face-veil, that is the local version of Muslim modest dress as a form of 'urban camouflage' to obscure the ethnic distinction that can put them at risk of attack and rape (Klemm 2013, 186). In less dangerous circumstances, the details of modest dress, are differently legible to those with the cultural and subcultural competency to recognize differences in style, or the significance of cut or forms of embellishment. In Muslim minority and majority contexts, the intent or 'piety' of a woman cannot be deduced by what she wears, even if the style or type of veil/modest attire provides some clues to informed observers.

Nuance in the design of garments or styling of clothes on the body may in some moments and places have been acutely legible to some, but this is becoming more complicated now that a greater range of garments are made available to wider markets through the globalized relations of fashion production. An ever proliferating range of styles is now disseminated and available across wider parts of the globe. With the pace of change in hijab styling increasing in rapidity and reach by online how-to hijab tutorials, longer established habits of generational distinction are now paired with micro-generational distinctions in taste that become even less legible to different categories of observer.

The inability to control entirely how our dressed bodies are read by those that encounter us is true for everyone, although many Muslim women in Muslim-minority contexts tell me they use fashion to communicate to majority observers that they are part of contemporary modern society, as also with women converts to Islam in France and Quebec interviewed by Mossière (this volume). For the researcher, it can be important to establish an ethical position that does not seek to arbitrate on which, if any, form of presentation is appropriate for modesty.

Modest fashion as fashion mediation: Communications, community, and conflicts

The growth of a market producing modest fashion has a social impact, legitimating practices that may previously have been seen as minority or extreme (and that may still be regarded this way by some). The market does not operate outside society; it actively shapes the society in which individuals and groups live, and is shaped by them in turn. Whilst some religiously identified people argue that modest dressing should not be commercialized and that fashion – with its inference of wasteful, unnecessary consumption – is inappropriate for modest social values, for many others, the availability of fashionable garments and accessories has assisted in the practice of modest dressing.

Into this domain falls fashion mediation in all its forms, from window dressing and visual merchandizing in Turkish tesettür stores, to fashion lifestyle magazines addressing Muslim, Jewish, and Christian women, and to blogs and social media. The Internet has played an essential role in the development of modest fashion as commerce and as commentary. Whilst the opportunities offered by e-commerce to specialist fashion start-ups could have been predicted, the enormous effect of online fashion mediation could not. Modest fashion blogging has grown communities of readers and practitioners within faiths and has gone beyond this to engender connections between modest dressers across faiths. Just as brands welcome consumers from different faiths, so too do modest fashion bloggers garner readers inside and beyond their religious community. Comment streams indicate a cross-faith religious range which is transnational in its geographical scope; guest posts and commercial collaborations instigate and celebrate inter-faith dialogue.

For many women who dress modestly for religious and spiritual reasons, the connections between faiths are a valuable form of mutual support. Forms of modest fashion mediation have been essential to the development of this sort of support, and have also provided the terrain for new forms of conflict and controversy, with new routes to criticism opening up within and between faiths.

Online communications have made modest fashion commerce and in-group commentary possible. Online media and the advent of affordable portable smart phones and devices have given the largely youthful demographic of modest fashion early adopters access to international communications that are not subject to local intimate oversight, as was the case with early Internet website and blogs when viewed on the family desktop. As with other sectors of digital life, the affordances of new developments in information and communication technologies (ICT) have a tremendous impact on the form, effect, and use of communications: this applies to affordable smart phones and it also applies to the development of new social media platforms.

The transition from blogs in the mid-2000s, which often had significant literary textual components, to visually-led social media platforms such as Tumblr and Instagram at the end of the decade, facilitated participation across language divides. This is assisted by the take-up of emojis as a transnational youth language, and the development of Google translate, permitting a British follower to participate across national and linguistic borders by 'liking' posts from bloggers in Indonesia, Turkey or Iran. With star bloggers, such as Indonesian designer Dian Pelangi, counting the number of their social media followers in the millions,[3] a sense of participation is opened up to ever-increasing numbers. But so too do ICT developments open the field of modest fashion to critics of all sorts and from further away.

Anti-fashion, anti-consumerism

In the early–mid-2000s, before the advent of widespread online communication, earlier phases of Muslim and modest fashion appeared in the new genre of Muslim lifestyle magazines. In contrast to previous Muslim community publications, the lifestyle titles foregrounded fashion content and faced immediate criticism. Hostility to the presentation of fashion as a topic of interest to Muslims was often filtered through two key lenses: criticisms about the representation of the female body, and criticisms of excessive spending and waste (a concern rarely applied to features on other consumables such as cars, associated with men, or holidays, associated with families, see Lewis 2015).

One response to criticisms of over-consumption has been to promote so-called ethical fashion, an area of widespread and growing concern among many fashion consumers in the 2000s and 2010s. Indeed, for some professional marketers in the growing field of Islamic branding and Muslim marketing, Islamic values per se can be leveraged as ethical to appeal to consumers (of finance, food, or fashion) and to create advantage in the market when operationalized as part of Corporate Social Responsibility plans and communications (Temporal 2011). Muslim consumers also face potential ethical dilemmas when brands supported by a mainstream market model, such as Dolce & Gabbana, enter the Muslim fashion market, creating a threat to small-scale Muslim businesses such as the already established local market for high-end abayas. Despite that Muslims feel underserved by the fashion industry, it may be an issue for Muslim consumers to support big brands which are driven by commercial imperative rather than by community or religious or spiritual motives. For Muslims, as for most people around the world, the experience of being positioned by participation in, or exclusion from, globalized consumer cultures has become largely unavoidable.

For women in Muslim-majority countries where gender-segregated spaces are a normative part of sociality, the impact of consumer culture can be particularly trying, raising the bar for women of lesser financial means and further entrenching elaborate high feminine codes of beauty and appearance. Writing about pre-civil war Syria, Salamandra (2005) points to the anti-fashion sentiment of some young women, frustrated at the (personal and financial) drain of having to appear suitably coiffed and elaborately dressed at the many women-only wedding parties that were essential to young women's chances of securing for themselves a 'good' marriage and advancing family status. In Saudi Arabia, as le Renard (2014) discusses, the new spaces of women-only malls can provide Islamically acceptable opportunities for socializing outside the home and chances to interact with women not already known to the family, but this welcome component of modern urban life comes at the cost of having to undertake the elaborate make-up and hair styling required to withstand the gaze of female scrutiny: women sometimes shun the mall in favour of mixed-gender public spaces where the compulsory abayas and face cover means they can avoid the cost and time required to achieve high maintenance grooming.

This is the double edge of being constructed as a religious consumer segment. In Muslim-minority contexts too, whilst Muslim women have long complained about being underserved by the fashion industry, if modest presentation becomes a facet of fashion, some may find themselves priced out of modesty if wearing the on-trend hijab is the tacit ticket to admission at the new halal café or restaurant.

Another form of Muslim anti-fashion is the development of styles of dress which respond to the appeal of clothes associated with the Arabian Peninsula of the time of the prophet (Tarlo 2013b). Like all origin myths, these garments can be conceptualized as 'pure' and, in this case, Islamic, and presented as an antidote to commercialized 'Western' fashion.[4] Nonetheless, such garments can also be commercially manufactured and retailed, as is done with considerable success by several companies, including British brand Shukr, whose advocacy of Arabic style garments for women and for men (thobes, abayas) is rendered modern with cool, clean design and graphics, in a suitably restrained palette (Tarlo 2010).

An affective relationship to the transnational ummah – community of Muslim believers – can enhance participation in Muslim modest fashion, and can encourage followers for social media around the world. But for designers, the commercial limits of the ummah are often revealed when local aesthetics and taste limit sales (Lewis 2016).

On the other hand, wardrobe options that move away from ethnic clothing are often welcomed by converts to Islam (a more significant demographic than converts to Judaism, for example, and more likely than converts to Christianity to be immediately concerned with revisions to their attire). As Mossière discusses (this volume), Muslim converts in France or Quebec may embrace selected elements of 'oriental' cultures, such as mint tea or Turkish slippers, at the same time as wanting to purify Islam of inappropriate or insufficiently 'strict' practices that they see as cultural accretions within local established Muslim communities. Nuanced in each case by the ethnic, national and cultural character and mix of proximate Muslim communities and families (especially for converts who marry men born Muslim), the exotic consumption of practices and commodities that can be coded as Islamic may exist alongside wardrobe strategies that ensure continuity with pre-conversion dress choices. As Mossière points out, some women regard their pre-conversion dress style as already modest.

As with converts, those born Muslim may shop around for different Islamic interpretations that support their particular choices, with modes of modest dressing understood as a journey into piety that is supported by peer groups rather than parents among migrant and convert youth in Berlin as Bendixsen describes (this volume). Yet in the process of coming to modest dress, including coming to the hijab, young Muslims in Berlin, as elsewhere, are acutely aware that they are judged not only by majority observers but also by other Muslims. They know this because they do it too, worrying that young women in hijab on the streets hanging out with men are bringing the community into disrepute.

Modest fashion on and offline has in some instances provided routes to social and economic development for women. In a context where women wearing modest Muslim attire face obstacles in education and employment whether in Muslim-minority Canada (Zine 2006), Britain (Kariapper 2009), or Muslim-majority secular Turkey (Gökarıksel 2012), the retail and leisure spaces of Islamic consumer culture can provide jobs and social opportunities (Sandıkçı and Ger 2005). The potential of fashion to be a route to social empowerment is manifest in the range of political and social topics covered in modest fashion-related social media across the faiths. Offline, the proliferating numbers of modest fashion events serve as a gathering point for women entrepreneurs and their clients; catwalk glamour and buying opportunities are combined with motivational speakers who provide guidance on access to education and jobs as part of a programme of women's capacity development that extends into and beyond the fashion industry.

Future developments in the research field

As the pioneering generation of modest dressers across the faiths matures, there will probably be changes in how they present themselves, as they move out of young adulthood into other life stages. Modesty and religiosity, may indeed remain a core practice, or it may not, but either way these women will definitely not be dressing in the same way in their 30s, 40s and 50s.

One development that is already discernible is the growing number of women who are electing not to cover their hair or heads. Sometimes referred to as dejabis for the conscious decision to remove the previously chosen hijab, similar developments are apparent among modern orthodox Jewish women who had covered their hair on marriage. The ways in which this change repositions gender, and ethnic as well as religious components of identity, widens the critical frame back to the body in its entirety. Given that disproportionate academic research, media attention and market activity has been focused on these most spectacular forms of religiously related presentation, I think that the move to consider less visible markers of religious dress will be fascinating.

The rise of the Religious Rights, plural, in many ostensibly secular and Muslim-minority countries also provides an important context for future research. As familiarity with different forms of Muslim practice and interpretation widens, I hope that nuanced understandings of distinctions within different Muslim populations and approaches will inform research into the relationship of religion to society. Researchers may find that it becomes more routine to consider a range of Muslim opinion, including those sometimes grouped as Progressive Muslims (Safi 2003; Sahar 2014), rather than being driven by a media and political agenda that sends funding to topics promising insight into 'extreme' forms of Muslim cultural politics. The same may also come to be true for other religiously related dress cultures, as collaborations between the right-wings of different religions and denominations become more prevalent and widely known. If I sometimes seem utopian about the potential of fashion to provide a conduit for women's cross-faith connectivity, given that we know there can be conflict within and between faiths as much as there can be harmony, I do remain convinced that the women who are influencers in the fashion sphere have potential to be influencers in other parts of the social world. Whilst most of the young women I have spoken to in the course of my research would reject the idea that they were religious authorities or even that they were engaging in forms of religious interpretation, many do accept that they are role models, taking seriously their responsibilities to other, especially younger, women. Their status as inspirational role models, is widely acknowledged on social media, shown through sales figures for designers, and known to extend beyond their faith community. Interest in Muslim men and modesty is also now developing, providing opportunities to focus on parallel issues of body management such as facial hair, with opportunities for further research into other religions such as Sikhism and forms of Judaism where male body management and presentation features prominently.

Modest fashion, as with Muslim fashion, may become an obsolete term in the market and in the media, and the styles familiar to me will certainly change, but I predict that practices relating the body to faith, to spirituality, to religious community and to the market will continue and will continue to provide a rich field for research.

Notes

1. Available at www.washingtonpost.com/news/acts-of-faith/wp/2015/12/21/as-muslim-women-we-actually-ask-you-not-to-wear-the-hijab-in-the-name-of-interfaith-solidarity (accessed 5 April 2016).
2. Da'wa (literally the call or invitation), applies both externally to invite conversion into Islam and internally in the obligation to 'urge fellow Muslims to greater piety' by teaching 'one another correct Islamic conduct' (Mahmood 2005:57–60).
3. See www.instagram.com/dianpelangi/?hl=en (accessed 19 April 2016).
4. Christian communities such as the Amish or Mennonites display an antipathy to fashion as part of industrialized modernity that parallels some approaches to 'Islamic' fashion in a desire to avoid the temporality and change of fashion as a potential threat to community cohesion. Whilst generally avoiding industrialized production, the styles and manufacture of Amish garments and Mennonite plain dress do themselves change over time and in relation to mainstream garment trends (see Arthur 1999).

References

Amer, Sahar. 2014. *What is Veiling?* Edinburgh: Edinburgh University Press.

Amir-Moazami, Shirin and Armando Salvatore. 2003. 'Gender, Generation, and the Reform of Tradition: From Muslim Majority Societies to Western Europe'. In *Muslim Networks and Transnational Communities in and Across Europe*, edited by Stefano Allievi and Jorgen S. Nielsen, 52–77. Leiden and Boston, MA: Brill.

Ammerman, Nancy T. 2007. 'Introduction: Everyday Religion: Observing Modern Religious Lives'. In *Everyday Religion: Observing Modern Religious Lives*, edited by Nancy T. Ammerman, 219–38. Oxford and New York: Oxford University Press.

Arthur, Linda B. ed. 1999. *Religion, Dress and the Body*. Oxford: Berg.

Cameron, Jane. 2013. 'Modest Motivations: Religious and Secular Contestation in the Fashion Field'. In *Modest Fashion: Styling Bodies, Mediating Faith*, edited by Reina Lewis, 137–57. London: I.B.Tauris.

Dwyer, Claire. 1999. 'Veiled Meanings: Young British Muslim Women and the Negotiation of Differences'. *Gender, Place and Culture: A Journal of Feminist Geography* 6(1):5–26.

Entwistle, Joanne. 2000. *The Fashioned Body: Fashion, Dress and Modern Social Theory*. Cambridge: Polity Press.

Gökarıksel, Banu. 2012. 'The Intimate Politics of Secularism and the Headscarf: The Mall, the Neighbourhood, and the Public Sphere in Istanbul'. *Gender Place and Culture: A Journal of Feminist Geography* 19(1):1–20.

Graham-Brown, Sarah. 1988. *Images of Women: The Portrayal of Women in Photography of the Middle East 1860–1950*. London: Quartet.

Kariapper, Ayesha Salma. 2009. *Walking a Tightrope: Women and Veiling in the United Kingdom*. London: Women Living Under Muslim Laws.

Katebi, Hoda (blogging as JooJoo Azad) 'Feminism, Orientalism, Asra Nomani, and the Hijab: An Open Letter', 2 June 2016, accessed 28-4-17: http://www.joojooazad.com/2016/06/feminism-orientalism-asra-nomani-and-hijab.html

Klemm, Peri M. 2013. '"We Grew Up Free but Here We Have to Cover Our Faces": Veiling among Oromo Refugees in Eastleig, Kenya'. In *Veiling in Africa*, edited by Elisha P. Renne, 186–204. Bloomington, IA: Indiana University Press.

Leach, William. 1989. 'Strategists of Display and the Production of Desire'. In *Consuming Visions: Accumulation and Display of Goods in America, 1880–1920*, edited by Simon J. Bronner. New York: Norton.

Le Renard, Amelie. 2014. *A Society of Young Women: Opportunities of Place, Power, and Reform in Saudi Arabia*. Stanford CA: Stanford University Press.

Lewis, Reina. 2004. *Rethinking Orientalism: Women, Travel, and the Ottoman Harem*. London: IB.Tauris.

Lewis, Reina. 2007. 'Veils and Sales: Muslims and the Spaces of Postcolonial Fashion Retail'. *Fashion Theory* 11(4):423–41.

Lewis, Reina. 2013a. 'Fashion Forward and Faith-tastic! Online Modest Fashion and the Development of Women as Religious Interpreters and Intermediaries'. In *Modest Fashion: Styling Bodies, Mediating Faith*, edited by Reina Lewis, 41–66. London: I.B.Tauris.

Lewis, Reina 2013b. 'Hijab Stories: Choice, Politics, Fashion'. In *Fashion Cultures Revisited*, 2nd edition, edited by Stella Bruzzi and Pamela Church Gibson, 305–21. Oxford: Bloomsbury.

Lewis, Reina. 2013c. 'Insider Voices, Changing Practices: Press and Industry Professionals Speak'. In *Modest Fashion: Styling Bodies, Mediating Faith*, edited by Reina Lewis, 190–220. London: I.B.Tauris.

Lewis, Reina, ed. 2013d. *Modest Fashion: Styling Bodies, Mediating Faith*. London: I.B.Tauris.

Lewis, Reina. 2016. 'The Commercial Limits of the Ummah? National and Regional Taste Distinctions in the Modest Fashion Market'. In *Islam, Marketing and Consumption*, edited by Aliakbar Jafari and Ozlem Sandıkçı, 83–101. London: Routledge.

Lewis, Reina and Nancy Micklewright, eds. 2006. *Gender, Modernity and Liberty: Middle Eastern and Western Women's Writings: A Critical Sourcebook*. London: I.B.Tauris.

McGuire, Meredith B. 2008. *Lived Religion: Faith and Practice in Everyday Life*. Oxford and New York: Oxford University Press.

Mahmood, Saba. 2005. *Politics of Piety: The Islamic Revival and the Feminist Subject*. Princeton, NJ: Princeton University Press.

Micklewright, Nancy. 2000. 'Public and Private for Ottoman Women of the Nineteenth Century'. In *Women, Patronage, and Self-Representation in Islamic Societies*, edited by D. Fairchild Ruggles, 155–76. New York: State University of New York Press.

Moors, Annelies. 2007. 'Fashionable Muslims: Notions of Self, Religion, and Society in San'a'. *Fashion Theory: The Journal of Dress, Body & Culture* 11(2/3):319–46.

Moors, Annelies. 2013. '"Discover the Beauty of Modesty": Islamic Fashion Online'. In *Modest Fashion: Styling Bodies, Mediating Faith*, edited by Reina Lewis, 17–40. London: I.B.Tauris.

Morey, Peter and Amina Yaqin. 2011. *Framing Muslims: Stereotyping and Representation after 9/11*. Cambridge, MA: Harvard University Press.

Osella, Caroline and Filippo Osella. 2007. '*Muslim Style in South India*'. *Fashion Theory: The Journal of Dress, Body & Culture* 11(2/3):235–52.

Safi, Omid, ed. 2003. *Progressive Muslims: On Justice, Gender and Pluralism*. Oxford: Oneworld Publications.

Saktanber, Ayşe. 2002. "'We Pray Like You Have Fun": New Islamic Youth in Turkey between Intellectualism and Popular Culture'. In *Fragments of Culture: The Everyday of Modern Turkey*, edited by Deniz Kandiyoti and Ayşe Saktanber, 254–76. London: I.B.Tauris.

Salamandra, Christa. 2005. 'Cultural Construction, The Gulf and Arab London'. In *Monarchies and Nations: Globalisation and Identity in the Arab States of the Gulf* edited by Paul Dresch and James Piscatori, 73–95. London and New York: I.B.Tauris.

Sandıkçı, Özlem and Güliz Ger. 2005. 'Aesthetics, Ethics and Politics of the Turkish Headscarf'. In *Clothing as Material Culture*, edited by Susanne Küchler and Daniel Miller, 61–82. Oxford and New York: Berg.

Secor, Anna. 2002. 'The Veil and Urban Space in Istanbul: Women's Dress, Mobility and Islamic Knowledge'. *Gender, Place and Culture: A Journal of Feminist Geography* 9(1):5–22.

Shaarawi, Huda. 1987. *The Memoirs of an Egyptian Feminist (1879–1924)*, translated by Margot Badran. New York: The Feminist Press.

Tarlo, Emma. 2010. *Visibly Muslim: Fashion, Politics, Faith*. Oxford and New York: Berg.

Tarlo, Emma. 2013a. 'Meeting through Modesty: Jewish–Muslim Encounters on the Internet'. In *Modest Fashion: Styling Bodies, Mediating Faith*, edited by Reina Lewis, 67–90. London: I.B.Tauris.

Tarlo, Emma. 2013b. 'Landscapes of Attraction and Rejection: South Asian Aesthetics in Islamic Fashion in London'. In *Islamic Fashion and Anti-Fashion: New Perspectives from Europe and North America*, edited by Emma Tarlo and Annelies Moors, 73–92. London: Bloomsbury.

Tarlo, Emma and Moors, Annelies, eds. 2013. *Islamic Fashion and Anti-Fashion: New Perspectives from Europe and North America*. London: Bloomsbury.

Temporal, Paul. 2011. *Islamic Branding and Marketing: Creating a Global Islamic Business*. Singapore: John Wiley & Sons (Asia).

Uddin, Asma T. 2011. 'Conquering Veils: Gender and Islams'. In *I Speak for Myself: American Women on Being Muslim*, edited by Maria M. Ebrahimji and Zahra T. Suratwala, 36–41. Ashland, OR: White Cloud Press.

Zine, Jasmin. 2006. 'Unveiled Sentiments: Gendered Islamophobia and Experiences of Veiling among Muslim Girls in a Canadian Islamic School'. *Equity and Excellence in Education* 39:239–52.

12

VEILING, FASHION, AND THE (PER)FORMATIVE ROLE OF DRESS IN NIGER

Adeline Masquelier

Introduction

'All the women who take the plane to Mecca wear a *hijabi*. Women pilgrims leaving Mecca wear a *hijabi* all the way home. One shouldn't see the body of a woman, it is *haram* [forbidden]. It is God who said women should wear a *hijabi*. Even Christian women must veil. God said so.' Thus did Malam Adamou, a traditionalist Muslim preacher, intone during a sermon in Dogondoutchi, a Hausa-speaking provincial town of Niger. The year was 2000. Following admonitions by members of an Islamic reform movement colloquially known as Izala that male and female garb be modified so as to offer proof of the wearer's religious commitment, the *hijabi* – a tailored veil of varying length and coverage – was becoming thoroughly incorporated in the wardrobes of many pious Muslim women. Even women who did not belong to Izala had begun wearing *hijabai* (plural of *hijabi*) to attend a lecture at a mosque or minimize friction with abusive male colleagues at work (Alidou 2005). If the *hijabi* functioned as a kind of 'mobile' seclusion (see Papanek 1973), theoretically allowing women to move in previously inaccessible public spaces, it was also valued for the performative possibilities it enabled. Unmarried young women who neither prayed nor fasted told me they wore the *hijabi* to look modern (that is, to embody 'spiritual progress') or to earn the respect of the piety-minded young men who were courting them. Now that it was no longer scandalous for girls from traditionalist Muslim households to marry Izala reformists – as was the case in the 1990s when traditionalist Muslims and reformist Muslims actively fought over the definition of Islam and the merits of various forms of religiosity – the *hijabi* was a crucial means through which some young women strategically situated themselves so as to optimize their life options. By marking the wearer as a pious Muslim, it served as a sartorial alibi, helping women to conceal 'sinful' conduct, such as prostitution, or to advertise their conversion to a life of piety.

The *hijabi* was originally designed as a class-levelling device that signalled loyalty to a particular brand of Islamic piety. As the concrete materialization of virtue and frugality, it hid not only women's charms (hair, ears, neck, and in some case, much of the body) but also their (supposedly) profligate and frivolous nature under a cover of homogeneity. Initially it promoted sartorial uniformity. Soon, however, the *hijabi* acquired a fashionability that turned it into a critical tool for re-inscribing social distinctions. Thanks to the myriad details – tailoring, texture, trim, sequins, embroidery, and so on – that could add distinctiveness to a garment and set trends, *hijabai* became an indispensable fashion accessory for Muslim women and girls aiming for respectability yet reluctant to become totally invisible.

This is not to say that the generic *hijabi* devoid of distinctive decorations disappeared entirely from local shops. Increasingly, however, a diverse array of stylish *hijabai* emerged, that, in the words of a local critic, 'catered to women's vanity as much as to their virtue'. Some of those head coverings were heavily ornamented, others less so. Prices could vary widely depending on the level of ornamentation and the quality of the fabric and overall tailoring. Today just as wealthy Yemeni elites purchase 'chic chadors' to differentiate themselves from the pious masses (Meneley 2007), so Nigérien women negotiate the boundaries of up-to-date-ness through their consumption of Islamic chic. Far from being antithetical to religion, the cultivated capacity to project social differences – that which Bourdieu (1984) called 'taste' – has emerged as an important terrain for 'sorting out the terms of piety' (Jones 2010, 624).

In this chapter I consider how style has been variously mobilized to address the requirements of Islamic modesty in Niger in ways that highlight the inseparability of faith and fashion. Specifically, I examine the evolving place of the *hijabi* within an extensive, and occasionally fraught, moral aesthetics through which Nigérien women learn to articulate their sense of what femininity, piety, and elegance entails. Critical to my approach is an emphasis on dress as embodied practice. From that perspective, the signifying capacity of the *hijabi* and other types of modest attire cannot be assessed without taking into account the fleshy, phenomenological reality of the dressed body. But first some historical context is in order.

Religious reform and the normativization of public piety

Hijabai were introduced in Dogondoutchi in the early 1990s by members of the Jama'at Izalat al-Bid'a wa Iqamat al-Sunna (Society for the Removal of Innovation and the Restoration of Tradition). Informally known as Izala, this reformist association was founded in 1979 in Nigeria to foster a return to 'authentic' Islam, stripped of heathenism and innovations, and promote rigorous moral standards (Kane 2003; Loimeier 1997; Umar 1993). A decade or so later, in the face of diminished economic opportunities and growing disillusions about the future, many Nigériens joined Izala, convinced that immorality and profligacy were the root cause of the country's poverty. Aside from admonishing their audiences to abandon their supposedly incorrect religious practices, Izala leaders denounced the pursuit of worldly pleasures, the Westernization of local values, and the flaunting of ostentatious consumption in an effort to redirect Muslims on the right path (Grégoire 1992; Masquelier 2009; Sounaye 2005, 2009). Originally an urban movement, Izala eventually reached rural areas where it is now firmly entrenched. Izala activism remains nevertheless concentrated in urban areas.

Izala's campaign for a moral order structured around discipline, self-restraint, and frugality translated into an unprecedented concern for the definition of 'proper' Islamic dress. In their sermons Izala preachers tirelessly proclaimed that a modest appearance was the true reflection of a woman's inner piety, thus situating virtuous womanhood at the centre of the debate over what it meant to be Muslim. They invoked verse 31 in chapter 24 of the Qur'an in which God commands the Prophet to '[s]ay to the believing women that: they should cast down their glances and guard their private parts [by being chaste] and not display their beauty except what is apparent, and they should place their veil over their bosoms'. They also made reference to verse 59 in chapter 33 in which God similarly enjoins the Prophet to veil his wives: 'O Prophet! Say to your wives, your daughters, and the women of the believers that: they should let down upon themselves their outer garment'.

Izala preachers' stress on female modesty offered the 'newly pious' (Hefner 2005, 21) unprecedented control over the terms of moral regulations in the public arena. Women who wore revealing clothes were berated (and, at times, physically assaulted) for falling prey to Western fashions. In 1999 an African fashion festival held in Niamey, the country's capital, prompted violent riots (Cooper 2003). The display of scantily clad women modelling the couturiers' latest creations was deemed an affront to Muslim morality and an 'incitement to fornication' (Mayer 2000). Meanwhile the *hijabi* was described in newspaper editorials and sermons as offering both moral and physical protection against lecherous male spirits widely rumoured to target pretty schoolgirls throughout the country (Masquelier 2016a).

The policing of body coverage notwithstanding, wearing the *hijabi* was hardly a revolutionary practice in Niger. For one thing, sartorial modesty was already critical to women's definition of propriety and piety. Adult women in Dogondoutchi and elsewhere had been covering their heads all along. If schoolgirls and unmarried young women appeared bareheaded or with a simple headscarf (*diko*) in public, their married counterparts never left home without loosely draping a large cloth (*lullu'bi, mayafi* or *zane* in Hausa) over their *diko*. Head coverings thus participated in the definition of pious Muslim womanhood long before the introduction of *hijabai* by Izala tailors and clothing merchants.

In this context it makes little sense to refer to 'the veil' in the singular to designate the diverse array of head and body coverings Muslim women put on to satisfy God's commands. Women in Niger draw from a range of sartorial registers to fashion a respectable look. The extent to which 'modest' attire conceals body parts (neck, buttocks, and so on) said to arouse male desire varies widely. Some women play with the seductive potential of their prayer shawl, letting it slip so that it reveals what is should ideally conceal. Under their expert hands the diaphanous *lullubi* they wear often enhances the curve of a neck or a shoulder even as it ostensibly offers 'proper' coverage. On the other hand, a small minority of women who take Izala's injunction to cover the body literally may choose to wear socks and gloves as well as a *niqāb* (face-veil) to complement their *hijabi*. In the end, veiling practices are neither stable nor uniform. Not only does 'modest dress' mean different things to different people but a person's own definition of modesty may be subject to changes, shaped as it is by the global tides of fashion and religiosity.

The shift from wearing the *lullu'bi* to the *hijabi* is nevertheless significant for it exemplifies how religious reformers (such as Izala members) 'purify' Islam by ridding it of accretions and introducing practices supposedly aligned with the Qur'an and the hadith. Moreover, Izala's insistence that women cover themselves is a reminder not only that piety takes distinctly gendered forms (Masquelier 2016b; Renne 2013; Selby 2016) but also that the promotion and consumption of Islamic dress is explicitly feminized, 'making women bearers of heavier semiotic burdens than male subjects' in many parts of the world (Jones 2010, 624). Girls often face parental disapproval, not to mention outright condemnation from religious Muslim leaders, for openly flouting local norms of Islamic propriety by adopting clothes of Western inspiration (especially when these clothes cling to the body or reveal what should remain concealed). Their choices of fashion are closely scrutinized in ways that young men's are not – at least, not to the same extent.

Initially women and girls who wore the *hijabi* invariably signalled that their husbands or fathers belonged to Izala. Because they often invoked God in the defence of their modest attire – it was God who instructed them to cover their bodies in such a manner – the tailored veils they wore over wrappers and blouses were perceived by others as an attack on local Muslim traditions. Thus women who wore the traditional *lullu'bi* often fiercely disparaged *hijabi*-clad neighbours. They made fun of the tent-like garments reformist Muslim women put on and accused them of covering up sins and secrets behind their holier-than-thou looks. Women's wrangle over the definition of proper Islamic dress was part of a wider disagreement over the correctness of Islamic practice, a disagreement that, when it pitted sons against fathers, often split families apart.

As Malam Adamou's admonition, with which I opened this chapter, makes clear, however, traditionalist Muslims who initially objected to Izala preachers' fervent injunctions that women cover their bodies eventually came to share the reformist movement's vision of the *hijabi* as a divinely ordained means of ensuring moral order in Muslim communities. Though they might occasionally quibble over the precise sartorial terms through which propriety should be publicly manifested, many Muslims on both sides agree that women and girls must demonstrate compliance with Islamic norms by veiling. 'The differences [between head coverings] are not important', an Izala member explained. 'The *hijabi* that women wear [in Niger] is actually not the correct outfit. They should wear a *djellaba* [loose-fitting robe with full sleeves] and a scarf covering the neck. But with our lightweight fabric, the *djellaba* would be too revealing.'

When Muslim preachers from all stripes urged women to veil when they ventured in public spaces, the *hijabi* lost its exclusive association with Izala's strict regimentation of women's bodies. It came to instantiate piety in a more generic sense (Masquelier 2009). 'Before, if you wore the *hijabi*, every one called you a "Izala" [member of Izala]. But not anymore', is how a young woman put it. Many young women thus insist on wearing their *hijabi* when they are photographed: they are aware of the importance of presenting themselves as modest, respectable Muslims. Meanwhile many young men say they want their future wives to don *hijabai*.

In Niger recent efforts to police the moral boundaries of community have focused on the creation of the virtuous woman whose modest appearance instantiates both inner purity and compliance with Islamic regulations. Significantly, this concern over female dress and demeanour arose as women were becoming an increasingly visible presence in the workplace and in the classroom. Add to this the widely shared perception that looks can be deceiving – a well-known Hausa proverb states that 'even if the baobab is bigger, the acacia is stronger', implying that one should not base one's judgement on appearance – and you have the social backdrop against which to consider women's rumoured engagement in immoral activities behind the façade of respectability provided by the *hijabi*. Stories of women committing thefts, enjoying trysts with lovers, or hiding pregnancies while cloaked under their *hijabai* are legion. By giving shape to the scepticism some Muslims feel toward Izala (or female piety), these narratives of deviant and, at times, dangerous female agency exemplify the deceitful potentialities of veiling as a practice that no only shields women's charms, as the Qur'an instructs, but also disguises their 'wickedness' (Masquelier 2008).

It is worth stressing that not all Nigérien women and girls have adopted the *hijabi*. Many of them nevertheless routinely capitalize on the *hijabi*'s moral value, and their reasons for doing so are often far more mundane than the rumours suggest. The normativization of public piety has affected all women – not just those who grew up in Izala households and have worn a *hijabi* since toddlerhood. Mindful that modest dress neutralizes a woman's sexuality while heightening her respectability, mothers inculcate in their daughters the skills they need to navigate the fraught intersection of fashion and morality. Because the *hijabi* marks its wearer as inherently virtuous, non-Izala girls wishing to polish their reputation have adopted it. Some of them only put it on during Ramadan, the holy month of the Islamic calendar. A few Christian girls reportedly own *hijabai*. The extent to which the *hijabi* and other veils have redefined the boundaries of the fashionable and the modest means that one can no longer identify Nigérien women's religious affiliations at a glance depending on what type of head-covering they wear.

Young women looking for a husband have learned to project an image of modesty – matching local expectations of what a proper Muslim woman looks like – when the circumstances require it. Knowing that most men wishing to marry put a premium on sartorial modesty, they turn themselves into demure *budurwa* (unmarried girls) whose vestmental restraint connotes virtue and humility. In some contexts, the *hijabi* functions as an instrument of deceit (worn by girls whose parents, unaware of the 'sexy' outfits their daughters are wearing underneath, let them go out at night). In other contexts, it serves as a type of protection, signalling that its wearer is unavailable. By deflecting the male gaze, it enables women to enjoy 'civil inattention' (Goffman 1963, 84) as they negotiate public spaces. In recent years a type of *djellaba* known as *respectez-moi* (respect me) has become popular among some young urban women weary of attracting unwanted attention. As its name suggests, the *respectez-moi* attire casts the wearer as modest and virtuous regardless of what she might be wearing underneath. Initially it featured no distinctive decorations. Later the garment came with contrasting cuffs and hood made of flowery fabric and adorned with rhinestones, hinting at the fluid and flexible nature of modest styles. As we shall see, the fashionable potentialities of veils have broadened the *hijabi*'s significance and the 'work' it does, enabling it to penetrate the larger world of ambiguous fashion signs.

Fashion and the commodification of piety

The first *hijabai* to be worn by women in Dogondoutchi were locally manufactured. Supposedly modelled after Meccan fashions, they were made of brightly coloured cotton brocade and came with matching drawstring pants and a long-sleeved tunic. By casting their wearers as uniformly pious, they created a visible sense of shared religious identity among Izala households. Soon, however, new mass-produced designs appeared, that reflected the incipient commercialization of pious dress – a global trend that has been extensively documented in the anthropological literature (Meneley 2007; Moors and Tarlo 2007; Sandıkçı and Ger 2005; Tarlo 2010). Each season brought new styles and new trends destined to make the *hijabai* of the previous year less 'fashionable'. In the early 2000s *hijabai* were often adorned with lace trims of contrasting colour though plain ones made of lighter, more flexible fabric could also be purchased. A few years later, the fashionable *hijabai* were made of a synthetic blend and often came with tiny rhinestones, sequins or eyelets. Decorative touches also included tassels or embroidery while patterned fabrics eventually became popular. Not only did flowery or checked fabric often replace plain cloth, but *hijabai* came in two-colour head and body combinations. In 2013 lavish multi-coloured embroidery in the back of the garment was the latest rage (see Figure 12.1). In 2015 young women in Niamey wore a *hijabi* whose top section resembled a slouchy gnome's hat with the tip knotted (see Figure 12.2). Meanwhile *mayafai* (plural of *mayafi*) too have reflected evolving consumer trends through their incorporation of decorative touches of all kinds (eyelets, embroidery, fringes, and so on).

Earlier *hijabi* styles emblematized timeless rigor and economy – qualities reformist Muslim women ideally embodied through dress and deportment – and exemplified a kind of 'anti-fashion' (Heath 1992). In contrast, the more recent styles clearly signal that the *hijabi* is now thoroughly subjected to the rules of fashion. Whereas the *hijabi* was initially 'localized' by Izala tailors who made it into something distinctly Nigérien, today, its appeal is enhanced when it comes from abroad. As a religiously coded item, the *hibaji* remains a key component of pious identities but it is often treated as a fashion statement in itself. Ironically, by becoming an object of consumer desire, it undermined its own mission: initially designed to remedy the ills of consumption, the *hijabi* now relies on the logic of consumption for its own appeal (see Jones 2010).

Aside from generating anxiety about the dynamics of concealment and truth (not all women in *hijabi* are perhaps as devout as they appear), the contradictory potential of pious consumption has unleashed denunciations of women's shallow, materialistic nature. Women are criticized for

Figure 12.1 Nigérien woman wearing *hijabi* over a head scarf

Figure 12.2 Nigérien women wearing *hijabai*

veiling to 'follow fashion' and compete with one another. I have heard people disparage the way some young women supposedly collect *hijabai* like others collect handbags or shoes. What upsets some people is how a device originally aimed at preventing the sexualization of women has turned women's bodies into objects of visual consumption. Take for instance the *hijabi* that sports eye-catching embroideries on its backs (see Figure 12.1). A striking example of how dress functions as 'public display' (LeBlanc 2000, 448), it is disadvantaged when seen from the front since its best points are hidden. The back view of a woman wearing such a *hijabi* is arresting, however. Even when she turns her back to onlookers, she offers a perfect picture of grace and femininity. Indeed, her walking motions animate the embroidered design of her *hijabi* in such a way that, far from rendering her inconspicuous, they transform her into a spectacle.

Criticisms aside, the fashionable *hijabi* empowers Nigérien women who feel tasked with the moral responsibility of embodying both piety (through modest conduct) and modernity (through the up-to-date-ness of their attire). The strategies through which women balance the – occasionally conflicting – demands of trend-setting fashions and Islamic norms vary widely. A pious law student told me that she carefully chose her *hijabi* each morning so that it matched the rest of her outfit. For some of her peers, on the other hand, the *hijabi* was part of the special dress clothes one wore during Ramadan to demonstrate one's fashion-forwardness. Thanks to the proliferation of head coverings of diverse inspiration, women can make use of piously coded items to suit their own agenda.

If trendy piety has generated its own ambivalence, it has also been experienced by some women as liberating. A sociology student admitted that wearing a *hijabi* allowed her to skimp on clothes. The knee-length *hijabai* she purchased at the market were cheaper than the tailored outfits she used to order every so often from her tailor. Wearing a *hijabi* not only enhanced her confidence in public spaces but it also freed her from both the 'tyranny' of fashion and the need to constantly reinvest in her wardrobe. An older woman stressed the convenience the *hijabi* offered during the hot season: she often used the *hijabi* as both dress and outerwear, forgoing entirely the tailored blouse that is typically worn with a matching wrapper under the veil. Because it allowed air to circulate underneath, the roomy garment was a comfortable alternative to the more restrictive blouse she wore during the rest of the year.

Veiling as embodied practice

Much has been written about the significance of veiling as a symptom of patriarchal oppression, a sign of religious devotion, a means of creating social distinctions, an instrument of nationalist consciousness, and a tool of female emancipation. Increasingly, however, studies stress the 'impossibility of generalizing about the veil' (Rabine 2013, 103). The problem remains that as an idiosyncrasy that needs to be accounted for, veiling mobilizes explanations that typically cast the *hijabi* and other styles of modest dress as an expressive practice. In short: a matter of representation. By focusing exclusively on the social significance of veils, analysts have lost track of the materiality of clothing and of the critical role it plays in 'producing different types of bodies and demeanors' (Andrewes 2005, 15).

Clothes, it is worth noting, are designed to be worn on a live, moving body. Their presence on the body 'prompt[s], mould[s], and shape[s]' its movements and 'position[s] it into the conventional stance, allowing the wearer to experience and understand in a special way the ideas and notions which belong within that convention' (Andrewes 2005, 4). The way in which dress guides the body, instructing it on how it should sit, stand, restrain itself, or expand its stance ultimately means that we cannot understand how dress 'works' without taking into account 'what it means to be clothed, to experience clothing on one's body' (Bastian 1996, 100).

In other words, we must recognize that the body is 'the inevitable starting point of dress, as well as its inescapable partner' (Andrewes 2005, 31). Rather than claiming that veiling signifies this or that, I consider here how veiling can be said to instantiate a type of 'situated bodily practice' (Andrewes 2005, 32) in which dress and body work with each other, enabling the wearer to perform her expected role in public space.

Misty Bastian (2013, 17) writes of how unnatural it felt to be 'bundled into seven yards of fabric' in the traditional Igbo style for a special event soon after she arrived in Onitsha, Nigeria. At first the thick cotton wrapper she tied around her waist unravelled each time she moved; once it was securely fastened, however, she could hardly breathe. In a similar manner, Liza Dalby (1993, 325–6) describes how, when she started wearing a kimono in Kyoto, Japan, 'walking rendered [her] breathless, and moving around seemed an unnatural activity'. Dress does not automatically translate into a smooth bodily presentation, especially when it involves styles of clothes that feel uncomfortable, constraining the body in awkward, at times, painful ways. The way in which dress and body come together as situated bodily practice is the outcome of a learning process, what Joanne Entwistle and Elizabeth Wilson (2001) call 'embodied competence'. This competence relates to the skills with which people wear clothes so as to produce desirable 'embodied identities' (Hendrickson 1996). During this process a whole set of postures, movements and gestures are progressively sedimented as routine embodied practice; eventually dress and body 'work' together as if intuitively.

Many Nigérien girls start wearing a *hijabi* around the age of 4 or 5, sometimes earlier. One occasionally comes across a baby girl carried on her mother's back who is fitted with her own tiny *hijabi*. More than simply signalling her family's pious commitment, the *hijabi* a young girl wears is an intimate part of her religious training. 'Training' here refers to the process through which moral rules become internalized by the body, acquiring the status of embodied habits. It describes how the body comes to inhabit the *hijabi*, heightening the wearer's awareness of her moral selfhood. Instead of being given expression through verbal declarations of faith or religious acts, piety here is naturalized as a form of embodied competence. While initially serving as a means with which a woman or a girl trains herself to act modestly, veiling ultimately 'constitute[s] the very substance of her intimate, valorized interiority' (Mahmood 2001:214). Considering dress as a form of practice thus requires that we attend to the formative role of dress over time. For our current purposes, it further means asking how veiling, as an ethical practice, works to transform individuals into subjects of a particular moral discourse (Foucault 1997).

With time, our bodies come to adapt to the contours and constraints of dress and footwear. So comfortable do we become with our clothes, shoes and headwear that we expect their feel on our bodies and 'miss that constriction if it is absent' (Dalby 1993, 326). Saba Mahmood (2001, 214) describes how, for young reformist Muslim women living in Cairo, veiling exemplifies the mutually constitutive relation between 'body learning and body sense' in such a way that the 'body literally comes to feel uncomfortable if [one] were *not* to veil'. Similarly the *hijabi* many Nigérien women wear on a daily basis affect their embodied experience and the way they move in space so that they do not feel quite themselves without it. It is so integral to the contours of their selfhood, to the sense of agentive autonomy it helps to produce that its absence is experienced as a 'sense of incompleteness' (Fanon 1965, 59).

Conclusion: The work of veiling

In this chapter I have suggested how, to paraphrase Mahmood (20005, 56), the meaning of the *hijabi* is not exhausted by its significance as a sign but 'encompasses an entire way of being and acting that is learned through the practice of veiling'. In closing, I consider 40-year-old Halimatou's testimony of how veiling constitutes a 'way of being and acting'. Halimatou, a teacher and divorced mother of two who lived in her father's compound, put on a *hijabi* five times a day in preparation for the prayer she accomplished in her home. She wore modest attire when stepping outside but reserved the *hijabi* for her encounters with God. 'In front of God, I am all alone. He sees me completely, therefore I must be modestly dressed. The Qur'an tells women to cover themselves. During prayer, only God sees me. This is why I have to cover myself'. After each prayer, she took off her *hijabi* and folded it back into a large shopping bag.

It is a requirement for women to cover their heads during worship. For Halimatou, however, this requirement meant fully covering herself. She was so accustomed to put on a *hijabi* after performing her ablutions that she felt she could not pray unless she wore her special 'prayer' *hijabi*. Without the *hijabi*, she lacked the motivation to perform prayer. The importance of veiling and other ethical practices, Mahmood, following Foucault, argues (2005, 29), 'does not reside in the meanings they signify to their practitioners, but in the work they do in constituting the individual; similarly, the body is not a medium of signification but the substance and the necessary tool through which the embodied subject is formed'. The *hijabi* was central to Halimatou's definition of her pious subjectivity not because of what it signified but because of the work it performed, helping shape the corporeal sense of self-defined interiority that sincere, effective communication with God required.

References

Alidou, Ousseina D. 2005. *Engaging Modernity: Muslim Women and the Politics of Agency in Postcolonial Niger*. Madison, WI: University of Wisconsin Press.

Andrewes, Janet. 2005. *Bodywork: Dress as Cultural Tool*. Leiden: Brill.

Bastian, Misty L. 1996. 'Female "Alhajis" and Entrepreneurial Fashions: Flexible Identities in Southeastern Nigerian Clothing Practice'. In *Clothing and Difference: Embodied Identities in Colonial and Post-Colonial Africa*, edited by Hildi Hendrickson, 97–133. Durham, NC: Duke University Press.

Bastian, Misty L. 2013. 'Dressing for Success: The Politically Performative Quality of an Igbo Woman's Attire'. In *African Dress: Fashion, Agency, Performance*, edited by Karen Tranberg Hansen and D. Soyini Madison, 15–29. New York: Bloomsbury.

Bourdieu, Pierre. 1984. *Distinction: A Social Critique of the Judgment of Taste*. Cambridge, MA: Harvard University Press.

Cooper, Barbara M. 2003. 'Anatomy of a Riot: The Social Imaginary, Single Women, and Religious Violence in Niger'. *Canadian Journal of African Studies* 37(2/3):467–513.

Dalby, Liza. 1993. *Kimono: Fashioning Culture*. New Haven, CT: Yale University Press.

Entwistle, Joanne and Elizabeth B. Wilson. 2001. 'Introduction'. In *Body Dressing*, edited by Joanne Entwistle and Elizabeth B. Wilson. New York: Bloomsbury.

Fanon, Frantz. 1965. *A Dying Colonialism*, translated by Haakon Chevalier. New York: Grove.

Foucault, Michel. 1997. *Essential Works of Foucault, 1954–1984*, Vol. 1: *Ethics: Subjectivity and Truth*, edited by Paul Rabinow, translated by R. Hurley. New York: New Press.

Goffman Erving. 1963. *Behavior in Public Places: Notes on the Social Organization of Gatherings*. New York: Free Press.

Grégoire, Emmanuel. 1992. *The Alhazai of Maradi: Traditional Hausa Merchants in a Changing Sahelian City*, translated by Benjamin H. Hardy. Boulder, CO: Lynne Rienner.

Heath, Deborah. 1992. 'Fashion, Anti-Fashion, and Heteroglossia in Urban Senegal'. *American Ethnologist* 19(1):19–33.

Hefner, Robert. 2005. 'Introduction: Modernity and the Remaking of Muslim Politics'. In *Remaking Muslim Politics*, edited by Robert Hefner, 1–36. Princeton, NJ: Princeton University Press.

Hendrickson, Hildi. 1996. *Clothing and Difference: Embodied Identities in Colonial and Post-Colonial Africa*. Durham, NC: Duke University Press.

Jones, Carla. 2010. 'Materializing Piety: Gendered Anxieties about Faithful Consumption in Contemporary Urban Indonesia'. *American Ethnologist* 37(4):617–37.

Kane, Ousmane. 2003. *Muslim Modernity in Postcolonial Nigeria: A Study of the Society for the Removal of Innovation and Reinstatement of Tradition.* Leiden: Brill.

LeBlanc, Marie-Nathalie. 2000. 'Versioning Womanhood and Muslimhood: "Fashion" and the Life Course in Contemporary Bouaké, Côte d'Ivoire'. *Africa* 70(3):442–81.

Loimeier, Roman. 1997. *Islamic Reform and Political Change in Northern Nigeria.* Evanston, IL: Northwestern University Press.

Mahmood, Saba. 2001. 'Feminist Theory, Embodiment, and the Docile Agent: Some Reflections on the Egyptian Islamic Revival'. *Cultural Anthropology* 16(2):202–36.

Mahmood, Saba. 2005. *Politics of Piety: The Islamic Revival and the Feminist Subject.* Princeton, NJ: Princeton University Press.

Masquelier, Adeline. 2008. 'When Spirits Start Veiling: The Case of the She-Devil in a Muslim Town of Niger'. *Africa Today* 54(3):38–64.

Masquelier, Adeline. 2009. *Women and Islamic Revival in a West African Town.* Bloomington, IN: Indiana University Press.

Masquelier, Adeline. 2016a. 'Schooling, Spirit Possession, and the "Modern Girl" in Niger'. In *Femmes, générations et agency en Afrique subsaharienne: Vers de nouveaux défis,* edited by Muriel Gomez-Perez and Marie-Nathalie Leblanc. Paris: Karthala.

Masquelier, Adeline. 2016b. '"The Mouthpiece of an Entire Generation": Young Men, Islam, and Hip-hop in Niger'. In *Muslim Youth and the 9/11 Generation,* edited by Adeline Masquelier and Benjamin F. Soares, 213–38. Albuquerque, NM: University of New Mexico Press.

Mayer, Joel. 2000. 'Protest against FIMA'. *Niger News Kakaki,* 11 November. Available at http://users.idworld.net/jmayer/kakaki/k001111.htm (accessed 1 December 2000).

Meneley, Anne. 2007. 'Fashions and Fundamentalisms in Fin-de-Siècle Yemen: Chador Barbie and Islamic Socks'. *Cultural Anthropology* 22(2):214–43.

Moors, Annelies and Emma Tarlo. 2007. 'Introduction: Muslim Fashions'. *Fashion Theory* 11(2/3):133–42.

Papanek, Hanna. 1973. 'Purdah: Separate Worlds and Symbolic Shelter'. *Comparative Studies in Society and History* 34(1):66–109.

Rabine, Leslie W. 2013. 'Religious Modesty, Fashionable Glamour, and Cultural Text: Veiling in Senegal'. In *Veiling in Africa,* edited by Elisha P. Renne, 85–109. Bloomington, IN: Indiana University Press.

Renne, Elisha P., ed. 2013. *Veiling in Africa.* Bloomington, IN: Indiana University Press.

Sandıkçı, Özlem and Güliz Ger. 2005. 'Aesthetics, Ethics, and Politics of the Turkish Headscarf'. In *Clothing and Material Culture,* edited by Suzanne Küchler and Daniel Miller, 61–82. London: Berg.

Selby, Jennifer. 2016. '"The Diamond Ring Now Is the Thing": Young Muslim Torontonian Women Negotiating Mahr on the Web'. In *Muslim Youth and the 9/11 Generation,* edited by Adeline Masquelier and Benjamin F. Soares, 189–212. Albuquerque, NM: University of New Mexico Press.

Sounaye, Abdoulaye. 2005. 'Les politiques de l'Islam au Niger dans l'ère de la démocratization de 1991 à 2002'. In *L'Islam politique au sud du Sahara: Identités. Discours, et enjeux,* edited by Muriel Perez-Gomez, 503–525. Paris: Karthala.

Sounaye, Abdoulaye. 2009. 'Islam, État et société: À la recherche d'une éthique publique au Niger'. In *Islam, État et société en Afrique,* edited by René Otayek et Benjamin Soares, 327–352. Paris: Karthala.

Tarlo, Emma. 2010. *Visibly Muslim: Fashion, Politics, Faith.* Oxford: Berg.

Umar, Sani. 1993. 'Changing Identity in Nigeria from the 1960s to the 1980s: From Sufism to Anti-Sufism'. In *Muslim Identity and Social Change in sub-Saharan Africa,* edited by Louis Brenner, 154–78. Bloomington, IN: Indiana University Press.

13

THE 'DISCIPLINE OF THE VEIL' AMONG CONVERTS TO ISLAM IN FRANCE AND QUEBEC

Framing gender and expressing femininity

Géraldine Mossière

Introduction

In the course of the Islamic revivalism currently spreading across Muslim countries (Deeb 2006; Mahmood 2005; Shirazi 2000; Torab 1996), many women have adopted the veil as a symbol of negation of Western values and domination. However, in Europe and North America where Muslims live as minorities, what sorts of clothing practices do female believers display? What kinds of fashion style have they developed and how? What discourse on femininity do these strategies convey? The particular focus of this chapter is on women who embraced Islam in France and Quebec (Canada). For these converts, being Muslim does not necessarily mean wearing clothes with 'oriental' designs. Far from it, they are starting their own clothing companies so as to produce distinct Muslim-Western fashions that they promote through the Internet. By interpreting Islam in a context that is not framed upon Islamic standards, converts construct alternative religious and social representations of Muslim identity that accord with their own interpretation of the Qur'an while simultaneously incorporating the Western background within which they were socialized. In this regard, the many ways that they embody Muslim modesty and simultaneously integrate into their environment (family, workplace, and so on) make it clear that fashion, religion, culture and identity are interacting in multiple, creative ways. This contribution draws on an ethnographic case study that was conducted amongst female converts to Islam in France and Quebec between 2006 and 2008. As the data shed light on the various strategies new Muslims develop for combining Muslim dress codes with Western styles, I show how, for these women, negotiating Islamic dress codes help to embody Islamic gender discipline while developing innovative, creative and personalized fashion styles. New Muslims shape thereby a specific form of feminism aimed at re-moralizing the self and the society.

The convert women of the study

In Quebec, as in France, the number of converts to Islam is on the rise, as indicated by the current influx of non-Muslim Westerners to mosques, the increased enrolment in Arabic language courses, and the commercial success of the English version of the Qur'an. Furthermore, it has been observed that the number of women converts is notably higher than that of men. From 2006 to 2008, I conducted 40 interviews in France and 38 in Quebec with women who embraced Islam, in addition to a few informal meetings with members of their social circles, and with the significant actors who led their path in Islam. I focused on their conversion trajectories within their personal biographies. The decision to embrace Islam was thus situated in the new Muslim's personal trajectory, starting from childhood and (possible) first religious socialization until the first encounter and discovery of Islam, the *shahada* (formal ritual of conversion), the adoption of religious practices and rituals, as well as adhesion to a new community. Observations were carried out at Islamic learning centres for new Muslims during lessons on Islam addressed to converts as well as during social activities organized by the interviewees (dinners, social activities for matching potential partners, and so on). I also examined the social, religious and family trajectories of 5 of the 40 converts I met in each country. I participated in the converts' everyday lives that are mainly structured around gathering with other Muslims, either at the mosque or in their homes. I also had informal conversations with family members or people from their social circles, as well as with the contact persons who introduced them to Islam. My first participants were recruited by snowball method, and later, by means of advertisements shared by some converts on private Muslim forums. Apart from a handful of converts who refused to participate in the study for fear of a potential ideological and media instrumentalization of their narratives, the recruitment was unexpectedly highly successful. A lot of women expressed gratitude for the possibility to speak about their experience in a secure and non-discriminating environment.

All participants were socialized in France or in Quebec, most were in their 30s or younger, and the majority were homemakers or students. In both France and Quebec, the vast majority of my subjects resided in large cities although half of them grew up in rural settings (Paris, Lyon, Bordeaux, Rennes, Marseille, among others in France; Montreal and Quebec in the province of Quebec). Many of the women had relocated to cities to pursue post-secondary education and sometimes to escape from a closed or 'narrow-minded' rural environment. Although a few had converted to Islam more than ten years before our interview, most had converted after 9/11. A few interviewees had been divorced at least once, and nearly all of them had remarried Muslim partners at the time of the interview. Most of these partners were Muslim-born, and were not always as pious as their wives. Although their husbands were usually first or second-generation immigrants from North Africa and, to a lesser extent, from the Middle East, all respondents identified as both Muslim and French or Quebecois. Moreover, only a small number planned to move to a Muslim country in the future because, although some of these women were facing religious or social prejudice, liberal democracy remained, according to them, the best environment for everyday Muslim life that is, a life based on their interpretation of Islam.

Their conversion paths followed similar steps[1] in France as in Quebec although these patterns may have differed in chronology and intensity. The conversion experience of Amelie, a 30-year-old Quebecoise woman, exemplifies the first steps of this path: Amelie worked as the head of a call centre in Montreal while studying administration. When we met, she had embraced Islam for two years and asserted she had always believed in God although she had never 'really' practised any religion in particular. She had met Mourad, an immigrant of Moroccan descent four years earlier. Although Mourad was not a practising Muslim, he strongly abided by some values, like refusing cohabitation before marriage. Quite intrigued by his behaviour that she qualified as 'very quiet all the time', Amelie decided she wanted to know more about Islam. She then embraced conversation with a Muslim woman since she 'needed to know how it is to be Muslim for a woman. Because, whether you want it or not, there are more prescriptions for women. It is harder for women.'

Empirical observations show a series of common features among the women I met: all 80 women were passionate, committed, infatuated with justice, and pragmatic; they also often saw themselves as rebels and nonconformists. Most of them reported they had religious beliefs before their conversion or, at least, questions that made them receptive to Islam, a religion they perceived in continuity with their existing religious life. The religious education and experience of my interviewees varied from atheist, secular to pious Christian milieus, and diverse New Age trends. Some explored different religious traditions, so that they may have qualified as 'serial converts'. The testimony of a few women who quitted Islam soon after their conversion suggested that the Muslim option may only be a temporary stop in their overall trajectory. In spite of the diversity of the profiles and of the trajectories I describe, the women's narratives draw on a series of common themes that display their attraction to Islam, as well as disaffection for a Western lifestyle, notably the everyday discipline of religious life, the rationality of Islamic prescriptions, the spiritual path following conversion, the redefinition of the concepts of modesty and piety, the lifestyle centred on family, the importance of the role of spouse and mother and of conservative values, the strength of community ties, the excessive individualism in contemporary societies, the abusive patterns of sexuality prevailing in the West, the objectification of the Western female body, and existing discrepancies within Christianity and in the Catholic church.

These women try to navigate the extensive body of writing and the various Islamic schools of thought by appropriating a dress code that suits their own understanding of their aims. All the converts I met acknowledged the importance of wearing loose clothes that do not reveal their waistline, bosom, legs, arms and, for the majority, their hair. Although aesthetic concerns may influence their dress practices, their clothing is designed mainly to embody their new religious identity as well as to gradually construct the specific gendered structure new Muslims attribute to their religion. Since they have not been socialized in a Muslim context, converts usually learn Islamic dispositions by relying on a meticulous reading of the Holy Scriptures aimed at grasping the underlying logic of religious prescriptions. Their approach is therefore based on the acquisition of Islamic knowledge and on a process of rationalizing the Holy Scriptures.

The 'discipline of the veil':[2] Body and gender

Navigating between the manifold interpretations of the *Qur'an* and the diverse impacts of those interpretations on modesty as a lived experience for Muslim women, the converts I've met adhere to a strict and literal definition of clothing prescriptions that are shared by the main Sunni schools of law, among which are the following: woman's obligation to cover her body, excluding her face and hands, except in front of men to whom marriage is not permitted (*mahram*), and clothes should not be worn tight or show the outlines of the body.[3] These Islamic clothing regulations follow Muslim representations that frame women as objects of passion and symbols of carnal temptation. By contrast, men embody weakness but also reason as they are endowed with the propensity to control women's inner predisposition toward eroticism. These conceptions of gender that are governed by a perception of sexuality based on instinct hinge upon values of modesty, chastity and virtue as a way to literally and figuratively cloak the sexual identity of women by keeping it covered up with clothing. The hair of women particularly embodies this dangerous, seductive beauty.

In this context, a significant number of participants emphasized to me the need to cover all parts of the body except for the face and hands because they aimed at controlling the body and the variety of its experiences in earthly life: sexuality, virginity, cleanliness and maintenance. Their clothing choices are meant to de-eroticize and desexualize their female bodies, so as to channel their potential for chaotic passion towards helping to maintain social order. As one converted Quebecois explained:

> The veil brings a distance, it erases gender between men and women in that we are all human beings. With the veil, there is less to remind us that there is a difference and I believe that men are more easily distracted by a feminine presence than the other way around.

Later however, this same woman admitted that a modest dress code is not always an adequate safeguard against assaults by the opposite sex: 'Having said that, it does not prevent men to come and see you, whether you wear the veil or not. Sometimes when I go out, men look at me, they talk to me in Arabic . . . it doesn't prevent them.'

Generally speaking, newly converted Muslims shape their gender identity in relation to the Prophet's wives, who are seen as the ideal figure of maternity, sweetness, modesty, shyness and elegance. The Prophet's youngest wife, Aisha, is thought to represent the perfect seductive model that new Muslim women aspire to in regards to the private, intimate sphere that they share with their husbands. The attention that women pay to their clothing and appearance underlines the degree of virtue that they demonstrate in all aspects of their daily lives, in their effort to protect the honour of their menfolk and to help to maintain social harmony and order. A Quebecois woman, explained:

> It's a respect among women. We do not all share the same beauty and we always compare to each other . . . Of course some women are more pretty than others or when you are young, you're better shaped than when you're older. So when you're dressed and you can hardly see anything, it's like a mutual respect for other women. You could tell me that we're able to control our emotions. But to what extent are we really able to do so?

Accordingly, new Muslims often choose to wear loose-fitting pants or long skirts under tunics that are usually discrete in colour (dark or very light colours with minimal contrast), and fluid fabrics that ripple over their silhouette, revealing only a hint of their body shape. These women reported that the changes they have made to their wardrobe and habits of dress since their conversion are not always easy, but that they receive much support and advice from their new sisters in Islam, who accompany them during shopping excursions. Some have even learned to sew their own clothing so as to make sure that their body is properly covered.

When questioned about how they deal with the heat during the summer while wearing layers of fabric, converts' reply marked a consensus: 'anyway, when it's hot, it's hot for everybody, whether you wear long clothes or not'. For these women, the adoption of new dress codes does not necessarily imply a change in their everyday activities, but rather a change in their behaviours. In Quebec for instance, one respondent who has always been very athletic reported she continued to play volleyball after embracing Islam, though while wearing her veil and long pants and not hanging around with male members of the team. At first her attire was astonishing to her team-mates, but they soon accepted her as a member of the group. Other women barely changed their habits of dress, arguing that the clothes they used to wear before converting to Islam were already modest, thereby emphasizing a sense of continuity in their identity. They still shop in mainstream French and Quebecois clothing retailers, seeking regular pants or even a simple pair of large jeans that they match with a loose sweater, always remaining mindful of the necklines and lengths of their shirts, pants and skirts. Whereas a minority of converts are comfortable showing their hair, others wear only a headband, favouring authenticity of faith and spirituality over strict and orthodox obedience to prescriptions.

Beyond religious orthodoxy, compliance with the Islamic code of conduct may also open a space for stylistic innovations, occasionally in accordance with the cosmopolitan lifestyles and attitudes of openness that some, often young people, develop by being exposed to increased religious and ethnic diversity in European and North American large cities. In a Sufi mosque in Montreal for example, I saw a newly converted woman participating to *dikhr* rituals while wearing a colourful and light Caribbean *pareo* that she used for covering her hair. In the province of Quebec, this affordable piece of fabric is indeed widely used by young people as a fashion accessory, as a scarf, a turban or even to put around one's hips. In France as well, the dress code is interpreted as an opportunity for creativity regarding the shaping of feminine identity, as the following comment from a French convert exemplifies:

> As we embraced Islam, my friend and I, we didn't mind. At that time, we were at the university and we used to dress in large and ugly things. When we talk about it now, we still laugh, and I tell her: 'We used to dress like girls who had bought their clothes at a flea-market!' Gradually, we corrected ourselves.

Revisiting culture and religion by means of sartorial performances

The significant efforts that converts deploy to be as respectful as possible of the Holy Scriptures lead many Muslim-born individuals to blame them for being overzealous. In turn, converts often consider the interpretation of Islam by Muslim-born individuals to be perverted by their ethnic and social backgrounds. They comply for dress codes that are considered to be universal for all Muslims, as opposed to choosing local ones that they describe as 'culturally-oriented'. Power relationships between pious converts and their Muslim-born partners are negotiated through dress and hairstyle strategies among others, as I show in the following example. As soon as she converted to Islam, a Quebecois woman decided to wear the veil in order to 'express her devotion and piety'. At that time, she was engaged with a young man stemming from Tunisia's Westernized, secular social class, and when she was first introduced to her future in-laws, strong tensions emerged because they criticized her for displaying a 'backward' understanding of Islam. This led her fiancé's mother to devise all kinds of ingenious techniques aimed at getting the young woman to uncover her hair, including organizing a trip to the hairdresser.

In fact, converts often have high expectations regarding their Muslim-born peers' religious performances. Many new Muslims exert pressure on their husbands to more strictly abide by the Islamic dress code, like this woman who talked about her husband:

> Since he's not a very good practitioner, he isn't very strict, I'm a bit stricter than he is. So I'm the one who checks things he's supposed to check. For example, the man is supposed to report directly to Allah, to not let his wife go out unveiled ... But now, I'm the one who needs to tell him 'No! Those pants are really too tight, change them!'

Converts' narratives relate Muslim identity to a modern and active lifestyle. As a matter of fact, most of the converts claimed that they aim to modify Islamic dress requirements to fit with their Western background and environment. In this respect, many women developed innovative and creative Islamic styles of dress so as to dispel the exclusive link that is often mistakenly made between Muslims and 'oriental' or Arab identities. In France as in Quebec, they claim that 'being Muslim does not necessarily mean wearing a *djellaba*'. One woman reported that when she asked her North African Muslim friend to bring back Islamic clothes for her after a trip back home, she usually received such items as tunics decorated with numerous glittering faux-gems, to the point that in one case, she had to remove the gems one by one. Some have thus started their own clothing companies that promoted a specific 'Western' Muslim fashion. In both countries, they sought to manufacture clothes with 'excellence in quality with a high standard of style and beauty', and they organized sewing workshops and fashion shows that were only open to women. For instance, the Quebecois company *N-ti* proudly declares that its production activities are concentrated in Canada, where it tries to have a primarily Muslim workforce. The company places importance on meeting Islamic requirements as well as Muslim women's specific needs: large clothes that hide the contours of one's body, which can be used in professional settings, and that are compatible with other public spheres of life such as sports and vacations. Believing that Western Muslim women are 'too constrained by the oriental style', the designers use fabrics similar to jeans and stretchy materials with plain and sober colours, focusing not only on issues of modesty but also on aesthetic sensibilities. Their products are equally informed by Western dominant social and ecological concerns – for example, the French company *Al-furqane* offers clothes that are '100% made from natural products'.

Converts' production of Muslim fashion is aimed at ensuring continuity between their interpretation of Muslim dress codes and their inherited Western-style by creating new and innovative local styles, that they, however, depict as authentically Islamic. Living and interpreting Islam in a context where Muslims are a minority involves complex paradoxes. Ironically, since they were not brought up in the tradition, their knowledge of their new religion also rely on stereotypes about the so-called 'authentic' Muslim dress codes that have been constructed by the dominant society and conveyed by Western media. As a result, converts tend to embody the archetypal Muslim, that the Razanne doll best illustrates. 'Razanne' is the name of a doll created by a Palestinian expatriate living in the United States. Yaqin (2007) shows that this Muslim doll's lifestyle and fashion are depicted as a role model for Muslim girls living in the West, as well as an alternative to the hedonistic American Barbie. This polarized dress code requires women to wear long and discrete clothes for participation in the public sphere while the private realm is reserved for the exploration of fashion, for more relaxed clothing, and for sophisticated or seductive garments. Because the Razanne doll is marketed online, it contributes to the homogenization and spread of a transnational Islamic identity. It therefore works as a common global benchmark for many new Muslims who want to measure their adherence to Muslim ethical prescriptions.

In parallel to this appeal for a universal definition of Islam, other converts also expressed a profound attraction to the particular ethnic identities commonly associated with Islam, what one of them called the 'refined character of Oriental civilization and its original design'. As they embrace Islam, these converts often cultivate exotic representations of their new religion and adopt various habits or artefacts that they associate with it. For example, some women enjoy drinking Moroccan tea on special North African tea services and wearing *djellabas* or Turkish slippers at home, while others are proud to say that they import special fabrics from Arab countries. For these women who were raised in secular and diversified environments, playing on dress codes allows to participate to a cosmopolitan experience of globalization aimed at mixing alterities.

Veiling: Resistance and accommodation

Most participants admitted that they initially swore to never wear the veil after embracing Islam, nevertheless, nearly all have subsequently adopted the veil, as the achievement of a long process of dealing with their own personal perceptions and stereotypes regarding the adornment of their body and the transformation of their physical appearance. Conversion narratives that I collected in France and Quebec actually indicate the existence of a common hijab-adoption trajectory that parallels the conversion experience: converts initially rejected this Islam-labelled piece of clothing, then gradually began to wear it when going to the mosque or because of social and religious pressure, and finally appropriated it as part of their religious devotion practices. They usually claimed that in the end, they were hardly able to take it off. In Quebec, one woman remembered the first day that she 'tested' the hijab: 'People were staring at me and I wanted to tell them "it's not true that I'm veiled, I'm not really like that". I really needed to justify myself and for each look I got, to say "it's a joke, me, I'm not really like that, I'm cool".' New Muslims select between the different modes of veiling according to the way they understand their participation into public life ranging between active presence in public debates to seclusion in private sphere and virtual interactions through the web. These different strategies of veiling that display different views on ethics and morality are not without creating power relationships between Muslim women. What is more, one woman considers veiling in the Quebecois secular society that she comes from as a 'selfish choice', one that flouts her own social circle's sensibilities against otherness:

> Just to see people's reactions, it would break my career, that would be selfish, I would [only be doing] it for me. With my family, my uncles and aunts who don't know about Islam, it would make my grandparents sad. And I don't want to feel attacked, I don't feel strong enough.

By and large, whether collected in France or in Quebec, narratives show how resistance, pressures, discomfort and shame are involved in the (re)construction of one's self-image as Muslim in relation to parents, neighbours, friends and colleagues. Various technics are used to minimize the veil's stigma, such as wearing alternative head coverings that are more socially acceptable or that look exotic: hats, caps, African boubous, turbans or headbands are just some of the many compromises employed by converts. In France, one convert wore a cap when working as a postal delivery person during the summer. At the time when I collected data, these clothing practices were seen as just exotic in Quebec's multicultural context, and they allowed new Muslims to feel quite discrete or even fashionable in public. In the French more homogeneous system, however, non-Muslims instantly categorized wearers of the veil, or alternatives to the veil, as Muslims, and then ostracized them. It is worth noting that the differences in terms of how Muslims and Muslim converts were treated in Quebec and in France extended beyond judgements based upon veiling. In Quebec, Muslim populations were able to take advantage of various arrangements made for them in the workplace, such as prayer rooms or flexible work schedules during Ramadan. In France, on the other hand, legislation limiting the expression of religious belonging in public institutions, which was largely supported by public opinion, pushed individual religiosity into the private sphere. This means that French working converts planned to stay at home as soon as their husband's work revenues would provide sufficiently for their family. Others took off their veil when working, albeit reluctantly:

> I feel like I'm living a double life. I'm going to my parents, and I take the veil off, or when I'm going to work, I take the veil off. So I'm two different persons. Because if you see me veiled, you see me like that. But then you'll see me without my veil and you'll see me differently. See, when I'm veiled, people talk to me about Islam, when I'm not, they tell me dirty jokes.

Converts faced even more pressure to perform their Muslim identity when it came to legitimize their belonging to the Muslim community. Their new religious peers put indeed converts' strict compliance with the Islamic dress codes under high strict scrutiny. A significant number of newly converted women reported enduring comments from some of their sisters in Islam, who commented on the length of their skirts or of their shirt sleeves, or on their necklines, and constantly reminded them that being Muslim means committing one's self to a set of duties and codes of conducts. Because of these social controls and pressures, other more inconspicuous converts chose not to wear the veil thereby avoiding being identified as a peer by pious Muslims, this in spite of the fact that they acknowledged veiling to be an Islamic prescription. This shows that as symbols and bearers of Muslim moral ethics, Muslim women were supposed to monitor their sartorial behaviour as well as have their sartorial behaviour monitored.

Shaping modern and pious femininities

A significant number of converts were active in instrumentalizing their attire, as a way of promoting alternative representations of women and of sexuality or of challenging Islamophobic public opinion. This behaviour was more salient in France, where their lifestyles were more often targets of stigmatization. In Paris, one new Muslim who did not usually veil, decided once to wear the headscarf when she participated in a documentary about motherhood 'just so that they don't only show women wearing mini skirts'. In a more rural region of France, a physician began to wear the veil in the hospital where she was practising in order to dispel the stereotype that veiled women are uneducated, but also to clearly show that 'yes, one should be able to live as a Muslim in this society'. Feeling responsible for contributing to a positive representation of Islam transforms Islamic clothing practices into political gesture while it simultaneously reconstructs converts' own subjectivities as women.

Converts' reasoning draws on the assumption that Islam is a progressive ideology, as evidenced by its recognition of the fundamental equality of men and women, which was supposedly quite innovative at the time of the Prophet. It also posits that the lower status of female believers in Islam stems from erroneous, patriarchal interpretations of the Holy Scriptures that prevailed following Mohammad's initial Qur'anic revelations, particularly the conflation of Islamic teachings and tribal traditions. In this respect, converts' egalitarian interpretation of the Muslim Holy Scriptures subverts the liberal-secular stereotype whereby Muslim women are seen as victims of gender oppression. For instance, new Muslims argue that their adherence to Islam is a source of self-empowerment, just like their clothing strategies. Because they see Western women as victims of their own obsession with hair and body shape, these converts in turn regard hiding their silhouettes as an effective antidote to undesired male attention and sexual harassment. According to them, it also ensures that they are considered for their inner qualities and not simply for their physical appearance, allowing them to feel like more full-fledged persons rather than only physical beings.

The company *N-ti*'s commercial production draws on the idea that Western women are well equipped to embody this profile of the 'authentic' Muslim woman. Like *Al-furqane*, *N-ti* portrays its commodities as 'the perfect solution for Western Muslim women' whom it depicts as independent, working women: 'The *N-ti* woman is confident. The *N-ti* woman is active. The *N-ti* woman is intelligent. The *N-ti* woman is you'. This marketing slogan is to some degree echoed by a Quebecois convert who is married to a Muslim-born partner, and who defined her Western Muslim female identity in opposition to the 'typical Arab woman' living in the Arab homeland:

A Western woman has much more of a free attitude, [she is] very different from an Arab woman! She is ambitious, she wants a good job, she wants to study, to express herself openly, she can give conferences, she's strong, she earns her life, she's audacious. Arab women rely more on their husbands, they keep more in the background, they are less dynamic, they don't necessarily want to study or have a job.

In French and, more recently, in Quebecois societies, Islamic attire and the veil in particular have increasingly become prominent social and political issues and thus provided useful identity resources to display a clear opposition to secular 'modern moralities of the national femininity' (Lapeyronnie 2008, 529). Although French conversions have their own specificities (Mossière 2012), the fashion styles that Muslims develop in France and in Quebec show a common desire to combine Muslim piety and modesty with a Western-style based on individual agency and creativity, urban living, working, studying and sporting activities, as well as a quest for self-development and transformation. In this regard, most converts believe themselves to embody an idea of the woman that is different from that which prevails in their society of origin. They notably criticize the commodification of the female body (and its use for marketing purposes) as well as the role of the media in propagating hegemonic standards of beauty and grace. Sociologist Nilüfer Göle contrasts 'the Western woman's body, [which is] considered a symbol of aesthetic prestige and freedom, and is turned into an object for worship' to 'the Islamic body, in accordance with divine precepts, religious rituals, and the control of pleasures (*nefs*)' (2005, 125–6). As a result, sartorial performances like veiling, wearing modest clothes and fashion styles are designed to convey a morality that hinges on a conservative definition of family roles, control over the 'female sex' and enhancement of the role of mother. In this context, Western women with their often obsessive concern with their appearance, their games of seduction and their ambition for obtaining egalitarian status vis-à-vis men are regarded as obscene and shameful, likely to diminish a woman's value to society and negatively impact upon her role as a guardian of the home, as a wife and as a mother. Reminding the Prophet's hadith according to which 'paradise lies at the feet of the mothers', women contested the dominant representations of women that they characterize as 'hypersexualized' or 'commodified' like this woman explained:

You can be beautiful and modestly dressed at the same time. When I wear a large dress I tell myself 'I'm making efforts, I want to look nice', I have a certain way of presenting myself but I refuse to do some things, like to wonder 'am I the most beautiful? Do I want to be attractive to men?' That means you have to change your habits, some ways of thinking, of looking my best, I thought it was vain to behave like that.

Conclusion

As they embraced Islam in Europe and Quebec, the converts I met moved in a liminal space where they negotiated the tenets of their new religion with their cultural heritage. By rethinking dress codes and creating new Islamic fashion, these women displayed a feminist and egalitarian interpretation of the Islamic Holy Scriptures and built Muslim feminist subjectivities. While they borrowed a feminist Islamic discourse, these women aimed at shaping a universalistic vision of Islam, one that is disconnected from its traditional cultural and ethnic adaptations. At the same time, by developing various dress strategies in relation to the settings where they lived as religious minorities, converts produced alternative religious and social representations of Muslim womanhood identities that accorded with their feminist reading of sacred texts while continuing to accommodate their Western context and culture. As they came to embody their new religious and gendered identity through their respect for Islamic dress codes, converts committed themselves to new moralities that, in some cases, were instrumental in their original decision to embrace Islam.

The dress codes that converts adopted exemplified various combinations of these new Muslim feminist subjectivities, they also showed how they incorporated both their religious identity as pious and veiled Muslim women, and their position as modern and Western citizens. Unlike the secular feminist view that portrays dress codes related to religious traditions as an expression of women's subordination – especially in Islam – dress practices may represent strategies for empowering Muslim women in Western contexts and for redefining their roles, status and identities with the aim of reforming traditional Muslim patriarchal hierarchies from within. This argument is connected to Ahmed's (1992) historical analysis that posits Western and secular feminism as being based on 'the internalization of colonialism and of notions of the innate superiority of the European over the native – the colonization of consciousness' (178–9), as opposed to the Islamic feminism that is associated with Arab nationalism and is influenced by Zeinab Al-Ghazali's emphasis on women's education and respect for tradition. Latte Abdallah (2010) and her colleagues have delineated a third wave of feminism that started in the early 1990s as a result of a large-scale movement of individualization of religious trajectories and reconstruction of feminine subjectivities. This impetus toward a new version of feminism thrives through access to education as well as political, social and religious commitments. These Islamic trajectories also hinge on a global Islamic revival (Badran 2010) that revolves around techniques of individual development and processes of working on subjective piety. This movement is now widespread among younger generations of Muslims and suggests new ways of living and dressing as Muslim.

Notes

1. These steps are typically: (1) an encounter with a key person of Muslim obedience (friend, neighbour, colleague, lover); (2) a personal search for information on Islam essentially by means of an Internet resource, or reading of the Qur'an; (3) fears and hesitations with respect to the changes that Islam induces in one's everyday life and social relationships; (4) creation of social ties with practising Muslims be they Muslim-born or converts; (5) decision to embrace Islam and the declaration of faith; (6) socialization in Islam through an assiduous learning process of the Muslim system of beliefs and practices (lessons in the mosque), construction of a feeling of belonging with the new community, gradual change in behaviour and incorporation of social, ritual, clothing and eating practices; (7) announcement and display of one's new identity to the non-Muslim social circle (family, job milieu); (8) management of potential conflicts, identity negotiation with the environment of origin, adoption of the veil.
2. Following Brenner (1996).
3. Opinions still differ among Muslim experts about which parts of the body should be covered in front of other women.

References

Ahmed L. 1992. *Women and Gender in Islam: Historical Roots of a Modern Debate*. New Haven, CT: Yale University Press.

Badran M. 2010. 'Où en est le féminisme islamique?'. *Critique internationale* 46:25–44.

Brenner S. 1996. 'Reconstructing Self and Society: Javanese Muslim Women and "The Veil"'. *American Ethnologist* 23(4):673–97.

Deeb L. 2006. *An Enchanted Modern: Gender and Public Piety in Shi'i Lebanon*. Princeton, NJ: Princeton University Press.

Göle N. 2005. *Interpénétrations. L'Islam et l'Europe*. Paris: Galaade.

Lapeyronnie D. 2008. *Ghetto urbain. Ségrégation, violence, pauvreté en France aujourd'hui*. Paris: Laffont.

Latte Abdallah S. 2010. 'Le féminisme islamique, vingt ans après: économie d'un débat et nouveaux chantiers de recherche'. *Critique internationale* 46:9–23.

Mahmood S. 2005. *The Politics of Piety: The Islamic Revival and the Feminist Subject*. Princeton, NJ: Princeton University Press.

Mossière G. 2012. 'Modesty and Style in Islamic Attire: Refashioning Muslim Garments in a Western Context'. *Contemporary Islam* 6(2):115–34.

Shirazi F. 2000. 'Islamic Religion and Women's Dress Code: The Islamic Republic of Iran'. In *Undressing Religion: Commitment and Conversion from a Cross-Cultural Perspective*, edited by Linda B. Arthur, 113–30. New York: Berg.

Tarlo E. 2007. 'Islamic Cosmopolitanism: The Sartorial Biographies of Three Muslim Women in London'. *Fashion Theory* 11(2/3):143–72.

Torab A. 1996. 'Piety as Gendered Agency: A Study of Jalaseh Ritual Discourse in an Urban Neighbourhood in Iran'. *Journal of the Royal Anthropological Institute* 2:235–52.

Yaqin A. 2007. 'Islamic Barbie: The Politics of Gender and Performativity'. *Fashion Theory* 11(2/3):173–88.

14

MUSLIM YOUTH PRACTISING VEILING IN BERLIN

Modernity, morality and aesthetics

Synnøve Bendixsen

Introduction

When a Muslim girl arrives at school in a headscarf for the first time, many German teachers and her non-Muslim peers consider this an (unfortunate) continuity of her migrant background, and potentially a sign of parental control. It is also seen as a sudden change, where from one day to the other the girl moves from walking with her hair loose to covering it completely. Since the 1990s, veiling has become a matter of concern for state policy and has come to be the ultimate marker of the 'integration' of the so-called second and third generation migrants in European societies.

In this chapter I discuss how the veiling fashion of young Muslims in Berlin must be understood as a religious and social practice in which perceptions of Islam as a universal religion encounters local veiling practices. The political framing of the veil in European societies shapes how the veil and women with headscarves are viewed in everyday public life, and produces the headscarf as a particular symbol for non-Muslims and Muslims, albeit in different ways. For many Muslims in Berlin, wearing a headscarf brings forth a high degree of social solidarity and identification with other Muslims. Yet, as can be observed when walking in large European cities such as Berlin, there are a variety of ways to carry the veil. Walking through Oranienstrasse in Kreuzberg, an area with a high immigrant population, youths can be observed combining their veil with sexy dresses and make-up, smoking cigarettes and hanging out with boys. However, for the youth with whom I conducted fieldwork, and who are the focus of this chapter, veiling is part of a reflexive religious path in which veiling is about modesty. For these youths, veiling comes with obligations regarding how to comport the body in public, dressing modestly, and making internal religious reflections about being a 'good Muslim'. Veiling for them is both a continuity of their path towards becoming more pious Muslims, and a change of their social status, in that they are now representing Islam in public.

Data for this chapter is based on fieldwork in various periods during 2004–2007 and 2011–2012 with young Muslims participating in a religious youth organization Muslimische Jugend in Deutschland e.V. (Muslim Youth in Germany, henceforth MJD) in Berlin. I ask: how is their veiling fashion performed and given meaning in the particular context of their

Figure 14.1 At the Muslim youth summer camp

lives in Berlin? How are their relationship to a transnational *umma* (the worldwide Islamic community) and their local experiences of being a Muslim in Berlin made relevant in their veiling practice?

To veil or not to veil

One Monday during a weekly MJD meeting, a group of 15 young women are waiting to read the Qu'ran. Anne, a 12-year-old convert, is also participating in the group today. Anne has a German mother who, after divorcing Anne's father, married an Egyptian man four years before, and so, Anne explains, 'we converted to Islam'. She sounds apologetic when she says that she is not wearing a headscarf at school or in the street, and therefore does not have a headscarf at the MJD meeting. She continues: 'I don't think that I am ready to wear the headscarf now, I am only 12 years old. I am thinking of doing it when I am 18 or so.' She looks at Serap who smiles at her. Serap is 16 years old, has Egyptian parents who immigrated to Germany in the 1970s and she grew up in Berlin. Serap says that she started to wear the headscarf when she was 12 years old, to which Anne responds 'ahh' and looks impressed. Serap says:

> when I started to wear it, it was very clear why I was wearing it. But people would ask me if it wasn't warm and such ... And then to be honest, I had a period [after veiling] when I was using very tight clothes and such, and that was warmer than these loose cloths. [This kind of loose clothes] is also what they use in the desert.

175

This discussion illustrates the questions and concerns young women with whom I conducted fieldwork had before deciding whether or not to veil. During my fieldwork I frequently heard youth talking about 'not being ready' and referring to their fear and difficulties or a need to 'work on themselves' when discussing whether to start veiling. Given the current politicized and polarized situation of the veil in European societies, it should be no surprise that discussions of whether or not to veil and when to veil are common and emotional topics among young Muslims at certain stages of their lives.

The youths' statements are indicative of the importance of belonging to a community of believers when contemplating whether to veil, and of how religious peers encourage the youths' religious performance in a society where the majority is not Muslim. At another event, Aishegül, a 20-year-old woman born in Berlin to Turkish parents who arrived in the 1970s, discusses veiling with a young woman, Janna, who does not veil. Janna argues that it is not explicitly mentioned in the Qu'ran that women's hair should be covered, to which Aishegül answers: 'Yes, but it is very undisputable that it also meant the hair. You know that it says two times in the Qu'ran . . . Also, you should see what Mohammed did, because when something is unclear in the Qu'ran then one should see how Muhammad did it, and the women were covering up their hair in those times also.'

> *Janna persists:* 'Yes. But then, the point is that one should not be noticeable. And then I wonder. Because, like in Turkey you get harassed by men whether you are covering your hair or not! Like, if you have a pretty face, then they will harass you anyway, that is my experience. And here in Germany, they stare at you much more if you are wearing a headscarf than [if you are] not.'
>
> *Aishegül:* 'Yes, that is true. But there are two reasons why you should wear a headscarf: to show that you are a Muslim, and to not be harassed.'
>
> *Janna:* 'No one can see that I am a practising Muslim like this.'

During the weekly religious meetings, the youth were introduced to arguments for veiling which referenced both German society and the veil as a religious obligation. Among these youths, the decision to veil was seen as a duty to God – a duty found through references to the Qu'ran and by seeing women at the time of Prophet Muhammad as role models. These universal references were combined with discussions about the society in which they were living. 'What is important to you?' is one of the questions the youths are asked during meetings and events, 'this worldly life, or the one in the thereafter?' While they might face problems in Germany when veiling, as practising Muslims they should focus on their award for veiling in the afterlife. For these youths, Islam is considered a way of life where religious devotion is the only way to obtain the ultimate desire: to please God and to enter paradise on the 'Day of Judgement'.[1] During weekly religious MJD meetings, presentations, events, and casual conversation, the youths discuss and learn how to gain 'good points' (*hassanat*): by veiling and praying they increase their chances of entering the garden-like paradise after death.

The young women's favourite song, *Sister, dear sister*, by the German Muslim hip-hop singer Ammar 114, also alludes to this. The chorus goes as follows 'Don't give it up [the headscarf]. Paradise is lying in front of your feet.' In his lyrics, Ammar 114 encourages women to fight problems they will face in Germany because they will be rewarded in the afterlife. As women start veiling, they receive comments such as 'you wear it for *Allah*' and '*Allah* will reward you', and people wish them 'inner strength'. The youth also talked about the commodification of women and women's bodies in German society. They saw German society as secular and materialistic, characterized by immorality. By veiling, many youth argue, they will protect their body from commodifying gazes and add value to female bodies.

Reflections and discussions about the veil thus combine what is presented as universalized reasoning (Islamic verses from the Qu'ran and hadiths), and more localized arguments (sexualization of women and stigmatization of Muslims in Germany) in defining what behaviour and dress style are viewed as morally correct and necessary to fulfil the required modesty. These youths' veiling, I argue, should be understood as shaped both by their experience of membership in an imagined transnational community of Muslims (see Salih 2003, 102), as well as their belonging to a community of Muslims in Germany. For these youth, the *umma* symbolizes a form of belonging that transgresses national identities, and produces, as well as accentuates a transnational religious identity (see Göle 1996; Pedersen 2015; Roy 2004; Schmidt 2007). As Muslim women come to look similar across national settings, the veiling practices come to symbolize this imagined community (Göle 1996, 5; Pedersen 2015, 97). Yet the local context also plays a role in how the veil is performed, understood and perceived by young Muslims in Berlin.

Acquiring pious fashion

Serap's confession to Anne that she had not made the 'full change' at once when she started veiling, situates the practice of veiling within a larger process of becoming pious, which includes dressing more modestly. Veiling, as part of reaching piety, is not a settled state of mind. Starting to veil is viewed as only one (although important) step on a continuous religious path of crafting their selves as religious subjects (see also Mahmood 2005; Bendixsen 2013b). When a young woman dons the headscarf she will continue to learn and recognize the expectations attached to her new social position as a visible Muslim.

The headscarf, although part of a process of crafting a religious and virtuous self, becomes part of practices of consumption and an expression of identity in that its bearer reflects on the colours, textures and styles of their veil in combination with their dress and behaviour. On our way from the mosque to the metro, Naila (17) asks me, referring to her headscarf: 'I have a new style – you have not said anything. Do you like it?' Her younger brother had said that it looks like something on a fashion show. I tell her it looks nice. She says: 'I have seen how others do it, and thought about it for a long time, but didn't know how to do it.' She has not learned it from anyone, but tried by herself. She asks: 'Do I look as if I have an "egg-head"?' As I dismiss the idea, she says that her mother found it too large in the back. She tells me that she went to Hennes & Mauritz 'because there they have these mirrors where you can see the back' and she checked what it looked like. She continues: 'And the others at my school told me that I look cute like this, but I don't know. All these hairs coming out from the side, I look like Elvis!' We laugh.

How to wear the headscarf and which clothes to wear as a young Muslim are frequent topics of discussion. Wearing it too high in the back, as Naila alludes to, is from an Islamic perspective a possible sin if it is part of 'showing off' the length or thickness of one's hair. Here Naila also points to a potential criticism of the aesthetics of the shape it creates. The youths take seriously the role that the body plays in the expression of identity and the stylistic use of the body as a form of communication in Berlin streets.

Headscarf styles are inspired by popular online sites targeting young Muslims living in European societies (such as www.MuslimGear.com) and by German religious products, such as T-shirts with 'I love my prophet', but also by transnational sites and shows taking place in the Middle East and Turkey. For example, Dalal (19) tells me:

On Arabic television they have a show telling you different ways to put [the headscarf] on. There are women who show different ways you can have your headscarf. One day I had this with three different layers, it looked really professional! I had seen it on television.

TV shows, religious authorities and influential figures among youth in Europe and in the Middle East (including transnational charismatic figures, such as Tariq Ramadan, Amr Khalid and Yusuf al-Qaradawi) shape the religious knowledge of the youth. As Dalal's statement suggests, popular talk shows even form the basis for headscarf fashion in Berlin.

To dress fashionably in a modest way must be learned, desired and potentially also habituated. For women, certain comportments in the public sphere, like shouting or hanging around with boys, was discouraged during regular discussions and talks about living as a Muslim in Berlin. I noticed that veiled women generally started to gradually become more aware of their clothing and wore more modest and loose garments in order to not show their figure. This was encouraged by friends making comments, or adjusting each other's headscarves when some strands of rebellious hair appeared from underneath it. For example, one summer day I walked down the street with Nawar (17) and Somaya (17), headed to a picnic:

The two young women talk about how to dress for the celebration the day after, including what colour of headscarf, dress and shoes they are going to wear, when Nawar turns to Somaya:

> *Nawar:*   'You can wear the same colour of socks as your sandals – that is what I usually do.'

Somaya tells Nawar that she doesn't use socks in her sandals.

> *Nawar:*   'Sandals without socks is *haram*!'
> *Somaya:*   'What? I have never heard that before.'
> *Nawar:*   'Yes. Once I was going out without socks in my sandals, barefoot, and then my brother said, 'Hey, what are you doing, that is *haram*'.
> *Somaya:*   'Sorry, hey, but I am not doing that, I have so many sandals. I just bought a new pair.'

Then Somaya asks which school of (Sunni) Islamic thought allows one to not wear socks, and she says that she will follow that school on this issue.

Although she first brushed aside Nawar's 'correction' nonchalantly, Somaya next resituates her practice as religiously correct by finding out which school of Islam would allow her to not wear socks in her sandals. For Nawar and Somaya, veiling is part of crafting the self as a pious Muslim, but whether a particular style or aesthetic is against Islam and rules about modesty can sometimes be unclear (see also Gökarıksel and Secor 2015). While Somaya and Nawar strive for a universal understanding of modesty in the Qu'ran, Somaya here also displays ways of negotiating what Islamic modesty requires. Access to Islamic knowledge has created new spaces of religious contestation (Mandaville 2000, 283), and youth learn how to provide religious arguments for their choices and ways of acting. By expanding their knowledge, youth can compare religious interpretations and choose between them, which also partly strengthens their moral autonomy. Other youth wore the headscarf so that their earrings showed, although they would admit that it was not the 'real' Islamic way of dressing modestly and that they were still 'working on themselves' to become 'better'.

Perhaps ironically, given that religiously speaking the veil is supposed to make women less visible in public, the veil has become the ultimate visible sign of being a Muslim. Veiling marks women as visibly Muslim in the European public sphere: women are not becoming invisible when veiling – rather, they are made visible in a particular way (Tarlo 2010). This visibility is not only tied to the headscarf, but also to how the veil is combined with a particular style of clothing and ways of behaving in public. Adopting a veiled presentation in the public sphere is one way the youth visually represent their religious orientation, as not traditional (like their mothers' generation) or ethnically oriented (as peers who make use of more ethnic dress-markers, such as the *abaya* or *tesekür* – a long frock covering most of the shape of the body, popular among veiled middle-class women in Turkey, but also sold in Germany), but rather as modern and religious. As one youth self-ironically exclaimed among a group of friends: 'We have to be modern. After all, we are Muslims!' She then laughs. This short narrative of modernity, uttered half playfully and half seriously, should be understood within a context where Islam and Muslims are considered by the non-Muslim majority as 'traditional', backward and resisting the modern (secular) society. Rüya recognizes that the non-Muslim German majority consider religious adherence to Islam to be traditional. She promotes 'modernity' through her devotion to Islam as part of her spiritual and social self-fulfilment in Germany. Rejecting an Islam that is 'traditional' or 'cultural', the youth take on an Islam based on acquiring knowledge by going back to the scriptures and understanding Islamic laws, through which they situate their religiosity and Islamic fashion as part of 'modernity' (Bendixsen 2013a).

Fashion as a marker of distinction

The veil constructs and enables the individual to experience a community with other 'Muslims sisters' on her path to the faithful. The identification with Muslims sisters entailed an increased responsibility for improving the negative image of Islam and Muslims in Germany. In other words, a politics of representation affected their dress style and comportment. Many avoided black to 'avoid scaring non-Muslims', or worked on themselves to stop using make-up when veiling because this is viewed as religiously flawed. Many were conscious about being friendly, or of smiling while sitting on the metro or in the street to 'not look like a depressed veiled Muslim woman', but to give a positive image of Muslims to other non-Muslim Berliners.

Representing Islam in the public sphere also entails social control of how young women behave. The following exchange made me aware of this. During an Islamic wedding, a young man had asked Aishegül about a particular 'sister' [a woman who had been a member of the same religious organization as Aishegül] whom Aishegül knew. Aishegül tells me about the discussion afterwards: 'She wears the headscarf and she has a German boyfriend and they kiss and [hug] in the library and everywhere. Not even the Germans do that . . . What you do between four walls is your business, but not in public. He said that we should do something. She is damaging the community behaving like that. They are really angry with her.' Her friend had asked Aishegül 'whether I could call her and ask her to either stop it or to take off her headscarf. But I don't know. If I call her, she would probably just be angry at me, and she wouldn't listen. It's been going on for a long time, she doesn't care.' She continues: 'it gives the wrong impression; people see that she wears a headscarf and behaves like that. [They will] think that there is no difference. Either she should stop behaving like that or she should take off the headscarf. It's not good for our community.'

Indeed, veiling conveys social move this entire sentence to appear after . . . implications of veiling practices. The suggestion that a woman should remove her veil because she is not adhering to expected religious behaviour and dress is indicative of the moral implications of veiling practices.

Figure 14.2 Young Muslim women in Berlin

The difference sought by Aishegül is not only one between her and non-Muslims, but also between her and other Muslims who do not act or dress 'religiously correct' according their universalized definition of 'real' Islam. Dressing piously must be combined with particular forms of behaviour, otherwise the meaning of the headscarf changes. A fashionable headscarf and dress is not problematic as long as it is combined with modesty. Signalling to the German population that they are not 'traditional' and do not seek to segregate themselves, such fashionable yet modest presentations can be instead viewed as *da'wa* – invitations to Islam.

Combining fashionable Western-style urban clothing with an emphasis on modest behaviour, education and work, taking pleasure in Islamic hip-hop and distancing themselves from their parent's generation, links these young women to a 'vision of modernity' dissimilar to the Western models – an alternative modernity. Yet when other veiled women trespass the border for modesty, youths regarded this as working against their effort to create and sustain a particular image of veiled women. This was suggested the following Saturday, during an evening party with young practising Muslims who regularly attended MJD and Lifemakers. (Lifemakers was a youth group in various places in Germany influenced by the Egyptian Amr Kahlid. In Germany, it was concerned with improving the negative image of Muslims in Western Europe through practical initiatives.) During the evening, a group of young women discuss girls who veil, but do not behave 'according to Islam'. A new convert, Aishe (German parents, 20 years old), asks the other girls: 'What are the girls with headscarves thinking when they are in the street, joking and touching boys?' She later asks: 'Why are the girls with sexy clothes and headscarves and who chat with and make passes at young men not taking off their headscarf?' Fahra

(Arabic parents, 20 years old) tells her that: 'They are forced to wear the headscarf, you know.' Fahra mentions a video of a girl performing a blow job; the boy filmed her from above, and she is wearing a headscarf. 'You can see who it is, and now all of Kreuzberg knows it. So embarrassing!' Latifa says: 'They are ruining it for us. Why behave like that in the street when you have a headscarf?' Fahra continues: 'They can do it at home – whatever they like, at home it is between them and *Allah*. But not in the street! Now the foreigner girls have a worse reputation than the Germans! They are more bitches than the Germans.' Latifa protests: 'No, it's because you see them in the street. The Germans go to clubs and parties, so you don't see on the street what they do there.' Fahra tells us about a group of veiled girls who daily sit at a bench in Kreuzberg together with young men who sell drugs. 'Like the type of guys who would use any girl.' One day she went up to the girls, asking them why they sit there, that it is embarrassing and whether they are ashamed. She ends, 'and they didn't say anything, 'cause they were ashamed, they know that I am right.'

This conversation reveals the complexity and diversity of being Muslim and the role of the veil in negotiating religious identities through specific encounters in public places. It suggests that veiling fashion is not conventional fashion: veiling fashion includes 'a particular ethical practice' (Gökarıksel and Secor 2014, 185), that of an Islamic form of modesty. In their work on veiled women in Istanbul, Gökarıksel and Secor (2014, 188) have argued that the aesthetic ideal of veiling fashion is characterized by harmony: 'harmony between elements of the dress, harmony between appearance and conduct, and harmony between appearance and belief'.

Social control is here projected onto other 'incorrect' practising Muslims, who are 'destroying' the reputation linked up to the piousness of veiling for the religious youth. The disharmony between dressing in tight skirts or bright make-up while wearing a headscarf is not only one of aesthetic wrongdoing according to the youth, but also a morally and religiously flawed practice. While the answer to how and in which ways a woman should dress according to Islam is not singular and standardized, some believe their interpretation to be the most appropriate. In contrast to the young women who veil but do 'not behave modestly', these youth consider their own transition to veiling as including more care with their public appearance, both in terms of behaviour and in terms of combining it with a style of dress that is modern and pious.

If youths behave in 'undesirable' ways in public and the behaviour thus is brought to the attention of the public, it becomes relevant for all Muslims as it is thought to stain public perceptions of Muslims in Germany. The (public) front stage becomes particularly important for the Muslim youths because of their already spoiled (cf. Goffman 1963) image, whereas what a young woman does on the (private) back stage (Goffman 1959) is left to her own private consciousness. In light of the objective of rectifying the negative image of Islam in Germany, many practicing Muslims emphasize that young veiled women should conform to a universalized interpretation of Islamic morality. Wearing the veil should indicate to other Muslims that they are persons with a particular moral stance. When you have decided to veil, the women explained, you must also start to dress and behave modestly. The harmony of veiling encompasses a consistency of dress, and paying special attention to their way of moving and behaving to ensure that they conform to the required piousness of the look.

Conclusion

There is a variety of headscarf fashion among young Muslims in Berlin. Veiling while wearing sexy clothes is not the same as veiling with a *tesekür* or with modest, fashionable clothing. According to the youths with whom I conducted fieldwork, Islamic fashion has to be performed in a particular way, and requires a harmony between how the body and hair is covered and their public behaviour.

Starting to veil is one part of the process of becoming a pious, 'good Muslim', a step on a continuous path towards crafting a religious self. In order to be religiously correct, however, youths must adhere to religiously defined ideas and ideals of female modesty, the content of which was taught in a religious community by references to the Qu'ran, *ahadith* (records of the sayings and life of the prophet Mohammed) and other universal sources. Veiling practices in this life have consequences for the rewards or punishments in the afterlife. The emphasis on virtuous practices situates the veil as a feature of crafting a 'pious' self, simultaneously differentiating this self from the veil as a custom or symbol.

Yet veiling fashion in Berlin is also shaped by living as Muslims in a society where Islam is stigmatized and the veil is viewed as backwards at best and as oppressing women at worst. The urgency to change how Islam is perceived among non-Muslim Germans makes the youths conscious about their public appearance, their behaviour and dress. Veiling, in its various forms and shapes, makes the women visible as Muslims in the public sphere. Islam's role in Berlin, the particular socio-historical time/place in which they live, means that it becomes particularly important to project a 'correct' or idealized image of Muslim women in public. While smoking, combining sexy clothes with the headscarf and hanging out with boys contradicts the European stereotype of Muslim women as submissive and sexually 'un-liberated', these forms of behaviour also do not assert the 'ideal' image that the many practising Muslims struggle to project in their everyday practices. Donning the veil involves more than covering the hair. It includes being ready to present themselves as practising, pious Muslims, and dressing and behaving accordingly in public.

Note

1. In Islam, this present life is considered a preparation or test for life after death, the next realm of existence. A record (Book of Record of a Person's Life) or the angelic scribes record the person's faith (belief) and actions (deeds, including words spoken) during their life in this world. This record forms the basis for the judgement of where the person will go in the afterlife (the Next life). Further, Paradise and Hell have different levels, and punishment or rewards are given depending on one's actions (words, deeds and belief) while in this life (Murata and Chittick 1994, 208).

References

Bendixsen, Synnøve. 2013a. 'I Love My Prophet: Religious Taste as Social Boundary Marking in Berlin'. In *Islamic Fashion and Anti-Fashion: New Perspectives from Europe and America*, edited by Annelies Moors and Emma Tarlo, 272–90. Berg Publishers: London.

Bendixsen, Synnøve. 2013b. *The Religious Identity of Young Muslim Women in Berlin: An Ethnographic Study*. Brill: Leiden.

Goffman, Erving. 1959. *The Presentation of Self in Everyday Life*. New York: Anchor Books.

Goffman, Erving. 1963. *Stigma: Notes on the Management of Spoiled Identity*. New York: Simon & Schuster.

Gökarıksel, Banu and Anna Secor. (2015). 'The Veil, Desire, and the Gaze: Turning the Inside Out'. *Signs* 40(1):177–200.

Göle, Nilüfer. 1996. *The Forbidden Modern: Civilization and Veiling*. Ann Arbor, MI: The University of Michigan Press.

Göle, Nilüfer. 2003. 'The Voluntary Adoption of Islamic Stigma Symbols'. *Social Research*, 70(3):809–28.

Mahmood, Saba. 1998. 'Women's Piety and Embodied Discipline: The Islamic Resurgence in Contemporary Egypt'. Unpublished dissertation submitted for PhD, Department of Anthropology, Stanford University.

Mahmood, Saba. 2005. *Politics of Piety: The Islamic Revival and the Feminist Subject*. Princeton, NJ, and Oxford: Princeton University Press.

Mandaville, Peter G. 2000. 'Information Technology and the Changing Boundaries of European Islam'. In *Paroles d'Islam: individus, sociétés et discours dans l'islam européen contemporain*, edited by F. Dassetto, 281–99. Paris: Maisonneuve et Larose.

Murata, Sachiko and William C. Chittick. 1994. *The Vision of Islam*. St. Paul, MN: Paragon House.

Pedersen, Marianne H. 2015. *Iraqi Women in Denmark: Ritual Performance and Belonging in Everyday Life*. Manchester: Manchester University Press.

Roy, Oliver. 2004. *Globalised Islam: The Search for a New Ummah*. New York: Colombia University Press.

Schmidt, Garbi. 2007. *Muslim i Danmark – muslim i verden. En analyse af muslimske ungdomsforeninger og muslimsk identitet i årene op til Muhammad-krisen*. Uppsala: Universitetstryckeriet.

Tarlo, Emma. 2010. *Visibly Muslim: Fashion, Politics, Faith*. Oxford: Berg.

15

FASHIONING SELVES

Biographic pathways of hijabi women in Rio de Janeiro, Brazil

Gisele Fonseca Chagas and Solange Riva Mezabarba

Introduction

Islam in Brazil has been associated with distinct historical moments, dating back to the arrival of the 'Mouriscos' from Portugal in the sixteenth century, African Muslim slaves in the eighteenth century, and the various waves of Arab migration in the nineteenth and twentieth centuries. Although the majority of Muslim communities in the country are composed of Arabic-speaking immigrants from the Middle East (Syria, Lebanon, Palestine) and their descendants, there is a growing number of Brazilians without an Arab background, who converted to Islam during recent decades. According to the 2010 national census, there were 35,167 Muslims in Brazil. This number is contested by local religious leaders, for according to them, there are around 1,000,000 Muslims in Brazil. According to the views of local researchers, the reasonable estimate is between 100,000 and 200,000 Muslims (PINTO 2015).

These communities have very diverse social compositions, resulting from the Islamic schools of thought they belong to, their differing ethnic identities and institutions, and the ways in which they shape their visibility in local, national and transnational levels. In addition to the various historical, social and cultural elements which frame their Muslim identities and experiences, it is important to highlight that female participation in the everyday life of local religious institutions is very significant.

Muslim women attend and organize different religious, social and charitable activities in the mosques, Islamic centres and associations they belong to, as well as in various non-Muslim social arenas. Many of them wear the hijab in public, which creates a specific channel to communicate their religious identities, contributing to giving them visibility and shaping the dynamics of Islam in the local context. This chapter aims to focus on the ways in which Muslim women construct their religious identities and performances through veiling practices.

We also explore the different manners in which hijab and its multiple uses are managed in everyday lives of the women we worked with during our research, and how that religious symbol is enmeshed in their life histories, professional careers and social relationships. The following analysis is based on data collected through interviews and ethnographic research in Muslim communities in Brazil between 2013 and 2015, mainly in the city of Rio de Janeiro. It is estimated that there are a total of 5,000 Muslims in the state of Rio de Janeiro, and around 100 veiling hijabi women (Chagas 2012).

In order to address these issues, we will follow Emma Tarlo's (2007) notion of 'sartorial biographies' in order to analyse three biographical trajectories of hijabi women in Brazil. The first woman we talked to was Rafaela, 36 years old. Born in Rio de Janeiro, she converted to Sunni Islam 14 years ago. The second one was Dania, 32 years old, born in Florianópolis to Palestinian Sunni parents who came to the country in the 1970s, as a result of the 1967 Israel-Arab War. The third woman was Andiara, in her 30s, a convert to Shi'a Islam for ten years.

The context

One of the most symbolic aspects related to the mythologies about Rio de Janeiro is the 'love relationship' that local people have with the city's natural landscape, especially the beaches. The beach is a privileged locus of sociability, a meeting point, as well as an open air market where people can buy different kinds of food and drink. According to Mezabarba (2012), these connections between nature and bodies contribute to an ethos of informality in the city, which strongly produces an informal dress style in the public space.

In this way, the urban charisma (Hansen and Verkaaik 2009) of Rio de Janeiro is also embodied in dressing styles and practices, which can be observed chiefly in the streets of the city's *bairros da zona sul* (South zone areas), from the affluent neighbourhood of Leblon to the most popular one of Copacabana. There, we can find women in shorts, small sleeveless blouses, tight jeans, necklines, and other kinds of fashions which expose arms, legs and necks. Such styles are reproduced to other regions of the city, thus becoming part of Rio de Janeiro's way of life.

In this urban charismatic context, a hijabi woman has to develop creative competences and strategies to manage the way in which she presents herself in the everyday life, according to the 'situation' and the 'impression' that she desires to cause, even facing the problem of stigmatization (Goffman 1990). The three sartorial biographies presented below will shed some light on the complex processes through which those women deal with their public appearance in a city where bodily performances through dress styles are considered important.

Rafaela: 'In London, they don't wear that'

Rafaela was a fashion undergraduate student when she converted to Islam 14 years ago. She told us in an interview that she was raised in a Catholic family, but seldom went to church. She used to read about different religious conceptions and practices, and it was by reading on Islamic principles that she became interested in Islam. So, she decided to enrol in an Arabic language course. Her teacher, a Lebanese Maronite who immigrated to Brazil, told her about the existence of a Muslim community in Rio de Janeiro, and gave her the community's mosque address. Rafaela called the mosque, and the local imam invited her to visit them. As she was not feeling confident about her 'presentation of the self' for the occasion, the imam told her that she should wear whatever she felt comfortable in; so, she wore jeans and a smock. At the meeting, she did her *shahada*, declaration of belief, becoming a Muslim.

As soon as Rafaela converted, she decided to wear the hijab. She wore it for the first time during the Ramadan 2002. After that, she adopted the veil in her daily life. At that time, she worked as a hotel receptionist during the day, and at night, she studied at the university. According to her, she 'experienced some bad situations' in public places because of the hijab. She was a target of hostilities, such as being insulted in the subway queue, or hearing comments such as 'you don't need to wear that [the veil] in Brazil'. Rafaela interpreted those negative reactions to her veiled appearance as a result of a society that is not enough informed about Islam and Muslims. In her opinion, the religious bigotry enmeshed in the insults she received was a result of the pernicious stereotypes that surround Islam, mainly Muslim women, since the veil is generally perceived as the most salient symbol of the supposed female oppression suffered by them. 'Nobody was able to imagine that the hijab could be an option of life, and never an obligation', said Rafaela.

Moreover, her mother did not like her to go out wearing the hijab. Worried about violence, she was afraid of people's reactions on the streets after the events of 11 September, 2001. So, in order to avoid any annoyance for her mother, Rafaela usually took off the veil in the elevator of her building, before entering home.

Reflecting on the reasons why she decided to adopt the hijab as soon as she converted, she told us: 'I really don't know why I have started wearing the veil so early'. But she noticed that, inside the mosque, a symbolic distinction was structured among the women who attended the religious and social activities. The women who wore hijab were locally perceived as more religiously committed. Many of them were from Arab families, born Muslims, and this ethnic element was also an aspect of distinction between them and others. In Rafaela's view, as she was very confident about her conversion, the veil was a bodily proof of her commitment to Islam.

Rafaela married a Muslim man from Pakistan, whom she met through the Internet, and moved to London. Her experiences as a hijabi in this city are quite interesting. First of all, as a Muslim, she felt the enormous difference between living in Rio de Janeiro and in London, where the Muslim community is much larger compared to the Brazilian one. Some aspects about her lifestyle in London are remarkable. Observing that it was very common to meet Muslim women working in the police, supermarkets, banks and different kinds of offices, she concluded that in London she would not be considered 'odd' (as in Rio de Janeiro), and that she could live as a 'real' Muslim. As a result, Rafaela felt more 'socially comfortable' living in a cosmopolitan city, where Islam was not 'something from another world', as she put it. She also discovered London as a mature market for Muslim garments – in comparison to Rio de Janeiro – with a huge diversity of specialized stores. By the time of our last chat, Rafaela was excited about the spring collections at specialized stores in which hijabs, abayas and other Muslim garments were sold. Talking about a kind of brooch some girls in the mosque of Rio de Janeiro use with hijab in order to fix it properly, she observed: 'In London they don't wear that. It's considered old-fashioned!' She noticed that some Muslim women in London wore big brooches on the head, but she realized that they were from Asiatic countries. So, these ways of composing the presentation of the self in London show clearly the distinctions between all the ways of belonging to Islam expressed through the veil.

In this context, and with special interest for students of fashion, Rafaela developed some different ways to fold her hijab in London. She even worked for a fashion agency specialized in Muslim fashion, and produced some personal videos in YouTube, in order to help Muslim women in finding different ways to wear the veil in a charming manner. When she arrived in London, delighted with the new possibilities of colours and fashion, one of her first acts was to change her visual appearance. For that, she stopped using all the veils she had brought from Rio de Janeiro, which she now felt uncomfortable with and considered old-fashioned. Instead, she decided to update her wardrobe with other new styles of veil. When she came to visit her family in Brazil, a while after her marriage, she took more than 70 'old' veils to donate to the mosque in Rio de Janeiro. The hijab, she says, 'is not a sacred object', so the discard is not a delicate issue. It is an ordinary object that women wear, as part of a modest behaviour required

Figure 15.1 Veiled women praying in Rio de Janeiro. Photograph Solange Riva Mezabarba

by Islam. 'It's an ordinary piece of fabric', says Rafaela. The only exception was the hijab she wore in her wedding, which she kept because it was special for her. This statement allows us to think about the connections between the symbolic and material dimensions of the hijab. In her considerations, Rafaela speaks about fashion and trends and about her favourite veil fabrics (viscose and chiffon). So, for her, the symbolic weight of the hijab is not in its materiality, but on the female behaviour as a proof of love to God.

Dania: 'I don't wear the hijab to be ugly'

Dania is from a Muslim Palestinian family. In their youth, her parents fled from the 1967 Six-Day War and came to Brazil. Here, they met each other and got married. They had six children: four girls and two boys. According to Dania, the British domination of Palestine after the First World War affected negatively the way her ancestors practised Islam. For this reason, in Dania's opinion, her parents were not versed on the normative codes and ritual practices of the Islamic tradition. They used to pray, but neither her mother nor the female members of her family used to wear the hijab. In this sense, Islam was perceived more as a cultural heritage than as a lived practice inside her family. However, Dania and her sisters undertook a pathway to rescue the religious meanings of Islam inside their family. They decided to search for Islamic knowledge aiming to discover the religious 'specificity' of their family:

> My mother did not know if the *hijab* was mandatory. They came from generations, since 1918, when a process of detachment of people from their religion was already

in course. She told me that when she left her city in Palestine, just few women
wore the veil.

In the city where Dania lived as a teenager, there were no mosques. The only Muslims were
the members of her family. When she was 14 years old, one of her sisters wrote to an Islamic
Centre in Portugal, in order to get some information about Islamic normative codes. In response
to her letter, she received a big box by mail containing many books written in Portuguese,
which they used as a source to study Islam.

Delighted with what they learned from the books, the sisters decided to look for an Islamic
religious authority that could provide them with more orientation. In a nearby city, they found
another little, but organized, Muslim community. When they met the local shaykh, Dania and
her sisters asked him many questions about Islamic principles, including the use of the hijab by
women. The shaykh told them the hijab was obligatory, and taught them about the religious
and social reasons for that. This search for religious knowledge was a way of tracing back the
religious path of the family, as well as a personal reorientation towards Islamic principles.

Thus Dania decided to start wearing the hijab. When her uncle travelled to Jordan, where
the family had some relatives and friends, she and her sisters asked him to bring them some
'Muslim clothes'. So, he brought them some abayas and hijabs. But the girls were disappointed:
the abayas were too big for them, and the veils, which they expected to be more colourful,
came only in black, matching the abayas. They could not wear them, so their 'hijab project'
was postponed. However, the shaykh they had met told them about a camp organized by and
for Muslims in Brazil. The Muslim camp would take place in the city of São Paulo, and Dania
and her family decided to go. In an effort to be dressed as 'Muslims', Dania's mother ordered
a dressmaker to sew five hijabs (for herself and the four daughters). The girls swapped and
customized their four veils each day. From this moment on, Dania decided to always wear the
hijab, the garment that became part of her identity. She also changed her clothes, choosing to
wear long blouses with long sleeves over her tight jeans. By the beginning of this visual
transformation, she had to face the judgement of people in the public space or even of some
relatives. Dania's parents and sisters, on the other hand, had supported her decision. During the
period when the soap opera *O Clone*[1] was being broadcast on TV, Dania noticed that the negative
judgement concerning her clothes diminished. However, according to Dania, her mother worried
about her safety, since the Moroccan Muslim characters of the soap opera were presented as
very rich. Her mother was afraid that people could think that she was from a rich family and
could try to assault or even kidnap her.

As Brazil does not have a consolidated market for Muslim clothes, local Muslim women are
led to search for alternatives, wearing available items of clothing with an Islamic 'touch',[2] and
that was also Dania's strategy to create a 'Muslim wardrobe'. In our conversations, she pointed
to the fact that when she decided to don the hijab, the Brazilian fashion market offered 'baby
look' style blouses and tight jeans. There was the need to fit the requirements of hijab with the
available apparel. Thus the solution was to order smocks and tunics from a dressmaker, and
wear them over jeans. Dania also wore tight blouses with long sleeves underneath long dresses.
The scarves, normally worn by Brazilian women around the neck, were a freely available option
to create hijabs.

Dania married a Muslim man from a Syrian family when she was 22 years old, and moved
to Rio de Janeiro. As the Muslim community of Rio de Janeiro has its own mosque, Dania is
an active participant in the religious and social activities that occur at that sacred space. For
some time, she was the director of the Mosque's female department, being responsible for the
organization of the women activities in the institution. She is also a point of reference to the

girls and women in the mosque, and sometimes is asked by them to teach religious issues concerning Muslim women, including the best way to construct their presentation of the self through clothing.

According to Dania, if the hijab is part of Muslim women identity, it cannot be limited to an accessory. To wear a hijab, a woman has to be religiously convinced, otherwise the veil is reduced to a 'shell'. However, as a part of her subjectivity, Dania manages her preferences concerning the hijab, choosing among many kinds of fabrics, folding styles, pins, embroideries, and so on. As a local authority for converted women in Rio de Janeiro, she affirms that 'the hijab was not made to turn women ugly. If a woman is ugly in her clothes, she gets the attention of others in a negative way. But if she is pretty with the veil, everybody will notice [her] in a good way.'

For this reason, Dania dedicates attention to her individual aesthetic project. The hijab has to match with other clothes. When she started wearing the veil, she did not have any orientation as to how to do that. Her mother, knowing little about this way of dressing, taught her what she could remember from her life back in Palestine in the 1950s and 1960s. Dania, then, started wearing a square scarf, folded into a triangle, tied around the neck. Gradually, learning new ways of draping the veil and attaching it around the head, the knowledge of new options of fabrics, colours and shapes encouraged Dania to experiment with other possibilities. According to her, outside Brazil it is easy to recognize the origin of a hijabi woman just by observing the way she wears the veil. In Brazil, on the other hand, there is no easy trace of identification. The reason for this is the poor market for Muslim garments established in this country, in her perception.

Dania got more references on the different ways of wearing the hijab after meeting and socializing with other Muslim women in Brazil. When she adopted the veil, she did not have the expertise to tie and fix the veil, and the scarf slipped off frequently because she did not know how to fix it properly. Nowadays, according to her, it is easy to find in the Internet tutorials for many ways to wear the veil, with different shapes and folding styles. Dania's perception is that hijab fashion is timeless. There are many different models or ways to wear it, but it is never old-fashioned. According to Dania, many women use brooches, pins, prints, a bonnet under the veil, with fringes at the edge. Muslim women can choose among many different ways to wear the hijab in everyday life, or according to each different period of the day. Dania, for instance, changes the hijab when she changes her clothes during the day. The hijab has to go well with each aesthetic project of Dania. In her opinion, the 'wonderful' dress bought for the special party goes with a 'wonderful' hijab, and that is a good reason for an investment in an expensive veil, or even the effort to search for 'the right' hijab for such a wonderful dress. So, the carefully chosen clothes for a special occasion, a wedding party, for example, can encourage Dania to purchase other items to match with them, including a special veil.

This is the reason why Dania, among the endless number of hijabs inside her wardrobe, prefers the white ones. Because the white ones go with almost every kind of clothes, making it easier to creating an aesthetic project, diminishing the energy spent to prepare the presentation of the self. 'I like to feel beautiful wearing a hijab, and it has to go with my clothes', says Dania. Periodically, Dania discards some of her hijabs. According to her, this happens every time she realizes that 'they are not fitting inside the drawers anymore'. She organizes her hijab drawers according to the frequency she wears them (the veils that she wears the most are inside the most accessible drawers), and then according to the colours. The veils that she does not want anymore, she gives to the mosque for donation.

Dania knows that she 'gets the attention' when walking around the streets of Rio de Janeiro, but for her this is something positive, identification with her faith. At the university, she remembers, she felt like a 'celebrity', exactly because of what the veil revealed about her.

Andiara: 'I get others' attention when I wear the veil'

Andiara lives in Rio de Janeiro, but her Muslim paternal grandparents came from Saudi Arabia. After the oil crisis in the 1970s, they decided to come to Brazil, since they had some relatives who worked for pharmaceutical industry in the country. Her parents met and married in Brazil. Her mother's ancestry was Spanish Catholic. Thus Andiara could choose her religious pathway. She decided for Islam when she was 14 years, because, in her opinion, it is a more rational religion. So, she started to study Arabic and to attend the local mosque, where she met her husband-to-be.

When she was a teenager, Andiara and her family lived for a short period of time in Saudi Arabia, in the city of Riyadh. There, she usually wore a black abaya, the most common garment in the local public space. She wore it with a black hijab: her hair should be totally hidden. There were no special fabrics for the garments, but small details, such as discreet red or burgundy embroidery, made the difference. The mood of Andiara to 'fit in the situation' is clear in her speech:

> There was an imposition, a rule, we had to be in black. It was not such an obligation, but everybody wore that. There was a cohesion. If everybody wears that, I would not wear a red abaya.

As Andiara was careful about challenging the female clothing codes in Riyadh, she also took care about such codes in Rio de Janeiro. But this would be a complex negotiation. Questioned about the 'situations' in which she wears the hijab in Rio de Janeiro, she told us:

> Not in every place. For example, in very crowded places, such as Rio de Janeiro's downtown, I do not wear it. I wore the hijab every day during four years when I was an undergraduate student at a university located in downtown. But, I regretted that. I will explain why: I got more male attention wearing the hijab, than not wearing it. I usually heard things that you even couldn't imagine. So, the reason for the hijab is modesty, is to be unnoticed. But, at certain contexts, it is the opposite.

Later, as a member of the Brazilian Navy, Andiara asked for authorization to wear the hijab during working hours. It was granted, if the veil was white (like the uniform), and it could be worn during her professional activities, but not on marches and the rituals of the platoon's integration. In spite of evaluating as positive the assemblage of the Navy cap and the hijab, there was, according to Andiara's perception, an incoherence: a skirt is part of the uniform, obligatory for every woman in the Brazilian Navy, and it was short, coming only a little above over the knees. This was too short to be in accordance with the hijab, for the legs would be covered only with thin tights. After a short period, Andiara decided to leave the Navy.

After many embarrassing social situations, she decided to wear the hijab only when she went out with her husband. However, Andiara told us that she has to evaluate the situation: in situations of being alone in public places or going out with some friends, she ponders about her presentation of the self. She considers carefully places and persons with whom she will interact, because, at the end, the veil 'brings many things', she says. The symbolic elements that go with the presentation of the self in the context of Rio de Janeiro, mark the hijab as beyond a garment that is only part of a personal aesthetic project. It is necessary to have a coherence in the religious practices that concern the hijab. 'The hijab is not only a piece of fabric that can be worn in a casual manner', says Andiara. The hijab is 'behaviour'. 'It does not make sense, in the end, to wear the hijab and insult others, or argue, or even to defend the right to wear it. If it happens, it is better not to use the hijab but to keep the modesty, as recommended by the Qur'an', she added. She, thus, criticized Muslim women who wear the veil, but do not care about modesty or politeness: 'There are certain practices that are against Islam, and people do not notice that. Thus, they start a kind of performance. It's fake.'

Andiara prefers the *al-amira* hijab style for the everyday life (see Figure 15.2). She classifies the *al-amira* as a practical and 'easy to wear' garment. She does not want to think too much, or to elaborate a personal aesthetic project for different 'situations', such as leisure time, restaurants, cinema and theatre. In her personal hierarchy of clothing classification, Andiara separates hijabs for parties or formal occasions ('when I allow myself to shine') from the *al-amira* ones, which she uses on a daily basis. Andiara prefers neutral colours without embroidery, special pins, brooches and even prints. Beauty and vanity, however, are part of her criterion to choose what to wear in her presentation of the self. The dress for a party she went to in the city of Ribeirão Preto, for example, did not have a hijab to 'match with'. She told us that, then, she needed to reconsider the whole aesthetic project to match the dress with the hijab. 'The wrong hijab damages the combination', she added.

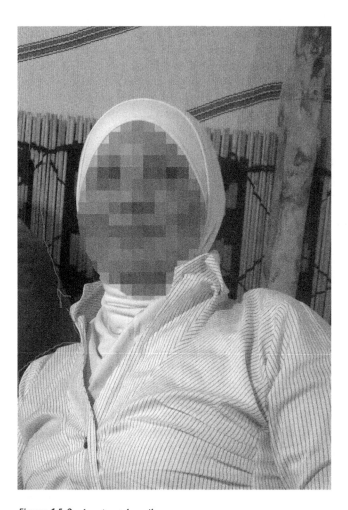

Figure 15.2 *al-amira* style veil

191

Andiara likes to wear hijabs in light fabrics, such as cotton and silk. The hot and humid weather in Rio de Janeiro influences her choices for fabrics: she prefers a kind of cotton similar to a sheet, and also materials as handcraft lace and macramé[2] from the Northeast of Brazil. Because of this, she has a special zeal for her hijabs, which she washes, irons and rolls to avoid wrinkles. They are kept inside a small cotton bag with a perfumed soap, placed far from her underwear in her wardrobe: 'the hijab reminds me of my religion, my submission to God', she said. For this reason, she classifies the hijab as a symbol of purity, which has to be apart from the ones classified as impure.

Conclusion

The comparison between the biographic pathways of Rafaela, Dania and Andiara shows the complex nuances through which the veil, as a powerful religious symbol, acquires meanings, and is used in everyday life. Living in Rio de Janeiro, these three hijabi women developed different strategies to deal with their appearance. In a Goffman (1985, 2010) perspective, their 'Muslim looks' challenge the established city's ethos, in which Islam and Muslims are generally perceived as 'other'. Although the women we worked with have in common the desire to follow what they understand as the path of God, as it comes to their ideas about making their involvement with religion public and clear, their pathways of veiling are quite different. Rafaela and Dania have a more linear narrative in their attachment to the veil than Andiara. For the former two, the hijab is part of Muslim identity: they use it in all different public arenas of their everyday life, since they work, study and perform leisure activities as hijabi women. They only remove the veil in the intimacy of their homes. Both have a preoccupation with their personal aesthetic projects, since the veil and other clothes must match in a way they consider religiously correct and modest, but also beautiful and fashionable.

In this sense, Rafaela's 'sartorial biography' (Tarlo 2007) as a Muslim woman shows that her conversion to Islam was a turning point in her life. It was not only about adopting a new religion, but also about adopting a new way of presentation of herself in the public space through veiling. On the one hand, this resulted in her facing religious bigotry in Rio de Janeiro's streets, that is, being stigmatized (Goffman 1990) because of her veil. On the other hand, she understands the use of the hijab as a means to be socially included in the dynamics of the local Muslim community, since hijabi women are appreciated in that context as the ones who are more committed to Islam. As a result, she tried 'to fit in' in the mosque space and in the local social networks by using her veil in a way very similar to other local hijabi women. However, when she moved to London, she became more aware of Islam's internal diversity, as well as of the plurality of ways in which a Muslim woman can elaborate a personal aesthetic project, in which religion, modesty, beauty and fashion are enmeshed in creative ways. In this sense, her experiences in London allowed her to classify the Rio de Janeiro's Muslim clothing market as incipient, and some pieces of clothing as old-fashioned.

Dania's biography showed us the possibility of turning the stigma of a veiled woman from a negative bias to a positive one, when she emphasizes the way she attracts attention in public spaces, which makes her feel sometimes like a 'celebrity'. For her, the hijab is a symbol of her religious identity, and a means of self-discipline, since it reminds her all the time who she is and what are her moral and religious commitments. Dania's biographic pathways allow us to understand how she adopted the hijab as a personal effort of being close to her family 'roots', as well as part of the reconfiguration of her religious self. According to her narrative, Islamic knowledge is a cumulative process, and in her case, the more she learns, the more she is committed to the hijab.

On the other hand, Andiara had some conflicts in her trajectory as a hijabi woman. She was worried about the way people would interact with her, fearing religious bigotry. She wears the hijab only in occasions and spaces where she feels confident. While Dania understood the veil as a form of protection even in the interactions with her non-Muslim colleagues at the university, Andiara felt exactly the opposite: she emphasized in her accounts the paradox of modesty, since in her interpretation the hijab in a non-Muslim context catches more attention, mainly the male gaze. Sandıkçı and Ger (2005) pointed to something similar in their fieldwork in Turkey, highlighting an important question about the 'fetish': even if the veil aims to denote modesty, in some contexts it can be a fetish in the same way as the hair it is intended to hide.

Apart from being an object indicating identity and religious belonging, it is important to highlight that for all the hijabi women we worked with, the hijab is also part of an individual aesthetic project. According to Rafaela's opinion, there is a fashion logic in the London market of Muslim garments. Prints and formats change each season in the same manner as other fashions. In this sense, Rafaela, as a fashionista, felt much more comfortable in creating her 'hijabi look' in London than in Rio de Janeiro, since she considers the Brazilian consumption of Muslim garments on the verge of improvization.

The practice of her hijab discard described above shows us how she separates the veil as a religious symbol on the one hand, when it is part of her religious identity and behaviour in a given social context, and as a garment, an object of Islamic material culture on the other. For all the religious meanings enmeshed in the adoption of the hijab by our interlocutors, we can infer that the veil is culturally transformed from a 'piece of fabric' into something 'pure' and valued when worn. In terms of fashion, the careful choices these three women make in combining their hijabs with the whole aesthetic project they pursue, takes for granted the idea of beauty. In this sense, the destiny of an old or ugly hijab can be the garbage bin. It is not an issue for the women we worked with.

In this analysis of the biographic pathways of hijabi women in Brazil we tried to follow Tarlo's argument (2007) concerning fashion in a plural way, since it is beyond the mainstream fashion industry. Biographical approach highlights individual tastes and the daily negotiation in the arenas of social life. In the case of hijabi Muslim women, we have to consider their relationship with their garments in terms of the plural experiences and reasoning, which connect them in creative, fashionable pathways. In this sense, this chapter has aimed to illustrate the biographic trajectories of three hijabi women in the city of Rio de Janeiro. Departing from narratives on their religious commitment to Islam, those women presented us their choices and reasoning for adopting the hijab in a context in which Muslims are a minority in the local religious field. These choices and reasoning are not only religiously oriented, but also a result of personal projects of self-presentation. In this way, if the hijabi women are important actors in the process of making Islam visible in the local context, they take this task as both a religious and an aesthetic duty.

Notes

1. *O Clone* (The clone) was a Brazilian soap opera whose yarn took place in Morocco and in Brazil.
2. Macramé is a form of textile-making using knots very typical in the north-east of Brazil.

References

Chagas, Gisele F. 2012. 'Preaching for Converts: Knowledge and Power in the Sunni Community in Rio de Janeiro'. In *Ethnographies of Islam: Ritual Performances and Everyday Practices*, edited by Baudoin Dupret, Thomas Pierret, Paulo G. Pinto and Kathryn Spellman-Poots, 71–9. Edinburgh: Edinburgh University Press.

Goffman, Erving. 1985. *A representação do eu na vida cotidiana*. Petrópolis-RJ: Vozes.

Goffman, Erving. 1990. *Stigma: Notes on the Management of Spoiled Identity*. London: Penguin Books.

Goffman, Erving. 2010. *Comportamento em lugares públicos*. Petrópolis-RJ: Vozes.

Hansen, Thomas Blom and Oskar Verkaaik. 2009. 'Introduction – Urban Charisma: On Everyday Mythologies in the Cities'. *Critique of Anthropology* 29(1):5–26.

Mezabarba, Solange Riva. 2012. *Vestuário e cidades: ethos, consumo e apresentaçao de si no Rio de Janeiro e em São Paulo*. Niterói/Rio de Janeiro: Tese de doutorado em antropologia/ UFF.

Pinto, Paulo G. 2015. 'Conversion, Revivalism, and Tradition: The Religious Dynamics of Muslim Communities in Brazil'. In *Crescent over Another Horizon: Islam in Latin America, the Caribbean, and Latino USA*, edited by María del March Logroño Narbona, Paulo G, Pinto and John Karam, 107–43. Austin, TX: University of Texas Press.

Sandıkçı, Özlem and Güliz Ger. 2005. 'Aesthetics, Ethics and Politics of Turkish Headscarf'. In *Clothing as Material Culture*, edited by Suzanne Küchler and Daniel Miller. New York: Berg.

Tarlo, Emma. 2007. 'Islamic Cosmopolitanism: The Sartorial Biographies of Three Muslim Women in London'. *Fashion Theory* 11(2/3):143–72.

PART IV

Industries, images, materialities

16

CULTURE INDUSTRIES AND MARKETPLACE DYNAMICS

Özlem Sandıkçı

Introduction

The global Islamic fashion market is estimated to be worth around $270 billion or 12 per cent of the global fashion industry. The fast-growing market is expected to reach $484 billion by 2019 and account for 14.4 per cent of global fashion expenditure (Thompson Reuters 2015). According to the leading consultancy agencies, given the increasing demand for stylish yet religiously appropriate clothing, modest fashion will remain as a lucrative segment of the emergent global Islamic economy and continue to attract new players. It is truly amazing that veiling, a practice that has been associated mostly with tradition, oppression, and resistance to modernity, is fast adopting the logic of consumer capitalism and getting integrated to the workings of the fashion industry.

Veiling and fashion are two terms that, until recently, seldom came together. A substantial body of work in the social sciences and humanities discusses the veil as a symbol of (Islamic) patriarchal domination and/or as a symbol of opposition against Western hegemony (e.g. Afshar 1998; Hoodfar 1993; Mernissi 1991). Rooted in the discussions of colonial domination and subjugation, this dichotomous framing conceptualizes the veil as a representational form – an abstract object full of political and social meanings but devoid of materiality and aesthetics. When the veil is defined as an over-determined cultural signifier, its shape, color, fabric, and design become ancillary, almost irrelevant to the practice of veiling. As such, in its abstract form, the veil exists outside the domain of fashion, consumption, and the market. Research on veiling fashion positions itself in relation to this prevailing analytical background and directs attention towards understanding the intricacies of the veil as a commodity form and the practices of producing, marketing, and consuming fashionable Islamic clothing.

In this chapter, I provide an up-to-date overview of the scholarship on the fashion and marketplace dynamics of veiling, and lay out an agenda for future research. Specifically, I outline the growth of the global Islamic cultural industry and the concomitant rise of fashionable veiling. The analysis locates the development of veiling fashion within the political economy of neoliberalism, delineates the institutional and individual actors involved in the manufacturing of modest fashions, maps out the changing practices and market dynamics, and elaborates on the tensions and contradictions between Islamic piety and marketing ethos. The overview of the literature reveals that there is multidisciplinary interest on the topic and scholars draw from a wide range of theoretical perspectives in their investigations. Such multiplicity offers conceptually and empirically rich and diverse analyses of the practices of Muslim consumers and marketers across the world.

Contextualizing the veiling market

The last decades have witnessed dramatic changes in the nature of veiling. Muslim women wearing stylish and expensive headscarves in various colors, designs, and shapes have appeared on the streets alongside women in the customary face-veil. Covered women donned in trendy, colorful, fashionable combinations of overcoats and trousers or skirts walk next to women in black chadors. Fashion shows promoting the latest trends in Islamic clothing styles, advertisements targeting fashion-conscious Muslim women, and magazines and blogs disseminating tips on modest outfits have become commonplace. The changes in the sartorial practices of Muslim women observed in contexts as diverse as Turkey, Pakistan, England, France, and Malaysia have unsettled the stereotypical representations of Muslim women and complicated the meanings of what constitutes religiously appropriate modest look. At a broader level, the proliferation of veiling forms and the emergence of faithful and fashionable clothing resonate with the rise of an Islamic consumption culture.

Indeed, many scholars note that, since the 1980s, new consumption practices that explicitly draw from Islamic references have become increasingly visible (Hasan 2009; Jones 2010a; Schulz 2006). People have always used religious commodities, such as prayer mats or rosaries. As Starrett (1995) argues, such objects typically have a direct association with acts of worship and serve a predominantly utilitarian function. However, the new 'Islamic' consumption styles are driven by market rather than religious logic and reflect a desire to construct and communicate identity rather than fulfill a practical function. The range of products and services sold with an Islamic accent includes magazines, novels, video and board games, pop music, toys, clothing, perfumes, nail polish, holiday packages, fitness and beauty salons, and even gated communities (e.g. Fischer 2009; Maqsood 2014; Navaro-Yashin 2002; Sandıkçı and Ger 2001; Wong 2007; Zaman 2008). The emergent Islamic culture industry and proliferation of the Islamic-labeled offerings signal the changing nature of the relationship between Islam and capitalism and the expansion of the market logic into the realm of religion.

Despite the prediction of secularization theory, religion has gained a new visibility and importance in the contemporary political economy (e.g. Gauthier *et al.* 2013; Wilson and Steger 2013). The changing role of religion in the everyday life and the political sphere is linked to the growing influence of neoliberalism, and in particular the globalizing media-sphere and the growth of consumerism (e.g. Ignatow *et al.* 2014; Martikainen and Gauthier 2013). A growing body of work in sociology and anthropology discusses 'the emergence of forms of religio-ethno-economic practice which are completely integral to consumer capitalism' (Gauthier *et al.* 2013b, 269; Comaroff and Comaroff 2001; Hefner 2010). In line with this research stream, several studies look into the relation between Islamism and neoliberal globalization and reveal how socioeconomic restructuring transforms everyday experiences of Islam and how new forms of piety inform marketplace dynamics (e.g. Fischer 2009; Jafari and Sandıkçı 2016; Osella and Osella 2009; Özyürek 2006; Pink 2009; Rudnyckyj 2009; Sandıkçı and Jafari 2013).

Scholars identify three structural developments as central to the growth of the Islamic culture industries and Islamic modes of consumption. First is the emergence of new Islamists movements – activist structures organized around loosely defined networks and groups that promote particular values through proper observance of Islam (Bayat 2005; Wiktorowicz 2004; Yavuz 2004). New Islamist movements parallel the logic of new social movements and seek to create 'networks of shared meaning' (Melucci 1996) through mobilization of various resources such as political parties, religious organizations, media, NGOs, schools, and business networks. In these communities, the feelings of belonging happen less through formal membership in a hierarchical structure and more through shared patterns of everyday life including consumption practices (e.g. Mandaville 2010; Karataş and Sandıkçı 2013; Yavuz 2004). Studies indicate that the new Islamists networks have been instrumental in both propagating the Islamic lifestyles and generating financial resources for the movements.

Second, important structural development is the growth of Muslim middle classes (Nasr 2009; Wong 2007). In the late 1980s and early 1990s many Muslim countries went through a process of economic liberalization that resulted in an influx of global brands, proliferation of advertising and marketing practices, and emergence of new spaces of shopping. These economic changes along with major socio-political transformations contributed to the development of a conservative but consumption-oriented segment. In countries such as Turkey, Egypt, Malaysia and Indonesia to name a few, accumulation of wealth concomitant with the increasing influence of Islamic movements has resulted in the creation of a new middle class 'conservative in values but avant-garde in consumption practices' (Sandıkçı and Ger 2002, 467; Nasr 2009; Wong 2007). As a result, a growing market that seeks to cater to the demands of new Muslim middle classes emerged and expanded from Muslim-majority to Muslim-minority contexts, reaching to the diaspora Muslim communities in Europe, North America and Oceania.

The growth of the new Islamic middle classes coincides with the emergence of new Muslim entrepreneurs. From Malaysia to Turkey, India, Syria, the UK, USA and Australia, these pious businessmen design, manufacture and market products that cater to the demands of modern Muslim consumer subjectivity (Adas 2006; Demir *et al.* 2004; Osella and Osella 2009; Sloane 1999). Some popular examples that received research attention include Turkish Tekbir, an Islamic clothing company; Syrian Newboy Design Studio, producer of *Fulla* dolls; Australian Ahiida, marketer of the modest swimsuit Burqini, a term derived from merging 'burqa' and 'bikini'; and the UK-based *emel*, a Muslim lifestyle magazine. In each case, an aspiration to achieve business success and enable Muslims to live properly Islamic yet modern lives underlines the entrepreneurial story (Sandıkçı 2011). These new Muslim entrepreneurs appear to be well connected to the networks of similar-minded business people and benefit from their connections within the new Islamist movements. Similar to the Calvinist work ethic, Muslim entrepreneurs 'sanctify hard work, economic success and pursuit of wealth as important religious obligations' and believe that 'a good Muslim should be an entrepreneurial Muslim' (Adas 2006, 129).

Overall, research conducted in different parts of the Muslim world shows that the growing prevalence of neoliberal values and the relentless expansion of market into every domain of life have been instrumental for the making of Islamic consumption culture and the production of religious subjectivities. The domain of fashion has been at the forefront for the public display of new forms of Islamic identification and lifestyles. Not surprisingly, the rise of Islamic fashions attracted the attention of scholars from a wide range of disciplines and studies investigating the dynamics of the veiling market proliferated in the last 20 years.

From selling headscarves to lifestyle marketing

Research on the aesthetics and economics of veiling began to appear in the late 1990s. In the initial phases, scholars concentrated more on analyzing the changes in the nature of the veiling practice and sought to explain the emergence of new forms of Islamic dressing styles in relation to the political and economic developments. Later, research interest has expanded to the actors involved in the production and marketing of Islamic fashions and their roles as well as the subjective experiences of women as they craft faithful and fashionable looks.

Supplying the uniform look

Early on researchers focused on countries, such as Turkey, Egypt or Indonesia, which have gone through a process of 'Islamization', and witnessed an increase in the visibility of urban covered women (e.g. Abaza 2007; Brenner 1996; Hasan 2009; Jones 2007; Kılıçbay and Binark 2002; White 1999). The common observation in these studies is that the rise of political Islam underlies the changes in the meanings, functions, and forms of veiling. For example, a number of studies analyze the emergence of *tesettür*, an emic term used to denote new forms of covering in Turkey, and discuss the role of veiling in distinguishing Islamic and secular sensitivities and identifications (e.g. Kılıçbay and Binark 2002; Navaro-Yashin 2002; Sandıkçı and Ger 2001, 2002; White 1999). Turkish women traditionally covered their heads using a *başörtüsü* – a scarf that covers loosely the head but not the neck. However, starting in the 1980s young, urban, educated women adopted *tesettür*, a combination of a large head scarf that fully covered the hair, neck, and the shoulders and a long, loose-fitting overcoat. *Tesettür* distinguished women who are ideologically committed to Islam from those who are covered out of tradition or faith and soon became the symbol of political Islam. Similar developments were observed in other countries such as Egypt, Syria, Kazakhstan, Azerbaijan, Indonesia, Malaysia, and among diaspora Muslim communities in the West. As many analysts observed, the increasing interest in veiling especially among the young, urban, educated women across Muslim geographies did not simply indicate a heightened religious sensitivity, but more so, a collective expression of the commitment to Islamism as a new global social movement (Brenner 1996; El-Guindi 1999; Göle 2003).

With the rise of political Islam, demand for headscarves, overcoats and other clothing items that came to be associated with new forms of veiling began to increase. Firms catering to this emergent consumer segment flourished. Many of these suppliers have adopted brand names that evoke Islam, such as 'Tevhid' (unity under one God), 'Ihvan' (Muslim brotherhood), and 'Hak' (one of the names of God). In the initial stages of market development, companies acted mostly as providers of religiously appropriate outfits rather than as marketers of fashionable veiling. Hence, promotion of Islamic clothing during the early years resonated more with propaganda than advertising, and sought to educate consumers on the benefits of veiling rather than stimulate consumer desire for fashionable and faithful styles and lifestyles.

Two studies, both focusing on the Turkish context, provide insights into the commercial dynamics of the veiling industry in its early stages. Kılıçbay and Binark (2002) report that some essential terms and concepts of fashion marketing were absent in the early promotional efforts of *tesettür* companies. As the authors explain, *tesettür* advertisements of the 1980s mostly use illustrations rather than photographs and provide information about items available and store location. Some include short texts emphasizing the duty of covering and remind women to fulfill their religious obligation. With their informational and simplistic nature, these advertisements assume a pedagogical function and depart from the conventions of fashion advertising that accentuate glamour, desire, and spectacle. At a broader level, the advertisements reflect the communicative goals of the magazines they are embedded in. As Kılıçbay and Binark (2002) argue, the Islamic women's magazines of the period address their readers as 'the fighters for religion' and seek to educate them on issues such as childcare, homecare, and health from an Islamic perspective. In general, the magazines adopt a discourse critical of Western capitalism and frame fashion as wasteful, materialistic, and contrary to Islamic principles. In line with the position of the magazines, advertisements take on a didactic approach and address their target consumers through a subdued, straightforward, and utilitarian message strategy (see Figure 16.1).

Sandıkçı and Ger (2007) find a similar commercial logic operating in veiling advertising in Turkey. In line with Kılıçbay and Binark's (2002) findings, the authors report that early advertisements are in the form of product announcements that talk to a prescribed 'pious' woman. The commercial representations of the pious woman highlight the moral necessity of covering and depict a subject who is committed enough to look different from uncovered or traditionally covered women. The authors argue that the pious woman is devoid of individual identity. The absence of the face of the models and photographic imagery erases subjectivity and ascribes anonymity to women. The target audience of these advertisements cannot decode the model's socioeconomic status, lifestyle, and aspirations. Hence *tesettür* operates as an equalizing and homogenizing factor that dissolves individual identity within a uniform Islamic identity.

Indeed, the analyses of the changes in the veiling practices in Turkey and other similar contexts indicate that the uniform veiling styles of the 1980s were instrumental in constructing a particular Islamic feminine identity vis-à-vis the Western/secular feminine identity (e.g., Abaza 2007; Hefner 2010; Jones 2007; White 1999). At the core of this distinction has been an opposition between (Islamic) modesty and (secular) indecency. Women adopted the new forms of veiling to communicate their commitment to Islam and quest for visibility in the public sphere. However, while the uniform attire enabled women to distinguish themselves from the 'less'

Figure 16.1 Advertisement for Altın İğne, Turkey, circa 1990

religious, it failed to create distinctions among those who are similar. Goods are always used to demarcate social relationships and hierarchies and this has also been the case with veiling. As wealth began to accumulate among the Islamic upper classes, the classificatory and discriminatory uses of consumption began to gain prominence over its homogenizing and equalizing uses (e.g. Abaza 2007; Navaro-Yashin 2002; Sandıkçı and Ger 2010). The initial uniformity in Islamic attire gradually gave way to heterogeneity in the dressing style, signaling the rising fashion and marketing consciousness.

Adoption of the marketing logic

In the 1990s, multiplicity took over uniformity. The 1980s' uniform veiling style had lost much of its attraction, and elegant, colorful clothes in various designs become popular. The changes in the sartorial practices of veiled women were visible across Muslim geographies. In Turkey, the original *tesettür* form came to be perceived, at least by some segments of the covered women, as a tasteless 'grandmother's overcoat' (Sandıkçı and Ger 2010). The normative long, dull colored overcoat and large scarves yielded to colorful, stylized pants and long jackets, skirts and blazers, long vests, above-the-knee coats, and smaller, more tightly tied scarves placed inside the jacket (see Figure 16.2). Covered women demanded more modern, fashionable, and youthful designs (Gökarıksel and Secor 2009; 2010a; Sandıkçı and Ger 2005; 2010). In Egypt, in the 1970s, Islamic attire was promoted as a practical solution to poverty and a comfortable way of escaping the acute class differences (Abaza 2007). Three decades later veiling 'has evolved from being identified with the underground, harsh-looking anti-establishment and pro-Iranian revolution movement, to being associated with a more prosperous, "Saudified", and petro-Islamized look' (Abaza 2007, 288). In Yemen, 'chadors designed to hide adornment were themselves adorned' (Meneley 2007, 235). As Meneley observes, by the end of 1990s, the pious dress had been commodified as fashion, and chadors had become items of consumption. Much like expensive cars or jewelry, chadors adorned with fancy buttons, colored embroidery, and even rhinestones, enabled wealthy Yemeni women to signal their status and distinction. Overall, processes of aesthetization and personalization led to the emergence of fashionable Islamic clothing styles and companies specialized in fashionable veiling (Sandıkçı and Ger 2010).

With the proliferation of veiling practices, research on manufacturing, marketing, and promotion of fashionable Islamic clothing intensified. Workshops and conferences on faith and fashion intersections started to take place in the 2000s. Studies exploring different aspects of veiling fashion published in journals in a variety of disciplinary areas, from fashion studies to geography, women's studies, marketing and anthropology. Special issues on Islamic fashion appeared in the journal *Fashion Theory* in 2007 and in the *Journal of Middle East Women's Studies* in 2010. Edited collections (e.g. *Islamic Fashion and Anti-Fashion* by Emma Tarlo and Annelies Moors 2013; *Modest Fashion* by Reina Lewis 2013) and books (e.g., *Visibly Muslim* by Emma Tarlo 2010; *Muslim Fashion* by Reina Lewis 2015) further advanced the debates over veiling fashion. Overall, studies offered detailed analyses of the changes in the veiling industry and discussed the roles of lifestyle magazines, Islamic fashion designers, and online media on production and dissemination of fashionable Islamic clothing.

The emergence of plurality in the veiling styles suggests the adoption of the marketing logic. Marketing rests on fabrication of difference. That is, through marketing practices, indistinguishable commodities turn into branded objects that connote a distinctive identity for their owners. As many scholars demonstrate, wearing a certain style of veiling communicates both a pious identity and social distinction in terms of class, taste, ethnicity or race (e.g. Abaza 2007; Gökarıksel and Secor 2009; 2010a; Lewis 2015; Moors 2007; Sandıkçı and Ger 2010; Tarlo 2010). The marketing of veil as a fashion item aims to turn difference into profit and integrate the iconic symbol of Muslim women into the cycles of the fashion industry. With the increasing market mediation of modest dressing, studies began to scrutinize the changes in the marketing practices of companies catering to the Islamic consumer. For example, Kılıçbay and Binark (2002) and Sandıkçı and Ger (2007) note the shift in the late 1990s in veiling advertising in Turkey from an informational approach to lifestyle orientation. Pedagogic and didactic tone underlying the 1980s and early

Figure 16.2 Tekbir, Turkey, 2005 catalog

1990s advertisements gives way to lifestyle depictions that invite consumers to be different from others; crude visuals gets replaced by professional fashion photography, and the image of a 'modern consumer' takes over the image of a 'pious woman'. In contrast to the subdued image of the pious woman, advertising imagery of veiled woman as the modern consumer highlight her aestheticized look (see Figure 16.3). Recent analyses of Turkey's *tesettür* industry reveals that veiling companies have now fully adopted conventions of fashion advertising and promote their collections on billboards, in magazines and catalogues, on television and online (e.g. Gökarıksel and Secor 2015; Lewis 2015).

Along with the changes in the nature of advertising, fashion shows and festivals emerged as common industry practices (Gökarıksel and Secor 2010a; 2015; Jones 2010b; Lewis 2015; Sandıkçı and Ger 2001). Turkey was one of the first countries where Islamic fashion shows were held. Later, such events became regular in countries such as Indonesia, Malaysia, and Iran. Several studies discuss Turkish Tekbir, the company that organized the first Islamic fashion show in Turkey in 1992, as a prime example of the prevalence of the marketing logic in the veiling industry (Gökarıksel and Secor 2010a; 2015; Sandıkçı and Ger 2001). Tekbir fashion shows orchestrate 'the image of veiling fashion as Islamic and modest but also chic and up to date' (Gökarıksel and Secor 2015, 134). The event combines Islamic referents with the tools of fashion

Figure 16.3 Setre, Turkey, 2004 Catalog

marketing. The music, choreography, décor, and ambiance suggest an unmistakably Islamic identity. Yet, cutting edge sounds, visuals and designs mediate the Islamic references, creating a hybrid form. Islamic fashion shows have become established practices and even got integrated into more institutional forms, such as Islamic fashion weeks. Examples include Islamic Fashion Festival Kuala Lumpur, Malaysia (since 2006), USA Islamic Fashion Week (2014), Banyuwangi, Java Islamic Fashion Week (2015), and Istanbul Modest Fashion Week (2016). However, fashion events still remain controversial, facing criticism from both secular and religious communities for promoting modesty through extravagance and showoff.

Another factor that contributed to veiling fashion has been the emergence of Islamic lifestyle magazines (e.g. Jones 2010b; Lewis 2010). These are available in both Muslim-minority and – majority contexts and target the urban, well-off, modern Muslim woman. Unlike the didactic and pedagogic women's magazines of the 1980s (Kılıçbay and Binay 2002), contemporary lifestyle magazines are glossy journals that function as mediators of taste and style. The Islamic lifestyle magazines constitute a major medium through which debates about modesty, piety, consumerism, and the female body take place. For example, in her study of the Indonesian Muslim women's lifestyle magazine *NooR*, Jones (2010b, 92) explores the disjuncture between piety as 'merely image' and piety as 'a reflection of deeper material and spiritual transformation'. Jones argues that images of women in fashionable Islamic dress in the pages of *NooR* complicate the relation between value and virtue. By framing fashion and beauty as an outward expression of piety, the magazine's editorial staff defend themselves against the criticism of superficiality directed against fashionable Islamic dress, and justifies promotion of consumption as a sign of piety. Similarly, Lewis (2010; 2015) argues that the new genre of Muslim women's lifestyle magazines that emerged in contexts such as the UK (*emel* and *Sisters*), the US and Canada (*Azizah* and *Muslim Girl*), Turkey (*Ala* and *Nisa*), and Kuwait (*Alef*) seek to meet the needs of an emergent international Muslim bourgeoisie. She shows how the fashion pages become an arena where 'style mediators' engage in the difficult task of mediating between the expectations of different faith communities, and the demands and limitations of the marketplace.

Islamic fashion shows and lifestyle media have been crucial not only in popularizing fashionable veiling but also in promoting Muslim designers as the new actors of the global modest fashion industry. A few studies examine Muslim fashion designers and their contribution to the development of modest fashions. For example, in his historical study of Turkish *tesettür*, Altınay (2013) uncovers the role of Şule Yüksel Şenler, an early iconic figure of Islamic fashion in Turkey, in creating a new interpretation of the Islamic dress code in the 1970s. The style that came to be known as 'Şulebaş' enabled urban Muslim women to combine the headscarf with the prevailing Western fashions of the time. While her interpretation has gradually disappeared and *tesettür* has developed its own trends and styles, the role of Muslim fashion designers in Turkey and elsewhere has become more prominent in the last decades. In Indonesia, for example, in 1993 an association of Indonesian fashion designers was established with the task of development of modern and sophisticated Islamic clothing designs. Indonesian Muslim fashion designers, such as Anne Rufaidah, Tuty Adib, and Sharifa, established transnational connections and exported their collections to Saudi Arabia, Malaysia, Singapore, India and Dubai (Amrullah 2008). There are also connections between Muslim fashion designers and the global centers of fashion. For example, in his study of *haute couture* designers in Tehran, Balasescu (2003) exposes the material and symbolic exchanges that take place between Tehran and Paris. Tehrani designers rework and reinterpret Iranian traditional aesthetics and Western sensibilities to produce designs that appeal to the upper-class Tehranis and the Iranian diaspora living in Paris. Moreover, some Iranian designers display their work in Paris, while Parisian designers consciously modify their designs to adapt to the tastes of their Middle Eastern clients. Such exchanges highlight the increasing interconnections between global and Islamic fashion networks and the potential for hybrid creations. Similarly, Tarlo's (2013) work on the South Asian diasporic population in London shows that, inspired by the multicultural environments in which they live in, young Muslim designers in England draw from clothing traditions from around the world and mix different patterns, shapes, textiles and decorative elements in their collections.

The growth of the veiling industry has been transnational, and the veiling market has developed through globally connected networks of production, distribution, marketing, and consumption. For example, Turkish *tesettür* style spread slowly to Egypt, Syria and diaspora communities in Europe, and companies such as Tekbir, Aker and Moda Nisa developed into multinational companies with subsidiaries in Europe, Middle East and Asia (Lewis 2015; Moors and Tarlo 2013). Dubai, Indonesia, and Iran developed as important centers of fashionable veiling industry. In Muslim-minority contexts the growth of the Islamic fashion industry has happened in a more piecemeal way (Tarlo 2013). In most of these contexts, a well-established Islamic fashion industry has been absent or limited; hence, young Muslims who wanted to look fashionable and faithful had to rely on personal experimentation and adapt mainstream fashions to modest styles of dressing. As proper Islamic ways of dressing are interpreted in multiple ways, fashionable veiling has varied significantly across different diaspora communities and ethnicities. Online technologies have been instrumental in creating a unifying identifiable Muslim sensibilty of modest fashion by enabling the exchange of ideas as well as access to products.

Indeed, the online spaces of veiling fashion have received increasing research attention in recent years. The Internet has become a key domain for selling, advertising, and promoting Islamic clothing and fashions particularly in Europe, America, and Australia. In the last decade, online stores selling modest fashion have emerged. These stores sell a wide variety of products ranging from conventional *abayas* to new inventions such as the burqini (Moors 2013; Lewis 2013). With the development of online media, Islamic fashion blogs, Facebook communities, discussion forums, and YouTube videos of *hijab* tutorials gained importance as sources of advice and commentary on fashionable and faithful dressing styles (Akou 2007; 2015; Tarlo 2010; 2013; Lewis 2013; Moors 2013). As Moors and Tarlo (2013) note, online media encourage interaction and dialogue between Muslims from different backgrounds, traditions and locations. For Muslims in Muslim-minority contexts, the resources available through the Internet help overcome isolation and lack of local support in dressing choices and practices (Akou 2015).

The physical retail spaces of veiling fashion have also received some research attention. In particular, scholars have examined shopkeepers and their roles as style mediators. The speed and extent with which new styles emerge and proliferate make fashionable veiling a highly laborious and complex 'beauty work' (Sandıkçı and Ger 2005). Sales assistants help customers navigate through products on offer and advise them on new styles, trendy colours, and 'it' products and brands (Lewis 2010; 2015; Sandıkçı and Ger 2005). In Muslim-minority contexts, such as London, veiled shopkeepers who work in high street fashion stores function both as consumers and marketers of veiling fashions (Lewis 2013). Their bodies serve to demonstrate possible Islamic ways of wearing the outfits they sell and help connect with a large Muslim consumer base. However, research also indicates that veiled shopkeepers might face discrimination in the labor market and suffer from exclusionary practices. While Islamic clothing stores create work environments for covered women, such opportunities do not seem to extend to mainstream stores in countries such as Turkey. Both Lewis (2015) and Sayan-Cengiz (2016) report that women wearing head-scarves are excluded from employment in chain stores of global and national brands, and work in small-scale retailers and *tesettür* companies instead. Such discriminatory practices reproduce the view that women with headscarves are more suitable for the world of local, traditional market places rather than global networks of fashion, and confine these women in insecure, dead-end jobs.

Overall, as fashion sensitivities of Muslim consumers developed and the veiling industry became more globally connected, a cosmopolitan aesthetic and style began to emerge (Moors and Tarlo 2013; Sandıkçı and Ger 2010). Young women drawing from multiple sources of fashion, and mixing popular high street outfits with headscarves and mainstream brands with Islamic ones, create new hybrid forms of modest looks (Christiansen 2013; Salim 2013). However, not everyone agree with the fashioning of veiling and the emergence of trendy and attractive styles of Islamic attire. There are groups that exhibit strong anti-fashion and anti-consumption attitudes and choose to continue to wear large veils, long loose overcoats, and *abayas* in dark and subdued colors (Bendixsen 2013; Moors 2013). Studies conducted in Muslim majority and minority contexts highlight the diversity of the interpretations and experiences of fashionable and faithful covering and the ongoing debate over what constitutes the proper Islamic dress.

Navigating through piety, beauty, and profit

The past 20 years have witnessed the development of veiling fashion as a globally connected and lucrative market. However, marketing and consuming faithful and fashionable looks have been full of tensions and contradictions. The difficulties consumers and marketers encounter as they juggle religious, aesthetic, and commercial concerns are significant and have been an underlying theme in much of the existing literature (Abbas 2015; Gökarıksel and Secor 2010a; 2010b; Jones 2010a; Sandıkçı 2005; 2010). A major criticism against the rise of Islamic fashion industry has targeted commodification of religion. While veiling is essentially linked to Islamic morality, fashion is an indispensable component of consumer capitalism. Critiques of the veiling fashion call into question the compatibility of Islamic and capitalist moralities, and regard fashion as antithetical to modesty. Fashionable dress practices of Muslim women are often condemned by religious authorities or orthodox groups, and invalidated by secular observers as failed fashion (Gökarıksel and Secor 2010a; Jones 2010a; Lewis 2007, 2010; Sandıkçı and Ger 2010). However, research on veiling fashion indicates that the relationship between piety, beauty, and profit is complicated and cannot be reduced to a commodification framework and interpreted simply from an Islam versus capitalism dichotomy.

For example, in Turkish context, appearing well-groomed and neat, and presenting a pleasant and harmonious look can be considered as an act which pleases God (Sandıkçı and Ger 2005). Hence, wearing aesthetically appealing, beautiful forms of Islamic dress can take a religious mission, encouraging women towards covering, inviting others to Islam, and producing a positive image of the religion (also Moll 2010; Tarlo 2010). However, what constitutes an aesthetically appealing and modest look is a contentious issue and varies contextually and temporally. In the Turkish case, the shift from the uniformity to the multiplicity of *tesettür* indicates the change in how women construe and negotiate the demands of Islam and the demands of a modern life (Sandıkçı and Ger 2010). These negotiations suggest that different and conflicting interpretations of proper Islamic dress co-exist and shape women's sartorial choices. These negotiations are enabled and constrained by a dynamic and complex network of actors beyond the individual consumer (Sandıkçı and Ger 2005; 2010). Theologians, intellectuals and feminists often engage in heated debates over what constitutes proper female Muslim clothing. Television channels, radio stations and publishing houses, affiliated by different religious orders, broadcast divergent views. Clothing stores and fashion designers introduce new styles that expand the heterogeneity in attire. Lifestyle magazines and online media circulate diverse views and looks to a transnational audience. All of these factors help women negotiate and justify different interpretations and practices of *tesettür*. As Sandıkçı and Ger (2005; 2010) argue, the often-heard statement 'everybody shapes their own *tesettür*' provides the grounds for heterogeneous covering styles and justification for fashionable veiling. Ultimately, clothing practices of veiled women indicate both acceptance and negotiation of restrictions, and juggling of religious norms and aesthetic concerns.

Jones (2010a), in her study of Indonesian middle-class women, reports a similar tension between the appeal and anxiety surrounding fashionable veiling. According to Jones, pious commodities construct virtue through, rather than outside, consumption, and frame the path to piety through consumption. Yet this path is also devalued as 'vain and superficial'. Fashionable forms of Islamic dress appeal to middle-class Indonesian women by promising virtue through modesty and beauty; yet this very promise also makes fashionable garments vulnerable and even subject to rejection by their target consumers. Jones argues that religious consumption operates in the space of anxiety and, especially for women, lifestyle consumption is a risky game. Indeed, the risks can be quite substantial and consequential for women. As for example, Kelly (2010) notes, in Kuwait, women dress to impress in the knowledge that one will be scrutinized by one's peers and any dress code violations will be widely noted. The clothes that Kuwaiti women wear comfortably abroad may become a source of anxiety and rejected as unsuitable for use at home. Such observations indicate the shifting boundaries of acceptable and unacceptable styles of fashionable veiling and its contingent and precarious nature.

Veiling fashion companies play an important role in both easing and intensifying such anxieties. As Gökarıksel and Secor (2010a) argue, some leading *tesettür* firms in Turkey claim that by putting fashion in the service of an Islamic ideal of covering, they serve the Islamizicing agenda. These companies market *tesettür* as seamlessly combining piety and fashion and justify their promotion of fashionable veiling in reference to Islamist politics. Yet women question the relationship between fashion and *tesettür* and the acceptability of the lifestyle and Muslim womanhood that advertising images evoke. Similar to the tensions discussed by Sandıkçı and Ger (2005; 2010), Gökarıksel and Secor (2010a) observe that women recognize the disjuncture between the ideal of Islamic modesty and the spectacle of fashion. They too engage in a constant mediation of the tension between piety and beauty and seek to find ways to accommodate aesthetic considerations, personal desires and religious norms.

The tensions and contradictions women encounter, and the multiplicity of the sartorial choices of covered women across different localities, draw attention to the complexity of the signifier 'Islamic'. In their case study of three veiling fashion firms in Turkey, Gökarıksel and Secor (2010b) focus on this very complexity and raise the question what makes a commodity 'Islamic'. The authors argue that the Islamic-ness of a commodity cannot be fixed but is instead best understood as a mode of insertion into socio-spatial networks. In other words, Islamic-ness cannot be located in the moment of production or use; 'Islamic-ness is like a holograph in the life of the commodity – one minute present, the next not' (314). Veiling fashion enters into and helps form broader social and spatial networks, such as financing and retailing, in different ways at different moments in its life as a commodity. As veiling fashion is a product of multiple relations and significations, the meaning of Islamic-ness is never finally established. Gökarıksel and Secor argue that 'across this shifting terrain of Islamic and class distinction, the commodity contributes to the emergence of particular kinds of subjects, sites and relations' (329).

Ultimately, then, marketing and consumption of veiling fashions and the lifestyles promoted by the Islamic culture industries reflect an ongoing search to fix, even temporarily, a particular notion of Islamic-ness and related forms of consumption as appropriate and essential for construction of a modern Muslim identity. However, claims to fix the meaning of proper Islamic consumption seem to fail and instead only contribute to multiplying identifications as well as disidentifications. Marketers and consumers of veiling fashions do not counter modernity, but particular expressions of it, and craft new, hybrid identities that are both modern and religious, feminine and wholesome, tasteful and moral, pious and entrepreneurial.

Conclusion: Further explorations

Research on the marketing and consumption dynamics of veiling fashions draws attention to the complex interconnections between religion and market in the contemporary political economy and urges us to rethink fashion and anti-fashion in today's networked, digitalized, and multicultural world. As Moors and Tarlo (2013) note, the existence and growth of Islamic fashion, 'an oxymoron' for many, 'contributes to the breaking down of systems of classification by which the world is divided into the fashionable West and unfashionable rest whose only access to fashion is by emulation or insertion within a pre-existing frame' (26). However, it continues to be the case that modest fashion is excluded from style pages of daily newspapers while women in black chadors and burqas are frequently featured in the news section and often in relation to Islam-terrorism connections (Hoggard 2013).

The small but growing literature on the veiling fashion reveals the complicated, layered, and multidimensional nature of marketing and consuming Islamic clothing and highlights the need for further research in the area. As the current overview indicates, a significant amount of interest has been on Turkey. Turkey has a long and thriving history in manufacturing and selling textile products. This experience in combination with the increasing role of Islam in the everyday life and politics has contributed to the development of the Turkish *tesettür* market as a leader in international context. Accordingly, many scholars have sought to understand the dynamics of this market. While there are a few studies that look into the development of Islamic culture industries and veiling market in other geographies such as Indonesia, Yemen, Egypt, and diaspora communities of Europe and North America, more research on different contexts is needed. Given the transnational nature of the fashion industry in general, and the veiling industry in particular, our existing knowledge of the interconnections between different countries and the nature of the networks of relationships among different actors remains rather sketchy. Such a focus can uncover the power dynamics across different countries that assume a leadership position in fashionable veiling and among Muslim-majority and minority-players. For example, studies that explore the competitive dynamics between Turkish and Arabic styles of Islamic fashions can provide many insights into the flows of financial, marketing and creative resources as well as the legitimization of different actors.

Our knowledge of the interconnections between the Islamic and world fashion also remains limited. While a few studies allude to the borrowings between the two systems of fashion and reveal some instances of hybridity, how and to what extent Islamic fashions and global/Western fashions cooperate, compete, and integrate remains unknown. Some global fashion brands now collaborate with Muslim fashion designers. But we need more research to understand the workings of this cooperation and its implications for marketers and consumers of Islamic clothing. On the other hand, how non-Muslim consumers perceive such collaborations constitutes an interesting avenue of research. There is some indication that, given the increasing Islamophobia in the West, some non-Muslim consumers express antagonism toward brands that are associated with Islam. While this research tends to focus on consumer goods and halal labeling, similar hostile attitudes might also arise in the context of clothing.

Finally, more research is needed on the emerging subdomains of the Islamic fashion industry. Given the historical political connotation of the Islamic veil, much of the existing research focuses on the head-covering and dressing practices of women. Research on male Islamic fashions is almost non-existent. The lack might be due to difficulties in collecting data (i.e. researcher-informant gender dynamics) or the still prevailing view of the feminine nature of fashion. In either case, studies on marketing and consumption of male Islamic fashions will enrich the area. Furthermore, as with the general dynamics of the fashion market, the boundaries of the Islamic fashion market have been expanding. How faith, fashion, and profit intersect and inform each other in new domains such as the markets for Islamic bridal gowns, maternity clothing, children's clothing, and lingerie remain overlooked. The expansion of Islamic fashion logic to related domains can provide fresh insights into the current maturing phase of the veiling market. Overall, the veiling market and Islamic culture industries continue to grow and attract new players. Multidisciplinary research that draws upon a rich theoretical toolkit and data from diverse contexts will continue to provide stimulating, exciting, and challenging insights to our existing knowledge of religion-market interactions.

References

Abaza, Mona. 2007. 'Shifting Landscapes of Fashion in Contemporary Egypt'. *Fashion Theory* 11(2–3):281–98.

Abbas, Saba. 2015. "'My Veil Makes Me Beautiful": Paradoxes of Zeena and Concealment in Amman'. *Journal of Middle East Women's Studies* 11(2):139–60.

Adas, Emin Baki. 2006. 'The Making of Entrepreneurial Islam and the Islamic Spirit of Capitalism'. *Journal for Cultural Research* 10(2):113–25.

Afshar, Halef. 1998. *Islam and Feminisms*. London: Macmillan.

Akou, Heather Marie. 2007. 'Building a New "World Fashion": Islamic Dress in the Twenty-First Century'. *Fashion Theory* 11(4):403–22.

Akou, Heather Marie. 2015. 'Becoming Visible: The Role of the Internet in Dress Choices among Native-Born Converts to Islam in North America'. *Hawwa* 13(3):279–96.

Altınay, Rüstem Ertuğ. 2013. 'Şule Yüksel Şenler: An Early Style Icon of Urban Islamic Fashion in Turkey'. In *Islamic Fashion and Anti-Fashion: New Perspectives from Europe and North America*, edited by Emma Tarlo and Annelies Moors, 107–22. London: Bloomsbury.

Amrullah, Eva F. 2008. 'Indonesian Muslim Fashion Styles & Designs'. *ISIM Review* 22:2.

Balasescu, Alexandru. 2003. 'Tehran Chic: Islamic Headscarves, Fashion Designers, and New Geographies of Modernity'. *Fashion Theory* 7(1):39–56.

Bayat, Asef. 2005. 'Islamism and Social Movement Theory'. *Third World Quarterly* 26(6):891–908.

Bendixsen, Synnøve. 2013. '"I Love My Prophet": Religious Taste, Consumption and Distinction in Berlin'. *Islamic Fashion and Anti-Fashion*, edited by Emma Tarlo and Annelies Moors, 272–90. London: Bloomsbury.

Brenner, Suzanne. 1996. 'Reconstructing Self and Society: Javanese Muslim Women and "the Veil"'. *American Ethnologist* 23(4):67–3-97.

Christiansen, Connie Caroe. 2013. 'Miss Headscarf: Islamic Fashion and the Danish Media,' *Islamic Fashion and Anti-Fashion*, edited by Emma Tarlo and Annelies Moors, 225–239. London: Bloomsbury.

Comaroff, Jean and John L. Comaroff. 2001. *Millennial Capitalism and the Culture of Neoliberalism*. Durham, NC: Duke University Press.

Demir, Ömer, Mustafa Acar and Metin Toprak. 2004. 'Anatolian Tigers or Islamic Capital: Prospects and Challenges'. *Middle Eastern Studies* 40(6):166–88.

El-Guindi, Fadwa. 1999. *Veil, Modesty, Privacy, and Resistance*. New York: Berg.

Fischer, Johan. 2009. *Proper Islamic Consumption: Shopping among the Malays in Modern Malaysia*. Copenhagen: NIAS Press.

Gauthier, François, Tuomas Martikainen and Linda Woodhead. 2013. 'Acknowledging a Global Shift: A Primer for Thinking about Religion in Consumer Societies'. *Implicit Religion* 16(3):261–76.

Gökarıksel, Banu and MacLarney, Ellen. 2010. 'Muslim Women, Consumer Capitalism, and the Islamic Culture Industry'. *Journal of Middle East Women's Studies* 6(3):1–18.

Gökarıksel, Banu and Anna J. Secor. 2009. 'New Transnational Geographies of Islamism, Capitalism, and Subjectivity: The Veiling-Fashion Industry in Turkey'. *Area* 41(1):6–18.

Gökarıksel, Banu and Anna J. Secor. 2010a. 'Between Fashion and Tesettür: Marketing and Consuming Women's Islamic Dress'. *Journal of Middle East Women's Studies* 6(3):118–48.

Gökarıksel, Banu and Anna J. Secor. 2010b. 'Islamic-ness in the Life of a Commodity: Veiling-fashion in Turkey'. *Transactions of the Institute of British Geographers* 35(3):313–33.

Gökarıksel, Banu and Anna J. Secor. 2012. "'Even I Was Tempted": The Moral Ambivalence and Ethical Practice of Veiling-Fashion in Turkey'. *Annals of the Association of American Geographers* 102(4):847–62.

Gökarıksel, Banu and Anna J. Secor. 2015. 'Islam on the Catwalk: Marketing Veiling-Fashion in Turkey'. In *The Changing World Religion Map*, edited by Stanley D. Brunn, 2581–2595. Springer Netherlands.

Göle, Nilüfer. 2003. 'The Voluntary Adoption of Islamic Stigma Symbols'. *Social Research* 70(Fall):809–27.

Hasan, Noorhaidi. 2009. 'The Making of Public Islam: Piety, Agency, and Commodification on the Landscape of the Indonesian Public Sphere'. *Contemporary Islam* 3(3):229–50.

Hefner, Robert W. 2010. 'Religious Resurgence in Contemporary Asia: Southeast Asian Perspectives on Capitalism, the State, and the New Piety'. *The Journal of Asian Studies* 69(4):1031–47.

Hoggard, Liz. 2013. 'Modesty Regulators: Punishing and Rewarding Women's Appearances in Mainstream Media'. In *Modest Fashion*, edited by Reina Lewis, 175–89. London: I.B.Tauris.

Hoodfar, Homa. 1993. 'The Veil in Their Minds and on Our Heads: The Persistence of Colonial Images of Muslim Women'. *Resources for Feminist Research* 22(3–4):5–18.

Ignatow, Gabe, Lindsey Johnson and Ali Madanipour. 2014. 'Global System Theory and "Market-friendly" Religion'. *Globalizations* 11(6):827–41.

Jafari, Ali and Özlem Sandıkçı. 2016. 'Introduction: Islam in Consumption, Marketing and Markets'. In *Islam, Marketing and Consumption: Critical Perspectives on the Intersections*, edited by A. Jafari and Ö. Sandıkçı, 1–14. London: Routledge.

Jones, Carla. 2007. 'Fashion and Faith in Urban Indonesia'. *Fashion Theory* 11(2–3):211–31.

Jones, Carla. 2010a. 'Materializing Piety: Gendered Anxieties about Faithful Consumption in Contemporary Urban Indonesia'. *American Ethnologist* 37(4):617–37.

Jones, Carla. 2010b. 'Images of Desire: Creating Virtue and Value in an Indonesian Islamic Lifestyle Magazine'. *Journal of Middle East Women's Studies* 6(3):91–117.

Karataş, Mustafa and Özlem Sandıkçı. 2013. 'Religious Communities and the Marketplace: Learning and Performing Consumption in an Islamic Network'. *Marketing Theory* 13(4):265–84.

Kelly, Marjori. 2010. 'Clothes, Culture, and Context: Female Dress in Kuwait'. *Fashion Theory* 14(2):215–36.

Kılıçbay, Barış and Mutlu Binark. 2002. 'Consumer Culture, Islam and the Politics of Lifestyle'. *European Journal of Communication* 17(4):495–511.

Lewis, Reina. 2007. 'Veils and Sales: Muslims and the Spaces of Postcolonial Fashion Retail,' *Fashion Theory*, 11(4):423–41.

Lewis, Reina. 2010. 'Marketing Muslim Lifestyle: A New Media Genre'. *Journal of Middle East Women's Studies* 6(3):58–90.

Lewis, Reina, ed. 2013. *Modest Fashion: Styling Bodies, Mediating Faith*. London: I.B.Tauris.

Lewis, Reina. 2015. *Muslim Fashion: Contemporary Style Cultures*. Durham, NC: Duke University Press.

Mandaville, Peter. 2010. *Global Political Islam*. London: Routledge.

Maqsood, Ammara. 2014. '"Buying Modern" Muslim Subjectivity, the West and Patterns of Islamic Consumption in Lahore, Pakistan'. *Cultural Studies* 28(1):84–107.

Martikainen, Tuomas and Francois Gauthier. 2013. 'Introduction: Religion in Market Society'. In *Religion in the Neoliberal Age: Political Economy and Modes of Governance*, edited by Tuomas Martikainen and Francois Gauthier, 1–20. Farnham: Ashgate.

Melucci, Alberto. 1996. *Challenging Codes: Collective Action in the Information Age*. Cambridge: Cambridge University Press.

Meneley, Anne. 2007. 'Fashions and Fundamentalism in fin-de-siecle Yemen: Chador Barbies and Islamic Socks'. *Cultural Anthropology* 22(2):214–43.

Mernissi, Fatima. 1991. *The Veil and the Male Elite*. Reading, MA: Addison-Wesley.

Moll, Yasmin. 2010. 'Islamic Televangelism: Religion, Media and Visuality in Contemporary Egypt'. *Arab Media & Society* 10:1–27.

Moors, Annelies. 2007. 'Fashionable Muslims: Notions of Self, Religion and Society in Sana'a'. *Fashion Theory* 11(2–3):319–46.

Moors, Annelies. 2013. 'Discover the Beauty of Modesty'. In *Modest Fashion*, edited by Reina Lewis, 17–40. London: I.B.Tauris.

Moors, Annelies and Emma Tarlo. 2013. 'Introduction: Islamic Fashion and Anti-Fashion: New Perspectives from Europe and North America'. In *Islamic Fashion and Anti-Fashion*, edited by Emma Tarlo and Annelies Moors, 1–37. London: Bloomsbury.

Nasr, Vali. 2009. *Forces of Fortune: The Rise of the New Muslim Middle Class and What It Will Mean for Our World*. New York: Free Press.

Navaro-Yashin, Yael. 2002. 'The Markets for Identities: Secularism, Islamism, Commodities'. In *Fragments of Culture: The Everyday of Modern Turkey*, edited by Deniz Kandiyoti and Ayşe Saktanber, 221–53. New Brunswick, NJ: Rutgers University Press.

Osella, Filippo and Caroline Osella. 2009. 'Muslim Entrepreneurs in Public Life between India and the Gulf: Making Good and Doing Good'. *Journal of the Royal Anthropological Institute* 15(1):S202–21.

Özyürek, Esra. 2006. *Nostalgia for the Modern: State Secularism and Everyday Politics in Turkey*. Durham, NC: Duke University Press.

Pink, Johanna, ed. 2009. *Muslim Societies in the Age of Mass Consumption*. Newcastle upon Tyne: Cambridge Scholars.

Rudnyckyj, Daromir. 2009. 'Spiritual Economies: Islam and Neoliberalism in Contemporary Indonesia'. *Cultural Anthropology* 24(1):104–41.

Salim, Degla. 2013. 'Reading Islamic Fashion Imagery in Sweden'. In *Islamic Fashion and Anti-Fashion*, edited by Emma Tarlo and Annelies Moors, 209–24. London: Bloomsbury.

Sandıkçı, Özlem and Güliz Ger. 2001. 'Fundamental Fashions: The Cultural Politics of the Turban and the Levi's'. *Advances in Consumer Research* 28:146–50.

Sandıkçı, Özlem and Güliz Ger. 2002. 'In-Between Modernities and Postmodernities: Investigating Turkish Consumptionscape'. *Advances in Consumer Research* 29:465–70.

Sandıkçı, Özlem and Güliz Ger. 2005. 'Aesthetics, Ethics, and Politics of the Turkish Headscarf'. In *Clothing as Material Culture*, edited by Susanne Küchler and Daniel Miller, 61–82. New York: Berg.

Sandıkçı, Özlem and Güliz Ger. 2007. 'Constructing and Representing the Islamic Consumer in Turkey'. *Fashion Theory* 11(2–3):189–210.

Sandıkçı, Özlem and Güliz Ger. 2010. 'Veiling in Style: How Does a Stigmatized Practice Become Fashionable?'. *Journal of Consumer Research* 37:15–36.

Sandıkçı, Özlem and Ali Jafari. 2013. 'Islamic Encounters in Consumption and Marketing'. *Marketing Theory* 13(4):211–20.

Sandıkçı, Özlem. 2011. 'Researching Islamic Marketing: Past and Future Perspectives'. *Journal of Islamic Marketing* 2(3):246–58.

Sayan-Cengiz, Feyda. 2016. *Beyond Headscarf Culture in Turkey's Retail Sector*. Springer.

Schulz, Dorothea E. 2006. 'Promises of (Im)mediate Salvation: Islam, Broadcast Media, and the Remaking of Religious Experience in Mali'. *American Ethnologist* 33(2):210–29.

Sloane, Patricia. 1999. *Islam, Modernity, and Entrepreneurship among the Malays*. New York: St. Martin's Press.

Starrett, Gregory. 1995. 'The Political Economy of Religious Commodities in Cairo'. *American Anthropologist* 1997(1):51–68.

Stephan-Emmrich, Manja and Abdullah Mirzoev. 2016. 'The Manufacturing of Islamic Lifestyles in Tajikistan through the Prism of Dushanbe's Bazaars'. *Central Asian Survey* 35(2):157–77.

Tarlo, Emma. 2010. *Visibly Muslim*. Oxford: Berg.

Tarlo, Emma. 2013. 'Landscapes of Attraction and Rejection: South Asian Aesthetics in Islamic Fashion in London'. In *Islamic Fashion and Anti-Fashion*, edited by Emma Tarlo and Annelies Moors, 73–92. London: Bloomsbury.

Tarlo, Emma and Annelies Moors, eds. 2013. *Islamic Fashion and Anti-Fashion: New Perspectives from Europe and North America*. London: Bloomsbury.

Thompson Reuters. 2015. 'State of the Global Islamic Economy'. *Thompson Reuters's Zawya*. Available at www.zawya.com/ifg-publications/ IslamicEconomy15–251114170832G (accessed 8 February, 2016).

White, Jenny B. 2002. *Islamist Mobilization in Turkey: A Study in Vernacular Politics*. Seattle, WA: University of Washington Press.

Wiktorowicz, Quintan. 2004. *Islamic Activism: A Social Movement Theory Approach*. Bloomington, IN: Indiana University Press.

Wilson, Erin K. and Manfred B. Steger. 2013. 'Religious Globalisms in the Post-Secular Age'. *Globalizations* 10(3):481–95.

Wong, Loong. 2007. 'Market Cultures, the Middle Classes and Islam: Consuming the Market?'. *Consumption Markets & Culture* 10(4):451–80.

Yavuz, Hakan. 2004. 'Opportunity Spaces, Identity, and Islamic Meaning in Turkey'. In *Islamic Activism: A Social Movement Theory Approach*, edited by Q. Wiktorowicz, 270–87. Bloomington, IN: Indiana University Press.

Zaman, Saminaz. 2008. 'From Imam to Cyber-Mufti: Consuming Identity in Muslim America'. *The Muslim World* 98:465–74.

17

IMAGES OF DESIRE

Creating virtue and value in an Indonesian Islamic lifestyle magazine

Carla Jones[1]

Introduction

The recent and highly visible rise of Islamic consumer culture in contemporary urban Indonesia is a source of both pleasure and anxiety for many Indonesians, figuring in debates about the appeal of a new piety there in the past decade. At the centre of these debates is the image of the piously dressed woman. Simultaneously a consumer and a sign of piety, modest yet attractive, she seems to blur assumptions about the boundaries between image and substance, and in so doing generates anxiety. A booming Islamic fashion industry and Islamic fashion media traffic in this space, are turning virtue into value and vice versa by deploying the image of the pious feminine to incite consumer desire while denying accusations that this is simply capitalism with a religious face. Based on research and interviews with the editorial staff of one Islamic fashion magazine, *NooR*, this article traces how Indonesia's rising Islamic fashion industry and lifestyle media have placed women at the centre of broader cultural debates about the relationship between devotion and consumption. Since the original publication of this essay, the Islamic fashion industry in Indonesia has grown substantially. The Indonesian government has directed funding and logistical assistance towards key Islamic designers and event planners with a view to using Islamic dress as an engine for national economic development. *NooR* and its sister magazines have only increased in circulation, ad revenue and visibility. Young fashion designers such as Dian Pelangi style themselves as modest lifestyle leaders, using Instagram, blogs and other social media in particular to distribute their reputations, which are then parlayed into advertisements for companies like Wardah. Multiple fashion events in Jakarta compete through the year to be the authoritative venue for the Islamic runway scene. And elite social clubs such as Hijabers Community have formed in major Indonesian cities as venues for religious study, dress tips and private trunk shows. In spite of, or perhaps because of, this substantial commercial growth, the themes identified in this chapter remain true. Debates about the sincerity of women's simultaneous modesty and beauty have only become more frequent, turning the very ubiquity of attractive piety into a site of mediation.

NooR: Islamic piety as consumer thrill

Perhaps no figure better captures the ambivalence of the possibility of value and virtue co-existing than the fashionably dressed pious Muslim consumer. A woman who embraces both the promise of piety and the thrill of being attractive, expressed through purchasing power, embodies the tensions of these debates in urban Indonesia today. She is also the target reader and buyer of an increasingly crowded and competitive fashion media market. Creating her, speaking to her, and defending her are all part of creating a fictional, typical reader, which is standard practice in media marketing around the world. Yet this woman also stands at the centre of highly loaded public conversations, a figure whose modesty should quell desire yet who seems unable to manage her own desire for beauty and consumer goods. As a medium for desire, she is both object and subject, making critiques about women's dress especially loaded. When conversations about the insincere use of signs of Islamic piety occur, they very often start or stop with references to the fashionably dressed Muslim woman who is accused of merely performing a consumer role of piety, of buying an identity rather than being sincerely devout.

Indonesia has a long history of vibrant media production, even despite intense state censorship during the 32-year Suharto administration. Print media for women in particular had been dominated by a group of magazines headed by the ubiquitous *Femina* which enjoyed a high profile and was trusted both by the Indonesian state and by readers to take a mature, comfortable, educational tone even when discussing topics deemed sensitive, such as marital communication or balancing motherhood with career demands. *Femina* had and continues to have a reputation for professionalism and 'world class' production. The Asian economic crisis was a key factor in the environment that allowed the Islamic fashion media to develop. With the effect the crisis had in encouraging political dissent in the streets of Jakarta and other cities in 1998, which resulted in Suharto's resignation; the eventual closure of the infamous Ministry of Information, which had policed media expression; and the economic squeeze that diminished advertising revenue and increased the cost of paper, the Indonesian magazine industry was heavily transformed during the early 2000s. Notably, smaller magazines often tended to have a shorter lifespan, while major magazines were able to survive. The latter included *Femina* and its sister magazines as well as the global franchise magazines that had entered Indonesia at the beginning of the crisis, such as *Bazaar*, *Her World*, *Cosmopolitan* and, notoriously, *Playboy*.

The editors of *NooR* created their lush, colourful and somewhat expensive monthly magazine in 2003 in response to a void they perceived in the media landscape. This void was both moral and market, one they identified as having been created in part by the editors of *Femina* and the arrival of global magazines. Readers of *Femina* frequently wrote letters to the editor during the 1990s, borrowing authority from the discourse of consumer choice to demand recognition by asking that examples of Muslim dress be included in the journal's fashion spreads (Jones 2007). The exclusion of pious dress, they asserted, denied them the pleasure and edification of being treated as consumers. Invisibility in the fashion media, they suggested, echoed the more general disdain women who chose to wear Muslim dress felt on the street, i.e. that they were unfashionable, uncool and undesirable. Their exclusion could be rectified through mass mediated representation in which models in work and leisure settings in both pious Muslim and more typical Indonesian business-style dress would appear in the same frame, suggesting that either style of dress was an equivalent, personal, consumer choice. *Femina* responded to these letters by doing just that, commissioning fashion spreads for approximately one issue in four that placed Muslim dress on an equal footing with comparatively more exposed and explicitly non-religious dress styles.

Although *Femina* did respond to these requests, the staff also felt under pressure to compete with the globally franchised magazines that generally recycled both photos and articles from their offices headquartered in Paris or New York. Not only was such content more cosmopolitan in orientation but it was often more racy than *Femina*'s relatively conservative fare. According to Sri Artaria Alisjabhana, one of two founding co-editors of *NooR*, *Femina*'s response to this pressure was misguided. Instead of realizing that Indonesian readers are unique and that it had an established reputation with its readership, *Femina*'s editorial choices veered toward the more salacious and the less 'Indonesian' as it attempted to compete with more global content (Alisjabhana 2008). Those decisions meant that the growing audience of pious women readers who wanted media recognition was abandoned to essentially one other publication, a more traditional Muslim family life magazine called *Ummi* which, as Jetti Hadi (2008), the other founding co-editor of *NooR*, explained, positions Islamic lifestyle as a derivation of Middle Eastern culture. There was no magazine and therefore no image-generating, mediated commodity to speak to and make visible the unique figure of the globally oriented yet authentically Indonesian pious Muslim female consumer. In so identifying her, *NooR* called her into being.

NooR's Indonesian orientation in no way suggests that the magazine is provincial. To the contrary, much like the student activists Brenner (1996) studied, *NooR*'s editorial staff see themselves as connected to the world through international travel and Internet research. That world is complex, comprising the Islamic *umat* (*umma*) and the global fashion scene, bringing both together for their readers. There are few inspirational examples of this type of creative mediation in the world, although the editors know of and admire other Islamic lifestyle magazines from Europe and North America, specifically *emel* (London), *Muslim Girl* (Toronto), and especially *Azizah* (Atlanta). From articles dedicated to Qur'anic interpretation, to tourism to other Islamic countries, to reports from current non-Islamic fashion shows, *NooR* assumes that its readers care about the world of faith and fashion beyond Indonesia. Its 'Indonesian' orientation refers to a commitment to caring for one's husband and children and prioritizing family and faith above other concerns. Indeed, during the first year of publication, the magazine was sold exclusively in domestic settings, at private, upscale Qur'anic study sessions in Jakarta's elite neighbourhoods. On the assumption that the sort of woman who would be interested in *NooR* would probably never alight from her chauffeured car to buy it at a streetside kiosk, as most newsstand sales occur in Indonesia, this choice made the magazine seem exclusive and contributed to its early word-of-mouth praise.

In short, the founding editors had a strong vision for the magazine based on the assumption that to publicly express an Islamic identity is a purely personal choice, and that once made, that decision should be supported and encouraged. *NooR* was there to provide that support through the argument that while globalization might threaten Indonesian tradition, Indonesians themselves have a priceless, historically proven, globally valued resource for dealing with that threat, in the form of the holy Qur'an. No contemporary problem a reader might face would be too great for a Qur'anic solution. This mission has remained at the core of the magazine's official description. Editor Jetti Hadi travels Indonesia regularly to offer workshops on this concept for readers, arguing that although a thousand-year-old text might seem out of date for the challenges Indonesian women face, when consulted seriously, it can provide answers.

Images of desire

This powerful commitment to education and Islamic guidance operates in an equally powerful media marketplace. *NooR* is not the only magazine angling for reader loyalty. It shares newsstand space with four other large-circulation Islamic women's magazines (*Paras*, *Ummi*, *Muslimah* and *Alia*), while several similar publications have launched and failed. And like any magazine, religious or not, it faces the demands of attracting advertising revenue and increasing readership. As a result, *NooR* traffics in images. Essentially, that is what fashion magazines do: from commissioning photography, to selling imagery to aspirational readers, to soliciting image-based advertising pages, imagery is central to the appeal of a fashion magazine. Unlike magazines such as the British *emel*, in which fashion photography is constrained by Islamic prohibition against human representation which forces editors to crop out models' faces, *NooR*'s staff sees itself as relatively more free and potentially more able to participate in making Indonesia a centre of the Islamic fashion world. This role held out a related promise, that the Muslim fashion industry could help Indonesia achieve what it never quite seemed to do under secular developmentalism, i.e. link Indonesia's low-wage, outsourced global garment industry to real national growth. The steady supply of inexpensive labour and the demands of heavy beading and elaborate work on many of the newest styles of Islamic fashion provide what the editorial staff imagine could be the conditions for uplift, both moral and economic.

Yet the fundamental fact that magazines traffic in images ultimately steered *NooR* in a direction the founding editors had not originally intended, that of fashion magazine. While their orienting vision focused on the power of Qur'anic interpretation for the twenty-first-century Indonesian woman, the editors were quickly confronted, in their first few issues, with the fact that their readers and advertisers were fascinated with the thrill and pleasure of creating an entirely new fashion universe, complete with designers dedicated to Islamic dress, accessories, styling, salons and, importantly, buyers. Comparable magazines in Europe or North America have struggled to put fashion and Islam comfortably in the same sentence, in part because of the profoundly stigmatized associations of political and racial identity with immigrant Islam in these regions. By contrast, because *NooR* was based in Muslim-majority Indonesia, the environment was quite different. Indonesian readers were enthusiastic about the possibility of seeing themselves as both pious and attractive, giving the magazine early success, and Indonesian designers soon caught on.

Describing the intense advertising scene of 1980s consumer culture in the US, media scholar Stuart Ewen (1999) has argued that the commodification of images, and the marketing of commodities via images, turned contemporary culture into a landscape of surfaces. The religious nature of celebrity, he argues, creates an economy in which the more one's image circulates, the more one's celebrity value increases (93), producing the alienating effects of capitalist exchange. That increase in value is the opposite of what Walter Benjamin (1968) famously described as the loss of 'aura' or the authentic essence of a great image, which occurs when images are mechanically reproduced and endlessly circulated. Both arguments, however, belie the assumption that image and matter are fundamentally opposite, and that consumption, and consumption of images, can never satisfy the desires they inspire but can only result in destructive alienation. More recently, the anthropologist William Mazzarella (2003), studying the advertising industry of late-1990s Bombay and also using Walter Benjamin, has argued that the murky space between image as ephemeral and image as substance is in constant flux, making consumer participation in that space thrilling and hence generating the pleasure of consuming, whether that consumption is of images or commodities. Yet I would argue that none of these interpretations makes sense without considering the vital role of gender, and the feminine, in making both images and commodities appealing, because those consumer spaces, the buyers and the images used to incite transactions are all feminized. As Victoria de Grazia and Ellen Furlough (1996) have argued for European capitalist history, consumer culture has fundamentally relied on an easy blurring of the female body as object of desire to create consumer desire, associating femininity with both image and object, and stigmatizing consumption as feminine lack of control in the process.

Fashion magazines rely on all these dynamics: the promise of satisfaction, the pleasure of participation, and the murky space between image and matter. Yet Islamic fashion magazines occupy a unique position at the crux of the relationship between the image and the sacred nature of celebrity, while their religious identification distinguishes them from ordinary fashion magazines. When, in its first year of publication, *NooR* found itself in the middle of a growing fashion industry, it simultaneously found itself in the centre of a broader process, one in which religious substance was transformed into aesthetic style. This process required images and incited consumption in the pursuit of personal image management, linking consumption to personal expression, aspiration and the promise of actualization.

Whereas Indonesian fashion designers, whose own success had been linked to the cultural politics of national development (Jones 2003) in the 1980s and 1990s, had eschewed Islamic dress for its dowdiness and its association with the non-elite, by the early 2000s, they began producing secondary lines for the busana Muslim market. These lines follow different seasonal calendars, with major shows and releases typically timed for the month preceding Ramadan, which means that fashion shows occur in different calendar months from one year to the next. And while European designers might take Orientalist inspiration from travels abroad, adding touches of exoticism to their collections, Indonesian Islamic fashion designers use such references to impute authenticity and cosmopolitaneity ('I just came back from Dubai and this embroidery is all the rage'), to a certain extent reinforcing the idea that true Islam is Middle Eastern.

Magazines such as *NooR* have been absolutely central to the growth of the Islamic fashion industry in Indonesia, through sponsoring designers' shows, reporting on them, and, importantly, publishing photographs of their work. Much of the ad space in *NooR* is bought by fashion houses or producers of related accessories such as halal (religiously permissible) make-up, or children's clothing lines. The editorial staff seem ambivalent about this, proud of the way in which what was once a minority style has flourished in the past decade, yet concerned that the proliferation of Islamic dress as fashion might distract readers from pursuing the highest ideals of true piety. Two comments from one editor are illustrative. On the one hand, she proudly informed me that the Austrian crystal company Swarovski now considers Indonesia a major market because of the spectacular beading on the highest-end designer lines of busana Muslim. Indonesia, as a consuming nation, is now legible in the eyes of a reputable, historic, pedigreed, European company, thanks largely to the growth of the Islamic fashion industry. Swarovski now sponsors major fashion events in Jakarta and provides private showings of new crystal designs to Islamic fashion editors. On the other hand, according to this editor, the notion of halal, ethical consumption is missing from this hopeful narrative in which Islamic fashion stimulates Indonesia's transnational legibility and national development. Unlike editors at *emel* (see Lewis 2010) who argue that Islam provides the ethical resource for conscious consumption, and who link the green of Islam to the green of the eco-style movement, few if any Indonesian consumers of pious fashion consider working conditions for those who manufacture the goods they purchase. Instead, the emphasis on natural ingredients in halal make-up, for example, is linked to the Prophet's prescient advice, guiding women away from synthetic ingredients and preservatives that are ultimately destructive to the skin and personal health, rather than to the product's effects on the environment or fellow humans.

The problem of *imej* and the solution of spiritual beauty

It would be easy and tempting to read a particular interpretation from the history I have just sketched, one that in fact partly informs popular anxiety about Islamic fashion and the assertion that public piety in contemporary Indonesia is merely *imej*, or the pursuit of piety through surface rather than depth. That interpretation would argue that commodified forms of devotion do not represent a new Islamic subjectivity, but rather the objectification of Islam. This popular interpretation shares space with a frankly cynical secular view which denies that users of pious goods might experience genuine devotion in that use. Such interpretations imply scandal, an illicit and improper use of the sacred. They also rely on a notion of Islam as singular, which Talal Asad (1986, 14) has argued fails to recognize that Islam, like any discursive tradition, is and always has been a shifting complex of beliefs, politics and histories, some of which have become powerful precisely through disavowing this complexity. The illusion of a singular Islam can overlap with the motivations of *ulema*, those charged with verifying the accuracy of claims about what is and what is not Islamic. Neither perspective allows space for the consuming masses to avert the scandal of mistaking image for piety.

Analysing a related concern in artistic production, Kenneth George (2009) has recently argued that scholarship on Islamic art has failed to attend to the problem of the production of pious art. While the category of 'Islamic art' is classified as calligraphic rather than representational, calligraphy creates its own challenges, especially if it is used without attention to meaning or correct inscription, as George illustrates through his analysis of the scandal that followed Karl Lagerfeld's use of a Qur'anic quotation on a bustier in his 1994 collection. Indonesian clerics, and later, *ulema* in other countries including France and Britain, took the designer to task for using sacred text without recognizing its meaning and in the service of stimulating sexual desire with the exposed form of the woman (Claudia Schiffer) who modelled his strapless top on the catwalk. In this sense, the problem of production in Islamic representations is especially potent when it brings together the substance of the word of God and the image of the female form. The editorial staff of *NooR*, who one might think would only stand to gain from being at the centre of Indonesia's Islamic fashion boom, in fact find themselves negotiating similar terrain carefully, yet with pride. The magazine relies on the ease of circulation of the image of the pious feminine, but this ease implies another one, that of being too desirable, too accessible, too easily consumed, too comfortable straddling the line between image and human being. And that risk is much greater for the feminine than for the masculine in this discourse. Indeed, famous Indonesian *ustadz* (preachers) are far more likely than women to have their images circulate without risk to their reputations.

One tactic for operating in the fraught space where virtue and value would coalesce, while avoiding the scandal of confusing image with substance, is to generate an alternative discourse in which 'spiritual beauty' is deeper and more compelling than its projected opposite, secular beauty. So appealing is this line of thinking that *NooR* has collaborated with a leading designer of busana Muslim, Itang Yunasz, to produce a book on the subject. Spiritual beauty explicitly frames piety as an inner state that compels outer modesty but does not prevent also creating a beautiful exterior. 'True beauty is not just a physical matter, but is found inside in inner beauty. Yet, when that inner beauty is surrounded by beautiful designs, it can radiate even more, Insya Allah' (Yunasz 2005, 11). Spiritual beauty promises to realign image and substance in a morally true order that allows value to endure through virtue and reminds pious women that creating an attractive image of oneself can be both hard work and pleasurable.

Given this problem of production, circulation and consumption of the image of the pious feminine, editorial staff at the magazine have gone to impressive lengths to differentiate between the pious feminine as commodified female and the piety of real women, distinguished as originating in an inner life and moving to outward, attractive expression. If women are a charged space on and through which debates about the moral state of Indonesian public culture are taking place, then the solution to that problem is twofold: to humanize pious women through examples of women consuming Islamic fashion, and to produce the magazine in a manner consistent with Qur'anic teachings about modesty and propriety.

For the first several years, *NooR*'s editorial staff pursued these goals through a variety of methods. For example, the magazine's cover girls were rarely professional models who by definition commodify their bodies for visual consumption. Instead, they were accomplished white-collar professionals who had chosen to wear Muslim dress. Each was described in a prominently placed profile of her background, career and family status. As Sri Artaria Alisjabhana explained, such women could serve as inspiring role models for readers, showing that one could be covered, professionally active, and attractive. This would imply that professional models are not suitable role models for pious readers.

Professional models – who might only don a headscarf for a cover shoot and leave the studio in tight-fitting or more exposed clothes – are part of a category of publicly visible women in Indonesian media and entertainment frequently glossed as *selebriti, peragawati, dan artis*, or celebrities, models and artists (typically singers). This class of performer is notable for its combination of female form and public desire. Actresses in soap operas, spokeswomen for high-profile commodities and generally ubiquitous figures in Indonesian mass media, such women are considered beautiful yet separate from respectable middle-class life. While their images circulate almost promiscuously in the media landscape, appearing practically everywhere at once, the tabloid media gossip and report on their social world as if it were free of ordinary social mores.

As women who wear more exposed styles of clothing than is standard in polite company or professional life, female celebrities are imagined to engage in an alternate universe where sex is casual, alcohol is consumed, and smoking is common. The proliferation of their images in the public sphere allows audiences to imagine a similar and, significantly, scandalous corporeal promiscuity in the private sphere, whether that is true or not.

NooR implemented its original plan to use non-professional cover models along with a policy of using female stylists and photographers whenever possible, preferably women who respected or who chose to adopt Islamic dress themselves. The theory was that that technicians who understood the aspirations and limits that Islamic dress represented would be able to make up, light, and pose a model in ways that would not offend her, e.g. through contact with or objectification by strange men, and who might even emphasize the angles most attractive for a woman wearing a headscarf. Male grips handling heavy lighting gear and being physically assertive could be off-putting for amateur models, especially if they were novices in the world of commercial photography. The overall setting could be traumatizing to a sensitive woman, as one editor explained to me.

In spite of their good intentions, these policies did not last. Most non-professional models were uncomfortable posing, unskilled in thinking of their body as an image, even though such thinking is part of ordinary feminine cultivation. Their discomfort was apparent and it took repeated efforts to get a usable image. A photo shoot that should have taken an hour or two took a whole day or more, costing the magazine more in time and fees than they had budgeted. It was especially difficult to find female photographers and stylists with pious sensibilities. Commercial photography is dominated by men; booking a female team is a challenge. Ultimately, they had to resort to professional models and photo crews, which is also how most Islamic fashion shows operate. It is not uncommon to see models in tank tops and short denim skirts weave their way through a crowd of well-to-do, piously dressed women as they exit a five-star hotel lobby after working an Islamic fashion show.

This reliance on non-pious models and production teams to create the aura of fashionable Islamic dress feeds a suspicion that the public display of Islamic identity may be nothing more than a fashion statement. The very trafficking in images of piety through the bodies of professional models keeps the possibility of piety as mere *imej* just below the surface, always almost revealed. The model who covers in her offstage life is rare. She is the figure who redeems the life of the model through an unusually authentic performance of pious display on the runway. I have attended fashion shows where fellow attendees whispered to me that a particular model, known for wearing Muslim dress in her daily life, is obviously more gifted in displaying the beauty of her garment because she understands the disciplinary demands of wearing pious clothing.

There is perhaps no better way to redeem the inappropriate life of a model or a celebrity who has allowed unlimited circulation of the image of her body, than to adopt pious Islamic dress. This is becoming a common trajectory for many former models and actresses whose stories are chronicled in both religious and secular media. Their narratives frequently focus on an awakening, often around marriage, as the woman feels increasingly uncomfortable, even undressed, and the crisis is resolved when she chooses to cover her head, if only in a makeshift way, and feels immediate, almost palpable relief. Her adoption of pious dress is usually associated with her retreat from the entertainment world she formerly inhabited (which is why covered, active models are rare), but that does not mean she is out of public view. Instead, such women are highly visible on television and in the print media, describing their decision to adopt Islamic dress and taking up new roles in the growing Islamic entertainment field. In this way, a woman's pious identity mitigates and even inoculates against her continued visibility. Lila Abu-Lughod (1995), in describing a similar phenomenon among retired actresses in Egypt, has argued that their narrations of moving into piety and out of regret for the entertainment business rest on the assumption that piety is available to any woman, a path one simply chooses. Yet that assumption belies the class privilege of seclusion enjoyed by former stars who can afford to maintain the domestic boundaries necessary for pursuing piety, a privilege that working-class women – many of whom form the audience base for these celebrities – do not enjoy. This description captures, at least in part, the narrative of the transformed celebrity in Indonesian public life. The main difference is that Indonesian celebrities often do not retreat to a life of domestic seclusion, and they frequently continue to work.

Perhaps no figure better exemplifies the life journey from celebrity star to pious celebrity than Inneke Koesherawati, spokesmodel for the halal make-up company Wardah. Described as a former actress, Koesherawati in fact still regularly acts in Indonesian Islamic soap operas, many of which focus on the drama, pain and, ultimately, peaceful beauty of living in a polygynous marriage. Koesherawati's departure from secular entertainment coincided with her decision to begin wearing Islamic dress, linking being uncovered to the sins of the entertainment industry. Her case is unique, because the sort of films in which she appeared prior to her decision to cover ranged from conventional domestic dramas to soft-core pornography, a genre in which the thrill of the visual form of the female body is most obviously scandalous. Koesherawati frequently describes her decision to adopt the jilbab (headscarf) as increasing her ability to circulate publicly: 'Before I wore a jilbab, I had this feeling inside myself of having done wrong. Now, it is much easier for me to mingle with others.'

The problem of the image of femininity remains no less a problem in its pious aspect, and the image of the converted celebrity is alluring precisely because of its promise to bring apparently contradictory states into harmony, that is, the scandal of feminine commodification and the purification of Islam. This promise itself rests on the illusion that the converted celebrity is purifying, through her dress, the prior commodification of herself, and transforming that self into the virtuous form of the covered woman. The underlying logic of this promise once more resurrects the idea that virtue and value cannot co-exist in the same form. Yet the popular image of Koesherawati's adoption of public piety circulates in media much the way her prior image did, widely and for exchange value. In fact, I would argue that while her current popularity is due at least in part to the dramatic nature of her pious transformation, it is also due to the fact that she convincingly promotes the pleasure of being even more beautiful than the woman who does not wear Islamic dress. Her appeal is broad; college students, designers and magazine editors frequently state that her facial shape is so well suited to the jilbab that she looks far more attractive wearing it than she did without it. This narrative suggests that by covering, Koesherawati finally reconciled her selves, bringing her character into harmony with her natural beauty. Her popularity has not only endured but increased through the circulation of her image as a covered woman, revealing that the converted star is simultaneously a sign of capitalist excess and religious restraint, and suggesting that these qualities are not mutually exclusive. Readers of magazines like *NooR*, in admiring her pious form, actively participate in generating the alchemy of virtue and value, thereby creating the very pleasure that makes consuming as rewarding as it is alienating.

Note

1   This is an extract of an article, with a new introduction written for this volume, that originally appeared in *Journal of Middle East Women's Studies* 2010 6(3):91–117.

References

Abu-Lughod, Lila. 1995. 'Movie Stars and Islamic Moralism in Egypt'. *Social Text* 42(Spring):53–67.

Alisjabhana, Sri Artaria. 2008. Interview with the author, Jakarta, 19 August.

Asad, Talal. 1986. 'The Idea of an Anthropology of Islam'. Occasional Papers, Center for Contemporary Arab Studies, Georgetown University, Washington, DC.

Benjamin, Walter. 1968. *Illuminations*, translated by Harry Zohn. New York: Harcourt, Brace & World.

Brenner, Suzanne. 1996. 'Reconstructing Self and Society: Javanese Muslim Women and "the Veil"'. *American Ethnologist* 23(4):673–97.

De Grazia, Victoria and Ellen Furlough, eds. 1996. *The Sex of Things: Gender and Consumption in Historical Perspective*. Berkeley, CA: University of California Press.

Ewen, Stuart. 1999. *All Consuming Images: The Politics of Style in Contemporary Culture*, revised edition. New York: Basic Books.

George, Kenneth. 2009. 'Ethics, Iconoclasm, and Qur'anic Art in Indonesia'. *Cultural Anthropology* 24(4):589–621.

Hadi, Jetti. 2008. Interview with the author, Jakarta, 19 August.

Jones, Carla. 2003. 'Dress for Sukses: Fashioning Femininity and Nationality in Urban Indonesia'. In *Re-Orienting Fashion: The Globalization of Asian Dress*, edited by Sandra Niessen, Ann Marie Leshkowich and Carla Jones. Oxford: Berg.

Jones, Carla. 2007. 'Faith and Fashion in Urban Indonesia'. *Fashion Theory* 11:211–31.

Lewis, Reina. 2010. 'Marketing Muslim Lifestyle: A New Media Genre'. *Journal of Middle East Women's Studies*, 6(3):58–90.

Mazzarella, William. 2003. *Shoveling Smoke: Advertising and Globalization in Contemporary India*. Durham, NC: Duke University Press.

Yunasz, Itang. 2005. *Spiritual Beauty*. Jakarta: Dian Rakyat Press.

18

SMART-ENING UP THE HIJAB

The materiality of contemporary British Muslim veiling in the physical and the digital

Shehnaz Suterwalla

Introduction

In contemporary style, the hijab is a long scarf worn by Muslim women that is tied around the head and shoulders. It can be made from a range of materials, from luxurious silk to cotton; it can be any colour, either plain or printed. Most often it is draped around the head so that an end tucks under the chin to stay in place, or is held in place by a pin. It is rare that the hijab is worn as a turban, although this can be the case. More often it is folded over the head in layers to cover the hair or the skin of the neck or chest, in line with Islamic edicts relating to modesty. Muslim women interpret ideas of modesty differently according to their religious affinity and cultural backgrounds and all have different ways of veiling. In Britain, many young Muslim women create their own hijab styles by adopting and adapting scarves and material from British high street shops. Motifs, fabrics and colours from mainstream fashions are rendered 'Muslim' through the way in which they are shaped and draped on the head. As such, the aesthetic and cultural politics of the hijab simultaneously defy and enforce continuous engagement with the mainstream: the hijab, while fashioning otherness, at the same time constantly borrows from global fashion industries. It thus creates a double discourse: one that seems to resist the mainstream but at the same time forms part of it, and in turn, of modernity.

The contemporary Muslim veil is in fact so full of diverse interpretation, myriad expressions and individual style, as well as religio-cultural history, that as a topic it engenders limitless analysis. In this chapter, I will concentrate on the hijab's materiality and affect. This means that I will explore how the material handling of a piece of cloth or scarf, how its feel and its texture, allows Muslim women to create a Muslim identity through embodiment based on their feelings, desires and subjectivity. I will discuss how the manipulation of the cloth, its folding and draping, transforms the wearer's identity into a Muslim 'look', and allows for expressions of subjectivity: philosophically as well as physically. I will unravel some of the ways in which the crafting of the hijab exposes a wearer's skill and dexterity to create different affects that in turn reflect more closely their own, personal, social, cultural and political experiences and motivations. The chapter also looks at technological innovation and tech-inspired design change, and the way that these factors are creating even more new opportunities for Muslim women to subvert stereotypes and fashion systems though 'smart' hijab-wearing.

Let us talk about scarves . . .

The main aim of this chapter is to pull apart some of the generalizations and misconceptions about the hijab, many of which have caused alarm since the attacks on New York's twin towers in 2001, and the subsequent 'war on terror' that followed.[1] Since that date, the hijab in Western cosmopolitan and metropolitan centres has become a highly visible, contentious and public issue that has sparked a range of debates about women's bodies and sexual politics, race, notions of national identity, and affiliation with terrorism, tradition and modernity. Moreover, in recent times, the hijab's role in Muslim feminist emancipation – where the emphasis has been on how Muslim women feel empowered by the hijab to express their identity – has morphed into a poetics of terror with the rise of the so-called Islamic State group, and the number of women who have left the UK to join ISIS wearing hijab. Recent female recruits were three girls from Bethnal Green: Kadiza Sultana, Amira Abase and Shamima Begum. In February 2015, the girls ran away from home and were reportedly smuggled into Syria via Turkey. CCTV footage of the runaways at Gatwick showed two of the three wearing a hijab. One had created layers with a black cloth, and had a leopard-patterned scarf around her neck and draped down her torso; the other had scooped her hair into a scarf, tied at the back, with some of the scarf and its trim hanging over the shoulders of her bright yellow top. Of note is the fact that rest of the girls' attire looked as if it was from the high street: jeans, T-shirts, jackets and trainers.[2] In many ways subcultural, and in others so mainstream, the narratives of the contemporary hijab remain challengingly complex.

Of course the wearing of the contemporary, cosmopolitan hijab as a highly styled, urban Muslim 'look' is as much about contemporary bodily performance as it is about object. The hijab must be considered not as inanimate cloth but as an embodied appendage brought to life by its wearer. In its limp, impotent form it could be just another rag; this does not evoke its symbolic meaning which has proved, throughout history, to be charged with social and cultural significance (El-Guindi 1999; Scott 2009; Mernissi 1987). Controversially, the hijab is as much about the erotic body as the modest, concealed one, with its play on notions of revealing and concealing.

Meanwhile, the semiotics of the hijab, particularly in contemporary Anglo-American popular culture, shapes discourses about both Muslims and non-Muslims, with the hijab as the signifier that pits one against the other in mutually generative definitions of modern, progressive, tolerant versus oppressed, terrorist. Desire, affect, 'Britishness', 'Westernness' come to be constituted through interpretations of the hijab and its highly gendered female wearer. While the metaphoric and symbolic charge of the hijab is limitless, it cannot be fully interpreted without analysing its materiality, its 'thingyness' (Brown 2004),[3] its texture and tightness. The surface of the hijab is as important as its semiotic vibe, for it sits on the skin in intimate contact with the wearer. 'Materiality is not a question of materials but rather concerns the substance of material relations' (Bruno 2014, 2). The hijab must be viewed not just as an object but also as a site of mediation and projection: mediation because it involves haptic manipulation, that is, the handling of the material by the wearer creating reciprocal contact between the wearer, the object, and their environment; projection because through the layering of the cloth on the head, the scarf represents the particular identity of its wearer. The process of veiling enfolds, unfolds, represents the inner world of the hijabi as a subjectively designed space.

Handle with care

We handle the hijab. The haptic becomes the process of making as a direct intervention to the process of looking. In this instance we make the veil by draping the scarf to conceal parts of the body from view by bringing into view the hijab as highly conspicuous. The hijab as subcultural dress resists techniques of mainstream corporeal inscription and normalization because it represents the direct interest of the wearer: it is made directly through her skill and design. Reina Lewis has explored Muslim hijab-wearing as both a subcultural style and popular mainstream fashion (Lewis 2015). To add to this, it is important to note that an alternative embodied hierarchy of the senses unfolds in the individual construction of the hijab where through the haptic a personal immersion into a private dimension is created specifically for public view and consumption. This creates a simultaneous hiding alongside exhibitionism, where the reciprocity of touch – cloth to skin and vice versa – are no longer just about looking and to-be-looked-at-ness but also about sensation. Richard Shusterman (2000) defines two types of body consciousness. One is an awareness of the external form of the body, which projects it into visual representation as image. The other is a somatic awareness, in Shusterman's terms 'somaesthetics', which concerns how the body feels in terms of lived experience and 'its kinaesthetic sense of itself' (2000, 149). In the haptic making of the hijab, what follows can include the pleasure of touch.

Pull tight

The folding and draping of the headscarf requires dexterity. With hijab, it is not enough to loosely rest a scarf on the head. At a physical level hijab involves the acts of pinning, knotting, tucking tightly. Tightness in the case of the hijab ensures concealment. Creating tightness involves stretching the material of the hijab to ensure it folds closely to the head. The act proves transformative, physically and existentially, the sense of touch negates any separation between subject and object since they are in direct proximity to each other, blurring the border between the self and the other. Touch represents 'an orientation to sensuality as such that includes all the senses' (Young 1994, 204), and the wearer transforms into a Muslim subject.

The process of transformation through folds is a theme that is central in Gilles Deleuze's *The Fold* (1993). The text explores, through an analysis of philosophy and art, the movement of thoughts and a philosophical approach to folding, with close reference to the work of German philosopher and mathematician Gottfried Wilhelm von Leibniz. The book is about culture only by implication, yet in it Deleuze explains that a fold is not a line that dissolves into independent points but more like a continuous labyrinth: the fold can never be accepted as a singular event, but rather as a population of many folds. Even its antonym, 'unfolding', is not to be understood as the opposite of the fold, but as a movement up to a containing fold. It is itself a derivative of the fold. 'Folding-unfolding no longer simply means tension-release, contraction-dilation, but enveloping-developing, involution-evolution' (1993, 9).

Deleuze interprets folding as a series of potential expressions of pure movements, defined as differentiations. Folding presents another concept of space and time: folding across lines creates impermanent configurations instead of defined boundaries of separation. In this way, Deleuze's analysis suggests that folds create a blurring of inside and outside, solid and void, absence and division. The fold is thus a critique of accounts of ontology or subjectivity that presume a simple interiority and exteriority, such as appearance and essence, or surface and depth. Deleuze's philosophical interrogation offers a model in which to understand the British hijab in terms of its never-ending potential for transformation: the wearer's identity is not bound by the object but in constant movement through its folds.

The idea of movement is particularly significant when considering Deleuze's philosophy directly in relation to cloth or textiles. Pennina Barnett uses Deleuze's presentation of the fold to reconceptualize what she calls 'the poetics of cloth' as ' "soft logics", modes of thought that twist and turn and stretch and fold' (1999, 26). The scarf as head-covering, twisted and folded and stretched, matches Barnett's description exactly. Barnett adds later that:

[t]he poetics of cloth are composed of folds, fragments and surfaces of infinite complexity. The fragment bears witness to a broken whole; yet it is also a site of uncertainty from which to start over; it is where the mind extends beyond fragile boundaries, beyond frayed and intermediate edges, expanding in the fluidity of the smooth. The surface is a liminal space, both inside and out, a space of encounter.

(1999, 31–2)

The idea of 'encounter' again raises questions about new possibilities. It reminds us that the manner in which the surface of the hijab drapes and covers the head and neck, how it meets the body and thereby creates a haptic experience, and its protection of the wearer from immodesty or inappropriate gaze, are all performative articulations: this means that they happen as an action within a particular time and space to present the identity of the wearer at that moment. Encounter also raises the idea of an interface, where a Western scarf, that is, a mass-produced object that forms part of the fashion system and its cycles, meets the Muslim wearer. This is a point of creative consumption, of modernity, where objects from within the fashion system act as a prism for mainstream values and trends, but also of individuality and subjective desire.

And yet drapery also has a long tradition in histories of Western idealized body fashioning. Anne Hollander has discussed its place in Western art, where the nude body and draped cloth 'became essential elements of idealised vision; they came to seem correct for conveying the most valid truths of life' (1993, xiii). Gen Doy notes that 'the lack of drapery in the image of the nude woman . . . reveals that she has not been treated as an "aesthetic object", draped, idealised and distant' (2002, 103). The Western concept of dress, from the time of Christianity, has been defined in opposition to a naked body (Mascia-Lees 1992, 93), and covering has been predicated on a disavowal of the organic form to create highly gendered bodies defined through normative dress functions. Paradoxically in the Western context, the more that female fashions have disavowed the organic forms of the body, the more tantalizing the body has proven to be, with women's clothing historically, and somewhat uncritically, associated with sexual attraction and eroticism (Kidwell and Steele 1989; Wilson 2003).

The British hijab has its own logic, one of draping, layering and pleating: like the Indian sari, for example. Interestingly the hijab's folds and pleats also correspond with highly futuristic technological fashion developments. The work of Issey Miyake, a Japanese designer, relies on pleating to stimulate an active interaction between the clothes he designs and the body of the wearer and its movements. His shapes are dynamic rather than pinned, tucked, sewn and finished (like many rigidly shaped garments such as suits). He likes to give an impression that his clothes are unfinished, leaving it to the wearer to complete the look through embodied performance. Parallels between the hijab and the way that fabrics are wrapped to form the kimono are also evident.

While Miyake is famous for his pleats,[4] he uses these innovatively with new materials that heighten the tactile experience, such as vinyl. He – and others like Rei Kawakubo and Yohji Yamamoto – exaggerate a manufactured aesthetic, often combining industrially inspired looks with elements of futurism. While the designers are loyal to their raw materials and traditional fabrics, they promote still an interest in the evolution of fibre technology. For example, Miyake has used heat-embossing and synthetic coating textile processes to effect more modern sculptural forms, while Kawakubo, referencing historic fashions, incorporates cold synthetic fibres in her designs.

The idea of folds, and the layers and pleats inherent in the fold, are thus shown to be modern and technologically driven. Moreover, while technology determines how some of the hijab scarves are manufactured, it is through digital life that hijab-wearing as subcultural practice or as modern, mainstream fashion practice has proliferated over the last decade or so.

Smarten up!

Through the Internet, all and every dimension of hijab-wearing occurs: production, consumption, embodied identity politics and representation, to name but a few, and the websites pertaining to the British hijab amount to more than 500,000 results in a Google search.[5] The timing of the rise of the Internet alongside the rise of British hijabi identity politics has proved fortuitous not only because it has facilitated subcultural and fashion momentum, but also because of how developments in technology and the web have been associated with various freedoms for individuality and self-expression. The current Maker Movement and the rise of DIY culture in digital life are contemporary examples of self-fashioning, but it is also the broader discourse of the merging of humans and technology into transhumans – which refers to the way in which science and technology pushes us beyond our human limits though augmentation and digital innovation – that offers exciting scope to rethink embodied identity, generally. In the new world of skin and digital circuitry, everyone is, to some degree, a data body. But it was in 1960, as a product of early cybernetic theory, that the term 'cyborg' was coined, to refer to a being with both organic and biomechatronic parts. It was precisely this kind of idea that heralded the new frontier where humans were going to have their bodily and cognitive functions enhanced by technology. Twenty years later, theorist Donna Haraway (2006) sequestered the term into feminist theory, marking a turning point for thinking about gender. In her very famous essay, 'A Cyborg Manifesto', she used the idea of the cyborg to reject that gender is confined or based solely to the body. Instead she wanted us to rethink ourselves as the fusion of self and machine as a way of transcending the physical body, and in turn its social and political limitations. Haraway presented a gender theory and politics for the information age.

While she has been critiqued, Haraway's ideas have also been heavily developed by successors, particularly in the 1990s, when British cultural theorist Sadie Plant (1997) argued that the 'digital revolution' marked the decline of masculine power structures. Plant's 'cyberfeminist' vision saw the web as fractured and diffuse structures: ones that she argued were aligned with women's fluid identities. In her book *Zeros and Ones* (1997), she identifies women's natural relationship with modern technology, one that she argues would lead to a sexual revolution. Within her utopian polemic, she also connects the development of code – that is the binary of zeros and ones – with weaving. Plant suggests that weaving and textile production, specifically the development of string, are a foundation for society's further invention, innovation and entrepreneurial advances in the information age. She makes much of the connection between the computer and the loom, arguing that the structure of the computer, which is controlled by the two digits, zero and one, is closely related to the construction of the loom.

The critical fact about the cyber-discourse of the 1990s was that it was, for the most part, premised on disembodiment through technology: it mapped the Internet as a disembodied cyberspace and this is where, for its proponents, utopianism lay: through liberation from the constraints of physical, gendered reality. Undisputedly, one of the key signifiers about the hijab is that it fixes Muslim women into a gendered position, that of 'female', reinforcing a gender hierarchy rooted in traditional and historic texts and mores.

But as digital subjects, hijabi women face a new frontier: one where wearable technology and smart fabrics might be embodied as hijab, potentially throwing into crisis the meaning behind the historic definitions of 'woman', 'female', let alone 'hijab' or 'hijabi'. Our posthuman and artificially augmented futures offer a fascinating turning point regarding ontological definitions and uncap myriad potentialities to express our digital subjectivities beyond any that, to date, we have recognized.

Conclusion

Considering that many hijabs are made from globally produced scarves, it is noteworthy that in January 2015, Microsoft researchers prototyped SWARM, an emotion-sensing scarf that can be commanded to heat up and vibrate via a smartphone app, part of an exploration of how the accessory could eventually work with emerging biometric- and emotion-sensing devices. The current prototype is a flexible laser-cut garment made of hexagons of industrial felt overlaid with conductive copper taffeta. Some of the modules can heat up, while others can vibrate.[6] Elsewhere, there is Veil, a Kickstarter project with the tag line, 'The Future of Modesty' and a homepage tile that reads: 'Hijab meets Technology'. The company has developed a crowdsourced hijab that is climate-adaptive with water repelling technologies. The hijab is called 'Cool Dry' and the founder, Ahmad Ghanem, says his motivation for the smart scarf is that he wants:

> to continue to innovate, revolutionise, and change the way people see the hijab. These women are the strongest and steadfast, and they deserve everything. The hate and verbal abuse many of them receive is wrong and unfair, and I hope my brand can inspire them to go out and become what they want to be.

While still in its infancy, smart textiles and wearable technology have strong growth predicted over the coming years and success for mainstream adoption. In a report in 2014 about market trends, Beecham Research predicted that the wearable technology market is expected to be worth almost $3bn by 2018,[7] and it is also likely that more women will be the founders of the start-ups producing these sorts of objects.

The idea of the hijab as vibrant matter[8] creates a new arena to think about potentiality and affect beyond historical reduction of gender, race and religio-ethnic identities that has traditionally held notions of the body as stable matter and ontologically defined. Smart-hijabs raise a host of new questions about definitions, and ideas about materiality and sensuality of the British Muslim woman. Stretching further, in a world of posthumans and artificial intelligence, should we also ask: might robots wear hijab in the future, and to what affect?

Notes

1. There are no accurate statistics about the number of women wearing Muslim head coverings in the UK. The rise in newspaper, television and radio footage about the topic in the last decade, or more, is one measure of how veiling has become a significant public issue, as is the rise in hate crimes against Muslim women wearing the veil. Hate crimes against Muslims in the United Kingdom have jumped nearly 275 per cent since the 13 November Paris attacks, according to a Reuter's report on 23 November 2015. A couple of years prior, in August 2012, Anne Marie Waters, a council member of the National Secular Society, made the claim that 'The number of women wearing the burka and niqab has exploded in Britain in recent decades'. Available at www.secularism.org.uk/blog/2012/08/women-can-choose-to-wear-the-burka--but-can-they-choose-not-to (accessed 16 April 2016).
2. For a still of the footage see www.bbc.co.uk/news/uk-31650985 (accessed 16 April 2016).
3. While there is much writing about the 'thingyness' of things, Brown's (2004) text offers a contemporary theoretical overview of the materiality of things.
4. Issey Miyake's London store is called Pleats Please Issey Miyake. Available at http://pleatspleaseshop.com/storeinfo.html (accessed 16 April 2016).
5. About 564,000 results on 16 April 2016.
6. Available at www.technologyreview.com/s/534261/microsoft-researchers-get-wrapped-up-in-smart-scarf/ (accessed 16 April 2016).
7. Available at http://www.beechamresearch.com/download.aspx?id=29 (accessed 16 April 2016).
8. For a discussion of new theories of materialism and vibrant matter, see Bennet (2009).

References

Barnett, Pennina. 1999. 'Folds, Fragments and Surfaces'. In *Textures of Memory: The Poetics of Cloth*, 25–34. Nottingham: Angel Row Gallery.

Bennet, Jane. 2009. *Vibrant Matter: A Political Ecology of Things*. Durham NC: Duke University Press.

Brown, Bill. 2004. *Things*. Chicago, IL: University of Chicago Press.

Bruno, Guiliana. 2014. *Surface: Matters of Aesthetics, Materiality, and Media*. Chicago, IL: University of Chicago Press.

Deleuze, Gilles. 1993. *The Fold: Leibniz and the Baroque*. London: Athlone Press.

Doy, Gen. 2002. *Drapery: Classicism and Barbarism in Visual Culture*. London: I.B.Tauris.

El-Guindi, Fadwa. 1999. *Veil: Modesty, Privacy, and Resistance*. London: Bloomsbury.

Haraway, Donna. 2006. *A Cyborg Manifesto: Science, Technology, and Socialist-Feminism in the Late 20th Century*. Dordrecht: Springer.

Hollander, Anne. 1993. *Seeing through Clothes*. Berkeley and London: University of California Press.

Kidwell, Claudia B. and Valerie Steele. 1989. *Men and Women: Dressing the Part*. London: Booth-Clibborn Editions.

Lewis, Reina. 2015. *Modest Fashion: Styling Bodies, Mediating Faith*. London: I.B.Tauris.

Mascia-Lees, Frances E. 1992. *Tattoo, Torture, Mutilation, and Adornment: The Denaturalization of the Body in Culture and Text*. New York: SUNY Press.

Mernissi, Fatima. 1987. *Beyond the Veil: Male–Female Dynamics in Modern Muslim Society*. Bloomington, IN: Indiana University Press.

Plant, Sadie. 1997. *Zeroes and Ones: Digital Women and the New Technoculture*. London: Fourth Estate.

Scott, Joan Wallach. 2009. *The Politics of the Veil*. Princeton, NJ: Princeton University Press.

Shusterman, Richard. 2000. 'Somaesthetics and Care of the Self: The Case of Foucault'. *The Monist* 83(4):530–51.

Wilson, Elizabeth. 2003. *Adorned in Dreams: Fashion and Modernity*. London: I.B.Tauris.

Young, Iris. M. 1994 'Women Recovering Our Clothes'. In *On Fashion*, edited by Shari Benstock and Suzanne Ferris, 197–210. New Brunswick, NJ: Rutgers University Press.

PART V

Gender, space, community

19

VEILING, GENDER AND SPACE

On the fluidity of 'public' and 'private'

Anna-Mari Almila

Introduction

Veiling has in the 'Western' mind been associated with the mysterious *harem* for centuries. Over-eroticized ideas about harems and public baths in the 'Orient' appear in traveller narratives, art and literature alike. For centuries, Muslim women (and Muslim men) have been created through romantic, exotic, erotic, sensual, sensational stories by Europeans (Haddad 2007). Yet it is indeed the case that veiling and *harem* have been intimately connected in many locations across the Middle East and North Africa. While the nature of these spaces and practices has often been misunderstood, the interconnectedness of dress, construction of space, and gender is undeniable in practices of veiling (e.g. Fay 2012; vom Bruck 1997).

It has been recognized that sartorial fashion and architecture in Europe have tended to follow similar aesthetic trends (McLeod 1994). Even more fundamentally, any spatial practice must be in balance with the built environment (Lefebvre 1991 [1974]). If dress is understood as a spatial practice, it follows that dress systems must be in balance with architecture and the built environment. The interesting question, then, becomes this: what kind of adaptations are needed when a 'foreign' dress practice, following 'foreign' spatial logic, is brought into a different environment? In other words, how do veiling women manage European spaces and spatial practices?

In this chapter I consider veiling as dress, and as spatially located practice. This means that I consider veiling as a phenomenon that is socially meaningful, embodied and contextual. Dress is always defined according to social situation and social environment, and according to who is present; shared socio-moral norms define the acceptability of dress in a situation and in society. One important element of such norms is sexual morality, and related norms that define the acceptability of exposure of the gendered body (Ribeiro 2003 [1986]). Scott (2007), for example, has argued that the French headscarf debates in the early 2000s were partly framed through French idea(l)s of sexual liberation, and through what such liberation meant to the exposure of the female body. Thus, one element of 'foreignness' of the hijab in Europe is the perceived difference in terms of which parts of the body are customarily covered. But beyond this element, I shall argue, there is also a deeper, spatial level of difference, which requires various adaptation strategies from veiling women in Europe.

Therefore I seek to understand what happens to a dress phenomenon when it is taken from one kind of spatial structure, allowing for following certain spatial practices in order to pertain to moral order, into a different set of spatial logics. It has been argued by many that the 're-veiling' emerging in the 1970s was a new form of veiling rather than return to 'traditional' veils (e.g. Duval 1997; MacLeod 1987; 1992; Zahedi 2007). The reason for this was clear: the new phenomenon was driven by working and studying middle classes, rather than largely connected to elite women, as was the case with 'traditional' veiling practices. These women lived in socio-spatial conditions very different from the 'traditional' elite veilers, and therefore had very different requirements for their dress. As the need and desire for new forms of veiling emerged, also a supply market of such garments developed, and this market with time became internationalized, serving consumers across countries and continents (Abaza 2007, Gökarıksel and Secor 2010; 2013; Jones 2007).

Today, veiling has been fetishized and politicized on the one hand, and normalized and com-modified on the other. The veil is a symbol of Islamism! The veil is fashion! The veil is a human right! The veil is oppression! But at a fundamental, everyday level, veiling is a dress practice, shaped by its environment. Veiling women manage and produce space through their practices, and they also produce gender order which corresponds to their religious beliefs about morality. It is these concerns I focus on in this chapter. I first discuss what space, public, and private have been taken to mean particularly in Europe, and how they have been theorized. I then proceed to discuss how space, dress and gender have been constructed in North Africa and the Middle East, before discussing the challenges and solutions to spatial practices that veiling women face in Finland, where I have conducted extensive ethnographic fieldwork within local Muslim communities.

Space, public and private

Many conventional ideas about public versus private, and public versus domestic in Europe are based on nineteenth-century ideas. A new public sphere emerging in the eighteenth century emphasized openness instead of secrecy in governance and ruling (Habermas 2011 [1989]). While this sphere was characteristically open, masculine and political, it was only after the French Revolution that fundamental, gendered opposition between public/male versus private/domestic/female came to be established. Indeed, the public and private spheres were largely overlapping in the eighteenth century (Goodman 1992). The emergence of the 'modern' city as a masculine space in the nineteenth century, and the commitment to the domestic sphere of bourgeois women, were elementary to new understandings of public and private (Walker 1998). Male workplace in the city as a separate space from the female domestic environment was characteristic of the century (Sciama 1993). Such gendered division and opposition, still partly surviving today, is both based upon, and contributes to, the social, cultural and psychological organization of societies, whereby higher value is placed on male-dominated, culturally legitimated public activities (Rosaldo 1974). The gendering of space reflects society, and re-creates society at the same time (Massey 2002 [1994]). Yet this theory of separation of spaces, that is, that women were excluded from the public sphere, was not the full reality. Instead, women's practices in the public sphere happened in various forms throughout the nineteenth century (Balducci and Jensen 2014).

It is important here to remember how complex these overlapping concepts are. Public and private spheres of activities partly correspond to, but are not fully defined by, spaces considered public or private. Gendered practices may be theoretically limited to certain spaces only, but in reality are far more flexible. It is not my intention here to go into detailed discussion of such historical nuances. Rather, it is important to remember that 'public' and 'private' are historically constructed concepts, and as many critics have pointed out, are often not very suitable for analysing societies that subscribe to different ideas of privacy and public (e.g. Abraham 2010; El-Guindi 1999; Sciama 1993).

An alternative way of looking into arrangement of domestic and other spaces is 'interior' versus 'exterior'. In Bourdieu's (1970) famous interpretation of the Berber house, he sees the house (interior) as symbolically opposite to the exterior – the market, the café, the mosque. While this difference is gendered – female, sanctuary and the interior associated with each other – the house is not exclusively female space, but is instead transformed into male–female space or all-female space according to necessity. Symbolic meanings in such spatial arrangements are not inherent to the space but are instead socially produced, and all such ideas to do with public/private and outside/inside can be tracked back to ancient Greece (Ardener 1993).

Spaces can either be open to everyone, or restricted through different mechanisms and forms of gatekeeping. Spaces are also defined by individuals present, behaviours of individuals, and objects in space. Thus, the entry of a stranger changes private space into public, and furniture and other objects in space indicate its intended uses. Gender matters in some spaces (or can be an entry requirement to some spaces) and is considered irrelevant in others (Ardener 1993). Such restrictions and exclusion strategies bring us nearer to the concept of privacy defined in a more inclusive manner than equating 'domestic' with 'private'. Sciama's (1993, 87) often-cited definition considers privacy as 'the need for individuals, families or other social groups, to separate themselves from others at various times, or for certain well-defined activities'. It is important to remember that while the association of women with privacy and men with public is often assumed, in reality privacy is a far more flexible concept: 'Privacy can . . . be seen as a continuum, and it may be very difficult indeed for the anthropologist, faced with the complexities of human interaction, to say at just what point the private turns into its opposite, the public' (Sciama 1993, 93). When exploring privacy in everyday life, it is less contrasted with the political than the social. Indeed, political and economic power are often hidden and surrounded with the privilege of privacy (Sciama 1993). Such privileged privacy is a form of creating social distance, and can occur also in intimate relations. Rosaldo (1974, 27) uses the example of 'the veil of a newspaper' to illustrate how men may be creating social distance to their wives and children by retiring behind their newspaper in the breakfast table, avoiding intimacy, and creating 'sacredness' through separation. This is an important point to remember later when I discuss the problematics of face-veiling, privilege, and privacy.

Dress has been intimately linked to special structures, which in Europe has involved the considerations of public/private and public/domestic. Thus, in the nineteenth century, when public and private domains became gender-segregated, also male and female dress came to be strictly separate, and visually and materially differentiated. While female dress-making of the 19th century borrowed details and materials from male tailoring, it was middle-class women's entry to the labour market in the twentieth century that produced a new kind of female dress suitable for work purposes (Hollander 1994). Similarly, veiling has been deeply embedded in architecture and the organization of space, and the 'new veiling' that emerged in 1970s was fundamentally different from 'traditional' forms of veiling due to different spatial necessities associated with it (MacLeod 1987; 1992). When talking about dress, space and the cultural understandings of public and private are, therefore, essential to the discussion.

According to Schmid (2008, 29), 'space and time do not exist universally. As they are socially produced, they can only be understood in the context of a specific society'. In other words, space is produced over a course of location-specific history. Therefore space must be understood as a history that is both formulated by and formulates the very social history of the particular location. Consequently, understanding space 'calls for an analysis that would include the social constellations, power relations, and conflicts relevant in each situation' (Schmid 2008, 29). This point will, again, prove to be extremely relevant for understanding the position of face-veiling women in Europe.

According to Henri Lefebvre (1991 [1974]), space can be understood as a triad: it is simultaneously perceived, conceived and lived. Space is hegemonic, but it allows for re-imagining, and counter-hegemonic activities – therefore space is dialectical. Space is also always a historical process, and each form of socio-cultural production creates its spaces. In addition to the obvious fact that human action happens in space, space also shapes human action: space sets the limits for possible actions, and guides spatial practices. At the same time, space *itself* is shaped by human action. According to Lefebvre (1991 [1974], 57), space pre-exists its actors and this pre-existence 'conditions the subject's presence, action and discourse', yet space is produced by humans through the production of society, knowledge and institutions (Elden 2004, 184). In the words of Schmid (2008, 29), space and time 'are both result and precondition of the production of society'. It is from this point of view that I start considering the historical formulation of space and veiling, and how veiling and space have transformed with 'modernity'.

Veils and spaces in North Africa and the Middle East

In North Africa and the Middle East, veiling and spatial seclusion have for a long time been a mark of status and respectability. Indeed, the veil was a privilege of elite women far before Islam, in various societies that practised forms of gender segregation (Ahmed 1992; Fay 2012). Veiling can in some ways (although not exclusively) be considered an urban phenomenon; certainly it has taken different, and often stricter, forms in urban environments from rural customs. Full veiling has been historically practised by elite women in urban environments, whilst poor and rural women have followed far less strict veiling customs that allow for participation in labour (Fay 2012; Rostam-Kolayi and Matin-Asgari 2014; Wide 2014). The 'new veiling' emerging in the 1970s was an urban phenomenon as well, albeit in a different manner: it was driven by new forms of middle-class participation in work life and education (MacLeod 1987, 1992). I will consider both these veiling phenomena in terms of space and the organization of urban environment. It will become evident that forms of gender segregation are achieved through architecture as well as dress and behaviour.

'Traditional' veiling and harem

Harem, haram, forbidden, inviolable. According to Leila Ahmed (1982, 524):

> [t]he harem can be defined as a system that permits male sexual access to more than one female. It can also be defined, and with as much accuracy, as a system whereby the female relatives of a man – wives, sisters, mother, aunts, daughters – share much of their time and their living space, and further, which enables women to have frequent and easy access to other women in their community, vertically, across class lines, as well as horizontally.

This point about the dual character of the harem system is echoed by others. On the one hand, the control of female reproductive capacity is crucial for a kinship system to develop. In such a system, women are ultimately a form of property. On the other hand, gender segregation is not necessarily a system of seclusion, but tends to give certain women considerable power and influence both within their parallel, female sphere, and through their links to influential men (Fay 2012). Indeed, the elite harem as a space is forbidden to all men, including the master of the house, when unrelated women are present, which also allows women to keep their conversations private (Ahmed 1992; vom Bruck 1997). But in less privileged households, women may have less power over their privacy. If the master of the house is allowed to enter when he pleases (albeit giving an appropriate warning that he is approaching), women must check their dress, behaviour and topics of conversation with very short notice. Gender segregation is then upheld more through norms of gendered behaviour and practices of avoidance, rather than through strict spatial separation. In such circumstances, it is likely that male guests are rarely invited to the house (Buitelaar 1998), while in a more affluent household, there are separate guest reception rooms for men and women (Fay 2012; Kotnik 2005; vom Bruck 1997). In this section, I draw upon scholarly work focusing on certain specific locations, but also on more general characteristics of 'Islamic' organization of space. It is not my intention to claim that nineteenth-century Cairo (Fay 2012), mid-twentieth-century Morocco (Buitelaar 1998) and late twentieth-century Yemen (Kotnik 2005; vom Bruck 1997) would be directly comparable and without specific local characteristics. Nevertheless, as Abu-Lughod (1987) has argued, there are similarities between these locations and historical moments that can be considered 'Islamic', particularly in terms of gender segregation and how gendered space is organized and practised.

Not only have 'Western' travellers and scholars had highly misleading ideas about the harem and about (elite) women in North Africa and the Middle East, but they have often also failed to understand the key spatial characteristics of the 'Islamic city'. Janet Abu-Lughod (1987) has traced back 'Western' scholarship on the topic and argues that a tendency to reproduce 1920s ideas from one scholar to another is a great flaw in seeking to understand 'Islamic' urban space. Based on a limited number of examples – first North African (French scholarship), then Syrian – generalizations were made about characteristics that were not related to Islamic doctrines, but rather were connected to climate, politics and cultural factors. But, one crucial religious element shaping 'Islamic' space and urban environment was the ideal of gender segregation. This had consequences to architecture and spatial practices likewise.

> [B]y encouraging gender segregation, Islam created a set of architectural and spatial imperatives that had only a limited range of solutions. What Islam required was some way of dividing functions and places on the basis of gender and then of creating a visual screen between them. This structuring of space was different from what would have prevailed had freer mixing of males and females been the pattern. Such spatial divisions were a functional supplement to alternative patterns of person-marking which were also used but often not fully satisfactory. Semiotics of space in the Islamic city gave warnings and helped persons perform their required duties while still observing avoidance norms.
>
> *(Abu-Lughod 1987, 163)*

What this meant in practice must be clarified. Segregation between genders was primarily visual, and required little spatial distance. Unrelated men and women could be in close proximity as long as they were not in direct physical contact, and the man could not see the woman (Abu-Lughod 1987). While visual segregation worked in one way only, both genders had equal responsibility in securing it. Architecture helped them in this. Bending corridors at the entry to a house ensured that an outsider could not accidentally glimpse the residents of the house. The visitor would first reach a courtyard from which doors led to other parts of the house. The placement of windows, the height of buildings, and the placement of doors was so regulated that visibility from outside, and from the neighbours, was restricted (Abu-Lughod 1987; Buitelaar, 1998; Fay 2012). In addition to such stable measures to provide visual privacy, one important element of architectonic solutions were portable wooden screens that were flexibly used to provide women free movement inside and outside the house (for example on a boat deck) (Abu-Lughod 1987; Fay 2012). Such architectural structures and strategies provided certain freedom of movement for elite women, which fully veiling women in Europe sometimes lack, as we will see later on.

Veiling is an intimate part of such a system of gender segregation. The veil in this context is simply another screen, a portable form of visual privacy, which guarantees woman's inviolability when moving out in public. In fact, it is possible to see the veil as a tool of creating and securing harem, rather than seeing the veil and harem as complementary. According to Fay (2012), harem was not a location in a house, but rather was a space created by moving female bodies. Where the elite female body went, harem had to go with her – hence the screens that could be moved, and provided one-way (in)visibility; hence the veil that provided similar one-way means of seeing. Both allowed the woman to see, but not to be seen. In other words, 'the veil functions as a movable interior space that allows women to penetrate exterior space' (Kotnik 2005, 480). Clearly, the association of private with domestic is not fitting for understanding such a spatial arrangement as this. Quite the contrary, domestic space transforms into public (albeit still gender-segregated) with the entry of guests (vom Bruck 1997).

It must be remembered that such levels of privacy for elite women were only possible in a society where slave and lower-class women were not similarly protected against (male) gaze, and thus could perform tasks that the elite women never could have done (Fay 2012). But the urban poor were not completely without means to secure gender segregation. While they had less space at their disposal, and had to perform a variety of work tasks, there were nevertheless ways to protect the neighbourhood women from outsider gaze. Spatial codes and signals were used to uphold gender segregation in Muslim neighbourhoods. In 'Islamic' cities, where neighbourhoods were cell-like entities with one entrance only, the shared space of the neighbourhood was treated as semi-private by the residents. This allowed local women to perform tasks outside their domestic space, without wearing veils that would have hindered their performance. Such 'semi-private space, a third category between public and private . . . is found infrequently in sex-integrated societies but is often found in sex-segregated societies' (Abu-Lughod 1987, 168), and is protected by a (male) gatekeeper located near the entrance. It is his duty to approach strangers who intend to enter the neighbourhood enquiring his business, giving alert to local people and gaining information for everyone's benefit. But this space was also a space of community control, where especially women's behaviour was closely monitored by the community and the gatekeeper (Abu-Lughod, 1987).

Another space of privacy, upheld by signs and social customs, was the public bath. A sign at the entrance would indicate ladies' day, when no man would dare to enter (Abu-Lughod 1987). This constructed an inviolable female space, which for some women was the only space where they could not be interrupted by men, and could freely interact beyond family networks. As mentioned above, not all houses in all places were large enough to pertain to full gender segregation. For women in such domestic settings, the public bath was the only space where their husbands could not reach them (Buitelaar 1998).

'New veiling' in the city

Towards the late nineteenth century, ideas to do with 'modernisation' (Europeanization) of state institutions and architecture had taken root in many places around the Ottoman empire. More or less successful attempts to 'modernise' cities by state and colonial powers changed the nature of urban space, the location of power, and consequently spatial practices (see e.g. Gul 2009; Sutton and Fahmi 2002). It is not my intention here to trace down these changes, or to seek to understand how exactly they were linked to anti-veiling campaigns and discourses that emerged across the region. Suffice to say that there were active attempts to change both urban environments and dress styles of men and women, and these followed European ideas of 'modernity'. For example, the French built new, European areas in North African cities, which resulted to political and economic power shifting geographically, and led to the abandonment of 'Islamic' areas of the city (Sutton and Fahmi 2002). In Turkey, the 'modernization' of Istanbul was a long-standing project that only succeeded after the Second World War (Gul 2009). Cairo was an early 'moderniser': during the nineteenth century, the city's European-style extensions attracted business and administration, thus shifting the centre of power of the city (Sutton and Fahmi 2002). Cairo was, of course, also central to 'new veiling' in the 1970s. Increasing rural–urban migration, improved opportunities to study at the university, crowded public transportation and university lecture halls, limited economic capital of the newly migrated students to invest in fashionable garments, and increasing need for lower middle-class women to contribute to the income of their family, were all factors behind the new forms of veiling that emerged during that decade (Abaza, 2007; El-Guindi 1999; MacLeod 1987; 1992). The crucial point here is that the change was by no means exclusively driven by increasing religiosity, but instead was linked to socioeconomic factors, as well as spatial and geographical issues.

Therefore the 'new veiling' that emerged in the 1970s was born in completely different spatial conditions from 'traditional' veiling phenomena. Urban space had transformed, and women were participating in new kinds of activities. They moved in public places far more regularly than elite women of the past. They went to spaces that would have been exclusively considered male beforehand. And like the poorer women of the past, they could not afford such protection and privacy as wealthy women could. Therefore the veil became a protector of another kind, which allowed middle-class women to perform tasks they needed to perform and still enjoy a certain level of protection, privacy, and even untouchability.

The entry of veiled women into the public sphere has resulted in certain allowances for the sake of practicality. For example, female factory workers can relax dress rules in front of their male colleagues in a similar manner as less strict veiling in front of neighbourhood men was allowed before. Similarly, communication with male colleagues may be allowed for upper middle-class women who at home would follow much stricter norms of segregation (vom Bruck 1997). 'Traditional' forms of veiling are simply not possible in spatial settings that are not 'traditional'. Even if all garments may not have changed much, their use, and behaviour associated with them has radically transformed which changing urban space and new female activities. And even more so, the new, fashionable forms of hijab that have emerged during the last decades are all highly suited for public, gender integrated environments. They follow a different spatial logic while seeking to keep up some levels of gender distance.

Veils and spaces in Finland

Spaces are gendered also in Europe, and different standards about modesty and nudity are in place across the continent. So, for example, nudity in front of others is framed differently in public baths and swimming halls across the continent. In Germany, public saunas are mixed-gender spaces, and swimwear is often banned. In Finland, while swimwear in many public saunas is banned, these spaces are gender-segregated. In Italy, washrooms for public swimming halls are gender-segregated, and nudity is banned (Karlsson Minganti 2013). Swimwear would be condemned in most social settings. 'Too revealing' outfits, especially worn by young girls or older women cause moral and social concern (Duits and van Zoonen 2006; Twigg 2013). The list could be continued endlessly: clearly, ideas about the appropriate coverage of the body vary vastly, and are defined through gender and environment, among other things.

The complexities to do with public and private apply to European contexts as well as to the 'Muslim world'. Domestic spaces are rarely exclusively private. There are windows that provide visibility, and there are also people who request admittance, and are indeed often admitted: friends of family members, readers of electricity meters, deliverers of goods, and various people carrying out surveys. While some spaces can be considered 'back stages' allowing for relaxation from public roles (Goffman 1990 [1959]), these spaces may still be stages for other kinds of roles. Consider, for example, the ladies' room. While women fix their appearance in front of mirrors, they are perfectly visible to other women, and therefore have only a partial level of privacy. In certain ways, this is still a 'front stage'.

This part of the chapter draws upon ethnographic fieldwork I conducted in Finland in 2011–2012. Based on this empirical material, I argue that semi-private spaces can be, and are, created through gatekeeping processes and collective spatial practices, but also that even in spaces that seem public, the nature of the space may provide temporary privacy for veiling women in 'Western' environment. But, how different forms of gendering spaces are viewed by veiling women themselves differs widely. While some women seek to 'fit' hegemonic spatial organization, others' views on space and spatial resistance are leaning towards counter-hegemonic activities. As we will see, these views are linked to how different veiling styles are perceived by Muslim women themselves and by others.

Pragmatics of veiling in Finland

The largest Muslim group in Finland today is Somali, who arrived from the early 1990s on, fleeing the Somalian Civil War (Tiilikainen 2003). Somalis are a highly distinctive group, whose prominent veiling style is often more conservative and covering than many other Muslims' in Finland. The commonly donned veils worn by Finland's Somalis today are in fact Arab-influenced, and 'traditional' Somali dress was far more revealing than today's strictly covering styles (Isotalo in this volume). Before the 1970s, Arab-style veils were worn in Somalia by Arab and Persian settlers only (Akou 2010).

Somalis were placed around Finland upon their arrival, but often moved afterwards to the Greater Helsinki area – presumably because of better chances for studying and employment, networks of friends and relatives, more open-minded environment, and access to goods such as halal meat. Somali families are typically large, and tend to live in council houses, usually in flats in block houses, and the population is concentrated in certain areas of the town (Virtanen and Vilkama 2008). Finnish block house flats have been largely standardized since the late 1960s on, due to great rural-to-urban migration at the time, and the consequent need to provide housing. The predominant types of flats are one- or two-bedroom flats (Kaasalainen and Huuhka 2016), which causes challenges for large families. Gender segregation, practised with Somali children over 7 years old, places requirements for flats that the Finnish Council officials rarely understand (Virtanen and Vilkama 2008).

Gender segregation causes also other challenges when living in Finnish flats. Popular open kitchens are highly problematic for Somali families for whom the kitchen operates as female space where guests of the family can temporarily remove their veils without fear of disruption. In Somalia, many of these families had houses with more than one entry, so that male and female guests could each use a different one. There were also separate guest rooms for male and female guests. In Finland, the kitchen (with a door) is primarily used for female guests, and the living room for men (Dahlmann 2011).

Also large windows, often facing other block houses nearby, cause concern. Somali families prefer to have two kinds of curtains in all the windows: light curtains that during the daylight hours let the light in, and are kept closed at all times, and thicker curtains that are drawn for the night. Such arrangement ensures that the light from outside can enter, while privacy of the apartment against gazes from the outside is ensured (Virtanen and Vilkama 2008). Not all Muslims are equally concerned with visibility to outsiders, however. When visiting an Afghan woman in a new area of single-family houses, most of which were still under construction, I noticed that my hostess's living room had a façade wall of large windows. I could see construction workers building another house not far from the curtainless living room windows. Yet my hostess was not veiled. Later, I asked her whether she ever felt that she was too visible because of the windows. She told me that 'men in Finland don't look into other people's houses' and hence she does not need to worry about the windows, even if she is not wearing her hijab. She also stated that in Afghanistan it would be quite another matter. According to her, if the Afghan homes had large windows, every passer-by would peek in. Her adaptation to the local situation was based upon her observations and ideas as to how the concept of domestic privacy operates in Finland.

Moving in a neighbourhood holds different kinds of challenges to different groups of Muslims, too. In the neighbourhoods where the majority of Somalis live, harassment and verbal abuse are very common, restricting individual mobility. The commonness of such abuse is related to the general deprivation of these areas (Virtanen and Vilkama 2008), but it may also be directly linked to the individual woman's veiling style. It is a common consensus among Muslims in Finland that face-veiling provokes far more hostile reactions than any other type of veiling. Indeed, one of my face-veiling Somali informants told me that she consciously limits her spatial mobility in order to avoid hostility. Such limitations included avoiding shopping in any other time than late morning, which she perceived as the 'safest' hour to leave the house.

In Finland, there is no chance of such extension of (semi-)private space as the less affluent households exercised in 'traditional' Islamic urban settings (Abu-Lughod 1987). The space behind the front door is out of bounds for a woman who is not veiled. Here again we see a difference between more and less affluent neighbourhood. Single houses with space around them may provide partial privacy which is not possible when the front door opens into the staircase of a block house. Streets and paths near the property increase the risk of accidental visibility in densely populated areas. It is no surprise, therefore, that Somali families are known to avoid ground-floor flats (Dahlmann 2011).

While areas of Helsinki are in many ways defined by affluence and deprivation, and while this shapes significantly different Muslim women's life, there are also spaces that are less defined by the geographical location. For example, playgrounds are relatively similar across the city. Playgrounds are also in practice, if not in principle, often gender-segregated. This allows for relaxation of veiling rules. Spending time in a public playground in a residential area in Eastern Helsinki with a Somali woman who often brought her small children there, I noticed that she liked lifting her niqab when in the playground. This particular playground had a relatively large area of sparse woods around it that enabled her to see around. Also the paths around the playground were located quite far from the playground itself which meant that no one would be passing very nearby. Thus she enjoyed a wide visibility that enabled her to decide flexibly whether she needed to lower her face-veil or not.

Finland is, in fact, somewhat specific case in terms of uninhabited, unbuilt space. There are relatively large areas of woods that provide temporary protection against gaze and visibility practically everywhere. Spending time in the woods is a popular way of relaxing, but the likelihood of meeting anyone is significantly reduced especially if the area is large. This provides opportunities for relaxing the hijab, as explained by one Finnish woman:

A couple of times I've gone to the forest somewhere to pick berries or mushrooms. If I'm almost hundred per cent certain that no people will come there, or at least I'll hear from afar if someone's coming, I might push the hem of the abaya in [the waist of] my trousers and just wear the trousers.

Therefore there are ways in which an individual can through certain security mechanisms ensure her appropriate veiling in all occasions, whilst safely relaxing her outfit in others. These strategies have a lot to do with the arrangement of space both in the domestic setting and in the surroundings. Yet there are also restrictions to veiling women, which, as seen above, have to do with the social environment, and often face harder the less privileged women.

The front door is the most crucial point of negotiation in the Finnish setting. Contrary to the 'Islamic' architectonic solution of bending corridor, which places a large part of the responsibility of ensuring privacy to the (male) guest, the front door is negotiated by the inhabitants of the house through a variety of means. The following narrative illustrates some of these practices:

> *Interviewee:* If I go to visit either friends or relatives, close relatives, [I take my scarf off]. If my friends' husbands are not at home – and they normally don't invite [me around] if he is. Though a friend of mine, she has teenage sons so it's a bit [different]. I said last summer when I visited her on a really hot day: 'Are your boys at home, I'd like to take my scarf off?' So she shouted upstairs that they mustn't come without announcing they want to come, that I can remove my scarf. And she telephoned the other son: 'Ring the doorbell when you come.' . . .
>
> *Interviewer:* If your doorbell rings and you don't know who it is, do you check?
>
> *Interviewee:* I check through the peephole. If it looks like it's a woman I open . . . Sometimes when [I expect] things [to be] delivered . . . I'm quite a long time before it [already wearing] my scarf. Or I shout behind the door 'wait a bit' and put it on.

Peepholes, doorbells, mobile phones, and other means of alerting – these are modern versions of the spatial system of one-way visibility, and the male responsibility to alert women to their approach. While Muslim family members and friends are expected to respect these rules automatically, the responsibility of ensuring one's appropriate bodily coverage is exclusively the veiling woman's concern when dealing with Finnish men.

Yet in some environments, partial privacy can be ensured by a sympathetic gatekeeper. Resident houses in Helsinki are places for local activities directed mainly to youth, families with small children, immigrants and the elderly. They are city-sponsored and run by a small number of paid workforce and volunteers. Some of them are particularly popular among women of ethnic minorities, including Muslim women. Due to the demographic of users, these spaces are often temporarily gendered. A gatekeeper in such a setting may manage the space so that especially face-veiling women will know whether they can lift their veil or not: she gives hand signs to the face-veiling women as to whether there are men present, or if a man is about to enter. Such pre-arranged signals and warnings are necessary in the absence of culturally agreed spatial warning signals that are in use in many Muslim-majority societies, and can temporarily transform a resident house into a gendered, semi-private space.

Symbolic veiling in Finland

The Roihuvuori mosque in Eastern Helsinki attracts primarily young worshippers: Somalis and Finnish converts to Islam. Like other mosques in Finland, it is not specifically built for its purpose, but is instead in a building originally designed for commercial use. The large front windows, desirable for a shop, are covered, and the space converted into a prayer room with two entries, for men's and women's sides, respectively. The women's side, presumably preferable for them due to a lack of windows, is also smaller and has no wash facilities. Therefore when women arrange their evening activities, it is typically agreed that certain nights belong to them exclusively.

I happened to be present during a women's Qur'an study group in the larger side of the mosque when three 'brothers' needed to go through the room in order to enter the back of the mosque. Unsurprisingly, they requested permission to pass by calling out from outside, and were then allowed to walk through the room. This they did very swiftly, keeping their eyes high in order not to look at the women sitting on the floor. The women kept their eyes firmly on the floor, and some covered their face with their hand. In other words, their behaviour was remarkably similar to that of the young members of new mosque movement in Egypt where such movements emerged from 1970s on (El-Guindi 1999). Like in Egypt, these young Muslims in Finland are self-imposing certain spatial and behavioural norms that they consider religiously necessary and desirable.

In this particular mosque, face-veiling women can be seen relatively often. While face-veiling is not common in Finland, in some communities it is more accepted than in others (see Almila 2018). The niqab is associated by strict standards of gender segregation by many, and this makes them object the garment itself. One Finnish convert woman disagreed with such gendered spatial separation:

> I don't personally support segregation between genders . . . I rather suffer from it; I consider it embarrassing and demeaning . . . I'm strongly against it . . . and related to this I don't support [the niqab] at all . . . And I was quite shocked when my daughter a couple of years ago seriously thought [of wearing the niqab] – she's now 16. A couple of years ago when we were in Morocco the last time, there was a wife of a relative, a German who wears the niqab and doesn't go much outside the home. And she wore the niqab and that looked somehow hip and cool, and [my daughter] speculated aloud that perhaps she [will], too. And I tried to my best ability diplomatically express why it in my opinion isn't reasonable especially in Finland.

This association between the face-veil, gender segregation and home-boundedness is indeed reality to some face-veiling women, who, as discussed above, may be limited in their mobility outside the home due to their veil, and who often have preference for stricter religious interpretations of gender segregation. Culturally this is a particularly foreign concept for Finnish women, since the society is operating on a concept of (presumed) gender 'neutrality' and integration (Julkunen 2010). Another Finnish woman stated that while she can somehow understand Somali women's face-veiling (for she considered it 'traditional'), she cannot stand Finnish converts isolating themselves: wearing the niqab and 'speaking through letterboxes' – meaning that these women allegedly refuse to open the door for many people and communicate by speaking through a letterbox in the door. Again, her expression indicates not only an idea of gender segregation but also of homebound self-imposed seclusion.

While the association between the face-veil, strict gender segregation, and domestic isolation is strong, it is nevertheless the case that many face-veiling women do not wish to seclude themselves at all. Face-veiling for them is a personal choice that enhances their God relationship. Many face-veiling women also wish to participate in work life and are acutely aware that face-veiling significantly reduces their chances of employment. These women are usually willing to remove their face-covering during the work hours, but they typically prefer female-dominated work environments. It is worth considering here the specificities of privacy in 'female' and 'male' work environments. Spain (2002 [1985]) has argued that women and men typically have different levels of privacy in their occupational roles. Women, who tend to hold lower occupational roles, are often working in open spaces and have less control over space than men who tend to hold higher status positions. Typically 'female' occupations, such as teaching, nursing and secretarial roles, are performed in spaces where the staff is visible and available, and the organization of space provides limited privacy. These forms of employment are overwhelmingly typical also for working Muslim women in Finland, and this means that their veiling practices have to adapt to the relative lack of privacy at the workplace, as well as to the expectations of non-Muslim Finns whom they meet at work. While veiling is sometimes considered as resistance to hegemonic social norms, many veiling women in Finland are actually willing to conform to spatial rules, and adapt them only as far as necessary (Almila 2018).

The contradictory nature of 'private' is again apparent here. Privacy in a workplace is a privilege, but domestic privacy for women is often considered negative, indicating powerlessness and seclusion. But veiling has historically meant privilege and high social status. Similarly as 'the veil of a newspaper' created social distance and 'sacredness' (Rosaldo 1974, 27), the (face-)veil is often intended to indicate sacredness (El-Guindi 1999). That the face-veil is perceived to create social distance in Europe is undeniable, but it also indicates the privilege of privacy that is deemed ill-fitting to those that the majority would perceive as very low in social hierarchy (Almila 2018). So, the power relations and conflicts between groups of people (Schmid 2008) create conflictual spaces for face-veil wearers. On the one hand, they enjoy an extreme privilege, on the other, they suffer extremely hostile responses and are often home-bound as a consequence. This is partly because their choice of an outfit is not matching the spatial organization surrounding them, and is therefore interpreted in different terms than they themselves see their appearance. The act of face-veiling is resistant to hegemonic spatial practices (Lefebvre 1991 [1974]), whether the face-veiling women themselves consider it as such or not.

While face-veiling can be seen as creating an extreme form of privacy, also other forms of veiling are connected to ideas about private and public. A Finnish woman who described her hijab style as 'Western' considered the privacy provided by her veil as an important factor for her public presentation.

> You'll have more clearly a public self and a private self. When you cover yourself in the public it's also a way of saying I'm to be taken seriously, even if it's not perceived as such in our Western culture. I'm an active woman in the society.

In a strong contrast with common 'Western' ideas about veiling, for this woman her veil is actually an indicator of her contribution to society. Her thoughts echoed ideas expressed by many others as well: the veil is understood to make male–female relations less complicated, and to remove any sexual references from public environments. Therefore it allows the woman's entry into the public sphere, not (only) by reassuring her family, but because she herself chooses to keep her body, and therefore part of her self, private.

Conclusion

The primary point that this chapter makes is that veils and veiling are far more than political or fashion phenomena only, for they are also spatial phenomena, too. Analysis of veiling practices is incomplete if it does not take into account the relations that pertain between particular types of veils and veiling, and specific sorts of space. Scholarship on veils needs to concentrate much more on spatial dynamics than it has done until now. What must be brought into analysis of particular veiling practices is a consideration of how particular sorts of spaces have been involved in the creation and operation of particular sorts of veils and the uses to which they have been put. As the nature of space changes in particular locations, veiling practices either adapt to those changes or begin to come into conflict with the changed spatial settings. Spatial analysis of veils and veiling therefore must be centrally concerned with analysing the extent to which particular types of space and specific sorts of veils and veiling activities 'fit' with each other or not. The key questions, then, are – do veils and veiling operate in ways that are congruent with specific spatial locations, or are they in conflict, and if so, how and for what reasons? Such general questions are thoroughly bound up with issues of social change and so-called modernization. Veils in the 'Islamic' tradition were created and initially worked within urban and rural contexts with which they were generally congruent. But as the internal dynamics of Muslim-majority societies became more complex over time, and as processes set in train by Western colonialism impacted on those societies, the relationships between veils and spaces themselves became more complex and more potentially ambiguous. Throughout the nineteenth and twentieth centuries, the relations between veils and spaces became ever more complex, especially in relation to large-scale migration of Muslims to Europe. European urban space was based on principles in some ways very different from those which structured 'Islamic' forms of space in earlier centuries. Much of the controversy in Europe and in European-influenced societies around the world over veils and veiling derives at a deep level from divergent forms of mismatch between urban spatial principles embedded in space and embodied in veils. Built into both buildings and streets on the one side and veils and veiling on the other are different cultural principles concerning appropriate modes of visibility, bodily comportment and, ultimately, morality. Thus controversies about veils in general, and face-veiling in particular, are based on more than just obvious and observable political dynamics; they are also founded in very long-standing, deeply rooted sets of spatial assumptions. Those assumptions are expressed in the material environment and in objects such as veils, and so at one level, are highly visible and constantly surround us. But at another level, spatial principles are often far from obvious to the people whose actions are deeply shaped by them, because they are so taken for granted that they are rendered partly invisible. It is the task of the spatial analysis of veils and veiling to reveal the deep generative principles of space that underpin particular practices, and render veiling either a very natural or highly unnatural practice within a particular spatial environment.

References

Abaza, Mona. 2007. 'Shifting Landscapes of Fashion in Contemporary Egypt'. *Fashion Theory* 11(2/3):281–98.

Abraham, Janaki. 2010. 'Veiling and the Production of Gender and Space in a Town in North India: A Critique of the Public/Private Dichotomy'. *Indian Journal of Gender Studies* 17(2):191–222.

Abu-Lughod, Janet L. 1987. 'The Islamic City – Historic Myth, Islamic Essence, and Contemporary Relevance'. *International Journal of Middle East Studies* 19(2):155–76.

Ahmed, Leila. 1982. 'Western Ethnocentrism and Perceptions of the Harem'. *Feminist Studies* 8(3):521–34.

Ahmed, Leila. 1992. *Women and Gender in Islam: Historical Roots of a Modern Debate*. London: Yale University Press.

Akou, Heather Marie. 2010. 'Somalia'. In *Berg Encyclopedia of World Dress and Fashion*, Vol. 1: *Africa*, edited by Joanne B. Eicher and Doran H. Ross, 413–20. Oxford: Berg.

Almila, Anna-Mari. 2018. *Veiling in Fashion: Space and the Hijab in Minority Communities*. London: I.B.Tauris.

Ardener, Shirley. 1993. 'Ground Rules and Social Maps for Women: An Introduction'. In *Women and Space: Ground Rules and Social Maps*, 2nd revised edition, edited by Shirley Ardener, 1–30. London: Berg.

Balducci, Temma and Heather Belnap Jensen. 2014. 'Introduction'. In *Women, Femininity and Public Space in European Visual Culture 1789–1914*, edited by Temma Balducci and Heather Belnap Jensen, 1–16. Farnham: Ashgate.

Bourdieu, Pierre. 1970. 'The Berber House or the World Reversed'. *Social Science Information* 9(2):151–70.

Buitelaar, Marjo. 1998. 'Public Baths as Private Places'. In *Women and Islamization: Contemporary Dimensions of Discourse on Gender Relations*, edited by Karin Ask and Marit Tjomsland, 103–23. Oxford and New York: Berg.

Dahlmann, Hanna. 2011. 'Yhden uhka, toisen toive? Somalien ja venäläisten asumistoiveet etnisen segregaatiokehityksen valossa'. PhD thesis, University of Helsinki.

Duits, Linda and Liesbet van Zoonen. 2006. 'Headscarves and Porno-Chic: Disciplining Girls' Bodies in the European Multicultural Society'. *European Journal of Women's Studies* 13(2):103–17.

Duval, Soroya. 1997. 'New Veils and New Voices: Islamist Women's Groups in Egypt'. In *Women and Islamization*, edited by Karin Ask and Marit Tjomsland, 45–72. Oxford: Berg.

El-Guindi, Fadwa. 1999. *Veil: Modesty, Privacy and Resistance*. Oxford: Berg.

Fay, Mary Ann. 2012. *Unveiling the Harem: Elite Women and the Paradox of Seclusion in Eighteenth-Century Cairo*. New York: Syracuse University Press.

Goffman, Erving. 1990 [1959]. *The Presentation of Self in Everyday Life*. London: Penguin.

Gökarıksel, Banu and Anna Secor. 2010. 'Between Fashion and Tesettür: Marketing and Consuming Women's Islamic Dress'. *Journal of Middle East Women's Studies* 6(3):118–48.

Gökarıksel, Banu and Anna Secor. 2013. 'Transnational Networks of Veiling-Fashion between Turkey and Western Europe'. In *Islamic Fashion and Anti-Fashion*, edited by Emma Tarlo and Annelies Moors, 157–67. London: Bloomsbury.

Goodman, Dena. 1992. 'Public Sphere and Private Life: Toward a Synthesis of Current Historiographical Approaches to the Old Regime'. *History and Theory* 31(1):1–20.

Gul, Murat. 2009. *Emergence of Modern Istanbul: Transformation and Modernisation of a City*. London: I.B.Tauris.

Habermas, Jürgen. 2011 [1989]. *The Structural Transformation of the Public Sphere*. London: Polity.

Haddad, Yvonne Yazbeck. 2007. 'The Post 9/11 Hijab as Icon'. *Sociology of Religion* 68(3):253–67.

Hollander, Anne. 1994. *Sex and Suits: The Evolution of Modern Dress*. New York: Alfred A. Knopf.

Jones, Carla. 2007. 'Fashion and Faith in Urban Indonesia'. *Fashion Theory* 11(2/3):211–32.

Julkunen, Raija. 2010. *Sukupuolen järjestykset ja tasa-arvon paradoksit*. Tampere: Vastapaino.

Kaasalainen, Tapio and Satu Huuhka. 2016. 'Homogenous Homes of Finland: "Standard" Flats in Non-Standardized Blocks'. *Building Research & Information* 44(3):229–47.

Karlsson Minganti, Pia. 2013. 'Burqinis, Bikinis and Bodies: Encounters in Public Pools in Italy and Sweden'. In *Islamic Fashion and Anti-Fashion*, edited by Emma Tarlo and Annelies Moors, 33–54. London: Bloomsbury.

Kotnik, Toni. 2005. 'The Mirrored Public: Architecture and Gender Relationship in Yemen'. *Space and Culture* 8(4):472–83.

Lefebvre, Henri. (1991 [1974]) *The Production of Space*, translated by D. Nicholson-Smith. Oxford: Blackwell.

MacLeod, Arlene Elowe. 1987. *Accommodating Protest: Working Women, the New Veiling and Change in Cairo*. New York: Columbia University Press.

MacLeod, Arlene Elowe. 1992. 'Hegemonic Relations and Gender Resistance: The New Veiling as Accommodating Protest in Cairo'. *Signs* 17(3):533–57.

McLeod, Mary. 1994. 'Undressing Architecture: Fashion, Gender, and Modernity'. In *Architecture: In Fashion*, edited by Deborah Fausch, 38–123. New York: Princeton Architectural Press.

Massey, Doreen. 2002 [1994]. 'Space, Place and Gender'. In *Architecture: An Interdisciplinary Introduction*, edited by Iain Borden, Barbara Penner and Jane Rendell, 128–33. London: Routledge.

Rendell, Jane. 2002. 'Introduction: "Gender, Space"'. In *Architecture: An Interdisciplinary Introduction*, edited by Iain Borden, Barbara Penner and Jane Rendell, 101–11. London: Routledge.

Ribeiro, Aileen. 2003 [1986]. *Dress and Morality*. Oxford: Berg.

Rosaldo, Michelle. 1974. 'Woman, Culture and Society: A Theoretical Overview'. In *Woman, Culture and Society*, edited by Michelle Rosaldo and Louise Lamphere, 17–42. Stanford, CA: Stanford University Press.

Rostam-Kolayi, Jasamin and Afshin Matin-Asgari. 2014. 'Unveiling Ambiguities: Revisiting 1930s Iran's Kashf-i Hijab Campaign'. In *Anti-Veiling Campaigns in the Muslim World*, edited by Stephanie Cronin, 121–48. London: Routledge.

Schmid, Christian. 2008. 'Henri Lefebvre's Theory of the Production of Space: Towards a Three-Dimensional Dialectic', translated by Bandulasena Goonewardena. In *Space, Difference, Everyday Life: Reading Henri Lefebvre*, edited by Kanishka Goonewardena, Stefan Kipfer, Richard Milgrom and Christian Schmid, 27–45. Abingdon: Routledge.

Sciama, Lidia. 1993. 'The Problem of Privacy in Mediterranean Anthropology'. In *Women and Space: Ground Rules and Social Maps*, 2nd revised edition, edited by Shirley Ardener, 87–111. London: Berg.

Spain, Daphne. 2002 [1985]. 'Excerpts from "The Contemporary Workplace"'. In *Architecture: An Interdisciplinary Introduction*, edited by Iain Borden, Barbara Penner and Jane Rendell, 118–27. London: Routledge.

Sutton, Keith and Wael Fahmi. 2002. 'The Rehabilitation of Old Cairo'. *Habitat International* 26:73–93.

Tiilikainen, Marja. 2003. *Arjen Islam: Somalinaisten elämää Suomessa*. Tampere: Vastapaino.

Twigg, Julia. 2013. *Fashion and Age: Dress, and the Body in Later Life*. London: Bloomsbury.

Vilkama, Katja, Mari Vaattovaara and Hanna Dhalmann. 2013. 'Kantaväestön pakoa? Miksi maahanmuuttajakeskittymistä muutetaan pois?'. *Yhteiskuntapolitiikka* 78(5):485–97.

Virtanen, Hanna and Katja Vilkama. 2008. 'Somalien asuminen pääkaupunkiseudulla: Suurperheiden arki suomalaisessa lähiössä'. In *Islam Suomessa: Muslimit arjessa, mediassa ja yhteiskunnassa*, edited by Tuomas Martikainen, Tuula Sakaranaho and Marko Juntunen, 132–56. Helsinki: Suomalaisen kirjallisuuden seura.

vom Bruck, Gabriele. 1997. 'A House Turned Inside Out: Inhabiting Space in a Yemeni City'. *Journal of Material Culture* 2(2):139–72.

Walker, Lynne. 1998. 'Home and Away: The Feminist Remapping of Public and Private Space in Victorian London'. In *New Frontiers of Space, Bodies and Gender*, edited by Rosa Ainley, 65–75. London: Routledge.

Wide, Thomas. 2014. 'Astrakhan, Borqa', Chadari, Dreshi: The Economy of Dress in Early-Twentieth-Century Afghanistan'. In *Anti-Veiling Campaigns in the Muslim World*, edited by Stephanie Cronin, 163–202. London: Routledge.

Zahedi, Ashraf. 2007. 'Contested Meaning of the Veil and Political Ideologies of Iranian Regimes'. *Journal of Middle East Women's Studies* 3(3):75–98.

20

HINDU AND MUSLIM VEILING IN NORTH INDIA

Beyond the public/private dichotomy

Janaki Abraham[1]

Introduction

Veiling produces space, as it does gender, not only through the ideas which inform its practice but also through the ways in which women practise veiling, and negotiate the rules of veiling. While much of the discourse on veiling has reinforced the idea that veiling critically marks out spaces as either public or private, I would like to argue in this chapter that practices of veiling among both Hindus and Muslims complicate this idea and points to the need for a more nuanced understanding of veiling, space and power. This chapter is based on fieldwork done in the town of Bikaner, Rajasthan in north-western India for a study that seeks to explore how spaces in a town are gendered and how space and gender are mutually produced in everyday life.

In looking at space, I am influenced by theorists who have looked at the ways in which space is produced or created through practices that occur in it (Bourdieu 1977; 2003; Lefebvre 1991; Foucault 1975; Certeau 1984). This is in contrast to some earlier studies that saw physical space as reflecting social structure and conceptualized space as given and fixed in time. These theorists and others, such as geographers Edward Soja (1989) and Doreen Massey (1994), have been concerned with making central the category of space and exploring the relationship between spatial relations and the production of power. In particular, there has been a growing body of work that focuses on how space and gender are mutually constituted (Ardener 1993; Moore 1986; Rose 1993; McDowell 1999; specifically on India: Niranjana 2001; Phadke 2007; Ranade 2007; Khan 2007; Phadke *et al.* 2011).

However, long before scholarship on space became popular, feminists and feminist scholars had engaged with these issues through the debate on the public/private dichotomy.[2] The public/private dichotomy was one frame through which feminists in the 1970s and 1980s explained what they saw then as the 'universal subordination of women' (Rosaldo and Lamphere 1974; Reiter 1975). This position gave way to one in which feminists challenged the idea of the universal subordination of women and turned to looking at socially, culturally and historically specific understandings of 'public' and 'private' that changed over time (Rosaldo 1980). Scholars have stressed that understandings of these domains needed to be grounded in the material realities of class, race, caste, and sexuality. Simultaneously, feminists argued that much of the cultural construction of gender was and is tied to the assumption of separate spheres, and further argued that the categorization of public and private was a means of circumscribing women's actions and an excuse for the social control of women.

In looking, then, at Hindu and Muslim veiling practices (or *gunghat* and *purdah*) in this chapter, I argue that the a priori categorization of spaces as 'public' and 'private' has not only prevented a full exploration of the ways in which these categories are socially and culturally defined, but has prevented a fuller understanding of veiling practices in relation to social relationships, hierarchies and power.

A brief introduction to Bikaner town

Bikaner is a medium[3] sized town located in the western part of Rajasthan. In the 500-plus years since it was established, the city has expanded considerably beyond the walled city and the palace in the Junagarh Fort: erstwhile village areas have become part of the municipality, new colonies have been formed, and dramatically different living spaces modelled on global apartments have appeared just outside the city.

The space of Bikaner's walled city is organized on the basis of caste and religion. Muslims belonging to different occupational groups[4] and privileged Hindu castes such as Brahmins and Baniyas (traders) including Jains live in the walled city, and the *mohalla*s (neighborhoods) are named by caste, lineage (within the caste) or occupational group. Dalits (former untouchables) live just outside the walled city in seperate settlements, while Rajputs live around the Fort and palace where the Rajput Royal family continues to live. Newer colonies are far more mixed in social composition, and among them there is a considerable variation based on class, caste, religion and a degree of cosmopolitanism. What is critical for the discussion in this chapter is that there is considerable diversity in the culture of many neighbourhoods, and correspondingly veiling regimes vary considerably by the neighbourhhood in question. This is highly relevant for the discussion of Hindu and Muslim veiling (referred to here as *gunghat* and *purdah*, respectively) in Bikaner town.

Veiling and the spaces of the *sasural* and *pihir*[5]

Both in social science scholarship and in popular discourse much of the focus on veiling has tended to be on practices of *purdah* among Muslims. In particular, veiling practices among Hindus has been a somewhat neglected area in the literature.[6]

The first principle of veiling of Hindu women in north India is that only married women practise *gunghat* – this may range from covering the face up to the chin, or just covering the head. Dress expectations vary across caste groups, as does the clothing married women are expected to wear and veil with. For example, married upper-caste Hindu women in the walled city are expected to wear saris and use the end of the sari (*pallu*) to do *gunghat*. The traditional *ghagra* and *odhni* (skirt, blouse and shawl draped on the head and shoulder and tucked into the skirt at one end) are strongly associated with Rajput women who wear them every day or at least used to. Dalit women in Bikaner most often also wear the *ghagra and odhni*.

Married women observe *gunghat* in their husband's house, and in front of older male and female relatives of their husband. Thus, a newly married woman is to cover her face in front of her mother-in-law and father-in-law, her older sisters-in-law and older brothers-in-law as well as in front of all older kin and non-kin. Such veiling often extends from sartorial veiling to not being seen at all – so that the daughter-in-law will hide behind a door or a wall in the presence of those she is expected to veil in front of. While she will speak in a hushed voice with her mother-in-law, she may not speak directly to her father-in-law at all. *Gunghat* then entails not only covering the body, but effacing the self in other ways – by not being seen at all in some contexts, by not making eye contact (*ankhe ka purdah*, 'veiling of the eyes') or through the veiling of the voice (*awaz ka purdah*)[7] including suppressing sounds such as of laughter or the expression of anger (Sharma 1989) and even sounds made by a woman's slippers as she walks. That her voice should not be heard means that she is not expected to express her opinion. *Gunghat* or the covering of the head and/or face is thus part of a larger complex of veiling. Veiling here symbolizes the deference and respect (*izzat*) a woman is to show towards her in-laws, and more generally the relatives of her husband. Rules of veiling are one way in which familial hierarchy is enforced. The idea of 'modesty' (*sharam*) which *gunghat* is often explained as, is thus linked to the expression of her subordination in her marital home and kin group. This is similar to what Lila Abu-Lughod describes in the case of Bedouins: '[T]he denial of sexuality that is a mark of *hasham* [modesty] is a symbolic means of communicating deference' (1986, 119). *Gunghat* and idea of 'modesty' are linked to denial of sexuality, so that a married couple are not expected to be seen speaking to each other in front of elder in-laws, and previously could not be seen leaving the house together, walking together in the neighborhood square of the husband's parental home, or driving together on a scooter. As mentioned earlier, this idea of 'modesty' also often acts as a pretext for the larger complex of veiling which limits a woman's ability to participate equally in political life or to claim her right to resources in her conjugal home. As Sharma argues, *gunghat* is best understood as a 'means of controlling the behaviour of in-marrying women' (1978, 219).

Practices of veiling are, however, always negotiated by women themselves. Radha (35), for example, lived with her parents-in-law, husband and two children. She had married at 25, and in her initial years of marriage would cover her face in front of her mother-in-law, and speak through the veil. She explained to me that since women need to learn the work of the house from their mothers-in-law, it is necessary to speak, even if mostly in a hushed voice. After Radha gave birth to her first child, a son, she pulled her *gunghat* back to just cover her head in front of her mother-in-law. Some years later she stopped doing this as well. However, with her father-in-law she continued to cover her head and often her face and did not speak to him directly. She would often stand behind a wall or a door when her father-in-law entered the area of the house. She would never be part of a conversation when he was present, and would also speak in whispers with me if he was in the near vicinity. Practices of veiling are part of a public performance, and while a woman negotiates the everyday practice, this practice is also critically tied to who else is present. Thus, while in everyday life a woman may negotiate how much of her face her *gunghat* covers, in front of other people she may ensure that her practice of *gunghat* conforms to what is expected or what is considered 'proper'. The idea expressed here then of 'public' and 'private' is less tied to the nature of the space – domestic or outside – and more to the presence of others who are witness to the interaction.

The place of a woman's *sasural* (marital home) extends beyond the house to the whole neighbourhood. People in the neighbourhood are the fictive kin of her husband's family. This practice of *gunghat* with neighbours may extend also to non-Hindu neighbours and to those from castes considered as 'inferior'. In fact, people say that previously a new daughter-in-law would observe *gunghat* in front of the Dalit woman who swept the street outside the house. So when the daughter-in-law went out to give the Dalit woman *rotis* (bread), she would cover her face. A woman had to veil in front of all male and female elders in her *sasural* irrespective of caste, class or religion. Women were also meant to wear what is called an *odhni* – a kind of shawl made with one and a half or two metres of cloth worn over the sari when they go outside the house. Older women still wear an *odhni*, while others do so only after a death in the family, to express a state of mourning.

But practices of veiling have changed dramatically in Bikaner. Men often say that *gunghat* hardly survives now, by gesturing with their hands to indicate that the *gunghat* has shifted from being worn pulled down below the chin to now above the forehead. The dramatic change is illustrated through the changes in veiling practices in the neighbourhood square. At the centre of the upper-caste Hindu *mohallas* are wooden platforms called *patas* on which men, mostly elderly men, sit. There was a time when every married woman would have to cover her face with the end of their sari (the *pallu*), wear an *odhni*, pick up her slippers and walk barefoot past the *patas* where men were sitting. They would walk in a way that made them as invisible as possible, walking close to the buildings and exiting into a by-lane as quickly as possible.

Walking with a woman through the walled city, one can observe the shifting relationship that she has with different 'public' spaces. On a number of occasions, when walking with Radha for example, I observed this. She would ensure that her head was well covered when she stepped out of her husband's house, and constantly re-covered her head when the end of her sari covering her head slipped off. But I noticed on more than one occasion that when we entered the *mohalla* of her *pihir* (parent's house) she did not bother to pull the sari *pallu* back up to cover her head. Not only this, but her whole persona seemed to change – she talked openly and animatedly with people she met on the road, including men, both younger and older. In this neighbourhood, she was the daughter, the sister – fictive or otherwise. The only situation in which a woman observes *gunghat* in her parent's house is when her husband or an elder in-law is with her. The covering of her head in this context is a sign of deference to her husband.

Age does not necessarily blunt the relationship a woman has to her *sasural*'s *mohalla*. Walking one day with a woman in her 70s, a widow dressed in a white sari and carrying a white *odhni*, I noticed that just before we entered a particular *mohalla* she opened up the white cloth and wrapped it around herself and pulled her sari *pallu* over her head and eyes. When I asked her why she was doing this, she explained that this was the neighbourhood of her husband's family. Fifteen years after her husband's death, this relationship to her husband's neighbourhood persisted.

Similarly, while a woman may let her sari *pallu* slip off her head when in a market some distance from the neighbourhood of her husband, the space of the market is also inflected by the particular individuals in it and their relationship to the woman. When walking in the market with Radha, I would notice that she would suddenly pull her sari *pallu* over her head. For example, she did this just before entering a shop run by a relative of her husband. Thus, even spaces that are comparatively anonymous in a town are altered by the presence of individuals and the particular relationship a woman may have with them. This then means that market spaces are produced in unique ways for different women. Characterizing these spaces as 'public' does not help understand whether a Hindu woman will veil or not.

Thus, the relationship that a woman has to the space of a neighbourhood or to the street is linked to her kinship relationship to others in that neighbourhood. 'Public' spaces, and women's presence in them, I argue, need to be seen in relation to each woman's kinship relationship to those in the space. This relationship, or complex of relationships, is what produces the space. While the mapping of women in different places and at different times of day reveals interesting conclusions (see e.g. Ranade 2007), such a mapping does not tell us about the quality of women's interactions with others in these spaces.

How do women experience practices of *gunghat* (and *purdah*) and in turn experience different spaces? Many of the women I interviewed used the term *gutan* (suffocation) to describe the experience of the *gunghat* (and *purdah*) in the *sasural*. 'I feel suffocated', one woman said when telling me about how she has stopped observing *gunghat* in front of her mother-in-law and only covers her eyes (rather than her whole face) in front of her father-in-law. But the word suffocated is sometimes used more generally to describe the space of the *sasural* – the place where a woman has to veil, and where she is constrained and subordinated. I met Ayesha, a Muslim woman in her mid-20s, at an NGO in Bikaner a few days after she had joined the organisation. I asked her how she was liking it and she said 'very nice – I feel like I am in my natal home – that I have come out of the suffocation of the house and neighbourhood of my in-laws'. For women, then, different spaces may not be seen within the frame of what is 'public' or 'private' but instead may be articulated through the categories of the natal and the conjugal houses and neighbourhoods. Ayesha's words also indicate the similarity in this respect between Hindu and Muslim veiling regimes. In fact, Ayesha indicated the stricter veiling regime in her *sasural* by pointing out that she had never owned a burqua[8] nor worn one before she got married. However, a cousin marriage among Muslims considerably diminishes this experience in the *sasural*, although women will often follow normative practices of veiling in the presence of outsiders.

In looking at how women negotiate the veil, it is important to also consider how women use the practice of veiling to their advantage. I am interested in exploring what kind of space the veil creates for women within contexts that are seen as necessitating veiling. What are the tactics used by women in a context of constraint? In talking about the *gunghat*, Radha explained that it was very useful on specific occasions. When a death occurs in a family, it is customary to sit in mourning for 7 or 11 days. And every time someone comes in, women have to cry out loudly. This performance, Radha said, is enabled through veiling, whereby no one can see the face and the dramatic change of emotion reflected on it! She also told me that observing the customary *gunghat* where the veil is drawn down to the chin communicates on the one hand respect and at the same time has enabled her to say exactly what she wanted, to an elder in her husband's family. While Radha does not speak to her father-in-law directly, with other elder members of the family she often observes the *gunghat* but speaks through it. This is one of the many ways in which different kinds of veiling are negotiated. As Ann Grodzins Gold writes, 'Women may think of *purdah* as a cover behind which they gain the freedom to follow their own lights, rather than as a form of bondage or subordination' (1996, 167).

The example of Sakina Begum, a Muslim woman now in her 80s, and one of the first women in Bikaner to become a teacher, is a case in point. When she told me her life story, including how she came to be educated in spite of opposition, she said her mother insisted that she covered her head when she went to school and walked through the small lanes of Bikaner to get to school. She said that both as a student and as a teacher she has always covered her head. This seemed to be a strategy to continue her education and later her job as teacher, which included teacher training courses in Jaipur and later in her life involvement in adult literacy in the neighbourhood. Thus, conforming to expectations of veiling enabled Sakina Begum to pursue an education. Therefore veiling may be seen as enabling a subversion of normative regimes, and in a context of constraint, actually opening up spaces.

The space a woman has to negotiate these rules depends on a complex set of factors – the social environment she lives in, the bargaining power she feels she has, her level of education, the status of her natal family in relation to her husband's, the number of children she has, whether she has a son or not, her relationship with her in-laws, the views of her husband and the family on veiling, the nature of the neighbourhood they are living in and so on. While some women spoke about the *ghutan* (suffocation) they feel when they wear their *gunghat* down to their chins, and present this as the reason for why they slowly stopped observing *gunghat*, others did not mention the reason explicitly but spoke about the time when the shift was achieved. For instance, this time is often marked by the birth of a child or the arrival of a younger daughter-in-law who did not observe *gunghat*. What is important to recognize is that women constantly negotiate creatively veiling expectations and the ideals.

In this section I have tried to show that marriage patterns and kinship relationships are critical to understanding how spaces are gendered in India, and how both gender and space are produced through veiling practices in everyday life. Given the dramatic difference in the ways in which a woman relates to the neighbourhood of her parent's house in contrast to that of her husband's, a mapping of women (and men) in 'public' spaces will not express the sharp differences in her interactions with people in different spaces and her experience of each space. Considering married women in Bikaner thus points to the limitation of the 'public/private' division as an analytical category and indicates instead the need to consider the kinship relationship that a particular woman has with those who occupy the space, especially whether it is an affinal or natal relationship. Thus, contrary to studies that have pointed to the 'veiling regimes' in a city that are fixed (see e.g. Sharma 1989; Secor 2002), I am arguing that a gendered geography of a town needs also to be conceptualized in terms of the subjective mapping of a woman with respect to her veiling and, linked to this, the quality of her interactions with people.

Veiling and the culture of neighbourhoods

In Bikaner veiling practices also differ between different neighbourhoods. Different communities and caste groups have different regimes of veiling – garments used for veiling may have different names (see Palriwala 1990), and different conventions to indicate respect and *sharm* (modesty). For example, in the Dalit *basti* (tenement colony) just outside the walled city, veiling regimes seemed stricter than in other *mohallas*. Young women would wear their *gunghat* down to their chins in front of their mothers-in-law, and would not speak in their presence. Further, certain caste groups and corresponding neighbourhoods were pointed out as having relaxed veiling regimes because of significant changes in residency. Neighbourhoods also differ on the basis of whether they are old or comparatively new spaces of residence. Thus, the *mohallas* in the walled city differ from the new colonies on the basis of the degree of anonymity, although colonies themselves are differentiated in this respect. Furthermore, colonies are far more heterogeneous in caste and religious composition in comparison with the *mohallas* in the walled city, and this has a bearing on veiling regimes. Additionally, household composition is an important feature that marks out the difference. Many houses in colonies are nuclear families in which a couple have built their own house and moved out of the walled city.

The importance of considering the culture of the neighbourhood in understanding different spatial practices of veiling became clear through the consideration of different *mohallas* in the walled city that are predominantly Muslim. In the discussion of practices of the *purdah*, variations based on the different sects and regional communities of those who follow Islam has been noted (Jeffery 1979; Khan 2007), as has also variation deriving from differences in wealth (Jeffery 1979). What has received insufficient attention, is the differences based on the history and culture of a neighbourhood. I seek to highlight these by focusing on two predominantly Muslim[9] *mohallas* in the walled city in Bikaner.

The Choongara *mohalla* is known for its very high level of literacy, particularly among women. Women are not only literate but they are also well educated, with degrees, especially teacher's training certificates or degrees. Many women work as school teachers, and this in turn is seen as what has altered the culture of *purdah*, practised both as seclusion and through clothing. As one woman said, 'by and large no one wears the burqua here anymore'. The culture of this *mohalla* is seen as resulting from a high level of education in the *mohalla*. This kind of environment that stresses education's importance for women is traced back to two individual women considered to have been the first Muslim girls to have gone to school in Bikaner, and then, as adults, to have been the first women to get jobs as teachers.

These women, Sakina Begum and Amina Begum became important role models in the *mohalla*. Their getting an education and achieving employment opened up this kind of possibility for many other women. Women and their families discovered that a woman could get a 'good' and 'respectable' job as a teacher if she was educated. This then caused the snowball-effect that has contributed to a *mohalla* culture in which women's education is now the norm, as is also women being employed as teachers in schools. This *mohalla* stands out as a contrast to other *mohalla*s (both Hindu and Muslim), not only in terms of education and employment of women, but also in the culture of *purdah* in which few women use the burqua.

By contrast, in another *mohalla* in the walled city, young girls often do not study beyond Class 8. The two young women I have come to know well were both engaged to be married fairly young (17 and 20) and do not go out of the house often – they rarely visit even their aunt's house across the main square near their *mohalla*, and only once a year before the Eid celebration (at the end of Ramadan fasting month) they go to the Bada Bazaar in Bikaner. When I spoke to Sara Bano (who was 20 years old then) and her mother, about Choongara *mohalla* and the large number of women teachers there, they said 'this [our] *mohalla* is full of uneducated people'. For them, the lack of 'educated people' in their *mohalla* meant that not only was education, especially for women, not encouraged, but the neighborhood as more conservative about women observing *purdah*.

Thus, while neighbourhoods may be divided by caste and religion, they are further differentiated by their particular culture – here, Ioca history and culture of women's education, and, linked to this, very different *purdah* practices. Correspondingly, while veiling practices differ across community, caste, and class, they also vary across neighbourhoods. Therefore, the ways in which spaces in a town are gendered is critically tied to the culture of the neighbourhoods. This presents us with a radical potential for transformation at the local level. What needs to be understood in greater depth are the processes of transformation and the ways in which multiple influences – local, national and global – intersect and are negotiated and articulated in socio-cultural rules and in everyday practices.

Conclusion

Although practised variously, veiling among both Hindus and Muslims is linked to ideas of seclusion in which through the covering of the face or the body, the attempt is to achieve an effacement or invisibilization of the woman. This was most clearly seen in palaces in north India where royal women witnessed public events, ceremonies or performances from behind a fine latticework screen made in stone. The latticework enabled them to see through it, but prevented others from seeing them. Houses of the wealthy were often divided between the women's side of the house and the side of men respectively. For lower-caste or working-class Hindu women, there was of course no such luxury of separate spaces or seclusion.

Further, veiling is linked to what constitutes the 'modesty' of a girl or a woman, or in turn the 'honour' of a family or community. Decisions to withdraw a girl from school or from some forms of work outside the house may be informed by these ideas of maintaining 'honour'. These ideas of 'modesty' and 'honour' are a masquerade for the larger complex of veiling which controls a woman's ability to participate equally in political life (Sharma 1989), limits her ability to claim her right to resources (Chowdhry 1994) or prevents the exercise of her own volition, especially in matters of sexuality. Veiling therefore needs to be seen as critically linked to power.

The idea of veiling as seclusion has resulted in the overwhelming association of veiling with ideas of public and private. Thus, by focusing on practices of veiling among both Hindus and Muslims in Bikaner, I argue that other axes of differentiation, such as between *sasural* and *pihir* for a married woman, are important for our understanding of the nature of spaces. A woman's relationship to people in a particular space is crucial to her experience of that space and to her practice of veiling. Further, the individual experience of a woman varies not only on the basis of her kinship relation with people in that space at different times, but is also based on the history and culture of the neighbourhood. Thus, veiling practices vary not only by religion and community but also by the culture of neighbourhoods. Consequently, moving away from looking at veiling through the categories of 'public' or 'private' can enable a more nuanced understanding of veiling, women's negotiation of rules of veiling, and power. The idea of veiling as seclusion does not adequately capture critical aspects of veiling: power and deference, but also the ways in which women negotiate veiling regimes to create spaces for themselves.

Notes

1. Some elements of this chapter appeared previously in the *Indian Journal of Gender Studies* (17:2, 2010). I am grateful for the comments I received at the seminars I have presented this chapter at and would also like to thank Mary John, Radhika Chopra, Rajni Palriwala, Ravinder Kaur, Vijay Shanker Vyas and Sumandro Chattapadhyay for reading the chapter and commenting on it. I thank Navdeep Kaur for assistance. I am particularly grateful to people in Bikaner, and those who live outside, who welcomed me into their homes and supported this research in a range of ways.
2. The public/private dichotomy has a long history in social science scholarship. Briefly, the use of these terms can be traced back to the ancient Greek writers such as Socrates, Plato and Aristotle whose ideas were organized on the basis of a division between what was common or public and that which was domestic or individual. This distinction is fundamental to much political theory written in the West, especially liberal political thinkers concerned to protect some part of social life from state intrusion.
3. In the 2011 census, its population counted 644,406.
4. Of course, not everyone in these neighbourhoods is or was engaged with these occupations, rather the names indicate *biradiri* (extended kin) or *jati* (caste) groups among Muslims.
5. The area of the marital house and the area of the parental house. This includes the neighbourhood in which the house is located.
6. Some exceptions to this are the work of Ursula Sharma (1978), Hanna Papanek (1982), Rama Mehta (1982), Sylvia Vatuk (1982), Doranne Jacobson (1982) and Prem Chowdhury (1994) and Raheja and Grodzins Gold (1996).
7. This effaced body language can be seen practised by men as well (Chopra 2006) when in the company of another man or woman who is hierarchically placed higher in relation to caste and class status. This is visible in everyday life in Bikaner.
8. A two-piece black garment that covers the body, the head and maybe the face.
9. The majority of Muslims in Bikaner are Sunni.

References

Abu-Lughod, Lila. 1986. *Veiled Sentiments: Honour and Poetry in a Bedouin Society*. California and London: University of California Press.

Ardener, Shirley, ed. 1993. *Women and Space: Ground Rules and Social Maps*. Oxford: Berg.

Bourdieu, Pierre. 1977. *Outline of a Theory of Practice*. Cambridge: Cambridge University Press.

Bourdieu, Pierre. 2003. 'The Berber House'. In *The Anthropology of Space and Place: Locating Culture*, edited by Setha M. Low and Denise Lawrence-Zunigo. Oxford: Blackwell.

Certeau, Michel de. 1984. *The Practice of Everyday Life*. Berkeley, CA: University of California.

Chowdhry, Prem. 1994. *The Veiled Woman*. Delhi: Oxford University Press.

Foucault, Michel. 1975. *Discipline and Punish: The Birth of the Prison*. New York: Vintage.

Gold, A. G. 1996. 'Purdah is as Purdah Kept: A Storyteller's Story'. In *Listen to the Heron's Words: Reimagining Gender and Kinship in North India*, by Gloria Goodwin Raheja and Ann Grodzins Gold, 164–81. Delhi: Oxford University Press.

hooks, bell. 1984. *Feminist Theory: From Margin to Center*. Cambridge, MA: South End Press.

Jacobson, Doranne. 1982. 'Purdah and the Hindu Family in Central India'. In *Separate Worlds: Studies of Purdah in South Asia*, edited by H. Papanek and G. Minault, 81–109. Delhi: Chanakya.

Jeffery, Patricia. 1979. *Frogs in a Well: Indian Women in Purdah*. London: Zed Press.

Khan, Sameera. 2007. 'Negotiating the Mohalla: Exclusion, Identity and Muslim Women in Mumbai'. *Economic and Political Weekly* 42(17):1527–33.

Lefebvre, Henri 1991. *The Production of Space*. London: Blackwell.

McDowell. Linda. 1999. *Gender, Identity and Place: Understanding Feminist Geographies*. Cambridge: Polity Press.

Massey, Doreen. 1994. *Space, Place and Gender*. Cambridge: Polity Press.

Mehta, Rama. 1982. 'Purdah among the Oswals of Mevar'. In *Separate Worlds: Studies of Purdah in South Asia*, edited by H. Papanek and G. Minault, 139–63. Delhi: Chanakya.

Moore, Henrietta L. 1986. *Space, Text and Gender: An Anthropological Study of the Marakwet of Kenya*. Cambridge: Cambridge University Press.

Niranjana, Seemanthini. 1997. 'Femininity, Space and the Female Body: An Anthropological Perspective'. In *Embodiment: Essays on Gender and Identity*, edited by Meenakshi Thapan, 107–24. New Delhi: Oxford University Press.

Niranjana, Seemanthini. 2001. *Gender and Space: Femininity, Sexualization and the Female Body*. New Delhi: Sage.

Palriwala, Rajni. 1990. 'Production, Reproduction and the Position of Women in a Rajasthan Village'. Unpublished PhD thesis, University of Delhi.

Papanek, Hanna. 1982. 'Purdah: Separate Worlds and Symbolic Shelter'. In *Separate World: Studies of Purdah in South Asia*, edited by H. Papanek and G. Minault, 3–53. Delhi: Chanakya.

Patel, Sujata and Jim Masselos, eds. 2003. *Bombay and Mumbai: The City in Transition*. New Delhi: Oxford University Press.

Phadke, Shilpa. 2007. 'Dangerous Liaisons: Women and Men: Risk and Reputation in Mumbai'. *Economic and Political Weekly* 42(17):1510–18.

Phadke, Shilpa, Sameera Khan and Shilpa Ranade. 2011. *Why Loiter?: Women and Risk on Mumbai Streets*. New Delhi & Mumbai: Penguin Books.

Raheja, Gloria Goodwin and Ann Grodzins Gold. 1996. *Listen to the Heron's Words: Reimagining Gender and Kinship in North India*. Delhi: Oxford University Press.

Ranade, Shilpa. 2007. 'The Way She Moves: Mapping the Everyday Production of Gender and Space'. *Economic and Political Weekly* 42(17):1519–26.

Reiter, Rayna R., ed. 1975. *Toward an Anthropology of Women*. New York: Monthly Review Press.

Rosaldo, Michelle Z. 1980. 'The Use and Abuse of Anthropology: Reflections on Feminism and Cross-cultural Understanding'. *Signs* 5(3):389–417.

Rosaldo, Michelle Zimbalist and Louise Lamphere, eds. 1974. *Woman, Culture, and Society*. Stanford, CA: Stanford University Press.

Rose, Gillian. 1993. *Feminism & Geography: The Limits of Geographical Knowledge*. Cambridge: Polity Press.

Secor, Anna J. 2002. 'The Veil and Urban Space in Istanbul: Women's Dress, Mobility and Islamic Knowledge'. *Gender, Place and Culture* 9(1):5–22.

Sharma, Ursula. 1978. 'Women and their Affines: The Veil as a Symbol of Separation'. *Man* 13(2):218–33.

Sharma, Ursula. 1989. 'Women and Public Space'. In *Women in Contemporary India and South Asia*, edited by Alfred de Souza, 214–39. New Delhi: Manohar.

Soja, Edward. 1989. *Postmodern Geographies: The Reassertion of Space in Critical Social Theory*. New York: Verso.

Vatuk, Sylvia. 1972. *Kinship and Urbanisation: White Collar Migrants in North India*. Berkeley, Los Angeles and London: University of California Press.

Vatuk, Sylvia. 1982. '*Purdah* Revisited: A Comparison of Hindu and Muslim Interpretations of the Cultural Meaning of *Purdah* in South Asia'. In *Separate Worlds: Studies of Purdah in South Asia*, edited by H. Papanek and G. Minault, 54–78. Delhi: Chanakya.

21

HUI WOMEN AND THE HEADSCARF IN CHINA

Xiaoyan Wang

Introduction

Gaitao, an old style of headwear, is the one which I was familiar with when I was a child, the one which my grandmother donned sometimes – and I never thought I would focus on it as a scholar one day. *Gaitao* is a 'traditional' ethnic headdress style, which elderly Hui Muslim women don when they are praying, participating in religious activities, meeting someone outside the family, or visiting someone's house, in my city Lanzhou. In everyday life, they prefer to wear a 'white hat' (see Figure 21.1). This garment covers hair, and is almost always white. Since the 1990s on, however, more women wearing a new style of covering – headscarf (see Figure 21.2) – have appeared in the streets of Lanzhou.

In community, women present their piety and belief through actions such as dressing, speech and behaviour, when they participate in religious activities. The dress of a woman reflects her Hui identity and faith. In this chapter I discuss the construction of gender within Hui communities, in terms of embodying faith in everyday life. The chapter is divided into two sections, the first focusing on gender ideology, and the second on veiling.

Gendered division of labour in family

Nowhere is the gender ideology clearer in the lifestyle of rural Hui people, than in how labour is strictly divided. Man's work is outside the home, earning money. A common saying states: 'man be in charge of the outside, woman be in charge of the inner'.

At home, the woman is in charge of all the housework, such as cleaning yards and rooms, washing up, cooking for the family (including parents-in-law, husband, children and sometimes, sisters/brothers in law), raising chickens and geese, feeding the babies, taking care of the elderly, and educating children in terms of appropriate manners. Women devote all their energy towards domestic work every day, and therefore are expected to not have time to feel lonely or regret the constant absence of their husbands. Men's responsibility is to earn money, and they never perform tasks such as washing and cleaning.

On occasion, I visited Lin, a rural housewife living two hours from my city by car. She is in her mid-50s with two daughters and a son. She has never been formally schooled, but she goes to the mosque of her community to learn the Qur'an from the imam every weekend, and studies very hard. Now she lives with her husband, son and daughter-in-law, elder

Figure 21.1 Hui housewives with white hats. Photograph courtesy of Jinsuo Zhao

daughter, and two grandchildren: her elder daughter's 5-year-old daughter, and her son's 4-year-old daughter. Lin's son works in the county. Her husband used to be a peasant, but later became a businessman, and further a labour contractor. Lin's family is a typical example of the gendered division of labour, but also of how Islamic faith constructs Hui women's responsibilities towards their family. Let us follow her through an ordinary day of domestic labour.

As usual, she got up at 5 o'clock and started her daily duties. After washing herself according to Islamic requirements, she donned a robe and a gaitou, and performed the first morning prayer at around 5:30. Her gaitou is used specifically for praying. It covers all the hair, ears, forehead, and chest. The white hat she dons at home, or when she leaves the house to visit a neighbour or to go shopping, only covers her hair.

At 6 a.m., she was in the kitchen preparing breakfast for the family members. She told me, as she shaped dough into rounded dollops, that she had to do a full cauldron of steamed breads for her family of seven. Half an hour later, the steamed breads were ready. At that time, her daughter-in-law, Mei, stepped into the kitchen greeting her and begun to assist her in the breakfast preparations. Mei is a teacher at a secondary school in the county town, and often works late to perform her domestic duties in the evenings, so Lin does not want her to get up early. Mei peeled and sliced several potatoes in silence, washed a cabbage and leeks, and arranged them in plates, ready for Lin to stir-fry. The potato dish is their daily main breakfast dish.

When breakfast was ready at 7:10 a.m., Lin woke up her granddaughters, for it was time to prepare them for kindergarten. After the breakfast, her husband, son and daughter-in-law went to work, and granddaughters to kindergarten, and Lin began the washing. She told me that on weekends, her elder daughter is at home to help with the washing, but the daughter works at a distant town and cannot come home every day.

Around half an hour later, she left the tidy kitchen and started to clean the foreyard and backyard, then the bedroom, sitting room and bathroom. She carefully washed all the furniture, and all the floors. In her social circle, it is important that the house be spotlessly clean, so she took care not to miss a speck of dirt. Around 10 a.m. Lin went out to buy vegetables and some washing products. An hour later she was back, and immediately began to prepare the lunch. Noodles are the main dish for lunch, and unlike her sister and cousin, Lin does not like to use a noodle machine. She prefers to make noodles with a rolling pin, because she thinks that hand-made noodles taste better than machine-made ones. By noon she had rolled two sheets of noodles ready to be boiled. Next, she stir-fried the meat and vegetables to be served with the noodles. When the working family members came home for lunch, all dishes had already been set on the table. Mei helped her mother-in-law to boil the noodles bowl after bowl for each individual family member. Right after finishing her dish, Lin left the table and went into the bedroom, to wash and perform

Figure 21.2 Hui woman with headscarf. Photograph courtesy of Xuejun Ma

the second praying at 1:20 p.m. Meanwhile, Mei did the dishes, and the workers returned to their workplaces again at 2 p.m.

Lin could now have an afternoon nap for an hour. After this, there was a short span (3–5 p.m.) of leisure time. She took her knitting, locked the door, and went to visit her cousin Mai, who lives about ten minutes away on foot. There were two women already visiting Mai, her two sisters-in-law, and the women sat on the couch chatting and knitting. Lin was knitting a woollen sweater for one of her granddaughters. She loves knitting for herself, her husband, children, brother, sister, nephew and niece. Her knitting works are admired and prized, and she is considered to be a handy woman.

The women shared neighbourhood chat; Lin enjoys this time of leisure with other women. Around 5 p.m. she departed to go to the kindergarten to pick up her granddaughters and return home. Then she washed to perform the third prayers of the day. Around 5:40 she began to prepare the dinner: she picked and washed green beans, celery and green peppers and rolled noodles again, while talking with the granddaughters, teaching them good manners. Then the whole family had dinner together. After dinner, she prayed for the fourth time at 7:20 p.m. Before the fifth prayer at 8:40 p.m., she joined her husband watching TV, still unceasingly knitting.

According to the traditional view, the woman's work is in the family, which is considered her natural responsibility and obligation. This kind of division of labour, which most women never question, is prevalent in north-west rural China, where housewives are seeking to fulfil their traditional role in the family. But in the city, things have been changing, and husbands of professional women are performing more household tasks nowadays. But although men share a part of the housework, women still spend more time doing, and pay more attention, to domestic tasks: a professional woman often spends three to four hours a day in domestic tasks. According to research, in 56.9 per cent of cases, women perform the majority of domestic tasks, compared to only 3.5 per cent of men doing so, in Linxia Autonomous Prefecture of the Hui (Xiaoxia Ma 2009, 40). Many women consider domestic labour as women's 'natural' tasks.

Economic dependency and family status

The cultural and social changes that have happened in China have also changed Hui women's views and behaviour. However, there was no change in the principle of the 'male centred' world view (Wen 2010, 63). Within the family, the principal income is still provided through male labour and the woman belongs to the family and remains financially dependent on her husband (Yingna Ma 2013, 54–7). The husband is always in control of money and the wife has no right to dispose of family possessions. All important decisions are made by the husband. Besides everyday expenses, the woman has no extra money to spend as she pleases, for example, to support her mother's family. When a woman needs money, she has to ask her husband. Lin told me her husband seldom gave her extra money for fear that she would spend it on 'excessive consumption'.

One Hui woman in employment explained: 'I think it is important and good for a woman to have a job. If you could bring money to the family, you would [not have to ask anyone else for it]. Also you would gain respect and proper status within family.' Meihua, a Hui woman in her 30s, had no job in the five first years after she married, but has found employment recently. She said: 'I feel that if I go out to work, it is good for my economic independence. When the huband is happy, it's okay [to ask for money]. But when he is unhappy, it is tough for the wife to get money she needs. That situation is too inconvenient for me'. She continued: 'Since I have earned money, I can do many things I want to do, if there is enough money. I can demonstrate more respect and piety to my parents, and can keep peace with my parents-in-law. Buying something I need freely is the life I want.' One woman told me that she used to even not have the right to cut a watermelon without a nod of approval from her husband or mother-in-law. After starting to work in the city two years after her marriage, she divorced. Afterwards she married again and worked in a factory, so that she can buy fashionable clothing and cosmetic products on her own income.

Wei, a 35-year-old Hui woman, is a manager of a company. Her husband and parents-in-law were against her working, because her work meant that she could not cook for the family and spend time with her son. After many quarrels with her husband, she chose to divorce two years ago. She said that for a woman, pursuing a career is hard: 'I have gone through a span of tough time. As a woman, I didn't get trust from my superior, or from the family. Family or career, I chose career and I have never regretted it.'

These cases demonstrate how economic independence brings individual independence. When women get their own income, they make their own decisions, gain more freedom, and the right to decide about family and personal consumption. Now that more and more women have learned lessons of their own lack of schooling and income, they have realized that education matters to girls' futures. Consequently, they support their daughters or granddaughters in gaining schooling and education.

Piety and obedience

In Chinese Muslim communities, women are taught that they must demonstrate piety, respect the elderly and obey their husbands. Yang, a female imam in my neighbourhood mosque, explained:

> A woman should show piety, and respect for parents and parents-in-law. A woman must bring up children [with good manners], and respect her husband. In this manner, there will be no quarrel in the family, and her parents-in-law will show regard for her, and her husband will give her the respect she deserves. As long as women are studying the Qur'an, they will know how to behave. Otherwise, they will lose both on the earth and in the afterlife.

In the past, parents used to arrange marriages, and women never enjoyed the same status as their husbands. Fang, a 63-year-old Hui woman, remembers that when she got married at the age of 19, she used to do all the housework. When she struggled to perform some tasks, such as lighting the coal fire appropriately, nobody helped her. Despite the kitchen being filled with smoke, her mother-in-law grunted and walked away. In some cases, neighbourhood gossip and collective shaming obliged women to remain in dysfunctional marriages, even when suffering domestic violence.

Lian, now in her 60s, married at 16, and had four children. But when her husband was arrested and convicted for drug dealing, she had to earn money to support her children's schooling. She started running a small eatery in the alley, while taking care of her 80-year-old mother and her children. When her children were already grown-up, her husband was released from jail, but died of cancer soon afterwards. Despite her rather miserable existence, Lian never complains. Instead, she finds refuge in worship and daily prayer. She meticulously fasts during every Ramadan, and is never absent from the activities in the local mosque. She has performed the hajj pilgrimage twice. She is enthusiastically looking forward to her third hajj, which she is due to perform soon, and plans to send pictures and videos to her children from the trip. She keeps reminding her children to follow Qur'anic teachings, and uphold good manners as pious Muslims. Like Lian, many Hui women have strong religious beliefs, and they demonstrate their piety both in actives and in thoughts. Their behaviour abides with what they have been taught is religious and morally correct. To follow Islamic teachings and customs is to be welcome and popular in the community.

Gender expectations

Thus gender expectations shape women's lives, as the cases above demonstrate. Parents hope to bring up their daughters to be good, dutiful and smart. Husbands expect their wives to be kind, handy in the household, beautiful, decent, and pure in thought. A common saying states that a good woman can sew like a tailor and cook like a chef. Parents-in-law expect the daughter-in-law to be a person who can bear hardships and perform hard work, a person who is pious and obedient. A woman is expected to be mild-mannered, affable and polite rather than self-assured, brusque in manner or bad-tempered. A woman who wants to be considered a 'nice' woman must obey the gender expectations of her community, or her community will seek to correct her behaviour. In the rural Hui community, judgements of a woman's value are communicated through constant talk about 'right' and 'wrong'.

In the rural Hui communities, and in some urban communities in the autonomous Hui area, husbands also expect their wives to dress like other Hui women, and obey the rules of Islam: no short skirts, short sleeves or uncovered hair. But in cities where Hui are living scattered, husbands, especially among the younger generation, usually do not make requirements for Islamic dressing. While the society has increasingly industrialized, also the family structure has changed from extended family towards nuclear family. This has had an impact on women's lives: some young women have entered paid employment and found new positions in society, while others have engaged in studying Islam in mosques and found new understandings of the religion. These different environments have vast influence upon whether they don the white hat or the new style of headscarf, or not.

Headscarf and identity

The requirement that Hui women are asked to conceal their body and hair comes from the Qur'an. The Quran instructs both Muslim men and women to dress in a modest way:

> Tell the believing men to lower their gaze and be modest.
>
> And say to the believing women that they should lower their gaze and guard their modesty; that they should not display their beauty and ornaments except what (must ordinarily) appear thereof; that they should draw their veil over their breasts and not display their beauty except to their husband, their fathers, their husband's fathers, their sons, their husbands' sons, their brothers or their brothers' sons, or their sisters' sons, or their (Muslim) women, or the slaves whom their right hands possess, or male servants free of physical needs, or small children who have no sense of the shame of sex; and that they should not strike their feet in order to draw attention to their hidden ornaments.
>
> *(Qur'an 24:30–1)*

Headwear and 'jiaomen'

So, Muslim women are urged to cover their heads and part of their chests. Following Islamic rules, the believing women in traditional Hui communities wear *gaitou*, or white hat (see Figure 21.1), and people consider it the appropriate way of covering for married women.

The wearers are seen to transmit the meanings of belief, respect and identity. First, wearing the *gaitou* or white hat demonstrates the wearer's belief in the Islamic faith. Wearing no *gaitou* or white hat shows that the woman's *jiaomen* is lacking. *Jiaomen* refers to abiding strictly to Islamic law, and is required in 'traditional' Hui communities. Second, veiling communicates respect to others, and modesty. Wearing the *gaitou* or white hat shows the moral accomplishment of a person, demonstrated in her respect to others and modest behaviour. Third, the veil communicates the wearer's identity. Wearing the *gaitou* or white hat expresses specifically Hui identity among Muslims, and distinguishes the wearer from other ethnic groups.

Dresses and headscarves

In the beginning of the 1980s, only Han women in Linxiao wore skirts. If someone was seen wearing a skirt, she was considered weird and mocked accordingly: 'Look! Not wearing pants!' (Xiaoxia Ma 2009, 45). In that time, girls of traditional Hui families in Lanzhou were not allowed to wear a skirt, and married women, especially the ones who did not work outside the home, usually wore the white hat. But times have changed. Now many Hui women wear short-sleeved dresses, and some of these, worn by young women, are very tight-fitting at the waist, with hems above the knee – people have come to accept women in the all kinds of skirts, including mini-skirts. Hair styles have changed, too. Younger Hui women wear diverse, colourful hairdos in cities, or some of them even in rural areas. Although a new fashion of the headscarf has been rising since the 1990s, not all Hui women cover their head. Actually, many Hui women, especially younger and working women, do not differ from Han women in terms of their dress. But women who do not go to work and stay at home still must wear the white hat, *gaitou* or headscarf, lest their neighbours regarded their *jiaomen* not good, which might result in shunning within the community.

The new headscarf fashion can help us understand the characteristics of new times of religious life. When the Sahwa movement was rising in Egypt in the 1980s and 1990s, headscarf fashions spread also in China, through people who had gone to work or study in Egypt, Saudi Arabia and Malaysia. Soon some college women in China were wearing the headscarf, which they never had donned before. This headscarf is a large square of fabric that covers the hair low to the forehead, comes under the chin to conceal the neck, and falls down over the chest and back (see Figure 21.3). In recent years, with the headscarf fashion growing in popularity, the headscarf has also become a hot product in the clothing market. There are currently over 1,300 'Muslim headscarf' products available at the online stores of Taobao, which is China's largest retail website. Headscarf styles have become more diverse: besides a square scarf, a long variant of the headscarf has appeared, which is fastened using pins (see Figure 21.2), as well as a sewn, shaped headscarf, fastened with a button (see Figure 21.4). These headscarves are very different from the old styles of *gaitou* and white hat. First in campuses, this new headscarf was soon appearing in metropoles and communities everywhere. The wearers of the new headscarf express a new kind of religious identity. They seek to rededicate themselves to the faith through the ways they choose to dress and exhibit their faith to others. They also seek to be seen as a symbolic icon of faith, in order to distinguish themselves from others. They also wish to re-establish Muslim identity, and to practise their faith in every aspect of their lives.

One college girl explains: 'if I did not wear the headscarf, nobody would know I am a Muslim, and if I did something bad, no one could blame Islam for it. But now that I've put on the headscarf, I have responsibility to do something good, and, then, I pay attention to my words and behaviour.' The headscarf is not only a symbol for Muslim women, but also a visual reminder

Figure 21.3 Hui women with headscarves in an Arabic language school.
Photograph courtesy of Linsuozhao

Figure 21.4 A girl wearing a headscarf in a Muslim-articles store.
Photograph courtesy of Xuejun Ma

of a collective consciousness of being a Muslim. The women recognize that through their actions, they have responsibility towards Muslim identity and towards Muslims collectively.

Yan, a second-year student from Gansu, north-west China, said: 'my headscarf shows my Muslim identity that I am proud of it. Nowadays, many people are eager for some sort of faith. I have mine, and I feel enriched and satisfied.' Juan, a junior student from Ningxiao, north-west China, explained: 'the headscarf is a Fard [a religious duty], that every Muslim woman should perform as obligation. The headscarf is my best reverence toward Allah, it makes me obey Allah's rules.'

I asked another girl, working in an elementary school, what changes the headscarf has brought her. She explained:

> I was from a rural village. The year I graduated from the university, I set my goals high for my future. But I ran into snags, and failed everywhere in my pursuits. After I encountered some unhappiness, it hit me especially badly when my boyfriend left me, I turned to religion and put on the headscarf, so that I would find calm and peace. Then I chose the teaching profession, which is the best job for me because I needed a quiet environment and simple interpersonal relations. All my behaviour and thinking is now led by my faith. I can be inclusive and tolerant of things or people, which I couldn't do before. My faith's made me gain a new mind-set.

Education and headscarf

Since the 1990s, mosques have begun to run Arabic language schools everywhere in China. In my hometown, the biggest mosque runs an Arabic language school that teaches working women Islamic knowledge, including how to perform prayers and how to read Surahs of the Qur'an and the Hadith (the oral tradition of Muhammed) using standard Arabic, as well as Arabic language, grammar and pronunciation. The women spend every weekend morning studying. There are two classes, each with around 50 women. Most of them are professional women with high education and university background, and a few with lower, elementary school background. These women are of all ages: around 30 per cent in their 20s, 50 per cent in their 30s and 40s, 20 per cent over 50.[1]

All of them came to the Arabic language school in order to learn to pray: to learn correct positions and words. Some came in order to learn correct pronunciation for prayers, because believers must read the Qur'an with accurate pronunciation of Arabic. To learn grammar and Arabic pronunciation helps them to develop the skills needed to read Surahs. The school has taught the women knowledge of Islam.

Hong, a Hui woman from the school run by the mosque, said:

> I was born in a traditional family. When I was a child, my father taught me strictly that I'll never wear a skirt or a short-sleeved top. In the past I didn't understand why my father wouldn't allow me to put on a dress. I even admired others' dresses, until I came in the Arabic language school where I learned the knowledge of Islam. Now I look at the colourful headscarves, so beautiful, I love my headscarf.

Zhang, another student at the School said: 'My father is an engineer. I did not know much about Islam before I came here. Now I wear the headscarf, I pray every day, and fasted in the holy month of Ramadan, which I have never done before'.

A great change has happened to them. One woman, Xiaoxue, said that after five months studying in the School, she realizes that believers should seek to meet the rules of Islam in deeds and words. But religion must keep up with the times, it cannot just be as in the past. She told me:

> [T]he teachers have taught us the moral code of conduct revealed in the Qur'an. It is apparently different from what they were told by their grandmothers and mothers. That was outside the [Islamic] law, or erroneous knowledge, in which customs and habits of the Han [majority] were mixed.

Another woman said that:

> [i]n every class by the teachers, I have learnt a lot of knowledge of Islam, and how to conduct myself in society, such as respect towards parents in studying the 17:23–24 of the Qur'an. The teachers use original texts of the Qur'an and Hadiths to explain how to deal with the relations between parents and children, wife and husband, family and neighbours.

The teachers tell the women which parts of the body should be washed before prayer, which parts of the body can be shown in public: the face between ears, below brow and above chin, but the rest, called private parts, must be covered. Although the teachers never instructed the women to put on the headscarf, in the class every elderly woman is wearing a *gaitou*. These *gaitous* are beautiful, with new pattern designs. Every younger woman wears a colourful, beautiful, and fashionable headscarf. The two styles are different: *gaitou* for the elderly, headscarf for the young. A teacher said to the students: 'you will put on the headscarf after you learn more. But if you are in a job, if you put it on, it will bring you a lot of inconvenience, so you all have a choice.' The female teachers, who wear colourful headscarves and beautiful clothes, seek to shape the image of professional Hui woman, to give example of veiling to the students. 'All younger teachers dress themselves beautifully, so that they would display a kind of new figure of Muslim professional female', Xiaoxue explained.

With their studies, these women have discovered the religious reason why Muslim women wear the headscarf, and they have persuaded their family members to not oppose their veiling. People in the circle of believers constantly discuss the importance of the headscarf for women, and encourage and promote young girls to don the veil.

Headscarf: Choice and ambivalence

Although in recent years there has been an increase in the number of Hui women who have chosen to wear the headscarf, they still are in the minority. Actually, most of the professional Hui women do not want to wear it. Ming, a woman working in a mall, said:

> My parents and my parents-in-law asked me to put on the *gaitou* or the white hat when I married at the very beginning, but I refused. Because I am a vocational woman, and I think it is a visual way to tell people you have Islamic faith. That I don't wear it does not mean that I am not pious in the religion. But, I think that if I will retire one day, I might put it on.

Many Hui women like Ming do not begin to wear the headscarf, although elderly family members urge or persuade them to put on it.

On the other hand, Feira, a senior student from Qinghai, said:

> Before I put on the headscarf, much needed to change in my life . . . I cried sometimes, because there was pressure from people around me, parents, elder brother, who disagree with me about wearing the headscarf. And I was uncertain about my future. My friends persuaded me to 'think it over if you propose to wear the headscarf'. My mother preached at me that if I would wear the headscarf there would be muttering: 'a girl who isn't married but wears the headscarf'. I hesitated for a long time. Finally, I made my decision of wearing the headscarf. After wearing it I found I couldn't take it off, because this was the right life I pursued. Anyway, I was worried about too many things before I wore it.

Why did these women hesitate and even refuse to wear the veil? Because it is inconvenient for the women, for veiled women to encounter indirect discrimination when they look for jobs, or in their social lives. For this reason, some women have taken off their headscarves. They feel they have no choice because they want to have a satisfying job. 'Allah would punish me for this, perhaps,' one girl said. 'No headscarf means I have hidden my Muslim identity. But I am still a Hui Muslim, it is just not so visible, that's it.' These women long for economic independence. After graduating from university, they hope to be teachers, or office clerks, which they find as the best jobs. But some of them would like to work in a Muslim enterprise somewhere, so that it will be convenient for their Muslim lives (Hei 2011, 56).

Conclusion

The traditional division of labour makes women stay in the home in rural areas, but university education and employment enable others to move into cities. But although these women participate in work life, religious gender ideology still influences their ideas as to what Muslim women should look like. The pursuit of goodness is one of the parameters of gender expectations. Seeking to fulfil such expectations, young Muslim women favour colourful and beautiful headscarves.

The headscarf indicates a manner of life, in which women face difficulties bravely, and choose a positive outlook on life. Because veiling women are assisted by their faith, they hold different values from the mainstream views. The headscarf brought them some suffering, but more happiness, and therefore social pressure did not change their decision to don the veil.

Whichever veiling style the women prefer – the headscarf, *gaitou* or white hat – the veil is a tool for protection for women. It brings them God's blessing; they gain God's protection. From a social point of view, it offers women not only a kind of protection against men who are not their immediate relatives, but also a feeling of security and a sense of belongingness into their communities.

Acknowledgments

The research presented in this chapter was supported by the National Funds Program of Philosophy and Social Science (13BSH066).

Note

1. The data come from the Arabic language school of Xiguan, Great Mosque of Lanzhou.

References

Hei, Zhiyan. 2011. 'Hijab Wearers' Religious Life and Muslim Identity: Based on the Interviews with Universities Hijab Wearers in Beijing'. Master's thesis, Minzu University of China. Available at www.cnki.net/KCMS/detail/detail.aspx?QueryID=46&CurRec=1&recid=&filename=1011165552.nh&dbname (accessed 28 January 2017).

Ma, Xiaoxia. 2009. 'A Case Study of Female Hui's Culture – Taking Female Hui of Linxia Bafang Area as an Example'. Master's thesis, Northwest University, China. Available at www.cnki.net/KCMS/detail/detail.aspx?QueryID=0&CurRec=9&recid=&filename=2009203438.nh&dbname (accessed 28 January 2017).

Ma, Yingna. 2013. 'A Study on the Shadian Area Muslim Women of Social Life'. PhD thesis, Minzu University of China. Available at www.cnki.net/KCMS/detail/detail.aspx?QueryID=4&CurRec=1&recid=&filename=1013317174.nh&dbname (accessed 28 January 2017).

Wen, Wenfang. 2010. 'A Study about Hui Women's Behavior and Conception on Process of Modernization and Social Transformation: Based on the Investigation of Xi'an and Lanzhou'. PhD thesis, Lanzhou University (China). Available at www.cnki.net/KCMS/detail/detail.aspx?QueryID=2&CurRec=1&recid=&filename=2010131940.nh&dbname (accessed 28 January 2017).

22

CONSTRUCTIONS AND RECONSTRUCTIONS OF 'APPROPRIATE DRESS' IN THE DIASPORA

Young Somali women and sartorial social control in Finland[1]

Anu Isotalo

Introduction

I contemplate in this chapter the meanings associated with the dress styles of young Somali women living in Finland. I particularly focus on how female reputation is constructed through socially shared meanings of appropriate and inappropriate everyday dress in public spaces. However, I do not argue that appropriate dress is all that is required to have good reputation. The chapter is based on my PhD dissertation in which I discussed the meanings of good and bad reputation in everyday life of adolescent girls and young Somali women (Isotalo 2015). The ethnographic fieldwork upon which this chapter draws took place in the city of Turku in 2003–2006. During these three years I interviewed first-generation Somali immigrant girls and women and observed their life. The women were 17 to 35 years old and had arrived in Finland in the 1990s. Most of the informants were not older than 24 years.

Turku is located at the south-west coast of Finland and was, during my fieldwork, the fifth biggest city of Finland with its 175,000 inhabitants. At that time there lived approximately 450 Somalis, of whom half were women. At the same time in Finland there were approximately 8,600 Somalis, of whom over 90 per cent lived in the Greater Helsinki area where the total population was 980,000 (OSF 2006; 2015a; 2015b). Thus the Somali population in Finland was centralized around the Greater Helsinki area and the Somalis of Turku were a small minority.

I focus on three specific viewpoints:

1   How was 'appropriate dress' defined in relation to young unmarried women's reputation?
2   Were the dress customs in pre-civil war Somalia different from the customs in Finland, and how?

3   How did fashion and individual preferences influence everyday dress choices of young unmarried women?

I analyse, on the one hand, forms of social definitions and control practiced by the Somali community, and on the other, self-control and agency of the young women. I argue that although the expectations and definitions related to young women's 'respectable dress' were often constructed in terms of religious and cultural tradition, they were also formulated through and in opposition to 'Western' and Finnish majority culture.

The interviewees' ideas as to what was considered (in)appropriate dress varied according to situation and individual. Personal opinion and social expectations could differ significantly. I seek to represent this multi-vocality of viewpoints. I stress that my intention is not to define what counts as right or wrong interpretation of Islam or Islamic dress. When I use such definitions, I talk about the interviewees' understandings of a dress being 'Islamic' or 'according to Islam'.

What is good reputation?

Reputation is something fundamentally social. It is constructed in social networks and necessitates some kind of a community, which recognizes the reputation. In this chapter I refer to good reputation as positive social value attached to an individual and her family. In collectivistic cultures, this evaluation of reputation based on behaviour of one individual not only affects parents and their children, but other relatives, too. In this chapter, however, I use the term 'family' mainly to refer to relatives living in the same household in Turku, as this was something the interviewees mainly focused on when they gave examples of good and bad reputation and described consequences of a young unmarried woman's dress styles to her family.

Although reputation and honour are sometimes used synonymously, in fact they have different connotations. While reputation may be good or bad, honour is usually something positive, indicating good social reputation. In cultures that hold honourability as a central social value, an individual's behaviour is considered to express also something about her family's social position and moral state. For a family to be impeccably honourable, its members have to be honourable.

According to the interviewees, Somali and Islamic idea of a family is based upon the idea of genders complementing each other in family life. Men and women have their own roles and areas of responsibility. The man is responsible for the family and decisions about the family's relations to the community and wider society. Man's honourability is shown in how he manages his task as the head of the family. Man's honourability is also considered to be expressed in the honourable behaviour of other members of the family. The woman is responsible for caring for the family and children, and for domestic decisions. The mother is expected to be a role model of good womanhood for the daughter. Her task is to bring up a daughter who behaves honourably – knows her religion, wears a skirt and a scarf, cherishes her pre-marital virginity and sexual purity, and is capable of taking care of a home and a family.

A daughter's modesty is particularly important for her family as a public sign of the honour of the family. Vice versa, her doubtful or shameless behaviour would harm the family reputation. Moreover according to the interviewees, female character was considered to be lost more easily and retained more difficultly than male reputation. From the point of view of the daughter, her impeccable behaviour was a sign of her self-respect, sense of responsibility and self-control. If honour was lacking, also self-respect was lacking: a young woman was treating herself, and allowing herself to be treated, in disrespecting ways. Self-control combined with chastity indicated that she was not lowering herself to deeds that harmed her reputation.

Communal care-taking and social control

During my fieldwork the Somali community in Turku was small. Approximately 50% of the population consisted of children under 15 years old (OSF 2015a). According to the interviewees, almost all Somalis older than 15 knew or recognized each other in Turku. Therefore, the social networks were rather tight-knit. As one informant put it, 'the Somalis are such a small community, and Turku is such a small place, and as we're like a small village, everyone is where everyone else is'. Therefore it is essential to understand how important the communal information-sharing was. The possibility of following the Somali youths' behaviour – both girls and boys – was a means of social care-taking and an element of security in the city space. The young women considered such care-taking precious and a part of 'being a Somali' (see Fangen 2007).

The relatively small centre area around the market square of Turku was the stage of mutual recognitions, appointments and casual meetings for Somalis. Around the square are located local bus stops, shopping malls, fast-food restaurants, cinemas and cafés in which Somali men gathered to meet each other. The area enabled watching behaviour of other Somalis without the observer necessarily being observed himself or herself. The young women were conscious of this possibility, which had become an efficient means of social and spatial control in the centre. It was sometimes necessary for young women to avoid 'invisible eyes' observing one's steps in the centre in order to 'preserve one's honour', as one of my informants said. From the interviewees' point of view, young men who spent time in public places like cafeterias were not targets of similar evaluative attention by the Somalis than they were. The consciousness of the possibility of being seen and evaluated in a specific way because of one's gender both restricted and produced behaviour in a gendered way (Foucault 1995).

Simultaneously good reputation was important for the young women themselves. Not dressing or behaving against norms of appropriateness was a question of both honour and conventionality. The women were agents seeking to play their part according to community norms (Mahmood 2005). Those few young women who did not wear the scarf regularly or wore trousers justified their choices on personal preferences as well as considering the scarf and skirt as not necessary high morality and being a Muslim. Also their decisions expressed agency, directed against the expectations set for them (Butler 1993).

At the time of the fieldwork, there was a visible difference in clothing styles in Helsinki and in Turku. In public places in Helsinki, it was much more common to see young women wearing no scarves and skirts but 'Western' or 'Finnish' clothes, as the informants described tight jeans, T-shirts and tops. According to them, this phenomenon reflected more rapid cultural change in Helsinki than in Turku. For them, it was also a sign of more lenient social control in Helsinki compared to Turku: because young Somali women living in Helsinki were not recognized as easily by the Somali community, individual variation in clothing was more possible and less socially controlled than in Turku. Some of the interviewees also took benefit of this freedom from communal observation and social control by experimenting with 'Western' clothing styles while they spend time in Helsinki during weekends or holidays. Altogether, some of the informants interpreted the Westernized clothing in Helsinki as a sign of moral degradation in Finland, others regarded this phenomenon as an acceptable and understandable change in the diaspora. Even if this 'cultural change' had taken place much more quickly in Helsinki, most of the interviewees thought that in the future, similar change and variation in young women's dress styles would take place in Turku, as well.

Reputation, dress and sexual morality

> Some people gossip that that girl misbehaves, that her whole body is naked. Though she has clothes, but she's naked, that's talked about, it's not good. It's said, wishing she'd understand. Or some say straight to her face 'What are you wearing?'

When justifying girls' and women's covering dress all the interviewees referred to Islamic regulations aiming to reduce sexual attraction between genders. Due to associations with sexual chastity, interpretations of dress were closely linked to honour and reputation. Dress style was considered one defining factor for a young woman's reputation, for it was seen as reflecting the woman's values and attitudes. A woman without a scarf would attract curious attention of other Somalis which could be socially harmful for her and her family. Therefore some young women wore the scarf especially to avoid gossip that would damage their reputation (cf. Karlsson Minganti 2007; Tarlo 2010; Moors and Tarlo 2013; Valentine *et al.* 2009).

Everyday dress choices were also situational. On one occasion, I met a young woman after her graduation in the city centre. She had not worn the scarf in the graduation and did not put it on when we went out, either. I brought the topic up out of interest and asked if she often goes out without the scarf. She said it doesn't matter if she is 'once a year' in the centre without it. However, soon she took her scarf from her bag and put it on. I was left wondering whether this was due to her uncertainty of being seen without it, due to my question, or perhaps due to the ambivalence of being seen without the scarf with me in particular. Maybe being observed like this by other Somalis would have given reasons to speculate that I as a Finnish researcher wearing 'Finnish' clothes had got something to do with her 'changed' behaviour?

There were also multiple and mixed opinions on young Somali women wearing trousers. Although the skirt was considered more appropriate, the fact that some adolescent girls wore trousers was seen as age-related and experimental. Some said that Islam did not forbid trousers per se, but tight trousers were not acceptable. Yet these young women did not wear trousers themselves because they considered them a less reputable form of dress than the skirt (see Almila 2016). By contrast, one informant who wore trousers and no scarf justified her choice according to ethical principles: 'I know what my heart is like'. For her the Islamic ideal of decency, restraint and piety was primarily realized in pure thoughts and heart, not through clothing practices (Isotalo 2007; cf. Fadil 2011; Karlsson Minganti 2007; Moors and Tarlo 2013; Roald 2012).

In gossip among community members, young women's negative reputation in terms of everyday dress choices was determined according to two lines. On the one hand, donning trousers and removing the scarf was considered a possible sign of abandoning one's religion and culture, and 'becoming Finnish'. On the other hand, tight and revealing 'Western' or 'Finnish' clothes were considered a sign of questionable sexual morals or excessive sexual openness (see Tarlo 2010; Dwyer 1999b). This interpretation was particularly obvious in cases where young women who were regarded as 'too Western' or 'too Finnish' by appearance of clothing were called whores by (some) members of the community. According to my informants, this kind of name-calling was not uncommon among those Somalis who disapproved of this kind of behaviour.

Despite some accepting individual comments about trousers, in the community's social definitions, wearing them was considered one clear example of 'crossing the line' that would influence female reputation negatively (cf. Dwyer 1999a):

> Of course a person who herself wanted to wear trousers, how she thinks is better. Really, she's proud of it. If she wasn't proud, she wouldn't do so. She's proud and doesn't listen to what others say. But ok, she accepts what everyone else is saying.

And it gets worse slowly and she hears every day 'they said this of you' . . . It can be that she just wears trousers, hasn't done anything bad. Just that the skirt's gone and trousers instead, nothing doing. It can be that she's just changed her style. But if they say she's changed to trousers and at the same time she's changed her religion. Or that she's changed from good girl and become a whore. She wasn't a whore but if some people [call her] 'whore, whore, whore', then it can be that this person gets fed up with what others say. And then it can even be that she goes and becomes a whore, what she's already been named.

According to the interviewees dressing in a manner 'too Finnish' or too revealing was sometimes interpreted as incapability of understanding that one has gone too far, or as a lack of religious understanding. Circulating gossip shared by the small community was expected to change the undesirable dressing of a young woman whose family heard about the gossip (Akou 200; Moors 2009). If her behaviour did not change despite the gossip and her dress was interpreted as a sign of 'changing one's religion' or 'becoming a whore', her reputation was practically gone. In other words, a 'whore' was made by naming and repeating this social label through gossip. As a consequence, this interpretation of bad reputation became generalized and well known in the community (Andersson 2003).

In the quotation above, whore-calling becomes a self-fulfilling prophecy (Merton 1968). Also in this way, whore-calling becomes performative, functioning as a method of labelling that creates the phenomenon that it names (Austin 1962; Butler 1993; Foucault 1981). From the young woman's point of view, labelling can lead to a loss of social position and moral self-esteem, and lead to behaviour that 'confirms' the whore-calling.

Although the interviewees recognized these social practices to label young women, they stressed that it was against Islam to gossip about presumed behaviour of others, or to whore-call anyone. One young woman considered unjustified and insulting use of the word based on dress only in the following way:

If a girl wears trousers or short skirts, I don't say she's a whore. For everyone behaves according to her own opinion, what she has in her heart. Every time someone says that's a whore, I say 'were you an eye-witness when she did it with a man?' 'No, it was just said.' I say: 'Don't say that, it's offensive. If you haven't seen her doing it with a man, why do you say so?'

It is notable that the interviewee defines a 'whore' as referring to a girl with any pre-marital sexual experiences. This makes sense in the context of the ideal of pre-marital virginity, central to Islamic and cultural values. In addition to interpretations about sexual reputation, another re-occurring theme in the interviews was the reconstructed social meanings of young women's appropriate dress in the diaspora. I will discuss such meaning-making in the next section.

Memories of homeland, interpretations of change

The interviewees compared the dress customs in Finland to their memories of or knowledge about dress in Somalia. They noted that covering dress deemed appropriate in Finland was not necessarily based upon Somali traditions but was rather following a stricter religious interpretation (cf. Berns McGown 1999; De Voe 2002; McMichael 2002). One interviewee described a common female dress style in Somalia before the Civil War:

> When I was in Somalia, I wore the *Dirac*, the Somali dress. It's thin, you can see where the line of the bra and the petticoat goes. And then, before, the fabric was also thinner so that you could see everything. And a small scarf . . . I wore that in the homeland, and no one looked at me that I'm bad. And arms were bare and all.

Dirac is a full-length, sleeveless, quadruple-shaped dress-like garment, often made of translucent fabric. According to the interviewees, it revealed more than was desirable from a religious point of view, but wearing it had been part of the customs in Somalia (cf. Abdi 2007; Berns McGown 1999; Talle 2008). Wearing the translucent *Dirac* and baring one's arms in Turku would certainly have drawn attention. The sexual and moral connotations of a revealing dress style were reflected in the statement that unlike in Finland, in Somalia 'no one looked at me that I'm bad'. Another interviewee stressed that despite revealing dress styles, 'we were honourable girls and we didn't do anything [bad], and we got respectably married' (see also Fadil 2011).

In Somalia, the variation of female dress has been great depending on age, social class, educational level and the place of residence (Akou 2011). Consequently, individual memories of dress norms could vary widely according to timeframe, region and personal background. Presumably also the age of arriving in Finland and marital status influenced interviewees' ideas and experiences of dress practices in Somalia before arriving. Those interviewees with memories or knowledge about the early 1990s Somali dress in Finland described it 'more European' than more recent styles. Married women wore trousers and did not necessarily don the scarf. Trousers were considered a pragmatic garment: they allowed easier movement than a skirt, and they were warmer during the winter. Some women wore them to increase their sense of security in a foreign environment and stressful life situation, especially in terms of fears of assault or rape (cf. Abdi 2007).

Female dress in Somalia took a turn towards more covering styles along with the breakout of the Civil War in 1988 (Abdi 2007; Akou 2011; Haga 2010; Roald 2012; Talle 2008). Towards the mid-1990s, interpretations and expectations about female dress changed also in Turku. Scarfless and trouser-driven 'European' styles were seen as contradictory to 'Islamic' Somali styles (cf. Dwyer 1999b). One interviewee explained this by saying that 'after the Civil War people understand religion and culture more than ever'. As religious interpretations appeared and became dominant, a dress style previously considered casual came to be defined as un-Islamic, and consequently as inappropriate (Moors and Tarlo 2007; Tarlo 2010). According to my informants, women were increasingly defined within the community as 'good' or 'bad' according to their dress style (cf. Abdi 2007; McMichael 2002). In the process, the skirt became prominent and replaced the trousers.

At the same time, wearing a full body-covering veil (which the interviewees called *jilbab*) became a 'fashion phenomenon', as one woman put it. Many married women donned the *jilbab* despite not wearing it previously in Somalia (Akou 2011; Berns McGown 1999; Tiilikainen 2003). According to my informants, these women attempted to make the *jilbab* as common a style as possible for the Somali women in Turku. Not all women took on these persuasion attempts, however. One woman justified her decision of not wearing *jilbab* by stating: 'I said it's not my style. My mother didn't wear it, my grandmother didn't wear it, why should I?' (cf. Berns McGown 1999; Tiilikainen 2003). Another interviewee had responded to women who wore *jilbab* and criticized her dress that Islamic doctrine did not require veiling head-to-toe, but covering the shapes of the female body with sufficiently loose garments. This was what she already did, and therefore she had no intention of changing her style.

In the 2000s the situation changed again. In Turku, wearing full-body veils was not as usual anymore as it had been before. Yet the scarf and the skirt retained their importance. The scarf was (and still is) an important religious, moral and ethnic signifier. However, not everyone considered this a positive development:

> In Somalia, as long as you weren't married, you didn't need to put the scarf on. Here, even if you're a young girl, you immediately had to put it on. People are so scared . . . I'm not sure what they're so scared of. For me, I don't want to forget my upbringing and my culture. I'm a Muslim alright and I try to accommodate all rules. But I don't want to change everything in my life, that I'd have to awfully try to be something I'm not. I can't really live a life like that. But there are some people who try to show that they're Muslims [*claps her hands*], they're so strong [*claps her hands*], and blaah blaah. I really can't stand that at all!

According to her interpretation, girls' and women's increasingly strict dress expectations were influenced by fears of change, and loss of culture and tradition in the diaspora (cf. De Voe 2002). She considered such fears pointless. The same fear of change she considered to be the reason for some women underlining their female Muslim belonging in ways she considered an overdone performance (Butler 1990; 1993).

The differences between past Somalia and present Finland created an interesting field of contradiction between a desire to experiment by the youth and principles of upbringing by their parents. One woman told me that some young women knew about their mothers' and other female relatives' more revealing dress styles in pre-war Somalia:

> When teenagers hear these kinds of things about their parents, and when the parents try hard to say 'don't go this way!', well, you've done it yourself . . . I'm a human, too, can't I experiment myself for a time?

According to the interviewee the conflict was essentially about parents trying to prevent the youth dress getting more 'Western', that is, more revealing, while it was known that dress customs in Somalia had been freer than what was expected of the daughters in Finland. By challenging the parental limits with questions such as described above, the young gained the chance of re-negotiating and widening the limits of their freedom of choice as young generation living in the diaspora (Peltola 2014).

From an ideal to fashion: Varying practices of everyday dressing

Interviewer: What do you think of it yourself that sometimes you don't cover your neck?

Interviewee: I really should, it's compulsory to cover the neck all the time.

As already noted, Islamic dress style was presented as a norm to be followed by my informants. Although recognized and followed by many, such norms were also ideals aimed at but not necessarily realized in individual dressing. The citation above tells of such choices and agency. The young woman knew how she should act – her neck should be covered with a scarf. She nevertheless did not necessarily do so if a different dress style felt more applicable (see Strandbu 2005). Thus, the variations of everyday dress are partly to be understood through the difference between ideal and practice. Doing things differently repeatedly enables change: if one 'really should', but is acting in an alternative manner, one is creating a distinction from the constructions of 'expected'.

The informants considered a variety of points important for their dress styles: religion, cultural background, comfort, functionality, fashionability and fit with the body and face (in terms of the scarf). But fulfilling all these criteria simultaneously was not necessarily possible or even desired. Also, some young women only mentioned religion as an influencing factor but nevertheless dressed in a manner indicating fashionable influences of youth styles. Because individual preferences guided dressing, for example daughters of a same family sometimes followed very different styles.

A rather common scarf-binding style at the time of the interviews was binding the scarf as a bun on the back of the head. This style left the neck visible, which according to the interviewees was not in accordance with Islam. One young woman commented: 'I've been wondering if it's somehow wrong, but I don't know. At least my parents don't react to it as other young [women] have it, too.' Were it religiously acceptable or not, the style was in fashion among young women. Where this fashion initiated was difficult to say. Some had chosen the style because they felt it fitted the shape of their face, others liked it because it allowed ear rings to show and displayed make-up better. A scarf could also be bound in a manner that the ends of it were hanging in the back as 'bunny ears', as they were called by one of my informants.

Islamic interpretations were also followed thoroughly by many interviewees. Some of them wore another scarf in addition to the headscarf, because the small scarf around the head did not cover enough. Such a scarf could easily be lifted to cover the head when needed. I also observed teenage girls wearing a combined style where a cap was worn over the scarf. Some others favoured a large *shalmat*-scarf that was wrapped around the head and neck, and needed to be 'fixed' time and again by its loose end over the shoulder. Yet another style was to wear a small headscarf covered with a larger scarf so that it covered the neck and left the under-scarf visible on the forehead. The top scarf was fastened with a pin on one side. Such side-fastened scarves were also worn without the under-scarf. This style, I was told, was fashionable in Arab TV channels at the time. Also scarves imported from Arab countries by relatives brought seasonal fashions into Finland (Almila forthcoming). The scarves were of different fabrics, patterns, sizes and shapes, depending on current fashion. Seasonal changes in the weather influenced dress choices, too. Some young women changed their style so that they wore neck-covering scarves in the winter and smaller headscarves in the summer.

Other garments worn included ankle-length skirts and long-sleeved tops. At the time of the interviews, skirts tightly hugging hips, bottom and thighs were fashionable among young women. In their opinion, this style was too tight from the religious point of view, but loose and large skirts did not look as nice. Because the young women bought many of their garments in shops favoured by all youth, their cardigans, tops, jewellery, bags and shoes did not differ much from those worn by Finnish young women (cf. Abdi 2007; Almila 2016; Moors and Tarlo 2013). In case they wished to wear more loose and covering skirts that were long enough, they couldn't find these skirts in the garment stores in Turku but had to buy them from somewhere else. Nowadays, there are also many online stores offering Islamic garments in seasonal styles. However, such shopping possibilities were not yet widely available when I conducted my interviews.

In everyday life, there may be an observable difference between 'ideally Islamic' and 'practically Islamic' clothing styles. However, this did not seem to cause internal conflicts among the interviewees. For many of them, it was not an either-or choice – 'I either respect and follow or deny and break a norm' – but instead a choice of both: knowing the ideals and acting according to one's own judgement, if not always perfectly according to ideals. Also interpretations as to what was in accordance with Islam varied (see Akou 2011; Moors 2009). It seems that in Turku, at the time of the fieldwork, it was more important to wear a scarf than how the scarf was bound. Same was true of the skirt as well: it was more important to wear one than how tight the skirt was. In public space, a skirt and a scarf worn by young women were visible signs of belonging to Islamic Somali community, as well as manifestations of maintaining and reproducing the ethnic minority community in the diaspora.

Conclusion

In this chapter I have explored how young Somali women's dress choices were defined in terms of good reputation in Turku, Finland. I have argued that dress codes were strongly constructed in terms of Islam on the one hand and Somali identity on the other. In such interpretations, appropriate dress was an indicator of chastity and morality, and also of belonging to the Somali and Muslim communities. Moral interpretations of young women's behaviour in public space were important for them and their family also in terms of maintaining the social status of the family in the small Somali community.

Life in the diaspora has also led to a reconstruction of certain dress ideals and expectations. One example of this is the increased stress placed upon religious values and covering dress, as a consequence of a heightened religious consciousness (Akou 2011; Berns McGown 1999; 2013; Johnsdotter 2002; Talle 2008; Tiilikainen 2003). This was particularly visible when the women compared dress styles in pre-war Somalia and today's Finland. In Finland, much more covering dress was expected. Ideal dress styles are also constructed in terms of passing on cultural traditions, and in comparison to Finnish majority dress styles and behaviours. Sharply distinguishing between 'Finnish/Western' and 'Somali' dress is also aimed at protecting community values in a minority position (Yuval-Davis 1997; Nagel 2003).

Irrespective of this communal status of female covering dress, clothing styles are also constantly negotiated in the Finnish context. Young women's dress is influenced by both locally adopted ways of dress and transnationally communicated dress styles and fashions. The women participate in these dress negotiations through their own choices and interpretations. Their agency is performed in the borders between self-control and social control, through norm-conforming and norm-challenging actions. One example of the latter was descriptions of how some young women from Turku would wear trousers or would not wear scarf when visiting Helsinki. In Turku, vice versa, such behaviour would have drawn negative attention. They themselves did not interpret such dress choices in terms of infamy or losing reputation, but in terms of experimenting and contextual fit. What was inappropriate in Turku was less inappropriate in Helsinki. In this sense, Helsinki was a place for cultural change and new experiences for the young women of Turku.

A decade has passed since my fieldwork period in Turku. During this time, the local Somali population has tripled from 450 to 1,200 (OSF 2015a). Have dress practices become more 'Western', as predicted by some of my informants? Are there more obvious fashion trends to be observed? Looking around in the centre of Turku one sees that the scarf and the skirt persist as elements of adolescent female dress. Yet one of my former informants, whom I met when writing this chapter, insisted that the young women today dress in a much more fashion-conscious manner than her generation ten years back. She found that fashion was far more central for young women's dress than it used to be a decade ago.

It is also fair to say that social control and experiences of being observed have changed during these years. Because there are far more Somalis living in Turku in 2015 than there were in

2005, girls and young women cannot be as quickly and accurately recognized as daughters of a certain family. I do not mean to say that this would have removed social control and opportunities for community observation, but such a change may have influenced how strictly the control is experienced. Yet one woman I met recently told me that in Turku, young female dress is still a matter to be evaluated and monitored according to religious and cultural values. Not wearing a scarf and a skirt is still considered a message of not valuing one's background and not 'belonging in the community' in the deepest sense of the term. Thus, the young women's dress is one visible means to perform communality and Somali community in the diaspora. From this viewpoint, no matter how covered in public, young women's corporeality is not at all a private matter.

Translated by Anna-Mari Almila and Anu Isotalo.

Note

1. This chapter was written in the project 'Generational Negotiations, Social Control and Gendered Sexualities' (GENESO) coordinated by the Finnish Youth Research Network and financed by The Academy of Finland.

References

Abdi, Cawo Mohamed. 2007. 'Convergence of Civil War and the Religious Right: Reimagining Somali Women'. *Signs* 33(1):183–207.

Akou, Heather Marie. 2011. *The Politics of Dress in Somali Culture*. Bloomington & Indianapolis, IN: Indiana University Press.

Almila, Anna-Mari. 2016. 'Fashion, Anti-Fashion, Non-Fashion and Symbolic Capital: The Uses of Dress among Muslim Minorities in Finland'. *Fashion Theory* 20(1):81–102.

Almila, Anna-Mari. Forthcoming. *Veiling in Fashion: Space and the Hijab in Minority Communities*. London: I.B.Tauris.

Andersson, Åsa 2003. *Inte samma lika. Identifikationer hos tonårsflickor i en multietnisk statsdel*. Stockholm/Stehag: Brutus Östlings bokförlag Symposion.

Austin, John Langshaw. 1962. *How to Do Things with Words: The William James Lectures Delivered at Harvard University in 1955*. Oxford: Clarendon Press.

Berns McGown, Rima. 1999. *Muslims in the Diaspora: The Somali Communities of London and Toronto*. Toronto, ON: University of Toronto Press.

Butler, Judith. 1990. *Gender Trouble: Feminism and the Subversion of Identity*. New York: Routledge.

Butler, Judith. 1993. *Bodies that Matter: On the Discursive Limits of 'Sex'*. New York & London: Routledge.

de Voe, Pamela A. 2002. 'Symbolic Action: Religion's Role in the Changing Environment of Young Somali Women'. *Journal of Refugee Studies* 15(2):234–46.

Dwyer, Claire. 1999a. 'Contradictions of Community: Questions of Identity for Young British Muslim Women'. *Environment and Planning* 31(1):53–68.

Dwyer, Claire. 1999b. 'Veiled Meanings: Young British Muslim Women and the Negotiation of Difference'. *Gender, Place and Culture* 6(1):5–25.

Fadil, Nadia. 2011. 'Not-/Unveiling as an Ethical Practice'. *Feminist Review* 98(1):83–109.

Fangen, Katrine. 2007. 'Citizenship among Young Adult Somalis in Norway'. *Young* 15(4):413–34.

Foucault, Michel. 1981. *The History of Sexuality*, Vol. 1: *The Will to Knowledge*. Harmondsworth: Penguin.

Foucault, Michel. 1995. *Discipline and Punish*. New York: Vintage Books.

Haga, Rannveig Jetne. 2010. 'Piety and Trade: A Somali Woman Trader in Dubai'. In *Perspectives on Women's Everyday Religion*, edited by Marja-Liisa Keinänen, 219–32. Stockholm: Stockholm University.

Isotalo, Anu. 2007. 'Did You See Her Standing at the Marketplace? Gender, Gossip, and Socio-Spatial Behavior of Somali Girls in Turku, Finland'. In *From Mogadishu to Dixon: The Somali Diaspora in a Global Context*, edited by Abdi M. Kusow and Stephanie R. Bjork, 181–206. Trenton, NJ: The Red Sea Press.

Isotalo, Anu. 2015. 'Mistä on hyvät tytöt tehty? Somalitytöt ja maineen merkitykset. [What are good girls made of? Somali girls and meanings of reputation]'. PhD dissertation, University of Turku.

Johnsdotter, Sara. 2002. *Created by God: How Somalis in Swedish Exile Reassess the Practice of Female Circumcision*. Lund: Department of Sociology, Lund University.

Karlsson Minganti, Pia. 2007. *Muslima. Islamisk väckelse och unga muslimska kvinnors förhandlingar om genus i det samtida Sverige*. Stockholm: Carlssons.

McMichael, Celia. 2002. '"Everywhere is Allah's Place": Islam and the Everyday Life of Somali Women in Melbourne, Australia'. *Journal of Refugee Studies* 15(2):171–88.

Mahmood, Saba. 2005. *Politics of Piety*. Princeton, NJ, and Oxford: Princeton University Press.

Merton, Robert K. 1968. *Social Theory and Social Structure*. New York: Free Press.

Moors, Annelies. 2009. '"Islamic Fashion" in Europe: Religious Conviction, Aesthetic Style, and Creative Consumption'. *Encounters: An International Journal for the Study of Culture and Society* 1(1):176–201.

Moors, Annelies and Emma Tarlo. 2007. 'Introduction'. *Fashion Theory* 11(2/3):133–42.

Moors, Annelies and Emma Tarlo. 2013. 'Introduction: Islamic Fashion and Anti-Fashion: New Perspectives from Europe and North America'. In *Fashion and Anti-Fashion*, edited by Emma Tarlo and Annelies Moors, 1–30. London and New York: Bloomsbury.

Nagel, Joane. 2003. *Race, Ethnicity, and Sexuality: Intimate Intersections, Forbidden Frontiers*. Oxford: Oxford University Press.

OSF Official Statistics of Finland. 2006. Väestörakenne: Pääkaupunkiseudun väkiluku. Helsinki: Tilastokeskus.

OSF Official Statistics of Finland. 2015a. Väestörakenne: somalinkieliset Turussa. Helsinki: Tilastokeskus.

OSF Official Statistics of Finland. 2015b. Väestörakenne: somalinkieliset Suomessa. Helsinki: Tilastokeskus.

Peltola, Marja. 2014. 'Kunnollisia perheitä. Maahanmuutto, sukupolvet ja yhteiskunnallinen asema'. PhD dissertation, Helsinki, Nuorisotutkimusverkosto/Nuorisotutkimusseura.

Roald, Anne Sofie. 2012. 'Expressing Religiosity in a Secular Society: The Relativisation of Faith in Muslim Communities in Sweden'. *European Review* 20(1):95–113.

Strandbu, Åse. 2005. 'Identity, Embodied Culture and Physical Exercise'. *Young* 13(1):27–45.

Talle, Aud. 2008. 'Precarious Identities: Somali Women in Exile'. *Finnish Journal of Ethnicity and Migration* 3(2):64–72.

Tarlo, Emma. 2010. *Visibly Muslim: Fashion, Politics, Faith*. Oxford and New York: Berg.

Tiilikainen, Marja. 2003. *Arjen islam. Naisten elämää Suomessa* [*Everyday Islam. The Lives of Somali Women in Finland*]. Tampere: Vastapaino.

Valentine, Gill, Deborah Sporton and Katrine Bang Nielsen. 2009. 'Identities and Belonging: A Study of Somali Refugee and Asylum Seekers Living in the UK and Denmark'. *Environment and Planning D: Society and Space* 27(2):234–50.

Yuval-Davis, Nira. 1997. *Gender and Nation*. London & Thousand Oaks & New Delhi: Sage.

23

COVER THEIR FACE

Masks, masking, and masquerades in historical-anthropological context

David Inglis

Whatever is profound loves masks . . . there is not only guile behind a mask – there is so much graciousness in cunning . . . Every profound spirit needs a mask: even more, around every profound spirit a mask is growing continually, owing to the constantly false, namely *shallow*, interpretation of every word, every step, every sign of life he gives.

(Nietzsche 1918, 45)

Never did mine eye see anything so motley-coloured! I laughed and laughed, while my foot still trembled, and my heart as well. 'Here forsooth, is the home of all the paint-pots' – said I. With fifty patches painted on faces and limbs – so sat ye there to mine astonishment, ye present-day men! And with fifty mirrors around you, which flattered your play of colours, and repeated it! Verily, ye could wear no better masks, ye present-day men, than your own faces! Who could recognise you! Written all over with the characters of the past, and these characters also pencilled over with new characters – thus have ye concealed yourselves well from all decipherers! . . . Out of colours ye seem to be baked, and out of glued scraps. All times and peoples gaze divers-coloured out of your veils; all customs and beliefs speak divers-coloured out of your gestures. He who would strip you of veils and wrappers, and paints and gestures, would just have enough left to scare the crows.

(Nietzsche 2009, 80)

Introduction

The nature of both masks, and also the masking and masquerading practices which involve them, are in many, if not indeed all, human cultures characterized by fundamental ambivalences. In the Western tradition, this situation is nicely caught by Nietzsche in different places in his writings. On the one side, the masks worn by the people that the sage Zarathustra confronts indicate their shallowness and lack of depth – they are nothing more than mere masks, with no inner life of their own. Conversely, elsewhere Nietzsche claims that 'every profound spirit' dons a mask, partly to protect its great wisdom but also because the inadequate understandings of that spirit by other people place a mask upon it, forcing the spirit back into itself, making it ever more mysterious and hidden. Masks, then, are signifiers and generators of both profundity and superficiality. They have the capacity to hide and to reveal, and to connote wisdom and the lack thereof. They are inescapably multiplicitous in nature and deeply ambiguous (Napier 1986).

The works of anthropologists and other scholars across the world have indicated that the covering of the face by a mask betokens multiple ramifications and consequences (Napier, 1986; Pernet, 1992b; Mack, 2013), all of which are to do with identity, both of the person and of the groups to which they belong or exist in relation to (Tseëlon 2001). 'Simulacrum and concealment, protection and belligerence, nature and anti-nature, lament and celebration, men and women – these and other alliances of symbol and actuality constitute a complex labyrinth of the meanings of masks' – a comment that Heath (2008, 102) points out applies also to veils and veiling.

Putting on a mask can connote the obliterating, transforming, feigning, displaying or construction of identity. Masks both make some things present while occluding others. Their powers of affordance are great: they can bring forth and disguise, often at the same time. As such, in most societies across human history masks have been sources of veneration on the one side and fear on the other (Eliade 1992). They have been regarded as remarkably powerful objects, often hedged around by taboos and avoidances (Grimes 1975). They have evoked feelings of awe and terror, joy and amusement, worship and suspicion. Undoubtedly the power of masks is fundamentally connected to the work they do in covering the human face and head. But how they cover it is historically highly variable, and dependent on broader cultural assumptions held by particular social groups, about what is deemed to be worth covering, and what is less interesting or meaningful to cover.

Some groups have believed that the eyes are the most revealing parts of the face and head, and so it is especially powerful and meaningful to mask them. This seems to have been a particularly integral part of Western thinking for several millennia, going back at least to the time of Aristotle (Synnott 1989, 1990). Diverse cultural constellations – including ancient Greek science, ancient and medieval Christian moral philosophy, and early modern science – have all contributed to a remarkably ingrained, pervasive and long-standing set of assumptions about the face in general, and the eyes in particular, as 'windows to the soul' (Synnott 1989; 1990). In Western masking practice, more minimal masks conceal the eyes but not the whole face, indicating the importance of the eyes in Occidental thinking – a mask is not really a mask unless the eyes are dealt with in some way (Barthes 1991). It is partly out of these assumptions that spring present-day Western fears about veils and headgear, generally associated with Islamic practices, which are felt to be threatening because of the disappearance of the eyes from view (Scott 2007). But other groups have thought that the mouth, the nose, or even the ears, are far more symbolically and practically important, and that the covering of those features by masks, veils or other means is more efficacious for either more ritualistic or more practical and mundane reasons (Edson 2005, 47, 91; Seeger 1975). The mouth, rather than the eyes, is construed by some groups as the access point to the interior of a being and/or to their soul (Pollock 1995, 585, 587). It is also culturally variable whether a given masking culture defines the upper or lower part of the face as the more important area to cover or to reveal (Edson 2005, 47).

Consequently, one important lesson to be drawn from the analysis of masking practices is that particular covering methods and objects may seem deeply sinister to some groups, but there is nothing intrinsically 'natural' about such fears, because the anthropological record shows that it is entirely possible for particular groups of people to be very unconcerned about the covering of the eyes and to be much more concerned, positively or negatively (and often both simultaneously), about other face and head parts being disguised or hidden. It seems that there is not a cultural universal involving concerns about the covering of the eyes, even if some current anti-Islamic discourse is partly based on essentialist claims that the disappearance from view of the eyes is somehow simply 'unnatural' and thus intrinsically 'wrong'.

In this chapter, I will consider both the history of masks and masking in different parts of the world, the complexities of such practices, and also how masking activities compare to veiling practices, giving special attention to considerations of ritual, religion and gender. We will see that while there are often great differences both between the uses of masks and veils and between how they have been interpreted, nonetheless there are various ways in which veiling and masking practices have historically overlapped in terms of what they achieve and how they have been construed by people in particular cultural settings. A consideration of masks and masking illuminates both the particularities of veils and veiling, and also what these have shared with other means of covering the face and head.

What are masks and what do they do?

Masks, masking practices (whether sacred or secular, and whether taking place in specified ritual settings or in quotidian realities), and masquerades (which often occur at times and in events particular societies mark out as somehow 'special') involve a dizzying array of historical and cultural variability (Tseëlon 1995, 2001; Urban and Hendricks 1983). Masks have played, and continue to play, roles in rituals of every kind, including initiation ceremonies, the ministrations of secret societies, fertility rites, festivals and celebrations of many types, dramas both sacred and secular, and preparations for war (Eliade 1992; Pernet 1992b; Edson 2005, 67). Thus 'putting on a mask can mean many different things . . . [there are] many reasons for publicly covering the face' (Twycross and Carpenter 2002, 7).

Yet at the same time masks and masking exhibit some broad patterns across time and space. As Oettinger and Kenagy (1988, 9) have put it:

> Masks are universal. In cultures all over the world masks [were and are] worn to protect, to provoke fear, to symbolize, to exalt, to mock, to amuse. [They are] vehicles through which tensions are relaxed, dilemmas resolved, social taboos bridged, and communications established.

How masks look is very varied across time and space. Masks used by people in West Africa 500 years ago, for example, look very different indeed from those used in the Pacific at the same time (Jedrej, 1980; Edson 2005; Pernet 1992a, 1992b). The variety of mask styles across human history has been vast: 'some masks are more transparent than others. Some are more permanent. Some cover more of the body. Some are carried. Some are worn on top of the head so they can be seen by the deities above' (Grimes 1975, 509). Studies of the range of mask types over the course of planetary history have shown that some have been held in front of the face, or have covered the front of the face or part of the face, some have covered the whole head, others have been worn on top of the head, while others again have been located on superstructures placed upon the head (Mack 2013). This is in addition to half masks, which cover either the upper or lower parts of the face. Masks in miniature have always been worn as amulets and badges on other parts of the body (Edson 2005, 22).

Materials that masks have been fashioned from include paper, cloth, wood, gourds, metal, plant fibres, leather, clay, and bamboo, and have involved surfaces of varying smoothness and roughness (Edson 2005, 24). Masks have often been designed to create effects within the play of light and shadow arranged in ritual and theatrical spaces, creating bold effects for the edification of onlookers (Twycross and Carpenter 2002). The efficacy of masks rests in the fact that they can conceal or draw attention to different parts of the face, hiding some elements, accentuating others (Edson 2005, 47). In cultural contexts where the masking of the eyes is seen to be particularly significant, masks have been fashioned to change the nature of both the eyes of the wearer and of the eye contact with others that s/he is capable of. For example, a mask's eyes can be greatly accentuated, making them into a powerful source of energy, while observers' attention can either be drawn to the actual eyes of the wearer – as if they were burning through the mask – or they can be hidden altogether (Twycross and Carpenter 2002, 9).

Despite the massive variation in the appearances of masks across the world, there have been some discernible similarities in terms of the uses to which they were put – to invoke and body forth the gods or spirits, to call upon the ancestors, to frighten enemies in battle, and so forth. Masking practices have often involved attempts to gain control over something, be that everyday social life, or nature, or the realm of the supernatural (Dagan 1992, 13). The task of the anthropological or sociological analyst of masks is therefore to remain deeply sensitive to the nuances and enigmas of masking practices in particular times and places, while attempting to draw out broader patterns shared at some level across (at least some) cultures and time periods (Napier 1986; Pernet 1992; Pollock 1995). When masks and masking are considered as features of human existence known in most societies, then masking can be defined as 'any behaviour in which people are led to transform their normal selves, to transcend everyday roles, or to soar beyond the level of commonplace reality' (Honigmann 1977, 278). If that definition is accepted, then masking may be considered cross-culturally as fundamentally involving phenomena to do with *identity* and *performance* (Tseëlon 1995, 2001, 2014).

As Pollock (1995, 594) argues, 'the first problem of the mask is the problem of identity in general, in its social and cultural construction, attribution, display and transformation'. In many contexts, 'the mask is a technique for transforming identity, either through the modification of the representation of identity, or through the temporary – and representational – extinction of identity' (Pollock 1995, 582). Masks 'work' by taking conventional signs of identity – i.e. how persons present their faces to others in ways that are regarded as conventional in a particular cultural context (Goffman 1990 [1959]) – and replacing these with other conventionalized signs which are represented on the surface, and perhaps in the texture and shape, of the mask (Pollock 1995, 584). It is not simply that the uncovered face is 'natural' and that the masked face is 'unnatural' – which is in fact a view that has been proffered by moralists in some societies who have been concerned with what they see as the duplicitous and fictitious nature of masking the face.

Instead, considered anthropologically and sociologically, both face and mask are phenomena that are culturally shaped. A mask obviously bears within and upon it the traces of cultural construction – it is a highly stylized representation of some sort of face, be it of a human, or a spirit, or a god, or an animal, or whatever (Grimes 1975). But the culture of a given group also stylizes the face, and the rest of the body, creating distinctive patterns of facial disposition and presentation. If the work of culture is fundamentally to stylize – that is, to sculpt the human body in certain ways, and to render the world intelligible for the person that is that body (Mauss 1973; Inglis 2005) – then it follows that the mask is a stylized entity put onto the head and face of an organism that is already highly stylized. Thus the mask may be defined as a *double stylization* mechanism. Culturally shaped faces are covered by culturally shaped masks. In more homogeneous cultural contexts, it is the same cultural ensemble which 'makes' both the face and the mask. In more heterogeneous contexts, characterized by multiple and possibly conflicting forms of cultural stylization, one may find differing stylization techniques at work on the face and on the mask, with complex cultural results (for example, if a contemporary Japanese youth were to wear an American Halloween mask, then different forms of cultural sculpting of the face would be at work simultaneously).

It is also the case 'almost all public covering of the face involves some push towards performance' (Twycross and Carpenter 2002, 7). Masking is usually, explicitly or implicitly, a public statement about identity, and such statements usually involve performances of one sort or another (Tseëlon 2001). The nature of masked performances of course varies hugely within and across societies.

Masks can be deployed as crucial components in the performance of rituals, sacred or quasi-sacred. Within a very broad array of rituals and ceremonies, masks have been and can be powerful conveyers of spiritual significance (Eliade 1992; Edson 2005, 5). Masks have been important around the world for playing out the ceremonies associated with both *rites de passage* at important stages in a person's life course, and also times of death and bereavement, making difficult periods more bearable by the donning or ritualized faces expressing variously loss, tragedy and transcendence (Napier 1986; Pernet 1992b; Edson 2005, 6).

For example, a death mask worn by the deceased both allows the latter's passage into the afterlife, while also storing the power of the deceased in this life, by collecting in concentrated form the essence of their being as manifested in their face before decomposition (Heath 2008, 111). Masks have also been strongly associated with rites concerning sterility and fertility (Pernet 1982, 55). More generally, as Heath (2008, 102) points out:

> Masks are lenses for peering into the spiritual unknown . . . one of their jobs is to unlock the door that separates the daily from the divine. In all human societies, masks play an essential part in rites of passage and renewal, as decoys or disguises, for blessings and fertility. They perform in the borders between so-called reality – this world – and the supernatural . . . masks are instruments for metamorphosis.

The mask often affords the 'ritual transformation of the human actor into a being of another order', such as a spirit or ancestor (Tooker 1983). The donning of a mask by participants in a ritual allows the connection of quotidian reality to either the worlds of spirits and deities, or to what is understood to be the natural world of plants, animals and living beings. Masks allow supernatural beings to present themselves to human onlookers, while also being means for ritual participants to master those beings, creating a sense of cosmic order and control (Edson 2005 46, 85). Masks can operate as forms of protection for ritual participants – as Nunley (1999, 7) argues, when 'we compare a shaman's mask and an astronaut's helmet, we find that they are not so dissimilar if we understand them both as protective armour' from potentially hostile external forces. Likewise, women who veil often understand the veil as a means of protecting themselves from the impurities of the social environments in which they are compelled to operate (Almila 2018).

Masks can also allow for the (re)enactment of myths and historical dramas important to the group, making myths and foundation stories come dramatically and vividly to life, thus connecting the past, present and future of the group in concrete and graspable ways (Eliade 1992). More broadly, symbolic dramas played out by masked participants have served as forms of collective memory and inter-generational communication in non-literate cultures, where remembrance of times, beings and events past must be constantly iterated and played out in public settings (Edson 2005, 28, 41).

The particular power of the mask in ritual settings derives from its hyper-stylization of the face: it directs onlookers' attention to certain features (e.g. heightened eyes, exaggerated ears, protruding nose – all of which are laden with significance), and so arouses curiosity, stimulates the imagination, and provokes a range of emotional and intellectual responses (Edson 2005, 7).

Masks have often been used in performances which engage the various senses of participants and audiences. One powerful capacity of the mask rests in its unyielding rigidity, for the interplay of the latter with the kinetic dynamism of its dancing wearer can effect a powerful spell over observers, entranced by the interaction of facial stasis and bodily movement (Tseëlon 2001; Grimes 1975, 514). Wearing masks can in addition mutate the voice of the wearer, allowing him or her to impersonate the register of a different order of being, or to create nonsense words and noises that can create rich cognitive associations, or to create striking and uncanny forms of silence (Twycross and Carpenter 2002, 8).

Masks are not necessarily simply pictures of the spirits, animals or other beings that they represent in ritual contexts. They can also be what Pollock (1995, 594) calls icons and indexes of identity. That is, in ritual settings, masks may be not just pictures of other beings, but are more fundamentally considered to be ways in which the identity of those beings is attributed to or predicated of the mask-wearer as well. The mask can render, at least temporarily, the wearer into the being it points to. The mask can be both iconic representation and indexical conjuror-up of that being. The wearer's usual identity is disguised and disavowed at the same time as a new identity is brought into existence – a thoroughly ambivalent situation, and one which informs the donning of masks in less heavily ritualized contexts as well as explicitly ritualistic ones (Mesnil 1976, 12). The putting on of the mask can be a rich means of articulating power, including the power of the wearer to invoke the potencies of the being s/he is masked as (Tonkin 1979).

However, not all ritual uses of masks involve belief in the transformation of the wearer into that which the mask represents – the power of masks in that regard is as culturally variable as how they look and how they present the face (Pernet 1992). Even in what we may (dubiously) regard as less sophisticated cultural contexts than our own present-day ones, the level of belief afforded by participants and onlookers in the transformative power of masks is an empirical question and cannot be assumed. As Twycross and Carpenter (2002, 7) argue, 'television audiences today readily distinguish the heavy shades that signify the Mafioso from those that indicate "a celebrity keeping the press at bay" . . . There is no reason to assume that [other societies] were not equally adept at understanding masking signals.'

Those signals could involve beliefs locatable anywhere on a spectrum running from outright acceptance of the identity-transforming power of masks, through to complete disavowal of their properties in that regard and no sense at all of the wearer's alteration by the masking actions. The anthropological record indicates that there is no necessary connection between, on the one side, the physical object called the mask and the social acts of masking involving these, and on the other, any particular use made of these by specific groups of people. What is believed and done as regards masking is always contingent on local circumstances (Napier 1986; Pernet 1992).

Beyond explicitly ritualistic and sacred contexts, it is also the case that masks and masking contribute 'to play all of kinds – popular and courtly, spiritual and worldly, sporting and theatrical' (Twycross and Carpenter 2002, 1). As particular societies have complexified over time, moving away from a situation where religious beliefs were inextricably part of every sphere of social action, towards the emergence of more secular domains of thought and practice, masks and masking have taken on new roles and forms of significance. As particular social spheres move from more sacred to more secular bases, there often goes with this trend a multiplication of different types of mask and masking (Edson 2005, 51).

For example, in ancient Greece, the masks of the earliest historical periods were wholly religious in nature, deployed in sacred rites; but in later periods, with the emergence of secular theatre and performance, the masks used in dramas took on different forms and different purposes. While connected to earlier masking forms, and still retaining ritualistic significance (albeit within a markedly more secular cultural framework), the masks of Greek, and later Roman, theatre were used to signify the character types of the *dramatis personae*. The masks of Comedy and Tragedy more broadly connoted the genre of the play being performed, a more mundane use and understanding of masks than had been the case in archaic ritual contexts (Jenkins 1994).

It is worth noting here that the modern Western notion of 'persona', referring to self and self-image, uses a word that in Latin originally meant 'actor's mask'. This is a word that in turn may possibly have more ancient roots in the Etruscan word 'phersu', which also meant 'mask'. We know that in Rome by the first century BCE, the word 'persona' had broadened out from its original literal meaning of 'mask' to encompass a wider range of connotations, pointing to the role in life assumed by a particular individual (Edson 2005, 46). By the European Middle Ages, the word 'persona' had been widened in its sphere of reference to indicate both the appearance, qualities and 'personality' of an individual (Twycross and Carpenter 2002, 284). Thus in the Western tradition, the connections between masks, faces and personalities are long-standing and profound, and indicate different sorts of ambivalence about the role of masks in hiding or revealing both the 'true' face and 'real' nature of an individual. It is striking that it should be a word meaning 'mask' that is at the root of such important contemporary words as 'personal' and 'personality', and the concepts they represent about a very wide range of matters, especially to do with the integrity of selfhood and identity. Connections between masking and selfhood run long and deep.

The ambivalences of masks

The meaning for people of masks, masking and masquerades of course varies greatly from one cultural context to another. However, we can identify certain recurring themes that exist across at least some cultures in terms of the fundamental ambivalences masks have been and are felt to possess in human social life (Napier 1986; Mack 2013).

In at least some cases, it has been and is believed by some people that the person with the mask 'ceases to be himself . . . he [*sic*] seemingly, if not actually, becomes another' (Eliade 1964, 522). Thus the mask has the potential power of transmutation – to make someone into someone or something else, at least temporarily. In at least some cultures, the mask is associated with twin potential disasters. First, that during the wearing (especially in ritualized settings), the mask comes off and is revealed as a mere lifeless thing with a prosaic person underneath wearing it. Second, that during the period of the donning of the mask, it takes over the person who wears it, in ways that are out of their control, rendering them into the unwilled vehicle of the being or force that the mask represents and embodies (Grimes 1975, 511). Depending on the context, a mask may or may not be understood to be able to capture the soul of its wearer (Walens 1983).

The duality of masks also seems to be a feature of thinking about and using them in various cultures. The mask has two sides and two faces. It encompasses both the seen and unseen. It has the potential to represent and instantiate both outer and inner realities (Edson 2005, 30). It can be understood in some cultures as an oscillating mechanism: on the one hand, it can obliterate the identity of its wearer and create forms of facial, bodily and psychological inscrutability. But on the other hand, the mask can create and possibly impose a new identity on those who don it. Impersonation through masking exists in the middle of these extremes – it involves the partial denial of the wearer's primary identity, in the service of a make-believe presentation of being something or someone other. Acting using masks can therefore be understood as a delicate balancing act between denial and adoption of identities, going so far as to be convincing to an audience or to the wearer themselves, but not going so far as to give the impression of total possession of the wearer by the persona being impersonated, for the latter situation would imply madness or demonic possession (Twycross and Carpenter 2002, 12). Powers invoked from other worlds by the wearing of masks must not be allowed to take over the quotidian world, and the mask's powers must be carefully controlled and calibrated (Werbner 1989).

The same sorts of problems appear in sacred rituals as well as secular theatre, albeit in differently inflected ways (Grimes 1975). The mask-wearing initiate must become the god or spirit, but not fully and only temporarily. The actor with a mask must not allow the persona of the character to take them over fully, but the 'possession' must be capacious enough to seem convincing to an audience that somehow they are doing more than only watching an actor with a mask. In ritual performance, the wearer and the entity that the mask points to may be united as one temporarily, as far as the audience is concerned. But in at least some forms of secular theatre (as in classical Greek theatre, where each character type had its own conventional mask), the mask is meant to promote a certain distance between actor and audience. The character portrayed by the mask is presented by and through the masking as a generic character type, and not as a 'real' individual. In secular contexts, including the theatrical, the gaming and fantasy senses of masking are heightened, whereas in sacred-ritualistic contexts, masking is meant to fuse audience and mask-wearer, not separate them (Edson 2005, 197, 208; Twycross and Carpenter 2002, 13). But in both ideal-typical cases, the sacred ritual and the secular theatre, the ambivalence of masking as a human endeavour seems to be its most notable feature.

One of the major sources of the oscillating, dual and often uncanny nature of masks rests in the contrast between the relative mutability and changeable character of the human face, and the generally high level of immutability of the mask (Twycross and Carpenter 2002, 8). Masks involve processes of what Grimes (1975) calls 'concretion'. As seen very clearly in both theatrical and death masks, their fixity and rigidity involve the concretizing of otherwise dynamic facial and bodily forces. They fix into unchanging place what would normally be processes – the opening and closing of eyes and mouth, the moving of the head, the alteration of facial gestures, movements and tics, and so on. The mask reduces to one dimensionality living facial movement. The mask's uncanny nature takes wing from the fact that it is a dead thing impersonating a living being. Impersonation by a mask-wearer can seem to be either harmless pretence, or incarnation, either beneficial or maleficent.

Grimes (1975, 511) proposes a major division between 'non-modern' and 'modern' forms of masking:

> To don a mask is to don an other and doff a selfhood. But if the act is incomplete, if there is a disjunction of interior and exterior, rather than a seizure of interior by exterior, dissimulation is the result. In such a case pretending does not lead to possession but to pretence . . . [T]here are . . . two kinds of fear involved in masking: one, more dominant in tribal and pre-industrial societies, that exterior powers will take over and run wild; and the other, found primarily in industrial, urban societies, that a mask will only partially take hold of the wearer, thus allowing him [*sic*] to become merely a manager of images . . . When masking becomes manipulation, the wearer threatens his [*sic*] viewers, as well as the very notion of cultural roles. From his hidden position behind, he can scoff at the very exteriority which evokes fear in the beholder. He uses roles instead of playing them or becoming subject to them.

One must of course be wary of sweeping generalizations, especially based on unexamined assumptions about the 'modern' and whatever is construed as its antitheses (for an interesting if problematic periodization of different sorts of masking practices, see Tseëlon 2014). Nonetheless, the point made by Grimes holds if we take it not to refer to different 'types' of societies but to different sorts of social context, more sacred and more secular, which could co-exist within one particular society. In sacred-ritualistic settings, where supernatural forces are assumed, then the power of masks to invoke supernatural entities would logically involve as a corollary the fear that that power may run out of control. By contrast, in secular-quotidian settings, the power of the mask to disguise a person and dissemble identity has as a corollary the fear not that identity may be obliterated but that an ill-intentioned identity hides behind, and is either made possible, or is certainly greatly accentuated, by the mask. The fear in such settings is a) that an evil-doing persona skulks behind the mask, and that the mask may afford it *carte blanche* to do as it pleases, and/or b) that an erstwhile innocent persona is corrupted into carrying out wicked acts by the donning of the mask and the invisibility – physical and moral – which it allows or promotes. Thus when the face is masked, or when the face *is like* a mask, the potential for dissembling, un-truth and wickedness can be thought to be immense (Goffman 1959).

Masks and social (dis)order

It is well documented that in Western Europe since at least the Middle Ages there have been fears about the power of masks to create social disorder because of their capacities to change the behaviour of individuals, from law-abiding to law-breaking (Tseëlon 2001). At certain times, social elites and the authorities which police the social world for them have seemed most concerned about the potential of masking to encourage disorderly conducts ranging from theft, sacrilege and sedition, to sexual licentiousness and gender swapping (Honigmann 1977, 269). For Honigmann (1977, 275–6):

> [t]he facial disguise temporarily eliminates from social intercourse that part of the body through which, people [in the West, at least] have long believed, the individual's personal feelings and attitudes are revealed or can be deliberately communicated to others. The face is the organ by which self and society carry on the largest portion of the communication in which they engage, not only linguistic communication but paralinguistic as well. It is by sundering self and society that masks act on the sense of personal identity, including feelings of responsibility individuals have toward social conventions   The mask acts to disjoin personal identity from the behaviour being enacted   masking, by distantiating identity through concealing the face, overcomes some of the responsibility and conformity to convention that a person's sense of personal identity normally incorporates.

While Honigmann erroneously attributes this sort of facial communication, and its 'distortion' by masking, to all human societies, nonetheless his point seems to hold at least for the medieval and modern West. If the face and unmasked face-to-face interactions are fundamental bases of social order, then in masking lies the potential for social disorder, as normal forms of self-restraint are thrown off during the period of the masking, whether this is done as a purely individual act or (likely with more striking and powerful consequences) collectively in groups, as in the famous case of the masquerades of carnival time in the later medieval and early modern periods.

Thus masks in the Western tradition – and no doubt in some others too – possess a further sort of ambivalence: while they may create symbolic and cosmic order in the context of controlled rituals, they can also be involved in the creation of disorder and havoc. As Grimes (1975, 513) notes, masks used to conceal the face seem consistently to appear in circumstances in which 'anomalous, asocial forces (dead men, deities, demons, wild animals, bandits) are breaking through classificatory grids or are being brought under social control'. Masks are involved both in people 'enforcing social order and in challenging it or being in a temporary state of release from it' (Edson 2005, 22).

On the side of enforcement of the status quo (or the creation of a future one) can be secret societies, the rites of which are enacted by masked figures, and whose purposes are the maintenance of social order, including sometimes by means of the intimidation and terrorizing of non-initiates. In both Africa and Euro-America, much evidence exists as to the male-dominated nature of secret societies, both historically and in the present day (Nunley 1999, 37). This in turn points to a broader gender imbalance in masking rituals, with men tending to be the wearers of masks and females either the passive onlookers or the victims of intimidation by the masked male initiates (Eliade 1992). However, as Pernet (1982) points out, there is also evidence to show that the real picture may be more nuanced throughout most societies than a simple case of masked males dominating non-masked females, for the latter are often more complicit, and involved in more complicated ways, in masking rituals than early students of such phenomena had assumed (Tseëlon 1995).

In the Western context, masks have played a prime role in the social dramas concerning law enforcement and criminal deviance (Smith 2008). It is not an accident that avengers of wrongdoing like the Lone Ranger, Batman, and Zorro are masked, their righteousness signified by their fully or partly hidden faces. This indicates that in the West, a mask – especially one which covers only the eyes – need not necessarily connote something sinister but can point to valour and righteousness too. The masked, blinded female persona of Justice, holding the scales in her hand, also raises interesting questions about the semiotics of righteousness in the West and how these intersect with notions of gender. Conversely, the villainy of the Klansman and the oscillating perfidy and heroism of the highwayman are represented and made possible in part by full-face and half-face masks respectively (Barthes 1991). It would seem that that the mask's affordance of impersonality and anonymity has made it a vital vehicle for playing out the rituals and representations of social enforcement and violation. Both the masked executioner and the highwayman stand outside the law, but one exists above it and the other below it, and in both cases their symbolic positioning is made possible by their masked features (Grimes 1975, 512).

Much masking takes place in times and places collectively set aside for it, either in terms of rituals or secular masquerades (see also Tseëlon 2014). This raises questions of what Nunley (1999, 66) calls the various forms of 'agency of the masquerade'. In the much discussed case of late medieval and early modern carnivals in Catholic Europe, the mask worked as a public signal. The masked person signifies s/he is entering a world of play where normal social rules are – at least partly – suspended, and to a certain extent s/he cannot be held fully responsible for his or her actions as they are 'not themselves' during the masking period. In carnival conditions, 'covering the face, and thereby symbolically denying or inverting roles and normally constituted facial communication, becomes more important than bodying forth a deity or a type. Who one *is not* becomes more important than who one *is*' (Grimes 1975, 512, emphasis added).

There seems to have been marked ambivalence at the time about carnival masking and its social consequences (Stallybrass and White 1986). On the one hand, for the few advocates of the pleasures of carnival whose thoughts and feelings have been transmitted down to us today, the masking of carnival – where people would disguise their faces and bodies in different sorts of colourful costume – allowed for a merry celebration of the relativity of identity, the pleasures of metamorphosis, and the joy of role-play (Twycross and Carpenter 2002, 305). We could add that masking in carnival is deeply communal, for everyone is masked, and unlike in ritual, there is not a performance between masked figures and an unmasked audience. It was the pervasiveness of masking among throngs of people that gave carnival its distinctive forms of collective effervescence, and thus its power to provoke new energies and forms of collective movement.

But for Christian and secular moralists who condemned the festivities of carnival time, masking allowed anonymity, which in turn de-individualized, and freed the individual from a sense of moral responsibility for their actions. That in turn was thought to allow for all sorts of regrettable forms of licence to take place, as normal moral conventions were thrown off, albeit briefly (Heath 2008, 108). For those moralists who condemned carnival in general, and masking in particular, otherwise 'serious people can be transformed into clowns and otherwise timid people can become leaders', with grave consequences for the preservation of social order (Ancelet 1989, 2). The anonymity afforded by masking seemed particularly scandalous as it allowed for symbolic inversions of all sorts, with (it was feared) men dressed as women, prostitutes disguised as men, the poor disguised as the rich, and vice versa. In the frenetic atmosphere of masked crowds, sexual excitement was thought to be heightened, wives cuckolded husbands, and all sorts of inappropriate liaisons were instigated. Thus the gender, sexual and familial social orders were jeopardized. Masking was thought to make both women and men promiscuous, and that was why it was to be utterly condemned.

The discourse of moralists and (some) elites in this regard derived from the teachings of the early Church Fathers, who had condemned the ostensibly similar Roman Kalends celebrations as being unfit for Christian believers in the earliest days of the Church (Napier 1986). In the Christian tradition that built up over a millennium and more, masks had a very bad reputation. The Devil was thought to be the pre-eminent masker, hiding his evil wiles beneath an apparently beneficent mask. Masks thus were understood to be devilish in themselves. Good Christians were urged not to mask the true face that God had given them. This was especially the case with women. Women's bodily adornments, especially facial ones, were deeply distrusted by both the early Christian Fathers and later theologians. The painting of the face was seen as a wicked adornment, and by extension masks were wicked too. This viewpoint was one of the wellsprings from which derived the vehemence of Christian condemnation of popular carnival practices (Twycross and Carpenter 2002, 300–4).

Masks and veils: Contrasts and comparisons

It is impossible to compare 'the veil' and 'the mask' per se, for there are no such entities in the abstract. Both masks and veils are too multiple in their forms and ambivalent in their varied cultural meanings to allow for any grand statements about what each of them 'is' or entails. The existence of crossover phenomena – such as the mask-cum-veil of traditional Spanish penitents, as well as the Ku Klux Klan – also complicates the picture. But it is possible to contrast different, historically located conceptions and practices of masks and masking and veils and veiling, and to outline some broad trends and tendencies which traverse time and space at least to some degree.

At a very basic level, while veils are made of more soft materials, masks are usually but not always of more rigid construction. Veils certainly connote meanings to onlookers, but are not representational in the way many masks are, at least those which are meant to portray some sort of being or entity. However, the blank eye or mouth mask also lacks representational capacities, again muddying the borders between veils and masks. Heath (2008) claims that masks imply or require an audience, whereas veils do not. But this ignores the possibility that the wearer of a veil may believe that the eye of God, or some equivalent, is always upon them, and thus constitutes a constant and unwavering audience for the performance of wearing the veil, as can also be seen in the notion that Muslim women should veil while praying alone. It is better to say that both masks and veils involve performances, but to whom and involving what cannot be defined in essentializing ways.

Looking through the anthropological and historical record, we can see that there is certainly no neat dividing line between veiled women and masked men – for in societies throughout the world at different times, women have masked and men have veiled (Tseëlon 1995). Nonetheless, in patriarchally organized societies, there is a tendency for masks and masking rites often to be the primary prerogative of males, because of their centrality in rituals which are either directly controlled by men or are strongly masculine in orientation. The ranks of male-dominated or male-only secret societies have gained much of their symbolic power, and potential to instil awe or fear in others, through their monopoly control of certain kinds of highly charged masks. But male authority has also been achieved through different forms of veiling too (Murphy 1964). The mask is certainly not an essentially 'male' tool for displaying and gaining power, but it has been used as such by many male groupings throughout history.

Both masks and veils have been imbued strongly with multiple forms of religious significance. Masks have often been used in religious rituals throughout the world, being used to invoke and embody gods, spirits and other supernatural forces. The mask of the priest and shaman has the capacity to call forth powers and also to protect the wearer from them. Here some kinds of masks overlap with some types of veils, where the latter are to do with protecting believers from external impurities and dangers, and the former are concerned with protection against powers that are not fully within the control of the mask's wearer. Masks can invoke and channel the sacred, while veils tend more towards protecting the sacred, from either pollution internal to the wearer or external to him or her (El-Guindi 1999). Masks tend towards being a proactive and productive device in ritual, while veils tend towards a more negative role, excluding problem elements from the ritual.

Comparing societal concerns about masks in one society and veils in another reveals more about both cases, and illustrates unexpected resonances and overlaps. In early modern Europe, the carnival mask was believed to be a mechanism for the allowing of all sorts of undesirable licence, especially sexual in nature. In some Muslim-majority countries today, face-veiling is also considered to enable various types of clandestine sexual behaviour (Moors 2007). In both cases, the face-covering is understood both to facilitate wrongdoing and also to encourage or create it. Masks and veils, protectors and invokers of the sacred, are in both cases suspected of encouraging profanation, such is the power inherent in facial concealment. It is no surprise that throughout the history of certain societies, both masks and veils have been thoroughly bound up with imaginings of what constitutes sound social order and chaotic disorder. Both have made possible and potentially undo bodily regimes of control in general and facial ones in particular.

Examining the history of masks and masking in a particular society helps one to understand better the concerns and fears about veils and veiling in that society, in times both past and present. We have seen that there is a long tradition in Christian thought of suspicion towards masks and facial disguising, sometimes turning into outright denunciation. This suspicion is rooted in a long-standing metaphysics to do with the apparent truths to be found in looking into another person's face directly, and in particular seeing into their eyes. Here then is one of the historical roots – as distant and mediated as it may be – of contemporary Euro-American fears about Islamic veiling (see also Tarlo 2010, 133–4). The early modern carnival mask was denounced by moralists, and was to a certain extent feared by authorities, in large part because it hid the eyes. It is instructive to juxtapose this case with that of the burqa today. It has become the popular symbol in the West of face-veiling, precisely because it touches on a cultural raw nerve by hiding the eyes. The niqab, which usually leaves the eyes visible, is much less commented upon, and has come to lack the symbolic resonances that Westerners – or at least the politicians and others who claim to represent them – associate with the burqa, particularly in terms of terrorist threats and 'enemies within'. The security of the state or the West in general is metonymically threatened by a veil that covers the eyes, connoting something sinister because invisible and thus unknowable. A mask that covered the eyes was subjected to analogous fears and denunciations in Europe some 500 years before. In both cases, a masked or veiled female concentrates a range of imagined horrors into one iconic image, of a face whose eyes are inscrutable and whose motives perforce must be malicious. The inability to look into the eyes of the woman so as to fix her with authority's stare unites the secular mask and the religious veil in a Western history fundamentally characterized by a patriarchal insistence on peering into the soul.

References

Almila, Anna-Mari. 2018. *Veiling in Fashion: Space and the Hijab in Minority Communities*. London: I.B.Tauris.

Ancelet, Barry Jean. 1989. *'Capitaine, Voyage Ton Flag': The Traditional Cajun Country Mardi Gras*. Lafayette, LA: Center for Louisiana Studies.

Barthes, Roland. 1991. 'The Face of Garbo'. In Mythologies, 56–57. New York: Noonday Press.

Dagan, Esther A. 1992. *The Spirit's Image: The African Masking Tradition – Evolving Continuity*. Montréal: Galerie Amrad.

Grimes, Ronald L. 1975. 'Masking: Toward a Phenomenology of Exteriorization'. *Journal of the American Academy of Religion* 43(3):508–16.

Edson, Gary. 2005. *Masks and Masking: Faces of Tradition and Belief Worldwide*. London: McFarland.

El-Guindi, Fadwa. 1999. *Veil: Modesty, Privacy and Resistance*. Oxford: Berg.

Eliade, Mircea. 1992. 'Masks: Mythical and Ritual Origins'. In *Encyclopedia of World Art* 9:521–26. New York: McGraw-Hill.

Goffman, Erving. 1990 [1959]. *The Presentation of Self in Everyday Life*. London: Penguin.

Heath, Jennifer. 2008. '"What is Subordinated, Dominates": Mourning, Magic, Masks and Male Veiling'. In *The Veil: Women Writers on Its History, Lore, and Politics*, edited by Jennifer Heath, 99–118. Berkeley, CA: University of California Press.

Honigmann, John J. 1977. 'The Masked Face'. *Ethos* 5(3):263–80.

Inglis, David. 2005. *Culture and Everyday Life*. London: Routledge.

Jedrej, M. C. 1980. 'A comparison of some masks from North America, Africa, and Melanesia'. *Journal of Anthropological Research* 36:220–30.

Jenkins, Ian. 1994. 'Face Value: The Mask in Greece and Rome'. In Masks and the Art of Expression, John Mack, 50–167. New York: Harry Abrams.

Mack, John. (ed.) 2013. *Masks: The Art of Expression*. 2nd edition. London: British Museum Press.

Mauss, Marcel. 1973. 'Techniques of the Body'. *Economy and Society* 2(1):70–88.

Mesnil, Marianne. 1976. 'The Masked Festival: Disguise or Affirmation?' *Culture* 3(2):11–29.

Moors, Annelies. 2007. 'Fashionable Muslims: Notions of Self, Religion, and Society in San'a'. *Fashion Theory* 11(2/3):319–46.

Murphy, Robert F. 1964. 'Social Distance and Veil'. *American Anthropologist* 66(6):1257–74.

Napier, A. David. 1986. *Masks, Transformation, and Paradox*. Berkeley and Los Angeles, CA: University of California Press.

Nietzsche, F. 1918. *Beyond Good and Evil*. New York: Boni and Liveright, The Modern Library.

Nietzsche, F. 2009. *Thus Spake Zarathustra*. New York: Cosimo.

Nunley, John W. 1999. 'Introduction'. In *Masks: Faces of Culture*, edited by John W. Nunley and Cara McCarty. New York: Harry N. Abrams.

Oettinger, Marion and Suzanne Kenagy. 1988. 'The Many Faces of Mexico: Masks in Cultural Context'. *Masterkey* 62(2/3):9–22.

Pernet, Henry. 1992a. 'Masks and Women: Toward a Reappraisal'. *History of Religions* 22(1):45–59.

Pernet, Henry. 1992b. *Ritual Masks: Deceptions and Revelations*. Eugene. OR: Wipf and Stock.

Pollock, Donald. 1995. 'Masks and the Semiotics of Identity'. *The Journal of the Royal Anthropological Institute* 1(3):581–97.

Scott, Joan Wallach. 2007. *The Politics of the Veil*. Princeton, NJ: Princeton University Press.

Seeger, A. 1975. 'The Meaning of Body Ornaments: A Suya Example'. *Ethnology* 14:211–24.

Smith, Philip. 2008. 'Durkheim and Criminology: Reconstructing the Legacy'. *Australian & New Zealand Journal of Criminology* 41(3):333–44.

Stallybrass, Peter and Allon White. 1986. *The Politics and Poetics of Transgression*. London: Methuen.

Synnott, Anthony. 1989. 'Truth and Goodness, Mirrors and Masks Part I: A Sociology of Beauty and the Face'. *The British Journal of Sociology* 40(4):607–36.

Synnott, Anthony. 1990. 'Truth and Goodness, Mirrors and Masks Part II: A Sociology of Beauty and the Face'. *The British Journal of Sociology* 41(1):55–76.

Tarlo, Emma. 2010. *Visibly Muslim: Fashion, Politics, Faith*. Oxford: Berg.

Tseëlon, Efrat. 1995. *The Masque of Femininity: The Presentation of Woman in Everyday Life*. London: Sage.

Tseëlon, Efrat. 2001. 'Introduction: Masquerade and Identities'. In Masquerade and Identities: essays on Gender, Sexuality and Marginality, edited by Efrat Tseëlon, 1-37. London: Routledge.

Tseëlon, Efrat. 2014. 'Fashion and the Orders of Masking'. *Critical Studies in Fashion and Beauty* 3:3-9.

Tonkin, E. 1979. 'Masks and Powers'. *Man* 14:237–48.

Tooker, E. 1983. 'The Many Faces of Masks and Masking'. In *The Power of Symbols*, edited by N. Ross Crumrine and Margorie Helpin, 12–18. Vancouver, BC: University of British Columbia Press.

Twycross, Meg and Sarah Carpenter. 2002. *Masks and Masking in Medieval and Early Tudor England*. Aldershot: Ashgate.

Urban, G. and Janet W. Hendricks. 1983. 'Signal Functions of Masking in Amerindian Brazil'. *Semiotica* 47(1):181–218.

Walens, Stanley. 1983. 'Analogic Causality and the Power of Masks'. In *The Power of Symbols*, edited by N. Ross Crumrine and Margorie Helpin, 70–8. Vancouver, BC: University of British Columbia Press.

Werbner, Richard P. 1989. *Ritual Passage, Sacred Journey: The Form, Process and Organization of Religious Movement*. Washington DC: Smithsonian Institution Press.

24

THE AMISH PRAYER CAP
AS A SYMBOL THAT BOUNDS
THE COMMUNITY

Jana M. Hawley

Introduction

Amish dress serves as both a separator and an identifier. As a primary tenet, the Amish strive to be separate from the world and believe that appearance serves as a constant reminder of their beliefs. They also believe that the Church, rather than fashion designers and business owners, should control identity. Dress also serves as a form of boundary maintenance and contributes to the notion of community and belonging. Like other aspects of their material world, dress is plain. Amish clothing represents several dimensions of their cultural values, including religious convictions, humility, modesty, and group conformity. It is also functional, economical to produce, and relatively uniform among wearers within the same community. For nearly a century, Amish clothing has changed very little.

While this chapter will provide a cultural overview of the Old Order Amish and discuss Amish clothing in general, the focus will be on the Amish prayer cap. Depending on the relative orthodoxy of the community, the prayer cap (or *kapp* in their Pennsylvania Dutch dialect) serves as a unique identifier of the Old Order Amish and, as will be discussed, also serves as an identifier of geography, community membership, level of religious convictions, age, and marital status. A description of the production and distribution of Amish prayer caps is also presented.

Amish culture

The Old Order Amish are a large Christian-based group whose core values focus on separateness from the world, commitment to tradition, family, and community. They are an outgrowth of the sixteenth-century Swiss Anabaptist movement, in turn a product of the Protestant Reformation. They split from the Mennonites in the seventeenth century, but both groups have been relentlessly persecuted and came to be viewed as separatists from the dominant society. The Amish immigrated to the United States in the 1600s as part of William Penn's promise for religious freedom and settled initially in the Lancaster, Pennsylvania area. In the 1800s, some Amish groups split away from the Pennsylvania group and migrated to the Midwest and other parts of North America. Today, the Midwest Amish remain divisive with the Pennsylvania groups (Hostetler 1980).

Many demographers anticipated that the Amish would eventually assimilate into mainstream society, but surprisingly the opposite has occurred (Hostetler 1980). True, some Amish decide to leave the church when they become adults, but most find that their lives are deeply embedded with their families and culture, and choose to stay committed to the Amish faith. Today, the Amish population continues to grow, with approximately 300,000 Old Order Amish living in more than 750 congregations scattered throughout North America. The Young Center (2015) reports that the largest populations are located in Ohio, Pennsylvania, Indiana, Wisconsin, New York, Michigan, and Missouri (in descending order of population). Amish settlements typically have several church districts, each comprising about 30–40 people, small enough to fit within an Amish home during church services (J. Hartman, personal communication 2002).

Today, millions of tourists flock to Amish communities often claiming afterward that they now 'know' all about Amish (Trollinger 2012). But in a brief encounter with an Amish person, it is not possible to really understand what it means to be Amish. The media has objectified the Amish including a feature film, *Witness* (Feldman and Weir 1985), and various editorial spreads are found in *Vogue Taiwan* (Hardt 2014), *Vogue Italia* (Meisel 2008), and *Elle Ukraine* (Dementyeva 2013). These spreads often depicted models wearing plain clothes and framed with Amish props such as buggies, fields, bales of hay, one-room school houses, and horse-drawn equipment.

The Amish follow a strict church discipline that demands excommunication of wayward members, authority of the scriptures in matters of faith, separateness from mainstream society, and conscientious objection (Hamilton and Hawley 1999). Two important concepts that contribute significantly to Amish culture are their rejection of *Hochmut* (vanity and conceit) and a high value placed on *Gelassenheit* (self-control and tranquility) (Kraybill 1989). These core values are expressed through group norms rather than the individualized norms that are obvious in the wider American culture. This attention to humility and group conformity also helps to explain their rejection of modern technologies. In other words, when labor-saving technologies are not adopted, they must rely on members of the group to help with tasks such as harvest, quilting, or barn raisings. These values set them apart from the rest of contemporary American culture, making them a curiosity to many.

Central to Amish culture is a commitment to family, community, and a reliance on local Church leaders for regulating individual behavior. There is no central church bureaucracy from which the Amish are provided rules. Instead, the Amish live by a moral code or set of locally made rules called the *Ordnung*. The *Ordnung* controls such cultural behaviors such as whether or not community members can use diesel-powered milking machines to whether or not women use straight pins or snaps as dress closures. The *Ordnung* follows the specific congregation and the specific rules may vary along a continuum of conservative (low churches) to progressive (high churches). Even within the same settlement area, the *Ordnung* can vary from church to church. This helps explain why some Amish are seen using tractors while others use only horse-drawn equipment.

Amish families are arranged around traditional gender and age roles including power lying within the male gender and increasing with age. Amish men are responsible for the spiritual welfare of the family and women are expected to carry out the domestic chores. Large families are considered an asset, not only providing labor for the family farm but also as a perpetual assurance of Amish culture into the future.

The research process

This research is based on 11 months of participant observation where I lived among the Old Order Amish in the largest Missouri Amish settlement of Jamesport, Missouri. Participant observation research has long been the hallmark of anthropological method as a tool for collecting data about people, processes, and cultures in a qualitative form. When conducting participant observation, the researcher sets out to learn about the activities of the people under study in the natural setting through observing and participating in those activities. In other words, it is the process of learning through exposure to day-to-day activities (DeWalt and DeWalt 2002). This proved to be the most peaceful, reflective, and revealing year of our lives and resulted in lifelong friendships with several people of Amish faith with whom I remain in contact to this day. Jamesport is in Daviess County, Missouri in the northeast quadrant of the state. The Missouri Amish population has seen rapid growth in recent years, in part due to Amish migration from other states. Today, Missouri is home to over 11,000 Amish in 96 church districts and 43 settlements. Daviess County currently has 29 districts and a population of 4,570 (Young Center 2015). It has grown significantly since my year of data collection in 1992 when there were six districts and a population of c.1800 (Hawley 1993).

When one lives and works among a group of people distinctly different from one's own culture for an extended period of time, stark contracts become readily apparent and we learn all kinds of things about the group. Although my research question had to do with Amish business practices, I learned and have since written about many other aspects of Amish life.

At the time that I did my research, I was divorced and my children were 10- and 11-year-old boys. Even though many have wondered how I gained access to this closed community, I quite frankly found it easy. True, there were times when the bishops thought I was spending too much time with my new Amish friends, but this did not hinder my data collection process. Perhaps the reason it was so easy for me to gain access was because I grew up on a farm in rural Kansas giving me legitimacy in knowing the ways of farm life as I lived and worked among the 1,800 Amish people that lived in the rural area surrounding the community of Jamesport. In addition, I adjusted my own appearance by forgoing make-up and the latest fashion trends or my favorite jeans in lieu of adopting plain skirts and blouses. Shortly after I arrived, I found myself working alongside the Amish as we worked to make apple cider on an oak hand press, pies for bake sales, bread on a wood-fired oven, or candy on a kerosene stove. During the year I put 55,000 miles on my car as I served as the 'taxi' driver for the Amish who hired me to drive them to doctor appointments, shopping expeditions, and family weddings. By the end of the year, I had attended Amish church services, birthday parties, auctions, weddings, singings, volleyball games, work bees, quilt frolics, hospital visits, barn raisings, and a multitude of mundane daily chores. We gained mutual respect for each other and the Amish gave me a remarkable level of acceptance. At the same time, I grew to understand their world view, social structure, and unique (and sometimes subtle) levels of technology.

Amish dress

The history of Amish clothing is hard to establish. Some of it can be traced back to European peasantry, some to early American colonial times, and some can be traced to early rural America. Over the years only minor changes have evolved, but change undoubtedly does occur.

Amish dress reflects their faith and serves as a way to remain distinct from mainstream society. Dress rules serve as a way to strengthen the group by fostering conformity, simplicity, and humility. Dress serves as a way to build solidarity among the group so that when everyone conforms to the rules of dress, the emphasis is placed on the group instead of the individuals. Their simple clothing has contributed to their nickname of the Plain People. As in other parts of their material world, their dress clearly indicates humility. Their clothing also serves a functional role in that it can be produced economically and uniformly among members of the same community. Amish dress is outwardly observable which contributes to their notion of separateness from the rest of the world, in other words, dress provides a boundary maintenance (Hawley 1995).

Members within the same Amish congregation are easily recognizable from within the group, though outsiders may not notice the subtle differences of one Amish group to another. During my research year, I sat next to an Amish friend at a horse auction. In the center of the arena was a young Amish boy and I asked my friend whether he was from Jamesport. My friend said, 'No, can't you tell by his hat? The brim is much smaller!' To my untrained eye, the hat looked the same as those worn in the Jamesport community, but to my Amish friends, they could easily see the subtle distinction.

During my research year, I drove my Amish friends to a wedding in Iowa and took note of nearly a hundred straw hats that were thrown under a tree when everyone went inside for dinner. I wondered, 'How will they ever know which hat belongs to whom when they come out?' To me, they all looked alike. Yet, after dinner, each man easily retrieved his own hat from under the tree. These stories provide examples of how insiders fully comprehend the dress cues, but outsiders seldom see the differences.

Dresses for Amish women range in color but must be of *plain fabric*, in other words, fabric that is solid without print or unusual weaves. The fabric is often of poplin, percale, broadcloth weave or jersey knit. While the traditional fabric would have been woven of 100 per cent cotton, today's Amish women typically use fabrics that do not need ironing such as a blended fabric of cotton and polyester or knits. Some less conservative groups allow pastel colors, but more traditional colors are limited to shades of dark blue and black. Most Amish women make their own clothing, purchasing fabric from local stores usually run by women in their church community. The dresses are calf-length and often covered with an apron – serving as a utilitarian tool for wiping, holding items, and protecting the clothing. For church, women often wear a white organdy cape, or in winter months a woolen cloak. In the community where this research was done, the rules for the dress style dictate an open front bodice, elbow-length or long sleeves, and a fitted bodice with a narrow band collar. A self-fabric belt attaches to a dirndl, center-front opened skirt. The dress is designed to allow for change in body girth and is held closed with straight pins. In other communities the pattern/style might vary slightly, including dresses that are closed with snaps rather than straight pins. Married women use dull colors of burgundy and navy while unmarried girls are permitted to wear lighter values of greens, lavender, and blues. Women do not cut their hair and wear it parted down the middle and combed away from the face. It is twisted at the nape of the neck into a bun.

For Amish men, the garb focuses on practicality and includes both Sunday garb and work garb. For Sundays, men wear a simple black coat with no lapels that is fastened with hooks rather than a button. Black broadfall trousers are sewn from a traditional pattern and are often held with suspenders. Typically, the men have plain buttons on their shirts. For work, dark denim broadfall trousers are common. The male hairstyle is bowl-cut with bangs. Married men keep a beard, but no mustache. Single Amish men keep a clean-shaven face until their wedding day, or in the case of those who do not marry, they start growing a beard when they are baptized into the church.

Amish head coverings

A most distinguishing and critically important part of the Amish garb is the head-covering or prayer *kapp* (cap) which serves as part of their convictions of being Amish. The adult cap is made of white organdy and varies in style depending on the community and level of orthodoxy.

Amish caps are similar to the ones worn as early as the fifteenth century by Palatine women (Hostetler 1964). This headpiece has had several names including *Haubchen, Kappe, Ziehaube, Nebelkapp,* and more casually *Betz,* and *Saumagen* (Hostetler 1964).

The head-covering is steeped in Paul's teachings to the church at Corinth:

> But every woman who has her head uncovered while praying or prophesying disgraces her head, for she is one and the same as the woman whose head is shaved. For if a woman does not cover her head, let her also have her hair cut off; but if it is disgraceful for a woman to have her hair cut off or her head shaved, let her cover her head.
>
> *(1 Corinthians 11: 5–6, New American Standard Bible)*

For Mennonite women, the cap is typically worn only at times of worship or when in public, as compared to Amish women who wear it at all times except when sleeping. This is based on the notion that women should 'pray without ceasing'. For men, the rule follows the seventh verse, 'For a man ought not to have his head covered, since he is the image and glory of God; but the woman is the glory of man' (1 Corinthians 11:7). Hence, the head-covering provides a daily reminder of the concept of male leadership and the submission of woman to the man. Corinthians also discusses hair to which it makes clear that men's hair should be short and women's hair should be long.

Most Anabaptist groups (e.g. Amish, Brethren, Hutterites, Mennonites, Bruderhof, Quaker) mandate a head-covering but the type varies. The Amish prayer cap is typically made of white Swiss organdy and must always be worn in public. The style of the prayer cap and how it is worn varies depending on the level of orthodoxy and the *Ordnung* rules. The most conservative Amish groups are called Schwartzentruber or Nebraska Amish. These conservative or low churches wear unstarched prayer caps with strings that are often tied close to the chin. In progressive or high communities, the strings are tied low or not at all – or even are non-existent. The cap is often highly starched resulting in a cap with more form. Amish in the Pennsylvania region often wear a heart-shaped style with a narrower brim and gentle gathers to form a heart shape along the crown. This style is worn back on the head. Below are drawings of prayer caps and how they vary from low to high churches. The style of prayer cap also is determined or influenced by the region. See Figure 24.1 for examples of types based on community or geographic region.

Typically, an Amish woman will wear a black bonnet that covers the prayer cap when in public, travelling, or in cases of inclement weather. Again, the bonnet style also varies from region to region or from church to church. Married Amish women are supposed to always wear their black bonnet when in public, but many do not. The bonnets are hot and cumbersome. Occasionally, church leadership strengthens the policing of *Ordnung* rules, but this is often not lasting. During the period of social enforcement, the women are often seen carrying their black bonnets so that they can quickly don them if they spot a bishop or minister nearby. In fact, most Amish settlements have self-appointed 'police' who quickly report to the church hierarchy if someone is behaving outside the *Ordnung* rules.

There exists a private/public notion of place when it comes to covering the head. During the year I was in Jamesport, I established close relationships with several Amish women. At first the women would wear their prayer caps in my presence, even when in their homes. As the year passed, their trust and comfort with my presence resulted in the prayer caps being taken off as soon as we entered the privacy of their homes. One Amish woman spent an extended stay in my home while a family member was in the regional hospital. During that time, she often wore her long hair loose and uncovered when inside our homes.

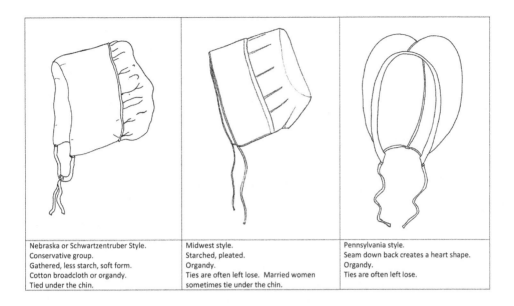

Nebraska or Schwartzentruber Style.	Midwest style.	Pennsylvania style.
Conservative group.	Starched, pleated.	Seam down back creates a heart shape.
Gathered, less starch, soft form.	Organdy.	Organdy.
Cotton broadcloth or organdy.	Ties are often left lose. Married women	Ties are often left lose.
Tied under the chin.	sometimes tie under the chin.	

Figure 24.1 Styles of prayer caps vary by community. Illustration by Jonathan Garcia Gutierrez, 2016.

On average, most Amish women own two or three prayer caps each costing just less than $20. In the past, Amish women often sewed their own prayer coverings and bonnets, but today many will order from either their local seamstress, through mail order, from a website, or even on eBay. Examples of companies that produce Amish head coverings are shown in Table 24.1. While most Amish do not own computers, they have English[1] friends who provide access to the Internet, or do ordering for them. In some communities, the Amish are permitted basic computers with very small screens (Kraybill 1998). Amish also are known to use the computers at the local libraries. Two nationally distributed Amish newspapers provide additional information for ordering clothing. Those newspapers are *The Budget* and *Die Botschaft*.

Easter Beachy, of Mount Eaton, OH, owns The Cap Shack, a small manufacturing facility that makes Amish prayer caps. She has been making prayer caps since she was a girl. It is Esther's attention to detail that has helped her grow her business. She ships community-specific prayer caps all across the country. Attention to pleating detail can determine whether the cap is made for Indiana, Ohio, or Missouri Amish. Her husband, a machinist, created a machine that pleats fabric for her. Before her husband's invention, she used a paring knife to fold the tiny one-eighth inch pleats so that they could be pressed with an iron. Esther's manufacturing facility is attached to her home. She now employs five women and they produce 150 caps per week (Ditlevson 2010). Table 24.1 provides a list of some companies that produce and distribute Amish head coverings.

Hats distinguish Amish men from the outsider, symbolize status within the group, and indicate *Ordnung* rules of the settlement. Boys as early as the age of 2 will begin wearing a hat with three or more inches of brim. A grandfather, on the other hand, has a four-inch crown and a four-inch brim. Failing to follow these age-related rules can result in sanctions from church elders. If a family moves from one settlement to another, one of the first adaptations

Table 24.1 Companies that sell Amish clothing

Company	Product offerings	Distribution method
Mennonite Maidens http://mennonitemaiden.com/	Specialize in prayer coverings, hair pins. Made in USA or by the staff of Mennonite Maidens.	Web-based
Quaker Anne http://www.quakeranne.com/	All types of Christian head coverings.	Does not sell directly. Offers websites of other companies.
Gohn Bros. http://www.gohnbrothers.com/	Men's clothing and hats.	Mail order from website.
The Amish Clothesline http://www.amishclothesline.com/	All Amish clothing. Sized by body measurements only.	Ordered and paid over email. Body measurements must be sent.
The Cap Shack Mount Eaton, OH	Custom-made prayer caps.	Word of mouth.
Mosses Stolzfoos Irishtown, PA	Men's straw and fur hats.	Ordered through post letters. Shipped via UPS.
Bollman Hat Company	Produces a wide range of contemporary and traditional hats, including Amish hats for men.	Web-based and other distribution centers. Sold wholesale and retail.

that must occur is making the appropriate adjustments to the size of crown and brim. While outsiders may not see the difference, they are very real distinctions within the Amish church.

Moses Stolzfoos, an Amish hat maker in Irishtown, Pennsylvania, makes and sells Amish fur and straw hats using equipment that is powered with diesel, kerosene, and foot-power. His black fur hats sell for around $80. He also reconditions hats and sells them for about $40. Mr. Stolzfoos ships the hats via UPS. Amish also purchase hats from the Bollman Hat Company, from Adamstown, Pennsylvania. Bollman was established in 1868 and recently re-shored some of its operations back to the United States. It now makes hats under a variety of labels and for celebrities as well as the Amish (http://www.bollmanhats.com/).

Amish children are taught the ways of the Amish from the time they are very little. Around the age of 4, children start dressing like their adult counterparts, including the head-covering. Unmarried girls starting at age 14 will wear black caps to church on Sundays as an indicator that they are single and available to be courted. Black caps also indicate that the girl is in *rumspringa* phase. *Rumspringa* refers to a time when Amish adolescents experience greater freedom from the Amish cultural rules. During this time, the youth have less control from parents and often experience 'worldly' activities such as buying a car, wearing non-Amish clothes, and listening to popular music. During my research year, a group of Amish girls came to my house late one night, wanting to borrow my clothes and make-up because they were going to the nearby town to 'party'. The practice of *rumspringa* varies from community to community with some more conservative churches still maintaining considerable control over their adolescent children.

In Jamesport, where I conducted research, the level of orthodoxy fell just right of center on the orthodoxy continuum. Prayer caps in Jamesport had a medium level of starch, strings made of the same fabric, and often worn untied. As suspected, however, the older the woman the more often the strings were not only tied, but tied closer to the chin. Teenage girls were seen flipping their cap strings as a method of flirting.

During my research year, I drove an Amish family to Kolona, Iowa for a wedding. The 16-year-old daughter in our group pouted on the way home because she wanted a prayer cap like her cousin's – more starch and therefore more progressive. Her mother argued, 'a cap like that, with all that starch, shows way too much pride. The church elders would have a fit!' But the daughter argued that the Iowa caps were so much 'more modern and stylish' and that it wasn't fair that she couldn't have one like her cousin's. She even threatened that she would move to Iowa! (Hawley 2013).

As indicated above, Amish women do not cut their hair. But when young people go through *rumspringa* many of the young girls will cut their bangs and wear non-Amish clothes that they consider more stylish. When they revert to Amish ways a few years later, or on Sundays when they attended Amish church, they have to bobby pin their bangs under their cap so that it is (hopefully) hidden from the elders. One group of girls were admonished by their mothers because even though the bangs were pinned back, there was too much pouf in the bang, clearly indicating that the bangs had been cut. *Rumspringa* is an institutionalized custom so Amish elders remember well their own period of *rumspringa* and are savvy to the rule-breaking that occurs. Regardless, it is always the mother's role to make sure the daughters remain respectable, especially during Sunday services. The Jamesport dry goods store, H&M Country Store, sold stacks of bandanas in a wide variety of colors. The teenage girls would wear bandanas to cover their hair, often in colors that matched their dresses.

Conclusion

After a year of living among the Amish, I concluded that for many, the convictions to head coverings is more cultural rather than religious. If one asks nearly any Amish person the purpose of wearing the prayer cap, they would say that it is because 'that's what Amish do' rather than citing scripture. For the Amish, sacred symbols of everyday dress, including the prayer cap, fulfils and reflects both micro and macro (Ritzer 1994) objectives. The form and function of sacred symbols are intimately related to the belief system and ideological commitment of 'being Amish'. Often, however, an Amish person cannot verbalize *why* they wear certain things. Instead, when asked, they would simply say, 'because we're Amish'. This is best explained because Amish theological and community commitment is so intimately entwined.

At the macro level, sacred dress for the Amish serves as a constant reminder of the personal spiritual commitments that have been made and as a reminder of social identification. Faithful adult members literally clothe themselves daily in items that represent spiritual and cultural commitment. Failure to dress in their Amish clothing represents a breach of the rules and sends a warning sign to family, community, congregations and the church leadership. *Tattletale* enforcement in these circumstances results in church leadership paying a visit to correct the behavior (Hamilton and Hawley 1999).

For the Amish, wearing of the prayer cap and other Amish garments provides a form of protection from that which they fear most – contamination from the outside world. With a basic tenet to be separate from the world, the dress announces who they are and suggests that outsiders should maintain a social distance. Thus, dress keeps them separate from the world and protects them from worldly influences.

The Amish continue to draw interest from outsiders in part because of their steadfast resistance to modernization and commitment to their cultural traditions. For those of us who belong to mainstream lifestyle we often are attracted to the nostalgia of what seems to be a step back in time. After living among the Amish for nearly a year, I realized that it was perhaps the most peaceful year of my life. As I teach fashion at a major university, many are fascinated that I was able to escape to a year of plain living. Among other things, I now understand that the Amish commitments to their lifestyle, including their tenets of dress, are really an index of their commitment to all things Amish. They succeed when their dress communicates that they are humble, conforming, loyal, thrifty, and faithful. Ironically, both the Amish and I use dress as a way to separate and integrate ourselves to and from our surroundings.

Note

1. The Amish refer to the non-Amish as 'English'. Because the Amish come from Dutch descent, the others around them often spoke English. This came to be the term used for all non-Amish.

References

Brown, Joshua R. 2011. 'Religious Identity and Language Shift among Amish-Mennonites in Kishacoquillas Valley, Pennsylvania'. PhD dissertation, The Pennsylvania State University, State College, PA.

Dementyeva, Yuliana. 2013. 'Simple Life'. *Elle Ukraine*. Available at www.trendhunter.com/trends/elle-ukraine-august-2013 (accessed 6 February 2017).

DeWalt, Kathleen and Billie R. DeWalt. 2002. *Participant Observation: A Guide for Fieldworkers*. Walnut Creek, CA: AltaMira Press.

Ditlevson, Jennifer. 2015. 'Putting a Cap on It – Local Amish Woman Manufactures Necessary Head Coverings for Holmes, Wayne Counties'. *Amish Heartland*. Available at https://m.amish-heartland.com/amish%20culture/2010/08/01/putting-a-cap-on-it-local-amish-woman-manufactures-necessary-head-coverings-for-holmes-wayne-counties (accessed December 21).

Hamilton, Jean A. and Jana M. Hawley. 1999. 'Sacred Dress and Public Worlds: Amish and Mormon Experiences and Commitment'. In *Religion, Dress and the Body*, edited by Linda B. Arthur and Joanne Eicher, 31–51. New York: Berg.

Hawley, Jana M. 1993. 'Amish/English Entrepreneurial Activity as a Function of Culture and World View: Conceptions of Responsibility, Cooperation and Competition, and Success'. PhD dissertation, University of Missouri, Columbia, MO.

Hawley, Jana M. 1995. 'Maintaining Business While Maintaining Boundaries: An Amish Woman's Entrepreneurial Experience'. *Entrepreneurship, Innovation and Change* 4(4):315–28.

Hawley, Jana M. 2013. 'The Amish Veil: Symbol of Separation and Community'. In *The Veil: Women Writers on Its History, Lore, and Politics*, edited by Jennifer Heath. Berkley, CA: University of California Press.

Hostetler, John A. 1964. 'The Amish Use of Symbols and Their Function in Bounding the Community'. *Journal of the Royal Anthropological Institute of Great Britain and Ireland* 94(1):11–22.

Hostetler, John A. 1980. *Amish Society*. Baltimore, MD: The Johns Hopkins University Press.

Huber, Tim. 2015. 'Beachy Amish Define Beliefs'. *Mennonite World Review*. Available at http://mennoworld.org/2014/04/16/news/beachy-amish-define-beliefs (accessed December 21).

Kraybill, Don. 1989. *The Riddle of Amish Culture*. Baltimore, MD: The Johns Hopkins University Press.

Kraybill, Don. 1998. 'Plain Reservations: Amish and Mennonite Views of Media and Computers'. *Journal of Mass Media Ethics* 13(2):99–110.

Meisel, Steven. 2008. 'Country Style'. *Vogue Italia*, February. Available at https://agnautacouture.com/2012/02/05/amish-influence-on-fashion/ (accessed 6 February 2017).

Ritzer, George. 1991. *Metatheorizing in Sociology*. Lexington, MA: D.C. Heath and Co.

Trollinger, Susan L. 2012. *Selling the Amish: The Tourism of Nostalgia*. Baltimore, MD: The Johns Hopkins University Press.

Witness. 1985. (Film) Directed by Peter Weir. Paramount Pictures.

Yang, Naomi. 2014. 'Simple Story'. *Vogue Taiwan*, 324. Available at http://www.fashiongonerogue.com/lena-hardt-wears-simple-style-vogue-taiwan-naomi-yang/ (accessed 6 February 2017).

Young Center for Anabaptist and Pietist Studies. 2015. *Statistics*. Available at http://groups.etown.edu/amishstudies/statistics/population-by-state (accessed December 21).

25

VEILING STUDIES AND GLOBALIZATION STUDIES

The promise of historical sociologies

David Inglis and Anna-Mari Almila

As this handbook amply demonstrates, the range and variety of veiling practices across the world is partly matched by the number and diversity of different sorts of scholars and analysts who work on veiling matters. The field of veiling studies has grown exponentially over the last few decades, encompassing forms of analyses from a broad range of disciplinary perspectives. But the apparent variety also tends to occlude the gaps and absences in the field. Works by individual scholars often tend to be of the case study type, examining in detail the micro-level practices of particular groups in specific locations. Of course, such analyses are absolutely vital for the purposes of understanding the nuances and subtleties of veiling activities and the sense made of them by particular people. But the case study approach too often remains rather unconnected to more systematic, long term, historical and macro-level ways of thinking (for recent notable exceptions, see e.g. Ahmed 1992, 2011), and it is precisely these frameworks that now need to be brought much more into the field of veiling studies, so that they may more rigorously inform case study material in the future and locate specific veiling practices within much broader geographical and historical contexts than they often hitherto have been placed. This way the field can further push and develop the wider approaches and historical considerations that only some scholars have hitherto fully engaged with.

A related problem is that edited books and special editions of journals have tended towards a regional focus, dealing with, for example, veiling in Europe (e.g. Ferrari and Pastorelli 2013), Euramerica (e.g. Tarlo and Moors 2013), or Africa (e.g. Renne 2013), rather than taking a broader comparative perspective and locating their objects of analysis within large-scale social processes that can be conventionally called the phenomena of globalization. When issues to do with globalization are mentioned, it is often in a rather rudimentary manner, and the insights to be gleaned from globalization theory and the field of globalization studies go relatively untapped. Therefore we suggest that what is needed is a much more systematic interpenetration of the concerns of veiling studies with those of globalization studies. Scholars of veiling would find many useful concepts, ideas and analytical orientations within the realm of globalization analyses. That field itself is highly diverse, and some of the most intellectually satisfying paradigms within it are drawn from the disciplines of history and historical sociology. The contribution of these areas to the understanding of globalization rests partly in their capacity to connect the micro-level world of actors' experiences and actions together with the macro-level dynamics of globalizing processes, networks, institutions and structures. This is precisely the micro-macro linkage that veiling studies now needs to develop more. Therefore what we call for here is not simply that theories of globalization be utilized more in the understanding of veiling practices, for that is a necessary but not sufficient condition for the intellectual enlargement of the field. Instead, what we are calling for is a more fruitful and deep engagement between veiling scholars and those, like historical sociologists, who have at their disposal a wide range of ways of understanding what globalization is, that go well beyond often glib assertions of more presentist and simplistic accounts of globalization (Inglis 2014).

It is inevitable that any sophisticated understanding of globalization is dependent upon an equally nuanced conception of modernity. It would seem impossible to understand any aspect of social reality, including veiling, without a sophisticated understanding of what the terms 'modern' and 'modernity' mean, both at the level of scholarly analysis and at the level of people's experiences, understandings and political orientations. A crucial step for veiling studies is to avoid simplification and reification of those terms, precisely the point raised by historical sociologists and others when they address the broader social sciences. Some scholars have indeed already embarked on this kind of work (e.g. Göle 1996, 2003). It is clear that political discourses and ideologies tend towards radical simplifications of what 'modern' and 'modernity' connote, heralding them either as wonderful achievements and conditions to be aspired to, or as disastrous innovations that need to be contested, avoided or destroyed. The modern/anti-modern dyad structures much of contemporary political discourse around the world, and has done so for several hundred years, a situation ripe with multiple contradictions. Those who denounce modernity most vehemently are themselves products of conditions that others would easily call 'modern'. Tradition, heritage and orthodoxy are invoked precisely when perceived modernity is felt to be encroaching on particular lifeworlds and lifestyles, and new traditions are invented as a consequence, and presented as solutions to a felt sense of danger and crisis (Castells 2009). Veiling practices and the discourses surrounding them of course have been located within these sorts of dynamics. But beyond that, the analyst must operate with a sense of the complexities of what the modern and modernity are or can be construed as being. Is there one modernity or multiple kinds? If the latter, what are the factors that create different sorts of modernities? What factors unite and are common to different versions of modernity? The historical sociological literature on multiple modernities tends to focus on different national forms of modernity (Eisenstadt 2000), for example examining the similarities and differences, and indeed empirical cross-border connections, between the French version of the modern and the Turkish variety. That veils and veiling are hugely important in both national contexts illustrates the need for analysis of veiling to be very sensitive to the multiplicitous forms of modernity that exist within and across particular national spaces.

Scholars also need to pay attention to how particular discourses about modernity, which in turn lead to programmes of institution building as regards both the state and civil society, have travelled from one national site to another. Thus, for example, Turkish modernity is in part constituted out of discursive and institutional elements that primarily began in France and then were taken up by Turkish elites after the First Word War. So it is not just that there are different national versions of modernity, but also that they have influenced each other in ongoing processes of emulation, imitation and hybridization carried out mostly, but not exclusively, by political and economic elites. Within each particular national form of modernity, there have come to exist complex but structured relations between the state and its institutions, religion and its institutional manifestations, the domestic sphere, the gendered division of labour, and civil society. Veiling practices have to be located within these complex contexts, and those contexts themselves have to be understood over long periods of development. Additionally, those periods themselves have to be analysed in terms not only of the creation of national social spaces, but also in terms of how those spaces were themselves created through complicated cross-border and transnational dynamics. In essence, if a comprehensive picture is to be gained, veiling has to be understood against very complex historical and institutional backgrounds, which only an inter- and trans-disciplinary approach can begin to grasp. How veiling is thought of, and the means by which it is practiced, are very much informed by the complex of conditions that have arisen within particular national territories and the forms of modernity they have entailed.

Veiling also has much to do with social and political dynamics that both transcend the borders erected through processes of state and nation creation, and also sometimes involve counter-movements that seek to challenge or disrupt the state and nation-building activities of elites. In other words, veiling must be seen as being informed both by the creation of national spaces and modernities, and also movements ranged against them. National projects have unintentionally led to and fostered the creation of transnational counter-projects, the most spectacular case in our period being that of radical Islamism. Veiling exists at the intersection between these two great sets of processes, each of which encompasses particular ideologies, affectivities and calls to mobilize millions of people (Roy 2004). Such processes can only be adequately understood within the sorts of global frames of reference developed by historical sociologists and cognate others.

These sorts of reflections take us in terms of intellectual complexity and depth well beyond any tendencies towards superficial appropriations of concerns from globalization studies into veiling studies. Much of the scholarly literature on veiling rightly deals with transnational connections, and indeed it is difficult to see how it could ignore them, when, for example, it is so obvious that veiling practices in Germany are highly influenced by those in Turkey, given the large-scale migration that has occurred between the two countries over the last several decades. But such transnational connections are still too rarely thought about in terms of globalization theory and wider globalization dynamics. The oft-used case study approach notes some phenomena of cross-border movement, but it does not go far enough. It needs to consider particular forms of mobility – of people and objects of various sorts – within a much broader, planetary level of movement across borders, the multiple strands of which have been occurring over the last 500 years or more (Urry 2007). Only within that much wider context can more specific practices be adequately located and understood.

It is a very noteworthy feature of the field of veiling studies that particular investigations offered by different scholars from around the world tend to converge around common findings as regards how women talk about veiling and how they understand what they are doing when they veil. Women in very different geographical, cultural and religious contexts tend to say the same sorts of things and offer the same sorts of justifications for why they veil. These have been noted as 'stock responses', for example in early studies of veiling in Egypt (El-Guindi 1999, see also Ahmed 2011), and the same sorts of responses certainly circulate more globally too (see Chapter 1). Yet it is not enough simply to note on a piecemeal basis that understandings of veiling are often very similar in particular countries. Rather, the important thing is to be aware of more global similarities, and to account for the complex reasons as to why they have come to exist. Only a more global analytic perspective can identify such phenomena and account for the reasons for their genesis. Such an analytic framework looks not only at particular forms of migration and intercultural influence, but also locates those within the broader planet-spanning processes of globalization that have been occurring for the last half millennium (Holton 2005). Therefore simply comparing particular national experiences of veiling is insufficient, as is just looking at particular forms of migration and movement in isolation from much broader patterns that have structured the entire world over the last several centuries. A more global, or truly cosmopolitan, frame of reference is needed to understand more specific and micro-level practices in their entirety (Beck 1999).

The points we have just made are ultimately to do with the problems attendant upon particular scholarly divisions of labour and the need to reconfigure them in more helpful directions. This applies not just at the level of the general relationship between veiling studies and globalization studies, but also at the level of the division of labour within veiling studies itself. Different sorts of specialists do refer to each other's works, but often in rather limited ways. For example, those who study veiling as fashion do refer to, and to some extent draw upon, the analyses offered by those who look at the political phenomena associated with veiling (e.g. Lewis 2015; see also Lewis 1999). But the structures of intellectual production often prevent a fuller interpenetration of ideas and insights drawn from each subfield. Thus edited books on veiling and fashion tend to focus on the fashion elements and give only a sketchy sense of the politics, while conversely books and special editions of journals oriented to politics tend to refer to fashion phenomena only in passing, when they do so at all. In this way, the totality of veiling is underplayed or lost altogether. This is another reason for drawing upon globalization studies, especially its more historically informed versions, for it has been the aim of the latter to try to think through how the political, cultural, social and economic aspects of globalization fit together in multiple and shifting ways. There are not just many different theories of globalization, it is also the case that there are multiple *globalizations* (or forms of globalization), ranging across every dimension of human existence, from the most material to the most ethereal. Those different forms of globalization operate at multiple levels and scales (Brenner 1999), and it is precisely these that veiling studies would benefit from attending to more. The most impressive works in globalization studies are able to model how, for example, the aesthetic and political dimensions of globalization have been articulated in varying but recurring manners (Holton 2005; Axford 2013). Indeed, the whole point of studying globalization is to seek to understand the complex but patterned interplay of all dimensions of human life, and to refuse to isolate particular realms of human practice from each other. In that sense, globalization theory is a very important contribution to general social theory, because the latter (at its best) is an attempt to build ways of understanding all the various facets of human existence considered together and not partitioned off into different discipline-based forms of expertise. That is why globalization studies and theory can be so useful for veiling studies scholars, because they provide resources to connect social spheres and sets of phenomena that are currently dealt with in ways that sequester them more than connect them. Globalization theory, as a form of general social theory, attempts to create synoptic visions of how the world works in all its manifold complexity, and the complexities of veiling can only be fully grasped when such synoptic visions are used and indeed are further developed through thinking about veiling. Therefore it is not just that globalization theory holds out the promise of more joined-up thinking in veiling studies, it is also the case that the application of such theory to veiling matters will help extend the analytical reach of the theory itself, deepening its grasp of the interpenetration of such factors as religion, fashion, aesthetics and identity. If there is one undoubted quality common to all forms of veils and veiling, it is their extraordinary multiplicity, and that quality is also true of the vast range of phenomena that we can put under the heading of 'globalization'. That is why the two fields of study should now come into much more systematic dialogue with each other, for the multifariousness of each can productively inform the comprehension of the other.

References

Ahmed, Leila. 1992. *Women and Gender in Islam: Historical Roots of a Modern Debate.* London: Yale University Press.
Ahmed, Leila. 2011. *A Quiet Revolution: The Veil's Resurgence, from the Middle East to America.* London: Yale University Press.

Axford, Barrie. 2013. *Theories of Globalization*. Cambridge: Polity.

Beck, Ulrich. 1999. *What is Globalization?* Cambridge: Polity.

Brenner, Neil. 1999. 'Globalisation as Reterritorialisation: The Re-scaling of Urban Governance in the European Union'. *Urban Studies* 36(3):431–51.

Castells, Manuel. 2009. *The Information Age: Economy, Society, and Culture*, Vol. 2: *The Power of Identity*, 2nd edition. Oxford: Wiley-Blackwell.

Eisenstadt, S. N. 2000. 'Multiple Modernities'. *Daedalus*, 129(1):1–29.

El-Guindi, Fadwa. 1981. 'Veiling Infitah with Muslim Ethic: Egypt's Contemporary Islamic Movement'. *Social Problems* 28(4):465–85.

El-Guindi, Fadwa. 1999. *Veil: Modesty, Privacy and Resistance*. Oxford: Berg.

Fair, Laura. 2013. 'Veiling, Fashion and Social Mobility: A Century of Change in Zanzibar'. In *Veiling in Africa*, edited by Elisha P. Renne, 15–33. Bloomington, IN: Indiana University Press.

Ferrari, Alessandro and Sabrina Pastorelli, eds. 2013. *The Burqa Affair across Europe: Between Public and Private Space*. London: Routledge.

Göle, Nilüfer. 1996. *The Forbidden Modern: Civilization and Veiling*. Ann Arbor, MI: University of Michigan Press.

Göle, Nilüfer. 2003. 'The Voluntary Adoption of Islamic Stigma Symbols'. *Social Research* 70(3):809–28.

Holton, Robert J. 2005. *Making Globalization*. Basingstoke: Palgrave.

Inglis, David. 2014. 'What is Worth Defending in Sociology Today? Presentism, Historical Vision and the Uses of Sociology'. *Cultural Sociology* 8(1):99–118.

Lewis, Reina. 1999. 'On Veiling, Vision and Voyage'. *Interventions: International Journal of Postcolonial Studies* 1(4):500–20.

Lewis, Reina. 2015. *Muslim Fashion*. Durham, NC: Duke University Press.

Renne, Elisha B, ed. 2013. *Veiling in Africa*. London: Bloomsbury.

Roy, Olivier. 2004. *Globalized Islam: The Search for a New Ummah*. New York: Columbia University Press.

Urry, John. 2007. *Mobilities*. Cambridge: Polity.

INDEX

abayas 44, 127, 141, 144–5, 147, 179, 186, 188, 206–7, 240; all-encompassing Saudi-style 91; and hijabs 188; wearing of 141

Abaza, Mona 6, 15–16, 200–2, 232, 237

Abdi, Cawo Mohamed 272, 274

Abraham, Janaki 4, 232, 246–53

Abrahamic religions 3–4

Abu-Lughod, Janet 235–6

Abu-Lughod, Lila 5, 8, 30, 46–7, 50, 220, 239, 248

abuse 69, 103–4, 113, 130, 239; of children 66, 68, 71; mental 104; physical 102, 104; verbal 103, 227, 239; and violence 104

Act Prohibiting the Concealment of the Face in Public Space 2010 58

activists: anti-religion 87; communist 87, 91, 119–20; political 6; and the rights of Afghan women 46; Uzbek anti-religious 87

adult women in Dogondoutchi 154, 156

advertisement for Altin İğne, Turkey **201**

advertisements 164, 200–1, 204, 213; fashion 16; for the Swedish fashion chain H&M 133; targeting fashion-conscious Muslim women 198

Afghan women 44, 46–7, 239; and the generic sufferings around the brutality of the Taliban 46; rights activists 46; and the *Time Magazine* article 44

Afghanistan 5, 45–7, 49–50, 103, 239; American invasion of 44–5, 49; children and women in 45; and Iran 5; and war 47

Afghans 45–6; burqas 9; children and women 45; homes of 239

Africa 4, 10, 287, 301; and European-inspired debates about the necessity and meaning of veiling 5; fashion festivals 154; and Muslims 184; and security concerns about Boko Harem 9; styles and fashions 14

Ahmed, Leila 4–6, 30–1, 44, 172, 234, 301, 303

Akou, Heather Marie 14, 16–17, 206, 238, 271–2, 275

AKP 29, 31–6, 121–2; government 31; lifting of the ban on the veil 31; reshaping of a neoliberal knowledge structure 36

Aktas v. France 56

al-amira style veil **191**

Alevism 119

Alexander, Chris 81

Ali, Hasan 118

Alimen, Nazli 112, 116–22, 145

Aliullin (activist) 87

Allah 3, 36, 39, 167, 176, 181, 263, 265

Almila, Anna-Mari 1–18, 231–43, 270, 274, 276, 282, 301–4

Alvi, Anjum 10, 12

Aly, Waleed 126–7

American culture 293

American values 49

American women 49

Amish 292–300; adolescents 298; children 298; churches 294, 298–9; clothing 292, 294, 298–9; commitments 293, 300; culture 292–3; dress 292, 294–5; elders 299; faith 293–4; families 293, 299; girls 298; head coverings 295, 297; prayer caps 292–3, 295–7, 299; women 295–7, 299

Anabaptist groups 296

Anatolian women 35, 37, 39

Andrewes, Janet 159–60

anti-fashion 15, 17, 137, 139, 141, 143, 145–7, 149, 156, 202; and anti-consumer culture 143; sentiment 147; strong 207; styles 17; veiling 17

anti-Muslim violence 82

anti-veiling campaigns 6–7, 236

anti-woman culture 81–2

Arab 14–16, 65–6, 68, 70–1, 238; countries 168, 274; culture 14; families 186; homeland 170; identities 65–6, 71, 167; language schools 262–3; parents 180; style garments 147, 209; women 65–6, 170–1

Ardener, Shirley 233, 246

Asma Bougnaoui, Association de défense des droits de l'homme (ADDH) v Micropole Univers SA 57

Atasoy, Yildiz 10–11, 29–41

Atatürk, Mustafa Kemal 118

Australia 1, 8–10, 125–30, 134, 141, 199, 206; calls for a 'burqa ban' 127; and the criticisms of Cory Bernadi 127–8; and the *Daily Telegraph* article titled 'The Silent Sufferers' 128; designers 129; hijabi bloggers 134; Muslims 125, 127–8, 131; news and current affairs programmes 125–7, 129–30; newspapers 128; values and ways of life 126; women 127, 129–30

Ayatollah Ali Khamenei 105, 108

Baby Loup Association 57–8

Baby Loup case 57

Balasescu, Alexandru 15–16, 205

'ban the burqa' 125, 127–9, 131, 133

Bandar Langeh 100–2

banning 7–10, 59, 77, 82; of headscarves 9; of niqabs 82

Bartkowski, J. 10–12

Bashir, Zarifa 86, 119

Bastian, Misty 159–60

Bayrak v. France 56

beards 116–18, 120–2, 144, 295

Beck, Lois 104, 303

Begum, Amina 251

Begum, Sakina 250–1

Beit Shemesh 63–8, 70–1; 'abuser' 68; events in 68; women of 64, 71

beliefs 54, 84, 91, 181, 185, 255, 261, 278, 283, 292; individualized pious 36; strong religious 259; wearer's 261

Bendixsen, Synnøve 11, 148, 174–82, 207

Berber House 233

Berlin 148, 174–82

Bible 3

Bikaner 246–8, 250–2

Billaud, Julie 11–12

Binark, Mutlu 16–17, 200, 203

blogs and bloggers 14, 125, 130–1, 133, 144, 146, 213

Borbieva, Noor 84–92

Bourdieu, Pierre 153, 233, 246

boys 47, 67, 85, 141, 174, 178, 180–2, 187, 294, 297; religious 67; young Amish 295

Brazil 2, 142, 184–90, 192–3; and body conscious cultural fashion norms 142; fashion market 188

Brazilians 184, 186, 188

Brenner, Suzanne 6, 10–13, 200, 215, 304

British hijab 224–6

British Muslims 222, 227

Buitelaar, Marjo 235–6

Al-Bukhari, Muhammed ibn Ismail 118

burqa 44, 47–8, 58, 77, 91, 108, 126; 'debate' concerning 128; dehistoricizes the veiling practice 44; in Europe 9; head-to-toe 44; issue 128; and niqab 127; representations 45; wearers 46, 79, 128

burqini swimsuits 10, 129, 199, 206

Bush, Laura 45–6, 50

Butler, Judith 269, 271, 273

Byng, Michelle D. 8, 12

Cairo 160, 235, 237

Callinicos, A. 29, 41

Calvinist work ethic 199

campaigns 5–7, 81, 86, 121; global marketing 145; political 74; women-led 6

Canada 9, 73–7, 79–81, 163, 168, 205; citizenship 73–4, 76–7, 80, 82; consensus on the issue of minority rights 80; debates 79; electorate 81; federal elections 80; 'identity' 76, 80, 82; law 81; multiculturalism, acceptability and citizenship in 73–82; and Muslims 73, 82; press coverage 76–7; values 73, 77, 81–2; veiling cases 8, 79

Canadian Charter of Rights and Freedoms 78, 80

capitalism 35, 75, 198, 213

Carland, Susan 126–7, 130

Carpenter, Sarah 280–5, 287–8

Carrel, Barbara Goldman 3, 14, 16–17

case law: *Aktas v. France* 56; *Asma Bougnaoui, Association de défense des droits de l'homme (ADDH) v Micropole Univers SA* 57; *Bayrak v. France* 56; *Dogru v. France* 56; *Gamaleddyn v. France* 56; *Ghazal v. France* 56; *Jasvir Singh v France* 56; *Kervanci v. France* 56, 78, 80; *Ranjit Singh v. France* 56

Catholic Church 4, 54, 165, 185, 190, 287

censorship 98, 111, 214

Central Asia 1, 5, 46, 84–5, 87, 89, 91; anti-veiling debates and campaigns 6; Muslims 7, 84, 87–92; and the Soviet Union's Communist Party 86; urban and agricultural Uzbek and Tajik ethnic groups 84; veiling as both a practice and symbol 88

chachvon 84, **86**, 87, 89–91

chadors 50, 98–9, 102–3, 106, 108, 111, 198, 202, 209; black 102, 198, 209; chic 153; and head scarves 103, 106; and niqab 99; traditional 104; usage of 102

Chagas, Gisele Fonseca 142, 184–93

Chambers, Clare 48–9

Charter of Quebec Values 80

chastity 13, 64, 69, 165, 268, 275
child abuse 66, 68, 71
children 45, 63–5, 67–9, 71, 248, 250, 255, 258–9, 264, 268–9; abandoned 88; adolescent 298; educating 255; endangered 68; and women 45; young 58, 142, 239–40, 260
China 2, 6–7, 255, 257–9, 261, 263, 265; college women in 261; headscarf wearing in 257, 259, 261, 263, 265; and Muslims 259; north-west rural 258
Choongara *mohalla* 251–2
Christianity 148, 165, 225
Christians 1, 3–5, 143, 146, 148, 152, 155, 165, 288–9, 292; and forms of veiling and modest dress 14; and girls 155; in the Middle East 4; and Muslims 117; and veiling 3
churches 3, 185, 288, 292–3, 295–6, 298; community 295; and dresses with short sleeves 142; early 3; and the elders 298–9; and leadership 296, 299; separated from the state 80
Çinar, Alev 120–1
Civil War (Somalia) 271–2
cloth 44, 63, 71, 97, 102, 104, 144, 175, 222–5, 248; black 223; draped 225; inanimate 223; plain 156; the poetics of 224; white 249
clothes 102, 141–2, 145, 154, 159–60, 165–8, 175, 188–9, 225, 298–9; beautiful 264; colorful 202; discrete 168; exposed 219; and forms of body management 142; matching 16; sexy 180, 182; special dress 159; traditional 48; uniform 15; wearing of 163, 171, 293
clothing 55, 64–5, 76–7, 142–3, 165–6, 178–9, 188–9, 197–8, 269–70, 294–5; children's 210; conservative 47; fashionable 181, 198, 259; female Muslim 207; improper 112; maternity 210; modest 133; non-Amish 298–9; practices 163, 169, 208, 270; religious 53, 55–6, 90; styles 202, 269, 274–5; traditional 47; of Western inspiration 154, 180
co-religionists 139, 144
Cola Turka 121
Cole, Darnell 11, 13
colonial powers 5, 236
colonial times 5, 294
Comaroff, Jean 198
Commission for Reflection on the Application of the Principle of *Laïcité* in the Republic (Stasi Commission) 55
communications 64, 139, 145–7, 177, 237, 280, 286; inter-generational 282; international 146; linguistic 286; marital 214; personal 293; technologies for 146
communist activists 87, 91, 119–20
communist moustaches 119
Communist Party (Soviet Union) 7, 86

companies 54, 57, 147, 170, 200, 202, 204, 206, 213, 297–8; and the emergence of fashionable Islamic clothing styles 202; multinational 206; that sell Amish clothing 163, 168, *298*; veiling fashion 204, 208
compulsory hijab 97–9, 101, 103–5, 107, 109, 111, 113; following the Islamic Revolution 97; in Iran 97; issue of 104; *see also* hijab
consumers 16, 142, 144, 147, 200, 204, 206, 208–9, 213–14, 216; fashion-conscious 109; female 215; high-end luxury Gulf 145; Mormon 144, 214; Muslim 109, 147, 198, 207; non-Muslim 209; ultra-orthodox Jewish 144
Corinthians 3, 296
Council of State, France 54–6, 59
Council on American-Islamic Relations 50
court cases 57, 140
Court of Cassation 54, 57–8
covered women 39, 198, 200–2, 206, 208
'Creil case' 53–5
cross-faith connectivity 141, 146, 149
culture 4–5, 75–6, 108–9, 141, 251–3, 268, 272–3, 280–1, 284, 293–4; ancient 75; anti-consumer 143; archaic 76; and citizenship 75; collectivistic 268; human 278; and identity 163; industries 197, 199, 201, 203, 205, 207, 209; local 5, 101; of neighbourhoods 247, 251, 253; non-literate 282; oriental 148; patriarchal 30, 49; public 144, 218; of purdah 251–2; and religion 141; religious 143; of sexual discrimination 108; traditional 30, 118; and values 109; of women's education 252

Dahlab v Switzerland 60
Dahlmann, Hanna 238–9
Daily Telegraph 128
Dalit woman 247–8
Daoud, Hassan 117
de Castro, Christina Maria 6, 10
de Voe, Pamela A. 271, 273
death masks 282, 285
debates 1, 4–10, 73–82, 125, 127, 202, 205, 207, 213–14, 218; in France 65; on minority rights in Quebec 79; on reasonable accommodation in Quebec 79
Delina on the streets of Jakarta **133**
Delina on the streets of Newtown **132**
Delina on the streets of Sydney **132**
designs 109, 129, 145, 168, 197–8, 202, 205, 224–5; beautiful 218; control hijab fashion 97; embroidered 159; new mass-produced 156; new pattern 264; oriental 163; youthful 202
diaspora 206, 209, 267, 269, 271, 273, 275–6; Iranian 205; Muslim communities 199–200; Somali 16; Turkish 145

discourses 10, 51, 73–4, 78, 82, 218, 223, 226, 234, 236; anti-Islamic 280; cross-faith 14; individual rights and freedoms 32, 34; new religious 14; securitising 144
Dogondoutchi 152–4, 156
Dogru v. France 56
dress 89–91, 141–2, 159–61, 166–7, 177–82, 231–5, 260–1, 270–2, 294–5, 299–300; conservative 14, 108; covering 14, 270–1, 275; decent 7; ethnic 141; everyday 267, 273, 299; and hairstyle strategies 167; long 87, 188; low-necked 120; male orthodox 3; neutral 7; pious 156, 202, 214, 220; religious 148; sacred 299; sexy 174; wearing short-sleeved dresses 261
dress codes 51, 63, 98, 100, 104–5, 108, 165, 167–8, 171–2, 275; authentic Muslim 168; in Finland 271; local 141; male 5; modest 166; new 101, 166; polarized 168; religious 54–5, 61; un-Islamic 112; violations 208
dress styles 13–15, 177, 179, 185, 237, 267, 270, 272–5, 295; common female 271; informal 185; non-religious 214; pre-conversion 148; young unmarried woman's 268–9
Droogsma, Rachel Anderson 12–13
Dubai 205–6, 217
Duval, Soroya 6, 232
Dwyer, Claire 9, 141, 270, 272

ECtHR 8, 38, 56, 58–60
Edmunds, June 7–8
Edson, Gary 279–85, 287
education 5–7, 30, 32–5, 37–41, 47–8, 54–5, 85, 90, 148, 250–2; and careers 48; and employment of women 32, 38, 41, 148, 251–2; high quality 36, 263; and jobs 148; post-secondary 164; and public-sector employment 33–4; religious 10, 165; university 265; women's 30, 91, 172, 252; and women's rights 7
Egypt 29, 199–200, 202, 206, 209, 220, 241, 261, 303; conservative styles 14, 16; early studies of veiling in 303; feminists 143; parents 175; universities 16; women 143
El-Guindi, Fadwa 2–3, 10, 200, 223, 232, 237, 241–2, 289, 303
Elor, Tamar 63–72
emancipation 97–8, 102, 104, 113; female 159; Muslim 45, 223; periods 113; of women 97
Emirates 144–5
Emirati citizens 144–5
Entwistle, Joanne 142, 160
environment 163, 167, 214, 216–17, 223, 231–2, 237, 240, 251, 260; gender-mixed 141; hostile media 130; multicultural 206; social 122, 231, 240, 250, 282; urban 234–5, 237

Ershad e Eslami/Irshad Islami 99, 107
Esposito, J.L. 12, 131
EU 31, 57
European 1–2, 7–10, 13, 15, 141, 206, 215–16, 231–3, 236–7, 242–3; capitalist history 216; countries 8–9, 16; cultural norms 30; designers 217; female dress 5; gender norms 31; gender relations 8; headscarf disputes 7; hijab styles 14; ideals of secularism and modernity 5; influenced societies 12, 243; societies 8, 174, 176–7; standards 32, 35
European Court of Human Rights *see* ECtHR
European Union *see* EU

face-veiling 4, 9, 87, 91, 233, 241–3, 289; banning of 7; debates 9; politics of 9, 29; women 9, 233, 240–2
Facebook communities 130–1, 206
facial hair 116–22, 145, 149; fashions 116, 121–2; male 1; of Muslims 116; politics of 116–17, 119, 121; styles 117, 122; traditional 119; in Turkey 116, 118, 122
Fadil, Nadia 8, 12, 270, 272
Fahmi, Wael 236–7
'Faith Fashion Fusion' Exhibition (Sydney) 129
Fanon, Frantz 5, 30, 160
fashion blogs 130–1
fashion markets 15, 133, 209; global Islamic 16, 197; thriving online 97
fashion media 131, 133, 214
Fashion Theory 202
fashions: Asian 14; controlled hijabi 113; development of modest 146, 205; and facial hair 116, 121–2; and female dress in Somali 238, 272, 275; hijab 129, 140, 189; and politics of facial hair 117, 119, 121
Fay, Mary Ann 231, 234–6
feminism 6, 12, 64, 130, 163, 172; Islamic 172; secular 12, 172
Fethullahçilar (mass-based religious civil society movement) 36–8
fine ticket for wearing improper hijab **107**
Finland 232, 237–42, 267, 269, 271–5; pragmatics of veiling in 238–43; social control in 267; symbolic veiling in 240–2; young Somali women in 269, 271, 273, 275
First World War 187
Fitzpatrick, Shanon 8, 10, 17
flirting 12–13, 298
forced marriages 81
Fornerod, Anne 53–61
Foucault, Michel 160–1, 246, 269, 271
France 7, 9, 56, 59–60, 65, 70–1, 144–5, 163–5, 167, 169–71; and Britain 218; Council of State 54–6, 59; and Quebec 164, 169; and Turkey 65

freedom 36, 38, 44–5, 48–51, 53–61, 78, 87–8, 90–1, 103–6, 128; cultural 70; of education 54; human 38; individual's 8, 36, 39, 91; for Iranian woman 106; personal 29; religious 58, 79, 92, 292; for woman 106
French-Canadian identity 9
French headscarf debates 231
Frontbek, Jamal 87, 89, 91
Furseth, Inger 11–12

gaitao (old style headwear) 255–6, 260–1, 264–5
Gamaleddyn v. France 56
Garcia, Jonathan 297
Gauthier, François 198
gender 4, 165–6, 226–7, 231–3, 235, 237, 241, 246–7, 269–70, 287–8; and dress 232; equality 8, 55, 59–60, 75–8, 80, 82, 108, 126; expectations 260, 265; hierarchy 226; ideology 255; male 293; oppression 8; and space 233, 235, 237, 239, 241, 243, 250; and veils 10
George, Kenneth 218
Ger, Güliz 15–17, 121, 148, 156, 193, 198–200, 202–4, 206–8
Germany 7, 174–7, 179–81, 237, 303; community of Muslims in 177; Muslim youth in 174; negative images of Islam in 179, 181; public perceptions of Muslims in 181; religious products (T-shirts with slogan) 177
Ghazal v. France 56
Gillette, Maris 7, 15–16
girls 64–5, 67, 85–7, 152–6, 180–1, 186–9, 223, 261–3, 265, 297–9; adolescent 267; college 261; first-generation Somali immigrant 267; teenage 274, 298–9; unmarried 156, 295, 298; veiled 181; wearing a headscarf in a Muslim-articles store **262**; and women 65, 189
globalization 2, 18, 168, 215, 301–4; studies 301, 303–4; theory 301, 303–4
God 10–12, 36–9, 88–9, 104, 152–4, 161, 176, 192, 265, 288–9
Goffman, Erving 156, 181, 185, 192, 238, 281, 286
Gökariksel, Banu 11, 13, 15–17, 148, 178, 181, 202, 204, 207–8, 232
Göle, Nilüfer 10, 177, 179, 200, 302
government fashion shows **110**
Government of Iran 109
Gramsci, A. 38, 41
Grimes, Ronald L. 279–81, 283–7
Gul, Murat 236–7
Gülen community 37, 121
Gulf countries 6, 15–16, 144–5
Gurbuz, Mustafa E. 11–12

Haaretz 63, 66
hadiths (oral tradition of Muhammed) 3, 87, 117–18, 140, 154, 177, 263–4
hajj pilgrimage 14, 16, 259
HALDE 57–8
Hamilton, Jean A. 293, 299
Haredi (feminism) 64–6, 69–71
harems 8, 143, 231, 234–6
Hasan, Noorhaid 198, 200
Hasanov 84–5
Hasidic women 16
Hawley, Jana M. 3, 292–304
head coverings 40, 78, 100, 153–5, 159, 167, 169, 297, 299
headscarf 8–9, 32–5, 37–40, 56–7, 174–82, 205–7, 219–20, 255, 257, 259–65; banning of 29, 31–2, 37–8, 40–1, 120; in China 257, 259, 261, 263, 265; colourful 263–4; controversies 7; controversies in Europe 7; debates 8–9; expensive 198; fashion 178, 181, 261; fashion in Berlin 178; fashionable 180, 264; and identity 260; Islamic 53, 55, 57; issues 40–1; wearing of 32, 206; for women 264
Heath, Deborah 156, 279, 282, 288
Hefner, Robert 154, 198, 201
Helsinki 238–40, 267, 269, 275; Resident houses in 240; social control in 269; Westernized clothing in 269
High Authority for the Struggle against Discrimination and for Equality *see* HALDE
hijab 2–3, 84–7, 90–1, 97–9, 101–7, 111–13, 127–31, 140–1, 184–93, 222–7; abolition of 99; black 190; contemporary 223; cosmopolitan 223; crowdsourced 227; and dress codes 98, 112; fashions 129, 140, 189; improper 107; and modest dress 143; obligatory 105; on-trend 147; physical level 224; styles 142, 145, 191, 222, 242; unauthorized 109; wearing of 88, 130, 223; and woman's responsibilities 105; and women's emancipation 97
hijabi 125, 130–1, 152–7, 159–61, 186, 223, 226; bloggers 125, 127, 129–31, 133–4; couture 109; crime of bad 106; and Muslim women 184–5, 189, 192–3, 226; women in Rio de Janeiro 185, 187, 189, 191, 193
Hindu women 247, 249; married upper-caste 247; veiling of 4, 247; working-class 252
Hindus 1–2, 246–7, 252; and Muslims in Bikaner 252; and Muslims veiling 246–7, 249–53
Hirschmann, Nancy J. 5–6
Ho, Christina 30, 126, 128
Hochel, Sandra 10–11
Hollander, Anne 225, 233
Holton, Robert J. 303–4

Honigmann, John J. 281, 286
Hostetler, John A. 117, 292–3, 296
Hui 256, 258, 260; communities 260–1;
    housewives with white hats **256**; identity 255,
    261; Muslims 265
Hui women 255, 257–65; changing views and
    behaviour 258; with headscarf **257**; with
    headscarves in an Arabic language school **262**;
    prefer not to wear headscarves 264; wearing
    short sleeved dresses 261
Hujum 86–7, 91
Hurufism 119

identity 17, 70–1, 75, 77, 79–80, 177, 260–1,
    279, 281–4, 286–7; cosmopolitan 17; cultural
    129, 131, 134; distantiating 286; distinctive
    202; female 170; gendered 172; hybrid 208;
    ill-intentioned 286; individual 14, 201;
    national 53, 177, 223; personal 286; pious
    121, 156, 202; primary 284; racial 216;
    religio-ethnic 142, 227; rightist 120; sexual
    165; wearer's 222, 224, 261
Indonesia 131, 146, 199–200, 204–6, 209,
    213–18, 220; business-style dress 214;
    contemporary urban 221; fashion designers
    205, 217; and Islamic consumer culture
    213–21; Islamic fashion boom 218; Islamic
    fashion designers 213, 217, 220; magazine
    industry 214; mass media 219; and middle-
    class women 208; readers 215–16
Inglis, David 278–90, 301–4
Internet 14–15, 73, 97, 111, 139, 146, 163, 186,
    206, 226
Internet research 215
Iran 1, 5–6, 16, 91, 97–9, 101–13, 140, 146,
    204, 206; clergy and devout Muslims 99; and
    the compulsory hajab 97; and France 1; post-
    revolution 98; secular 106; Shah of 98, 106;
    theocratic 106
Iranian 97–8, 109, 112; authorities 98; chadors
    91; fashion designers 109, 111, 205;
    government 109; Islam 113; street fashion
    110; traditions 99; women 9, 97–8, 104–6,
    110; youth 111
Iraq 47–8
Iraqi women 47
Islam 10, 36, 104–6, 125–8, 163–72, 178–82,
    184–7, 190–3, 216–18, 263–4; attitudes and
    behaviors 88; in Brazil 184; and capitalism
    198; clothes 165, 168, 170, 198–9, 205–6;
    clothing 200, 206, 209; code of conduct 167;
    consumer culture 148, 213; consumption
    culture 198–9; culture industries 198,
    208–10; in Europe and Quebec 171; in
    France and Quebec 145, 163, 165, 167, 169,
    171; and Muslim cultures 8, 12, 74, 179, 186,
    192; and Muslims in Germany 179; and

neoliberalism 40; and socialism 87; values and
    practices of 30; for veiling 127; and women's
    role 8
Islamic dress 58, 89, 104, 154–5, 207–8, 213,
    216–17, 219–21, 268; codes of 163, 167, 170,
    172, 205; emergence of new forms of 199,
    205; fashionable 205, 219; interpretations of
    proper 207; pious 220; styles of 199, 273;
    wearing of 220
Islamic faith 37, 256, 261, 264
Islamic fashion 108–9, 116, 179, 181, 199, 202,
    204–5, 209, 216–17, 219; blogs 206; and
    clothing festival 109; creating new 171;
    designers 89, 202; editors 217; and
    global/Western fashions 209; holding regular
    shows 109; industry 109, 206–7, 209, 213,
    217; and Islam attires 116; magazines 213,
    217; male 209; media 213–14; production and
    marketing of 199
Islamic Fashion and Anti-Fashion 202
Islamic feminism 172
Islamic knowledge 39, 165, 178, 187, 192, 263
Islamic law 87, 100, 105, 179, 261
Islamic learning centres for new Muslims 164
Islamic lifestyle magazines 205, 215
Islamic modesty 153, 178, 208
Islamic morality 32, 181, 207
Islamic piety 89, 152, 197, 214
Islamic political parties 117
Islamic principles 185, 188, 200
Islamic Republic of Iran 97–9, 102, 104–6, 109
Islamic revivalism 143, 163
Islamic Revolution 6, 97, 99, 104
Islamic rules 108, 116–20, 122, 260
Islamic veiling 55–6, 90, 105, 126, 209, 238,
    289
Islamism 65, 122, 198, 200, 232; authentic 71;
    radical 13, 303
Islamist parties 121
Islamist politicians and supporters of Islamist
    politics 120
Islamist politics 116, 120, 208
Islamization 200; agenda 208; of Turkey 121
Islamophobia 131; and anti-Muslim violence 82;
    attacks 13; increasing 209
Isotalo, Anu 238, 267–76
Israel 63–5, 67, 69–71
Istanbul 181, 237
Izala (Islamic reform movement) 152–6

Jafari, Ali 198
Jakarta 133, 213–14, 217
Jamesport 293–6, 298–9
Jasvir Singh v France 56
Jewish 63, 65, 68, 70–1, 131, 146; and Christian
    forms of veiling 14; fashion 16, 144; groups
    17; women 3–4, 14, 63, 65, 70, 148

Jews 1, 4, 14–17, 71, 117; and early Christians 4; and Muslims 15–16
jilbab (cloaks) 3, 141, 220–1, 272
Jiwani, Yasmin 75, 78
Jones, Carla 14–15, 129, 153–4, 156, 198, 200–1, 204–5, 207–8, 213–21, 232
Journal of Middle East Women's Studies 202
Judaism 14, 148–9
Justice and Development Party *see* AKP

Kabul 44, 46, 48, 63
Kamp, Marianne 5, 7, 84–92
Karlsson Minganti, Pia 10, 237, 270
Kassam, Shelina 16, 73–82
Kazakh women 85
Kazakhstan 90–1, 200
Kenney, Jason 80, 280
Kervanci v. France 56, 78, 80
Khamenei, Ayatollah Ali 105, 108
Khamis, Susie 10, 125–34
Khan, Reza 12, 97–100, 103–6, 111, 113, 246, 251
Khomeini, Ayatollah 104–6, 113
Killian, Caitlin 11–12
King Solomon 67
Koran 176, 191
Korteweg, A.C. 30
Kotnik, Toni 235–6
Kraybill, Don 293, 297
Kuwaiti women 205, 208
Kyrgyz woman's headwear **85**
Kyrgyz women 85, 89
Kyrgyzstan 84–5, 87–91

Lacayo, Richard 47–8
Lafontaine, Laurence M. 3–4
laïcité (legal principle) 53–61, 65, 71
Lamphere, Louise 246
Lefebvre, Henri 231, 234, 242, 246
legislation 5, 58, 77, 79–80, 90, 140, 169; in France 140; in Quebec 77; on veiling regulations in Europe 8
Lentin, Alana 7–8
Lewis, Reina 5, 12, 14–16, 133, 139–49, 202, 204–7, 217, 224, 304
lifestyles 118, 165, 170, 186, 199–201, 208, 255, 300, 302; magazines 202, 205, 207; marketing 199; media 16, 205, 213

Mackey, Sandra 99–100
MacLeod, Arlene Elwoe 6, 11, 13, 30, 64, 232–4, 237
magazines 45, 133, 198, 200, 204, 213–19, 221; and blogs disseminating tips 198; and catalogues 204; in Europe 216; expensive monthly 214; franchised 214; global 214;
humour 121; pedagogic women's 205; traditional Muslim family life 215
Mahmood, Saba 11, 40, 46, 160, 163, 177, 269
mainstream media 49, 125–6, 128–31, 134
Maker Movement 226
Makover-Belikov, Sari 63, 65–6
Malaysia 108–9, 131, 198–200, 204–5, 261; government of 109; and Saudi Arabia 261; and Turkey 109, 199
male Islamic fashions, research on 209
Malkoçoğlu moustache 122
Mamdani, Mahmood 75, 81
marketing 1, 144, 197, 199, 202, 206–9, 216; and anthropology 202; of commodities 216; and consumption of veiling fashions 208; and creative resources 209; practices 199, 202–3; slogans 170
Martin Place, Sydney 130
Mashhad 101–2, 108
masking 278, 280–9; ambivalence of 285; culture 279; duplicitous and fictitious nature of 281; and masquerading practices 278, 284; practices 279–81; rituals 287; and selfhood 284
masks 283; ambivalences of 284; appearances of 281; of Comedy and Tragedy 284; death 282, 285; donning of 283; duality of 284; efficacy of 281; of Greek 284; half-face 287; and helmets 126; history of 280, 289; human history of 279; and masking rites 280–1, 283, 288–9; in miniature 280; power of 279, 283, 286; and veils 280, 288–9
masks and masking, practices of 288
Masquelier, Adeline 11, 14, 141, 152–61
Massey, Doreen 232, 246
McBrien, Julie 88–9
McGown, Berns 271–2, 275
McLarney, Ellen 9, 17
McMichael, Celia 271–2
Mecca 152
Meccan fashions 156
media 2, 51, 58, 74, 81–2, 129–31, 139, 149, 214, 220; American news 46; Anglo-Saxon mainstream 8; and the burqa debate 128; Canadian coverage 76–7; discourse 9, 76–9, 81–2; global 9; headlines 47; Islamic fashion 213–14; news 45, 145; and public discourses 74, 82, 149; for women 214
Meneley, Anne 153, 156, 202
Mennonite women 296, 298
Mernissi, Fatima 3, 12, 30–1, 197, 223
Metinsoy, Murat 5, 15
Mezabarba, Solange Riva 142, 184–93
middle classes 31, 68, 232; new Islamic 199; new Muslim 199; veiling 179; women 6, 98, 237
Middle East 1, 5, 14–15, 89, 140, 143, 177–8, 184, 231–2, 234–5; culture 215

Milliyet Newspaper 32
mini-skirts 120, 261
Minister of Citizenship and Immigration, Canada 81
Ministry of Education, France 55–6
Ministry of Education, Tajikistan 90
minorities 139, 145, 163, 166, 168, 193, 264; Christian women 5; religious 171; rights in Quebec 79
mixed-gender gatherings 106
modernities 5, 7, 29–31, 48, 88, 179–80, 222–3, 225, 234, 302–3; countering of 208; multiple 302; perceived 302; and tradition 109
modest fashion: and anti-fashion 139–49; Baraka label 130; bloggers garner readers inside and beyond their religious community 146; brands 143; pioneers 139
modesty 128–9, 144–5, 147–9, 165–6, 178, 180–1, 190–3, 205, 248, 251–2; and beauty 208; daughter's 268; female 2, 90, 154, 182; issues 102, 168; and nudity 237; and piety 165; practice symbolizes women's 46; and propriety 219; religious 7; sartorial 141, 154, 156; wearer's 129
Moghadam, V. 29, 98
Mohammad, Reza (Shah) 98
Mohanty, Chandra 30, 48
Montreal 79, 164, 167
Moors, Annelies 9, 11–12, 15–17, 143, 156, 202, 206–7, 209, 270–2, 274–5
Mormon women 142
Morocco 235, 241
mosques 6–7, 163–4, 169, 177, 184–6, 188–9, 240–1, 255, 260, 263; in Islam 260; local 190, 259; in Rio 186; Roihuvuori (Finland) 240; Sufi 167
Mossière, Géraldine 16, 145, 148, 163–72
moustaches 116–22; bushy 119, 121; communist 119; horseshoe 119; nationalist 120; in Turkey 119; well-trimmed 119–22
movements 5–6, 10, 38, 41, 98, 159–60, 224–5, 236, 241, 303; collective 287; early piety 143; eco-style 217; free 235; global Islamic 172; Islamic 10, 92, 199; mass-based religious civil society 36; nationalist 119; new global social 200; new Islamists 198–9; new mosque (Egypt) 241; new veiling 15; rational dress 97; re-Islamization 10; reform 10–12; religious 11; sixteenth-century Swiss Anabaptist 292; social-change 38; women's 6–7, 98
Muhammed 3–4, 17, 263
multiculturalism 73–7, 79, 81–2; Canadian understandings of 74, 82; limits of 78, 82; and Muslims 77; and secularism 73
multidisciplinary research 210
Muslim 1–17, 73–82, 125–34, 139–49, 163–72, 174–82, 184–93, 198–200, 205–9, 259–65;

anti-colonial resistance 30; anti-fashion 147; Australians 126, 129, 131; bodies 74–6; consumers 109, 147, 198, 207; dress codes 16, 108, 140–1, 145, 163, 168, 214, 219–20; and Hindu 2; identity 11, 163, 167, 170, 184, 192, 208, 261, 263, 265; and Jewish T-shirts 17; and non-Muslims 140; Tuareg men 4
Muslim communities 11, 14, 79, 81, 146, 148, 155, 184, 186, 188; in Brazil 184; and the diaspora 199–200; local 192; and Somalia 275
Muslim fashion 15–16, 109, 140–1, 144, 149, 168, 186; bloggers 130–1; contemporary 140; designers 205, 209; entrepreneurship 17; garments 186, 189, 193; imagery 16; industry 216; market 147; and veiling 139
Muslim minorities 145, 205; in Canada 148; in Europe 141
Muslim societies 30–1, 128; contemporary global 112; spending power and contribution 109
Muslim veiling 1, 3, 29–30, 64, 74, 79–80, 246–7, 249, 251, 253; practices 247; regimes 250; styles and fashions 14
Muslim women 5–8, 30–1, 48, 50–1, 73–82, 126–8, 139–42, 168–70, 186, 222–3; in Australia 127–8; authentic 170; body coverings 154; in Brazil 189; in Canada 81; "depressed veiled" 179; devout 142; discriminations 45, 51; enabled urban 205; fashion-conscious 198; fashionably dressed 214; framed veiled 125; garments reformist 154; imperilled 73–5, 78, 81; liberated 5; niqab-wearing 78; pious 152; veiled 74, 76, 125–6, 128–30, 172; young reformist 160
Muslim youth 109, 181; in Germany 174; practising veiling in Berlin 174; summer camp **175**; and veiling in Berlin 174–82
Muslimische Jugend in Deutschland (MJD) 174
Muslims 7–10, 13–17, 38–9, 73–7, 116–19, 139–41, 144–9, 167–72, 174–82, 184–6; in Berlin 174; in Brazil 184, 188; in Canada 76; female 273; in Finland 239; in Germany 177, 181; and Jews 17; in Muslim-minority contexts 145, 147, 199, 206; new 163–70; traditionalist 152, 155; urban 223
Mustafa, Naheed 73–82

Navaro-Yashin, Yael 15, 17, 198, 200, 202
negative image of Muslims, in Western Europe 180
negative images: of Islam and Muslims 179; of Islam in Germany 179, 181
New York terror attacks 8, 223
newspapers: daily 209; *Daily Telegraph* 128; *Milliyet Newspaper* 32; *Zaman Newspaper* 32
Niger 141, 152–5, 157, 159, 161; dressing and fashion in 152–61; the veil in 141; women in 154

Nigérien woman wearing *hijabi* **157**
Nigérien women 153, 155, 157–60
Nigérien women wearing *hijabai* **158**
Nile, Fred 126
niqab/burqa, banning of in public spaces 77
non-Muslims 81, 117–18, 140, 169, 174,
    179–80, 184, 223
Nunley, John W. 282, 287

Old Order Amish (Christian-based group)
    292–3
Osella, Caroline 6, 11, 16, 198–9

Pakistan 46, 186, 198
palaces 247, 252
Palatine women 296
Palestine 184, 187–9
pallu (sari) 247–9
Papanek, Hanna 2, 152
paranji 84–5, **86**, 87, 89–91
parents 56, 58, 148, 169, 187, 190, 258–60,
    264–5, 268, 273–4
parents-in-law 248, 255, 259–60, 264
parliament 58–9, 98, 102, 106, 118, 121–2
Pashtun women 46
Pastorelli, Sabrina 9, 301
Patel, David S. 6, 11, 13
Paulo 188
Pernet, Henry 280–3, 287
Peshkova, Svetlana 88–90
Pew Research 109
Pham, Minh-Ha T. 133–4
Plant, Sadie 226, 282
political Islam 119, 200
political powers and structure in Iran 105, 107
politics of face-veiling 9, 29
Pollock, Donald 279, 281, 283
Posetti, Julie 126–7
pragmatics of veiling in Finland 238–43
prayer caps 292, 296, **297**, 298–9
prejudice 51, 128; anti-Muslim 141; social
    164
Prodanovic, Branka 125–34
Psalms 38, 63, 66, 68
PSB (public service broadcasters) 127
public baths 8, 231

Qom 99–100
Quebec 77–80, 82, 145, 148, 163–7, 169,
    171
Quebec Charter 78–9
Quebec Council for the Status of Women 78
Quebecois 79, 164, 170; clothing retailers 166;
    company 168; converted 166; secular society
    169; societies 171; women 164, 166–7
Qur'an 2–3, 87, 153–5, 161, 163–5, 175–8, 182,
    255, 259–60, 263–4

'Rabbanit' 63, 66–7
Rabia Balhi Hospital 47
Rabine, Leslie 6, 14–15, 159
Rajput Royal family 247
Rajput women 247
Ramadan 155, 159, 169, 185, 217, 259, 263;
    Tariq 178
Ranjit Singh v. France 56
Razack, Sherene 74–5, 78, 81
Razanne doll 168
re-Islamization and reform movements 12
reforms 15, 91, 118; modernization 118; state-
    issued dress 15
religious convictions 59, 292
religious rights 8, 80, 149
religious studies 1, 38, 213
Renne, Elisha 10, 16, 154, 164, 301
research 31, 34, 40–1, 139–40, 149, 197, 199,
    206–7, 209, 293–5; ethnographic 184;
    informant gender dynamics 209; internet 215;
    and interviews 213; multidisciplinary 210
Rio de Janeiro 184–93
Roald, Anne Sofie 270, 272
Roihuvuori mosque 240
Rosaldo, Michelle 232–3, 242, 246
Rostam-Kolayi, Jasamin 5, 234
Rotem, Tamar 63–8
Roy, Oliver 177, 303
Ruby, Tabassum F. 2, 11–12, 44–51
Ruhani, Hassan (President of Iran) 97, 105,
    108
rules 35, 45, 54–5, 57, 99–101, 104–5, 250, 252,
    293–7, 299; age-related 298; authoritarian 37;
    cultural 298; of hygiene 57; of Islam in deeds
    and words 112, 260, 264; law-ordained 104;
    moral 160; social 287; of veiling 239, 246,
    248, 253
Russia 84–5, 89
Ryskulov, Nimatulla 88

Sahwa movement 261
Sandikçi, Özlem 15–17, 121, 148, 156, 193,
    197–210
São Paulo 188
sari *pallu* 247–9
Saudi Arabia 6, 147, 190, 205; influenced
    religious movements 6, 14; and Iran 140; and
    Malaysia 261
SBS 127
Schmid, Christian 233–4, 242
School for Educational Leadership, Jerusalem
    69
Schulz, Dorethea E. 14, 198
Schwab, Wendell 88, 90
Sciama, Lidia 232–3
Scott, Joan 2, 7, 45, 70, 223, 231, 279
Second World War 7, 237

Secor, Anna 11, 13, 15–16, 142, 178, 181, 202, 204, 207–8, 232
secularism 5–6, 73–4, 79, 81; and Canadian identity 79; and citizenship 81; feminism 12, 172; and modernity 5; and multiculturalism 73; state 78; Turkish 32
Sedghi, Hamideh 4, 6
segregation 235, 237; between genders 6, 241; gender 6, 234–6, 238, 241; ideal of gender 235
Setre, Turkey, 2004 Catalog **204**
settlements 247, 294, 297–8; Missouri Amish 293, 296
sexualization of women 159, 177; and stigmatization of Muslims 177
Shah of Iran 98, 106
Sharma, Ursula 248, 251–2
Shi'a Islam 119, 185
Shirazi, Faegheh 6, 97–113, 116–17, 163
Shodiyev, Shuhrat 89–90
Sikh men 4, 55, 79
Sikhism 149
Smith, Adam 36, 38, 49, 287
Smith, Courtney 49
Somalia 238–40, 267–73, 275; communities 268–9, 275–6; families 238–9; female dress in 238, 272, 275; identity and Islam 275; and Muslim communities 275; and the population in Finland 267; pre-war 273, 275; and Somalis in Turku 267; traditions 271; women 239, 241, 272; youths 269
Soviet state 6, 46, 92
Spinner, Jackie 47–8
Staniczia, Dr Rahima Zafar 47
State of Khorasan 103
Stephan, Manja 88–9
students 29, 32–3, 38–40, 49, 55, 90, 99–100, 122, 141, 263–4; banned 90; college 47, 221; deprived 37; female 29, 49, 70, 89–90; female Palestinian 70; headscarf-wearing 39; junior 263; law 159; undergraduate 190; university 29, 32, 47, 89, 120
studies 1, 18, 49, 163–4, 171, 198–200, 202–5, 207–9, 246, 251–2; globalization 301, 303–4; on marketing and consumption of male Islamic fashions 1, 209; religious 1, 38, 213; veiling 1, 18, 301–4
Sufi mosque, Montreal 167
Sunni Islam 118–19, 178, 185
Sunni schools 165
Sunni villages 119
Supreme Court, US. 50
Supreme Court of Canada 81
Suterwalla, Shehnaz 222–7
Sutton, Keith 236–7
Sydney 127–8, 130, 132; based Muslims 129; and the outbreak of terrorism 125

Sydney Morning Herald 128
Sydney Powerhouse Museum 129
symbolic veiling in Finland 240–2
Syria 184, 188, 199–200, 206, 223

Tajik women 87, 89, 91
Tajikistan 90–1
Taliban 44–6, 48, 50; regime 45–6; women 65
Talle, Aud 272, 275
Tarlo, Emma 11–17, 141, 147, 156, 202, 206–7, 209, 270, 272, 274
Tehran 100, 102, 105, 109, 112, 205
Tekbir, Turkey, 2005 catalog **203**
Tekbir fashion 204
Thobani, Sunera 75, 82
Tiilikainen, Marja 238, 272, 275
Tong, Joy Kooi-Chin 10–11, 13
Torah 3, 16, 38
traditions 45, 48, 75, 79, 109, 118–19, 168, 172, 197, 200; cultural 75, 78, 268, 275, 299; of Islam 119; liberal 30; local Muslim 154; long-standing veiling 46, 225, 289; oral 3, 263; religious 78, 81, 165, 172; Somali 271; tribal 170
Turkey 15–17, 29–33, 36–7, 41, 65, 116, 118–22, 145–6, 176–7, 198–209; and Arabic styles of Islamic fashions 209; and categories of women in 39; and dress reform 5; headscarf-wearing practices in 29; Islamic fashion in 205; and the Islamist movement in 119; Islamization of 121; and Malaysia 109, 199; membership bid for the EU 35; neoliberalism in 41; and neoliberalization 31; and the politics of women's veiling in 29–41, 200
Turku 267–9, 272–6
Turner, Bryan S. 4, 10–11, 13
Twycross, Meg 280–5, 287–8

Ummi (Islam magazine) 215
United States *see* US
university students 29, 32, 47, 89, 120
unmarried women 90, 268
unveiling 5, 7, 12, 84–7, 89, 91, 98–100, 102, 104, 106; associated with freedom and women's individual rights 91; campaigns and bans on veiling 7; compulsory 97–8, 100–1, 104; forced 98; Iranian women 104; order of 100; Reza Khan's forced 98; supported by the Soviet state 92; of women 98
US 8, 16, 44–7, 49–51, 168, 205, 216, 292, 298; and Canada 205; news media 45, 48; women 45
Uzbek Communist Party 87
Uzbekistan 2, 84, 86–7, 89–91; agricultural 84; anti-religion activists 87; and Kazakh women 85, 87; and Tajik women 89

Vagheh e kashf e hejab 100, 102
Vakulenko, Anastasia 3–4, 8
van Santen, José C. M. 6, 10, 14, 16
veiled women 11, 13, 63–71, 90–1, 98–9, 102, 107, 126, 178, 180–1; clothing practices of 208; praying in Rio de Janeiro **187**; standards of 71
veiling 1–8, 10–15, 73–82, 84–92, 174–9, 197–203, 231–43, 246–8, 250–3, 301–4; banned in Albania 7; in Canadian political and media discourse 76; compulsory 29, 97, 104; defended by Muslim feminists 12; early studies of 303; emerges as a powerfully political symbol since late colonial and post-colonial times 4; fashion firms in Turkey 208; fashion of young Muslims in Berlin 174, 182; fashions 197; in France 70; and globalization studies 301–4; Hindu and Muslim in north India 246–53; Islamic 55–6, 90, 105, 126, 209, 238, 289; and modernity 88; and Muslim Tuareg men 4; and Muslim women 81; of Muslim women in Australia 126, 128, 130; narratives in Canada 75, 77, 79, 81; and non-veiling Muslim peers 13; practiced by only certain Jewish groups 16; practised in a number of cultures, kingdoms and areas 4; in public institutions 54; in public schools 54–6; and spaces in North Africa and the Middle East 234; strongly connected to gender and the regulation of sexuality 4; studies 1, 18, 301–4; and unveiling in Central Asia 85, 87, 89, 91; of women in Central Asia 91; women in Europe 231, 236; women in Finland 242; of women of Beit Shemesh 64–6; in the workplace 56–7
veiling practices 1–2, 10, 44–6, 48, 50–1, 177, 201–2, 242–3, 246–53, 301–3; Bikaner 251; change in individual 10; Hindu and Muslim 247
Vilkama, Katja 238–9
Virtanen, Hanna 238–9
Volpp, Leti 51, 75–6
vom Bruck, Gabrielle 231, 234–7

Walker, Lynne 126, 232
Walton, Susan 117
Wang, Xiaoyan 255–65
Washington Post 45, 50, 140
Western clothing 51, 100, 225, 269
Western Europe 7, 9, 126, 140, 180, 286
Western-style clothing 48, 74, 101, 111, 118, 163
Western values 49, 88, 163
Western women 48–9, 170–1
Westernization 30; of the hijab 113; of local values 153
Wilson, Elizabeth 160, 198, 225
women 3–15, 29–35, 44–51, 84–9, 97–108, 139–49, 152–6, 163–8, 232–8, 246–53; abusing of 102; Anatolian 35, 37, 39; of Beit Shemesh 64, 71; in Bikaner 250; in Britain 144; and children in Afghanistan 45; covered 39, 198, 200–2, 206, 208; enabled wealthy Yemeni 202; in Iraq 47; living in Finland 267; Mennonite 296, 298; middle-class Indonesian 208, 216; in Muslim-majority countries 147; non-Western 30; in North Africa 235; post-Victorian 97; ultra-Orthodox 68, 71; unmarried 90, 268; veiled Oriental 74; of Yazd 102; young Central Asian 87
Wong, Loong 198–9

Yaqin, A. 17, 168
Yavuz, Hakan 198–9
Yemen 202, 209; late twentieth-century 235; wealthy elite of 153
young Muslims 10, 108, 148, 174, 176–7, 180–1, 206, 241; in Berlin 148, 174, 177, 180–1; in Finland 241; women 16–17, 222; women in Berlin **180**
young Somali women 267, 269–71, 273, 275
Yumul, Arus 119–20

Zahedi, Ashraf 5–6, 232
Zaman Newspaper 32
Zine, Jasmin 11–13, 148